# UNDERSTANDING JURISPRUDENCE

*'Do not weep; do not wax indignant. Understand.'*

*Baruch Spinoza*

# Understanding Jurisprudence

## An Introduction to Legal Theory

*Fourth edition*

## RAYMOND WACKS

*BA, LLB, LLM, LLD, MLitt, PhD*
*Emeritus Professor of Law and Legal Theory*

OXFORD
UNIVERSITY PRESS

# OXFORD
## UNIVERSITY PRESS

Great Clarendon Street, Oxford, OX2 6DP,
United Kingdom

Oxford University Press is a department of the University of Oxford.
It furthers the University's objective of excellence in research, scholarship,
and education by publishing worldwide. Oxford is a registered trade mark of
Oxford University Press in the UK and in certain other countries

© Raymond Wacks 2015

The moral rights of the author have been asserted

First edition 2005
Second edition 2009
Third edition 2012
Impression: 1

Public sector information reproduced under Open Government Licence v2.0
(http://www.nationalarchives.gov.uk/doc/open-government-licence/open-government-licence.htm)

Published in the United States of America by Oxford University Press
198 Madison Avenue, New York, NY 10016, United States of America

British Library Cataloguing in Publication Data
Data available

Library of Congress Control Number: 2014949671

ISBN 978-0-19-872386-8

Printed in Italy by
L.E.G.O. S.p.A.—Lavis TN

# Contents

# Detailed Contents

# New to this Edition

- Expanded chapters on natural law, legal positivism, realism, rights, and theories of justice.
- New and enhanced discussions of the rule of law, global justice, virtue ethics, human and animal rights, the economic analysis of law, and postmodernist theories.
- Updated suggested further reading lists and questions at the end of each chapter.

# Preface

A new edition is more than an exercise in textual addition or subtraction. It affords a valuable opportunity to assess whether a book's principal goal continues to be achieved. That goal is straightforward: to provide a lucid guide to a subject that often generates confusion, even apprehension. Consequently I have searched for passages that could be rendered even clearer than before. Where detected they have been overhauled.

Students have remarked that they enjoy the book's informal style; its purpose is to establish a—congenial—conversation between teacher and student. As previously, this edition concentrates on those subjects that my own students have found particularly challenging. The space devoted to a specific topic is therefore proportionate to its relative degree of difficulty, or the adequacy of its treatment by other texts.

The manuscript has been scrupulously reviewed by an anonymous band of distinguished jurists from law schools in a number of jurisdictions. I have been quick to adopt their constructive suggestions which, I am sure, have improved this edition. I am greatly indebted to them all.

My gratitude is owed also to a number of co-conspirators who have so capably assisted in this enterprise. I am especially grateful to Abbey Nelms and Amarpreet Pannu of Oxford University Press, and to Deborah Hey.

A number of readers have generously expressed their thanks for the helping hand that the book has lent them. I fervently hope that this salutary state of affairs continues to apply to students, and teachers, who have invested in this new edition.

Raymond Wacks
August 2014

# Preface to First edition

In the course of writing this book, Lily and Willy would often peer through my study window. Though intelligent, these doves exhibited an extraordinary curiosity in the words flickering across my monitor. And in the garden, as I sat proofreading, my plucky hens displayed an equally remarkable interest in the fluttering pages I was correcting. One afternoon, Ruby leapt on to the table and pecked 'Dworkin' once and 'Coleman' twice. I have no idea what she was trying to tell me. This avian enthusiasm, I am bound to say, far exceeded that evinced by many of my pragmatic law students who may perhaps have been right: jurisprudence is strictly for the birds.

I hope not. The concept of law lies at the heart of our social and political life. Jurisprudence illuminates it and its relation to the universal questions of justice, rights, and morality. It analyses the nature and purpose of our legal system, and its practice by courts, lawyers, and judges. Or so I told them. Frequently, however, it is only after they have studied legal theory that even students of the strongest black-letter disposition come to recognize how rewarding it was. Or so they told me. Indeed, it may be the lone opportunity in a crowded curriculum for reflection upon, and critical analysis of, law and the legal system. Given proper guidance and encouragement, even the least compliant, most vocationally oriented student may develop a genuine interest in, and even affection for, jurisprudence.

But here lurks a significant difficulty. Much of the literature is an impenetrable thicket to all but the professional jurist, or wholly dedicated and gifted student. It is the chief object of this book, without avoiding the subtleties and complexities of legal theory, to provide such guidance and encouragement. The perplexed and occasionally bewildered faces of my long-suffering students over the years have been in my mind's eye throughout the writing of the pages that follow.

Jurisprudence teachers harbour few illusions about the place of the subject in students' hearts or in the pecking order of most law school curricula. What was once, in many common law jurisdictions, a compulsory course, has, in our anti-authoritarian age, become a forlorn elective. Nor, incomprehensibly, do many American students reap the rich rewards of a discipline in which so many of their professors excel. This is a crime against philosophy. If the approach adopted in this book can contribute even in small measure towards reversing this pernicious drift, my exertions may be justified.

Legal theory is, of course, a demanding discipline. Several dangers lie in wait for anyone injudicious enough to endeavour to condense or elucidate its primary concerns. In embarking upon this imprudent course, I have been alert to these perils. But I have been fortified by the guidance and encouragement I have received from friends and colleagues who have been charitable enough to suppress their misgivings about my attempts to identify and unravel some of the mysteries I have selected for analysis. This has sustained me during periods when I feared that the task I had undertaken was a hopelessly intractable one.

In writing this book I have inevitably drawn on both the earlier incarnation of this work and other published work (listed in the acknowledgements overleaf). In the case of the former, I was fortunate to have received comments, often painstaking, from Roger Cotterrell, Ronald Dworkin, John Finnis, the late Eugene Kamenka, Katherine O'Donovan, Joseph Raz, and the late Alice Tay. In respect of the latter, other debts have—felicitously—been incurred. Friends and colleagues have been humane enough to indulge my attempts to make sense of the questions I consider in my writings on legal theory and privacy that I have drawn on in this book. They have done so over the years by providing generous encouragement, assistance, or (most sensibly) by signalling my many errors. For these, and other, favours I am most grateful to Mick Belson, Colin Bennett, Peter Birks, Michael Bryan, Tom Campbell, Ann Cavoukian, Albert Chen, John Dugard, David Dyzenhaus, John Eekelaar, David Flaherty, Michael Freeman, Jim Harris, Michael Hayes, Alan Hunt, Ellison Kahn, Michael Kirby, Monnie Lee, Eddie Leung, Neil McCormick, Alistair MacQueen, David McQuoid-Mason, Roda Mushkat, Steve Nathanson, Charles Raab, Megan Richardson, Michael Robertson, Wojciech Sadurski, Heather Saward, Scott Shapiro, Jamie Smith, Nico Steytler, Peter Wesley-Smith, and David Wood. None, needless to say, should be indicted as a co-defendant for the transgressions I have committed.

My publishers prudently enlisted a detachment of distinguished legal scholars from both sides of the Atlantic to review my manuscript. I was, needless to say, quick to adopt many of their valuable suggestions. And, since their identity is unknown to me, I can, with complete insouciance, hold these anonymous individuals jointly and severally liable for what follows.

The questions that conclude each chapter serve a threefold purpose. First, they identify the central problems in each of the areas analysed. Secondly, they provide fodder for reflection and discussion in seminars or study groups, and, thirdly, they should, I hope, assist students in revising for the examination or other forms of assessment. Most are borrowed from the course materials, essay questions, and examination papers that my students at the University of Hong Kong were compelled to endure. I am grateful to the Faculty of Law for permission to use them here.

This book began life almost twenty years ago as a modest attempt to clarify some of the fundamental concerns of the philosophy of law. Though its ambitions remain modest, it, like many of us, has grown stouter. There are, nevertheless, vestiges of the book's earlier Blackstonian manifestation in these pages. But a great deal is new, for academic ingenuity endlessly slouches toward jurisprudence to be re-born.

I am grateful to those at Oxford University Press who helpfully steered this project from my mind, via my screen, to these pages. Especial thanks to Angela Griffin, Sarah Hyland, Melanie Jackson, Catherine Kernot, Sarah Nattrass, Nicola Rainbow, and Penelope Woolf (who twisted my arm to undertake this project).

This book could not have been written without the love, patience, and support of my wife, Penelope Wacks (who twisted my arm not to undertake this project). My gratitude to her for all she has given me cannot be expressed adequately in words.

This is unashamedly a book for students. It is not, however, a textbook. I have selected its subject-matter on the simple ground that it reflects what tends to be taught in most jurisprudence courses in the common law world. Inevitably, a number of subjects have had to be omitted; it is therefore neither comprehensive nor exhaustive. Nor is it intended to replace the books and essays to which reference is made throughout, and to which all serious students will want to turn. My principal objective is to point students of jurisprudence in the right direction, soaring above needless deviation, mystification, and impediment—not unlike my discerning doves.

Raymond Wacks
October 2004

# List of Tables and Figure

## Tables

## Figure

# Acknowledgements

I am grateful for the kind permission of the publishers listed below to draw on the following material:

**Oxford University Press**

Richard Nobles and David Schiff, 'Debating with Natural Law: The Emergence of Legal Positivism' in James Penner, David Schiff, and Richard Nobles (eds), *Introduction to Jurisprudence and Legal Theory: Commentary and Materials* (Oxford: Oxford University Press, 2002). Figure 3.1 on page 78 is adapted from the diagram on page 106.

**Hong Kong University Press**

Raymond Wacks, 'Are Judges Morally Accountable?' in Raymond Wacks, *Law, Morality, and the Private Domain* (Hong Kong: Hong Kong University Press, 2000) pp 91–111.

Raymond Wacks, 'Do Animals Have Moral Rights?' in Raymond Wacks, *Law, Morality, and the Private Domain* (Hong Kong: Hong Kong University Press, 2000), pp 153–7.

Raymond Wacks, 'Can "Human Rights" Survive?' in Raymond Wacks, *Law, Morality, and the Private Domain* (Hong Kong: Hong Kong University Press, 2000), pp 179–209.

Raymond Wacks, 'Sacrificed for Science: Are Animal Experiments Morally Defensible' in Gerhold K Becker (ed), in association with James P Buchanan, *Changing Nature's Course: The Ethical Challenge of Biotechnology* (Hong Kong: Hong Kong University Press, 1996), pp 37–57.

Raymond Wacks, 'One Country, Two *Grundnormen*? The Basic Law and the Basic Norm' in Raymond Wacks (ed), *Hong Kong, China and 1997: Essays in Legal Theory* (Hong Kong: Hong Kong University Press, 1996), pp 151–83.

**Sweet & Maxwell Asia and *Hong Kong Law Journal***

Raymond Wacks, Review of Michael Moore, *Objectivity in Ethics and Law* (Aldershot: Dartmouth, and Burlington, VT: Ashgate, 2004) in (2004) 34 *Hong Kong Law Journal* 429–32.

Raymond Wacks, 'The End of Human Rights?' (1994) 24 *Hong Kong Law Journal* 372.

**Editions Rodopi BV**

Raymond Wacks, 'Judges and Moral Responsibility' in W Sadurski (ed), *Ethical Dimensions of Legal Theory*, Poznan Studies in the Philosophy of the Sciences and Humanities (Amsterdam: Rodopi, 1991), pp 111–29.

**Franz Steiner Verlag**

Raymond Wacks, 'Law's Umpire: Judges, Truth, and Moral Accountability' in Peter Koller and André-Jean Arnaud (eds), *Law, Justice, and Culture* (Stuttgart: Franz Steiner Verlag, 1998), pp 75–83.

**Palgrave Macmillan**

Alan Hunt, *The Sociological Movement in Law* (London: Macmillan, 1978). Tables 7.3 and 7.4 on pages 199 and 201 are adapted from diagrams on pages 107 and 119, respectively.

# 1

# What's it all about?

Jurisprudence seeks to answer fundamental questions about law.[1] What *is* law? What is its purpose? Does it consist merely of rules? Can anything be law? What has law to do with justice? Or morality? Democracy? What makes a law valid? Do we have a duty to obey the law? These, and many other, 'theoretical' questions suffuse the fabric of jurisprudence and legal theory. Nor are they restricted to the philosophical reflections of contemplative jurists. Every substantive or 'black letter' branch of the law generates queries about its own meaning and purpose. Can the law of contract be properly understood without an appreciation of the concepts of rights and duties? How is the law of tort to be explained in the absence of economic theories of compensation? Is property law not founded on certain conceptions of private property that are steeped in theory? Can criminal law dispense with philosophies of punishment? And so on. Your negative responses to all these questions will, I hope, be deafening and unequivocal.

Jurisprudence is consequently ubiquitous. Its concerns are an inescapable feature of the law and legal system. But it is more. As will soon be evident, it is both informed by, and has significant implications for, economic, political, and social theory. Drawing the boundaries of this vast terrain is therefore a challenging exercise. Most university courses conceive the purpose of jurisprudence to include an examination of leading legal theories and selected legal concepts and an attempt to place them in the context of the legal system. This entails developing the intellectual skills essential to an evaluation of the acceptability or otherwise of ideas of law, justice, and the legal system. It requires an analysis of general theoretical questions about the nature of laws and legal systems in modern societies and the relationship of law with justice and morality.

---

[1] Throughout this book, I use the words 'jurisprudence', 'legal theory', and 'legal philosophy' interchangeably, though, strictly speaking, 'jurisprudence' concerns the theoretical analysis of law at the highest level of abstraction (eg, questions about the nature of a right or a duty, judicial reasoning, etc) and are frequently implied within substantive legal disciplines. 'Legal theory' is often used to denote theoretical enquiries about law 'as such' that extend beyond the boundaries of law as understood by professional lawyers (eg, the economic analysis of law, Marxist approaches to legal domination, etc). 'Legal philosophy' or the 'philosophy of law', as its name implies, normally proceeds from the standpoint of the discipline of philosophy (eg, it attempts to unravel the sort of problems that might vex moral or political philosophers, such as the concepts of freedom or authority). For a preliminary account of the nature of law, its past, present, and future, see Raymond Wacks, *Law: A Very Short Introduction* (Oxford: Oxford University Press, 2008). See too John Gardner, *Law as a Leap of Faith: Essays on Law in General* (Oxford: Oxford University Press, 2014).

Many courses seek also to examine the function of law in society with particular reference to the relations of law and power, and the concepts and techniques characteristically used in the operation of developed legal systems. And some endeavour to apply philosophical and sociological theories and methodologies to problems of and problems about the law.

## 1.1 An analgesic?

Jurisprudence is, for some students, pain. Given the choice, they would not choose to take the subject at all. And it is little consolation for them to be told that one day they will look back and recognize the value of their exposure to legal theory. Unlike most 'black letter' law courses, this one requires you to think, to read a copious assortment of often turgid—and even impenetrable—writing which appears to have little connection with 'the law', and frequently presumes an understanding of philosophy, sociology, economics, and even anthropology. There is little security here; you long for the friendly reassurance of a statute, or the simple pleasures of the judgment of a court. Suddenly you are plunged into the perilous depths of grand theory, a world inhabited by epistemology, teleology, and metaphysics. And your apprehension is compounded by the fact that some of your peers actually give the impression of understanding it!

A great deal of the literature is highly technical, some of it simply unreadable; its intended audience is a professional one: other jurists rather than the harassed student. Indeed, one distinguished philosopher himself laments the depressing tendency of these analytical debates

> to be flat and repetitive...revolving in smaller and smaller circles among a diminishing band of acolytes. Worse still, they are in danger of becoming uninterestingly parochial from a philosophical point of view, as we distance ourselves from the intellectual resources that would enable us to grasp conceptions of law and controversies about law other than our own conceptions and our own controversies, and law itself as something with a history that transcends our particular problems and anxieties.[2]

In these pages I attempt to avoid these indefensible lapses into obscurity. (And a glossary of the philosophical terms you are most likely to encounter in your jurisprudential journey is provided at the end of the book. The abbreviated definitions are intended both to ring a bell and to assist you to comprehend them when they appear before their more detailed discussion in the appropriate chapters.)

This book is not, however, intended to be a substitute for your reading of the materials prescribed for your course. Unfortunately no single text could achieve that Utopian ideal. Nor should it. Jurisprudence is a rich and diverse subject which is in a constant state of growth; most textbooks (and, indeed, courses) cannot aspire to a great deal more than an eclectic skimming of its vast depths. And the book in your hands is not

---

[2] Jeremy Waldron, 'Legal and Political Philosophy' in Jules Coleman and Scott Shapiro (eds), *The Oxford Handbook of Jurisprudence and Philosophy of Law* (Oxford: Oxford University Press, 2002), 352, 381.

a textbook. Nevertheless, while its purpose is modest, I trust that what follows contains enough detail to be a reliable, helpful, and congenial guide to the major themes of this field of study. Limitations of space called for hard choices. This required concision, excision, and even omission. The editorial axe had to fall somewhere; its blade was stayed where the material in question struck me as essential or intractable, or both, and therefore clamouring for more space and, I hope, illumination.

Secondly, and almost as obvious, no two courses in jurisprudence are the same. There are a number of theorists and theories that are common to most university syllabuses—the core of this book—but beyond that, every teacher has his or her own preferences, conditioned by a wide range of factors, and you will inevitably be required to consult several books, essays, and articles which pertain to these topics. This book is intended to develop your skills in getting to the heart of the matter and, though it deals only with the major strands of legal theory, it aims to equip you to apply similar techniques in respect of the more exotic issues covered in your particular course.

Thirdly, the affliction most commonly associated with the study of jurisprudence is lack of confidence. Overwhelmed by the enormity of the subject and its attendant reading materials, many students experience a combination of frustration and despair. Having ploughed through the often rarefied works of leading legal philosophers, they throw up their hands in exasperation at their complexity, density, or their sheer incomprehensibility. It is hoped that the chapters which follow may, while avoiding oversimplification, facilitate a better understanding of the ideas so as to increase your confidence both in reading and writing about them.

Fourthly, this book will help you to think more clearly about jurisprudence. It should encourage you to approach the literature with greater insight and understanding. To this extent, a great deal of your pain may be relieved, and the pages that follow may even assist you to enjoy this absorbing and important subject.

## 1.2 Reading

Jurisprudence has a prodigious literature. Most teachers, especially in the United States, eschew textbooks, and prepare their own, often comprehensive, materials tailored to their courses. There are, nevertheless, some useful works recommended by instructors in American law schools. Among them are George C Christie and Patrick H Martin (eds), *Jurisprudence: Texts and Readings on the Philosophy of Law*,[3] Robert Hayman, Nancy Levit, and Richard Delgado, *Jurisprudence, Classical and Contemporary: From Natural Law to Postmodernism*,[4] and Mark Murphy, *Philosophy of Law: The Fundamentals*.[5] Undergraduate classes in the philosophy of law often use Joel Feinberg and Jules Coleman (eds), *Philosophy of Law*[6] and Brian Bix, *Jurisprudence: Theory and Context*.[7]

---

[3] 3rd edn (St Paul, Minn: West Publishing, 2008).
[4] 2nd edn (St Paul, Minn: West Publishing, 2002).     [5] (Hoboken, NJ: Wiley, 2006).
[6] 7th edn (Belmont, Calif: Wadsworth/Thomson Learning, 2003).
[7] 5th edn (Durham, NC: Carolina Academic Press, 2009).

Elsewhere in the common law world, the prescription of textbooks that include extracts and commentaries is more common. Among the most widely used are MDA Freeman (ed), *Lloyd's Introduction to Jurisprudence*[8] and James Penner, David Schiff, and Richard Nobles (eds), *Introduction to Jurisprudence and Legal Theory: Commentary and Materials*.[9] Yet another helpful collection is *Jurisprudence: Texts and Commentary* by Davies and Holdcroft.[10] Many students like JW Harris's *Legal Philosophies*,[11] McCoubrey and White's *Textbook on Jurisprudence*,[12] and NE Simmonds *Central Issues in Jurisprudence: Justice, Law and Rights*.[13] Also popular is the British version of Brian Bix's *Jurisprudence: Theory and Context*.[14] For a thematic approach to the subject, look at Denise Meyerson's *Jurisprudence*.[15] Another intelligent, lucid introduction to the subject from an explicitly philosophical perspective is Mark Tebbit, *Philosophy of Law: An Introduction*.[16] You may also find useful S Veitch, E Christodoulidis, and L Farmer, *Jurisprudence: Themes and Concepts*[17] and Suri Ratnapala, *Jurisprudence*.[18]

A handy series of readers on a wide range of theoretical subjects has been published by Dartmouth. Called the *International Library of Essays in Law and Legal Theory*, it is divided into three sections: schools, areas, and legal cultures. Each volume contains about twenty essays. The books are fairly expensive, but it is likely that your library will have copies. New titles are constantly being added to the large number already published. There are, of course, a number of more specialist works (to which reference is made in the chapters that follow), and if you are a keen student—or simply an affluent one—it would be very useful to own copies of them. Full details of books are given in the 'Further Reading' sections at the end of each chapter. You will certainly be expected to read parts or all of them. Much depends, of course, on what your course attempts to cover. No course in legal theory is, in my experience, ever large enough. There is never enough time to devote to this vast and ever-expanding subject.

Articles in journals and essays in collections are, of course, every bit as important as books. Apart from the leading law reviews and journals, there are a number of specialist journals to which you may be referred. These include *Jurisprudence*, the *American Journal of Jurisprudence*, *Legal Theory*, the *Juridical Review*, *Philosophy and Public Affairs*, the *Philosophical Quarterly*, the *Journal of Law and Society*, the *Law and Society Review*, *Political Studies*, *Ratio Juris*, and the *Proceedings of the Aristotelian Society*. The *Oxford Journal of Legal Studies* devotes a fair number of its pages to essays legally philosophical and jurisprudential. There is also, needless to say, an abundance of material available at the click of a mouse on the Web.

---

[8] 8th edn (London: Sweet & Maxwell, 2008).    [9] (London: Butterworths, 2002).
[10] (London: Butterworths, 1991).    [11] 2nd edn (London: Butterworths, 1997).
[12] 5th edn (Oxford: Oxford University Press, 2012).
[13] 4th edn (London: Sweet & Maxwell, 2013).    [14] 6th edn (London: Sweet & Maxwell, 2012).
[15] (Melbourne: Oxford University Press, 2011).    [16] 2nd edn (London: Routledge, 2005).
[17] 2nd edn (London: Routledge, 2012).
[18] 2nd edn (Melbourne: Cambridge University Press, 2014).

## 1.3 Why jurisprudence?

As already mentioned, jurisprudence has generous frontiers. It accommodates copious subjects of intellectual enquiry. And the magnitude of this expanding discipline explains, in part, my disclaimer above. These pages attempt to identify and elucidate several of the major preoccupations of legal theory. And I cannot repeat too often that they are not a substitute for the reading of the primary sources themselves. My overriding purpose is, by distilling the essential questions of legal theory, to encourage you to read and reflect upon their original exposition and the controversy they have engendered.

No society can properly be understood or explained without a coherent conception of its law and legal doctrine. The social, moral, and cultural foundations of the law, and the theories which both inform and account for them, are no less important than the law's 'black letter':

> Legal and political theories are not descriptions of brute facts. Nor are they merely postulated ideals or aspirations. Theories reflect and are reflected in our social relationships. And the historical development of our social life is itself a part of the intellectual evolution of our ideas…And, if understanding a moral or political concept is a matter of understanding the 'form of life' to which it belongs, an articulation of this or that conception may well require attention to its history. Moral and political values thus cannot and should not be discussed in isolation from the institutions and social histories that shaped them.[19]

The import and validity of this claim will become evident, I hope, as you read the pages that follow.

Among the many topics within legal theory's substantial precincts is that of the definition of law, as well as legal concepts. It stands to reason that before we can begin to explore the nature of law, we need to clarify what it is we mean by this elusive concept. We can barely begin our analysis of the law and legal system without some shared understanding of what it is we are talking about. Or can we? Richard Posner, a leading theorist and judge (whose economic theories are described in 9.2) pours scorn on this simple goal:

> If someone said to you 'time is an incredibly important and fundamental feature of the universe and human life, and therefore it is very important that we define it' you would be nonplussed…I react the same way to efforts to define 'law'.[20]

Yet jurisprudence—and the law itself—is haunted by questions of definition. This problem is, however, easier to state than resolve. Nevertheless, there is a relatively painless means by which you can begin to clarify your thoughts on this important question: read Professor Hart's 'Definition and Theory in Jurisprudence'.[21] The fact that

---

[19] NE Simmonds, *The Decline of Juridical Reason* (Manchester: Manchester University Press, 1984), 13.
[20] Richard Posner, *Law and Legal Theory in the UK and the USA* (Oxford: Clarendon Press, 1996), 1.
[21] (1954) 70 *Law Quarterly Review* 37, reprinted in his *Essays in Jurisprudence and Philosophy* (Oxford: Clarendon Press, 1984).

Hart devoted his inaugural lecture (after being elected to the Chair of Jurisprudence at Oxford in 1953) to this question gives you some indication of the importance he attached to the matter. In this essay, Hart warns against the danger of 'theory on the back of definition'. By this he means that we should not confuse the act of attempting to *define* a legal concept with an account of what one might call its *ideological function*; to do so conflates logical and political criteria.

Broadly speaking, there are three main approaches to the problem of definition in general. The first argues that 'to mean is to denote'.[22] In other words, all significant expressions are proper names—what they are the names of are what the expressions signify. But this raises immediate difficulties when it comes to, for instance, fictitious or non-existent things (Mickey Mouse or a unicorn). Surely, it cannot be correct (as Ryle puts it) 'that to every significant grammatical subject there must correspond an appropriate *denotatum* in the way in which Fido (the dog) answers to the name "Fido"'.

A second approach therefore has emerged that rejects this 'denotationist' view; it is associated with the Cambridge philosopher, Ludwig Wittgenstein, who said: 'Don't ask for the meaning, ask for the use.' The use of an expression is the *function* it is employed to do, as opposed to any thing or person or event which it is supposed to *denote*. Thus, to use one of Wittgenstein's own examples, a 'knight' has meaning only once we know the rules of chess; unless we know these rules, it is merely a piece of wood in the shape of a horse. The chief attraction of this approach is that it enables us to fix a meaning to certain legal concepts without the need to employ fictions to correspond with the meaning of certain concepts.[23]

A third position, known as 'essentialism' argues that particular things have essences which serve to identify them as the particular things they are. Thus Austin and Kelsen sought to define law by reference to its fundamental nature (as commands of the sovereign or a normative system, respectively).

You will, of course, realize that in seeking 'definitions' of law or legal concepts, several difficulties lie in wait. Our political or ideological preferences will inevitably intrude, as will historical, social, and moral considerations. Provided we are alive to these issues, we should not shy away from elucidating the ideas that infuse the legal system. Indeed, unless we do so, conceptual confusion may actually inhibit our attempt to improve the law.

## 1.4 Descriptive, normative, and critical legal theory

Descriptive legal theory seeks to explain what the law is, and why, and its consequences. Normative legal theories, on the other hand, are concerned with what the law ought to be. Put differently, descriptive legal theories are about facts; normative legal

---

[22] G Ryle, 'The Theory of Meaning' in CA Mace (ed), *British Philosophy in Mid-Century* (London: George Allen & Unwin, 1957).
[23] See Hart's discussion of a 'corporation' in the essay mentioned at n 21.

theories are about values. Critical legal theory (the subject of Chapter 13) questions the very foundation of jurisprudence.

Descriptive legal theory may, first, be 'doctrinal'. It provides a theory to explain a particular legal doctrine. For example, freedom of expression might be justified by decisions of the courts on the limits of free speech. Doctrinal legal theory seeks to answer questions such as 'Can these cases be elucidated by some underlying theory?' Secondly, descriptive legal theory may be 'explanatory'; it attempts to explain why the law is as it is. Marxist legal theory, for example, is 'explanatory' in this sense, for it offers an account of law as expressing the interests of the ruling class. A third form of descriptive legal theory concerns the consequences that are likely to follow from a certain set of legal rules. For example, economic analysts of law (see 9.2) might use their tools of analysis to assess the probable behavioural effects of a strict liability regime on manufacturers.

Normative legal theory, on the other hand, is concerned with values. Such a theory may, for instance, seek to establish whether strict liability ought to be adopted in order to protect consumers. Normative legal theories tend inevitably to be associated with moral or political theories. In pursuing an evaluation of the law, normative legal theories might be either 'ideal' or 'non-ideal'. The former relate to what legal rules would create the best legal system if it were politically achievable. The latter presuppose an assortment of constraints on the choice of legal rules, such as the difficulty in enforcing such rules.

But there is no clear-cut distinction between these two categories of legal theory. A normative theory may rely on a descriptive theory to obtain its purchase. Thus, it is hard to sustain the normative theory of utilitarianism (see 9.1) without a descriptive account of the consequences of the application of a specific rule. How would a utilitarian know whether rule X causes the greatest happiness (result Y) without a description of these consequences? Similarly, a descriptive legal theory may, on the basis of predictions about the likelihood of success of, say, law reform, put a brake on the normative legal theory that gave birth to the improvement.

You will also perceive (especially in Chapter 5) how normative and descriptive theory may be grafted together to yield a sort of hybrid legal theory. In Dworkin's theory of 'law as integrity', for example, there is an amalgamation of the goals of descriptive doctrinal theory and normative theory. By claiming that a theory of law should both 'fit' and 'justify' the legal materials, his theory appears to allow descriptive doctrinal theory to coalesce with normative theory.

Critical legal theory has deep misgivings about the concept of a universal foundation of law based on reason. Jurisprudence, it argues, endows the law and legal system with a spurious legitimacy. The very notion of law as a unique and distinct discipline is doubted, for it overlooks the fact that, far from being autonomous, the law is inseparable from politics. Indeed, the law, in the minds of critical legal theorists, is anything but a determinate, coherent body of rules and doctrine; it is uncertain and indefinite. Nor is the law inevitably rational, neutral, or objective: it is expressive of political and economic power.

## 1.5 Is eating people wrong?

A popular launching pad for the comprehension of legal ideas is Lon Fuller's entertaining hypothetical 'Case of the Speluncean Explorers'.[24] It contains five judgments of the Supreme Court of Newgarth in the year 4300. Four members of the Speluncean Society were trapped in an underground cave. Huge efforts were made to rescue them, at a major financial and human cost (ten lives had been lost). On the twentieth day of their ordeal the ill-fated explorers decided that they could avoid death by starvation before they could be rescued only if they killed and ate one of their number. It was proposed by Roger Whetmore, one of the explorers, that they should cast dice to determine who should be eaten. After considerable vacillation, this was accepted, whereupon Whetmore declared that he withdrew from the agreement. The others nevertheless decided to proceed, and one of them cast the dice on Whetmore's behalf. The throw went against him, and he was duly killed and eaten. The survivors were eventually rescued, and charged with murder.

Each of the five judges adopts a different approach and conclusion to the case. And, not unlike judges in the real world, each emerges as a distinct personality. The Chief Justice, Truepenny, is a self-important formalist. Keen J is an unyielding positivist. Tatting J is indecisive and rather tortured. Handy J is an arch-realist. Foster J adopts a purposive vision of law, a thinly disguised version of Fuller's own position.[25] The import of each of these positions will become clearer when you have studied the various theories embodied in each of these judicial positions. It would therefore not be a bad idea to return to the Spelunceans when you have completed your study of natural law, positivism, and realism in the following chapters of this book.

The central issue confronted in the case is the extent to which conflicting legally protected values (human lives) can be reconciled. This dilemma provides a vehicle for Fuller's deeper belief concerning the very nature of legal theory, for, as he points out, 'the case was constructed for the sole purpose of bringing into common focus certain divergent philosophies of law and government... [which] presented men with live questions of choice in the days of Plato and Aristotle and which are among the permanent problems of the human race.'[26] Hence, as Professor Twining shows, the case reveals the Fullerian perspective of jurisprudential enquiry. He boils it down to the following sorts of questions:[27]

---

[24] Lon L Fuller, 'The Case of the Speluncean Explorers' (1949) 62 *Harvard Law Review* 616. The facts are based on the two leading common law decisions on cannibalism and the defence of necessity in criminal law: *R v Dudley & Stephens* [1884] 14 QBD 273, affirmed [1885] 14 QBD 560, and *US v Holmes* 26 Fed Cas 360 (1842).

[25] 'It may startle my hearers for me to say so, but in many ways I feel myself closer to Foster than to anyone else on this court. If he could only rip off that metaphysical jacket he has put on himself, and gain a little more freedom of action, I think we might get along very well indeed.' Ibid.     [26] Ibid, 645.

[27] William Twining, *Law in Context: Enlarging a Discipline* (Oxford: Clarendon Press, 1997), 217. I have slightly amended his formulation.

1. Is it ever morally
   (a) justifiable
   (b) excusable
   to kill and eat a human being?

2. Whether or not it is *morally* justifiable or excusable, is it *legally* justifiable to kill and eat a human being in order to save one's life? Alternatively, is necessity a defence to the charge of murder?

3. What is the connection, if any, between 1 and 2?

4. What is the proper role of an appellate judge in deciding a difficult case on a question of law? How does this differ from the role of other officials?

5. What kind of reasons are admissible, valid, and cogent in
   (a) reaching
   (b) justifying
   a judicial decision in a hard case? What is the relationship between (a) and (b)? In particular, should public opinion be taken into account in reaching and justifying such decisions? Do (a) citizens (b) judges owe an indefeasible duty of fidelity to the law?

Three of the judges in the case accept that Whetmore's killing was, to some extent, defensible. Keen J appears to regard it as entirely justifiable. The somewhat gauche Tatting J is uncertain of the morality of the defendants' actions. Truepenny CJ and Keen J conclude that the defendants were, despite the circumstances, guilty of murder. Handy and Foster JJ would overturn the conviction. Tatting J finds the case too difficult, and withdraws. As a result, the court is split and the conviction of the defendants is upheld.

Truepenny CJ and Keen J justify their decisions by focusing on what they conceive to be the clear language of the legislature. Tatting J prefers to rely on precedent and analogy. Foster J naturally appeals to the purpose of the law, which he regards as at variance with the statute. Handy rests his decision on 'common sense' supported by articulated public opinion. The most significant and instructive contrast is, I think, between the standpoints of Handy and Foster JJ. The former is a realist who conceives of the law as a matter of practical politics. He enjoys belittling Foster J's efforts to defend a middle ground between politics and formalism.[28]

The contest between Handy and Foster exposes the nerve of Fuller's own equivocation about realism (see Chapter 6). It reveals his conviction that law cannot be considered as either 'is' or 'ought': normative or descriptive. Hence Handy J holds that 'government is a human affair' and bemoans the propensity to analyse a situation 'until all the life and juice have gone out of it and we have left a handful of dust'. He

---

[28] 'Formalism' emphasizes law's formal properties rather than its content. For further insights into this approach, see Frederick Schauer, 'Formalism' (1998) 97 *Yale Law Journal* 509. There is also a useful symposium, 'Formalism Revisited' in (1999) 66 *University of Chicago Law Review* 934.

urges an awareness of substance, popular will, and practical politics. Nevertheless, he acknowledges that substance is inadequate; there is frequently a need for form.

You will almost certainly be expected to read the 'Speluncean Explorers' in full. It provides, for many teachers of legal theory, an entertaining and valuable means of introducing their students to a number of the fundamental concerns of the subject, including the relationship between law and morality; legal positivism and natural law; the nature of the judicial function; the interpretation of statutes; the relationship between adjudication and legislation; the connection between law, democracy, and public opinion; whether law has a purpose; the concepts of justice and injustice; the process of legal reasoning, and many more. The case has retained its piquancy and relevance for more than half a century, and will, I believe, continue to do so for many more generations of students.

## 1.6  The rule of law

You will already have encountered this phrase in your constitutional law course or, if not, in the pervasive rhetoric of politicians, newspaper leader writers, and commentators. It is frequently used to champion a 'government of laws, not of men'.

### 1.6.1  Dicey

Though the concept dates back to ancient times, it is with the constitutional theorist, AV Dicey, that it is most closely associated, at least in its *formal* sense. Dicey, in his celebrated treatise, *Introduction to the Study of the Law of the Constitution*,[29] formulated three principles that stipulate the necessary institutional and constitutional requirements without specifying what the *content* of the law ought to be.

The first principle declares that 'no man is punishable or can be lawfully made to suffer in body or goods except for a distinct breach of law established in the ordinary legal manner before the ordinary courts of the land. In this sense the rule of law is contrasted with every system of government based on the exercise by persons in authority of wide, arbitrary, or discretionary powers of constraint'. This principle captures the important prerequisite that the laws under which individuals are punished should be enacted in accordance with proper legal procedures, and that guilt should be established only through the normal trial process. Dicey's reference to wide, arbitrary, or discretionary powers might extend to laws that violate certain fundamental rights, or it might describe laws properly enacted, but which are vague or uncertain so that citizens are unable to plan their lives in harmony with the law.

The second principle asserts that 'every man, whatever be his rank or condition, is subject to the ordinary law of the realm and amenable to the jurisdiction of the ordinary tribunals'. This affirms the significance of equal access to the courts. Again,

---

[29]  (1885) Classic Reprint, London: Forgotten Books, 2012.

Dicey here expresses a formal or institutional notion rather than a substantive concern with how judges actually *apply* the law to different individuals or social groups. The principle is therefore not incompatible with discrimination or special treatment. This is a far cry from contemporary theories of justice discussed in Chapter 9. Nor does it satisfy certain Marxist and Critical Legal Studies (CLS) theorists who contend that the rule of law is little short of a mask that conceals the oppression of the working class. See Chapters 7 and 13.

'We may say' Dicey stated thirdly, 'that the [British] constitution is pervaded by the rule of law on the ground that the general principles of the constitution (as for example the right to personal liberty, or the right of public hearing) are with us the result of judicial decisions determining the rights of private persons in particular cases brought before the courts'. This is a claim of superiority of the British unwritten constitution over those written constitutions of continental Europe. For Dicey, individual liberty was more secure where it was the product of judicial decision rather than being susceptible to repeal or abrogation by authoritarian governmental fiat.

### 1.6.2 Modern approaches

Legal theorists in several jurisdictions have sought to adapt the conception to contemporary questions of legality, authority, and other virtues of democratic governance. So, for example, Lon Fuller's idea of the 'inner morality of law' (discussed in Chapter 2) specifies eight desiderata with which the law should comply if it is to achieve 'excellence'. Joseph Raz (see Chapter 4) attempts to add flesh to the bare bones of Dicey's principles, while stressing that the rule of law is not the sole virtue of a legal system.[30] His organizing principle is that the rule of law performs a crucial role in facilitating individuals planning their lives.[31] To do so, he argues, the law ought to be prospective (as opposed to retrospective); relatively stable; that particular laws should be directed by open, general, and clear rules; that the courts should be independent and accessible; and that those who enforce the law should not have untrammelled discretion.

From the perspective of justice, however, an unjust legal system could satisfy these norms (or even Fuller's) while enacting wicked laws. See the case study of apartheid South Africa in Chapter 2. Nevertheless, as Raz insists, a formal (or content-neutral) conception of the rule of law permits us to evaluate the operation of a legal system *independently* of its political or moral quality.

---

[30] Joseph Raz, 'The Rule of Law and its Virtue' (1977) 93 *Law Quarterly Review* 195. See further J Raz, *Ethics in the Public Domain* (Oxford: Oxford University Press, 1994) at 362; John Gardner, 'Rationality and the Rule of Law in Offences against the Person' (1994) 53 *Cambridge Law Journal* 502 at 511–20. For the perspective of a British judge, see Tom Bingham, *The Rule of Law* (Harmondsworth: Penguin, 2010). See too Paul Craig, 'Formal and Substantive Conceptions of the Rule of Law: An Analytical Framework' [1997] *Public Law* 467.

[31] 'The rule of law...implies the precept that similar cases be treated similarly. Men could not regulate their actions by rules if this precept were not followed', John Rawls, *A Theory of Justice* (Harmondsworth: Penguin, 1971) at 237. Rawls is discussed in Chapter 9.

A number of jurists have rejected this approach and look instead to the power exercised by the judiciary over the executive. Judicial review is an important means by which government is kept in check and thereby rendered more accountable, both procedurally and substantively. For example, Ronald Dworkin (the subject of Chapter 5) argues that 'propositions of law are true if they figure in or follow from the principles of justice, fairness and procedural due process that provide the best constructive interpretation of the community's legal practice'.[32]

Dworkin places the courts at the epicentre of the legal system. It is their function to decide what rights individuals have. In this endeavour, as we shall see, judges ought to select the interpretation of the law that best fits with the commitment of the law to justice, and displays the community's institutions in the best light. The formal (or 'rule book') notion of the rule of law, Dworkin contends, neglects the centrality of individual rights; citizens have moral rights and duties with respect to one another, and political rights against the state. Such rights should be recognized in positive law, in order that they can be enforced by the courts. The conception of the rule of law 'does not distinguish, as the rule book conception does, between the rule of law and substantive justice; on the contrary it requires, as part of the ideal of law, that the rules in the book capture and enforce moral rights.'[33]

You will want to return to this debate after you have studied the jurists mentioned above.

## 1.7 The point of legal theory

All things considered, the world is not a happy place. The cycle of injustice, war, hunger, exploitation, corruption, racism, sexism, disease, and poverty seems an inevitable feature of our planet, some 40 per cent of whose population—three billion people—live in poverty, earning less than US$2 per day.[34] The average Gross Domestic Product per capita in the north is almost twenty times that of the south. A quarter of the world's population enjoys the fruits of wealth and consumerism as it expends 80 per cent of the planet's resources. In developing countries, one person in

---

[32]  R Dworkin, *Law's Empire* (Cambridge, Mass: Harvard University Press, 1986), 225.

[33]  R Dworkin, *A Matter of Principle* (Cambridge, Mass: Harvard University Press, 1985), 11–12. See too TRS Allan, *Constitutional Justice, A Liberal Theory of the Rule of Law* (Oxford: Oxford University Press, 2001); J Jowell, 'The Rule of Law Today', in Jowell and Oliver (eds), *The Changing Constitution*, 5th edn (Oxford: Oxford University Press, 2000), Ch 1. TAO Endicott, 'The Impossibility of the Rule of Law' (1999) 19 *Oxford Journal of Legal Studies* 1.

[34]  *Human Development Report*, United Nations Development Programme, 27 November 2007, p 25. According to the United Nations Development Programme, 'There are still around 1 billion people living at the margins of survival on less than US$1 a day, with 2.6 billion—40 percent of the world's population— living on less than US$2 a day.' Ibid. The picture is somewhat brighter in the latest report which describes 'the rise of the South': 'For the first time in 150 years, the combined output of the developing world's three leading economies—Brazil, China and India—is about equal to the combined GDP of the long standing industrial powers of the North—Canada, France, Germany, Italy, United Kingdom and the United States. This represents a dramatic rebalancing of global economic power' *Human Development Report*, United Nations Development Programme, Summary, 2013, p 2.

five goes hungry every day. Two out of every three lack safe drinking water. Illiteracy and unemployment are rife. A quarter of adult men and half the women of the south are illiterate. One child in six is born underweight. Every year one child in ten dies from waterborne diseases or malnutrition.[35] Women constitute 70 per cent of the world's poor and, in much of the south, they work harder but earn less than men; they are more likely to be undernourished as a consequence of discrimination in the allocation of food.

There are some signs that this situation is improving, although famine, environmental degradation, disease (including the devastation wrought by AIDS), deforestation, natural disasters, and war are almost endemic to the Third World. These problems are aggravated by the displacement of millions of people as a result of war, terrorism, and religious and tribal conflict. Fighting in countries such as Somalia, Sudan, Syria, Iraq, are thought to have spawned more than 50 million refugees, many of whom are housed in squalid camps where disease is often rife. In the face of this agonizing misery and suffering, the futility of academic discourse often appears overwhelming, or worse. Noam Chomsky may be right:

> By entering the arena of argument and counter-argument, of technical feasibility and tactics, of footnotes and citation, by accepting the legitimacy of debate on certain issues, one has already lost one's humanity.[36]

We must hope that he is wrong, and that moral sensibility and rational argument can indeed co-exist. In the face of evil, it is all too easy to descend into tenuous simplification and rhetoric when reflecting upon the proper nature and function of the law.[37] Analytical clarity is especially urgent in times of turmoil when the voice of the demagogue is loudest. Scrupulous jurisprudential consideration of the most fundamental questions of law, justice, and the meaning of legal concepts is essential. Legal theory has a crucial role to play in defining, shaping, and safeguarding the values that underpin our society. These central questions arise in numerous chapters of this book, especially the account of natural law (Chapter 2), the philosophy of Ronald Dworkin (Chapter 5), social theory (Chapter 7), justice (Chapter 9), rights (Chapter 10), critical legal theory (Chapter 13), and feminist and critical race theory (Chapter 14).

---

[35] UNICEF claims that some 30,000 children die daily as a result of poverty. About 28 per cent of all children in developing countries are underweight or stunted. Infectious diseases continue to afflict the lives of the poor. An estimated 40 million people are living with HIV/AIDS. Annually between 350 and 500 million individuals contract malaria, with 1 million dying from the disease. Africa accounts for 90 per cent of malarial deaths and African children account for over 80 per cent of malaria victims internationally. See http://www.globalissues.org/TradeRelated/Facts.asp.

[36] N. Chomsky, *American Power and the New Mandarins* (Harmondsworth: Penguin, 1969), 11, quoted in S Clark, *The Moral Status of Animals* (Oxford: Clarendon Press, 1977), 1.

[37] See the discussion of socio-economic rights in Chapter 10. The recognition and enforcement of such rights have an important, if problematic, role to play in addressing poverty. See David Bilchitz, *Poverty and Fundamental Rights: The Justification and Enforcement of Socio-economic Rights* (Oxford: Oxford University Press, 2008).

# 2
# Natural law and morality

Are same-sex marriages immoral? Why is racism wrong? Should the law permit abortion? Are we exercising proper stewardship of the environment? Moral questions routinely tug at the sleeve of our legal and political practices. Their persistence is perhaps one of the hallmarks of a democratic, or at least an open, society. Nor are such enquiries confined to the armchair of philosophy: the vocabulary of ethics increasingly infuses the language of international relations. To postulate an 'axis of evil' presupposes a normative touchstone by which to judge the behaviour of states that, since the establishment of the United Nations, is partly embodied in an ever-growing cluster of international declarations and conventions. The ubiquity of ethical problems, from the quotidian ('Should I tell him the truth?') to the momentous (a declaration of war on ostensibly moral grounds) has, of course, preoccupied moral philosophers since Aristotle. Indeed, the recent renaissance in natural law theory may represent an acknowledgement that we have, over the centuries, come no closer to resolving these awkward questions.

There are, broadly speaking, two opposing positions. The first is known as 'moral realism', and proposes that certain moral virtues exist independently of our minds or of convention. Natural lawyers and those of a Kantian persuasion generally march under this banner—an approach that will be examined in this chapter.[1] Secondly, there is the sceptical path, most closely associated with utilitarians, such as Bentham, and legal positivists like Kelsen, who deny the existence of any deontological, mind-independent moral values. This position is discussed in 3.2 and 4.3.

The place and function of morals in the law has always been a focal concern of legal and political philosophers, and it is no exaggeration to say that it has become one of the most significant questions, indeed the fundamental question, that animates

---

[1] Ronald Dworkin nicely expresses what he calls 'Kant's principle' as follows: '[I]f the value you find in your life is to be truly objective, it must be the value of humanity itself. You must find the same objective value in the lives of all other persons. You must treat yourself as an end in yourself, and therefore, out of self-respect, you must treat all other people as ends in themselves as well'. Ronald Dworkin, *Justice for Hedgehogs* (Cambridge, Mass and London: The Belknap Press of Harvard University Press, 2011), 265. Dworkin's claim that '[l]aw is effectively integrated with morality', ibid, 414, could just as comfortably be considered in this chapter, but the significance and sweep of his argument, and the extent to which it constitutes an elaborate theory of law and morality, requires that it be considered in its own right in Chapter 5. But bear in mind that, though Dworkin is not, strictly speaking, a natural lawyer, his moral thesis often resembles a secular version thereof.

the debates of today's jurisprudence. The full extent of the disagreements between legal positivists who seek to maintain a sort of conceptual apartheid between law and morals, on the one hand, and those, including natural lawyers, on the other hand, who reject the idea of a law/morals separation, will become a great deal more comprehensible in Chapter 4. At this stage, it suffices to alert you to this crucial dispute that has come to dominate—not always beneficially—contemporary legal theory.

While reading what follows, bear in mind that, along with natural law (which I sketch first below), the views of theorists who regard law as an essentially moral concept, have, in recent years, shrunk to a minority. You may want to ponder why this is the case, and why legal positivism, once denigrated,[2] has become something of a growth industry.[3]

The contrasting approaches of two Cambridge colleagues provide a nice exemplar of the gulf between contemporary jurists. Nigel Simmonds mounts a careful, compelling case in support of the view that '"law" is an intrinsically moral idea, and that inquiry into the nature of law is ultimately a form of moral enquiry...and...that system specific debates about law's content can never wholly be separated from the philosophical inquiry into the nature of law as such.'[4] On the other hand, his colleague, Matthew Kramer, while conceding that law and morality occasionally intersect, robustly defends legal positivism against its detractors.[5] A healthy difference of opinion?

## 2.1 Classical natural law theory

'The best description of natural law', according to one natural lawyer, 'is that it provides a name for the point of intersection between law and morals.'[6] There is an unquestionable tension between what 'is' and what 'ought' to be; theories of natural law attempt to resolve this. Its principal claim, put simply, is that what naturally *is, ought* to be. But this apparently uncomplicated proposition has been widely misunderstood and misinterpreted. An understanding of the essentials of natural law theory is therefore important.[7]

---

[2]  In the early 1980s a professor—newly appointed to a law school abroad—was about to deliver his first lecture in jurisprudence. He was greeted by a horde of rowdy students who refused to allow him to speak. The clamour continued for several minutes. Eventually he managed to impose a modicum of order, and asked why he had attracted such hostility. The students explained that it was because one of their lecturers had described him as a legal positivist. 'But why would anyone think that?' he enquired of a sea of puzzled faces. They did not know. When he explained that, as far as he knew, he was not a legal positivist, the class quickly settled down. The professor was me.

[3]  Its extent should become evident in Chapter 4.

[4]  Nigel Simmonds, *Law as a Moral Idea* (Oxford: Oxford University Press, 2007), 6.

[5]  See, in particular, Matthew H Kramer, *Where Law and Morality Meet* (Oxford: Oxford University Press, 2004) and Matthew H Kramer, *In Defense of Legal Positivism: Law Without Trimmings* (Oxford: Clarendon Press, 1999).

[6]  A Passerin D'Entrèves, *Natural Law* (London: Hutchinson, 1970), 116.

[7]  A useful reader is *Natural Law*, edited (in two volumes) by John Finnis, in the *International Library of Essays in Law and Legal Theory*, published by Dartmouth in 1991. Most accounts of natural law to which you may be referred in your course normally sketch the 'development' of natural law thinking, starting with the

### 2.1.1 **Plato and Aristotle**

Among the Greek philosophers, it is particularly the ideas of Plato and Aristotle whose analyses of ethics are especially significant. For Plato the fundamentals of ethics lay in absolute values that things could emulate. For example, a beautiful object derives its beauty not from itself but from elements of beauty discovered within the object itself. We know beauty (a value) intuitively, although its precise content may be further extended by the application of reason. Another absolute Platonic value is justice which has an inherent connection to law: only laws that pursue the ideal of justice can be considered right. Indeed, according to Plato, justice is a universal value that transcends local customs or conventions.

Aristotle also sought to discover values by the application of reason. Unlike Plato, however, the source of these ideals is to be found in our human nature rather than in external, transcendent values. The natural world, Aristotle argues, contains elements of both stability and change. These conflicting forces are integrated by the concept of '*telos*': the object or purpose to which things inexorably evolve. Humans are no less susceptible to this teleological process. We are social animals and therefore in order to flourish we require family and social groups. But we are also political animals and hence the *polis*—or state—exists in nature. It is our nature to live in a *polis*: it is indispensable to our thriving as human beings. And this has certain consequences for the law which should, amongst other things, further those elements that facilitate social life.

In his *Nicomachean Ethics*, Aristotle suggests that 'justice' describes two different but related ideas: 'general justice' and 'particular justice'. Our actions are generally just when we are wholly virtuous in all matters relating to others. Particular justice, on the other hand, refers specifically to treating others fairly or equitably.

On this foundation, he develops the concept of 'political justice' which is derived partly from nature, and is partly a matter of convention. Natural justice is a thus a species of political justice. It is, in other words, the system of distributive and corrective justice that would be established under the best political community (see Chapter 9).

### 2.1.2 **St Thomas Aquinas**

Aristotle's ethical theory influenced the teachings of the Dominican, St Thomas Aquinas (1225–74), whose principal work *Summa Theologiae* contains the most

Greeks and the Romans, through the religious teachings of St Thomas Aquinas and its secular (and political) adaptation by Grotius, Hobbes, Locke, Rousseau, and Blackstone. The decline of natural law theory in the nineteenth century (and the rise of legal positivism after the attack by Hume) are then described—often to demonstrate that the 'debate' between natural lawyers and legal positivists, while important, is inconclusive. You will then learn of the 'revival' of natural law theory in the twentieth century. You will be expected to exhibit a knowledge of these developments, but too many students merely reel off these historical 'developments' (which they have committed to memory) without demonstrating a real grasp of what questions natural lawyers have sought to answer and explicate.

comprehensive statement of Christian doctrine on the subject. The thirteenth century witnessed the development of European city-states. The Pope's authority over these states was hampered through want of a theological stance in respect of the exercise of secular power. Previously, the foremost Christian thinker of the day, St Augustine, had merely endorsed the Biblical exhortation to 'render…unto Caesar the things which are Caesar's'. But Aquinas deployed Aristotle's philosophy in an effort to reconcile secular and Christian authority. He argued that Christianity was a stage in the development of humanity that was unavailable to the Greeks. The *polis* in which we were destined to live was therefore Christian.

For Aquinas natural law is merely one element of divine providence: it is a 'participation' in the eternal law—the rational plan that orders all creation. In other words, it is the means by which rational beings participate in the eternal law. Secondly, when human beings 'receive' natural law, its content comprises the principles of practical rationality by which human action is to be judged as reasonable or unreasonable. Indeed, for Aquinas it is this characteristic of natural law that justifies its description as 'law', for law, he claims, consists in rules of action declared by one who protects the interests of the community: since God defends and protects the universe, His decision to create rational beings with the capacity to act freely in accordance with reason entitles our regarding these principles as constituting 'law'.

The tenets of natural law are binding on us, Aquinas contends, because—as rational beings—we are guided towards them by nature; they point us toward the good, as well as certain specific goods. Moreover, these principles are known to us by virtue of our nature: we demonstrate this knowledge in our inherent aspiration to achieve the various goods that natural law exhorts us to pursue. We are able to discern the essence of practical knowledge, though the precise practical consequences of that understanding may often be difficult to determine. And, Aquinas acknowledges, our passion or malevolence may obstruct their application.

At the heart of Aquinas's elucidation of natural law is the elementary idea that good be done and evil avoided. Given his theological context of objective moral truth, Aquinas contends that we have a continuing duty to seek the good. We know intuitively what constitutes the good: it includes life, knowledge, procreation, society, and reasonable conduct. For him the good is prior to the right. Whether an act is right is less important than whether it achieves or is some good. We are, he suggests, capable of reasoning from these principles about goods to practical means by which to realize these goods.

But how do we know when an act is fundamentally unsound? There is no simple yardstick; we must scrutinize features of the acts in question, such as their objects, their ends, the circumstances under which they are carried out. For example, Aquinas contends that certain acts may be defective by virtue of their intention: acting against a good, as occurs when one commits a murder, tells a lie, or blasphemes. While he resists stating universal, absolute, eternal principles of right conduct, he does claim that natural law regards it as always wrong to kill the innocent, to lie, blaspheme, or to indulge in adultery and sodomy, and that they are always wrong is a matter of natural law.

The leading (and most accessible) contemporary proponent of natural law, John Finnis (discussed below at 2.6) expresses it as follows in *Natural Law and Natural Rights*: anyone who tries to explain law, makes assumptions, willy-nilly, about what is 'good':

> It is often supposed that an evaluation of law as a type of social institution, if it is to be under-taken at all, must be preceded by a value-free description and analysis of that institution as it exists in fact. But the development of modern jurisprudence suggests, and reflection on the methodology of any social science confirms, that a theorist cannot give a theoretical description and analysis of social facts, unless he also participates in the work of evaluation, of understanding what is really good for human persons, and what is really required by practical reasonableness.[8]

This constitutes an important challenge to the alleged 'objectivity' or scientific methodology of legal positivism. But it also represents an incisive philosophical starting point of the natural law approach. It suggests that when we are discerning what is *good*, we are using our intelligence differently from when we are discerning what *exists*. In other words, if we are to understand the nature and impact of the natural law project, we must recognize that it yields 'a different logic'.[9]

Aquinas distinguishes between four categories of law, as illustrated in Table 2.1. He contends that human posited law draws its power to bind from natural law. His 'definition' of natural law (above) speaks of participation of the eternal law in rational creatures ('*participatio legis aeternae in rationali creatura*'). This proposition is eluci-dated well by Finnis. Aquinas does not mean 'participation' in the normal sense of the word. As Finnis explains:

> For Aquinas, the word *participatio* focally signifies two conjoined concepts, causality and similarity (or imitation). A quality that an entity or state of affairs has or includes is partici-pated, in Aquinas's sense, if that quality is *caused by* a *similar* quality which some other entity or state of affairs has or includes in a more intrinsic or less dependent way. Aquinas's notion of natural law as a participation of the eternal law is no more than a straightforward applica-tion of his general theory of the cause and operation of human understanding in any field or inquiry.[10]

His theory of understanding may be very briefly summarized as follows: Aquinas (following Plato and Aristotle) postulates a 'separate intellect' which causes in us our own power of insight. Humans, as opposed to animals, 'participate' in natu-ral law in this sense: we are able to grasp the essential principles of natural law, that is, human nature's Creator's intelligent and intelligible plan for human flour-ishing. But we grasp it not by any kind of direct knowledge of the divine mind, but rather: 'all those things to which man has a natural inclination, one's reason

---

[8] John Finnis, *Natural Law and Natural Rights*, 2nd edn (Oxford: Oxford University Press, 2011), 3.
[9] Ibid, 34.       [10] Ibid, 399.

**Table 2.1** Aquinas's four categories of law

---

1. *Lex aeterna* (eternal law)
   Divine reason—known only to God. God's plan for the Universe. Man
   needs this law without which he would totally lack direction.

2. *Lex naturalis* (natural law)
   Participation of the eternal law in rational creatures.
   Discoverable by *reason*.

3. *Lex divina* (divine law)
   Revealed in the scriptures (God's positive law for mankind).

4. *Lex humana* (humanly posited law)
   Supported by reason. Enacted for the common good.
   Necessary because the *lex naturalis* cannot solve many day-to-day
   problems. Also, people are selfish; compulsion is required to force
   them to act reasonably.

---

naturally understands as good (and thus as "to be pursued") and their contraries as bad (and as "to be avoided")'.[11]

His analysis of natural law distinguishes between primary and secondary principles; the former may be supplemented by new principles, but not subtracted from. The latter may, in exceptional circumstances, be susceptible to change. But he does not tell us on what *basis* this distinction is drawn: which principles are primary? Nor does he explain how the secondary principles are *derived* from the primary ones.

An important claim routinely linked with Aquinas (and one which, according to Finnis, has been widely misconstrued) is that a 'law' which fails to conform to natural or divine law is not a law at all. This is normally expressed in the maxim '*lex iniusta non est lex*' (an unjust law is not law). It appears that Aquinas himself never made this contention, but merely quoted St Augustine. Certainly Plato, Cicero, and Aristotle expressed similar sentiments, yet it is a proposition that is most closely associated with Aquinas.[12] What Aquinas seems to have said was that laws which conflict with the requirements of natural law lose their power to bind morally. In other words, a government which abuses its authority by enacting laws which are unjust (unreasonable or against the common good) forfeits its right to be obeyed— *because it lacks moral authority*. Aquinas calls any such law a 'corruption of law'. But he does not suggest that one is always justified in *disobeying* it, for though he says that if a ruler enacts unjust laws, 'their subjects are not obliged to obey them', he adds 'except, perhaps, in certain special cases when it is a matter of avoiding "scandal"'

---

[11] *Summa Theologiae*, II/ I, 94, 2.

[12] See Finnis, *Natural Law and Natural Rights*, 363–6, for a powerful refutation not only of the view itself but also the suggestion that Aquinas held it in the naive sense in which many jurisprudence textbooks present it.

(ie a corrupting example to others) or civil disorder.[13] This is a far cry from the radical claims sometimes made in the name of Aquinas which seek to justify disobedience to law. In 2.11 I attempt to show the difficulties and limitations of natural law when invoked in an unjust society.

In his 2011 postscript, Finnis describes as 'loose' the proposition that natural law 'accords to iniquitous rules legal validity'. Natural law, he affirms, 'accepts that iniquitous rules may satisfy the legal system's criteria of legal validity, and where they do, it does not seek to deny that fact, unless the system itself provides a juridical basis for treating these otherwise valid rules as legally invalid (directly or indirectly) of their iniquity.'[14]

It would be illusory to seek or attempt a 'definition' of natural law, but Cicero's Stoic pronouncement in *De Re Publica*[15] contains the three main components of any natural law philosophy:

> True law is right reason in agreement with Nature; it is of universal application, unchanging and everlasting.... It is a sin to try to alter this law, nor is it allowable to attempt to repeal any part of it, and it is impossible to abolish it entirely.... [God] is the author of this law, its promulgator, and its enforcing judge.

This formulation stresses natural law's:

- universality and immutability;
- standing as a 'higher' law; and
- discoverability by reason (it is in this sense 'natural').

Any account of natural law should—at the very least—incorporate these three elements. But note Brian Bix's important observation:

> Contrary to a lay person's expectations, natural law often has little if anything to do with 'law' as that term is conventionally used. The 'law' in natural law theory usually refers to the orders or principles laid down by higher powers that we should follow.[16]

This has not, however, prevented natural law from being deployed in contemporary moral and political argument in respect of a range of issues from world government to oral sex.[17]

As you might expect, there are differences and disagreement concerning its fundamental principles. The classical natural law tradition accentuates the importance of reason. Thus Finnis emphasizes the centrality of reason in answering the question (posed by a conscientious individual, a group, or an official): 'What should I do?' This tradition, according to Finnis,

---

[13] *Summa Theologiae*, I/II, 96, 4.    [14] Finnis, op cit, 476.    [15] Book 3, Ch 22, sect 33.
[16] Brian H Bix, 'Natural Law: The Modern Tradition' in Jules Coleman and Scott Shapiro (eds), *The Oxford Handbook of Jurisprudence and Philosophy of Law* (Oxford: Oxford University Press, 2002), 70–1.
[17] See, eg, Robert George's closely reasoned arguments against 'non-marital orgasmic acts', pornography, abortion, and homosexuality from a natural law standpoint in Robert P George, *In Defense of Natural Law* (Oxford: Oxford University Press, 1999), Parts 2 and 3.

...has a clear understanding that one cannot reasonably affirm the equality of human beings, or the universality and binding force of human rights, unless one acknowledges that there is something about persons which distinguishes them radically from sub-rational creatures, and which, prior to any acknowledgement of 'status', is intrinsic to the factual reality of every human being, adult or immature, healthy or disabled.[18]

## 2.2 Contemporary natural law theory

There is some truth in the observation by Alf Ross (the Scandinavian realist, see 6.3.1) that 'like a harlot, natural law is at the disposal of everyone'.[19] The theory has been employed to justify both revolution and reaction. During the sixth century BC, the Greeks described human laws as owing their importance in the scheme of things to the power of fate which controlled everything. This conservative view could be (and presumably was) used to justify—however evil—features of the status quo. By the fifth century BC, however, it was acknowledged that there might be a conflict between the law of nature and the law of man.

With Aristotle there is less reference to natural law than to the distinction between natural and conventional justice. It was the Stoics who were especially attracted to the notion of natural law where 'natural' meant in accordance with *reason*. The Stoic view informed the approach adopted by the Romans (as expressed by Cicero) who recognized (at least in theory) that laws which did not conform with 'reason' might be regarded as invalid.[20]

It was, however, the Catholic Church that gave expression to the full-blown philosophy of natural law as we understand it today. As early as the fifth century, St Augustine asked, 'What are States without justice, but robber bands enlarged?'[21] In about 1140, Gratian published his *Decretum*, a collection of some 4,000 texts dealing with numerous aspects of church discipline which he sought to reconcile. His work begins by declaring, in keeping with the medieval conception of natural law: 'Mankind is governed by two laws: the law of nature and custom. The law of nature is contained in the scriptures and the gospel.' But he continues, 'Natural law overrides customs and constitutions. That which has been recognised by usage, or recorded in writing, if it contradicts natural law, is void and of no effect.'

As discussed above, the comprehensive account of the tenets of natural law by Aquinas has been most influential.

By the seventeenth century in Europe, the exposition of entire branches of the law (notably public international law) purported to be founded on natural law. Hugo de

---

[18] John Finnis, 'Natural Law: The Classical Tradition' in Coleman and Shapiro (eds), *The Oxford Handbook of Jurisprudence and Philosophy of Law*, 4.

[19] Alf Ross, *On Law and Justice*, transl Margaret Dutton (London: Stevens & Sons, 1958), 261.

[20] An interesting attempt to apply Cicero's conception of natural law to contemporary problems of justice and rights is made by Hadley Arkes in Robert P George (ed), *Natural Law Theory: Contemporary Essays* (Oxford: Oxford University Press, 1992), 245.    [21] *City of God*, Book 4, iv.

Groot (1583–1645), or Grotius as he is generally called, is normally associated with the secularization of natural law. In his influential work *De Jure Belli ac Pacis* he asserts that even if God did not exist (*'etiamsi daremus non esse Deum'*) natural law would have the same content. This proved to be an important basis for the developing discipline of public international law, though exactly what Grotius means when he postulates his *etiamsi daremus* idea is not entirely clear.[22] My own view is that he regarded certain things as 'intrinsically' wrong—whether or not they are decreed by God; for, to use Grotius's own analogy, even God cannot cause two times two not to equal four. In saying this, however, he is not denying the existence of God (as is sometimes suggested); he is stressing that what is right or wrong are matters of natural appropriateness, not of arbitrary divine *fiat*.

In England the high-water mark of natural law was reached in the eighteenth century with Sir William Blackstone's *Commentaries on the Laws of England*. Blackstone (1723–80) commences his great work by adumbrating classical natural law doctrine—in order, it has been argued,[23] to sanctify English law by this appeal to God-given principles. But, while he makes various claims about positive law deriving its authority from natural law and being a nullity should it conflict with it, these assertions do not actually inform Blackstone's analysis of the law itself. It was, of course, this attempt to clothe the positive law with a legitimacy derived from natural law that attracted the criticism (one might even say the wrath) of Bentham who described natural law as, amongst other things, 'a mere work of the fancy'. See 3.2.

## 2.3 Natural law in political philosophy

Aquinas is associated (as pointed out earlier) with a fairly conservative view of natural law. But the principles of natural law have been used to justify revolutions—especially the American and the French—on the ground that the law infringed individuals' *natural rights*. Thus in America the revolution against British colonial rule was based on an appeal to the natural rights of all Americans, in the lofty words of the Declaration of Independence of 1776, to 'life, liberty and the pursuit of happiness'. As the Declaration puts it, 'We hold these truths to be self-evident, that all men are created equal, that they are endowed by their Creator with certain unalienable rights.' Equally stirring sentiments were incorporated in the French *Declaration des droits de l'homme et du citoyen* of 26 August 1789, which speaks of certain 'natural rights' of mankind.

The *political* application of natural law theory is bound up with various 'contractarian' theories which conceive of political rights and obligations in terms of a *social contract*. This 'contract' is not an agreement in a strict legal sense, but contains the idea that only with his consent can a person be subjected to the political power of another.

[22] For differing interpretations contrast D'Entrèves, *Natural Law*, 53–6, and Finnis, *Natural Law and Natural Rights*, 43–4.

[23] See D Kennedy, 'The Structure of Blackstone's *Commentaries*' (1979) 28 *Buffalo Law Review* 205.

It continues to have a hold on contemporary liberal thought, notably in the work of John Rawls (see 9.3).

Some courses in jurisprudence deal only in passing with the thoughts of the leading social contractarians (Hobbes, Locke, and Rousseau) either in the present context or when discussing the revival of such theories in the work of Rawls. These theorists are, of course, not, strictly speaking, jurists, but they have exercised such an important influence on social and political as well as legal theory that you ought—at the very least—to be familiar with the essentials of their respective views. For present purposes it will suffice to give only the briefest outline of each of their analyses of natural law and the social contract. You would, however, be well advised to spend some time reading about these important theorists or, better still, consulting their own works.

### 2.3.1 **Hobbes**

For many students Thomas Hobbes (1588–1679) is summarily identified with his aphorism that life is 'solitary, poor, nasty, brutish and short', though more than one examination candidate has rendered this as 'nasty, *British* and short'. (He actually lived an extraordinarily *long* life and was something of a fitness fanatic!) What he actually said (in his famous work, *Leviathan*) was that this was the condition of man *before the social contract*, that is, in his natural state. Natural law teaches us the need for self-preservation: law and government are required if we are to protect order and security. We therefore need, by the social contract, to surrender our natural freedom in order to create an orderly society. Hobbes, it is now widely thought, adopts a fairly authoritarian philosophy which places order above justice. In particular, his theory (indeed, his self-confessed objective) is to undermine the legitimacy of revolutions against (even malevolent) government.

For Hobbes every act we perform, though ostensibly kind or altruistic, is actually self-serving. Thus when I give a donation to charity, it is in fact a means of enjoying my power. In his view any account of human action, including morality, must acknowledge our essential selfishness. In *Leviathan* (a book that Oxford University burnt as a seditious tract!) he wonders how we might behave in a state of nature, before the formation of any government. He recognizes that we are essentially equal, mentally and physically: even the weakest has the strength to kill the strongest. This equality, he suggests, generates disagreement. And we tend to quarrel, he argues, for three main reasons: competition (for limited supplies of material possessions), distrust, and glory (we remain hostile in order to preserve our powerful reputations). As a consequence of our propensity toward disagreement, Hobbes concludes in Chapter XIII that we are in a natural state of perpetual war of all against all, where no morality exists, and all live in constant fear:

> In such condition, there is no place for industry, because the fruit thereof is uncertain; and consequently no culture of the earth, no navigation, nor use of the commodities that may be imported by sea; no commodious building, no instruments of moving and removing such things as require much force; no knowledge of the face of the earth, no account of time, no

arts, no letters, no society; and which is worst of all, continual fear and danger of violent death; and the life of people, solitary, poor, nasty, brutish, and short.

Until this state of war ceases, everyone has a right to everything, including another person's life. Hobbes argues that from human self-interest and social agreement alone, one can derive the same kinds of laws which natural lawyers regard as immutably fixed in nature. He re-defines traditional moral terms (such as right, duty, liberty, and justice) so as to reflect his account of self-interest and the social contract. In order to escape the horror of the state of nature, Hobbes concludes in Chapter XIV that peace is the first law of nature:

> That every person ought to endeavour peace as far as he has hope of obtaining it; and when he cannot obtain it, that he may seek and use all helps and advantages of war; the first branch of which rule contains the first and fundamental Law of Nature, which is, To seek peace and follow it; the second, the sum of the right of nature, which is, By all means we can, to defend ourselves.

The second law of nature is that we mutually divest ourselves of certain rights (such as the right to take another person's life) so as to achieve peace. This mutual transferring of rights is a contract and is the basis of moral duty. I undertake to forfeit my right to steal your property in return for a similar promise from you. In this way we transfer these rights to each other and hence fall under a duty not to steal from each other. For purely selfish reasons we mutually transfer these and other rights, for this will terminate the state of war between us. Such contracts, he concedes, are not generally binding, for, if I live in fear that you will breach your side of the bargain, no genuine agreement exists.

When we covenant mutually to obey a common authority, we establish 'sovereignty by institution'. When threatened by a conqueror, and covenant for protection by undertaking to obey, we establish 'sovereignty by acquisition'. Both are, he points out, legitimate methods by which to institute sovereignty; they share the same rationale—fear—either of one's fellow man or of a conqueror. Political legitimacy turns not on how a government achieves power, but its capacity to protect effectively those who have consented to obey it. In other words, political obligation ceases when this protection terminates.

Hobbes derives his laws of nature deductively: from a set of general principles, more specific principles are logically derived. His general principles are:

- that people pursue only their own self-interest;
- the equality of people;
- the causes of quarrel;
- the natural condition of war;
- the motivations for peace.

From these five principles he derives the two laws mentioned above, as well as several others. He is under no illusion that merely concluding agreements can secure peace. Such agreements need to be honoured. This is Hobbes's third law of nature.

He acknowledges too that since we are selfish we are likely, out of self-interest, to breach contracts. I may break my agreement not to steal from you when I think I can evade detection. And you know this. The only certain means of avoiding this break-down in our mutual obligations, he argues, is to grant unlimited power to a political sovereign to punish us if we violate our contracts. And, again, it is purely selfish reasons (ending the state of nature) that motivate us to agree to the establishment of an authority with the power of sanction. But he insists that only when such a sovereign exists can we arrive at any objective determination of right and wrong.

Hobbes supplements his first three laws of nature with several other substantive ones such as the fourth law (to show gratitude toward those who comply with contracts). He concludes that morality consists entirely of these Laws of Nature which are arrived at through the social contract. This is, as you will have noticed, a rather different rendition of natural rights from that espoused by classical natural law. His account might be styled a modern view of natural rights, one that is premised on the basic, the mundane right of every person to preserve his own life: a free-market version of natural rights, one that may have a message for us in our turbulent world.

### 2.3.2 Locke

A different position is adopted by John Locke (1632–1704) who argued that far from being the nightmare portrayed by Hobbes, life before the social contract was almost total bliss! One major defect, however, was that in this state of nature property was inadequately protected. For Locke, therefore (especially in *Two Treatises of Civil Government*), it was in order to rectify this flaw in an otherwise idyllic natural state that man forfeited, under a social contract, some of his freedom. Strongly reminiscent of Aquinas's central postulates, Locke's theory rests on an account of man's rights and obligations under God. It is a fairly complex attempt to explain the operation of the social contract and its terms, but be sure to have, at least, a grasp of two important precepts in Locke's theory.

First, its *revolutionary* nature: when a government is unjust or authoritarian, Locke acknowledges the right of 'oppressed people' to 'resist tyranny' and overthrow the government: 'a tyrant has no authority'. Secondly, he attaches considerable importance to man's right to *property*: God owns the earth and has given it to us to enjoy; there can therefore be no right of property. But by mixing his labour with material objects, the labourer acquires the right to the thing he has created. This view exercised an important influence on the framers of the American Constitution with its emphasis upon the protection of property. Locke has thus at once been hailed as the source of the idea of private ownership and vilified as the progenitor of modern capitalism. For Locke, the state exists to preserve the natural rights of its citizens. When governments fail in this task, citizens have the right—and sometimes even the duty—to withdraw their support and even to rebel.

Though strongly influenced by Hobbes, he rejected his view that the original state of nature was 'nasty, brutish, and short', and that individuals through a social contract surrendered—for their self-preservation—their rights to a supreme sovereign who was the source of all morality and law. The social contract, in his view, preserved the natural rights to life, liberty, and property, and the enjoyment of private rights: the pursuit of happiness engendered, in civil society, the common good.

Whereas for Hobbes natural rights are logically prior and natural law is derived from them, Locke derives natural rights from natural law, that is from reason. While Hobbes discerns a natural right of every person to every thing, Locke's natural right to freedom is circumscribed by the law of nature and its injunction that we should not harm each other in 'life, health, liberty, or possessions'.

Locke espoused a limited form of government: the checks and balances among branches of government and the genuine representation in the legislature would, in his view, minimize government and maximize individual liberties.

### 2.3.3 Rousseau

Natural law plays less of a central role than does the social contract in the works of Jean-Jacques Rousseau (1712–78). More metaphysical than either Hobbes or Locke, Rousseau's conception of the social contract (in *Social Contract, Or Principles of Political Right*) inspired the ideological fervour that led to the French Revolution and rests on the idea that it represents an agreement between the individual and the community by which he becomes part of what Rousseau calls the 'general will'. He contends that as an individual, the subject may be selfish and decide that his personal interest should override the collective interest. But, as part of a community, the individual subject disregards his egotism to create this 'general will'—which is popular sovereignty. It determines what is good for society as a whole. The social contract is encapsulated in the following terms: 'Each of us puts his person and all his power in common under the supreme direction of the general will; and in a body we receive each member as an indivisible part of the whole.'

His concept of the general will is coupled with his notion of sovereignty which, in his view, is not merely legitimate political power, but its exercise in pursuit of the public good, and hence the general will unfailingly promotes the interests of the people. Its object, however, is 'general' in the sense that it can establish rules, social classes, or even a monarchy, but it can never specify the individuals who are subject to the rules, members of the classes, or the rulers. To do so would undermine Rousseau's central idea that the general will addresses the good of the society as a whole rather than an assembly of individual wills that place their own desires, or those of particular factions, above the needs of the people at large. Indeed, he distinguishes between the general will and the collection of individual wills:

> There is often a great deal of difference between the will of all and the general will. The latter looks only to the common interest; the former considers private interest and is only a sum of private wills. But take away from these same wills the pluses and minuses that cancel each other out, and the remaining sum of the differences is the general will.[24]

---

[24] *Social Contract*, Vol IV, p 146. Does this sound a little like Rawls's 'original position'? See 9.3.3.

Thus Rousseau's—notorious—proposition that man must 'be forced to be free' should be interpreted to mean that individuals surrender their free will to create popular sovereignty. Moreover, as the indivisible and inalienable 'general will' decides what is best for the community, should an individual descend into selfishness, he must be compelled to fall in line with the dictates of the community.

There are, in Rousseau's theory, certain natural rights that cannot be removed, but, by investing the 'general will' with total legislative authority, the law could infringe upon these rights. As long as government represents the 'general will' it may do almost anything. Rousseau, while committed to participatory democracy, is also willing to invest the legislature with virtually untrammelled power by virtue of its reflecting the 'general will'. It has become trite to remark that he is therefore a paradox: a democrat and yet a totalitarian. But since, in Rousseau's view, the general will is a foolproof touchstone, it intervenes only when it would be in the interests of society as a whole. It is therefore arguable that his apparently authoritarian position is tempered by the importance he attaches to equality and individual freedom.

Legitimate interference by the sovereign might thus be interpreted as required only in order to advance freedom and equality, not to diminish them. The delicate equilibrium between the absolute power of the state and the rights of individuals rests on a social contract that protects society against sectional and class interests.

## 2.4 The decline of natural law theory

Broadly speaking, two principal developments contributed to this decline. First, the rise of legal positivism (discussed in 3.1), and secondly, non-cognitivism in ethics (see below).

Chapter 3 will consider the assault on natural law led, in particular, by Bentham who was scathingly dismissive of Blackstone's espousal of natural law. For Bentham the assertion that human law derives its validity from natural law was a means of fending off the sort of criticism of the law that he so skilfully made. Yet even Blackstone was unable to provide an actual *instance* of the law of England being regarded as invalid because it conflicted with natural law. It is sometimes thought, therefore, that Bentham was attacking a paper tiger. Moreover, the reply of natural lawyers (and not merely natural lawyers: see 2.6) is that when we make a statement about the law we are normally also making a statement about morality. The question of what is the law is inextricably bound up with moral considerations. As Finnis puts it:

> The tradition of natural law theorising is not concerned to minimise the range and determinacy of positive law or the general sufficiency of positive sources as solvents of legal problems. Rather, the concern of the tradition…has been to show that the act of 'positing' law (whether judicially or legislatively or otherwise) is an act which can and should be guided by 'moral' principles and rules; that those moral norms are a matter of objective reasonableness, not of whim, convention, or mere 'decision'.[25]

[25] See Finnis, *Natural Law and Natural Rights*, 290.

The second development generally associated with the decline of natural law is the proposition that in moral reasoning there can be no rational solutions: we cannot *objectively* know what is right or wrong (non-cognitivism in ethics). It was David Hume (1711–76) who, in his *Treatise of Human Nature*, first remarked that moralists seek to derive an *ought* from an *is*: we cannot conclude that the law should assume a particular form merely because a certain state of affairs exists in nature. Thus the following syllogism, according to this argument, is *invalid*:

- All animals procreate (major premise).
- Human beings are animals (minor premise).
- Therefore humans *ought* to procreate (conclusion).

Facts about the world or human nature cannot be used to determine what *ought* to be done or not done.

Finnis agrees with Hume that arguments of the above type are invalid. He refutes the claim that classical natural law theory (as expounded by Aristotle and Aquinas) ever sought to derive an 'ought' from an 'is' in this way.[26]

## 2.5  The revival of natural law theory

A number of factors have contributed to a reawakening of natural law theory in the twentieth century. Without providing a comprehensive account of this development here, the following six factors (in no particular order) seem to constitute the major landmarks in this evolution:

- The post-war recognition of human rights and their expression in declarations such as the Charter of the United Nations, the Universal Declaration of Human Rights, the European Convention on Human Rights, and the Declaration of Delhi on the Rule of Law of 1959. Natural law is conceived of, not as a 'higher law' in the constitutional sense of invalidating ordinary law, but as a *yardstick* against which to measure positive law. Thus the Universal Declaration of Human Rights speaks of its terms merely as a 'common standard of achievement' (or, in the French text, a 'common ideal to be achieved').

- The impact of the Nuremberg war trials which established the principle that certain acts constituted 'crimes against humanity' regardless of the fact that they did not offend against specific provisions of the positive law. The judges in these trials did not appeal explicitly to natural law theory, but their judgments represent an important recognition of the principle that the law is not necessarily the sole determinant of what is right.

---

[26] Ibid, 33–42, for a defence of this position.

- The neo-Kantianism of Rudolf Stammler (1856–1938) and Giorgio Del Vecchio (1878–1970). Stammler developed the idea of natural law 'with a variable content' (its principles are relativistic and evolving)—a formal construct with no particular content. Del Vecchio's theory approximated to classical natural law 'in placing the autonomy of the individual in the centre of his theory of justice; the maximising of the human being's capacity for free development, and the protection of the rights which naturally belonged to him because entailed by this end, was the main business of the state; the state, indeed, had no title to, activity incompatible with this purpose, which was its only justification for existence; and he described a state which acted contrary to justice in this sense as a "delinquent state".'[27] Gustav Radbruch (1878–1949) was, until the horrors of the Nazi regime, a legal positivist. He had been briefly Minister for Justice under the Weimar Republic, and a draftsman of the Basic Law of the new German Federal Republic. In 1947 he condemned legal positivism for its failure to prevent the evils of Nazism and advanced the contention that 'the idea of law can be nothing but the achievement of justice . . . [which] like virtue, truth and beauty is an absolute value'.[28]

- The neo-Thomism now best known to English-speaking lawyers in the works of John Finnis (see 2.6).

- The development of constitutional safeguards for human or civil rights in various jurisdictions (eg, the American Bill of Rights and its interpretation by the United States Supreme Court, especially the Warren Court in the 1950s; and the West German Basic Law).

---

[27] JM Kelly, *A Short History of Western Legal Theory* (Oxford: Clarendon Press, 1992), 378.

[28] The approach adopted by Radbruch is discussed by Professors Hart and Fuller in (1958) 71 *Harvard Law Review* 593 and 630 respectively—the so-called Hart–Fuller debate. See 2.10.2. For a useful analysis of Radbruch's thoughts see B v D van Niekerk, 'The Warning Voice from Heidelberg: The Life and Thought of Gustav Radbruch' (1973) 90 *South African Law Journal* 234. These jurists were neo-Kantian in the sense that they developed, in different ways, theories of law as 'justice' which envisaged the historical realization of a community of rational, autonomous agents. For an interesting (if rather impenetrable) analysis of Radbruch's position, and a complex theory that argues, in part, that law has two dimensions, ideal and real that require elucidation by a conceptual analysis that distinguishes between the observer's and the participant's perspective, see the works of Robert Alexy. He champions a 'non-positivist' theory of law that is 'inclusive' in the sense that it classifies *some* unjust laws as laws, but not all (and is thus not 'super-inclusive'). Alexy repudiates the 'exclusive non-positivism' that treats every injustice in the law as denying its legal validity. See, especially, Robert Alexy, *The Argument from Injustice: A Reply to Legal Positivism*, transl Stanley Paulson and Bonnie L Paulson (Oxford: Oxford University Press, 2002); *A Theory of Legal Argumentation*, transl Neil MacCormick (Oxford: Oxford University Press 1989); *A Theory of Constitutional Rights*, transl Julian Rivers (Oxford: Oxford University Press, 2002); 'Some Reflections on the Ideal Dimension of Law and on the Legal Philosophy of John Finnis' (2013) 58 *American Journal of Jurisprudence* (2013) 97. Cf John Finnis, 'Law as Fact and as a Reason for Action: A Response to Robert Alexy on Law's "Ideal Dimension"' (2014) 59 *American Journal of Jurisprudence* 85. On the application of these questions to the unjust legal system of apartheid South Africa see Raymond Wacks, 'Judges and Injustice' (1984) 101 *South African Law Journal* 266. Cf J Dugard, 'Should Judges Resign?—A Reply to Professor Wacks' (1984) 101 *South African Law Journal* 286, and the other essays mentioned in 'further

- The natural law theory of Lon Fuller (see 2.6),[29] and Hart's 'minimum content of natural law'.[30] (See 4.2.1.1.)

## 2.6 John Finnis

Though he disclaims originality, and describes his book as 'introductory', Finnis's *Natural Law and Natural Rights* constitutes a major restatement of classical natural law theory. It is groundbreaking in its application of the methodology of analytical jurisprudence to a body of doctrine usually considered to be its polar opposite. There is no substitute for reading the original (though parts of the book are heavy going). A second edition appeared in 2011 with a 'postscript' in which the author (who modestly identifies a number of 'serious weaknesses' in the book) defends or elaborates upon several elements in his original text of three decades ago.[31]

The overarching purpose of the book is to continue the project begun by Plato, Aristotle, and Aquinas to consider and evaluate human choices, actions, institutions, and well-being. But students frequently tend to neglect this philosophical rationale of the undertaking and simply digest and regurgitate Finnis's seven 'basic forms of human flourishing' and his nine 'basic requirements of practical reasonableness'. This is plainly inadequate. It is essential that you grasp the *purpose* of the natural law enterprise. What is the point of the theory? In Finnis's words:

> A theory of natural law need not be undertaken primarily for the purpose of… providing a justified conceptual framework for descriptive social science. It may be undertaken, as this book is, primarily to assist the practical reflections of those concerned to act, whether as judges, or as statesmen, or as citizens.[32]

In particular, *Natural Law and Natural Rights* represents a rejection of Hume's conception of practical reason which holds that every reason for action is merely ancillary to our *desire* to attain a certain objective. Reason merely informs us how best to achieve our desires; it cannot tell us *what* we *ought* to desire. Instead, Finnis adopts an Aristotelian starting point: *what constitutes a worthwhile, valuable, desirable life?* This is his inventory of the seven 'basic forms of good':

---

reading' at the end of this chapter. On the dilemmas faced by judges in such a legal order, see the case study in 2.11.

[29] See LL Fuller, *The Morality of Law*, especially Ch 3, and (1958) 71 *Harvard Law Review* 630.

[30] See HLA Hart, *The Concept of Law*, 2nd edn by PA Bulloch and J Raz (Oxford: Clarendon Press, 1994), Ch 9, and (1958) 71 *Harvard Law Review* 593.

[31] The postscript constitutes an important clarification of the author's interpretation and development of the natural law tradition. It does not, however, make for easy reading; there are numerous references to the large body of writing— principally articles and essays—that Finnis has published since 1980. Few students will have the time, skill, or energy to read them—even though Oxford University Press has recently published five volumes of his collected essays.

[32] Finnis, op cit, 18. And, presumably, simply as ordinary human beings. See Ronald Dworkin's notion of living well and having a good life, discussed in Chapter 5. Do Finnis and Dworkin share a common idea here?

1. Life. The drive for self-preservation we all have, it includes health and the pro-creation of children.

2. Knowledge. It is a good in itself to be well-informed rather than ignorant or muddled.

3. Play. Recreation, enjoyment, fun.

4. Aesthetic experience. An appreciation of beauty in art or nature.

5. Sociability (friendship). Acting in the interests of one's friends.

6. Practical reasonableness. Employing one's intelligence to solve problems of deciding what to do, how to live, and shaping one's character.

7. 'Religion'. Our concern about an order of things that transcends our individual interests.

It is an attempt to answer Aristotle's question. And it is combined with his nine 'basic requirements of practical reasonableness':

1. The good of practical reasonableness structures the pursuit of goods. It shapes one's participation in the other basic goods, by guiding one's selection of projects, one's commitments, and what one does in order to carry them out.

2. A coherent plan of life. One ought to have a harmonious set of purposes as effective commitments.

3. No arbitrary preference among values. One ought not to omit or unreasonably exclude or exaggerate any of the basic human values.

4. No arbitrary preference among persons. One should maintain impartiality in regard to others and their interests.

5. Detachment and commitment. One should be both open-minded and committed to one's projects.

6. The (limited) relevance of consequences: efficiency within reason. One must not squander opportunities through inefficiency; actions should be reasonably efficient.

7. Respect for every basic value in every act. One should avoid acts that achieve nothing but damage or impede one or more of the basic forms of human good.

8. The requirements of the common good. One should act to advance the interests of one's community.

9. Following one's conscience. One should not do what one feels should not be done.

Together these constitute the universal and immutable 'principles of natural law'.

Finnis argues that this approach accords with the general conception of natural law espoused by Thomas Aquinas. It does not, he claims, fall foul of the non-cognitivist strictures of Hume (see above) for these objective goods are *self-evident*; they are not deduced from a description of human nature. So, for example, 'knowledge' is self-evidently preferable to ignorance. And even if one were to seek to deny this (how often is one tempted to assert that 'ignorance is bliss'?), it could only be done by accepting that one's argument is a useful one; one is therefore accepting that knowledge is indeed good! You thus apparently fall into the trap of self-refutation.

Some critics have, however, responded that in arguing against the proposition that knowledge is an objective good you could be accepting that knowledge is valuable when put to a certain *use* (ie instrumentally), but that when it consists in the acquisition of useless information it is not necessarily an objective good.[33]

Each of these principles is identified by Finnis in order to pursue the 'lines of thought about human choices, action, institutions, and well-being that were carried forward from Plato by Aristotle and Aquinas.'[34]

So, for example, the basic good of 'life' includes health, freedom from pain, and perhaps the 'transmission of life by procreation of children'.[35] In his 2011 postscript, Finnis adds to this basic good, the institution of marriage—'the committed union of man and woman with a commitment to expressing the good of marriage itself as both friendship and procreative.'[36] 'Religion' is tied to the notion that, whether or not we believe in God, we acknowledge that each of us is 'responsible'—ie obliged to act with freedom and authenticity—to choose what we are to be.

Do not simply swallow Finnis's assumptions unthinkingly. You will gain considerably more from a critical reading of his analysis (of which I have provided only the barest of bones) than from committing to memory his seven basic goods plus nine basic requirements of practical reasonableness as if it were a mathematical formula. Many students have found, for instance, Finnis's model of the family to be idealized, his politics too conservative, and his basic goods too restrictive (doesn't the common good require, for example, the right to work?). Finnis has conceded, in later writings, that his third basic good should have been: skilful performance in *work* or play. But do not lose sight of his general project.

The quotation from Finnis below illustrates his purpose: to understand 'what is really good for human persons'. For Finnis, before we can pursue human goods we require a *community*. This explains his view (mentioned earlier) that unjust laws are not simply nullities, but—because they militate against the common good—lose their direct moral authority to bind. Similarly, it is by an appeal to the common good that Finnis develops his conception of justice. For him, principles of justice are no more than the implications of the general requirement that one ought to foster the common good in one's community. The basic goods and methodological requirements are clear enough to prevent most forms of injustice; they give rise to several absolute obligations with correlative absolute natural rights:

[33] See NE Simmonds, *Central Issues in Jurisprudence*, 4th edn (London: Sweet & Maxwell, 2013), 118.
[34] Finnis, op cit, 425. Finnis contends that Aquinas's contribution has been misunderstood, thereby rendering the natural law tradition 'needlessly vulnerable and enfeebled in its response, to the crude attacks of Hobbes, Locke, and Hume, attacks to which Kant responded quite inadequately and Bentham by compounding their errors', 425. Both quotations appear in the 2011 postscript.          [35] Finnis, op cit, 87.
[36] Finnis, op cit, 447.

There is, I think, no alternative but to hold in one's mind's eye some pattern, or range of patterns, of human character, conduct, and interaction in community, and then to choose such specification of rights as tends to favour the pattern, or range of patterns. In other words, *one needs some conception of human good, of individual flourishing in a form (or range of forms) of communal life that fosters rather than hinders such flourishing.* One attends not merely to character types desirable in the abstract or in isolation, but also to the quality of interaction among persons; and one should not seek to realise some patterned 'end-state' imagined in abstraction from the processes of individual initiative and interaction, processes which are integral to human good and which make the future, let alone its evaluation, incalculable.[37]

This important passage encapsulates much of the essence of Finnis's conception of natural rights, including the rights not to be tortured, not to have one's life taken as a means to any further end, not to be lied to, not to be condemned on knowingly false charges, not to be deprived of one's capacity to procreate, and the right 'to be taken into respectful consideration in any assessment of what the common good requires'.[38]

Remember that a crucial element in Finnis's explanation of natural law is his insistence that its first principles are (contrary to the widely held view) *not* deductively inferred from facts, speculative principles, metaphysical propositions about human nature or about the nature of good and evil, or from a teleological conception of nature. *They are not derived from anything; they are underived.* Aquinas, according to Finnis, makes it clear that each of us 'by experiencing one's nature, so to speak, from the inside' grasps 'by a simple act of non-inferential understanding' that 'the object of the inclination which one experiences is an instance of a general form of good, for oneself (and others like one)'.[39] For Aquinas, to discover what is morally right is to ask, not what is in accordance with human nature, *but what is reasonable.*

This restatement of classical natural law theory has been (and will continue to be) considerably influential. Finnis brings his scholarship to bear on a subject that has for too long been surrounded in mystery and generality. Nevertheless, there have, inevitably, been a number of criticisms made of Finnis's views. Some have claimed that his interpretation of Thomist philosophy is mistaken; he has replied, and the argument continues. More importantly, there is a question mark that, for some critics, hangs over Finnis's account of *law.* Thus for Lloyd:

Finnis is a social theorist who wants to use law to improve society. His arguments for law thus, not surprisingly, centre on its instrumental value. The focal meaning of law concentrates on what it achieves, not what it is. As a result of this orientation we are left with the suspicion that Finnis gives us no substantial reason why social ordering through law is the most appropriate way of organising political life, that it has, in other words, the greatest moral value.[40]

I am not sure that this is a fair criticism, but it would be a provocative quotation as a seminar or examination question.

---

[37] Ibid, 219–20, emphasis added.     [38] At 225.     [39] At 34.
[40] *Lloyd's Introduction to Jurisprudence*, 8th edn (London: Sweet & Maxwell, 2008), 132.

## 2.7 Hard and soft natural law?

Contemporary natural law theory has achieved a level of sophistication to rival the controversies and complexities that currently bedevil modern legal positivism. See 4.5. For a taste of this refined fare, have a look at Robert P George's defence of the brand of natural law espoused by Finnis, Grisez, and their disciples.[41] Most of the debate within natural law itself appears to focus on the extent to which the Grisez–Finnis slant constitutes 'real' natural law mainly because some of its fundamental propositions are far from self-evident, and, secondly, because it is not based on factual statements about human nature.

I suppose one could fairly describe the Aquinian, Grisez–Finnis approach as 'soft' natural law, and those who regard their stance as inadequately grounded in strict Aquinian doctrine, as 'hard' natural lawyers.

Legal positivists, of course, take issue with natural lawyers at a fundamental level (and their case is considered in the next three chapters of this book), but there are non-positivist arguments against natural law on what might be called philosophical grounds. So, for instance, Jeffrey Goldsworthy is among several philosophers who deny the existence of objective moral values altogether. This non-cognitivist claim is based on the impossibility of genuinely rational, as opposed to merely emotional, motivation. Why? Because all human action includes emotional motivation.[42] This attack is overcome by those, like Michael Moore (see 2.8) to whom, the objectivity of morality is neither 'queer' nor untrue. Robert George defends this patch robustly:

> [O]ften our rational grasp of the intelligible point of certain possible actions (e.g., the exercise of our intellectual powers in an effort to understand whether morality is truly objective or necessarily merely subjective) is what stimulates the emotional support that is admittedly necessary for us to perform the actions....[O]bjective values are no less 'queer' than many other non-material phenomena whose existence we all recognise (e.g., meaning, consciousness, causation), and that it is, in fact, cognitivism, rather than non-cognitivism, which best explains people's own understanding of the evaluative practices they engage in when they conclude, for example, that gratuitous cruelty is wrong.[43]

Finnis's plea of innocence to the charge that natural law seeks to derive an 'ought' from an 'is' has already been mentioned. But some critics allege that this is precisely what classical natural law did: drawing on certain ontological features of human nature in order to obtain moral precepts. In other words, this assault, articulated, for example, by Weinreb,[44] is premised on the view that Grisez, Finnis, Boyle, and other 'neo-scholastics' (or what I have called 'soft' natural lawyers) misinterpret Aquinas.

---

[41]  Robert P George, *In Defense of Natural Law* (Oxford: Oxford University Press, 1999).

[42]  Jeffrey Goldsworthy, 'Fact and Value in the New Natural Law Theory' (1996) 41 *American Journal of Jurisprudence* 1.

[43]  Robert George, *In Defense of Natural Law*, 2. See too MC Murphy, *Natural Law in Jurisprudence and Politics* (New York: Cambridge University Press, 2006).

[44]  Lloyd L Weinreb, *Natural Law and Justice* (Cambridge, Mass: Harvard University Press, 1987).

In particular, Weinreb rejects the proposition that moral truths are 'self-evident' and argues that Finnis confuses his personal ethical convictions with self-evidence.

Hittinger[45] attacks the Grisez–Finnis account of natural law on similar grounds, arguing that by severing the classical natural law connection with human nature (and so deriving a normative 'ought' from a factual 'is'), the 'soft' natural lawyers effectively adopt a Kantian deontological view of morals that dispenses with the philosophy of nature.

In short, therefore, the charge is that their morality is no longer derived from nature. This is a grave indictment against which 'soft' natural lawyers present a powerful and exhaustive defence. Robert George's long essay, 'Recent Criticism of Natural Law Theory' (itself not so recent), is rather heavy going, but expounds a sustained argument against these assaults that will illuminate many of the questions that animate this debate.[46]

## 2.8 Moral realism

Is objectivity possible in morals? As already mentioned, many dispute this central principle of natural law. Its advocates maintain, however, that moral properties are indeed 'real' in the sense that they are not merely illusory, not simply reducible to the subjective affective experiences of individuals—as its detractors claim. For these sceptics, morality is simply a matter of personal preference and subjective taste. They cannot, it is argued, be demonstrated to be true or false. If this is so, it would gravely weaken the natural law position. And what of the law? If a convincing case can be made for moral objectivity, does this have any bearing on legal judgment?

Among the leading champions of secular moral realism is Michael Moore (the philosopher, not the subversive *enfant terrible* director and fashionable *auteur*). In his prolific writing on this subject, Moore constructs a sturdy moral realist fortress, and with considerable agility defends it against the assorted invaders at the gate. Among these are subjectivists, relativists, hard-nosed empiricists, and other miscellaneous sceptics.[47] His careful justification of moral realism affords, at the same time, a useful means of understanding the nature of moral scepticism.

Moore identifies no less than eight sceptical arguments advanced by those who contest the objectivity of value judgments. Only the following four arguments disturb his battlements—but not excessively.

---

[45] Russell Hittinger, *A Critique of the New Natural Law* (Notre Dame, Ind: University of Notre Dame Press, 1987).

[46] Robert P George, 'Recent Criticism of Natural Law Theory' (1988) 55 *University of Chicago Law Review* 1371.

[47] Several of Moore's articles on this subject were published in 2004 in an anthology entitled *Objectivity in Ethics and Law*. I draw here on my review of this work in (2004) 33 *Hong Kong Law Journal* 429. See too Michael Moore, 'Law as a Functional Kind' in R George (ed), *Natural Law Theories* (Oxford: Oxford University Press, 1992).

- *The argument from logic.* This is the claim that there are no logically compelling reasons to value anything. Thus the non-cognitivist theories of ethics adopted by logical positivists like AJ Ayer, assert that value judgments are not really judgments at all; they express merely emotion. A less extreme version of this argument is the proposition that there exist no self-evident first principles of morality from which all else may be derived.

- *The argument from meaning.* This is the belief that moral reality cannot exist because ethical words have no descriptive function. This position includes subjectivism (ethical statements express only an individual's subjective state of mind) and conventionalism (ethical statements express only a particular group's state of mind). Moore is disinclined to take either seriously. He does, however, regard emotivism/prescriptivism as a minor nuisance. This argument claims that the meaning of an ethical judgment is discovered when we know the typical 'job' that the expression is used to carry out. These 'jobs' include *expressing* but not *describing* the speaker's feelings toward a person or act. When you punch me and I cry, 'Ouch!' this exclamation does not describe my pain, it expresses it. The same is true, the emotivist/prescriptivist argument goes, when I describe David as a 'good' person, and Victoria as a 'bad' one.

- *The ontological argument that moral properties do not exist.* So, for example, JL Mackie's celebrated 'argument from queerness' rests largely on the empiricist claim that we don't *need* 'queer' entities of this kind, so why invent them?[48] They resemble what Oliver Wendell Holmes memorably called a 'brooding omnipresence in the sky' (see 6.2.1).

- *The argument from vagueness.* This form of scepticism concedes that there could be general moral truths (such as Kant's imperative to use others as ends, never means), but denies that they assist in resolving actual moral dilemmas. The American realist impatience with nebulous theory is a paradigm of this species of scepticism. See 6.1.

Each of these marauders is given short shrift by Moore.[49] In addressing the central problem of the relationship between law and morality, he develops his own account of natural law. He sets out the truth conditions of legal judgments which, he insists, are not exhausted by the truth conditions of certain moral judgments. He reasons that non-moral facts enter into the truth conditions of legal judgments; this explains why legal judgments might not be objective in the way moral judgments are. There

---

[48] JL Mackie, *Ethics: Inventing Right and Wrong* (Harmondsworth: Penguin, 1977, reprinted 1990).

[49] 'Moral Reality' (Ch 1 of *Objectivity in Ethics and Law*, originally published in (1982) *Wisconsin Law Review* 1061) contains a powerful assault on these detractors. He returns to the fray in 'Moral Reality Revisited' (published ten years later), Ch 2 of *Objectivity in Ethics and Law*, originally published in (1992) 90 *Michigan Law Review* 2424, but with a greater emphasis on the content and consequences of natural law. His adversaries here include judges (Bork, Burger, and Posner) as well as constitutional theorist, John Hart Ely, and an assembly of other legal theorists (including Schauer, Bix, Waldron, Rawls, Mackie, and Harman). The article is rather turgid, with more than 100 pages of dense argument. But it is a virtuoso piece of philosophical discourse—even if you find yourself unable to share his view of moral objectivity.

is, however, a close relationship between them, and, in pursuit of their objectivity, he applies the same tests for both. In other words, he enquires whether legal judgments are true in the sense that they correspond to certain kinds of facts that exist in the world—independently of whether we believe them to exist. And he concludes that the objectivity of legal judgments is, in part, attributable to the objectivity of moral judgments.

Rejecting the functional (or teleological) tradition of natural law that he discerns in the approaches of Fuller and Dworkin, Moore argues that they are too procedural to guarantee substantive justice in systems that comply with them.[50]

He contends also that historical, institutional, and semantic facts do not suffice to render legal judgments objective. His thesis is that it is because moral facts are partly constitutive of legal judgments that the latter can be objective. In other words, moral objectivity is a *requirement* of legal objectivity.[51]

What makes legal propositions true? Moore identifies no less than six possible candidates for 'legal truth makers'.[52] These include the 'ostrich position' (for its refusal to examine the ontological question), and the metaphysically realist view about what Moore labels 'legal kinds' (a mélange of historical semantic, causal, and moral facts). The argument here is based on an analysis of two legal phenomena. The first is the law of a case, or what legal theorists call singular propositions of law. Moore chooses the United States Supreme Court's decision in *Kirby* v *United States*,[53] to demonstrate how, in arriving at its judgment, the court applied the spirit rather than the letter of the law.

His second example is the Good Samaritan rule in tort. Its application is illustrated by the case of *Union Pacific Railway* v *Cappier*,[54] in which the court dismissed a suit for nonfeasance when a railway company whose train had collided with a child trespasser failed to render aid to him as he lay dying. The thrust of Moore's argument is that the case would be decided differently today. In the light of the law's 'greater experience with positive duties to those whose risk we have created, and … correspondingly greater insight',[55] the Supreme Court, if faced with a similar set of facts, he maintains,

---

[50] 'Law as Justice', Ch 4 of *Objectivity in Ethics and Law*, originally published in (2001) 18 *Social Philosophy and Policy* 115. But is this true of Dworkin's approach in *Justice for Hedgehogs*?

[51] 'The Plain Truth About Legal Truth', Ch 5 of *Objectivity in Ethics and Law*, originally published in (2003) 26 *Harvard Journal of Law and Public Policy* 23.

[52] 'Legal Reality: A Naturalist Approach to Legal Ontology', Ch 6 of *Objectivity in Ethics and Law*, originally published in (2002) 21 *Law and Philosophy* 619.

[53] 72 US 482 (1869). Kirby was a state sheriff who was arrested for 'obstructing or retarding the passage of the US mail'. He had, indeed, obstructed the mail by halting a riverboat transporting a federal mail carrier and his mail and removing both from the vessel. But he had done so because the mail carrier was wanted for murder and Kirby had arrested him under a valid arrest warrant. The Supreme Court held that he was innocent of the offence.

[54] 72 Pac 281 (Kan Sup Ct 1903). This involved a child trespasser on the defendant's railway line. The boy was hit and seriously injured by one of the defendant's trains. An engineer stopped the train, removed the boy from the tracks, and drove on. The boy bled to death. The Kansas Supreme Court held the defendant was not liable as it had not 'culpably' caused the boy's peril of bleeding to death. No duty of care was, at that juncture of American tort law, owed to trespassers, and hence the court was unable to find the defendant negligent in its failure to prevent the collision.

[55] Moore, 'Legal Reality: A Naturalist Approach to Legal Ontology', 329.

would overrule *Cappier*. This, he claims, is because the law of Kansas is not exclusively a function of historical fact, but 'a blend of such historical facts and certain *moral* facts'.[56]

## 2.9 Critique

As mentioned above, among the criticisms levelled at the 'new' (or soft) natural law theory defended by Grisez, Finnis, Boyle, and others is its alleged failure to integrate practical reason with a philosophy of nature. In other words, natural law is inadequately 'natural'. It departs from the ontological approach adopted by classical and medieval natural law theorists.[57] Instead of an ontological posture (based on human nature) it adopts a deontological standpoint (based on principles that are not derived from our nature) that asserts that certain normative propositions are self-evidently true.[58]

Soft natural lawyers reject this claim, largely on the ground that it commits the 'naturalistic fallacy' of deriving norms from facts (see 2.7). They argue that logically, a conclusion cannot validly introduce a proposition that is not in the premise. In other words, one can draw a moral conclusion only from a premise that includes a more basic reason in support of that conclusion. The justifications for moral action, they contend, are not derived from facts about human nature, but, as Finnis explains, from our knowledge of worthwhile ends. These are, it is argued, self-evident.

We are, however, entitled to ask why *this* catalogue of objective, non-inferred basic goods? Is it wrong for me to act merely because I enjoy the activity in question? What's wrong with my acting to advance my pleasure if it causes no one harm? And why, as the 'new' natural law asserts, are these basic goods incommensurable? If they are, how am I to decide whether to do X or Y? The soft response would be that I should never act directly against a basic good. This is a fundamental moral rule. These, and other, arguments are contested mainly within natural law. The critique, especially by legal positivists, of the central tenets of natural law is the subject of Chapters 3 and 4.

## 2.10 Law and morality

Moral questions invade the law at every turn. A rigid separation between morality and the law—even in pursuit of analytical clarity—is, to natural lawyers, highly improbable. The legal positivist's quest for a value-free account of law is countered by the natural lawyer's claim that it neglects the very essence of law—its morality—that 'the

---

[56] Ibid, emphasis added.
[57] This is the thrust of the criticism made by Weinreb and Hittinger. See nn 44 and 45.
[58] See George, *In Defense of Natural Law*, op cit, 84.

act of positing law...can and should be guided by "moral" principles and rules; that those moral norms are a matter of objective reasonableness, not of whim, convention, or mere "decision"'.[59]

To compound what has long been a perplexing question, legal positivists do not, however, deny that moral considerations are without truth or practical consequence. As HLA Hart declares:

> So long as human beings can gain sufficient co-operation from some to enable them to dominate others, they will use the forms of law as one of their instruments. Wicked men will enact wicked rules which others will enforce. What surely is most needed in order to make men clear-sighted in confronting the official abuse of power, is that they should preserve the sense that the certification of something as legally valid is not conclusive of the question of obedience, and that, however great the aura of majesty or authority which the official system may have, its demands must in the end be submitted to a moral scrutiny.[60]

This concession to a normative appraisal of legal rules cannot, however, extinguish the apprehension that a narrow positivism may engender, or at least support, unjust laws. Ideal fidelity to law, as Lon Fuller has shown, must mean more than allegiance to naked power.[61]

But, as we shall see, earlier versions of what has come to be called 'hard' positivism, have been widely traded for a kinder, gentler, 'soft' positivism (adumbrated even by Hart in his postscript to *The Concept of Law*). The former, exclusivist position, espoused most conspicuously by Joseph Raz, insists that only social sources can supply the criteria of legality. The latter, inclusive, view claims that where specified in the rule of recognition, morality may constitute a condition of legal validity (see 4.5).

While we cannot avoid encountering moral questions daily, the existence, or even the recognition, of moral values by which to live is far from uncontroversial. Being or doing good is not always synonymous with obeying the law. But there can be little doubt that the law, its concepts, and its institutions are frequently animated by moral values. It would be odd if it were otherwise. And it may sometimes appear that, as Dias puts it, the two sides are 'shadow-boxing on different planes'.

You will need to reflect upon a number of questions before deciding where you stand on this central issue. They will include: in what respects might it be said that the pugilists are not really landing blows? Do they genuinely join issue? If so, how? What precisely are the different positions adopted by the two theories in respect, say, of the moral attitude to law? Do the two accounts have more in common than they have in conflict?

---

[59] Finnis, op cit, 290. For a powerful defence of the 'separability thesis' see Matthew Kramer, 'Also Among the Prophets: Some Rejoinders to Ronald Dworkin's Attacks on Legal Positivism' (1999) 12 *Canadian Journal of Law and Jurisprudence* 53.

[60] Hart, *The Concept of Law*, 210.

[61] Lon L Fuller, 'Positivism and Fidelity to Law—A Reply to Professor Hart' (1958) 71 *Harvard Law Review* 630, 634.

## 2.10.1 **Natural law v positivism**

Legal positivism—both soft and hard—differs, of course, from the natural law theory espoused, say, by Finnis who, as we have seen, bases his conception of law on the requirements of practical reasonableness. Yet there are several respects in which the apparently conflicting theories of legal positivism (*à la* Raz) and natural law (*à la* Finnis) share a common ground. Four quick examples will suffice here. First, as Finnis himself acknowledges, his approach is informed by the tradition of analytical jurisprudence. Secondly, they both seek to examine and justify the authority of law. Thirdly, they both subscribe to the view that there is no prima facie moral obligation to obey an unjust law. Fourthly, they both accept the importance of the ideal of the rule of law.

There are, obviously, a number of key differences between the two approaches.[62] Three instances may be briskly mentioned. First, at the most general level, legal positivists contend that there is no necessary connection between law and morality (see 3.1). Natural lawyers, of course, reject this view. Secondly, most positivist accounts of law tend to be descriptive and analytical, while natural lawyers are concerned, in the main, with evaluating society and law. This leads, thirdly, to different views concerning the relationship between practical reason and the moral point of view as an aspect of practical reason (and this may have a number of practical consequences).[63]

Most students tend to be easily persuaded of the flaws or, at any rate, the limitations, of classical legal positivism as expressed in the theories of Bentham or Austin. (See 3.2 and 3.3.) No great rhetoric or sophistication is required to demonstrate the simple proposition that the 'external' point of view may offer an incomplete explanation of the complex phenomenon of law. But, as discussed in the last chapter, contemporary positivism has moved a long way from its original preoccupation with commands, sanctions, and sovereignty. And, as we also saw, the assault on classical positivism assumes a number of forms. Nevertheless, at least six related kinds of assault on the tenets of legal positivism—even in its more refined incarnations—persist, and underlie the naturalist unease with its approach. Each has a slightly different starting point and method of attack.

The first rejects the very project of a value-free account of law. It argues that the emergence of legal positivism coincided with nineteenth-century capitalism; it therefore represents and expresses a particular *ideology*. Such critics point not only to the formalism that lies at the heart of positivism (the separation between 'is' and 'ought'), but also to the essential individualism that the theory assumes. This view is further explored in Chapter 9.

Secondly, it is claimed that the central idea of *validity* cannot be neutral. So, it is urged, the attempts to base validity on sovereignty (Austin), efficacy (Kelsen), or even

---

[62] For a perceptive comparison see D Beyleveld and R Brownsword, 'The Practical Difference between Natural-law Theory and Legal Positivism' (1985) 5 *Oxford Journal of Legal Studies* 1.

[63] A good, short (and eminently readable) account of this question is Neil MacCormick's essay, 'Contemporary Legal Philosophy: The Rediscovery of Practical Reason' (1983) 10 *Journal of Law & Society* 1.

the 'internal point of view' and 'critical reflective attitude' (Hart) fail to take account of the *values* that underpin legal validity or explain why the law is regarded as valid. This view is examined in greater detail later, especially in 4.2.

Thirdly, the related concepts of *authority* and *discretion* are attacked. Hart, after rejecting Austin's 'gunman' theory and Kelsen's *Grundnorm*, proposes a *neutral* theory of authority. He gives the example of the rules of a game. They are not moral, but they nevertheless define a practice in terms of which 'rights', 'duties', and so on are *accepted*: the participants obey an authority (eg, the referee in a chess match) because they accept the *rules* of the game. Hart shows that the acceptance of rules from an 'internal point of view' leads to a need for secondary rules of change, adjudication, and recognition which, in turn, necessitate authority. There is, therefore, no necessary connection between authority (or law) and morality. For Hart it is thus possible for moral questions to be excluded from the definition of law. But—as will, I hope, become evident—this means that when a judge is required to make a decision on a matter where there is a 'gap' in the law, he exercises a strong discretion. And in so doing, it is argued by certain critics, moral questions *do* enter into the determination of what is law. Ronald Dworkin, the leading contemporary critic of legal positivism, would deny that judges have a strong discretion and thus goes even further in repudiating the separation between law and morality (see 5.2).

Fourthly, it is argued, rules, commands, or norms do not fully explain reality. These are, it is claimed, abstract concepts which provide only a formal scheme of the operation of law and the legal system. Can we, for instance, understand the judicial role without an explanation of the relationship between the judiciary and the legislature? In other words, don't we require a theory of democracy to explain law?

Fifthly, it is argued (often by students!) that despite its claim to the contrary by its adherents, legal positivism does *not* promote clear thinking about law. Modern positivists, it is sometimes said, have developed a highly complex, technical, and occasionally unintelligible account of law.

Sixthly, there is said to be a *necessary* connection between law and morality. The best-known version of this assault on legal positivism is Professor Lon Fuller's book *The Morality of Law*. This argument provoked the following debate.

## 2.10.2 **Hart v Fuller**

Lon L Fuller (1902–78), whose Speluncean explorers we encountered in Chapter 1, is principally associated with his secular natural law position that law has an 'inner morality', and that a legal system is the purposive 'enterprise of subjecting human conduct to the governance of rules' which is considered below. Instead of postulating a substantive natural law approach which proclaims a higher law than that enacted by the state (as adumbrated, for example, by the German legal positivist, Gustav Radbruch), see page 29 above. Fuller adopts a procedural natural law approach. The eight ways to make law are, in Fuller's theory, reflected in his eight 'desiderata': 'eight kinds of legal excellence toward which a system of rules may strive' embodied in the 'inner morality of law'.[64] It epitomizes what he calls 'a morality of aspiration and not of duty. Its primary appeal must be a sense of trusteeship and to the pride of the craftsman'.[65]

The first shot in this legendary contest was fired by Hart in his Holmes Lecture (entitled 'Positivism and the Separation of Law and Morals') delivered at Harvard Law School in April 1957 and published in the *Harvard Law Review* in 1958.[66] Professor Fuller responded in his article 'Positivism and Fidelity to Law—A Reply to Professor Hart', also published in 1958 in the *Harvard Law Review*.[67] The focus of the debate was a decision of a post-war West German court. Under the Third Reich the wife of a German in 1944, wishing to be rid of him, denounced him to the Gestapo for insulting remarks he had made about Hitler's conduct of the war. He was tried and sentenced to death, though his sentence was converted to service as a soldier on the Russian front. In 1949 the wife was prosecuted for procuring her husband's loss of liberty. Her defence was that he had committed an offence under a Nazi statute of 1934. The court nevertheless convicted her on the ground that the statute under which the husband had been punished offended the 'sound conscience and sense of justice of all decent human beings'.

Hart argued that the decision of the court, and similar cases pursuant to it, was wrong, as the Nazi law of 1934[68] was a valid law since it fulfilled the requirements of the 'rule of recognition'. Fuller, on the other hand, contended that, since Nazi 'law' deviated so far from morality, it failed to qualify as law, and therefore supported the court's decision. Both Hart and Fuller would have preferred the enactment of retroactive legislation under which the woman could have been prosecuted.

Fuller contends that it is possible to deduce normative conclusions *from the nature of the legal system*. The norms he deduces, however, are formal and procedural. In a nutshell, Fuller seeks to show that law has an 'internal morality'. A legal system, he argues, is the purposive human 'enterprise of subjecting human conduct to the guidance and control of general rules'.[69] Whatever its substantive purpose, a legal system is bound to comply with certain procedural standards. In the absence of this compliance, what passes for a legal system is merely the exercise of state coercion. He relates the sad tale of King Rex, and the eight ways in which he failed to make law. Of the routes to failure:

> The first and most obvious lies in a failure to achieve rules at all, so that every issue must be decided on an ad hoc basis. The other routes are: (2) a failure to publicise, or at least to make available to the affected party, the rules he is expected to observe; (3) the abuse of retroactive legislation, which cannot itself guide action, but undercuts the integrity of rules prospective in effect, since it puts them under the threat of retrospective change; (4) a failure to make rules understandable; (5) the enactment of contradictory rules or (6) rules that require conduct

---

[64] LL Fuller, *The Morality of Law*, revised edn (New Haven, Conn and London: Yale University Press, 1969), 39.    [65] Ibid.    [66] (1959) 71 *Harvard Law Review* 593.    [67] Ibid, 593, 630.

[68] Enabling Act of 12 July 1934 passed by the German Reichstag which amended the German Constitution by permitting Hitler to issue decrees inconsistent with the Constitution.

[69] Fuller, *The Morality of Law*, 106.

beyond the powers of the affected party; (7) introducing such frequent changes in the rules that the subject cannot orient his action by them; and, finally, (8) a failure to achieve congruence between the rules as announced and their actual administration.70

These failures, Fuller explains, are mirrored by eight 'desiderata' or 'eight kinds of legal excellence toward which a system of rules may strive'[71] and are embodied in the 'inner morality of law'. They are:

1. Generality.
2. Promulgation.
3. Non-retroactivity.
4. Clarity.
5. Non-contradiction.
6. Possibility of compliance.
7. Constancy.
8. Congruence between declared rule and official action.

Where a system does not conform with any one of these principles, or fails substantially in respect of several, it could not be said that 'law' existed in that community. Thus, instead of adopting a substantive natural law approach, Fuller espouses a procedural natural law approach. The 'internal morality of law' is essentially a 'morality of aspiration'. Nor does it claim to accomplish any substantive ends, apart from the excellence of the law itself.

Fuller refuses to regard the 'law' of the Third Reich as law, a view rejected by Hart who prefers the simple utilitarian position that 'laws may be law but too evil to be obeyed'. It is arguable that *compliance* with Fuller's 'internal morality' is no guarantee of a just order; the apartheid South African legal system probably satisfied all eight principles—though Fuller contends that its apartheid legislation revealed a gross departure from the demands of the internal morality of law on the ground that this legislation defined race arbitrarily.

Fuller's position is essentially that law is a 'purposive enterprise, dependent for its success on the energy, insight, intelligence, and conscientiousness of those who conduct it'. To count as an instance of that enterprise it must fulfil certain moral requirements. (He does not, however, make clear precisely how his eight principles are *moral*.) Summers points out that although Fuller argued for *necessary* connections between his principles of legality and moral values,

> [M]ost of Fuller's explicit arguments supported only a contingent connection. Thus he believed that the satisfaction of his eight principles of legality generally served moral ends. To be sure these principles were 'neutral' with regard to the substantive purposes of law (its 'external morality'), but observing them made it less likely that truly bad laws would be adopted.[72]

---

[70] Ibid, 41    [71] Ibid, 39.
[72] Robert S Summers, *Lon L Fuller* (London: Edward Arnold, 1984), 38.

It is important to recognize, therefore, that Fuller's position does not commit him to treat a legal system that *does* comply with his eight desiderata as necessarily immune to criticism. The Fullerian stamp of approval does not place a legal system beyond reproach. It may still be an unjust legal order, though this is less likely.

### 2.10.3  Hart v Devlin

Professor Hart engaged in an equally celebrated debate with the English judge, Lord Devlin. Sparked by a report in 1957 by a British committee, under the chairmanship of Sir John Wolfenden, appointed to examine the question of homosexual offences and prostitution, this issue has recently resurfaced in a number of Western societies that have embraced the ideal of multiculturalism. The committee concluded that the function of the criminal law was to preserve public order and decency, to protect citizens from what is offensive and injurious, and from exploitation and corruption of others, especially those who are especially vulnerable: the young, the inexperienced, and the frail. But

> Unless a deliberate attempt is to be made by society, acting through the agency of the law, to equate the sphere of crime with that of sin, there must remain a realm of private morality and immorality which is, in brief and crude terms, not the law's business.[73]

In reaching this view, and recommending that both consensual homosexual acts between adults in private and prostitution should be decriminalized, the Wolfenden Committee was strongly influenced by the views of the nineteenth-century liberal utilitarian, John Stuart Mill who, in 1859 argued that

> [T]he sole end for which mankind are warranted, individually or collectively, in interfering with the liberty of action of any of their number, is self-protection. The only purpose for which power can be rightfully exercised over any member of a civilized community, against his will, is to prevent harm to others. His own good, either physical or moral, is not a sufficient warrant.[74]

This 'harm principle' may appear to be a simple yardstick by which to establish the borders of the criminal law. But snags arise. First, is the criminal law not justified in punishing what another Victorian utilitarian, Sir James Fitzjames Stephen (uncle of the novelist, Virginia Woolf) called 'the grosser forms of vice'? And, secondly, who is to say what constitutes 'harm'?[75]

---

[73] *Report of the Committee on Homosexual Offences and Prostitution*, Chairman Sir John Wolfenden (Cmnd 247), para 61.

[74] John Stuart Mill, *On Liberty*, ed Gertrude Himmelfarb (Harmondsworth: Penguin Books, 1974), 72–3.

[75] But some argue that the harm principle sets the barrier too high. In the case of freedom of speech, for example, Joel Feinberg proposes what he calls an 'offence principle' to facilitate the prohibition of those forms of expression that are especially offensive. He maintains that causing offence is less serious than harming someone, and therefore the sanction ought to be less onerous than for actions that cause harm. He cites the example of consensual sodomy and incest where, in the USA, the continuum of sentences have ranged from twenty years' imprisonment to capital punishment. Since these are victimless crimes, he contends, the penalty is presumably based on the assumed offensiveness of the behaviour rather than the harm caused. See J Feinberg, *Harm to Others: The Moral Limits of the Criminal Law* (Oxford: Oxford University

These difficulties are the nub of the dispute between Hart and Devlin. In a series of lectures in 1959 Lord Devlin took issue with the Wolfenden Committee's position, arguing that society has every right to punish conduct that, in the view of the ordinary member of society ('the man in the jury box'), is grossly immoral. Harm, he contended, is irrelevant; the fabric of society is maintained by a shared morality. This social cohesion is undermined when immoral acts are committed—even in private, and even if they harm no one. Societies disintegrate from within, he contended, more often than they are destroyed by external forces:

> There is disintegration when no common morality is observed and history shows that the loosening of moral bonds is often the first stage of disintegration, so that society is justified in taking the same steps to preserve its moral code as it does to preserve its government... [T]he suppression of vice is as much the law's business as the suppression of subversive activities.[76]

But, though Lord Devlin concedes that only those acts that cause 'intolerance, indignation and disgust' warrant punishment, Professor Hart challenges the very foundation of his 'social cohesion' argument. Surely, Hart insists, a society does not require a shared morality; pluralistic, multicultural societies may contain a variety of moral views. Nor, even if there is a shared morality, is it obvious that its protection is essential to the survival of society. In respect of the first assertion, it does seem far-fetched to claim that a society's foundation is unable to withstand the challenge of a competing ideology or morality. Is a Western society gravely wounded by the Islamic prohibition of alcohol espoused by a significant proportion of its inhabitants? Equally, is an Islamic society unable to withstand the morality of a minority in its midst?

Hart does not, however, shrink from supporting a paternalistic role for the law. At odds with Mill, he acknowledges that there may be circumstances in which the law ought to protect individuals from physically harming themselves. The criminal law may therefore justifiably withhold the defence of consent to homicide and assault. Requiring seat belts in vehicles or crash helmets to be used by motorcyclists is a legitimate exercise of legal control.

Hart also draws an important distinction between harm that is caused by public spectacle, on the one hand, and offence caused merely through knowledge, on the other. Thus bigamy may justifiably be punished since, as a public act, it may offend religious sensibilities, whereas private consensual sexual acts by adults may offend—but only through knowledge, and thus do not merit punishment. Such acts are best addressed by legislation. In the words of the distinguished English judge, Lord Atkin:

> Notoriously there are wide differences of opinion today as to how far the law ought to punish immoral acts which are not done in the face of the public. Some think that the law already goes too far, some that it does not go far enough. Parliament is the proper place, and I am firmly of opinion the only proper place, to settle that. When there is sufficient support from

---

Press, 1984) and *Offense to Others: The Moral Limits of the Criminal Law* (Oxford: Oxford University Press, 1985).

[76] Patrick Devlin, *The Enforcement of Morals* (Oxford: Oxford University Press, 1965), 14.

public opinion, Parliament does not hesitate to intervene. Where Parliament fears to tread it is not for the courts to rush in.[77]

Analogous questions arise in the case of the following highly contentious issue.

### 2.10.3.1 A right to life?

The subject of abortion is guaranteed to provoke intense debate. This is especially true in the United States where its morality is fiercely contested. On the one hand, Christian groups condemn (sometimes violently) the practice of abortion, regarding it as the killing of a potential human. On the other hand, feminists, among others, consider the matter as fundamental to a woman's right to control her own body. There is no obvious middle ground. Ronald Dworkin vividly describes the vehemence and divisiveness of the skirmish:

> The war between anti-abortion groups and their opponents is America's new version of the terrible seventeenth-century European civil wars of religion. Opposing armies march down streets or pack themselves into protests at abortion clinics, courthouses, and the White House, screaming at and spitting on and loathing one another. Abortion is tearing America apart.[78]

At the heart of the matter is the United States Supreme Court's 1973 decision in *Roe v Wade*.[79] A majority of the court held that the abortion law of Texas was unconstitutional as a violation of the right to privacy. Under that law abortion was criminalized, except when performed to save the pregnant woman's life. The judgment established the right of states to prohibit abortion to protect the life of the foetus only in the third trimester. The case is concurrently supported by feminists, and condemned by many Christians. Overruling the decision is on the agenda of many Christian lobbyists and politicians, but it remains a fragile thread by which the right of American women to a lawful abortion hangs.

In the abortion debate the sanctity of human life has somehow to be morally weighed against the right of a woman over her body. Most European countries have sought to strike this balance by legislation that permits abortion within specified periods under certain prescribed conditions. In Britain, for example, abortion is lawful if it is certified by two medical practitioners that to continue the pregnancy would involve risk to the life of, or injury to, the pregnant woman or her existing children, and that the risk is greater than if the pregnancy were terminated; or there is a substantial risk that if the child were born it would suffer serious physical or mental handicap. It is a criminal offence to terminate a pregnancy when the child is capable of being born alive. This is normally after twenty-eight weeks. More recent legislation provides that a pregnancy that has not exceeded twenty-four weeks may

---

[77] *Shaw v Director of Public Prosecutions* [1962] AC 220 (HL) at 267.

[78] Ronald Dworkin, *Life's Dominion: An Argument about Abortion and Euthanasia* (London: HarperCollins, 1993), 4. This account of these intractable cases draws on my discussion in Raymond Wacks, *Law: A Very Short Introduction* (Oxford: Oxford University Press, 2008), 74–82.

[79] 410 US 113 (1973).

be terminated where its continuation would involve risk, greater than if the pregnancy were terminated; of injury to the physical or mental health of the pregnant woman or any existing children of her family, but no time limit is imposed where termination may be necessary to prevent grave permanent injury to the physical or mental health of the pregnant woman, or risk to her life, or if there is a substantial risk that if the child were born it would suffer from such physical or mental abnormalities as to be seriously handicapped.

In its quest for a conscientious resolution to this complex issue each society must assess its own moral norms. If, as most humans tend to believe, life is sacred, does a foetus count as a person capable of suffering harm? If it does, how is ending its life to be distinguished from the humane killing of a living human? Should the welfare of the as yet unborn prevail over the distress suffered by a woman compelled to bear an unwanted pregnancy or endure the anxiety, cost, and difficulty of bringing up a handicapped child?

### 2.10.3.2 Euthanasia

Similar problems inescapably attend the intractable matter of euthanasia. Doctors, lawyers, and eventually judges increasingly encounter the contentious question of an individual's 'right to die'. Often a distinction is drawn (not always convincingly) between active and passive euthanasia. The former entails the acceleration of a person's life by a positive act, such as an injection of potassium chloride. Most legal systems treat this as murder. The latter involves the curbing of life by an omission to act: a withdrawal of treatment which is increasingly accepted as humane by both the law and the medical profession in many jurisdictions. But courts have not always found it easy to determine the lawfulness of withdrawing life support from an incurably or terminally ill patient who is in a persistent vegetative state (PVS), unable to make an autonomous decision.

Nor are generalizations easy in respect of either the morality or lawfulness of ending the life of a patient. There is, for example, a significant distinction between a patient who is incurable, and one who is terminally ill. The latter continuum may extend between incapacity (a fully conscious patient who can breathe unaided), artificial support (a fully conscious patient attached to a ventilator), unconsciousness, to intensive care (where the patient is comatose and is attached to a ventilator). Different considerations arise in each of these situations.

The intricate distinctions generated when the law confronts awkward moral questions of this kind suggest that they are not susceptible to resolution by slogans such as 'the right to die', 'autonomy', 'self-determination', or 'the sanctity of life'. Courts may not be the most appropriate arbiters in these circumstances, but is there a realistic alternative? Two decisions of the courts (one English, the other American) illustrate the problems involved.

The English case arose out of an accident that occurred at a crowded football stadium in 1989. Anthony Bland sustained hypoxic brain damage which left him in a PVS. Though his brain stem continued to function, his cerebral cortex (the seat of consciousness, communicative activity, and voluntary movement) was destroyed through lack of oxygen, but he was not 'legally dead'. The judge, Lord Justice Hoffmann (as he then was) described his wretched state as follows:

> He lies in...hospital...fed liquid food by a pump through a tube passing through his nose and down the back of his throat into his stomach. His bladder is emptied through a catheter inserted through his penis, which from time to time has caused infections requiring dressing and antibiotic treatment. His stiffened joints have caused his limbs to be rigidly contracted so that his arms are tightly flexed across his chest and his legs unnaturally contorted. Reflex movements in his throat cause him to vomit and dribble. Of all of this, and the presence of members of his family who take turns to visit him, Anthony Bland has no consciousness at all...The darkness and oblivion...will never depart.[80]

There was no prospect of any improvement in Bland's condition that could endure for an extensive period. His doctors applied to the court for permission to withdraw his ventilation, antibiotic, and artificial feeding and hydration regime, while continuing otherwise to treat him so as to allow him to die with dignity and minimal pain and suffering. The Official Solicitor (who acts for those under a disability) maintained that this would constitute a breach of the doctor's duty to his patient, and a criminal offence.

The House of Lords accorded primacy to the right of self-determination over the right to life. A doctor, it held, should respect his patient's rights in that order. This, the judges said, is especially compelling where the patient has, in anticipation of his succumbing to a condition such as PVS, expressed his clear wish not to be given medical care, including artificial feeding, calculated to keep him alive. But, though all five Law Lords agreed that Bland's life should be allowed to end, there is no clear consensus in respect of precisely what the law was or should be. All recognized both the sanctity of life and the autonomy of the patient, but what remained unanswered was how these values were to be reconciled in the absence of an explicit expression of instructions by Bland. For Lord Goff the answer lay in protecting the best interests of the patient. But what interests can an insensate patient have? Lord Goff thought they consisted partly in the anguish and stress to others. Lords Keith and Mustill were doubtful, the latter declaring:

> [I]t seems to me to be stretching the concept of personal rights beyond breaking point to say that Anthony Bland has an interest in ending these sources of others' distress. Unlike the conscious patient he does not know what is happening to his body...The distressing truth which must not be shirked is that the proposed conduct is not in the best interests of Anthony Bland, for he has no best interests of any kind.[81]

A similar solution has been adopted by several courts in the United States and Canada. In the celebrated decision of the United States Supreme Court of *Cruzan*, for instance (involving a patient in a PVS whose parents sought to persuade the court that, though she had not expressed this in a 'living will', their daughter would not have wanted to continue living), it was held that the state had an interest in the sanctity, and hence, the preservation of life. Similarly, the state's interest in preserving life looms large in the judgments.

---

[80]  *Airedale NHS Trust v Bland* [1993] AC 789 at 824–5 *per* Hoffmann LJ.
[81]  At 859 *per* Mustill LJ.

In the event, the House of Lords ruled that the withdrawal of Bland's nutrition and hydration did not constitute a criminal offence because any hope of Bland recovering had been abandoned, and, though the termination of his life was not in his best interests, his best interests in being kept alive had also evaporated along with the justification for the non-consensual regime and the duty to maintain it. In the absence of this duty, the withdrawal of nutrition and hydration was not a criminal offence.

Courts cannot evade these painful quandaries. Their burden is considerably eased by the existence of a 'living will' in which an individual stipulates something along the lines of the following: 'If, as a result of physical or mental incapacity, I become unable to participate in decisions concerning my medical care and treatment, and subsequently develop any of the medical conditions described below (from which two independent physicians certify I have no reasonable prospect of recovering), I declare that my life should not be sustained by artificial means.'

## 2.11 Judicial morality: a case study

The following exercise in applied jurisprudence is designed to bring some of these key issues to life. It is hoped that it will generate discussion, disagreement, and debate.

Suppose we were to ask how Dworkin's superhuman judge, Hercules J, would fare in a society very different from the one in which his creator places him. What if, instead of his generally fortunate liberal democracy, this mythical member of the judiciary were to be appointed to the bench of a profoundly unhappy, unjust society. How might his constructive interpretation operate in this evil legal system? And, more importantly from a moral standpoint, would we regard him as morally accountable for his ostensibly immoral participation in injustice?[82]

We live in an age of public accountability. Or, more precisely, we prosecute selected crimes against humanity; and the impunity in which evil government officials and their collaborators and military commanders were once able to bask is increasingly circumscribed. The establishment of the International Criminal Court marks an important post-war recognition that gross injustice perpetrated by states should not go unpunished. Yet the conduct of judges—who often lend legitimacy and provide succour to wicked regimes—is rarely called to account.[83] Why should they escape moral scrutiny

---

[82] I draw here on 'Are Judges Morally Accountable?' in Raymond Wacks, *Law, Morality, and the Private Domain* (Hong Kong: Hong Kong University Press, 2000) and 'Injustice in Robes: Iniquity and Judicial Accountability' (2009) 22 *Ratio Juris* 128. Earlier versions of this essay are 'Judges and Moral Responsibility' in W Sadurski (ed), *Ethical Dimensions of Legal Theory*, Poznan Studies in the Philosophy of the Sciences and Humanities (Amsterdam: Rodopi, 1991), 111–29, and Raymond Wacks, 'Law's Umpire: Judges, Truth, and Moral Accountability' in Peter Koller and André-Jean Arnaud (eds), *Law, Justice, and Culture* (Stuttgart: Franz Steiner Verlag, 1998), 75–83. This may illustrate the difficulty of this subject—and how far I am from resolving it!

[83] Some judges of the Third Reich were, in fact, prosecuted in the so-called 'Justice Trial' at Nuremberg. In the film *Judgment at Nuremberg*, Burt Lancaster played the role of a German judge (Ernst Janning) that was based loosely on the prosecution of Franz Schlegelberger who served in the Ministry of Justice from 1931 to 1942. He argued in his defence that he was bound to follow the orders of Hitler, the 'Supreme Judge' of Germany, but that he did so only reluctantly. He asserted also that he had no animosity against the

and, where appropriate, reproach? Is it possible to establish the grounds upon which judges in evil societies may be held morally responsible for their acts or omissions?

### 2.11.1 Moral questions

Consider for a moment some of the many difficulties that face the moral or legal philosopher attempting to answer this question. First, moral or ethical evaluation is itself problematic. Merely by postulating the view that the exercise has some point, one is resisting ethical nihilism or non-cognitivism. And by suggesting, as one would clearly wish to do, that the matter may in several important senses, be universalized, one is rejecting relativist, emotivist, and existentialist arguments and by claiming that it has some practical value—which I assume it does—one is embracing some form of prescriptivism. (These terms are further explained in the Glossary.)

Secondly, a number of fundamental moral judgments turn on which conception of ethics one adopts. I think that this issue is best confronted by way of a deontological, or action-centred (rather than an outcome-centred) approach. Thirdly, though it is not especially controversial to focus on apartheid South Africa as an archetypal 'unjust society' (for it does capture certain critical features of unfairness: racism, minority domination), the selection of *any* society as a model is not free of difficulty. It requires, at the very least, an accurate account of its political and legal system. You will immediately appreciate that the predicament of the judge in such a system depends on several empirical observations about the regime which are neither uncomplicated nor uncontroversial.

Fourthly, it may be that the value of any consideration of the judge's moral dilemma is likely to be diminished without a credible theory of the judicial function in a common law context. So, for instance, a Hartian conception of the judge vested with strong discretion (though the nature and extent of this discretion is debated among contemporary positivists, see 4.5) may be expected to generate a different set of practical problems and solutions from a Dworkinian one (see Chapters 4 and 5).

### 2.11.2 Semantic questions

The quest for moral clarity in matters such as the present one is unlikely to be advanced by the proposition that what purports to be law (say, discriminatory Nazi or apartheid South African legislation) is not law. You will recall the maxim '*lex iniusta non est lex*' (an unjust law is not law) that is normally attributed to Aquinas (see 2.2) and adopted by Lon Fuller (see 2.5). Dworkin calls it an expression of a 'sceptical interpretive judgment that Nazi law lacked features crucial to flourishing legal systems whose rules

---

Jews. In fact, his personal physician was Jewish. He pleaded also that he opposed sending 'half Jews' to the concentration camps, proposing instead that they be given a choice between sterilization and evacuation. He contended as well that he remained in office because 'if I had resigned, a worse man would have taken my place'.

and procedures do justify coercion'.[84] Fuller's misgivings about the positivist alternative cannot, however, be lightly dismissed:

> One can imagine a case—surely not likely in Professor Hart's country or mine—where a judge might hold profound moral convictions that were exactly the opposite of those held, with equal attachment, by his supreme court. He might also be convinced that the precedents he was bound to apply were the direct product of a morality he considered abhorrent. If such a judge did not find the solution for his dilemma in surrendering his office, he might well be driven to a wooden and literal application of precedents which he could not otherwise apply because he was incapable of understanding the philosophy that animated them. But I doubt that a judge in this situation would need the help of legal positivism to find these melancholy escapes from his predicament. Nor do I think that such a predicament is likely to arise within a nation where both law and good law are regarded as collaborative human achievements in need of constant renewal, and where lawyers are still at least as interested in asking 'What is good law?' as they are in asking 'What is law'?[85]

For Fuller the choice between applying an 'amoral datum called law' and doing what is thought to be 'right and decent' is a nonsense. 'It is like saying I have to choose between giving food to a starving man and being mimsy with the borogoves.'[86] To call the 'amoral datum' law is to recognize the moral obligation of fidelity to law. The conceptual separation between law and morality severs the moral obligation to obey law from other moral obligations.[87] And this is precisely where our moral judge's dilemma is located. Let us call him Righteous J. He is obliged to apply a 'law' that conflicts with his moral convictions. Fidelity to law cannot be fidelity to injustice that parades as 'law'. The alleged semantic sterility of this question arises only at the descriptive level. On the practical or normative level, however, it may serve as a reminder to the judge that the obligation to apply the law has moral limits.[88] Consider David Lyons' example:

> So, even if an official has a general obligation of fidelity to law, we can assume it has moral bounds. If the law he is called on to enforce is sufficiently immoral, there may be no moral argument for his adherence to it—not even if he has sincerely undertaken to apply the law as he finds it. A misguided or naive official under the Third Reich who initially believes that the law he shall be called upon to administer will not be outrageously immoral, may find that it requires him to verify the eligibility of persons for extermination in the gas chambers because they are Jews. He may in good conscience have undertaken to apply the law as he finds it, but I see no reason to suppose that his resulting obligation of fidelity to law extends this far. Such an obligation has moral limits.[89]

---

[84] R Dworkin, *Law's Empire* (Cambridge, Mass and London: Belknap Press, 1973), 104.

[85] LL Fuller, 'Positivism and Fidelity to Law—A Reply to Professor Hart' (1959) 71 *Harvard Law Review* 630, 648. [86] Ibid, 657.

[87] See too LL Fuller, *The Morality of Law*, 2nd edn (New Haven, Conn: Yale University Press, 1969).

[88] According to Dworkin: 'We need not deny that the Nazi system was an example of law, no matter which interpretation we favour of our own law, because there is an available sense in which it plainly was law. But we have no difficulty in understanding someone who does say that Nazi law was not really law, or was law in a degenerative sense, or less than fully law', Dworkin, *Law's Empire*, 103.

[89] D Lyons, *Ethics and the Rule of Law* (Cambridge: Cambridge University Press, 1984), 85. As Thomas Nagel puts it, 'any view as absolute as this is mistaken: there are no such extreme obligations or offices to which they attach. One cannot, by joining the army, undertake an obligation to obey any order

Unless fidelity to law is merely naked subservience to rules, its moral content is con-fined to keeping one's promises or, more appropriately in respect of the judge, doing one's duty: he undertakes to apply the law and is therefore required morally (as well, of course, as legally) to do so. But what if the law is plainly unjust? Surely an abso-lutist claim of this kind cannot be sustained; it strips the judge's obligations of their moral content and renders his promise hollow. Even the most inflexible deontologist is unlikely to hold to this line.

The value of Fuller's position lies therefore not in its linguistic claims about the nature of law, but in its recognition of the moral sovereignty of the judge. His argu-ment is of course part of a general unease about the dangers of what is often perceived to be the positivist rejection of values, or, at least, the potential this approach has for the triumph of the will over virtue.

This, of course, is strenuously denied by legal positivists who argue that moral val-ues are not necessarily promoted by the formal features of the law and, indeed, that 'law *qua* law does not carry any inherent moral consequences'.[90] Exclusivist legal posi-tivists such as Joseph Raz (see 4.4) would, of course, claim that there are no grounds for holding that law and morality are necessarily connected; even inclusivist legal positivists, like Jules Coleman (see 4.2.6) concede only that the substantive moral-ity of a norm may be a precondition of its legality only if it is specified in the rule of recognition.

Can legal positivism provide a way out of this dilemma? Coleman and Leiter, seeking to explain the authority of the centrepiece of Hart's theory—the rule of rec-ognition—state that 'we all recognize cases of binding laws that are morally rep-rehensible (for example, the laws that supported apartheid in South Africa)'.[91] In attempting to show the incoherence of positivism, John Finnis postulates an official such as an advocate of the Supreme Court of South Africa. Suppose this advocate[92] enquires why the South African rule of recognition provides a reason of a kind that he could reasonably regard as authoritative. How does the rule of recognition (which 'is the prepositional content of the attitudes accompanying and supporting the mas-sive fact of convergent official behaviour')[93] render the law not merely *accepted* as legally authoritative, but actually *authoritative as law* for Mandela or anyone aware of its injustice? Finnis indicates that Coleman and Leiter would respond in the following way:

whatever from one's commanding officer', T Nagel, 'Ruthlessness in Public Life' in his *Mortal Questions* (Cambridge: Cambridge University Press, 1979), 80.

[90] Matthew H Kramer, *In Defense of Legal Positivism: Law Without Trimmings* (Oxford: Clarendon Press, 1999), 16. Kramer usefully distinguishes between three overlapping conceptions of morality: moral-ity distinguished from (a) evil, (b) factuality, and (c) prudence. We are here concerned with (a).

[91] Jules Coleman and Brian Leiter, 'Legal Positivism' in Dennis Patterson (ed), *A Companion to Philosophy of Law and Legal Theory* (Oxford and Cambridge, Mass: Blackwell, 1999), 243.

[92] Finnis casts Nelson Mandela in this hypothetical role, though, in fact, he practised as a solicitor, and hence did not have audience in the Supreme Court.

[93] John Finnis, 'Natural Law: The Classical Tradition' in Coleman and Shapiro (eds), *The Oxford Handbook of Jurisprudence and Philosophy of Law*, 21.

1. One's self-interest frequently requires one to harmonize one's behaviour with the official line. (But, says Finnis, Mandela wants to know, not about his self-interest, but about authoritative directions.)

2. If one believes that the officials are seeking to follow the requirements of morality, one has reason to follow their lead. (Mandela will not think so, avers Finnis, and he will be right.)

3. One may accept that the rule of recognition expresses the right standards for evaluating the validity of rules subordinate to it. (Mandela, claims Finnis, rightly does not.)

4. Despite one's misgivings about the substantive merits of the rule of recognition itself, the avoidance of disorder, and the conditions of liberal stability require coordination among officials. Here at last, exclaims Finnis, Coleman and Leiter 'offer a reason of the relevant kind, a reason which could be rationally debated by being confronted with reasons of the same kind'.[94] In other words, this imagined rejoinder expresses a genuinely *moral* requirement, for it acknowledges the importance of order, peace, and justice ('liberalism'). But it explains the law's authoritativeness,

> ...only if the 'separability thesis' is recognised as an equivocation between defensible and indefensible theses, and Coleman and Leiter's favoured, 'positivist' interpretation of it is abandoned as the mistake it is. In jurisprudence, there is a name for a theory of law that undertakes to identify and debate, openly and critically, the moral principles and requirements which respond to *deliberating persons'* request to be shown why a legal rule, validly enacted, is binding and authoritative *for them*, precisely as law. That name, for good and ill, is 'natural law theory.'[95]

In the approach adopted by positivists like Coleman and Leiter, so Finnis contends, unjust apartheid legislation was not binding, despite the fact that it was commonly so regarded. And this exposes the poverty of positivism:

> Positivism never coherently reaches beyond reporting attitudes and convergent behaviour...It has nothing to say to officials or private citizens who want to judge whether, when, and why the authority and obligatoriness *claimed* and *enforced* by those who are *acting* as officials of a legal system, and by their directives, are indeed *authoritative reasons* for their own conscientious action. Positivism, at this point, does no more than repeat (i) what any competent lawyer—including every legally competent adherent of natural law theory—would say are (or are not) intra-systemically valid laws, imposing 'legal requirements' and (ii) what any streetwise observer would warn are the likely consequences of non-compliance. It cannot explain the authoritativeness, for an official's or a private citizen's conscience (ultimate rational judgment) of these alleged and imposed requirements, nor their lack of such authority when radically unjust. Positivism is not only incoherent. It is also redundant.[96]

You will want to reflect upon the truth of this coruscating conclusion.

---

[94] Ibid, 22.      [95] Ibid.      [96] Ibid, 23.

### 2.11.3 Public or private morality?

What is it to claim that a judge caught in our dilemma ought to exercise his moral autonomy and, if necessary, disregard an unjust law? Is this a statement about the judge's public duty *qua* judge or is it addressed to him or her as an individual? I think it is the former for otherwise the question no longer concerns public accountability and collapses into individual responsibility. It might be based on a normative view of what is entailed in the business of judging. At its very thinnest (and most Utopian) such a theory might point to the image of the judge as repository of fairness, possessing what Rawls calls the 'judicial virtues' such as impartiality and considerateness which are 'the excellences of intellect and sensibility'.[97] It is true that the peculiar nature of the judicial function, as compared with other public officials, suggests that ethical consideration (in the widest sense) ought to figure prominently in the very exercise of judicial office. We want to believe that politicians behave ethically; we *do* believe that judges do. I think, however, that despite the congeniality of this Solomonic conception, any coherent thesis must turn on the judge's role as public official, though extra purchase might be sought in the fact that judges should be especially sensitive to problems of right and wrong, good and bad.[98]

What is the *source* of the judge's public morality? Does it derive substantively from *individual* morality? It appears right that 'we cannot establish [the] special responsibility of officials merely by applying our ordinary convictions about individual responsibility to the circumstances of their case'.[99] But we must seek a firmer foundation for this conviction than the peculiar nature of the judicial function. The institution of promise-keeping will not do.[100] Where should we look?

The duty may originate in two places. The first may be called the institutional source. Nagel[101] shows that, though private and public morality are clearly not independent of each other, public officials assume the special and specific obligations of their office. Their moral duty springs from their job description: the institution for which they work or represent. At first blush, this institutional approach appears problematic, at least as far as the judges in an unjust society are concerned. Nagel rests his conception of the distinctive character of public morality on the *limitations* of the office of public officials: 'they correlatively reduce their right to consider other factors, both their

    [97] J Rawls, *A Theory of Justice* (Harmondsworth: Penguin, 1973), 517. See Chapter 9.
    [98] Joel Feinberg devotes much of his analysis to this issue, and concludes too that there is a fundamental difference between a conscientious individual, on the one hand, and a public official such as judge, on the other, 'Natural Law: The Dilemmas of Judges Who Must Interpret Immoral Laws' in his *Problems at the Roots of Law: Essays in Legal and Political Theory* (Oxford: Oxford University Press, 2003).
    [99] Dworkin, *Law's Empire*, 174.
    [100] Dworkin argues, correctly in my view, that it is mistaken to argue that an official is under a special responsibility of impartiality 'because he has accepted his office subject to that understanding, so these responsibilities are drawn from ordinary morality after all, from the morality of keeping promises', *Law's Empire*, 174. This view, he suggests, 'reverses the order of argument most of us would endorse: we share an understanding that our officials must treat all members of the community they govern as equals because we believe they should behave that way, not the other way around', ibid, 174–5.
    [101] Nagel, op cit, 78–90.

personal interests and more general ones not related to the institution or their role in it'.[102] But this is no real limitation for it is hard to conceive of a question that would not fall into the category of general interests which the official may legitimately consider. Indeed, he acknowledges that where 'the limits imposed by public morality itself are being transgressed' (and he gives as an example the duty to carry out what would be a 'judicial murder') there is no substitute for refusal and, if possible, resistance.[103] This implies that such refusal springs from the official's general interest in the institution or his role in it.

A second origin of the duty may be called the community source. Rejecting the idea that officials' moral responsibility stems from individual morality, Dworkin finds it to reside in the view that 'the community as a whole has obligations of impartiality towards its members, and that officials act as agents for the community in acquitting that responsibility'.[104] An agreeable idea which, sadly, has an embarrassingly empty ring in the unjust society which I am discussing here. The 'community' must perforce be restricted to those who exercise political and legal control (ie, the white minority)— the major element of the society's injustice. But this is consistent, as we shall see, with Dworkin's sense of 'community morality' which, in apartheid South Africa, could only have meant the morality of the dominant political group.

### 2.11.4 The judge's duty

The judge's oath to administer justice according to the law therefore becomes the source of both moral responsibility and moral dilemma.[105] No judge in apartheid South Africa could have claimed ignorance of the injustices of the law. None could say: 'When I took the oath I was unaware of the fact that the legal system was the creation of a white minority, that the political system disenfranchised every black person, and that the law discriminated against black persons in several important aspects of social and economic life.' This acknowledgement gives rise to three related difficulties.

First, how is it possible then that a moral dilemma can suddenly surface for Righteous J? The answer must be because beliefs change, and if we are to talk sensibly about moral sovereignty we must allow moral agents the freedom to change their minds. Secondly, is he not part of the very system that he now calls unjust? Again, we must recognize the possibility of moral conversion; to do otherwise would, in any event, render the present analysis futile. An agent of injustice may come to see himself as that, even though this revelation may thus far have eluded him. Thirdly, what is he *doing* there? Would a good man accept appointment to the judiciary of an unjust society, or even one that contained unjust laws?

This problem arose, for example, in relation to slavery in the United States: 'More and more, it appeared the question ought not to be put, "How should a judge of integrity decide these cases?" but rather "How can a man of integrity judge these cases?".'[106]

---

[102] Ibid, 89.     [103] Ibid, 90.     [104] Dworkin, *Law's Empire*, 174–5.

[105] See Feinberg, op cit. His analysis is inconclusive, but his hypothetical conversation between two fictitious judges, one of a positivist persuasion, the other a natural lawyer, is illuminating.

[106] R Cover, *Justice Accused: Antislavery and the Judicial Process* (New Haven, Conn: Yale University Press, 1983), 178. These were the words of Judge Wendell Phillips who resigned in protest against the law

To frame the problem in these terms begs the question of what it means—especially for a judge—to be 'good' or 'moral'. Two sorts of answers might be suggested. First, it might be thought possible for him to be a fair, honest, and impartial judge—and yet to find apartheid morally defensible. Secondly, the judge may concede the system's injustice, but believe that in accepting appointment he might 'do good' by helping to ameliorate its unfairness. Each of these issues requires separate consideration.

Is it plausible for a judge to be described as 'moral' by virtue of the fact that he displays the judicial virtues of impartiality, neutrality, and reason? Is he, in other words, moral if he acts justly in applying the law? This immediately raises the distinction between substantive and procedural justice. Hart's fundamentally procedural standard has won fairly wide acceptance: justice consists in 'treating like cases alike'.[107] Is a judge 'moral' when he treats like cases alike? Hart accepts that he is. But justice may require that like cases are *not* treated alike. Faced with an unjust law, a judge who applies it to a like case does an injustice. At the same time, according to Hart's principle, an injustice is also done if the law is *not* applied, though the judge would presumably be justified—morally speaking—in abandoning a strict adherence to the law where the injustice would be reduced if it were not adhered to.

'Treating cases in a regular or uniform manner', David Lyons rightly maintains, 'may be a necessary condition of justice, but it is not a sufficient condition'.[108] It is indeed hard to perceive to whom an injustice is done if Righteous J *refuses* to apply a segregation statute. Not to the defendant who is charged with violating it. Not to racists who support the legislation (for their object is immoral). Not surely to previous defendants who were convicted under the legislation. And not even, in the apartheid South African context at least, to 'the law' on the ground that it is right to give effect to the wishes of the majority expressed in legislation. This suggests that, as with justice (see Chapter 9), we are unlikely to find a satisfactory conception of morality on a procedural plane. Mere compliance with the principles of formal justice is an inadequate threshold of what is morally correct. Thus, though he scrupulously complies with the requirements of due process etc, the judge who gives effect to the immoral statute fails to be moral and fails to do justice.

requiring 'delivery up' of fugitive slaves. For a discussion of morality and roles see Charles Fried, *Right and Wrong* (Cambridge, Mass: Harvard University Press, 1978), Ch 7. There are, of course, other reasons that a judge might have for remaining at his post, the evil of the legal system notwithstanding. Such justifications include the prudential (financial reward, status, absence of realistic alternatives, etc). Thus Matthew Kramer refers to such officials' 'selfish and nefarious ends' whose reasons for acting (and 'embracing the rule of law') 'are wicked and purely prudential. For them, the rule of law is nothing more (and nothing less) than an efficient means toward the sustainment [*sic*] and extension of their powerfully repressive reign', Matthew H Kramer, *In Defense of Legal Positivism: Law Without Trimmings* (Oxford: Clarendon Press, 1999), 197. Raz suggests another possible (but rather fanciful) explanation: 'An anarchist...may become a judge on the ground that if he follows the law most of the time he will be able to disobey it on the few but important occasions when to do so will tend most to undermine it', J Raz, *Practical Reason and Norms* (Oxford: Oxford University Press, 1990), 148. But how likely is an anarchist to be appointed to the bench in an unjust legal system? See Joel Feinberg, 'Natural Law: The Dilemma of Judges Who Must Interpret Immoral Laws' in his *Problems at the Roots of Law: Essays in Legal and Political Theory*.

[107] Hart, *The Concept of Law*, 155–7.      [108] Lyons, op cit, 83.

### 2.11.5 **The judge's choice**

Righteous J may conclude that he should stay at his post for one or more of three reasons. First, he regards the greater part of the law as just and that most (or even all) of his judging takes place on this morally neutral terrain. Secondly, he believes that there are opportunities for him to interpret the law humanely, frustrating, if necessary, the immoral intention of the legislature. Thirdly, that should he give up his job, he is likely to be replaced by a less moral judge. This was, you will recall, the position adopted by the Nazi judge, Franz Schlegelberger (see note 83).

The strength of these arguments rests partly on empirical facts about the political system in question. But it depends also on how the judicial function itself is explained. Legal positivism, as you know, vests the judge with a strong discretion to fill 'gaps' in the common law. Hart's version postulates a 'rule of recognition', compliance with which is a prerequisite for rules to be valid members of the legal system. Judges are bound to apply only those rules that satisfy the criteria of validity specified in the rule of recognition. Many rules, however, have what Hart calls an 'open texture' and judges are therefore inevitably presented with hard cases in which they do not merely discover the law, they actually make it.

Since the law does not, by definition, provide the answer in such cases, judges draw on moral principles in order to reach a decision. For Dworkin, as we shall see, a rule of recognition that serves to segregate law and morals is not possible (see 5.2). A legal system is a kind of moral system. Law consists, in addition to rules, of 'non-rule standards' like principles and policies. In a hard case, a judge draws on these moral and political standards, not because they are endorsed by any rule of recognition, but because it is part of the process of 'constructive interpretation' by which he pursues the best possible interpretation of what the law is.

Hart's version of the judicial enterprise gives Righteous J slightly thicker ice on which to skate. It preserves an area of strong discretion by which he might do good. And liberal academics and judges in apartheid South Africa did indeed attempt to show how, within the interstices of unjust law, humane interpretations were possible. By appealing to certain 'liberal' principles of the common law, it was frequently claimed, repressive legislation might be tempered, immoral laws averted. If, however, strong discretion is not part of the judicial armoury, as Dworkin argues, such a route would appear to be closed.

The matter may, however, not be quite so simple. The question is whether, on Dworkin's account, an unjust legal system is capable of generating in hard cases *any moral principles at all*. To qualify for membership of the interpretive set of principles, a principle must satisfy a minimal moral threshold. It must, he says, at least render the decisions it purports to support more attractive than the exercise of arbitrary power. We therefore need some principle to explain the unjust legal system in question. Unless he takes the view that the whole legal system is tainted by immorality (because, say, the majority have been deprived any participation in it), Righteous J will have little difficulty in justifying those branches of the law such as the law of contract, which fall for consideration. But, in respect of discriminatory legislation, he will have a more formidable task: he must ask 'which interpretation of his country's legal practices would put them in what we believe would be their least bad light'.[109]

The moral judge's predicament is nicely captured by Dworkin, though he does not develop it:

> Do our legal practices, though morally infirm, nevertheless generate some weak political or moral rights in those who have relied on them, so that they should be enforced except when some compelling moral case can be made against this? Or are these practices so wicked that they should be seen as generating no rights at all, even weak ones?[110]

Suppose Righteous J is faced with a hard case under a racial statute. He regards the system of racial segregation enshrined in the legislation as immoral. He is unable therefore to justify the statute either by reference to previous cases decided under it, or to 'community morality': the principles and policies that explain the 'fit' between the legislation and the 'institutional history' of his society. He finds, in other words, that apartheid is so wicked that it fails to generate even weak rights. His choice, according to Dworkin, is threefold: first, he may give a decision based on moral (rather than legal) grounds; secondly, he may lie and declare the law to be what he would prefer it to be; or, thirdly, he may resign.[111]

But then Dworkin allows the judge's dilemma to be resolved by reference to a consequentialist calculation of the likely outcome of his choice:

> If the judge decides that the reasons supplied by background moral rights are so strong that he has a moral duty to do what he can to support these rights, then it may be that he must lie, because *he cannot be of any help* unless he is understood as saying, in his official role, that the legal rights are different from what he believes they are. He could, of course, avoid lying by resigning *which will ordinarily be of little help*, or by staying in office and hoping, against odds, that this appeal based on moral grounds will have the same *practical effect* as a lie would.[112]

But consequentialism gives rise to a number of difficulties, not least the problem of attempting to predict the effects of our preferences (see 9.1.2). I return to the uncertainties of this calculation in 4.2.7. Can Dworkin's slide into consequentialism be avoided? Though his theory of adjudication offers a more plausible account than Hart's, it stumbles into awkward straits when applied to unjust legal systems. This is not surprising since it is founded on their opposite: the concept of 'constructive interpretation' is to be understood as an explanation for the process, or ideal, of 'law as integrity' (see 5.2.7).

But this process does not operate independently of the 'dimension of fit'. To have explanatory power an interpretation must be 'true': we are engaged in a quest for the 'right' answer. An answer is 'right' not only in the sense that it is morally the best justification of the law, but also that it 'fits' with 'institutional history'. The judge therefore expresses the values inherent in the legal system. Where such values are essentially just (as Dworkin assumes the values of the American legal system to be), integrity

---

[109] Dworkin, *Law's Empire*, 107.     [110] Ibid, 107–8.

[111] R Dworkin, *Taking Rights Seriously*, new impression with a reply to critics (London: Duckworth, 1978), 326–7.     [112] Ibid, emphasis added.

and fidelity to principle will normally secure a just outcome. In an unjust legal system, however, there appears to be a conflict between constructive interpretation and coherence.

One could resolve the conflict by salvaging some coherence by severing the unjust laws from the rest of the law and regarding them as aberrations that lack any justification.[113] But we can do this only to the extent that it is realistic to declare that the whole system is infected with injustice. If it is—and a credible case could be made out—then constructive interpretation is for Righteous J a tragic *cul-de-sac*. If it is not so contaminated, then in hard cases involving unjust laws, he must lie. Both the lying judge and the judge who decides hard cases on explicitly moral grounds place fidelity to justice above fidelity to law. But to be 'of any help' the lies, if they do not cost him his job, cannot be told or the moral appeals made, too often so as not to undermine the judge's competence and integrity.

## 2.11.6 **The judge's surrender**

Should Righteous J simply throw in the towel and resign? His most compelling moral argument for relinquishing office is that he has become (or only now perceives that he has been) a vehicle for injustice. This entails an acknowledgement not only that the apartheid laws are iniquitous, but that, because significant portions of his jurisdiction have been ousted, his 'moral' decisions annulled on appeal or by subsequent legislation, and his constructive interpretation of the law worthless, he has lost the capacity to do justice.[114] An additional ground for his moral discomfort is that as an official he lends the system legitimacy. He (or indeed you) might reply that other members of the community, especially lawyers, also confer legitimacy and respectability on the system by virtue of their participation in it. But if they do, it cannot surely be the same kind of support as judicial acquiescence. I return to this problem in 4.2.7.

Hard cases offer Righteous J his most effective prospects to 'do good'. His withdrawal from the system might therefore be considered to be an abdication, rather than an expression, of his moral responsibility. But this sort of assessment seems rooted in consequentialism that, as I have already said, is notoriously complex. How might he go about weighing up the consequences of his staying against going?

---

[113] E Mureinik, 'Dworkin and Apartheid' in H Corder (ed), *Essays on Law and Social Practice in South Africa* (Cape Town: Juta, 1988), 188–217, 209. See too D Dyzenhaus, *Hard Cases in Wicked Legal Systems: Pathologies of Legality*, 2nd edn (Oxford: Oxford University Press, 2010).

[114] All three were, alas, true of the judge's plight in apartheid South Africa: 'liberal' judgments were almost routinely reversed on appeal or their effect negated by legislation, and the court's power to enquire into widely used executive powers of detention under the Internal Security Act 1982 (and its predecessors) were in practice annihilated. If you are interested in how a legal system can succumb to ideological corrosion, see the so-called 'Wacks–Dugard debate': R Wacks, 'Judges and Injustice' (1984) 101 *South African Law Journal* 266. Cf J Dugard, 'Should Judges Resign?—A Reply to Professor Wacks' (1984) 101 *South African Law Journal* 286; R Wacks, 'Judging Judges: A Brief Rejoinder to Professor Dugard' (1984) 101 *South African Law Journal* 295; J Dugard, 'Omar: Support for Wacks's Ideas on the Judicial Process?' (1987) 103 *South African Journal on Human Rights* 295.

On the one hand, his remaining in office allows him the potential, by whatever route, of doing justice in hard cases—on the empirical assumption that he believes this still to be possible. Oppressed people may benefit; suffering may be reduced. He will also consider the likelihood that this opportunity, however remote, will be eliminated when he is replaced by a judge who supports the wicked system. On the other hand, his withdrawal may assist, albeit modestly, to undermine legitimacy: judicial resignations on conscientious grounds are exceptional occurrences. It may also encourage other judges to follow suit or at least critically to evaluate their predicament and as a consequence to seek ways of avoiding the effects of the law's injustice. And a judicial proclamation of the paralysis of the courts may result in legislative measures to reduce the law's inhumanity.

If there is some vestigial morality in the system, the balance seems to weigh against withdrawal. The arguments in support of Righteous J remaining at his post are constructive, charged with hope that palpable good may result. The case for resignation, however, speaks of despair and futility. It is not surprising that few would advocate so extreme a step. For Feinberg it is self-indulgent narcissism:

> If a judge's resignation is motivated entirely by his desire to preserve his own moral purity, so that his hands will not be soiled with the blood of others, then he makes a poor hero, though his action on his own behalf might have required considerable courage. But would not a more fruitful use of his courage and a craftier use of the power of his office, if any, be more commendable? . . . I suspect that efforts to preserve integrity in situations like these will inevitably be self-defeating, because true integrity requires more effective resistance and less narcissistic self-concern.[115]

But this consequentialist calculus is highly problematic because of difficulties intrinsic to both consequentialism and the moral responsibility of judges and other public officials.

To make Righteous J's determination of whether he should stay or go turn on which course of action he thinks will achieve more justice entails a questionable utilitarian calculation. Apart from the fact it is impossible to forecast what effect his withdrawal might have, a utilitarian reckoning seems, as Kant says, to strip his action of moral worth, because it is done for the sake of its consequences. Yet teleological theories (which define what is good by reference to the goals that are achieved) are often hard to resist. According to John Rawls such theories,

> . . . have deep intuitive appeal since they seem to embody the idea of rationality. It is natural to think that rationality is maximizing something and that in morals it must be maximizing the good. Indeed, it is tempting to suppose that it is self-evident that things should be arranged so as to lead to the most good.[116]

But this attraction may be deceptive. Do you think they provide a convincing moral resolution of Righteous J's dilemma?[117]

---

[115] Feinberg, op cit, 21.

[116] J Rawls, *A Theory of Justice* (Harmondsworth: Penguin, 1973), 24–5.

[117] You may want to think about other possible resolutions to this thorny problem. For example, could we perhaps develop the argument (adopted by Dworkin and Nagel) that the morality of officials derives

## 2.11.7 **The judge and the lawyer**

You may be wondering whether the moral quandary of Righteous J can be resolved without reflecting upon the predicament faced by all who inhabit an unjust society. Should the fact that Righteous J is a public official distinguish him from others who participate in the legal system or who simply derive benefit from its injustice? Are there compelling reasons for morally differentiating judges from others, particularly lawyers?

Righteous J attempts to do justice when he can, admitting that his autonomy is curtailed in several major areas of the law. But is a conscientious lawyer not in the same boat? He strives to do good, often at great personal cost, within the strictures of the legal system. He too lends legitimacy to the system. Is the moral imperative to withdraw not the same?

One could attempt to answer this question on at least three levels: the political, the functional, and the practical or consequential. Politically, judges are officers appointed by the government to implement its laws. Their legal duty is plain. Lawyers, on the other hand, are not state officials. They owe a strong duty to their clients. They must, of course, work within the system, but their obligation is to utilize the law, not to dispense justice (or injustice). They may find the law morally repugnant, but their role within an unjust legal system is easier to justify than that of the judge. Lawyers in apartheid South Africa themselves recognized this distinction, and several eminent senior counsel declared that on conscientious grounds they would decline appointment to the bench. Yet they continued as lawyers. And, though the temptation to withdraw was often powerful, many lawyers played a courageous, sometimes heroic, part in the struggle for justice.

A lawyer may, however, decide that his or her participation in the legal system serves to legitimate it. This is a perfectly proper moral response. But it does not, I think, follow that the dilemma is therefore the same as for the state official. This is because of the important functional differences between the two. In particular, lawyers, unlike judges, are not concerned exclusively with the forensic process. Indeed, lawyers do some of their most worthwhile work when they advise clients of their rights, whether or not litigation is intended or anticipated. Thus, while appearance before the court may be regarded as a more palpable acceptance of its legitimacy, advising clients may not.

This is an area of considerable complexity that entails reflection upon the third—consequentialist—level: is it the legitimacy of the court or the law or a law (or all) that the non-participating lawyer questions? Morally, each may call for different action.

from the obligations they undertake on our behalf? Is it feasible to apply a similar obligation-based test to the question of withdrawal? In other words, might we postulate the dilemma in terms not of its—always uncertain—*consequences*, but by reference to the judge's *obligations*? The argument would run as follows. A judge has a legal duty to apply the law; he has a moral duty to 'do justice'; in a just or nearly just society this is unlikely to give rise to problems; in an unjust society, however, a conflict arises between his legal duty to apply the (unjust) law and his moral duty to 'do justice'; if he can find no way to 'do justice', his moral duty requires him to resign.

How does the lawyer distinguish between participation of an advisory kind from forensic representation? Do not both help to legitimate the law (a law, court, legal system)? Does withdrawal constitute an abandonment of the client's interests, assuming the client wishes the lawyer to represent him or her? Will participation facilitate exposure of injustice? Do the oppressed not rely on effective legal advice and representation? And so on. These are questions for a lively seminar. A legal positivist, moreover, would address the issue in a rather different manner, as should become clear in the next two chapters.

## Questions

1. Is Aquinas's theory of natural law a restraint on unjust laws being enacted?

2. In what sense may a principle be said to derive from natural law?

3. Examine the view that the *ius gentium* drew on natural law principles.

4. Is Hume's non-cognitivism destructive of all natural law thinking?

5. Why did the nineteenth century see a quietus in natural law theories?

6. 'The weakness of [Finnis's] argument is not simply that one can find complex counterexamples. The belief that, if one reflects carefully about the human condition, the principles of moral action are a self-evident basis for the determination of concrete obligations, is itself mistaken. One is led to suspect that Finnis believes that there are ascertainable principles determinative of moral obligations because he believes that, at a deep level, unless there are such principles, none of our moral judgments make any sense—and of course, they do make sense. If he does in fact hold this belief, in that as in much else he and I agree. But the puzzle cannot be solved as he proposes.' (Weinreb, *Natural Law and Justice*, 115)

   Is this a fair criticism of Finnis's account of natural law?

7. Consider Finnis's 'basic forms of human flourishing'. Are they a realistic account of the human experience? What would you exclude/include? Are such catalogues helpful? Is Hart's 'minimum content of natural law' a better/worse catalogue? Is the 'natural law' description apposite?

8. What do you make of Finnis's observation that:

   '[T]he ruler has very strictly speaking, no right to be obeyed; but he has the authority to give directions and make laws that are morally obligatory and that he has the responsibility of enforcing. He has this authority for the sake of the common good (the needs of which can also, however, make authoritative the opinions—as in custom— or stipulations of men who have no authority). Therefore, if he uses his authority to make stipulations against any of the basic principles of practical reasonableness, those stipulations altogether lack the authority they would otherwise have by virtue of being his. More precisely, stipulations made for partisan advantage, or (without emergency justification) in excess of legally defined authority, or imposing inequitable burdens on their subjects, or directing the doing of things that should never be done, simply fail, of themselves, to create any moral obligations whatever.'

9. Does Finnis's assumption (335) that the lawgiver's authority derives from a normative framework not of his making which is a means of realizing the common good, overlook the immorality or injustice of the system?

10. What are the objections to moral realism? What does Moore regard as the relationship between moral and legal objectivity? Is this a convincing argument?

11. 'In "strong" versions of positivism, including Hart's, a necessary condition of making a rule of primary obligation a rule of law is that it be picked out by a legal system's rule of recognition. In "weak" versions, it is a sufficient condition. For the first type of positivist all the Nazi laws were indeed law but the law applied by the Nuremberg Tribunal was not, while for the second type of positivist, the "weak", the Nazi laws were law but the law applied by the Tribunal also may have been law. A "strong" natural lawyer insists that law is law only if it conforms to natural law. A "weak" natural lawyer, however, is indistinguishable from a "weak" positivist.' (Richard A Posner, *Law and Legal Theory in the UK and USA* (1996), 18)

Analyse this claim in the context of the Hart–Fuller debate.

12. Why should we assume that Dworkin's answer to the question about the contested concept of law should incorporate the rights thesis?

13. Would Mill's 'harm principle' permit laws to restrict or control pornography or hate speech?

14. Would it affect the moral argument if the law allowed abortions to be carried out only on victims of rape?

15. If we recognize the 'right to life' should active euthanasia be a criminal offence?

16. Is the moral dilemma of lawyers who practise in unjust societies any different from judges who occupy the bench in these societies?

17. Etienne Mureinik contends: 'If we argue...that moral judges should resign, we can no longer pray, when we go into court as defence counsel, or even as the accused, that we find a moral judge on the bench.' Is this a teleological (or consequentialist) argument or a deontological one? Of the other arguments of each kind that you have perceived in this debate, which do you find more persuasive, and why?

18. Is Fuller's 'inner morality of law' really moral or is Hart correct in characterizing his eight desiderata as relating to efficacy? Is the 'inner morality' simply the rule of law?

19. In what sense does Fuller describe his principles as 'the morality of aspiration'?

20. Nigel Simmonds claims, 'Fuller would probably say that compliance with the eight principles is logically consistent with the pursuit of evil aims in very much the same way that armed robbery is logically consistent with a scrupulous concern for paying one's debts.' (Simmonds, *Central Issues in Jurisprudence*, 4th edn, 236 )

Do you agree? South African law under apartheid may broadly have conformed to Fuller's inner morality. What follows from this?

# Further reading

ALEXY, ROBERT, *A Theory of Legal Argumentation*, transl Neil MacCormick (Oxford: Oxford University Press 1989).

ALEXY, ROBERT, *The Argument from Injustice: A Reply to Legal Positivism*, transl Stanley Paulson and Bonnie L Paulson (Oxford: Oxford University Press, 2002).

ALEXY, ROBERT, *A Theory of Constitutional Rights*, transl Julian Rivers (Oxford: Oxford University Press, 2002).

ALEXY, ROBERT, 'Some Reflections on the Ideal Dimension of Law and on the Legal Philosophy of John Finnis' (2013) 58 *American Journal of Jurisprudence* (2013) 97.

AQUINAS, ST THOMAS, *Summa Theologiae* in *Selected Political Writings*, transl JG Dawson, ed A Passerin D'Entrèves (Oxford: Basil Blackwell, 1970, reprint of 1959 edn).

ARISTOTLE, *Nicomachean Ethics*, transl H Rackham (London: William Heinemann, 1938) (Loeb Classical Library).

AUGUSTINE, ST, *City of God*, transl WC Greene (London: William Heinemann, 1960) (Loeb Classical Library).

AUGUSTINE, ST, *Confessions*, transl W Watts (London: William Heinemann, 1912) (Loeb Classical Library).

BECKWITH, FRANCIS J, *Defending Life: A Moral and Legal Case Against Abortion Choice* (Cambridge: Cambridge University Press, 2007).

BEYLEVELD, D and BROWNSWORD, R, 'The Practical Difference between Natural-law Theory and Legal Positivism' (1985) 5 *Oxford Journal of Legal Studies* 1.

CICERO, MT, De Re Publica, transl CW Keyes (London: William Heinemann, 1928) (Loeb Classical Library).

COLEMAN, JULES, *Markets, Morals and the Law* (Cambridge: Cambridge University Press, 1988).

COLEMAN, JULES and LEITER, B, 'Legal Positivism' in D Patterson (ed), *A Companion to Philosophy of Law and Legal Theory* (Oxford and Cambridge, Mass: Blackwell, 1966).

COVER, R, *Justice Accused: Antislavery and the Judicial Process* (New Haven, Conn: Yale University Press, 1983).

DETMOLD, MJ, *The Unity of Law and Morality: A Refutation of Legal Positivism* (London: Routledge & Kegan Paul, 1984).

DUGARD, J, 'Should Judges Resign?—A Reply to Professor Wacks' (1984) 101 *South African Law Journal* 286.

DUGARD, J, 'Omar: Support for Wacks's Ideas on the Judicial Process?' (1987) 3 *South African Journal on Human Rights* 295.

DWORKIN, RONALD, *Life's Dominion: An Argument about Abortion and Euthanasia* (London: HarperCollins, 1993).

DWORKIN, RONALD, *Justice for Hedgehogs* (Cambridge, Mass and London: Belknap Press, 2011).

DWORKIN, GERALD, FREY, RG, and BOK, SISSELA, *Euthanasia and Physician-Assisted Suicide (For and Against)* (Cambridge: Cambridge University Press, 1998).

DYZENHAUS, D, *Hard Cases in Wicked Legal Systems: Pathologies of Legality*, 2nd edn (Oxford: Oxford University Press, 2010).

FEINBERG, JOEL, *Harm to Others: The Moral Limits of the Criminal Law* (Oxford: Oxford University Press, 1984).

FEINBERG, JOEL, *Offense to Others: The Moral Limits of the Criminal Law* (Oxford: Oxford University Press, 1985).

FEINBERG, JOEL, 'Natural Law: The Dilemma of Judges Who Must Interpret Immoral Laws' in *Problems at the Roots of Law: Essays in Legal and Political Theory* (Oxford: Oxford University Press, 2003).

FINNIS, JOHN, *Fundamentals of Ethics* (Washington DC: Georgetown University Press, 1983).

FINNIS, JOHN, (ed), *Natural Law* (Aldershot: Dartmouth, 1991).

FINNIS, JOHN, *Aquinas: Moral, Political and Legal Theory* (Oxford: Oxford University Press, 1998).

FINNIS, JOHN, 'Natural Law: The Classic Tradition' in J Coleman and S Shapiro (eds), *The Oxford Handbook of Jurisprudence and Philosophy of Law* (Oxford: Oxford University Press, 2002).

FINNIS, JOHN, *Natural Law and Natural Rights*, 2nd edn (Oxford: Clarendon Press, 2011).

FINNIS, JOHN, BOYLE, JOSEPH M, and GRISEZ, GERMAIN, 'Incoherence and Consequentialism (or Proportionalism)—A Rejoinder' (1990) *American Catholic Philosophical Quarterly* 64.

FRIED, C, *Right and Wrong* (Cambridge, Mass: Harvard University Press, 1978).

FULLER, LON LUVOIS, 'Positivism and Fidelity to Law—A Reply to Professor Hart' (1958) 71 *Harvard Law Review* 630.

FULLER, LON LUVOIS, *The Morality of Law*, rev edn (New Haven, Conn and London: Yale University Press, 1969).

GEORGE, ROBERT P, 'Moralistic Liberalism and Legal Moralism' (1990) 88 *Michigan Law Review* 1421.

GEORGE, ROBERT P, 'Does the "Incommensurability Thesis" Imperil Common Sense Moral Judgements?' (1992) 37 *American Journal of Jurisprudence* 185.

GEORGE, ROBERT P (ed), *Making Men Moral: Civil Liberties and Public Morality* (Oxford: Clarendon Press, 1993).

GEORGE, ROBERT P (ed), *Natural Law Theory: Contemporary Essays* (Oxford: Clarendon Press, 1994).

GEORGE, ROBERT P (ed), *The Autonomy of Law: Essays on Legal Positivism* (Oxford: Clarendon Press, 1995).

GEORGE, ROBERT P, *In Defense of Natural Law* (Oxford: Oxford University Press, 1999).

GLOVER, JONATHAN, *Causing Death and Saving Lives: The Moral Problems of Abortion, Infanticide, Suicide, Euthanasia, Capital Punishment, War and Other Life-or-death Choices* (Harmondsworth: Penguin Books, 1990).

GRISEZ, GERMAIN, BOYLE, JOSEPH, and FINNIS, JOHN, 'Practical Principles, Moral Truth, and Ultimate Ends' (1987) 32 *American Journal of Jurisprudence* 99.

HACKER, PMS and RAZ, J (eds), *Law, Morality and Society: Essays in Honour of HLA Hart* (Oxford: Clarendon Press, 1977).

HART, HLA, *The Concept of Law*, 2nd edn, ed PA Bulloch and J Raz (Oxford: Clarendon Press, 1994).

HIGGINS, RUTH, *The Moral Limits of Law* (Oxford: Oxford University Press, 2004).

HOBBES, THOMAS, *Leviathan*, ed M Oakeshott (Oxford: Basil Blackwell, 1960).

HULL, NEH and HOFFER, PETER CHARLES, *Roe v Wade: The Abortion Rights Controversy in American History (Landmark Law Cases and American Society)* (Lawrence, Kan: University Press of Kansas, 2001).

HUME, DAVID, *A Treatise of Human Nature*, ed LA Selby Bigge, 3rd edn revised by PH Nidditch (Oxford: Clarendon Press, 1978).

HUXTABLE, RICHARD, *Euthanasia, Ethics and the Law: From Conflict to Compromise? (Biomedical Law & Ethics Library)* (London: Routledge Cavendish, 2007).

KEOWN, JOHN, *Euthanasia, Ethics and Public Policy: An Argument against Legalisation* (Cambridge: Cambridge University Press, 2002).

KRAMER, MATTHEW H, 'Also Among the Prophets: Some Rejoinders to Ronald Dworkin's Attacks On Legal Positivism' (1999) 12 *Canadian Journal of Law and Jurisprudence* 53.

KRAMER, MATTHEW H, *In Defense of Legal Positivism: Law Without Trimmings* (Oxford: Clarendon Press, 1999).

KRAMER, MATTHEW H, *Where Law and Morality Meet* (Oxford: Oxford University Press, 2004).

LEE, ELLIE (ed), *Abortion Law and Politics Today* (London: Palgrave Macmillan, 1998).

LEITER, BRIAN, 'The Demarcation Problem in Jurisprudence: A New Case for Skepticism' (2011) 31 *Oxford Journal of Legal Studies* 663.

LOCKE, JOHN, Two Treatises of Government, ed P Laslett (Cambridge: Cambridge University Press, 1964).

LYONS, D, *Ethics and the Rule of Law* (Cambridge: Cambridge University Press, 1984).

MACCORMICK, NEIL, *HLA Hart* (London: Edward Arnold, 1981).

MACCORMICK, NEIL, 'Contemporary Legal Philosophy: The Rediscovery of Practical Reason' (1983) 10 *Journal of Law & Society* 1.

MCLEAN, SHEILA AM, *Assisted Dying: Reflections on the Need for Law Reform (Biomedical Law & Ethics Library)* (London: Routledge Cavendish, 2007).

MOORE, MICHAEL, *Objectivity in Ethics and Law* (Aldershot: Dartmouth/Ashgate, 2003).

MUREINIK, E, 'Dworkin and Apartheid' in H Corder (ed), *Essays on Law and Social Practice in South Africa* (Cape Town: Juta, 1988).

MURPHY, MARK C, *Natural Law and Practical Rationality* (Cambridge: Cambridge University Press, 2001).

MURPHY, MARK C, *Natural Law in Jurisprudence and Politics* (Cambridge: Cambridge University Press, 2009).

NAGEL, T, 'Ruthlessness in Public Life' in *Mortal Questions* (Cambridge: Cambridge University Press, 1979).

OST, SUZANNE, *Analytical Study of the Legal, Moral and Ethical Aspects of the Living Phenomenon of Euthanasia: Questions of Law, Morality and Ethics within Contemporary Society (Symposium)* (Ceredigion: Edwin Mellen Press, 2003).

OTLOWSKI, MARGARET, *Voluntary Euthanasia and the Common Law* (Oxford: Oxford University Press, 1997).

PASSERIN D'ENTRÈVES, ALESSANDRO, *Natural Law: An Introduction to Legal Philosophy*, 2nd edn (London: Hutchinson, 1970).

PATERSON, C, *Assisted Suicide and Euthanasia: A Natural Law Ethics Approach* (London: Ashgate, 2008).

RAWLS, J, *A Theory of Justice* (Harmondsworth: Penguin, 1973)

RAZ, J, *Practical Reason and Norms* (Oxford: Oxford University Press, 1990).

REGAN, T, BEAUCHAMP, TL, CALLICOT, JB, RACHELS, J, BEDAU, HA, and LEVENBOOK, B, *Matters of Life and Death*, 3rd edn (Columbus, Ohio: McGraw-Hill Higher Education, 1992).

SIMMONDS, NIGEL, *Law as a Moral Idea* (Oxford: Oxford University Press, 2007).

SIMMONS, AJ, *The Lockean Theory of Rights: Studies in Moral, Political, and Legal Philosophy* (Princeton, NJ: Princeton University Press, 1994).

SIMMONS, AJ, *On the Edge of Anarchy: Locke, Consent and the Limits of Society: Studies in Moral, Political, and Legal Philosophy)* (Princeton, NJ: Princeton University Press, 1995).

SINGER, PETER, *Rethinking Life and Death: The Collapse of Our Traditional Ethics* (Oxford: Oxford Paperbacks, 1995).

SUMMERS, ROBERT S, *Lon L Fuller* (London: Edward Arnold, 1984).

WACKS, R, 'Judges and Injustice' (1984) 101 *South African Law Journal* 266.

WACKS, R, 'Judging Judges: A Brief Rejoinder to Professor Dugard' (1984) 101 *South African Law Journal* 295.

WACKS, R, 'Judges and Moral Responsibility' in W Sadurski (ed), *Ethical Dimensions of Legal Theory* (Poznan Studies in the Philosophy of the Sciences and Humanities) (Amsterdam: Rodopi, 1991).

WACKS, R, 'Law's Umpire: Judges, Truth, and Moral Accountability' in P Koller and A-J Arnaud (eds), *Law, Justice, and Culture* (Stuttgart: Franz Steiner Verlag, 1998).

WACKS, R, 'Are Judges Morally Accountable?' in *Law, Morality and the Private Domain* (Hong Kong: Hong Kong University Press, 2000).

WACKS, R, 'Injustice in Robes: Iniquity and Judicial Accountability' (2009) 22 *Ratio Juris* 128.

WILLIAMS, GLENYS, *Intention and Causation in Medical Non-killing: The Impact of Criminal Law Concepts on Euthanasia and Assisted Suicide (Biomedical Law & Ethics Library)* (London: UCL Press, 2006).

# 3

# Classical legal positivism

Among the many labels you will encounter in your jurisprudence course, few have generated the confusion and the controversy that are associated with the apparently innocuous phrase 'legal positivism'. Use it with caution. Until fairly recently, to call someone a 'positivist' may excite an unexpected reaction: in some quarters it is regarded as a fairly serious term of abuse![1]

We are, of course, concerned here less about such sensitivity than arriving at a reasonably clear understanding of this frequently abused term and the theories of law espoused by those jurists who might legitimately be described as 'positivists'. It is therefore important that the confusion attending the use of the term be clarified at once, particularly because a proper grasp of these theories is an essential prerequisite to an understanding of jurisprudence.

After attempting to clarify the term, this chapter examines the theories of the foremost legal positivists of the nineteenth century: Jeremy Bentham and John Austin. Chapter 4 then investigates contemporary legal positivism through the works of some of its leading exponents: HLA Hart, Hans Kelsen, Joseph Raz, Jules Coleman, and others.

## 3.1 What is legal positivism?

At the outset, it is important to recognize that positivism is not an exclusively jurisprudential approach. Its central claim—whether it is logical, scientific, philosophical, sociological, or legal positivism—is the view that the only genuine knowledge is scientific knowledge which emerges only from the positive confirmation of theory by the application of rigid scientific methods. Its originator was the nineteenth-century thinker, Auguste Comte (generally regarded as the founder of sociology) whose ideas influenced the so-called Vienna Circle of logical positivism that developed in the early years of the twentieth century. Its members sought to combine empiricism (the view that we can know things only through observation) and rationalism (the idea that what we know must include an element that is not derived from observation alone). In the 1920s and 1930s the movement grew in importance and spread to Britain and the

---

[1] See Chapter 2 n 2.

United States. Its fundamental principles included an antagonism towards metaphysics, particularly ontology and *a priori* propositions. In a nutshell, it held that all knowledge rests on logical inference from simple 'protocol sentence' grounded in empirical, observable facts. It emphasized the test of verifiability: the doctrine that a proposition is 'cognitively meaningful' only when there exists a finite means by which to determine conclusively its truth or falsity.

Legal positivism attempts to identify the key features of the legal system that are posited by legislators, judges, and so on. Yet the theory has generated substantial misunderstanding. Indeed the confusion is so acute that, in the view of at least one distinguished writer, the term 'legal positivism' ought to be abandoned altogether.[2] And Professor Summers was driven to this conclusion by identifying no less than ten different positions which are described as 'positivist'. It is, however, unlikely that, whatever the extent of the ambiguity surrounding the phrase, it will cease being a central term of art in jurisprudence. Having a clear idea of what it is the positivists say about law and (as will emerge later) how this differs from other views (especially the natural law approach: see Chapter 2) is therefore essential.

A valuable starting point is Professor Hart's important essay, 'Positivism and the Separation of Law and Morals'[3] where he enumerates five main views that are generally associated with legal positivism, as follows:

1. That laws are commands of human beings.

2. That there is no necessary connection between law and morals.

3. That the analysis of legal concepts is (i) worth pursuing, (ii) distinct from (though not hostile to) sociological and historical enquiries and critical evaluation.

4. That a legal system is a 'closed logical system' in which correct decisions may be deduced from predetermined legal rules by logical means alone.

5. That moral judgments cannot be established, as statements of fact can, by rational argument, evidence, or proof (this is known as 'non-cognitivism in ethics' and was discussed in 2.7).

While, in general terms, it is fair to describe certain jurists as 'positivists' (Bentham, Austin, Kelsen, Raz, and Hart himself are the most important), students are sometimes too quick to treat them as if they belonged to a largely undifferentiated 'school' which adheres to certain general views about the law. At a fairly high level of abstraction, this is not entirely inaccurate. But it is important to recognize that not only do each of these writers pose different questions, but their method of enquiry and general objectives are often as different as the features they share. This ought to become evident below.

---

[2] RS Summers, 'The *New* Analytical Jurists' (1966) 41 *New York University Law Review* 861, 889–90.
[3] (1958) 71 *Harvard Law Review* 593, 601 n 25. See HLA Hart, *The Concept of Law* (Oxford: Clarendon Press, 1961), 253. See too 2nd edn by PA Bulloch and J Raz (Oxford: Clarendon Press, 1994), 253. A third edition, introduced by Leslie Green, with a postscript edited by Joseph Raz and Penelope Bulloch was published by Oxford University Press in 2012. See 'Further reading' in Chapter 4.

If one were to express the highest common factor among these writers it would probably be their emphasis on describing law by reference to formal rather than moral criteria. In their pursuit of a 'scientific' analysis of law and legal rules, it is their contention that the law as laid down (*positum*) should be kept separate—for the purpose of study and analysis—from the law as it ought morally to be. In other words, that a clear distinction must be drawn between 'ought' (that which is morally desirable) and 'is' (that which actually exists).

### 3.1.1 **What legal positivism is not**

It does not follow from this (and this is a point that Professor Hart is at pains to stress in the essay mentioned earlier) that a legal positivist is unconcerned with moral questions or even that he rejects the important influence of morality on law. Indeed, all of these jurists have been deeply concerned to criticize the law and to propose means of reforming it. This normally involves moral judgments. But positivists do share the view that the most effective method of *analysing* and *understanding* law and the legal system involves suspending moral judgment until it is established what it is we are seeking to explain. In explaining the operation of the internal combustion engine, a positivist might argue, it would not help if we were to suggest alternatives to the carburettor or point out the limitations of the air filter. We should *first* want to know how the engine works. Criticism is a legitimate, but *separate* enterprise.

Nor do positivists necessarily subscribe to the proposition (often ascribed to them) that unjust or iniquitous laws must be obeyed—merely because they are law. Indeed even Austin (to say nothing of Bentham as utilitarian and Hart as moralist) acknowledges that disobedience to evil laws is legitimate if it would promote change for the good. As Hart puts it in a widely quoted statement:

> [T]he certification of something as legally valid is not conclusive of the question of obedience…however great the aura of majesty or authority which the official system may have, its demands must in the end be submitted to a moral scrutiny.[4]

And Kelsen insists that the difference between legal and moral discourse is so great that we cannot directly confront a legal 'ought' with a moral 'ought'. The important question of the relationship between legal positivism and natural law theory was considered in Chapter 2 where it was seen that the general philosophy of positivism represented, in large part, a reaction against the allegedly unscientific metaphysics of natural law doctrine. Legal positivism has, in turn, been criticized for its preoccupation with the question 'What is *the* law?' and its failure to address the more fundamental question 'What is law?'

To deny the enduring relationship between law and power would be folly. Those who exercise political power normally do so through the enactment of law, whether or not they are themselves subject to it. This inhospitable reality, while it may not take us

---

[4] *The Concept of Law*, 206.

very far, identifies an important distinction between the law and other forms of social control. In particular, law's fundamentally coercive nature.

But this generalization leaves unanswered many important, and often uncomfortable, questions about the nature of law. These issues cannot sensibly be considered, however, without an understanding of the claim itself. What does it mean to say that law is little more than the decisions of those in power? Is it to divest law of moral content? Does it entail a rejection of attempts to distinguish good law from bad, the just from the unjust? This chapter and the next consider the theories most closely associated with a purely analytical view of law: so-called legal positivism. As will be examined in greater detail in Chapter 4, contemporary legal positivism has two main factions. The former, 'hard' positivists (also known as 'exclusivists'), argue that legality does not depend on content or moral merit. 'Soft' positivists (or 'inclusive positivists' or 'incorporationists'), accept, however, that content or merit may be a condition of validity where the rule of recognition so specifies.

One should, as I said, always be suspicious of generalization. It is, however, possible to identify a cluster of relatively uncontroversial defining characteristics of both legal positivism and natural law theory. Thus Richard Tur has sketched the following spectrum:

> [C]lassical natural law and, perhaps Kant himself might be placed at the natural law extreme and Frank, if interpreted as an extreme particularist, and the early Ross, adjacent to the positivist extreme. Bentham, for whom everything must pay up in the hard currency of fact, and Austin occupy a position fairly adjacent to the positivist extreme but, in comparison to Frank, the commitment to some degree of legal system would justify a slightly more central position. Hart's theory would be even more centrally located, not so much because of the minimum core of empirical good sense which he perceives in the terminology of natural law but because his positivism purports to be normative rather than fact-based. Given, however, the facticity of the rule of recognition, Hart might properly remain nearer the positivist end of the continuum. Aquinas, as interpreted by Finnis, clearly cannot go too far out from the centre towards the natural law end partly because, apparently, he allows that an unjust law is still a law but primarily because he apparently rejects the rationalist stance that all decisions flow from logical deductions, allowing for 'determinations' in his system…[G]iven a stronger normativity than Hart's, [Kelsen] must be placed nearer to natural law than Hart's theory.[5]

The implications of this continuum should become clearer as you progress through the following pages.

## 3.2 Jeremy Bentham: the Luther of jurisprudence?

Bentham and Austin represent the classical school of English legal positivism, often disparaged by modern theorists as quaint or simply misguided. But they cannot sensibly be understood without an appreciation of the historical context in which they

---

[5] R Tur, 'The Kelsenian Enterprise' in R Tur and W Twining (eds), *Essays on Kelsen* (Oxford: Clarendon Press, 1986), 166.

wrote and the objectives they sought to achieve. In particular, they were (in different ways) apprehensive about the manner in which the common law was explained and justified as the expression of community needs and interests. For them, law is an expression of political facts, as will become evident below. I shall briefly describe the main elements of their theories and then suggest where their strengths and weaknesses might lie.

Jeremy Bentham (1748–1832) was a prolific author. His prodigious manuscripts lay unknown, gathering dust in the University of London for more than a century after his death in 1832. Especially since 1970, when Professor Hart published the first authoritative edition of Bentham's *Of Laws in General* (which Bentham completed in about 1782), it is clear that Bentham's work (including, in particular, *An Introduction to the Principles of Morals and Legislation*) constitutes a major contribution to positivist jurisprudence and the systematic analysis of law and the legal system. But it is a good deal more. With his 'extraordinary combination of a fly's eye for detail, with an eagle's eye for illuminating generalizations',[6] Bentham devoted himself to exposing what he saw as the shibboleths of his age and constructing a comprehensive theory of, *inter alia*, law, logic, politics, and psychology, founded on the principle of utility.

Little escaped his meticulous and scrupulous attention. He dealt with the courts, prisons, procedure, and reform of the law on almost every subject. And his sustained, often devastating, assault on the received wisdom of his day is magnificent in its destructive power, for, as Mill put it, Bentham found the battering-ram more useful than the builder's trowel.[7] But it is his critique of the common law and its theoretical underpinnings that are especially important to the student of jurisprudence. Moved by the spirit of the Enlightenment, Bentham sought to subject (some would say reduce) the common law to the cold light of reason.

He attempted to demystify the common law, to expose what lay behind its mask. The use of fictions, the confusion and inconsistency of the Draconian criminal law with its disproportionate sanctions, including capital punishment, legal jargon, and the complex writ system were some of the features of the common law that he attacked in his characteristically stinging and incisive manner. The law was a perplexing network of technical rules created by lawyers, conveyancers, and judges ('Judge & Co') which served their, usually corrupt, interests (see 3.2.2). Most people were too poor or ignorant to derive any benefit from a process which purported to be fair and rational:

> The techniques of manipulation of ignorance, complexity, and selective terror for sinister ends...could not be seen, according to Bentham, as mere aberrations of an essentially rational system of law. Rather, they comprised the latest expected chapter in a saga that had been written over the centuries. If society was to see any improvement, its law must be reformed; if its law was to be reformed it must be burned to the ground and rebuilt according to a new and rational pattern.[8]

---

[6] HLA Hart, *Essays on Bentham* (Oxford: Clarendon Press, 1982), 4.
[7] Quoted in Gerald J Postema, *Bentham and the Common Law Tradition* (Oxford: Clarendon Press, 1986), 148.          [8] Ibid, 267.

Bentham, says Hart, 'surely recognised in himself the Luther of jurisprudence'.[9] He derided not only lawyers' language (which was designed to render the law incomprehensible to the layman and hence multiply lawyers' fees) but also their wigs, robes, and anachronistic forms of address (which sought to lend legal proceedings 'lustre and splendour'), and the ambiguity, complexity, and irrationality of the rules of evidence. His critique inspired the major legislative reforms of the English law of evidence of 1843, 1851, and 1898.

There is, as has already been stressed, no substitute for the reading of primary sources (though the often turgid writings of Bentham and Austin demand a fair amount of patience and resilience). Indeed, Bentham himself described *Of Laws in General* as a 'dry cargo of speculative metaphysics'—not an entirely fair self-criticism, for there are certainly more laughs in Bentham than Austin. But you will find the principal features of Bentham's legal positivism (as well as other themes in his writings) analysed with characteristic clarity and elegance in Professor Hart's *Essays on Bentham*.

### 3.2.1 In search of determinacy

Bentham devoted a significant portion of his onslaught against the common law tradition to the 'theory' of the common law and the extent to which this theory differed from its practice. The common law was, in the eighteenth century, considered to be the expression of immemorial custom and long-standing practice which embodied natural reason. The law was thus legitimated by its historical (and hence popular) antecedents as well as its inherent rationality. Bentham regarded such ideas as dangerous fallacies: appeals to the Law of Nature were nothing more than 'private opinion in disguise' or 'the mere opinion of men self-constituted into legislatures'. The 'most prompt and perhaps the most usual translation of the phrase "contrary to reason", is "contrary to what I like".'[10]

> The only determinate, concrete content that can be given to natural law or reason is entirely private and subjective because of the abstractness of these notions. They offer no public shared standards for assessment of rules, laws, actions, or decisions. This has two disastrous consequences for law and adjudication. (*a*) Justification of judicial decisions is removed entirely from the public arena. Judicial decisions resting on appeals to natural law or reason rest entirely on private sentiment or whim. And, (*b*) this opens the door wide for corruption and the manipulation by sinister interests of those who are subject to law.[11]

Behind the mask of legal fictions (vaunted, especially by Blackstone, as the spirit of the common law) and the pretence of immemorial custom, lay an incomprehensible

---

[9] Hart, *Essays on Bentham*, 29.   [10] Quoted in Postema, op cit, 269 and 270.
[11] Ibid, 270.

web of unjust laws perpetuated in the name of 'precedent' which Bentham ridiculed as 'dog law':

> Whenever your dog does anything you want to break him of, you wait till he does it, and then beat him for it. This is the way you make laws for your dog: and this is the way the judges make law for you and me.[12]

Such 'superstitious respect for antiquity' ensures that senseless decisions of the past are repeated in the future. But times obviously change:

> [T]he more antique the precedent—that is to say, the more barbarous, inexperienced, and prejudice-led the race of men, by and among whom the precedent was set—the more unlike that the same *past* state of things…is the *present* state of things.[13]

And, paradoxically, the doctrine of *stare decisis* produces greater rather than less arbitrariness. This is because despite the apparent rigidity of the doctrine, to avoid following a precedent judges resort to legal fictions, 'equity', 'natural law', and other devices which render the law even more uncertain. Moreover, a judge is at liberty either to observe a precedent or to depart from it. The doctrine thus defeats its own avowed purpose.

The indeterminacy of the common law is endemic. Unwritten law is, in Bentham's view, intrinsically vague and uncertain. It cannot provide a reliable, public standard which can reasonably be expected to guide behaviour. Bentham's positivist conception of law, in other words, is a profoundly purposive or functional one, informed of course by the principle of utility. The common law falls far short of this conception not only because it fails to express rules with clarity, but because (and as a consequence) its very validity is suspect. So law's indeterminacy infects its legitimacy; to accept the authority of the rules themselves is often to accept the larger authority of the law itself. And this conflation results in a reluctance to question and criticize the law in general, to blind obedience.

### 3.2.2 Judge & Co

The role of judges in this disorder is especially pernicious. As already mentioned, 'Judge & Co' conspire to preserve the common law's delay, expense, and injustice. The judiciary was insufficiently accountable to the people and its method of resolving disputes unduly complex. The first deficiency could, he argued, be remedied by rendering the whole process of judging more open and public. Publicity, Bentham wrote, is 'the very soul of justice'. It ensured that judges were legally and morally accountable. But it was not enough for the courts to be accessible, they had to use language which was comprehensible to the ordinary person (an ideal which still shows little sign of realization!).

The second problem (which also continues to afflict modern courts) could, Bentham thought, be resolved by making judges more like fathers. He saw considerable merit

---

[12] Quoted in ibid, 277.　　　[13] Ibid, 278.

in employing the method by which domestic disputes are resolved: a father quickly, justly, and comprehensibly determines (without technical rules of evidence) whether a child (or perhaps a servant) has committed the act in question, and hands down the appropriate verdict and judgment or sentence. This cosy model of alternative dispute resolution assumes, of course, a number of social features from which it may seem dangerous to extrapolate a great deal, but it supplies a fairly graphic analogy in support of informal modes of adjudication.

Bentham's attack on the conventional common law model of the judicial function is entirely consistent with his argument for grounding the legitimacy of law in rationality, accessibility, and utilitarianism, see 3.2.1.

### 3.2.3 **Codification**

The chaos of the common law had to be dealt with comprehensively. For Bentham this lay, quite simply, in codification. Once the law is codified:

> [A] man need but open the book in order to inform himself what the aspect borne by the law bears to every imaginable act that can come within the possible sphere of human agency: what acts it is his duty to perform for the sake of himself, his neighbour or the public: what acts he has a right to do, what other acts he has a right to have others perform for his advantage.... In this one repository the whole system of the obligations which either he or any one else is subject to are recorded and displayed to view.[14]

Such a code would significantly diminish the power of judges; their task would consist less of interpreting than administering the law. It would also remove much of the need for lawyers: the code would be readily comprehensible without the help of legal advisers. Codification, in short, would wind up 'Judge & Co'.

The principle of utility dictated that the code be structured in the most logical manner and formulated in the simplest language. It would lay down general principles in a coherent and fairly detailed way, as well as justifications for these principles (these are particularly important for the judge).

For Bentham codification demanded the construction of a complete body of laws based on natural and universal principles. Indeed, his great work, *An Introduction to the Principles of Morals and Legislation*, was conceived of as an introduction to a penal code, and he pursued it in *Of Laws in General* where he concludes that its boundaries could not be properly drawn without tackling the distinction between civil and penal law:

> [T]he most intricate distinction of all, and that which comes most frequently on the carpet, is that which is made between the *civil* branch of jurisdiction and the *penal*, which latter is wont, in certain circumstances, to receive the name of criminal.[15]

[14] Bentham, *Of Laws in General* (London: Athlone Press, 1970), Ch 19, para 10, quoted in Postema, op cit, 423.

[15] Bentham, *An Introduction to the Principles and Morals and Legislation*, ed JH Burns and HLA Hart (London: Athlone Press, 1970) (*The Collected Works of Jeremy Bentham*, ed JH Burns), Ch 17, para 29.

And this, he maintained, raised the question of the individuation of law, which was central to the relationship between an individual law and the complete code:

> The wonder will cease when it comes to be perceived that the idea of a law, meaning one single but entire law, is in a manner inseparably connected with that of a complete body of laws: so that what is a law and what are the contents of a complete body of the laws are questions of which neither can be answered without the other.[16]

Bentham described civil law as primarily expository or 'circumstantiative' while penal law concerned sanctions and was 'comminative'.[17] We would today perhaps portray this distinction as one between substantive and procedural law. The importance in drawing these (and other) fine distinctions lay for Bentham in the fact that codification was not merely the division or control of sovereign power, but the very definition of law. Distinguishing the sort of acts that should attract criminal liability was closely related to that of distinguishing between particular criminal acts as a component of the correct promulgation of the law.

But this approach was not simple: to express all the elements of every individual law would be a taxing chore, since each individual law would need to include a complete account of the relevant rights, duties, exceptions, penalties, etc.[18] To simplify the formulation, the elements were broken up according to the nature of the rules, and expressed in separate and complementary codes of civil and criminal law.[19] But since not every law was criminal in nature, his classification distinction was based on its expression in specific legal systems: no unqualified boundary could be drawn.[20]

Though both branches of the law had common features, Bentham argued that it was vital to distinguish them for the purposes of 'intellection and enunciation'.[21] The distinction lay behind the idea of a natural and universal system of laws, the proposal to create a legislative digest of customary law, the explanation for the promulgation of the law, the form of legislative expression, and the enhancement of the science of legislation through the institution of a school to teach 'the art of legislation for the benefit of empires'.[22]

Though Bentham argued for codification with passionate conviction for most of his life, his views fell on deaf ears in both England and America.

## 3.3 John Austin: naive empiricist?

John Austin (1790–1859) was a disciple of Bentham as well as a friend and follower of both James Mill and his celebrated son John Stuart Mill. Austin's major work, *The Province of Jurisprudence Determined*, was published in 1832, the year of Bentham's death. A significant figure in legal theory and legal education throughout his life, Austin's influence on modern jurisprudence has declined considerably (indeed the bicentenary of his birth on 3 March 1990 passed virtually unnoticed in the common

---

[16] Ibid.    [17] Bentham, *Of Laws in General*, Ch 16.    [18] Ibid, 197.
[19] Ibid, Ch 17, paras 10–20.    [20] Ibid, Ch 11, para 18.    [21] Ibid, 234.    [22] Ibid, 244.

law world). For one of his most articulate admirers, however, Austin's contribution is not unlike Mozart's Clarinet Quintet, through which many people have been led to explore the world of chamber music:

> For all the unmusical qualities which many find in Austin's style and mode of presentation, it is through the gate of John Austin's work that thousands of people have been led to explore the world of jurisprudence in common law countries—and continue to do so.[23]

### 3.3.1 Imperatives

Like Bentham, Austin's conception of law is based on the idea of commands or imperatives, though he provides a less complex account of what they are (see 3.4.1 and 3.4.3). Both stress the subjection of persons by the sovereign to his power. Austin's definition is sometimes thought to extend not very much further than the *criminal* law, with its emphasis on control over behaviour; his identification of commands as the hallmark of law leads him, in the minds of most commentators, to a more restrictive definition of law than is adopted by Bentham who seeks to formulate a single, complete law which sufficiently expresses the legislative will. But both share a concern to limit the scope of jurisprudential enquiry. In the case of Austin, however, his map appears to be considerably narrower, as may be seen from Figure 3.1.

### 3.3.2 Laws properly so called

For Austin, therefore, 'laws properly so called' fall into two categories: the laws of God and human laws. Human laws (ie, laws set down by men for men) are further divided into positive laws or laws 'strictly so called' (ie, laws laid down by men as political superiors or in pursuance of legal rights) and laws laid down by men not in pursuance of legal rights. Laws 'improperly so called' are divided into laws by analogy (eg, laws of fashion and international law) and by metaphor (eg, the law of gravity). Laws by analogy, together with laws set by men not as political superiors or in pursuance of legal right are merely 'positive morality'. It is only positive law that is the proper subject of jurisprudence.

   And the central importance of definition and classification characterizes the work of both jurists. For Austin, in jurisprudence, 'there abide three things: faith, hope and clarity. But the greatest of these is clarity and it is all that is needed in definition.'[24] His concern with precision in the use of legal concepts does not, however, lead him to a linguistic analysis of the kind undertaken by Professor Hart (see 4.2.2). He is, in Morison's words, a 'naive empiricist' who regards the laws as an empirical reality rather than a 'concept'. But this does not mean that he neglects the subtleties of language:

> The naive empiricist does not say that words or other things which have meaning may not function in other ways than by presenting the addressee with pictures of observable reality.

---

[23] WL Morison, *John Austin* (London: Edward Arnold, 1982), 192.          [24] Ibid, 207.

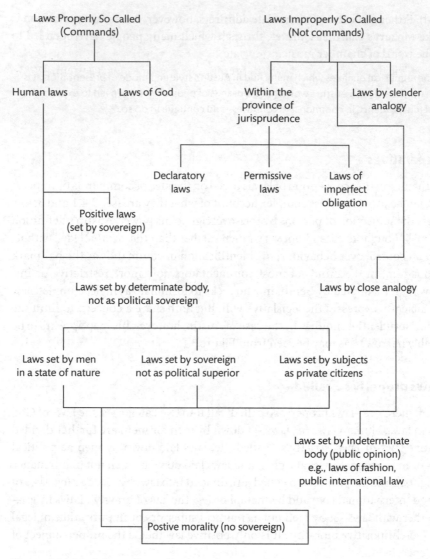

**Figure 3.1** Austin's province of jurisprudence

What he does say is that representing the other functions as conveying meaning is highly confusing, even though in popular language we may speak in this way, and that it does lead to confusion. Nor does the naive empiricist claim that there is any 'one to one' picture relationship between words that are commonly used and the observable reality which is pictured if the words have meaning....For the naive empiricist there is only one logic—covering the general propositional and implicational characteristics which everything we observe has—universally.[25]

---

[25] Ibid, 190.

Unlike Hart, therefore, who attempts to define legal terms by reference to the *context* in which they are used, naive empiricists such as Austin resist the temptation to develop particular forms of logic appropriate to specific legal statements or terms. Austin's empirical model of a legal system presupposes a single logical system.

### 3.3.3 Law and power

Yet, for all his empiricism, and even reductionism, Austin exhibits a shrewd understanding of the nature of politics and the relationship between law and power. Not for him the liberal doctrine of demarcating the scope of individual freedom by rules, or the natural law idea of fundamental rights. For Cotterrell:

> Austin…sees law as a technical instrument of government or administration, which should, however, be efficient and aimed at the common good as determined by utility.…All laws, rights and duties are created by positioning rules, the laying down of rules as an act of government. Consequently there can be nothing inherently sacred about civil or political liberties. To the extent that they are valuable they are the by-product of effective government in the common interest.[26]

The Austinian view of law is, on this account, anything but naive.[27] It represents an astute acknowledgement of 'the phenomenon of centralised modern State power in a way that classical common law thought seemed wholly ill-equipped to do'.[28]

## 3.4 Bentham and Austin compared

### 3.4.1 Their general approaches

Bentham is, of course, best known as a utilitarian (see 9.1) and law reformer. But he insisted on the separation (already identified above as the hallmark of legal positivism) between the 'is' and 'ought' of law, or what he preferred to call 'expositorial' and 'censorial' jurisprudence respectively. Austin was equally emphatic in maintaining this distinction, but his analysis is now generally regarded as much narrower in scope and objective than Bentham's. Even Professor Morison (who is Austin's most prominent contemporary fan) acknowledges this fact, conceding that 'Austin wished himself to construct a science of law rather than involve himself in Bentham's art of legislation'.[29] Nevertheless Morison is quick to defend Austin from the charge that Austin's concern

---

[26] Roger Cotterrell, *The Politics of Jurisprudence* (London: Butterworths, 1984), 60–1.

[27] Morison's notion of naivety is, of course, a different one and applied in a different context. See Morison, *John Austin*, 189.

[28] Cotterrell, *The Politics of Jurisprudence*, 82. Postema does not share this view: 'Austin, it seems, is closer to the Common Law tradition than would first appear. [Austin's] approach differs in motivation from the traditionalist Common Law approach only in the substitution of the wisdom of the utilitarian elite for the wisdom of the ages. Both define authorities which no individual citizen is regarded as competent to challenge. This departs radically from both the letter and the spirit of Bentham's utilitarian positivism.' At the same time, however, it is essentially anti-democratic, elitist, and not particularly concerned to postulate a system by which such power might be controlled. At 328.          [29] Morison, *John Austin*, 47.

with expository jurisprudence (as contrasted with Bentham's inclusion of censorial jurisprudence) renders his work less valuable than Bentham's; such a conclusion is, in his view, 'unfair'. The modern view is certainly that Austin was considerably more conservative politically than his mentor.[30] In fact, Austin eventually came to disown the principle of utility and to doubt the value of his own 'expository' jurisprudence.[31] Consider Rubin's argument that Austin's jurisprudence 'was designed to defend the stability of a particular economic system and protect the interests of the middle class. A legal theory built on these premises can hardly be called value-free or impartial'.[32]

Your reading of both jurists will benefit from comparing not only their differences in respect of the specific issues referred to below, but also their respective starting points and achievements. Though they both adhere to a utilitarian philosophy (which Bentham, Mills, and others propounded with varying degrees of success) and adopt broadly similar views on the nature and function of jurisprudence and the serious inadequacies of the common law tradition, there are a number of important differences in their general approach to the subject. In particular, Bentham pursues the notion of a single, complete law which adequately expresses the will of the legislature. He seeks to show how a single law creates a single offence defined by its being the narrowest species of that kind of offence recognized by the law.[33]

Austin, on the other hand, bases his idea of a legal system on the classification of rights; he is not concerned with the search for a 'complete' law.[34] Secondly, in his attempt to provide a comprehensive plan of a complete body of laws and the elements of the 'art of legislation', Bentham develops a complex 'logic of the will' (see 3.4.3). Austin, however, is more concerned to construct a science of law rather than involve himself in Bentham's art of legislation.[35] Similarly, while Bentham sought to formulate, in considerable detail, the means by which arbitrary power (exercised in particular by judges) might be checked, Austin did not really apply his mind to such questions.

Bentham regarded judicial law-making as a form of customary law with all its ambiguities and uncertainties (see 3.2.2). Austin, however, was willing to accept that judicial legislation was capable of providing a basis for codification of the common law.

### 3.4.2 The definition of law

Bentham's definition of law may be divided into the following six elements:

- an assemblage of *signs*;
- declaratory of a *volition*;
- conceived or adopted by the *sovereign*;
- concerning *conduct* to be observed by persons subject to his power;

---

[30] See E Rubin, 'John Austin's Political Pamphlets 1824–1859' in E Attwooll (ed), *Perspectives in Jurisprudence* (Glasgow: University of Glasgow Press, 1977).

[31] For an interesting account of Austin's politics, see Hamburger and Hamburger, *Troubled Lives* (Toronto and London: University of Toronto Press, 1985).          [32] Rubin, op cit, 38.

[33] Bentham, *Of Laws in General*, 170–6.          [34] Morison, *John Austin*, 44.          [35] Ibid, 47.

- such volition relying on certain *events* which it is intended such declaration should be a means of causing; and

- the prospect of which it is intended should act as a *motive* upon those whose conduct is in question.

Austin offers the following definition: 'a signification of desire by a party with a power to inflict evil if the desire be disregarded, thereby imposing upon the party commanded a duty to obey': command and duty are therefore correlatives. While their definitions of law are very similar (particularly in respect of their emphasis on the subjection of persons by the sovereign to his power), Austin's definition does not extend very much further than the *criminal* law. His identification of commands as the hallmark of law leads Austin to a far more restrictive conception of law than is adopted by Bentham who is concerned to arrive at the conception of a single, complete law which sufficiently expresses the legislative will.

Both jurists share a concern to *limit* the scope of jurisprudential enquiry (and this is illustrated by the very titles of their works: Austin's *The Province of Jurisprudence Determined* and Bentham's *The Limits of Jurisprudence Defined* (published under the title, *Of Laws in General*). Austin is the more doctrinaire (and restrictive) in the map he draws, which may be represented as in Figure 3.1 on p. 78.

### 3.4.3 **Commands**

The central feature of Austin's map of the province of jurisprudence is, of course, the notion of law as a *command* of the sovereign. Anything that is not a command is not law. Only *general* commands count as law. And only commands emanating from the sovereign are '*positive laws*'.

This insistence on law as commands has been a major focus of attack on Austin's theory. Not only does it require the exclusion of customary, constitutional, and public international law from the field of jurisprudence, but it drives Austin to the somewhat artificial conceptions of 'tacit commands', 'circuitous commands' (when a sovereign's 'desire' to require obedience to the commands of his predecessors is effected by his refraining from repealing them), and of nullity of, say, a contract, as constituting a sanction.

Bentham, on the other hand, argues that commands are merely one of four methods by which the sovereign enacts law. In developing his (far more sophisticated) theory of the structure of law, he distinguishes between laws which command or prohibit certain conduct (*imperative laws*) and those which permit certain conduct (*permissive laws*). In *Of Laws in General* Bentham is concerned with the distinction between penal and civil laws. Every law has a penal and a civil part; thus, even in the case of title to property there is a penal element. As Bentham puts it:

> Let the proprietary subject then be a certain piece of land, a field, the offence which consists
> in the wrongful occupation of this property will be any act in virtue of which the agent may
> be said to meddle with this field.... The offence then being the act of meddling with the field,

the act which is the object of the law, the act commanded is the negative act of not meddling with the field.[36]

In other words, the owner's title is derived from a general (penal) prohibition against 'meddling' with the field. The owner is himself, of course, exempted from this prohibition. What Bentham seeks to show is that laws which impose no obligations or sanctions (what he calls 'civil laws') are not *complete laws* (in the sense in which Austin uses the term, see below), but merely parts of laws. And, since his principal objective was the creation of a code of law, he argued that the penal and civil branches should be formulated separately.

The concept of a command was important for Bentham. It captured, in Professor Postema's words, 'the *artificial* character of law':

> Law conceived as command could not be regarded as some mysterious, unalterable fact of nature, as common law theorists often tried to portray it. To conceive of law as command invites the questions *who* issued it? and *when*? and with what authority? Law is clearly portrayed as an artificial creation of human society. The paradigm captures the related important idea that law is not just descriptive of social order, but is its 'cause'—not an expression of some deeper reality, but the *instrument* by which the social relations necessary for human life are constituted and sustained. This has important implications for Bentham. For once this view is adopted, no existing system of law and legal relations can be protected as sacred. All law, social relations, and institutions, are opened to critical assessment, challenge, and reform.[37]

And Bentham did not, of course, shrink from vigorously pursuing all three.

For Bentham, 'command' is merely one of four manners in which the sovereign's will is manifested. There are two *imperative* aspects (command and prohibition), and two *permissive* aspects (non-prohibition and non-command). Hart provides examples of each of these:[38]

- Command: 'Shut the door!'
- Non-command: 'You may refrain from shutting the door!'
- Prohibition: 'Do not shut the door!'
- Non-prohibition: 'You may shut the door!'

Bentham develops a complex system of what Hart suggests might be described by a logician as 'four imperative operators or deontic modalities'. This is difficult terrain; even Hart[39] confesses that *he* lacks the 'technical logical competence' to explain Bentham's complete 'logic of the will', so you are in distinguished company. You should nevertheless consider the relationship between the permissive aspects and the imperative (they release the subject from previously issued commands or prohibitions and are therefore dis-imperative) and reflect on Bentham's view that all 'complete' laws are imperative in form.

---

[36] *Of Laws in General*, 176.        [37] Postema, *Bentham and the Common Law Tradition*, 316.
[38] Hart, *Essays on Bentham*, Ch 5, 113.        [39] At 115.

For Bentham a law contains two parts: the *directive* part which announces the conduct to be done, not done, etc, and the *incitative* part which predicts the sanction. The sanction is, at this stage, merely a prediction; it becomes a reality only when a subsidiary law is addressed to an official ordering him to impose a sanction in the event of a breach of the first law. This subsidiary law requires the support of another law and so on. Every law therefore has a sanction, but unlike Austin's fairly crude account of sanctions (see 3.4.5) Bentham recognizes that a sanction may be not merely coercive, but may also be in the form of a reward. If it is coercive it may assume one or more of several forms: political, moral, or religious. And if it is a reward sanction (what he calls 'praemiary laws') it cannot be said to create an obligation; it is not therefore a 'complete' law (even though it is sufficiently similar to coercive sanctions to be called 'law').

This connection between sanction and obligation (the sanction creates or constitutes the legal obligation) is an important element in Bentham's theory and is, again, more sophisticated than Austin's account. You might here explore his distinction between *contrectation* (the power to handle persons or property, eg, the owner's power to walk on his land which is derived from a general prohibition against anyone else doing so) and *imperation* (the power to alter persons' legal position by making them subject to commands or prohibitions) to demonstrate the manner in which a particular sanction (eg, damages for breach of contract) may be used to make laws 'complete'.

As far as Austin's theory is concerned, the relationship between commands and sanctions is equally important. In particular, the fact that Austin's very concept of a command includes the likelihood that a sanction will follow failure to obey the command. A sanction is defined by Austin as an evil which is conditional upon the failure of a person to comply with the wishes of the sovereign. Thus unless a sanction is likely to follow, the mere 'expression of a wish' is not a command. Obligations are therefore defined in terms of sanctions: this is a central tenet of Austin's imperative theory. The 'likelihood' of a sanction is always uncertain, but Austin is driven to the position that a sanction consists of 'the smallest chance of incurring the smallest evil'.

His analysis of sanctions is adduced as evidence of the 'muddled, inconsistent and ambiguous' theory of Austin in general.[40] The whole question of the efficacy of sanctions in motivating obedience is controversial (you may want to consider Milgram's experiments and the general question of social and psychological factors explaining obedience).[41] 'Austin seems to assume', says Tapper 'that if evil is certain to be inflicted upon some who disobey, all who disobey run some risk of having it inflicted upon them. This is plainly false.'[42]

Moreover, if all laws are commands then how is one (or more especially Austin) to explain those rules which confer power on persons to alter their legal position (by contract, trust, etc)? Austin attempts to squeeze them into his scheme by suggesting that the sanction is nullity and the likelihood of this makes these rules duty-imposing in common with other commands. Hart, of course, demonstrates the artificiality of

[40] By Colin Tapper (1965) *Cambridge Law Journal* 270.
[41] See *Lloyd's Introduction to Jurisprudence*, 8th edn (London: Sweet & Maxwell, 2008), 264.
[42] At 281.

describing these 'secondary, power-conferring rules' as duty-imposing. This criticism of Austin's limited account of law as commands is an important element of Hart's critique in *The Concept of Law* (see 4.2). Despite Hart's attack on Austin, he acknowledges *The Province of Jurisprudence Determined* as constituting an important statement of legal positivism.

In spite of the importance of sanctions in any account of a legal system, it is highly questionable whether they ought to be accorded so central a place in the *definition* of an individual law and its accompanying obligation. In other words, there are many obligations imposed *by the law*, the breach of which carries no sanction at all. There are even situations in which there is *no* likelihood of the sanction being enforced (eg, the offender has died), yet we would not want to deny that the obligation exists.

You should be familiar with Bentham's strong views on codification (expressed, in particular, in *Of Laws in General*).[43] It would also be sensible to read the important section in *Of Laws in General*, pp 176–83, being careful to note that Bentham's usage of certain terms such as 'penal' and 'offence' often conveys something considerably broader than their contemporary meaning.

### 3.4.4 **Sovereignty**

For both Austin and Bentham, sovereignty is a key concept. They both regard sovereignty as a matter of the social fact of the *habit of obedience*. Again, Bentham's views turn out to be more sophisticated and less doctrinaire than Austin's. First, Austin defines sovereignty as follows:

> If a *determinate* human superior, *not* in a habit of obedience to a like superior, receive *habitual* obedience from the *bulk* of a given society, that determinate superior is sovereign in that society, and the society (including the superior) is a society political and independent.[44]

Bentham's definition is strikingly similar (and Austin's debt to him is plain):

> When a number of persons (whom we may style *subjects*) are supposed to be in the *habit* of paying *obedience* to a person, or an assemblage of persons, of a known and certain description (whom we may call *governor* or *governors*) such persons altogether (*subjects* and *governors*) are said to be in a state of *political* society.[45]

Notice how Austin refers to 'a society political and *independent*', while Bentham refers to 'a state of political society'. This explains why Austin's definition comprises two elements: one positive (the bulk of the population habitually obeys the sovereign) and the other negative (the sovereign is not in the habit of obeying anyone). Bentham, however, alludes only to the positive condition. This is only a minor difference and it is fairly likely that the issue of 'independence' (to which he refers elsewhere) is simply not germane to the point Bentham is making here.

---

[43] Especially 183, 232 ff.
[44] *The Province of Jurisprudence Determined* (London: Weidenfeld & Nicolson, 1954), 194.
[45] *A Fragment on Government*, 2nd edn (London: W Pickering, 1823), Ch 1, para 10.

The second difference is more significant. Whereas Austin insists on the illimitabil-ity and indivisibility of the sovereign, Bentham (alive to the institution of federalism) acknowledges that the supreme legislative power may be both limited and divided by what he calls 'an express convention'.

Both writers, by identifying 'commands' as an essential element of their theories of law, naturally require to explain *who* issues these commands and under what circum-stances. For Austin, to the four features of a command (wish, sanction, expression of a wish, and generality) is to be added a fifth, namely an identifiable political superior, or sovereign, whose commands are obeyed by political inferiors and who owes obedience to no one. But, as several critics have been quick to point out, this is a *theoretical* guide to the nature of law. It led Austin to give a distorted picture of legal systems which impose constitutional restrictions on the legislative competence of the legislature or which divide such power between a central federal legislature and law-making bodies of constituent states or provinces (such as obtains in the United States or Canada).

Bentham, however, recognizes not only that sovereignty may be limited or divided, but that limitation on the sovereign power is actually a correlative of limited obe-dience to the legislator's commands. What Bentham seems to be suggesting is that where the people decide not to obey a particular command this constitutes a limita-tion of sovereignty. This is not a wholly convincing argument (as Hart shows)[46] but it exhibits a willingness on Bentham's part to acknowledge political realities which often escape Austin. Indeed, Bentham goes so far as to accept (albeit reluctantly) the possi-bility of judicial review of legislative action. His conception of sovereignty is not a legal one at all: it is pre-legal: 'the logical correlate of an assumed factual obedience'.[47] In other words, the sovereign (person or body) is a more abstract idea: it is the source of political authority and legitimacy.

By confining 'laws properly so called' to the commands of a sovereign—who exists only 'if a determinate political superior, not in the habit of obedience to a like superior, receive habitual obedience from the bulk of a given society, and the society (including the superior) is a society political and independent'—Austin bases his idea of sover-eignty on the habit of obedience adopted by members of society. The sovereign must, moreover, be 'determinate' for 'no indeterminate sovereign can command expressly or tacitly, or can receive obedience or submission'. This logically leads Austin to exclude from his definition of law public international law, customary law, and much of con-stitutional law. He presents us with a conception of law which rests on a narrow con-ception of a sovereign—whose powers are illimitable and indivisible—and who is habitually obeyed.

It has been suggested[48] that Austin may have confused the *de facto* sovereign (or the body that receives habitual obedience) with the *de jure* sovereign (or the law-making body). And it has been pointed out[49] the Crown in Britain receives allegiance from its

---

[46] Hart, *Essays on Bentham*, 228–39.
[47] Manning, 'Austin Today: or "The Province of Jurisprudence" Re-examined' in WI Jennings (ed), *Modern Theories of Law*, 192 at 202, quoted by Cotterrell, *The Politics of Jurisprudence*, 70.
[48] By J Bryce, *Studies in History and Jurisprudence* (Oxford: Oxford University Press, 1901), vol 2, 51–60.
[49] By RWM Dias, *Jurisprudence*, 5th edn (London: Butterworths, 1985), 348.

subjects, while the Crown-in-Parliament is the supreme law-making body. When he refers to the un-commanded commander who makes laws, Austin means the *de jure* sovereign.

Other criticisms relate, of course, to the fact that by denying that the sovereign's power could be limited or divided, Austin (a) relegates large portions of constitutional law to 'positive morality', (b) ignores the possibility of limitations on the sovereign through disabilities rather than duties or by special procedures such as entrenchment, and (c) overlooks the possibility of vesting sovereignty in more than one body.

Bentham, on the other hand, offers a far more pragmatic conception of a sovereign which he defines as 'any person or assemblage of persons to whose will a whole political community are (no matter on what account) supposed to be in a disposition to pay obedience; and that in preference to the will of any other person'. This enables him to entertain the idea of a sovereign that, unlike Austin's, is not necessarily determinate. It is therefore possible for Bentham to explain the continuity of legal systems where the sovereign dies or the sovereign body is in recess. Austin is driven to the view that when the British Parliament has been dissolved, sovereignty resides with the Queen, the House of Lords, and the electorate. But, on this view, it is impossible to distinguish the commander from the commanded: it renders his general theory of sovereignty even more suspect. Bentham, however, allows that the sovereign's authority may be divided, he may even adopt the commands of his predecessor or a person to whom he has delegated his law-making power.

Joseph Raz[50] identifies a number of defects in Bentham's analysis of sovereignty, including the fact that it does not:

- fully explain *divided* sovereignty;
- account for the *relationship* between the various powers which constitute the single sovereign power;
- explain *how* sovereignty can be limited by the law; or
- explain how to decide whether a certain legal power is *part* of a sovereign power.

Your reading on this subject should include those decisions of the court which, if you are a student of law or government, you will have encountered in your course on the constitution. The question of the extent to which Parliament may bind its successor is an old chestnut that sheds considerable light on this contentious aspect of sovereignty.

### 3.4.5 **Sanctions**

Austin, of course, regards the sanction as an essential element in the definition of law. And he does so largely on the basis that if the sovereign expresses a wish and has the power to inflict an evil (or sanction) then a person is under a duty (or is 'obliged') to

---

[50] J Raz, *The Concept of a Legal System: An Introduction to the Theory of Legal System*, 2nd edn (Oxford: Clarendon Press, 1980), 10.

act in accordance with that wish. Duty is therefore defined in terms of sanction. This is another aspect of Austin's system which has been widely attacked.[51]

Though several major criticisms have been made, it is important to clarify exactly what Austin is saying. My own view is that (though he does occasionally suggest that the existence of a sanction supplies the motivation for obedience) his analysis of sanctions attempts to show that, in *a purely formal sense*, where there is a *duty* there is normally a *sanction*. In other words, he is not necessarily seeking to provide an explanation for *why* law is obeyed or whether it *ought* to be obeyed, but rather *when* a legal duty exists.[52] But this does not answer the more fundamental objection that *duty* is itself accorded undeserved importance by Austin: there are clearly many instances in the law where no legal duty arises at all (and hence there is no sanction) and yet we should not wish to exclude these examples from a sensible definition of law. The most obvious cases would be those laws which enable people to marry, to enter into contracts, or to make wills: no one is under a *duty* to do these things, yet they are obviously part of the law. Hart calls these 'power-conferring rules' (see 4.2.5).

Another objection is that, yet again, Austin's theory is too simple. The operation of law in society is a complex process which does not approximate to Austin's somewhat ingenuous explanation based on compulsion and coercion. This, as will be seen later, is the linchpin of Professor Hart's criticism of Austin, and, despite the spirited defence of Austin's 'naive empiricism' by Professor Morison,[53] it remains a pervasive weakness in Austin's command theory of law.

Bentham is willing to concede that a sovereign's commands would constitute law even in the absence of sanctions in the Austinian sense. For him law includes both punishments ('coercive motives') and rewards ('alluring motives'), but they are not the fundamental, defining characteristics of law that they are for Austin. Nor, therefore, is Bentham guilty of the limited social vision of law and the legal system that afflicts Austin in this respect.

Sanctions, as Lamond suggests, are best conceived of as disadvantages.[54] They entail some loss: the forfeiture or suspension of a benefit or expectation or right, or some extra burden like a penalty or duty. Bentham discarded this factor, and considered rewards as 'praemiary sanctions' because rewards could also induce compliance. In view, however, of the ordinary conception of sanctions, and their link to such concepts as coercion, deterrence, and punishment, Lamond contends that there is little reason to abandon this element. He also shows how sanctions are related to wrongs: they are imposed as a result of the commission of a wrong, that is, for the breach of a duty:

> More precisely, the reason for the imposition of the disadvantage is because of the breach of the duty. Not every disadvantage which is prescribed by law is thought to be a sanction. Taxes, for example, are not, nor is the necessity to fill in forms when claiming some benefit, nor the court fees for commencing a case, nor the attendance for an interview to obtain some status (such as marriage or a passport), although all of these requirements are, in various ways,

[51] An acute analysis may be found in the critique by Colin Tapper, 'Austin on Sanctions' [1965] *Cambridge Law Journal* 270.     [52] Cf Tapper, ibid, 282–3.     [53] Morison, *John Austin*, especially Ch 6.
[54] Grant Lamond, 'The Coerciveness of Law' (2000) 20 *Oxford Journal of Legal Studies* 39.

disadvantageous. The same is true of requirements such as jury service, giving evidence as a witness, and being conscripted to fight. Again, there seems no reason to modify this element of the conception of a sanction: it is only disadvantages which are imposed in virtue of the violation of some duty which constitute sanctions, rather than disadvantages which are imposed for other reasons. The reasons for which a disadvantage is prescribed is relevant to both our evaluation of the disadvantage itself and our evaluation of the person who renders themselves liable to it.[55]

# Questions

1. 'Bentham's positivism has a very special character. Although it embraces many of the properties of the model of rules, it rejects the crucial claim that legal standards supply a special sort of peremptory reason for action (at least for officials, and apparently for ordinary citizens as well). In this important respect Bentham's positivist jurisprudence not only differs from more recent positivist theories (for example, Hart's), but it also rejects an important assumption about the nature of authority and law running through British legal theory from Hobbes…through Hume.' (Gerald J Postema, *Bentham and the Common Law Tradition* (1986), 452)

   What are the main elements of Bentham's positivist account of law, and what, in your view, are its virtues and drawbacks?

2. What is Bentham's solution to the indeterminacy he identifies in the common law? Do you agree with his diagnosis and/or his treatment?

3. Is 'Judge & Co' a real or merely rhetorical description?

4. In what ways might Austin be seen as a 'naive empiricist'?

5. Austin's jurisprudence 'marks out the field of law—the province of the lawyer's concerns—with a rigour which is quite impossible within the framework of classical common law thought'. (Roger Cotterrell, *The Politics of Jurisprudence*, 80)

   In what way did the theories of Austin and Bentham differ from the ideas of classical common law thought?

6. Bentham's notion of a command is generally thought to be more sophisticated than Austin's. Why?

7. How do these two analytical jurists differ in respect of:

   • the definition of law?

   • the nature of the sovereign?

   • the role of sanctions?

---

[55] At 58.

8. '[F]or every legal positivist who regards his theory of law as therapeutic and progressive, there is a natural lawyer who sees it as desiccated and distorting. According to these critics, legal positivism is…a well-intentioned idea taken to absurd extremes. In its zeal to demystify, even shock, it trivializes and transmogrifies. Natural lawyers regard legal positivism as a sort of philosophical taxidermy: it hollows out and drains the law of its moral guts and lifeblood, then [like Bentham's preserved body on show in University College, London] wheels out and displays the stuffed mount as though it were the real thing.' (Scott J Shapiro, *Legality*, 388).

Is this a fair portrayal of natural lawyers' view of legal positivism? Does it accurately describe the perspective of John Finnis? (See Chapter 2.)

# Further reading

AUSTIN, JOHN, *The Province of Jurisprudence Determined and the Uses of the Study of Jurisprudence* (London: Weidenfeld & Nicolson, 1954).

BENTHAM, JEREMY, *A Fragment on Government; or, A Comment on the Commentaries*, 2nd edn (London: W Pickering, 1823).

BENTHAM, JEREMY, *An Introduction to the Principles of Morals and Legislation*, ed JH Burns and HLA Hart (London: Athlone Press, 1970) (*The Collected Works of Jeremy Bentham*, general ed JH Burns).

BENTHAM, JEREMY, *Of Laws in General*, ed HLA Hart (London: Athlone Press, 1970) (*The Collected Works of Jeremy Bentham*, general ed JH Burns).

GEORGE, ROBERT P (ed), *The Autonomy of Law: Essays on Legal Positivism* (Oxford: Clarendon Press, 1995).

HAMBURGER, LOTTE, and HAMBURGER, JOSEPH, *Troubled Lives: John and Sarah Austin* (Toronto and London: University of Toronto Press, 1985).

HART, HLA, *Essays on Bentham: Studies on Jurisprudence and Political Theory* (Oxford: Clarendon Press, 1982).

JORI, MARIO (ed), *Legal Positivism* (Aldershot: Dartmouth, 1992).

LEITER, BRIAN, 'The Demarcation Problem in Jurisprudence: A New Case for Skepticism' (2011) 31 *Oxford Journal of Legal Studies* 663.

LIEBERMAN, DAVID, 'Introduction' in *The Province of Legislation Determined: Legal Theory in Eighteenth-Century Britain* (Cambridge: Cambridge University Press, 1989).

MORISON, WL, *John Austin* (London: Edward Arnold, 1982).

POSTEMA, GERALD J, *Bentham and the Common Law Tradition* (Oxford: Clarendon Press, 1986).

WALDRON, JEREMY (ed), *Nonsense upon Stilts: Bentham, Burke and Marx on the Rights of Man* (London: Methuen, 1987).

# 4

# Modern legal positivism

Legal positivism is 'in'. Recent years have witnessed an explosion in the development and refinement of many of the ideas originally conceived, in particular, by HLA Hart. With its preoccupation with semantic and conceptual analysis, the source of authority, and objective reality, what was once considered to be rather conservative, dreary, and narrow has become sexy. In modern legal theory circles, it would seem that, in the words of the pop anthem of the nerd, 'it's hip to be square'.[1]

But though it may be trendy, the highly sophisticated and technical nature of most of this literature is slightly forbidding to all but the professional legal theorist, and even he or she may experience the occasional headache reading the incessant literature generated by its followers.[2] For the uninitiated, including the beleaguered jurisprudence student, it can be a disturbing phenomenon. This chapter is consequently rather long, but I hope it will escort you gently through the relentlessly enlarging thicket of contemporary positivism.

Dangers lie in wait for all but the energetic and industrious student; you are therefore advised to tread cautiously. Among the virtues of this remarkable development is that, if you are determined to master its particular intricacies, you will, willy-nilly have grasped several of the enduring and central ideas of jurisprudence. No mean feat.

---

[1] Indeed, our leading 'inclusive' positivist is flagrantly hip: 'I love rock, jazz, and blues music', and he flaunts his profound scholarship in respect of '"Acid Jazz" mavens Isotope 217 and Liquid Soul or blues unknowns like Honeybee Edwards, and rockers like the Chills and Yo La Tango…Good philosophy is like good blues…[it] penetrates the heart, touches the soul, turns pain into a form of pleasure…' He also confesses to being 'an avid, if by no means accomplished, blues guitarist', Jules Coleman, *The Practice of Principle: In Defence of A Pragmatic Approach to Legal Theory* (Oxford: Oxford University Press, 2001), ix–x. 'Hip to Be Square' is recorded by Huey Lewis and the News, composed by Bill Gibson, Sean Hopper, and Huey Lewis, and published by Cherry Lane Music Co. A philosophical question for you to ponder: is this song title a genuine paradox?

[2] It is hard to disagree with Ronald Dworkin's asseveration that many 'analytic positivists continue to treat their conceptual investigations of law as independent of both legal substance and political philosophy. But they talk mainly to one another and have become marginalized within the academy and the profession,' Ronald Dworkin, *Justice in Robes* (Cambridge, Mass: Belknap Press, 2006), 34. His conclusion as to their marginalization may, however, err on the side of sanguinity.

## 4.1 The foundations

Twentieth-century legal positivism is associated with the work of two exceptional, but very different, legal philosophers: HLA Hart (1907–92) and Hans Kelsen (1881–1973). Though they do—as legal positivists—subscribe to the view that an analytical distinction must be maintained between law and morality, between 'is' and 'ought', their starting points, methodology, and conclusions bear little resemblance to each other. As Professor MacCormick pithily puts it, 'Hart is a Humean where Kelsen is a Kantian'.[3] The piquancy (and accuracy) of this observation ought to become clearer in the course of this chapter.

While these two theorists are generally acknowledged to be the fathers of modern legal positivism, their theories have been subjected to comprehensive and scrupulous analysis by a number of distinguished contemporary jurists. As a result, the form, character, and implications of legal positivism have undergone significant revision and refinement—with profound implications for legal theory in general. Among these scholars are Joseph Raz, Neil MacCormick, Jules Coleman, and Scott Shapiro.

Contemporary legal positivism includes the following main claims about the nature of law.[4] These may be summarized as follows:

- *The separability thesis.* It denies the existence of necessary moral constraints on the content of law.[5]

- *The pedigree thesis.* It articulates necessary and sufficient conditions for legal validity in respect of how or by whom law is promulgated.

- *The discretion thesis.* It asserts that judges decide hard cases by making new law.

The first thesis is, of course, a critical component of the positivist refutation of the classical naturalist account of legal validity. Positivism supplies a rival explanation in the form of the pedigree thesis, which founds legal validity on the manner, form, and source of promulgated norms. Thus for Austin a proposition is legally valid only if it is promulgated by a 'sovereign' who is habitually obeyed, but who is not in the habit of obeying any other person; and is backed up by the threat of a sanction (see 3.4.5). Hart, as will become evident, is less concerned with who promulgates the law than with the manner of its promulgation.

Though classical positivists such as Austin differ in several respects from Hart and his account of the pedigree thesis, both subscribe to the view that law is created by

---

[3] N MacCormick, *HLA Hart* (Oxford: Oxford University Press, 2007), 26. Cf Alida Wilson, 'Is Kelsen really a Kantian?' in R Tur and W Twining (eds), *Essays on Kelsen* (Oxford: Clarendon Press, 1986).

[4] Kenneth Einar Himma, 'Judicial Discretion and the Concept of Law' (1999) 19 *Oxford Journal of Legal Studies* 72.

[5] This approximates to what is often called the 'social thesis': that law may be identified as a social fact, without reference to moral considerations. See J Raz, *The Authority of Law* (Oxford: Oxford University Press, 1979), 37 ff. For his own positivist triad, see 4.4.

human beings through acts that may be described as 'official'. For Austin, they are official because they have been performed by the sovereign; for Hart, because they meet the procedural (and perhaps also the substantive) requirements of the rule of recognition. The third thesis appears to entail that when a judge decides a 'hard case' (ie, one to which no rule is immediately applicable) he exercises discretion in order to fill the 'gaps' in the law (see 5.2.3).

These three claims do not exhaust the principal features of modern legal positivism. As will be seen later (in 4.4.), Joseph Raz probes the quintessence of positivist theory before expounding his 'social thesis'.

## 4.2 HLA Hart

Almost single-handedly, HLA Hart staked out the borders of modern legal theory by brilliantly applying the techniques of analytical (and especially linguistic) philosophy to the study of law. His work (largely, but by no means exclusively, *The Concept of Law*, published in 1961) has illuminated the meaning of legal concepts, the manner in which we deploy them, and the way we think about law and the legal system. His posthumous 'postscript' to this celebrated work was published in 1994.[6]

Despite its importance and accessibility, few students actually read *The Concept of Law* or, at any rate, the whole of it. This is unfortunate, for there are few better methods of familiarizing yourself with (what are still) the central questions of jurisprudence. And Hart's reflections are formulated so elegantly, coherently, and clearly that by reading it you will gain more than an 'understanding of law, coercion, and morality as different but related social phenomena' (as Hart, in his preface, modestly describes the aim of the book). Moreover, it is no exaggeration to say that *The Concept of Law* has been used as a springboard by several legal theorists (including Raz, Finnis, Dworkin, MacCormick) and has provided the inspiration for many more.[7]

### 4.2.1 Hart as legal positivist

Although he is unquestionably a positivist (particularly in the sense of maintaining, for analytical purposes, the separation of law and morality) Hart acknowledges the 'core of indisputable truth in the doctrines of natural law'.[8] You will have read in 2.1 that one of the hallmarks of the natural law tradition (attacked by Bentham and Austin) is the view that such a separation cannot be sustained. How then can the leading contemporary positivist concede that there is a 'minimum content' of natural law?

---

[6] HLA Hart, *The Concept of Law*, 2nd edn (Oxford: Clarendon Press, 1994).

[7] If you cannot read the entire book, you should, at the very least, digest Chs 4, 5, and 6. I strongly recommend Neil MacCormick's *HLA Hart* (the major part of which is devoted to an analysis of *The Concept of Law*) as a reliable and sympathetic account of Hart's contribution to legal theory. See too the excellent biography by N Lacey, *The Life of HLA Hart: The Nightmare and the Noble Dream* (Oxford: Clarendon Press, 2004) and my review of the book in (2004) 34 *Hong Kong Law Journal* 661.

[8] *The Concept of Law*, 146.

The answer is that Hart's positivism (though it follows very much in the tradition of classical English legal positivism, especially as developed by Bentham) is a far cry from the largely coercive picture of law painted by his predecessors. For Hart, law is a *social* phenomenon: it can only be understood and explained by reference to the actual social practices of a community.

### 4.2.1.1 'Minimum content of natural law'

Hart's formulation of the 'minimum content' of natural law is therefore a recognition of the fact that in order to survive as a community certain rules must exist. These are a consequence of the 'human condition' (he is strongly influenced here by David Hume) which Hart sees as exhibiting the following fundamental characteristics:

- 'Human vulnerability': We are all susceptible to physical attacks.
- 'Approximate equality': Even the strongest must sleep at times.
- 'Limited altruism': We are, in general, selfish.
- 'Limited resources': We need food, clothes, and shelter and they are limited.
- 'Limited understanding and strength of will': We cannot be relied upon to cooperate with our fellow men.

Because of these limitations there is a necessity for rules which protect persons and property, and which ensure that promises are kept. But, despite this view, Hart is *not* saying that law is *derived from* morals or that there is a necessary conceptual relationship between the two. Nor is he suggesting that if we accept his 'minimum content' of natural law this will guarantee a fair or just society. (How valid is this analysis? Are we really 'approximately equal'; what of minority groups, women, children? How complete is it; what about sex?)[9]

### 4.2.1.2 Breaking with Austin and Bentham

Hart severed positivism from both the utilitarianism (see 9.1) and the command theory of law championed by Austin and Bentham. In respect of the latter, his rejection rested on the view that law was more than the decree of a 'gunman': a command backed by a sanction. This imperative version of a legal order, moreover, located the sovereign beyond the law; this failed to account for the requirement that legislators comply with basic law-making procedures.

At the core of Hart's description of law and the legal system is the existence of fundamental rules accepted by officials as stipulating these law-making procedures. In particular, the 'rule of recognition' (see 4.2.6) which is the essential constitutional rule of a legal system, acknowledged by those officials who administer the law as specifying the conditions or criteria of legal validity which certify whether or not a rule is indeed a rule.

Another important feature of Hart's positivism is his approach to the central question of the extent to which the law is moral. The so-called Hart–Fuller debate concerning the 'morality of law' was examined in Chapter 2.

---

[9] See Simon Roberts, *Order and Dispute* (Harmondsworth: Penguin, 1979), 24–5.

## 4.2.2 **Law and language**

An important element in much of Hart's writing is the *linguistic* analysis of law. The influence of the work of, amongst others, the philosophers Gilbert Ryle and JL Austin (not to be confused with the jurist, John Austin) is apparent in *The Concept of Law* (in the preface to which JL Austin's aphorism that we may use 'a sharpened awareness of words to sharpen our awareness of the phenomena' is quoted) and other works by Hart (notably his inaugural lecture 'Definition and Theory in Jurisprudence').[10] The relationship between law and language pervades much of his thinking about law; this gives rise to questions such as: what does it *mean* to have a 'right'?, what is a 'corporation' or an 'obligation'? For Hart we cannot properly understand law unless we understand the conceptual context in which it emerges and develops. He argues, for instance, that language has an 'open texture': words (and hence rules) have a number of clear meanings, but there are always several 'penumbral' cases where it is uncertain whether the word applies or not.

Thus no set of rules can provide predetermined answers to every case that may arise. This does not mean, however (contrary to the claims of the American realists, see 6.2), that the meaning of words is completely arbitrary and unpredictable. In most cases judges have little difficulty in simply applying the appropriate rule—without any need to call in aid moral or political considerations. The importance Hart attaches to language is sometimes criticized as being rather one-dimensional: language is obviously important, critics have conceded, but when a model of law as a system of rules (see 4.2.3) is attacked (eg, by realists) it is not the law's linguistic uncertainty that is the target, but the process of precedential legal reasoning. It is argued that this process cannot be adequately accounted for by postulating a model of judicial decision-making that treats it as merely the laying down of rules which bind subsequent courts.

## 4.2.3 **Law as a system of rules**

All societies have *social rules*. These include rules relating to morals, games, etc, as well as *obligation rules* which impose duties or obligations. The latter may be divided into moral rules and legal rules (or *law*). As a result of our human limitations there is a need for obligation rules in all societies: the 'minimum content of natural law' (see 4.2.1.1). Legal rules are divisible into *primary rules* and *secondary rules*. The former proscribe 'the free use of violence, theft and deception to which human beings are tempted but which they must, in general, repress if they are to coexist in close proximity to each other'.[11] Primitive societies have little more than these primary rules imposing obligations. But as a society becomes more complex, there is a need to change the primary rules, to adjudicate on breaches of them, and to identify which rules are actually obligation rules. These three requirements are satisfied in each case in modern societies by the introduction of three sorts of *secondary rules*: rules of change, adjudication, and recognition. Unlike primary rules, the first two of these secondary rules do not

---

[10]  (1954) 70 *Law Quarterly Review* 37.     [11]  *The Concept of Law*, 89.

generally impose duties, but usually confer power. The rule of recognition, however, does seem to *impose duties* (largely on judges). This is considered further below.

In order for a legal system to exist, two conditions must be satisfied. First, valid obligation rules must be generally obeyed by members of the society, and, secondly, officials must accept the rules of change and adjudication; they must also accept the rule of recognition 'from the *internal point of view*'.

This is a bird's-eye view of Hart's picture of a legal system. Some of its more important (and controversial) features are now briefly examined.

### 4.2.4 **Social rules**

Hart rejects John Austin's conception of rules as commands and, indeed, the very idea that rules are phenomena that consist merely in externally observable activities or habits. Instead he asks us to consider the *social* dimension of rules, namely, the manner in which members of a society *perceive* the rule in question, their *attitude* towards it. This 'internal' aspect (see 4.2.8) distinguishes between a rule and a mere habit. Thus, to use his example,[12] chess players, in addition to having similar *habits* of moving the queen in the same way, also have a 'critical reflective attitude' to this way of moving it: they regard it as a *standard* for all who play chess; each 'has views' about the propriety of such moves. And they manifest these views in the criticism of others and acknowledge the legitimacy of such criticism when received from others. In other words, in order to explain the nature of rules we need to examine them from the point of view of those who 'experience' them, who pass judgment on them or, to use the language of hermeneutics, from the conceptual framework of the agent. It is particularly in respect of Hart's approach to the nature of rules that, though he is unashamedly positivist, Hart is to be distinguished from Austin and Bentham. He is concerned to demonstrate that far more significant than commands, sovereignty, and sanctions, is the *social* source of legal rules: they are a manifestation of our actual behaviour, our words, and our thoughts.

He also uses the concept of a 'rule' to distinguish between 'being obliged' and 'having an obligation'. The Austinian model cannot explain why if you are threatened by a gunman who orders you to hand over your money or he will shoot you, that though you may be *obliged* to comply, you have no *obligation* to do so—because there is no *rule* imposing an obligation on you.[13]

In the postscript to *The Concept of Law*[14] Hart acknowledges that the existence of social rules requires more than its general acceptance by most members of a group. He recognizes the relevance of Ronald Dworkin's distinction between conventions and concurrent practice. The former involves acceptance which is dependent upon its acceptance by *others*. In this sense, the rule of recognition (see 4.2.6) is conventional. On the other hand, 'the shared morality of a group' consists in a 'consensus of independent *convictions* manifested in the concurrent practices of the group'.[15]

---

[12] Ibid, 55–6.    [13] Ibid, 80.    [14] Ibid, 255.    [15] Ibid.

### 4.2.5 Secondary rules

It is important that you understand the nature and function of secondary rules. They play a leading role in Hart's system. Some encounter difficulty in respect of the three types of rules that Hart describes, and the relationships between them.

- *Rules of change*: Confusion sometimes arises as a result of Hart's use of this form of rule in *two* contexts. Rules of change are required in order to facilitate legislative or judicial changes to both the primary rules and certain secondary rules (eg, the rule of adjudication, below). This process of change is regulated by *rules* (secondary rules) which confer power on individuals or groups (eg, Parliament) to enact legislation in accordance with certain procedures. These rules of change are also to be found in 'lower-order' secondary rules which confer power on ordinary individuals to change their legal position (eg, by making contracts, wills, etc). Thus power-conferring secondary rules of change appear to have *two* meanings in Hart's model.

- *Rules of adjudication*: Certain rules confer competence on individuals to pass judgment mainly in cases of breaches of primary rules. This power is normally associated with a further power to punish the wrongdoer or compel the wrongdoer to pay damages. Further rules are required in this connection (eg, someone is under a duty to imprison the wrongdoer).

- *The rule of recognition* is essential to the existence of a legal system (and is considered further below). It determines the criteria by which the validity of the rules of a legal system is decided. As pointed out above, unlike the other two types of secondary rules, it appears, in part, to be *duty-imposing*: it requires those who exercise public power (particularly the power to adjudicate) to follow certain rules. This gives rise to an element of circularity[16] for the criteria for recognizing the validity of certain rules necessarily include—as a criterion of validity—the valid enactment of rules by the legislature in exercising its power conferred by the rule of change. But the rule of recognition presupposes the existence of judges whose duties are laid down by the rule of recognition. And these judges are empowered by a rule of adjudication. But this rule of adjudication is valid only if it satisfies some criterion of the rule of recognition. And, as just stated, the rule of recognition *presupposes* judges. And the existence of judges presupposes a rule of adjudication! 'Which member of this logical circle of rules', asks Neil MacCormick, 'is the ultimate rule of a legal system?'

### 4.2.6 The rule of recognition

Pointing to the serious limitations of the classic legal positivist theory of sovereignty (see 3.4.4), particularly the idea that legal authority is expressed in terms of a habit of obedience, Hart instead contends that rules are valid members of the legal system only

---

[16] Identified by MacCormick, *HLA Hart*, 108–9.

if they satisfy the criteria laid down by the rule of recognition. This secondary rule is a crucial aspect of Hart's model and you would be well advised to give it your closest attention. Not only is it important in its own right—as the centrepiece of Hart's positivism—but it provides the target of attack for several non-positivists, notably Ronald Dworkin, when they come to analyse, for instance, the judicial function (see 5.2.2).

Comparing it to the standard metre bar in Paris (the definitive standard by which a metre is measured), Hart says that the validity of the rule of recognition cannot be questioned: 'It can neither be valid nor invalid but is simply accepted as appropriate for use in this way.'[17] In the United Kingdom, he argues, the rule of recognition is 'what the Queen in Parliament enacts is law'. But the question of whether there is a *single* rule of recognition, whether it includes the doctrine of precedent (as it surely must) and whether there are several, perhaps graded rules of recognition is one which has not been adequately elaborated by Hart and which has generated considerable discussion.

Students generally find this the most perplexing aspect of Hart's theory. They often take the concept too literally. Hart certainly claims that for every developed legal system there is an 'ultimate rule of recognition' whose validity cannot be questioned and whose existence depends solely on the fact that it is accepted by officials 'from the internal point of view'. But Hart is not saying that the rule of recognition is merely a single rule or set of rules which, as if by some magical incantation, can supply the answer to the question: 'Which rules are legal rules?' It is more complex than that. The rule of recognition contains a set of different criteria of recognition which interact with each other in a variety of ways. A useful exercise is to attempt to set out the rule of recognition for a particular jurisdiction (which has certain constitutional and institutional features). MacCormick attempts such a formulation.[18] This is his fictitious rule of recognition for a state with a written constitution:

The judicial duty is to apply as 'valid law' all and only the following:

(i) Every provision contained in the constitution of 1950, save for such provisions as have been validly repealed by the procedures set in Article 100 of that constitution, but including every provision validly added by way of constitutional amendment under Article 100;

(ii) Every unrepealed Act of the Legislature validly enacted under, and otherwise consistent with, the provisions of the constitution of 1950;

(iii) Every provision by way of delegated legislation validly made under a power validly conferred by any unrepealed Act of the Legislature;

(iv) Every ruling on any question of law made by the Supreme Court or the Court of Appeal established by the Constitution of 1950, save that the Supreme Court may reverse any of its own prior rulings and those of the Court of Appeal, and the Court of Appeal may reverse its own prior rulings; and save that no judicial ruling inconsistent with any provision covered by criteria (i), (ii), or (iii) is valid to the extent of such inconsistency;

---

[17] *The Concept of Law*, 105–6.     [18] *HLA Hart*, 110.

(v) Every rule accepted as law by the custom and usage of the citizens of the State, either by way of general custom or local and particular custom, such being applicable either generally or locally so far as not inconsistent with (i)–(iv) above; and

(vi) Every rule in force in the State prior to the adoption of the Constitution of 1950, save for any such rule inconsistent with any rule valid under (i)–(v) above.

But this, you may cry, is simply a roll-call of the 'sources' of law. Surely, the rule of recognition is more intricate (and less obvious) than that! To this protest there are, I think, two answers. First, the connection between any 'acid test' of law and the 'sources' of law is a necessary and indeed inescapable one. It is clear that in applying the criteria of legal validity, a court (for it is normally courts that are called upon to decide such questions) is bound to accord validity to the enactments of the legislature, the judgments of courts, etc. It would be curious if this were otherwise. But the rule of recognition is more: it is 'a common, public standard of correct judicial decision'[19] which is binding *only if accepted by the officials in question*. Secondly, this is more than a *list* of formal standards of validity; in Hart's theorem this fictitious rule of recognition is actually a single rule which comprises six criteria ranked in order of importance. And each of them exerts complex mutual interrelations with one another.

If this strikes you as exasperating, you will not be alone. The precise (or even the least confusing) meaning of Hart's rule of recognition continues to perplex legal theorists.[20] In *The Concept of Law* he uses the phrase in two interrelated ways. First, he occasionally suggests that such rules are 'linguistic entities that designate what the primary rules of the system are … [by] designating the criteria for legal validity'.[21] When the concept is so employed he gives as an example 'an authoritative list or text of the [primary] rules to be found in a written document or carved on some public monument'.[22] Secondly, he frequently describes the rule of recognition as consisting in certain linguistic entities (such as those expressed in various sections of the United States Constitution). Here the rule of recognition constitutes those criteria that identify what primary rules of the legal system are. It operates as a barrier to exclude those rules that fail to satisfy the criteria contained in the rule of recognition.

Secondly, Hart most importantly characterizes the rule of recognition as a 'social rule': a particular kind of social practice. This formulation of the rule of recognition is a central feature of his account of law, and is endorsed by Hart in the postscript to *The Concept of Law*:

> My account of social rules is, as Dworkin has also rightly claimed, applicable only to rules which are conventional in the sense I have explained. This considerably narrows the scope of my practice theory and I do not now regard it as a sound explanation of morality, either individual or social. But the theory remains a faithful account of conventional social rules which include…certain important legal rules including the rule of recognition, which is in

[19] *The Concept of Law*, 116.
[20] Here it is Benjamin C Zipursky, 'The Model of Social Facts' in Jules Coleman (ed), *Hart's Postscript: Essays on the Postscript to* The Concept of Law (Oxford: Oxford University Press, 2001), 227 ff.
[21] Ibid, 227.        [22] *The Concept of Law*, 94.

effect a form of judicial customary rule existing only if it is accepted and practised in the law-identifying and law-applying operations of the courts.[23]

It is therefore unequivocally a *social* rule. This is well explained by Waluchow:

> In calling the rule of recognition a social rule, Hart means to distinguish it from rules whose existence is a result of official, rulemaking action(s) taken in accordance with secondary rules which establish and regulate this creative power. Unlike rules introduced by the formal actions of people in authority, social rules arise informally out of the complex practices of the members of the society or group in which they exist. In the case of a rule of recognition its existence is manifested in a complex general practice among the officials of a legal system and the general population. The former identify the valid rules of the system according to generally acknowledged and accepted criteria, while the latter acquiesce in, and conform with, the results of the rule of recognition's use by the officials.[24]

But, as Jules Coleman has observed, the rule of recognition cannot be equated with a social practice. The rule of recognition is a rule, and thus an abstract, propositional entity. A practice is constituted in part by behaviour, and is therefore not a propositional entity. The rule has conditions of satisfaction; the practice does not:

> The most important point about the relationship between rule and practice is that the rule of recognition comes into existence as a rule that regulates behaviour only if it is practised. The practice, we can say, is an existence condition of the rule of recognition. This feature falls out of the fact that the rule of recognition is a social or conventional rule: like the convention of driving on the right-hand side of the road, its claim to govern conduct depends on its being generally observed. By contrast, the legal rules that are validated by a rule of recognition purport to regulate behavior regardless of whether or not those rules reflect actual practice…Put precisely, while the claim to legal authority requires that all laws be capable of regulating conduct, the claim of legal norms generally to regulate conduct depends on the existence of a rule whose own claim to do so depends on its being practised.[25]

This ambiguity in the meaning of the rule of recognition impairs the authority of Hart's wider project, since several elements of his theory turn on the properties of the rule of recognition. How can so fundamental a conception simultaneously convey three different meanings? In the words of one critic echoing Coleman:

> [I]t is vital to Hart's theory that rules of recognition state criteria that primary legal rules satisfy or fail to satisfy. This feature seems to require the first or second version of 'rule of recognition' as something propositional. But it is similarly vital to Hart's rule of recognition that it is a social practice of judges. Yet a social practice is not something propositional, and a linguistic or propositional entity is not a practice of judges.[26]

Despite this impediment, you may conclude it is far from fatal to Hart's rule of recognition (as both a secondary rule and a social practice), and that the explanatory power of this central idea emerges relatively unscathed.

---

[23]  Ibid, 34.
[24]  WJ Waluchow, *Inclusive Legal Positivism* (Oxford: Clarendon Press, 1994), 235.
[25]  Coleman, *The Practice of Principle: In Defense of A Pragmatic Approach to Legal Theory*, 77–8.
[26]  Zipursky, 'The Model of Social Facts' in Coleman (ed), *Hart's Postscript*, 228–9.

### 4.2.7 **The existence of a legal system**

It has already been seen that it is Hart's view that a legal system may be said to 'exist' only if valid (primary) rules are obeyed and officials accept the rules of change and adjudication. In Hart's words: 'The assertion that a legal system exists is...a Janus-faced statement looking both to obedience by ordinary citizens and to the acceptance by officials of secondary rules as critical common standards of official behaviour.'[27] It is not clear whether these conditions are being postulated by Hart as a historical or developmental thesis (ie, primitive societies eventually develop by virtue of the emergence of secondary rules), or whether it is a purely hypothetical model to illustrate the function of these rules or as a heuristic device by which to recognize the existence of a legal system—as JW Harris puts it:

> If a country is in a state of turmoil and the political scientist is trying to assess whether it has that social grace commonly known as 'law', wheel in the patient and apply this two-pronged stethoscope—'Are your primary rules generally observed?' 'Do your officials accept your secondary rules?'[28]

Hart is not suggesting that *members of society* need 'accept' the primary rules or the rule of recognition; it is only the *officials* who need to adopt an 'internal point of view'. He acknowledges that if a legal system does not receive widespread acceptance it would be both morally and politically objectionable. But these moral and political criteria are not identifying characteristics of the notion of 'legal system'. The validity of a legal system is therefore independent from its efficacy. A completely ineffective rule may be a valid one—as long as it emanates from the rule of recognition. Nevertheless, in order to be a valid rule, the legal system of which the rule is a component must, as a whole, be effective.

### 4.2.8 **The 'internal point of view'**

It is important to grasp precisely what Hart means by this ubiquitous phrase (which appears in numerous guises throughout *The Concept of Law*). Let him speak for himself in a passage that is worth studying closely:

> What is necessary is that there should be a critical reflective attitude to certain patterns of behaviour as a common standard, and that this should display itself in criticism (including self-criticism), demands for conformity, and in acknowledgements that such criticism and demands are justified, all of which find their characteristic expression in the normative terminology of 'ought', 'must', and 'should', 'right' and 'wrong.'[29]

This 'internal' aspect of rules serves, of course, to distinguish social rules from mere group habits. You will notice, too, the emphasis on the language ('normative terminology') that is generated by the presence of rules. But a question that has been raised

---

[27] *The Concept of Law*, 113.
[28] JW Harris, *Legal Philosophies*, 2nd edn (London: Butterworths, 1997), 123.
[29] *The Concept of Law*, 56.

is whether by 'accepting' secondary rules, officials must 'approve' of them. The better view is that acceptance does not mean approval. In other words, certain judges in a wicked legal system (say, apartheid South Africa) may abhor the rules they are required to apply; this would nevertheless satisfy Hart's conditions for a legal system to exist. See the case study in Chapter 2. There is also a distinction between *accepting* the rules and *feeling bound* by them: see the discussion of the views of Alf Ross in 6.3.1.

### 4.2.9 **The judicial function**

In developing his theory of a legal system as a 'union of primary and secondary rules', Hart seeks to reject both the strictly formalist view (with its emphasis on judicial precedents and codification) and the rule-scepticism of the American realist movement (see 6.2). In so doing, he strikes something of a compromise between these two extremes: he—naturally—accepts that laws are indeed rules, but he recognizes that in arriving at decisions, judges have a fairly wide discretion. And he is, in any event, driven to this conclusion by virtue of the rule of recognition: if there is some 'acid test' by which judges are able to decide what are the valid legal rules, then where there is *no* applicable legal rule or the rule or rules are uncertain or ambiguous, the judge must have a strong discretion to 'fill in the gaps', in such 'hard cases'. The extent to which judges *do* have a discretion to decide—almost as they please—what the law is in these cases has, of course, become one of the most hotly contested subjects in contemporary jurisprudence (and hence popular examination question fodder; it is discussed at greater length in 5.2).

I have already mentioned that Hart recognizes that, as a consequence of the inherent ambiguity of language, rules have an 'open texture' (eg, what is a 'vehicle'?) and, are, in some cases, vague (eg, what is 'reasonable care'?). He therefore has no difficulty in accepting the proposition that in 'hard cases' judges *make* law. They will, of course, be guided by various sources (eg, persuasive cases from foreign jurisdictions), but, in the end, the judge will base his decision on his own conception of fairness or justice. Whether this is a valid way of describing the judicial function is examined in 5.2.

### 4.2.10 **'An essay in descriptive sociology'?**

In his preface to *The Concept of Law*, Hart says the book may be viewed in these terms. And the extent to which this is a justifiable claim is a matter that has attracted the attention of both jurists and social scientists[30] (as well as the occasional examiner). Lloyd prefers to regard it as 'an essay in analytical jurisprudence'[31] and Twining finds it difficult to support the claim 'not because it is wrong or misleading, but because the idea of a descriptive sociology of law is not developed in *The Concept of Law* nor in Hart's other writings'.[32] Yet Hart's insistence that officials accept the rule of

---

[30] See, for example, M Krygier (1982) 2 *Oxford Journal of Legal Studies* 155.
[31] *Introduction to Jurisprudence*, 2nd edn (London: Butterworths, 1997), 336.
[32] (1979) 95 *Law Quarterly Review* 557, 579.

recognition 'from the internal point of view' and his view that there should be a 'critical reflective attitude' to certain patterns of behaviour as a common standard echoes Max Weber's concept of internal legitimation. (See 7.5.) In her biography of Hart,[33] Nicola Lacey uncovers an intriguing mystery. When John Finnis borrowed Hart's copy of *Max Weber on Law in Economy and Society* he discovered that the pages had been heavily annotated by Hart. Beside one passage, in which Weber discusses the idea of law drawing its legitimacy from an 'internal' perspective, Hart had written, 'Good, like it, likely to be useful.' And useful it turns out to have been. Yet when, on two separate occasions, Finnis asked Hart whether this central idea in his concept of law had Weberian origins, Hart denied that he had been influenced by the German sociologist. One can only wonder: why? Lacey suggests that it may have been part of a general hostility among analytic philosophers towards modern social theory. We shall never know.

Stephen Perry has sought to show that Hart's substantive theory fails to provide a satisfactory conceptual analysis. Nor, he contends, does it account successfully for law's normativity. This is because Hart is committed to 'methodological positivism' which holds that a theory of law should provide external descriptions of legal practice that are morally neutral and without justificatory aims:

> Hart's own theory of law, being external, is admittedly without justificatory aims: it does not try to show participants how the social practice of law might be justified to them. But the theory is not, I have argued, morally neutral. Even so it does not offer a solution to the problem of the normativity of law in the way that, say, Raz's theory does. One reason for this is precisely that the theory is external; another is that it rests on a purely descriptive account of the concepts of obligation and authority. As far as these latter concepts are concerned, Hart is content simply to make the observation that officials and perhaps others accept the rule of recognition, meaning they *regard* it as obligation-imposing. This is to describe the problem of the normativity of law rather than to offer a solution.[34]

In other words, Hart's twin analytical ambitions of analysing both the concept of law and its normativity cannot be achieved by adopting an external, purely descriptive approach. The law, Perry argues, is not susceptible to a scientific method of investigation, for it is unable to address its normativity. A similar point is made by MJ Detmold:

> Hart's mistake…was to try to run two incompatible analyses together: the analysis of sociological statements, where existence can be separated from bindingness and thus from moral statements; and the analysis of internal normative statements, where it cannot. *The Concept of Law* suffers throughout from a failure to separate these things.[35]

This is a bold, provocative claim, but it is one that Detmold attempts to substantiate with largely philosophical evidence which is at once dense and difficult.

---

[33] Nicola Lacey, *A Life of HLA Hart: The Nightmare and the Noble Dream* (Oxford: Oxford University Press, 2004).

[34] Stephen Perry, 'Hart's Methodological Positivism' in Jules Coleman (ed), *Hart's Postscript: Essays on the Postscript to* The Concept of Law, 353.

[35] MJ Detmold, *The Unity of Law and Morality* (London: Routledge & Kegan Paul, 1984), 54.

### 4.2.11 **Critique**

It would be impossible to consider here the prodigious literature that Hart's work has generated. Nor could any student be expected to read even one tenth of it. But you may be certain that you will need to have a thorough understanding of *The Concept of Law* and probably also the later reflections of its author in the 1994 postscript (written when he was frail and unwell). Some of the criticisms that have been made of Hart's general thesis have already been referred to. There are many more (eg, Is the 'internal point of view' an oversimplification? Can people have an 'internal' attitude to rules of which they are unaware? Does Hart's system of rules ignore the concept of an institution? Is his anthropological evidence descriptive or analytical?). The most substantial and influential critique is the subject of Chapter 5.

Be sure you are acquainted with the principal criticisms that have been made of the thesis (from a variety of standpoints). Are you able to say whether and why you consider these attacks to be justified? Your analysis should exhibit, particularly in respect of this celebrated jurist, a 'critical reflective attitude'.

## 4.3 **Hans Kelsen**

Of all the legal theorists you will encounter, Hans Kelsen is probably the least understood (not only by students) and most misrepresented. I have therefore devoted more space to Kelsen than other positivists. This reflects my efforts, over many years, to reduce the pain and suffering that Kelsen has induced in my own students. Much of this is doubtless a consequence of his use of fairly difficult and abstract conceptual language which, especially to those unfamiliar with the Continental approach to philosophy, is not always congenial. Very few question his remarkable facility for critical exposition and inquiry, indeed, it has been claimed that 'no single writer... [has] made a more illuminating analysis of the legal process'.[36] His pure theory of law has become as important (if not nearly as influential) as Hart's theory, and represents a significant strand in modern legal positivism.[37] But, though the Kelsenian enterprise is not entirely painless, I hope the following discussion will assist your comprehension and appreciation of its principal features.

To the extent that he insisted on the separation of law and morals, what 'is' (*sein*) and what 'ought to be' (*sollen*), Kelsen may legitimately be characterized as a legal positivist, but he is a good deal more. The pure theory is a subtle and profound statement about the way in which we should understand law. And we should do so, he argues, by conceiving it to be a system of 'oughts' or *norms*. But Kelsen acknowledges that the law consists not merely of norms, but 'is made up of legal norms and legal acts

---

[36] *Lloyd's Introduction to Jurisprudence*, 8th edn (London: Sweet & Maxwell, 2008), 305.
[37] Dias describes Kelsen's writings as constituting 'the most refined development to date of analytical positivism', RWM Dias, *Jurisprudence*, 5th edn (London: Butterworths, 1985), 258.

as determined by these norms'.[38] In other words, legal norms (which include judicial decisions and legal transactions such as contracts and wills) when *acted upon* also describe actual human conduct. Even the most general norms describe human conduct. Thus:

> Kelsen's observation that the legal scientist is not concerned with human conduct but is only concerned with norms may have obscured from view the important point that so far as human conduct features in a norm as condition or consequence such conduct falls four-square within the concerns of the Kelsenian legal scientist.... Kelsen permits of a greater degree of reference to actual human conduct than is sometimes perceived by those who would label his contribution as 'sterile.' [39]

Indeed, it has been argued that Kelsen's attempt to understand and explain the 'science of the mind and of meaning and of values as instantiated in actual human societies' is 'the only jurisprudence ever to take sociology seriously'.[40] He was, it has been suggested, 'engaging in sociology when writing his *Pure Theory*, notwithstanding his indignant denials'.[41] The validity or otherwise of these claims should become clearer in the course of the following pages.[42]

As a follower of the great eighteenth-century philosopher, Immanuel Kant, Kelsen espouses the view that objective reality can be comprehended only by the application of certain formal categories like time and space. These categories do not 'exist' in nature: we use them in order to make sense of the world. Equally, to understand 'the law' we require similar formal categories, in particular the *Grundnorm* or basic norm which lies at the heart of the legal system (see 4.3.3).

Kelsen's project is thus a fairly ambitious one. He seeks, to use his own words, to raise jurisprudence 'to the level of a genuine science'. His theory is described by Richard Tur as 'a thoroughgoing attempt to develop an epistemology for jurisprudence. It is a recipe for legal knowledge'.[43] The ingredients are, however, often far from straightforward. And the result is not to everyone's taste.

### 4.3.1 Unadulterated law

Few have difficulty in grasping Kelsen's insistence on excluding the 'impurities' of morality, history, politics, sociology, etc. If we are to arrive at a *scientific* (as opposed to a subjective, value-laden) theory of law, says Kelsen, we need to restrict our analysis to the 'norms' of positive law: those 'oughts' which provide that if certain conduct (X) is performed, then a sanction (Y) should be applied by an official to the offender. If X

---

[38] *General Theory of Law and State*, transl Anders Wedberg (Cambridge, Mass: Harvard University Press, 1949), 39.                    [39] Tur and Twining (eds), *Essays on Kelsen*, 23–4.
[40] R Tur, 'The Kelsenian Enterprise' in Tur and Twining (eds), *Essays on Kelsen*, 150 at 182.
[41] G Sawer, *Law in Society* (Oxford: Clarendon Press, 1965), 5, quoted by Tur, op. cit.
[42] I draw here on my essay, 'One Country, Two *Grundnormen*? The Basic Law and the Basic Norm' in R Wacks (ed), *Hong Kong, China and 1997: Essays in Legal Theory* (Hong Kong: Hong Kong University Press, 1993).
[43] R Tur, 'The Kelsenian Enterprise' in Tur and Twining (eds), *Essays on Kelsen*, 149–83, 157.

then Y. The theory therefore rules out all that cannot be *objectively* known: the social purpose of law, its political functions, etc. Law has only one function: the monopolization of force.

Kelsen's pursuit of a 'science of law' is premised on the claim that an account of law can be disinfected from 'elements of psychology, sociology, ethics, and political theory'.[44] In his words:

> This adulteration is understandable, because [these] disciplines deal with subject-matters that are closely connected with law. The pure theory of law undertakes to delimit the cognition of law against these disciplines, not because it ignores or denies the connection, but because it wishes to avoid the uncritical mixture of methodologically different disciplines…which obscures the essence of the science of law and obliterates the limits imposed upon it by the nature of its subject-matter.[45]

By 'norms' Kelsen means that 'something *ought* to be or *ought* to happen, especially that a human being ought to behave in a specific way'.[46] Thus the statement 'the door ought to be closed' or a red traffic light are both norms. But a norm, in order to be *valid* (ie, binding), must be authorized by another norm which, in turn, is authorized by a higher norm in the system. The separation between law and morality means that the validity of legal norms can flow only from another *legal*, as opposed to a *moral* norm. Kelsen is profoundly *relativistic*: he rejects the notion that there are values 'out there'; all norms are relative to the individual or group under consideration. This point is well explained by Professor Raz[47] who shows that Kelsen is not a sceptic (ie, he does not take the view that all normative statements are necessarily *false*), he is a relativist or subjectivist:

> Normative statements can be true or false. It is merely that their truth depends on the existence of relativistic rather than absolute values: 'relativistic…positivism does not assert that there are no values, or that there is no moral order, but only that the values in which men actually believe are not absolute but relative values.'[48]

As Raz remarks, a conspicuous difficulty with this form of relativism is its assumption that any sincere moral statement I make about myself must be true; because I *believe* that there is a norm requiring me to perform a certain act such a norm *exists* and my statement is *true*. By the same process of reasoning insincere moral statements about myself are always false. And normative statements I make about *others* are true only if they conform to *their* beliefs about themselves. 'Thus', concludes Raz, 'it is true that a racist should behave in a racist way.'[49] This is clearly unacceptable.

Nevertheless Kelsen's relativist, value-free theory of law seeks to locate legal science in a world free of the 'impurities' of social science. It provides, in Stewart's words:

---

[44] *Pure Theory of Law*, transl Max Knight (Berkeley and Los Angeles: University of California Press, 1967), 1.  [45] Loc cit.  [46] *Pure Theory of Law*, 4.

[47] J Raz, 'The Purity of the Pure Theory' in Tur and Twining (eds), *Essays on Kelsen*, 79 at 87.

[48] H Kelsen, *What is Justice?* (Berkeley and Los Angeles: University of California Press, 1957), 179.

[49] Raz, 'The Purity of the Pure Theory', 88.

the basic forms under which meanings can be known scientifically as legal norms—which will have a content, although the particular content is empirically contingent, and which, once determined as having a particular content, can be morally evaluated. Far from being an attempt to exclude considerations of experience, content, and justice, the pure theory is intended to make attention to them more rigorously possible.[50]

The hierarchy of legal norms that forms a legal system is ultimately traced back to the *Grundnorm* or basic norm of the legal system. Its nature, function, and relationship to other norms will be examined later.

The law consists of norms used as a 'specific social technique' by politicians to determine how individuals ought to behave so as to promote social order and peace. This technique consists in the acts of will of individuals authorized by the law to create norms which render the behaviour of individuals lawful or unlawful by providing *sanctions* for failure to comply with the norms. Thus legal norms differ from other norms in that they prescribe a sanction. The legal system is founded on state coercion; behind its norms is the threat of force. This distinguishes the tax collector from the robber. Both demand your money. Both, in other words, require that you *ought* to pay up. Both exhibit a *subjective* act of will, but only the tax collector's is *objectively* valid. Why? Because, says Kelsen, the subjective meaning of the robber's coercive order is not interpreted as its objective meaning. Why not? Because 'no basic norm is presupposed according to which one ought to behave in conformity with this order'.[51] And why not? Because the robber's coercive order lacks the 'lasting effectiveness without which no basic norm is presupposed'. This illustrates the fundamental relationship in Kelsen's theory between validity and effectiveness which is discussed at 4.3.4.

Kelsen's reduction of all legislation to the form 'If X, then Y' (where X is certain conduct, and Y is a sanction) is widely regarded as unacceptably narrow. The *form* of law is given primacy over its *meaning*. It presumes (which, of course, Kelsen is content to do) that law is essentially coercion; many would want to argue that law has other functions, for example, regulatory purposes.

Other critics seek to show that Kelsen accords unwarranted importance to the role of sanctions in law. It results in a lopsided analysis of legal duty not only because a statute may impose duties *without* necessarily providing a sanction, but because, on the other hand, certain conduct may be made the condition of a sanction even though it is not the subject of a *duty*. Thus JW Harris points out that to measure effectiveness we need to know the content of the norm, that is, the nature of the duty involved. As he puts it, 'The concept of "duty" must...stand on its own feet, as something distinct from the concept of sanction. A theory of law must define duty and sanction separately.'[52]

---

[50]  I Stewart, 'Kelsen and the Exegetical Tradition' in Tur and Twining (eds), *Essays on Kelsen*, 123 at 128.
[51]  *Pure Theory of Law*, 47.          [52]  *Legal Philosophies*, 67.

### 4.3.2 **A hierarchy of norms**

Kelsen represents a legal system as a complex series of interlocking norms which progress from the most general 'oughts' (eg, sanctions ought to be effected in accordance with the constitution), to the most particular or 'concrete' (eg, David is contractually bound to mow Victoria's lawn). Each norm in this hierarchical system draws its validity from another—higher—norm. The validity of all norms is ultimately based on the *Grundnorm* (see 4.3.3).

This systemic, hierarchical model of law provides also the explanation for the dynamic creation of legal norms. The membership of norms in the legal system is determined by other norms in the hierarchy. Law is created by facts (eg, a judicial decision) which convey normative force from the authorizing norm to the authorized norm. The authorizing norm being valid and capable of endowing law-creating acts with status to create law, the norm so created is also valid. Law-creating acts thereby confer validity from one norm to another.

As has been pointed out, the validity of each norm is dependent on a higher norm in the system whose validity is in turn dependent upon a higher norm in the system and so on. A point is eventually reached beyond which this climbing cannot go. This is the basic norm or *Grundnorm*. All norms flow from it in increasing levels of 'concreteness': the basic norm expresses an 'ought' at the highest level of generality. Below it, in the hierarchy of norms, is the historically first constitution. Below it are laws enacted—by the legislature or judiciary—which are more 'concrete', all the way down to the most concrete, individualized norm such as: 'the bailiff is empowered to seize the property of the defendant who has been found by a court to be liable to the claimant and who is unable to pay what he owes'. The coercive act of the bailiff (or the prison warder in incarcerating a prisoner) is the ultimate stage in the progression from general basic norm to particular individuated norm.

### 4.3.3 **The *Grundnorm***

Since, by definition, the validity of the *Grundnorm* cannot depend on any other norm it must be presupposed. What does this mean? Kelsen seems to be saying (and this is a matter of some controversy) that we need this assumption in order to understand the legal order. As he says, disclaiming any originality:

> By formulating the *Grundnorm*, we do not introduce into the science of law any new method. We merely make explicit what all jurists, mostly unconsciously, assume when they consider positive law as a system of valid norms and not only as a complex of facts, and at the same time repudiate any natural law from which positive law would receive its validity. That the *Grundnorm* really exists in the juristic consciousness is the result of a simple analysis of actual juristic statements. The *Grundnorm* is the answer to the question: how—and that means under what condition—are these juristic statements concerning legal norms, legal duties, legal rights, and so on, possible?[53]

---

[53] *General Theory of Law and State*, 117.

This is a lucid statement of the role Kelsen assigns to his basic norm: it exists, but only in the 'juristic consciousness'. It is a presupposition which facilitates an understanding of the legal system by the legal scientist, judge, or lawyer.[54] But it is not chosen arbitrarily; it is selected by reference to whether the legal order as a whole is 'by and large' efficacious. Its validity depends on efficacy (see 4.3.4). The presupposed basic norm is characterized by Stewart as:

> the nodal point at which the *pure* part of legal science passes over into the *empirical* part; on the *pure* side, the basic norm stands in a relation of validity to the specific and generic formulations of the presupposition 'basic norm' and through them to the pure theory as a whole, while on the *empirical* side it stands in a relation of validity to the remainder of the legal order; its validity on the *pure* side cannot be questioned from the *empirical* side, since it is the condition of possibility, furnished by the *pure* side for the *empirical* side.[55]

In other words, the validity of the basic norm rests, not on another norm or rule of law, but is assumed—for the purpose of purity. It is therefore what Kelsen occasionally calls a 'juristic hypothesis', though it is sometimes described as a presupposition or even a fiction. According to its creator, it 'presents itself... not as a guess or hypothesis about the reality behind the law but explicitly as a methodological maxim, a norm of method which is ontologically neutral'.[56]

Consider his religious analogy:

> A father addresses to his son the individual norm, 'Go to school.' The son asks his father, 'Why should I go to school?' That is, he asks why the subjective meaning of his father's act of will is its objective meaning, i.e., a norm binding for him—or, which means the same thing, what is the basis of the validity of this norm. The father responds: 'Because God has commanded that parents be obeyed—that is, He has authorised parents to issue commands to children.' The son replies: 'Why should one obey the commands of God?' What all this amounts to is: why is the subjective meaning of this act of will of God also its objective meaning—that is, a valid norm? or, which means the same thing, what is the basis of the validity of this general norm? The only possible answer to this is: because, as a believer, *one presupposes that one ought to obey the commands of God*. This is the statement of the validity of a norm that must be presupposed in a believer's thinking in order to ground the validity of the norms of a religious morality. This statement is *the basic norm of a religious morality*, the norm which *grounds the validity of all the norms of that morality—a 'basic' norm*, because no further question can be raised about the basis of its validity. The statement is not a positive norm—that is, not a norm posited by a real act of will—but a norm *presupposed* in a believer's thinking.[57]

Kelsen's *Grundnorm* may therefore be an attempt to answer a more fundamental (perhaps the *most* fundamental) question of legal theory: why is law obeyed? His complex

---

[54] '[I]n the presupposition of the *Grundnorm* is the identification or fusion, in the juristic consciousness, of authorisation and rightness. The *Grundnorm* is, in this sense, the juristic God', John Gardner, 'Law as a Leap of Faith' in Peter Oliver, Sionaidh Douglas Scott, and Victor Tadros (eds), *Faith in Law* (Oxford: Hart Publishing, 2000), 19, 23–4.

[55] 'Kelsen and the Exegetical Tradition' in Tur and Twining (eds), *Essays on Kelsen*, 123 at 132, emphasis added.                                                                                          [56] Ibid, 170.

[57] 'The Function of a Constitution', transl I Stewart, in ibid, 112, emphasis added.

and controversial reply was: because legal norms are objectively valid. And they derive their ultimate validity from the *Grundnorm*, a neo-Kantian transcendental-logical condition of the interpretation of law-creating acts of wills as objectively valid legal norms. (On Kelsen's neo-Kantianism see 4.3.6.) It has two principal functions. First, it helps to distinguish between the demands of a robber and those of the law (see 4.3.1), that is, it makes it possible to regard a coercive order as objectively valid. Secondly, it provides an explanation for the coherence and unity of a legal order. All valid legal norms may be interpreted as a non-contradictory field of meaning.

What if I do not 'accept' the basic norm of the legal system? Suppose I consider the system immoral or unjust? Does the basic norm supply a *normative* or moral justification for law? The better view is that this is not Kelsen's purpose. He employs the idea of normativity in a *legal* sense only. Nevertheless, it is important, as Raz demonstrates,[58] to clarify precisely the nature of Kelsen's claim. Statements about the law may be 'committed', that is, they state what the law *ought* to be. Such moral statements are, of course, excluded by positivists like Raz from the proper realm of legal theory, and Kelsen's purity is bought at the cost of such exclusion:

> [L]egal theory to remain pure cannot study the law insofar as it is embedded in the moral beliefs of one person or another. That would violate the sources thesis [which claims that the identification of the existence and content of law does not require or resort to any moral argument] by making the identification of the law dependent on a particular set of moral beliefs. To be pure, legal theory must strictly adhere to the sources thesis and identify law by social facts only. Hence to describe it normatively it must non-committally or fictitiously accept the basic norm of the legal man, that is, the Kelsenian basic norm, for it is the only one to give validity to the *empirically established* law and to nothing else. This, then, is the sense in which the basic norm is the scientific postulate of legal thought.[59]

It is important to recognize, therefore, that Kelsen's conception of normativity is a narrow one. He repeatedly eschews moral absolutes. His theory, he says, 'cannot answer questions as to whether a particular law is just, or what is justice, because they cannot be answered scientifically at all'.[60] Such relativism strips his normativity of its usual moral connotations. This is not always grasped by commentators, though it is easy to see why this confusion should arise; it is often supposed that the 'ought' in the question whether an immoral law 'ought' to be obeyed is the same as the 'ought' in Kelsen's question whether the law 'ought' to be obeyed. The latter enquiry is, for him, expunged of moral considerations: it is a matter of determining whether the basic norm is valid; if it is, the *law* 'ought' to be *obeyed*.

The *Grundnorm* has two main features. First, it is *presupposed*. But, in Kelsen's words:

> The basic norm is…not a product of free invention. It refers to particular facts existing in natural reality, to an actually laid down and effective constitution and to the norm-creating and norm-applying facts in fact established in conformity with the constitution.[61]

---

[58] Tur and Twining (eds), *Essays on Kelsen*, 91–7.     [59] Ibid, 95.     [60] *What is Justice?*, 266.
[61] 'The Function of a Constitution', transl I Stewart, in Tur and Twining (eds), *Essays on Kelsen*, 115.

Secondly, it has no content. It is a purely formal category. Kelsen formulates the basic norm as follows:

> Coercive acts ought to be performed under the conditions and in the manner which the historically first constitution, and the norms created according to it, prescribe. (In short: One ought to behave as the constitution prescribes.)[62]

In *General Theory of Law and State*, he gives the following version:

> Coercive acts ought to be carried out only under the conditions and in the way determined by the 'fathers' of the constitution or the organs delegated by them.[63]

The basic norm's supposed 'neutrality' suggests that there is no *logical* reason why the basic norm of, say, a socialist legal system cannot be the basic norm of a capitalist one. Kelsen says: 'any kind of content might be law. There is no human behaviour which, as such, is excluded from being the content of a legal norm.'[64] And: 'The validity of a positive legal order cannot be denied because of the content of its norms.'[65]

Kelsen insists that his basic norm is unrelated to the political ideology of the legal system in question. As Honoré puts it:

> Legal theory has to be able to deal not merely with the law of democratic societies, but with dictatorships and one-party States. Many of the societies whose laws form the subject-matter of legal theory…are non-democratic. Of course different legal systems are bound to have different basic norms; at the very least they must be different in that they refer to the history or circumstances of different societies. But if the point of view of legal theory is itself to be a coherent one…these basic norms must be consistent with one another. Legal theory cannot simultaneously entertain the hypothesis, in relation to one system, that only laws proceeding from democratic institutions are valid and, in relation to another, that only laws proceeding from Marxist institutions are valid.[66]

Kelsen does, however, concede:

> A communist may, indeed, not admit that there is an essential difference between an organisation of gangsters and a capitalist legal order which he considers as the means of ruthless exploitation. For he does not presuppose—as do those who interpret the coercive order in question as an objectively valid normative order—the basic norm. He does not deny that the capitalist coercive order is the law of the State. What he denies is that this coercive order; the law of the State, is objectively valid. The function of the basic norm is *not* to make it possible to consider a coercive order which is by and large effective as law, for…a legal order is a coercive order by and large effective; the function of the basic norm is to make it possible to consider this coercive order as an objectively valid order.[67]

But, one is bound to say, by the same token, a 'capitalist' may be just as prone to deny that a socialist legal order is objectively valid. By Kelsen's own admission, this does not

---

[62] *Pure Theory of Law*, 201.     [63] *General Theory of Law and State*, 115–16.
[64] *Pure Theory of Law*, 198.     [65] Ibid, 267.
[66] AM Honoré, 'The Basic Norm of a Society' in his *Making Law Bind* (Oxford: Oxford University Press, 1987), 98–9.     [67] 'A Reply to Professor Stone' (1965) 17 *Stanford Law Review* 1144.

matter. However, as JM Eekelaar has argued,[68] it neglects the distinct social phenomena that differentiate the two societies.

To be fair, Kelsen (somewhat contradictorily) acknowledges that 'even an anarchist, if he were a professor of law, could describe positive law as a system of valid norms, without having to *approve* of this law'.[69] So, as Eekelaar puts it, 'a Communist professor might presuppose a capitalist basic norm in explaining a capitalist legal system'.[70] And the reverse would hold too. One way out of this dilemma is to *take neutrality seriously*. The notions of a 'capitalist basic norm' or a 'socialist basic norm' are themselves problematic if the basic norm is a purely *formal* construct. We might therefore seek instead a basic norm which is in some way independent of specifically ideological significance. Another solution is to reject Kelsen's pursuit of the will-o'-the-wisp of a basic norm of the legal system and instead postulate some general 'basic norm of society'. This is Professor Honoré's solution.[71] He acknowledges the need for a 'basic norm' of some kind, if we are to 'take law seriously'. He proposes instead a 'platitudinous basic norm' which 'will appear plausible to a variety of people living in societies with different social and political structures'.[72] He suggests: 'the members of a society have a duty to co-operate with one another'. It admirably captures a principle so bland that it cannot fail to win universal approbation. Nevertheless its purpose is not, as far as I understand it, to *authorize* the process of norm-creation (as Kelsen's *Grundnorm* seeks to do) but to justify every law: it therefore operates to fix the *content* of legal norms—however broadly. In this respect, as in several others, the *Grundnorm* differs from Hart's rule of recognition, as summarized in Table 4.1.

### 4.3.4 Validity, efficacy, and revolution

For Kelsen the *efficacy* (or effectiveness) of the whole legal order is a condition of the *validity* (or legitimacy) of every norm within it. In other words, implicit in the very existence of a legal system is the fact that its laws are generally obeyed. As Kelsen says:

> It cannot be maintained that, legally, men have to behave in conformity with a certain norm, if the total legal order, of which that norm is an integral part, has lost its efficacy. The principle of legitimacy is restricted by the principle of effectiveness.[73]

In *The Pure Theory of Law* he puts the matter plainly: 'Every by and large effective coercive order can be interpreted as an objectively valid normative order.'[74] But how is this to be measured? How do we *know* whether laws are actually being obeyed rather than ignored? How do we test whether the law is, in Kelsen's phrase, 'by and large' effective? Are, for example, one's motives for disobeying the law relevant?

JW Harris suggests that we might relate the number of laws in the system to the number of times that the specified sanctions have been or are likely to be applied. The ratio between the official acts and the acts of disobedience would provide an index

---

[68] 'Principles of Revolutionary Legality' in AWB Simpson (ed), *Oxford Essays in Jurisprudence*, 2nd series (Oxford: Oxford University Press, 1973), 27–30.
[69] *Pure Theory of Law*, 218 n, emphasis added.    [70] Ibid.    [71] *Making Law Bind*, 111.
[72] Ibid.    [73] *General Theory of Law and State*, 119.    [74] At 217.

**Table 4.1** The rule of recognition and *Grundnorm* compared

| Rule of recognition | *Grundnorm* |
| --- | --- |
| Does not depend on any aspect of coercion for its validity. | Based on coercion. |
| Its existence is a matter of fact. | A logical presumption of the 'juristic consciousness'. |
| Its function is to enable one to identify rules. | Functions to validate the Constitution and all norms in the system. |
| It may include several criteria of validity. | There is only one *Grundnorm*. |
| It imparts validity to rules within a legal system by enabling officials to recognize primary and secondary rules. | It imparts validity to a normative order, and is also the source of all norms. |
| It provides the unity in a legal system. | It enables the legal scientist to interpret all valid legal norms as a non-contradictory field of meaning. |
| Its own validity (which is meaningless in this context) cannot be demonstrated; it simply exists. | Pre-supposed in terms of efficacy, therefore it must be valid. |
| No necessary connection between the validity and efficacy of a rule (unless the rule of recognition contains such a provision amongst its criteria). | Its choice is not arbitrary and depends on the principle of efficacy. |

of effectiveness.[75] What Kelsen seems to be suggesting, therefore, is that for the legal order to be valid it is not necessary that every law be obeyed, but that there should be general adherence to the *Grundnorm*. Nor does a legal order cease being valid merely because a single norm loses its effectiveness. But if an individual legal norm is generally ineffective (because, eg, it is applied only occasionally), it does not lose its validity. If, however, it is *never* applied, it may cease to be valid.

An obvious difficulty arises. The extent to which a legal order is effective is primarily an empirical matter. Yet the pure theory spurns 'sociological' enquiries of this kind. Moreover, the *reasons* for the effectiveness of the law (its rationality, morality, etc) must similarly be excluded by Kelsen. If the validity of a legal order depends on the effectiveness of its basic norm, it follows that when that basic norm of the system no longer attracts general support, it may be supplanted by some other basic norm. This is precisely what occurs after a successful revolution. According to Kelsen when the new laws of the revolutionary government are effectively enforced, lawyers presuppose a new *Grundnorm*. This is because the *Grundnorm* is not the Constitution, but the presupposition that the new situation ought to be accepted in fact.

---

[75] *Legal Philosophies*, 1st edn, 103.

And this aspect of Kelsen's theory has been applied by courts in various jurisdictions which have undergone revolutions: the coup in Pakistan in 1958,[76] the Ugandan coup in 1965,[77] the Rhodesian UDI in 1965,[78] and, more recently, in the case of the revolution in Grenada.[79]

In all these decisions, the courts cited a passage from Kelsen which covers this very state of affairs, and (in all but the second Pakistani case) appear to have held that validity is indeed a function of efficacy. It should, however, be noted that the essential criterion of validity is what *the courts* regard as valid. In other words, in the hiatus between the overthrow of the old regime and its effective replacement by the new one, there is no longer a *Grundnorm*; nevertheless courts may continue to apply 'laws' which the courts recognize by reference to their *own* criterion of validity.

Thus in *Madzimbamuto* v *Lardner-Burke* the court held that the revolutionary 1965 Constitution was effective, yet for more than two years the Rhodesian courts had accepted the validity of certain of the revolutionary post-UDI 'laws'—even though they refused to recognize the legality of the revolutionary 1965 constitution. It is hard to see how this could be explained in simple Kelsenian terms. It suggests, says Dias,[80] that effectiveness is not the criterion of the *Grundnorm*, but what *courts* are prepared to accept as the basis of validity. It shows, too, that the validity of a law does not necessarily derive from an effective *Grundnorm*, but rather what *courts* are willing to accept as valid. Dias concludes that:

> Kelsen's theory does not apply in revolutionary situations, in which case it ceases to be a 'general theory'; or, if general, it ceases to be true. In settled conditions it teaches nothing new; in revolutionary conditions, where guidance is needed, it is useless, for the choice of a *Grundnorm* is not dictated inflexibly by effectiveness but is a political decision, as Kelsen has admitted.[81]

To some extent the Grenada Court of Appeal in *Mitchell* v *Director of Public Prosecutions*[82] seems to have accepted this view. Haynes P was reluctant to regard the revolutionary government as legal unless it complied with four conditions: (a) a successful revolution must have taken place, ie, the government is firmly established administratively; (b) the government is in effective control, ie, there is by and large conformity with its mandates; (c) such conformity was due to popular support not mere tacit submission to coercion; and (d) the regime must not be oppressive or undemocratic.[83]

Ask yourself the question whether Kelsen's theory may properly be used by judges to legitimate legal systems on the sole basis of their efficacy. Is efficacy the sole criterion employed by courts? What of other considerations such as 'justice'? John Eekelaar[84]

---

[76] See *The State* v *Dosso* PLD 1958 SC 180, 553, overruled 14 years later by the Supreme Court which rejected Kelsen's view in *Jilani* v *Government of Punjab* PLD 1972 SC 670.

[77] See *Uganda* v *Commissioner of Prisons, ex parte Matovu* [1966] EA 514.

[78] See *Madzimbamuto* v *Lardner-Burke* (1968) 2 SA 284, and see the decision of the Privy Council in [1969] 1 AC 645.            [79] *Mitchell* v *Director of Public Prosecutions* [1986] AC 73.

[80] *Jurisprudence*, 366.        [81] Ibid, 367.        [82] [1988] LRC (Const) 35.        [83] At 71–2.

[84] 'Principles of Revolutionary Legality' in Simpson (ed), *Oxford Essays in Jurisprudence*, 29.

argues that effectiveness is merely *one* of several criteria of the legal justification of a revolution; he suggests eight other factors (including legitimate disobedience to improper laws, necessity, the principle that a court should not allow itself to be used as an instrument of injustice, and the right to self-determination and the unacceptability of racial discrimination). Some would assert that the application of these kinds of criteria involve the courts in making 'political' judgments, but it is not easy to imagine how this can be avoided even if they ostensibly confine themselves to questions of effectiveness. Others suggest that merely by remaining in office, a judge gives tacit support to the effective legal order. See 2.11.

Kelsen defines a revolution as that which 'occurs whenever the legal order of a community is nullified and replaced by a new order...in a way not prescribed by the first order itself.'[85] Another definition he proposes is 'every not legitimate change of [the] constitution or its replacement by another constitution'.[86] If some *unlawful* or *unconstitutional* act is required to create a new, valid legal order then a peaceful transfer of sovereignty implies no change in the basic norm. 'A revolution is neither a necessary nor a sufficient condition for anything that should be described as a change in the identity of the State or the legal system.'[87] When does this come about? As discussed, effectiveness is, for Kelsen, a condition of validity. In the words of JW Harris:

> The *Grundnorm* does not change the moment the revolutionaries shoot the King...the *Grundnorm* changes when legal scientists make a new basic presupposition; but, as legal scientists, they must do this when the legal norms which are by and large effective within a territory can only be interpreted as a consistent field of meaning if a new *Grundnorm* (authorising a new ultimate source of law) is presupposed.[88]

In short, then, Kelsen's theory fails to account for the acceptability or otherwise of the new legal order. Such explanations lie—inevitably—beyond the horizons of a rule-bound landscape. In the end, questions about the validity of law must also be questions about its legitimacy. This is a question of a profoundly practical kind. 'To say this', as John Finnis states,

> ...is not to provide an answer to any concrete problem about the identity of any society or legal system. It is simply to say that the problem for the jurist is the same as the problem for the historian or for the good man wondering where his allegiance and his duty lie. From neither perspective is the thesis of discontinuity, as expressed by Kelsen, persuasive or acceptable.[89]

### 4.3.5 International law

Kelsen regards public international law as 'law' in the same sense as domestic law, though he concedes that the international legal order is a 'primitive' system which

---

[85] *General Theory of Law and State*, 117.    [86] *Pure Theory of Law*, 209.
[87] JM Finnis, 'Revolutions and the Continuity of Law' in Simpson (ed), *Oxford Essays in Jurisprudence*, 75.
[88] 'When and Why does the *Grundnorm* Change?' [1971] *Cambridge Law Journal* 103, 119.
[89] 'Revolutions and Continuity of Law' in Simpson (ed), *Oxford Essays in Jurisprudence*, 75.

lacks many of the institutions (especially for the enforcement of sanctions) to be found in domestic systems. He insists, however, on the need to conceive of both as a single, unified whole. This is based, he argues, on the fact that states recognize that each other's legal systems have equal force. This, in turn, suggests that they acknowledge the existence of a basic norm which is superior to the basic norm of their individual domestic legal systems. But what, asks Kelsen, provides the source of this notion of equality? It must come from a superior basic norm which, in the international context, takes the form of customary practice adopted by states expressed in normative language and backed by the threat of coercion: war and reprisals. But is there a shift in the meaning of the basic norm here?

> With reference to municipal law…the *Grundnorm* has to possess some basis in fact, namely, a minimum of effectiveness. It would seem that with reference to international law the *Grundnorm* is a pure supposition lacking even this basis. Assuming that a monist legal theory has to be offered to account for the present state of international society, then one way of explaining the assertion of equality by States would be by hypothesising a norm superior to that of each national order from which equality might be said to derive. It is open to doubt, however, whether even an attempt at a monist explanation is worthwhile, for one is entitled to question whether there is any *Grundnorm* which commands the necessary minimum of effectiveness demanded by Kelsen's theory.[90]

In other words, international relations are dictated by self-interest and fear. And appeals by revolutionary governments to ground the legitimacy of their regime in the fact that it has received international recognition have been given short shrift by courts.[91]

Kelsen's monism is frequently attacked also on the ground that it leads him to reject the possibility of a conflict between the norms of domestic law, on the one hand, and international law, on the other. In seeking to present a unified system of norms, he provides an analogy between an unconstitutional statute and a statute that contravenes the norms of international law. The former is valid until it is declared unconstitutional; it may, moreover, remain valid in circumstances where no procedure exists to declare it void. Nevertheless, those who passed the statute may be subject to sanctions. Equally, in the latter case, a statute in apparent breach of a norm of international law is valid though its passage may be the subject of sanctions (reprisals and war) under international law:

> The relationship of international law to a norm of national law which…is contrary to international law, is the same as the relationship of the constitution of a national legal order, which, for example in its provisions concerning fundamental rights, determines the content of future statutes to a statute which violates fundamental rights and is therefore considered to be unconstitutional—if the constitution does not provide for a procedure in which statutes, because of their unconstitutionality, may be abolished, but contains only the provision that certain organs may be tried in court personally for their part in the establishment of the 'unconstitutional' statute. International law determines the content of the national legal order

---

[90] Dias, *Jurisprudence*, 371.     [91] See *Jilani v Government of Punjab* PLD 1972 SC 139.

in the same way as the constitution, which does not establish a judicial control of the consti-
tutionality of statutes, determines the contents of future statutes.[92]

This ingenious comparison rests on somewhat special, not to say atypical, circumstances and, in any event, the alleged 'conflict' between domestic and international
law postulated by Kelsen is unlikely to lead to the sorts of consequences he suggests.
As one commentator points out, the more plausible result of the condemnation of a
state for passing legislation in violation of international law is either that the state will
recognize the existence of the international law on the point in issue (in which case it
will argue that the statute is not in breach of it) or it will declare itself not bound by the
particular norm of international law. In neither case will the international community
regard the statute as valid.[93]

What is the basic norm of this unitary world of domestic and international law?
Kelsen says the unity of the system may rest on the primacy of domestic law or, alternatively, on the primacy of international law. Either is acceptable; it is a matter of
ideology. If the latter is adopted (which seems to be his preferred view), it is necessary
both to specify the basic norm of the international legal order and its domestic coun-
terpart must stipulate that it is inferior to the supra-national presupposed norm, 'the
"constitution" of international law in a transcendental-logical sense'.[94] Kelsen defines
the basic norm of international law as follows:

> 'States—that is, the governments of the States—in their mutual relations ought to behave in
> such a way'; or: 'Coercion of State against State ought to be exercised under the conditions
> and in the manner, that conforms with the custom constituted by the actual behaviour of the
> States.'[95]

It is also necessary to substitute the domestic basic norm with one which recognizes
the validity of international law. As Kelsen says:

> [T]he reason for the validity of the individual national legal order can be found in positive
> international law. In that case, a positive norm is the reason for the validity of this legal order,
> not a merely presupposed norm. [This] norm of international law…usually is described by
> the statement that, according to general international law, a government which, independ-
> ent of other governments, exerts effective control over the population of a certain territory,
> is the legitimate government; and that the population that lives under such a government in
> this territory constitutes a 'State' in the meaning of international law…. Translated into legal
> language: A norm of general international law authorises an individual or a group of individu-
> als, on the basis of an effective constitution, to create and apply as a legitimate government a
> normative coercive order.[96]

This is all very well as a description of the criteria employed by international law to
establish the rights and duties of states, but Kelsen presents it as a justification for the
validity of domestic legal systems. This is considerably less compelling. As Professor
Hughes argues:

---

[92]  *Pure Theory of Law*, 331.
[93]  G Hughes, 'Validity and the Basic Norm' (1971) 59 *California Law Review* 695, 711.
[94]  *Pure Theory of Law*, 216.          [95]  Ibid.          [96]  Ibid, 214–15.

It is one thing to say that there is a system of international order which recognises for certain basic purposes any effective government as a participant in the system. Such a statement speaks only to the organs of international order. But it is a different matter to say that the reason for the *validity* of a *national* system is a norm of *international* law which somehow legitimises any effective, coercive order. Such a statement seems rather to speak to citizens of each State, telling them that because of a superior, supra-national norm, the system under which they live properly commands their respect so long as it can apply coercion effectively. Under Kelsen's position, if a citizen asks why a rule of the system under which he lives is to be regarded as valid, the ultimate answer would be that a norm of international law so provides because the system under which he lives is able to organise coercion effectively. Such an answer manages at once to be both dangerous and silly. It is dangerous because it appears to invest effective coercion with disproportionate value; it is silly because no one has ever been persuaded that the mere presence of effective coercion is sufficient to answer all inquiries about the validity of an order. [Apartheid] South Africa is a good example, for it is for some purposes recognised as a participant in the international system of order simply because it is an effective coercive government in a certain piece of territory. But a South African black would certainly not agree that the system under which he lives is valid because it monopolises effective coercion. Kelsen's presentation fails to distinguish between these quite different questions.[97]

Yet even here Kelsen's positivism is less than pure. His conception of international law as constituting a legal order, albeit a primitive one, seems frequently to advance less of an analytical than an ideological position. It is an expression of hope rather than a statement of fact or theory. In a number of his works (notably *Law and Peace, Principles of International Law,* and *The Law of the United Nations*) Kelsen advocates an evolutionary theory of international law which envisages a progression towards the centralization of sanctions by the international community. As Professor Bull comments:

Kelsen's doctrine that in international society there is a 'force monopoly of the community' strains against the facts. It is one of the most salient features of the modern international system that in it force is the monopoly not of the community but of the *sovereign States* of which it is made up. Kelsen's approach, like so much that was written by experts on international law and organisation in that period, was the product of wishful thinking.[98]

The 'idealist and progressivist assumptions'[99] that underlie his attempts to incorporate international law within a coherent, unified system of norms betray the limits of a theory which aspires to scientific inquiry in circumstances where the realities of power politics cry out for analysis and understanding.

### 4.3.6 Kelsen and Kant

The German philosopher, Immanuel Kant (1724–1804), developed a theory of knowledge which, like Hume, attacked metaphysics and sought to replace it with an

---

[97] (1971) 59 *California Law Review* 695 at 713, emphasis added.
[98] Tur and Twining (eds), *Essays on Kelsen*, 329, emphasis added.          [99] Ibid, 336.

explanation of knowledge based upon the categories we use in thinking about our experience. This is not uncomplicated territory, and it may well be circumvented in your jurisprudence course, but it does, I think, help to understand the philosophical roots of Kelsen's approach. To summarize the essence of Kant's theory very briefly, he attempted to show that our *a priori* knowledge (ie knowledge that is not derived from experience but is necessary and universal) falls into two groups: analytic and synthetic. The first consists of statements or judgments the truth of which can be established without reference to experience (eg, 'a green leaf is green'). Synthetic judgments, on the other hand, contain, as the predicate of the judgment, some information which is not contained in the subject (eg, 2 + 2 = 4): the judgment is a synthesis of two separate notions, one of which is the subject about which the other, the predicate, is asserted.

To explain what we can know, Kant employs two notions: first, 'the forms of intuition' by which we make *a priori* judgments (we impose them on everything we encounter: all things must have temporal and geometrical features) and, secondly, certain organizing principles, or 'categories' which enable us to make judgments about things we encounter in the world (they include causality, accident, substance, and possibility). These two notions facilitate knowledge of the phenomenal world (ie, the world we actually experience, as opposed to the noumenal or non-empirical world). But such knowledge is limited to the form, not the content, of the phenomenal world. Its content is determined by transcendental enquiries: they attempt to determine from our experience and judgments what their necessary features must be.

Kant was pessimistic about the prospect of metaphysical knowledge about reality beyond the world of experience. Our *a priori* understanding is limited to things we can actually experience. Nor can such understanding be inferred from what we know of the phenomenal world to the noumenal world. For Kant such inferences or applications are 'antinomies': conclusions which can be both proved and shown to be false. I argue that the world must have had a beginning in time; you argue that it cannot have. We cannot demonstrate conclusively which of two opposing arguments is 'true'. We cannot know whether the noumenal world has any of the features of the phenomenal world.

In developing his pure theory of law, Kelsen explicitly acknowledges the influence of Kant and he is frequently described as a neo-Kantian. In particular, his empirical and rationalist approach to law would seem to place him firmly in the Kantian epistemological tradition:

> Pure reason is the faculty of knowledge a priori. The critical philosophy reveals that knowledge is necessarily a synthesis of a priori form and a posteriori data. Consequently the *Pure Theory of Law* is not a book of knowledge but a book about knowledge. As a prolegomenon to all future jurisprudence which aspires to be scientific it must necessarily relate to the forms of knowledge and not provide legal knowledge itself.[100]

Yet in his pursuit of purity and, hence, his denial of any equation of law and 'justice', Kelsen parts ways with a Kantian ethics. Thus, while Kant conceived of law as part of

---

[100]  R Tur in Tur and Twining (eds), *Essays on Kelsen*, 160.

morals, Kelsen repudiates such impurity. Their similar, though different, approaches to the basic norm are well described by Richard Tur:

> [Kant's basic norm] is an impure material 'ought' from which normative conclusions may be drawn by logical deduction. This conflicts not only with the Kelsenian formulation of the basic norm as a logical, formal 'ought' providing no inference ticket to material normative conclusions, but also Kant's own critical philosophy. For Kant that knowledge is 'pure' which contains 'no admixture of anything empirical'. The distinction between form and content is central to Kant's critical enterprise. Kant holds that his formal category cannot tell us a priori what effects causes actually have in empirical reality... Kelsen holds that his formal category cannot tell us what consequences conditions have in the normative sphere. In both cases, therefore, it is a contingent matter of *fact* which provides the content of judgments, be they causal or normative. If one regards the Kantian epoch in the history of ideas as the critical synthesis of empiricism and rationalism then it is the absolutist, natural law ethics which falls to be discarded and the relativist epistemology, retained. This is Kelsen's option.[101]

It is therefore important to recognize the limitations of Kelsen's neo-Kantianism. In particular, Kelsen does not accept Kant's argument that practical reason is the source of norms. For Kelsen, moral judgments and values are not susceptible of rational knowledge. And he also rejects the material nature of Kant's 'ought': Kelsen's 'ought' is completely formal in nature.

Some would go further and deny a Kantian essence in Kelsen's theory. Alida Wilson argues that, notwithstanding Kelsen's explicit acknowledgement to Kant, the pure theory is informed by Kantian ideas considerably less than is generally believed. She concentrates her analysis on Kelsen's use of the concept of *Zurechnung* (usually translated as 'imputation'). Briefly, she challenges Kelsen's assumption that his *a priori* category of *Zurechnung* in the normative context is analogous to Kant's category of causation. When he attempts to apply Kant's method beyond the phenomenal world:

> [T]he charge against him is not merely that he endeavours to use the Kantian intellectual instrument and fails; not merely that he overlooks a prime fact about Kant's categories, that is, their definition in terms adapted to our understanding of natural phenomena; but rather that he supposed it possible to employ Kant's method on intellectual grounds where he had debarred himself from so doing. For, if we bar argument from the 'is' statement to a statement or prescription in terms of 'ought', it is hard to see how any useful connection could be found between such concepts as are involved a priori in our knowledge of what is and the type of concepts involved a priori in the normative view of the world. That is to say, talk of *analogy* between causality and *Zurechnung* is of no help with morality and law, if we insist that the essence of each of these is its normative character.[102]

Whether or not Kelsen succeeds in applying the Kantian method is ultimately a futile question; the pure theory falls to be evaluated in its own right. Does his non-cognitivist,

---

[101] R Tur and W Twining, 'Introduction' in ibid, 7, emphasis added. See H Steiner, 'Kant's Kelsenianism' in Tur and Twining (eds), *Essays on Kelsen*, 65.

[102] A Wilson, 'Is Kelsen Really a Kantian?' in Tur and Twining (eds), *Essays on Kelsen*, 56. Cf H Steiner, 'Kant's Kelsenianism' in Tur and Twining (eds), *Essays on Kelsen*, 65; Stanley L Paulson, 'The neo-Kantian Dimension of Kelsen's Pure Theory of Law' (1992) 12 *Oxford Journal of Legal Studies* 311.

relativist account of the normative basis of law have explanatory power? Is the presupposed transcendent *Grundnorm* a satisfactory heuristic device by which the unity and (following a revolution) the validity of the legal system may be understood? And so on.

### 4.3.7 **Democracy and the rule of law**

By refusing to recognize the state as an independent entity placed above the law, Kelsen effectively equates the state and the legal system. The institutions, powers, and functions of the state are defined by the law; their identity is determined by legal norms. He therefore concludes:

> If the identity of State and law is discovered, if it is recognised that the law—the positive law, not the law identified with justice—*is* this very coercive order in which the State appears to a cognition which is not mired in anthropomorphic metaphors but which penetrates through the veil of personification to the man-created norms, then it is simply impossible to justify the State through the law; just as it is impossible to justify the law through the law....And then the attempt to legitimise the State as governed by law, as a *Rechtsstaat*, is revealed as entirely useless because...every State is 'governed by law' in the sense that every State is a legal order. This, however, represents no political value judgment.[103]

In other words, Kelsen firmly rejects any Hegelian absolutist super-state and in so doing, exposes the coercive nature of law stripped of the sort of moral legitimacy provided by natural law theories.[104] Not every legal order is a *Rechtsstaat* (a democratic state governed by the rule of law which provides legal security), but little is required for a state to be a legal order: 'A relatively centralised, autocratic coercive order which, if its flexibility is unlimited, offers no legal security is a legal order too; and...the community, constituted by such a coercive order, is a legal community and as such, a State.'[105] And the equation of law and state is also the break between fact and value:

> From the point of view of a consistent legal positivism, law, like the State, cannot be comprehended otherwise than as a coercive order of human behaviour. The definition says nothing about the moral value or justice of positive law. Then the State can be juristically comprehended no more and no less than law itself.[106]

Kelsen's unwillingness to elevate the state above the law constitutes an important statement of his recognition of the need for controls over arbitrary power. For Cotterrell a 'major reason why he refuses to accept the State as an entity above law is because, when it is recognised as such, appalling things can be done in its name'.[107]

---

[103] *Pure Theory of Law*, 318–19.
[104] But see I Stewart in Tur and Twining (eds), *Essays on Kelsen*, 145, who argues that Kelsen 'tried to counter the State-absolutist substitute by constructing a basis, through an analogy, in a natural-scientific kind of objectivism'. Stewart believes Kelsen failed in this attempt and that the pure theory, along with legal positivism in general, is merely 'one of the frayed ends of ius naturalism', at 145–6.
[105] *Pure Theory of Law*, 319.      [106] Ibid.      [107] *The Politics of Jurisprudence*, 113.

## 4.3.8 **Critique**

As with Hart, the writings of Kelsen have provoked a considerable outpouring of critical literature. Both Joseph Raz[108] and JW Harris[109] have subjected the key elements of
the pure theory to rigorous analysis. Raz is unconvinced that Kelsen has developed the
positivism of Austin and Bentham. As he puts it (in a passage from *The Concept of a
Legal System* that is worthy of close scrutiny):

> Kelsen remains faithful to the principle of origin: The identity of a legal system, as well as the
> membership of a law in a system, is determined solely by the facts of its creation, by its origin.
> But the source of unity is no longer one legislative body, it is one power-conferring norm. The
> basic norm replaces the sovereign, otherwise nothing has changed.[110]

These two theorists tend to venture into territory which the average student of jurisprudence is likely to find fairly impenetrable and which he or she may not legitimately
be expected to traverse. Nevertheless, the effort will not be without its reward. And
even if this occasionally has the opposite effect, it may assist you to develop your ability to present your own arguments—especially in the examination—in a more refined,
sophisticated (though not, I hope, similarly inaccessible) style.

Kelsen's theory did not remain static and he attempted to modify or revise it over
the years.[111] Yet there seem, generally speaking, to be four main kinds of criticism
that have been levelled at various strands of the pure theory. You should be able to
discuss them (at greater length and in greater depth than the following outline). First
is the assault on the very notion of a 'pure' theory itself: is it really possible (let alone
desirable) to exclude from a model of law social and political factors? Harold Laski
described it as an 'exercise in logic but not in life'. It is even arguable that the concept
of efficacy, by which Kelsen sets so much store, can be measured only by reference to
the very sociological considerations which he is so determined to exclude. Secondly,
the *Grundnorm* as the progenitor of all other norms (even, in Kelsen's view, in the case
of international law: and you should be familiar with his ambitious claims in this area)
has been attacked largely on the ground that its existence cannot explain the validity
of what Dworkin calls 'non-rule standards', that is, policies and principles (see 5.2.1).

Thirdly, Kelsen's reduction of all legislation to the form 'If X, then Y' (where X is a
certain form of conduct and Y is a sanction) is widely regarded as unacceptably narrow. The *form* of law is given primacy over its *meaning*. It presumes (which, of course,
Kelsen is content to do) that law is essentially coercion; many would want to argue
that law has other functions. It neglects the regulatory function of law. A fourth kind
of assault seeks to show that Kelsen accords unwarranted importance to the role of
sanctions in law. It results in a lopsided analysis of legal duty not only because a statute
may impose duties *without* necessarily providing a sanction, but because, on the other

---

[108] *The Concept of a Legal System*, especially Ch 5, and *The Authority of Law*, especially Ch 7.
[109] *Law and Legal Science: An Inquiry into the Concepts Legal Rule and Legal System* (Oxford: Clarendon
Press, 1979).                                                                              [110] At 95.
[111] For a useful account of these developments, see Michael Hartney's introduction to his translation of
Kelsen's *General Theory of Norms* (Oxford: Clarendon Press, 1991).

hand, certain conduct may be made the condition of a sanction even though it is not the subject of a *duty*.[112]

## 4.4 Joseph Raz

Such is the breadth and depth of his scholarship, that Joseph Raz's philosophy is not easy to condense into a few pages.[113] For present purposes, however, the emphasis is on the essential elements of his hard (or 'exclusivist') legal positivism.

### 4.4.1 The 'sources thesis'

Raz argues that the identity and existence of a legal system may be tested by reference to three elements; efficacy, institutional character, and sources.[114] Thus, law is autonomous: we can identify its content without recourse to morality. Legal reasoning, however, is not autonomous; it is an inevitable, and desirable, feature of judicial reasoning.

For Raz, the existence and content of every law may be determined by a *factual* enquiry about conventions, institutions, and the intentions of participants in the legal system. The answer to the question 'What is law?' is always a fact. It is never a moral judgment. This marks him as a hard or exclusive positivist. 'Exclusive' because the reason we regard the law as authoritative is the fact that it is able to guide our behaviour in a way that morality cannot do. In other words, the law asserts its primacy over all other codes of conduct. Law is the ultimate source of authority. Thus, a legal system is quintessentially one of authoritative rules. It is this claim of authority that is the trade mark of a legal system.[115]

Raz identifies three principal claims made by positivists and attacked by natural lawyers:

- The '*social thesis*': that law may be identified as a social fact, without reference to moral considerations.

- The '*moral thesis*': that the moral merit of law is neither absolute nor inherent, but contingent upon 'the content of the law and the circumstances of the society to which it applies'.

---

[112] JW Harris says that to measure effectiveness we need to know the content of the norm, ie, the nature of the duty involved. As he puts it, 'The concept of "duty" must...stand on its own feet, as something distinct from the concept of sanction. A theory of law must define duty and sanction separately', *Legal Philosophies*, 2nd edn, 73.
[113] Merely to list his major books, let alone his extensive catalogue of articles, captures the range of Raz's scholarship: *The Authority of Law, The Concept of a Legal System, The Morality of Freedom, Practical Reason and Norms, Ethics in the Public Domain, Engaging Reason: On the Theory of Value and Action, Value, Respect, and Attachment, The Practice of Value, Between Authority and Interpretation: On the Theory of Law and Practical Reason*. On Raz's methodology, see Julie Dickson, *Evaluation and Legal Theory* (Oxford: Hart Publishing, 2001). For general assessments of his work, see Lucas H Meyer, Stanley L Paulson, and Thomas W Pogge (eds), *Rights, Culture and the Law: Themes from the Legal and Political Philosophy of Joseph Raz* (Oxford: Oxford University Press, 2003) and R Jay Wallace, Philip Pettit, Samuel Scheffler, and Michael Smith (eds), *Reason and Value: Themes from the Moral Philosophy of Joseph Raz* (Oxford: Clarendon Press, 2004).     [114] *The Authority of Law*.     [115] Ibid.

- *The 'semantic thesis'*: that normative terms such as 'right' and 'duty' are not used in moral and legal contexts in the same way.[116]

Raz accepts only the 'social thesis'. He does so on the basis of the three accepted criteria by which a legal system may be identified: its efficacy, its institutional character, and its sources. From all three, moral questions are excluded. Thus, the institutional character of law means simply that laws are identified by their relationship to certain institutions (eg, the legislature). Anything (however morally acceptable) not admitted by such institutions is not law, and vice versa. For Raz it is a stronger version of the 'social thesis' (the 'sources thesis') that is the essence of legal positivism. His principal justification for the sources thesis is that it accounts for a fundamental function of law, namely, the setting of standards by which we are bound, in such a way that we cannot excuse our non-compliance by challenging the rationale for the standard.

It is largely upon his acceptance of the social thesis (and his rejection of the moral and semantic theses)[117] that Raz builds his argument that there is no general moral obligation to obey the law. In arriving at this conclusion he rejects three common arguments made for the moral authority of law. First, it is often argued that to seek (as positivists do) to distinguish between law and other forms of social control is to neglect the *functions* of law; and because functions cannot be described in a value-free manner, any functional account of law must involve moral judgments—and so offend the social thesis. Raz shows that, while law does indeed have certain functions, his own analysis of them is value-neutral.

Secondly, it is frequently claimed that the *content* of law cannot be determined exclusively by social facts: so, for example, since courts inevitably rely on explicitly moral considerations, they insinuate themselves into what the law *is*. Raz, though he acknowledges that moral concerns do enter into adjudication, insists that this is unavoidable in any source-based system. But it does not, in his view, establish a case against the source thesis. Finally, it is sometimes suggested that one of the characteristics of law is that it conforms to the ideal of the rule of law. This, it is argued, demonstrates that the law is moral. Raz refutes this proposition by arguing that while conformity to the rule of law reduces the abuse of executive power, it does not confer an independent moral merit upon the law. For him the rule of law is a *negative* virtue, for the risk of arbitrary power is created by the law itself. Raz therefore concludes that even in a just legal system there is no *prima facie* duty to obey the law.[118]

## 4.4.2 **Practical reason**

Suppose I am faced with a choice between two courses of action, X and Y? It is clear that I *ought* to do X. Why? Because there is a *reason* for me to do it. When considering whether to do X or Y, I weigh up the various reasons that affect my decision. If there is a *rule* directing me to do X, this constitutes an 'exclusionary reason': a second-order

---

[116] Raz, *The Authority of Law*, 37 ff.    [117] Ibid, 155 ff.    [118] Ibid, 233 ff.

reason against doing Y—after I have weighed up my first-order reasons in favour of X. In the absence of this rule, I may decide to do Y, on, say, moral or prudential grounds, but, Raz argues, the presence of this rule supplies a strong reason to do what the rule requires, namely X.

What does this have to do with legal positivism? It would appear to support the hard or exclusivist version of positivism since it eliminates moral considerations from the concept of law. The law would fail in its vital function of providing authoritative guidance as to how we should behave. It would instead permit the choice to be made on the basis of weighing up first-order reasons. For Raz, Hart's secondary, power-conferring social rules provide reasons for action, but they are not 'exclusionary reasons'.

### 4.4.3 Committed and detached statements

According to Raz, laws do not simply require things to be done or not done; they impose *duties*. The concept of 'duty' has the same meaning whether it is used to denote a moral, religious, or legal duty. It must mean that there is a mandatory rule that excludes all first-order reasoning about the subject. How is it that I can accept that I am under a *legal* duty to do X, but deny that I am under a *moral* duty do it? This, Raz contends, is a 'detached' statement. On the other hand, when I unequivocally accept the authority of the legal rule in question, I am making a 'committed' statement. But this latter statement could also be a detached statement if made by a person who is merely *describing* the law. When we are engaged in the process of describing the law, we normally assume the position of one who acknowledges that his moral duties correspond to the requirements of positive law.

In other words, authoritative legal directives provide both first-order reasons for me to do X or refrain from doing X, and second-order reasons which exclude my 'dependent reasons'. These are right reasons, including moral reasons, that would otherwise affect my decision. By acknowledging the authority of the legal rule, I accept that I cannot base my decision directly on the dependent reasons that are excluded. Simply put, therefore, the authoritative rule turns into my reason for doing or not doing X. I accept authority because I know that by relying on its rules, I will benefit, which I will not do if I rely on my individual moral judgment.

Consider Raz's example of an orthodox Jew who asks his Catholic friend, an expert in Rabbinical Law, whether he should eat the bacon they have been served in a restaurant. The Jew's question relates to his own religious doctrine. Though his friend's personal view is that there is nothing wrong with consuming the meat of a pig, he recognizes that this is not the question he has been called upon to answer. By replying that the eating of bacon is prohibited by Jewish dietary laws, the friend does not endorse this norm, but merely states the view adopted by Rabbinical Law. This, according to Raz, is precisely the stance that is taken by a lawyer who advises his client that if he accepts the authority of the law, he should do X. This is a detached statement that in Raz's theory resembles Hart's 'internal point of view' (see 4.2.8), but differs from it. You may wish to reflect on where the distinction lies.

### 4.4.4 **Critique**

Raz's incorporation thesis has, not surprisingly, generated a spirited debate, especially within legal positivism. The following criticisms are a sample of the sorts of appraisal that Raz's ideas have provoked. Some challenge his claim that authoritative directives necessarily provide pre-emptive reasons.[119] Thus Hart, while remarking that Raz's theory 'holds out some olive branches to the natural law theorist', remarks that his insistence on this small moral component 'conveys an unrealistic picture of the way in which the judges envisage their task of identifying and applying the law'.[120] Hart is unpersuaded by Raz's notion that the concept of duty carries the same meaning in law as it does in morality. Legal duty, in Hart's view, describes only what is required by positive law.[121]

Secondly, some theorists are unconvinced by Raz's contention that it is a conceptual feature of law that it necessarily claims morally legitimate authority. Thus, Jules Coleman says,

> The fact that law can serve a variety of legitimate human interests may ground the claim that law must be the sort of thing that can possess a normative power to create genuine duties and responsibilities or confer genuine rights and privileges. From this it hardly follows that that normative power represents a moral authority.[122]

Thirdly, Coleman doubts whether legal authority functions in the manner Raz describes. The authority of law, Coleman suggests, may sometimes lie elsewhere, 'for example in its making clearer what the demands of morality are'.[123] Fourthly, Coleman rejects the idea that though conceptually law must claim authority of some sort, it therefore follows that 'each law must be able to make a practical difference in our reasoning about what to do'.[124] Why, he asks, should all rules, in order to qualify as law, be capable of guiding conduct, let alone of doing so in the manner Raz portrays?

Fifthly, another sort of assault is launched by critics who question the conceptual coherence of Raz's account of pre-emptive reasons. Thus Heidi Hurd argues that if Raz is right, then obedience to authority is irrational because it contradicts the principle that one ought to act in accordance with the balance of reasons.[125] Other attacks are made (none of which, I think, should unduly trouble Raz) on his analysis of the idea of authority itself. Thus, sixthly, Soper has imagined a government that declares that there was no duty to obey the law. This, he suggests, would alter nothing in the practice of the law as we understand it, because (a) the duty to obey the law is not normally

---

[119] See, eg, W Waluchow, 'Authority and the Practical Difference Thesis: A Defence of Inclusive Positivism' (2000) 6 *Legal Theory* 45, 58; Matthew Kramer, *In Defense of Legal Positivism: Law Without Trimmings* (Oxford: Oxford University Press, 1999), 83–92.

[120] HLA Hart, 'Legal Duty and Obligation' in his *Essays on Bentham*, 158.          [121] Ibid, 154.

[122] Jules Coleman, *The Practice of Principle: In Defence of A Pragmatic Approach to Legal Theory* (Oxford: Oxford University Press, 2001), 133.          [123] Ibid.          [124] Ibid.

[125] Heidi Hurd, 'Challenging Authority' (1991) 100 *Yale Law Journal* 1611. But see Kenneth Einar Himma, 'Inclusive Legal Positivism' in Jules Coleman and Scott Shapiro (eds), *The Oxford Handbook of Jurisprudence and Philosophy of Law* (Oxford: Oxford University Press, 2002), 151–3, and, in the same volume, Andrei Marmor, 'Exclusive Legal Positivism'.

expressed in a legal norm; (b) it does not follow from the state's position that there is no moral duty to obey the law or that it is abandoning its view of the moral virtues of the law; and (c) a legal system could survive by naked force.[126] But Himma effectively demolishes this assault:

> Soper's argument that abandoning the claim to moral authority would not result in any practical changes construes the Authority Thesis as a view about what a legal system must claim in order to be efficacious…But the Authority Thesis neither asserts nor implies that legal systems claiming authority are more likely to be efficacious than legal systems not claiming authority because the Authority Thesis is a *conceptual* claim—and not an empirical claim…Thus Raz can concede we would not notice any differences in the day-to-day functioning of a legal system S if it abandoned any claim to authority, but argue that the abandonment of that claim implies the abandonment of S's status as a *legal* system.[127]

Finally, it has been urged against Raz that the authority thesis is vulnerable if a system of rules existed that makes no claim to moral authority, but nevertheless looks like a legal system. Matthew Kramer offers the example of the Mafia, but this seems implausible.[128]

## 4.5 Hard and soft positivism

Contemporary legal positivism has grown increasingly technical and sophisticated. A split has developed between so-called hard and soft positivists. The former (who are often described as 'exclusive legal positivists') maintain that all criteria of legality must be what Joseph Raz calls 'social sources'. This means that the determination of whether something is 'law' cannot turn on a norm's content or substantive value or merit. The existence of a particular 'law', in other words, does not depend on whether it ought to be the law. Soft positivists (or 'inclusive positivists' or 'incorporationists'), on the other hand, accept that some principles may be legally binding by virtue of their value or merit, but morality can be a condition of validity *only where the rule of recognition so stipulates.*[129]

---

[126] Philip Soper, 'Law's Normative Claims' in Robert P George (ed), *The Autonomy of Law* (Oxford: Oxford University Press, 1999), 215.               [127] Himma, 156.

[128] Kramer, *In Defense of Legal Positivism*, 96. See Himma, 156–7 for a counter-example. See too Scott J Shapiro, *Legality* (Cambridge, Mass and London: Belknap Press, 2011), 214–16.

[129] Kramer distinguishes between 'inclusive legal positivism' and 'incorporationism' (as advanced by Jules Coleman). The former, Kramer claims, endorses the view that consistency with a moral principle can be a *necessary* condition of legality; the latter position accepts only that conformity with a moral principle can be a *sufficient* condition of legality. Kramer himself supports a 'moderate' version of incorporationism that 'duly acknowledges the indispensability of uniformity and regularity in anything that counts as a legal system', Matthew Kramer, 'How Moral Principles can Enter the Law' (2000) 6 *Legal Theory* 83. See too Matthew Kramer, *In Defense of Legal Positivism: Law Without Trimmings* (Oxford: Oxford University Press, 1999). This is by no means an easy read, but, if you persist, and overlook his somewhat laborious prose, especially some of his baroque adverbs, you will discover flashes of brilliance. For a feisty exchange of views on the proper principles of positivism, see David Dyzenhaus, 'Positivism's Stagnant Research Programme' (2002) 20 *Oxford Journal of Legal Studies* 703 (reviewing Matthew Kramer, *In Defense of Legal Positivism: Law Without Trimmings* (Oxford: Oxford: University Press, 1999)); Matthew H Kramer,

A soft positivist accepts that the rule of recognition may incorporate moral criteria (hence their often being dubbed 'incorporationists'). Therefore what the law is may sometimes rest on moral considerations. For example, where a constitution (or a bill of rights) requires a court to decide a case by reference to considerations of justice and fairness, he or she will be expected to determine the outcome by evaluating these moral values. Adjudication is therefore no longer confined to the exclusive applica-tion of *legal* rules. Hard positivists insist that the validity of a purported legal norm (its membership in the legal system) cannot turn on the moral merits of the norm in question. They therefore acknowledge that occasionally the law may incorporate moral criteria for ascertaining what the law is. In his 'postscript' to *The Concept of Law*, Hart himself seems to have gone soft by accepting that 'the rule of recognition may incorporate as criteria of legal validity conformity with moral principles or substan-tive values'.[130] In other words, moral issues seep into the process of determining what is 'law'. Or, to put it another way, soft positivists admit that judges employ moral rea-soning. This weakens the 'hard' positivist denial of the separation of law and morals. The significance of this concession—and the softness it has spread—will soon become evident.

Hart acknowledges that non-source-based moral criteria may be regarded by judges as legal rules—if this is expressly permitted by the rule of recognition (see 4.2.6). This concession has, however, been condemned by hard or exclusive positivists, such as Raz, who claim that these moral standards cannot be applied by a judge as law, for this would amount to a judge having the power to decide whether to apply norms according to his evaluation of their moral merit. It would annihilate the authority of the courts. Scott Shapiro has sought to supplement this objection by claiming that a necessary feature of the authority of law is that it be capable of making a 'practical difference' to decisions. In respect of both the judge and the ordinary citizen, Shapiro contends, the existence of a legal rule makes no practical difference. The citizen identi-fies authoritative rules only after, on the basis of some moral principle, he has decided to act. The legal rule, to repeat, makes no practical difference. In the case of the judge in a hard case who, in accordance with a rule of recognition that exhorts him to deploy moral principles, he need merely act morally and he will reach the same decision. The legal rule is, Shapiro argues, irrelevant.[131]

'Incorporationism' strikes a blow against this 'Practical Difference Thesis' (PDT), whereas inclusive legal positivism fares better. Thus Waluchow (an inclusivist) seeks to protect his position from Shapiro's argument by differentiating between the two.[132]

---

'Dogmas and Distortions: Legal Positivism Defended: A Reply to David Dyzenhaus' (2001) *Oxford Journal of Legal Studies* 673. Kramer's riposte is reproduced in Ch 5 of Matthew Kramer, *Where Law and Morality Meet* (Oxford: Oxford University Press, 2004).

[130] HLA Hart, *The Concept of Law*, 2nd edn (Oxford: Clarendon Press, 1994), 250. Should he have so conceded?

[131] Scott J Shapiro, 'Hart's Way Out' in Coleman (ed), *Hart's Postscript: Essays on the Postscript to* The Concept of Law.

[132] WJ Waluchow, 'Authority and the Practical Difference Thesis: A Defence of Inclusive Legal Positivism' (2000) 6 *Legal Theory* 45, 76–81. See too in Waluchow, *Inclusive Legal Positivism*); Kenneth Einar Himma, 'Inclusive Legal Positivism' in Coleman and Shapiro (eds), *The Oxford Handbook of Jurisprudence*

A rule of recognition that provides simply that compliance with morality 'as such' could be a sufficient ground for legal validity. You can see why this would undermine the PDT: the provision would make no 'practical difference' to a decision. But inclusive positivism—unlike incorporationism—claims only that a rule of recognitions *may* make moral compliance a necessary, not a sufficient, condition of legality. Only those decisions which are both 'moral' and meet the 'sources' test would fulfil the conditions for legal validity. Thus the authoritativeness of the law *would* make a practical difference. If, however, the sources-based condition is *immoral*, a judge cannot employ it. Shapiro argues that any appropriate criterion for determining whether to uphold the provision makes no practical difference because in these circumstances the judge must do what is unfair.

Waluchow maintains that these criteria are legal, because it is unlikely that such standards exist without some kind of pedigree. And it is certainly the case that moral principles are not generally unrelated to social sources. Nevertheless, as John Eekelaar points out:

> [T]he 'pedigree' of these principles seldom determines their ranking or weight in specific circumstances. As Shapiro puts it: in Dworkin's view such principles are not legal norms '*in virtue of* having these social pedigrees' but by virtue of their moral merit. It is hard therefore to see how Waluchow can embrace these within the ambit of law on the basis of social criteria. His determination to find a pedigree follows from his acceptance…of the distinction deriving from the Social Thesis between those elements of a legal decision based on law and those elements not so based. But under the judicial conception of law, appeals to prior statements of these principles may function more as reinforcements of a contemporary moral judgment than as authoritative stipulations of what is required for decision. Thus the distinction between them matters not for the conception of law used by judges.[133]

Scott Shapiro has recently postulated a different, highly original, account of the nature of law that seeks to demonstrate, from an essentially positivist standpoint, that legal activity is a form of social planning. Legal rules are fundamentally 'generalized plans' or 'plan-like norms' for a community originating from legal institutions vested with the authority to issue such plans. Far from being moral, however, a central objective of planning is to obviate or resolve moral problems that beset social life. His 'Planning Theory of Law' is an elaborate and intricate argument that:

> captures the power of the positivistic picture of law…[by showing] that there is another realm whose norms can only be discovered through social, not moral, observation, namely the realm of *planning*…[P]ositivism is trivially and uncontroversially true in the case of plans: the existence of a plan is one thing, its merits or demerits quite another.[134]

*and Philosophy of Law* (Oxford: Oxford University Press, 2002), 151–3, and, in the same volume, Andrei Marmor, 'Exclusive Legal Positivism'.

[133] John Eekelaar, 'Judges and Citizens: Two Conceptions of Law' (2002) 22 *Oxford Journal of Legal Studies* 497, 508.

[134] Shapiro, *Legality*, 119. But does law necessarily have a moral purpose? 'Shapiro's view commits him to the position that we cannot have law unless it is for the sake of solving some moral problem. So for Shapiro's view to be sustainable he needs to offer some reason to dismiss the notion that we have law in this scenario or some reason to believe that—contrary to appearances—our system of planlike norms has a moral aim,'

At the core of this deceptively uncomplicated claim is the proposition that life itself is an exercise in planning, whether it be our preparations for cooking dinner or the arrangements we make for our future. The very formation and persistence of rules of law are based upon the capacity of all individuals to make and execute plans which need not be 'good'. Even a bad plan is a plan which can engender the structure of hierarchy, authority, and institutional complexity that are the hallmarks of law. But is all law really plan-like? Is organizing a society really like preparing a meal?

> I cannot just *cook dinner*. Cooking dinner is not a simple action like raising my arm—it is a multistep process, requiring that I make preparations, string numerous actions together, and perform them in the proper order.[135]

Frederick Schauer criticizes Shapiro's 'relative inattention' to the role of coercion in law, arguing that:

> coercion is conducive to making plans, shared intentions, and cooperative behavior more effective. But coercion also serves to distinguish law from numerous other cooperative institutions that also have primary and secondary rules. It is not implausible to talk about the law of private clubs, nor is it silly to recognize that something law-like is in place in universities, corporations, condominium boards, and vast numbers of other complex nongovernmental institutions.[136]

In similar vein, Jeremy Waldron questions Shapiro's assumption that effective planning for a society is necessarily general, prospective, and stable:

> We know that managerial planning of large firms is not like that. The plans are usually not general; they solve particular problems of production or personnel on an ad hoc basis; they change from day to day or week to week, depending on various conditions, and they are not guided in that changeability by any general promulgated principles; some of these plans are communicated to all those who are affected by them; some are kept secret; some are passed on to managers and allowed to trickle down to the assembly line; some orders are issued not on the assumption that they are practicable but in order to test the limits of what is practicable; and so on. The same is true for military planning, both at the staff level and down the chain of command. So large-scale planning…sometimes…does not look like the rule of what we would call law.[137]

Notice that Shapiro's model of law rests on an explicitly exclusivist positivist view. And, not surprisingly, while doubting Lon Fuller's 'inner morality of law' (see 2.10.2), he suggests that regimes that violate Fuller's eight principles 'are simply not engaged in the basic activity of law: they are not engaged in social planning.'[138] This relationship

---

Mark C Murphy (2011) 30 *Law and Philosophy* 369, 375. I am grateful to Scott Shapiro for kindly answering my questions about his theory.

[135] Shapiro, op cit, 123. The cooking analogy is developed further to imagine a cooking club whose planning becomes more complex and demanding.

[136] Frederick Schauer, 'The Best Laid Plans' (2010) 120 *Yale Law Journal* 586, 620.

[137] Jeremy Waldron, 'Planning for Legality' (2011) 109 *Michigan Law Review* 883, 899. See too Stefan Sciaraffa, 'The Ineliminability of Hartian Social Rules' (2011) 31 *Oxford Journal of Legal Studies* 603, who argues that Shapiro fails to improve upon or supplant Hart's theory of social rules.

[138] Shapiro, op cit, 394.

between positivism and planning is intriguing, but in respect of the judicial function, the question is a rather different one. It concerns the very nature of law. Its practical importance is especially evident in a wicked or unjust society. Here the debate between inclusive and exclusive positivism assumes considerable purchase. This should become apparent in the next chapter.

## Questions

1. In what sense is Hart's description of social rules hermeneutic?

2. What are 'obligation rules'? Is Hart's idea of 'power-conferring rules' a satisfactory one?

3. 'While Hart was plainly correct in emphasizing the importance of the secondary rules, and thus greatly advancing our understanding of law, he was unfortunately less successful in explaining how these secondary rules are brought into existence ... [R]educing the fundamental rules of a legal system to the social practice of legal officials fails for the simple reason that rules and practices belong to different metaphysical categories.' (Scott Shapiro, *Legality*, p. 115)

   How might Hart have responded to this criticism?

4. What is the significance of Hart's 'existence thesis' in respect of legal systems? What purpose does it serve?

5. Legal positivism is sometimes described as insensitive to moral questions. Are such criticisms unfair?

6. Is Hart's description of the 'minimum content of natural law' an adequate one? What is a legal positivist doing talking about natural law?

7. It has been claimed that Hart's theory is a theory of rules, not of law, and that it fails to provide guidance to judges, one of whose primary tasks when settling disputes is to determine what is law. How might Hart defend his theory against this argument?

8. Is Kelsen's model of law as hierarchical system of norms more satisfying than Austin's system?

9. Does Kelsen adequately define his *Grundnorm*? Is it really 'meta-legal'?

10. How pure is the 'pure theory'?

11. Does Kelsen's exclusion of moral or social attitudes in relation to a law render his description of law unrealistic or artificial?

12. What role do sanctions play in Kelsen's system? How does his view differ from Austin's approach? Does Kelsen overplay the place of sanctions in law?

13. Should legality be measured by effectiveness?

14. How is 'by and large' effectiveness to be determined?

15. In what respects does Kelsen's *Grundnorm* differ from Hart's 'rule of recognition'?

16. What is the purpose of Raz's distinction between 'committed' and 'detached' statements?

17. 'Raz gravely threatens his own version of legal positivism when he insists that statements of legal obligations are statements of moral obligations' (Matthew Kramer, *In Defense of Legal Positivism: Law Without Trimmings*, 79 n 2)

   Do you agree?

18. How do Raz's detached statements differ from Hart's internal point of view?

19. 'Consider, then, a theorist who wants to elucidate and analyse the workings of an iniquitous legal system such as the Nazi system. Striving for a rich and accurate exposition he does his best to apprehend the beliefs and attitudes that impel the officials of the particular system to perform their roles in the ways that they do. He needs to gain a sense of the various major purposes which their regime pursues, in order to develop an awareness of the outlooks of the people who are engaged in advancing those purposes. Suppose, for example, that his study of the regime's workings—his study of its norms and decisions and of the officials' justifications for those norms and decisions—leads him to attribute to the officials a number of repugnant attitudes such as anti-Semitism, racism, intolerance, illiberality, servile deference to superiors, and so forth. Is he thereby obliged to endorse those distasteful attitudes? Must a theorist be sympathetic to Nazism if he is to produce an accurate exposition of Nazi law?' (Matthew H Kramer, 'Dogmas and Distortions: Legal Positivism Defended. A Reply to David Dyzenhaus' (2001) *Oxford Journal of Legal Studies* 673, 689)

   Is he? Must he?

20. Raz explains the social thesis as follows:

   [I]t is misleading to regard the [social] thesis and argument…as moral ones. The argument is indeed evaluative, but in the sense that any good theory of society is based on evaluative considerations in that its success is in highlighting important social structures and processes, and every judgment of importance is evaluative. (*Ethics in the Public Domain*, 235)

   What does he mean?

   Do you agree with Julie Dickson (*Evaluation and Legal Theory*, 120) that this does not commit Raz to attributing a single function to law? Return to this question after you have read Chapter 5 on Dworkin.

21. Neil MacCormick (*Institutions of Law: An Essay in Legal Theory*, 278) states that the dichotomy between positivism and natural law is 'rarely revealing of any important truth'. Is he correct?

22. 'Although it is not a particularly inspiring or romantic description, the law is, in the end, an instrument. And like all instruments, it can be used for good or bad purposes…As with all instruments, there are correct and incorrect ways to use the law; if we use it incorrectly, it will not do what it is supposed to do and authorities will not do what they are entitled to do.' (Scott Shapiro, *Legality*, 399)

   Is law simply an instrument? How might a natural lawyer respond to this claim?

# Further reading

CAMPBELL, TOM, *The Legal Theory of Ethical Positivism* (Aldershot: Dartmouth, 1996).

COLEMAN, JULES (ed), *Hart's Postscript: Essays on the Postscript to* The Concept of Law (Oxford: Oxford University Press, 2001).

COLEMAN, JULES, *The Practice of Principle: In Defence of A Pragmatic Approach to Legal Theory* (Oxford: Oxford University Press, 2001).

DETMOLD, MJ, *The Unity of Law and Morality: A Refutation of Legal Positivism* (London: Routledge & Kegan Paul, 1984).

DICKSON, JULIE, *Evaluation and Legal Theory* (Oxford: Hart Publishing, 2001).

DUARTE D'ALMEIDA, L, EDWARDS, J, DOLCETTI A (eds), *Reading HLA Hart's* The Concept of Law (Oxford: Hart Publishing, 2013).

DUARTE D'ALMEIDA, L, GARDINER, J, GREEN, L (eds), *Kelsen Revisited: New Essays on the Pure Theory of Law* (Oxford: Hart Publishing, 2013).

EEKELAAR, JOHN M, 'Principles of Revolutionary Legality' in AWB Simpson (ed), *Oxford Essays in Jurisprudence*, 2nd series (Oxford: Clarendon Press, 1973), 27–30.

EEKELAAR, JOHN M, 'Judges and Citizens: Two Conceptions of Law' (2002) 22 *Oxford Journal of Legal Studies* 497.

FINNIS, JM, 'Revolutions and the Continuity of Law' in AWB Simpson (ed), *Oxford Essays in Jurisprudence*, 2nd series (Oxford: Oxford University Press, 1973), 75.

FULLER, LON LUVOIS, *The Morality of Law*, rev edn (New Haven, Conn and London: Yale University Press, 1969).

GAVISON, RUTH (ed), *Issues in Contemporary Legal Philosophy: The Influence of HLA Hart* (Oxford: Clarendon Press, 1987).

GEORGE, ROBERT P (ed), *The Autonomy of Law: Essays on Legal Positivism* (Oxford: Clarendon Press, 1999).

HACKER, PMS and RAZ, J (eds), *Law, Morality and Society: Essays in Honour of HLA Hart* (Oxford: Clarendon Press, 1977).

HARRIS, JW, 'When and Why Does the *Grundnorm* Change?' [1971] *Cambridge Law Journal* 103.

HARRIS, JW, *Law and Legal Science: An Inquiry into the Concepts Legal Rule and Legal System* (Oxford: Clarendon Press, 1979).

HARRIS, JW, *Legal Philosophies*, 2nd edn (London: Butterworths, 1997).

HART, HLA, *The Concept of Law* (Oxford: Clarendon Press, 1961).

HART, HLA, *Essays on Bentham: Studies on Jurisprudence and Political Theory* (Oxford: Clarendon Press, 1982).

HART, HLA, 'Legal Duty and Obligation' in *Essays on Bentham: Studies on Jurisprudence and Political Theory* (Oxford: Clarendon Press, 1982).

HART, HLA, *Essays in Jurisprudence and Philosophy* (Oxford: Clarendon Press, 1983).

HART, HLA, *The Concept of Law*, 2nd edn by PA Bulloch and J Raz (Oxford: Clarendon Press, 1994).

HART, HLA, *The Concept of Law*, 3rd edn by PA Bulloch and J Raz, with an introduction by L Green (Oxford: Clarendon Press, 2012).

HIMMA, KENNETH EINAR, 'Judicial Discretion and the Concept of Law' (1999) 19 *Oxford Journal of Legal Studies* 72.

HIMMA, KENNETH EINAR, 'Inclusive Legal Positivism' in Jules Coleman and Scott Shapiro (eds), *The Oxford Handbook of Jurisprudence and Philosophy of Law* (Oxford: Oxford University Press, 2002).

HUGHES, G, 'Validity and the Basic Norm' (1971) 59 *California Law Review* 695.

HURD, HEIDI, 'Challenging Authority' (1991) 100 *Yale Law Journal* 1611.

JORI, MARIO (ed), *Legal Positivism* (Aldershot: Dartmouth, 1992).

KELSEN, HANS, *General Theory of Law and State*, transl Anders Wedberg (Cambridge, Mass: Harvard University Press, 1949) (*20th Century Legal Philosophy Series*, vol 1).

KELSEN, HANS, *What is Justice? Justice, Law and Politics in the Mirror of Science* (Berkeley and Los Angeles: University of California Press, 1957).

KELSEN, HANS, 'A Reply to Professor Stone' (1965) 17 *Stanford Law Review* 1144.

KELSEN, HANS, *Pure Theory of Law*, transl Max Knight (Berkeley and Los Angeles: University of California Press, 1967).

KELSEN, HANS, *General Theory of Norms*, transl M Hartney (Oxford: Clarendon Press, 1991).

KELSEN, HANS, *Introduction to the Problems of Legal Theory*, transl Bonnie Litschewski Paulson and SL Paulson (Oxford: Clarendon Press, 1992).

KRAMER, MATTHEW, *In Defense of Legal Positivism: Law Without Trimmings* (Oxford: Oxford University Press, 1999).

MACCORMICK, NEIL, *Institutions of Law: An Essay in Legal Theory* (Oxford: Oxford University Press, 2007).

MARMOR, ANDREI, 'Exclusive Legal Positivism' in Jules Coleman and Scott Shapiro (eds), *The Oxford Handbook of Jurisprudence and Philosophy of Law* (Oxford: Oxford University Press, 2002).

MEYER, LUCAS H, PAULSON, STANLEY L, and POGGE THOMAS W (eds), *Rights, Culture and the Law: Themes from the Legal and Political Philosophy of Joseph Raz* (Oxford: Oxford University Press, 2003).

PAULSON, STANLEY L, 'The neo-Kantian Dimension of Kelsen's Pure Theory of Law' (1992) 12 *Oxford Journal of Legal Studies* 311.

PERRY, STEPHEN, 'Hart's Methodological Positivism' in Jules Coleman (ed), *Hart's Postscript: Essays on the Postscript to* The Concept of Law (Oxford: Oxford University Press, 2001).

RAZ, JOSEPH, *The Authority of Law* (Oxford: Oxford University Press 1979).

RAZ, JOSEPH, *The Concept of Legal System: An Introduction to the Theory of Legal System*, 2nd edn (Oxford: Clarendon Press, 1980).

RAZ, JOSEPH, *The Morality of Freedom* (Oxford: Oxford University Press, 1986).

RAZ, JOSEPH, *Ethics in the Public Domain* (Oxford: Oxford University Press, 1994).

RAZ, JOSEPH, *Practical Reason and Norms* (Oxford: Oxford University Press 1999).

RAZ, JOSEPH, *Engaging Reason: On the Theory of Value and Action* (Oxford: Oxford University Press, 2000).

RAZ, JOSEPH, *Value, Respect, and Attachment* (Cambridge: Cambridge University Press, 2001).

RAZ, JOSEPH, *Between Authority and Interpretation: On the Theory of Law and Practical Reason* (Oxford: Oxford University Press, 2009).

SCIARAFFA, STEFAN, 'The Ineliminability of Hartian Social Rules' (2011) 31 *Oxford Journal of Legal Studies* 603.

SHAPIRO, SCOTT J., *Legality* (Cambridge Mass, and London: Belknap Press of Harvard University Press, 2011).

SOPER, PHILIP, 'Law's Normative Claims' in Robert P George (ed), *The Autonomy of Law* (Oxford: Oxford University Press, 1999).

TUR, RICHARD and TWINING, WILLIAM (eds), *Essays on Kelsen* (Oxford: Clarendon Press, 1986).

WACKS, RAYMOND (ed), *Hong Kong, China and 1997: Essays in Legal Theory* (Hong Kong: Hong Kong University Press, 1993).

WALLACE, R JAY, PETTIT, PHILIP, SCHEFFLER, SAMUEL, and SMITH, MICHAEL (eds), *Reason and Value: Themes from the Moral Philosophy of Joseph Raz* (Oxford: Clarendon Press, 2004).

WALUCHOW, W, 'Authority and the Practical Difference Thesis: A Defence of Inclusive Positivism' (2000) 6 *Legal Theory* 45.

ZIPURSKY, BENJAMIN C, 'The Model of Social Facts' in Jules Coleman (ed), *Hart's Postscript: Essays on the Postscript to* The Concept of Law (Oxford: Oxford University Press, 2001).

# 5

# Dworkin and the
# moral integrity of law

The debate surrounding the association between law and morality was explored in Chapter 2 where the principal tenets of natural theory were described and, I hope, elucidated. I suggested there that the position and operation of morals in the law has long generated a significant controversy among legal and political philosophers. Indeed, it continues to perplex jurists today. In Chapter 4, the central divergences between legal positivists—who seek to maintain a conceptual separation between law and morals, on the one hand, and those, including natural lawyers, who repudiate this philosophical dissection on the other—were considered.

Ronald Dworkin has long been the most tenacious and eloquent member of the latter group. 'Law,' he has recently written, 'is effectively integrated with morality: lawyers and judges are working political philosophers of a democratic state.'[1]

Dworkin's long campaign in support of 'the unity of value' began with an assault on legal positivism and, in particular, Hart's version of it.[2] His crusade has, however, enlarged to include not only a stimulating account of law and the legal system, but also an analysis of the place of morals in law, the importance of individual rights, and the nature of the judicial function. And all these elements are skilfully integrated into a single vision of law that purports to 'take rights seriously'.[3] Moreover, his theory has provoked an immense critical literature that shows little sign of abating; it continues to engender a veritable hullabaloo in the jurisprudential orchard.

---

[1] Ronald Dworkin, *Justice for Hedgehogs* (Cambridge, Mass and London: The Belknap Press of Harvard University Press, 2011), 414. This extraordinary book, masterful, rich, and elegant *tour-de-force* which, in its broad—and bold—sweep, enlivens and illuminates many of the central moral questions of our time, is prescribed reading for any serious student of legal or political theory. It is likely to stimulate debate for many years to come. Indeed, such is its breadth that limitations of space dictate that I focus only upon some of its most important arguments. For some spirited attempts to take issue with Dworkin see the conference papers published, with a response by Dworkin in the special issue: 'Symposium: *Justice for Hedgehogs*: A Conference on Ronald Dworkin's Forthcoming Book' (2010) 90 *Boston Law Review*.

[2] See 4.2. For a perspicuous and perspicacious account of the key issues in the debate between Hart and Dworkin, see Scott J Shapiro, 'The Hart–Dworkin Debate: A Short Guide for the Perplexed' in A Ripstein (ed), *Dworkin* (Cambridge: Cambridge University Press, 2007).

[3] Collected in *Taking Rights Seriously* (London: Duckworth, 1978) (hereinafter *TRS*) and in *A Matter of Principle* (Cambridge, Mass: Harvard University Press, 1985). See too *Law's Empire* (Cambridge, Mass: Harvard University Press, 1986).

A sensible first step is to read Dworkin's earlier classic, *Law's Empire*. This sounds like a tall order (the book has 453 pages). But, as it is the first comprehensive and systematic account of his jurisprudential position, the book provides an excellent insight into his exciting (if optimistic) vision of law and provokes one to rethink some of the assumptions one tends to make about law, justice, and morality. At the very least, read Chapters 6, 7, and 11. His more recent writings—and replies to critics—are collected in *Justice in Robes*,[4] which provides a valuable statement of how Dworkin's ideas have developed over the last three decades. And, of course, *Justice for Hedgehogs* is his latest (though not, I suspect, his last word on the subject of law as an interpretive process).

This chapter will give you the essential elements of Dworkin's theory of law. But, be warned! His is an intricate and subtle account which makes unexpected twists and turns into economics, politics, and even literary theory. It has, moreover, generated an enormous critical response, occasionally malevolent, which has, in turn, evoked spirited defences from Dworkin—and these are often the most illuminating—and entertaining—aspect of Dworkin's writing.[5] If this were an inadequate row of hurdles in your path, Dworkin has, over the last thirty years, not surprisingly, modified his position in a number of respects. You will therefore need to be sure that you have kept abreast of these moves. In order to diminish needless uncertainty, this chapter attempts to distil the most significant—and least variable—features of Dworkin's philosophy of law.

## 5.1 An overview

It might be useful if Dworkin's account of law—at its most general level—is summarized. I shall then consider some of its more important facets in slightly greater detail. Note that our principal concern here is Dworkin's assault on legal positivism; other aspects of his theory are considered elsewhere (eg, his argument for 'rights as trumps' is examined in 10.2.1).

Dworkin's starting point might sensibly be regarded as his attack on Hart's model of rules (see 4.2.3). You will recall that an article of Hart's faith is the conceptual

---

[4] Ronald Dworkin, *Justice in Robes* (Cambridge, Mass and London: Harvard University Press, 2006).

[5] A useful collection of criticism (including Dworkin's replies) is M Cohen, *Ronald Dworkin and Contemporary Jurisprudence* (London: Duckworth, 1984). For a lucid exposition of the central features of the Dworkinian landscape, be sure to consult Stephen Guest, *Ronald Dworkin*, 3rd edn (Stanford: Stanford Law and Politics, 2013). There is also much to be gained from the essays collected in Scott Hershowitz (ed), *Exploring Law's Empire: The Jurisprudence of Ronald Dworkin* (Oxford: Oxford University Press, 2006)—particularly Dworkin's coruscating response to his critics. See too Alan Hunt (ed), *Reading Dworkin Critically* (New York and Oxford: Berg, 1992) and Arthur Ripstein (ed), *Ronald Dworkin* (Cambridge: Cambridge University Press, 2007). A recent reviewer of yet another collection of critical essays on Dworkin's theory commented sardonically that Dworkin 'is one of the most cited and read legal philosophers alive. Yet this wide readership has not translated into more than a small number of disciples. It is quite rare to find anyone in the field identifying herself as a "Dworkinian." Indeed, Andrea Dworkin may well have the larger following', Thom Brooks (2006) 69 *Modern Law Review* 140, quoted in Tom Lininger, 'On Dworkin and Borkin' (2007) 105 *Michigan Law Review* 1315, 1318, n 8. Hmm...

apartheid of law and morality. For Hart (and other legal positivists) we gain a clearer understanding of law by maintaining, for the purpose of analysis, a separation between the law as it *is* and the law as it *ought* to be. To Dworkin this is unacceptable and, indeed, impossible. This is because law consists not merely of rules (as Hart would have us believe) but also of what Dworkin calls 'non-rule standards'. When a court has to decide a hard case it will draw on these (moral or political) standards—principles and policies—in order to reach a decision. There is no rule of recognition which distinguishes between legal and moral principles. A judge in a hard case therefore must appeal to principles which will include his own conception of what is the best interpretation of the 'great network of political structures and decisions of his community'.[6] He must ask 'whether it could form part of a coherent theory justifying the network as a whole'.[7] In other words, there is always one 'right answer' to every legal problem; it is up to the judge to find it. This answer is 'right' in the sense that it coheres best (or 'fits') with the institutional and constitutional history of the law. Legal argument and analysis is therefore interpretative (or, what Dworkin prefers to call, 'interpretive') in character.

The theory is premised on Dworkin's concern that the law ought to 'take rights seriously'. If (as Hart claims) the outcome of a hard case turns on the judge's own view or intuition or the exercise of his 'strong discretion', rights are rendered fragile things to be sacrificed by courts at the altar of community interests or other conceptions of the good. If individual rights are to be treated with the respect they deserve, they (ie, in effect, principles) are to be accorded proper recognition as *part of the law*. This leads Dworkin (*inter alia*) to deny the positivist separation between law and morals; to reject the proposition that judges either do or should *make* law; to argue that judges must seek 'the soundest theory of law' on which to decide hard cases; and to conclude that, since judges (who are unelected officials) do not make law, the judicial role is democratic and prospective.

This is merely the skeleton of the major characteristics of Dworkin's system. And most students gasp in disbelief (or is it bewilderment?) when they first encounter its provocative claims. Yet many is the student, in my experience, who, after the initial shock and some serious reading of Dworkin, finds himself or herself, if not a hard-line Dworkinian, then certainly sympathetic to the general tenor of the theory.

## 5.2 **The assault on positivism**

While his campaign against Hart's model of rules provides the springboard for Dworkin's denunciation of legal positivism, in *Law's Empire* he mounts a more comprehensive onslaught on what he calls 'conventionalism', which includes what he calls the 'semantic sting' of positivism (see 5.2.4). Conventionalism rests on two main claims. First, it argues that law is a function of *social convention* which it then

---

[6] *Law's Empire*, 245.     [7] Ibid.

designates as *legal convention*. In other words, it claims that law consists no more than in respecting certain conventions (eg, decisions of higher courts are binding on lower ones). Secondly, it conceives law as incomplete: there are 'gaps' in the law which judges fill by reference to their own predilections—ie, judges have a 'strong discretion'. In one sense, according to Dworkin, the semantic theories of legal positivists (see 3.1 and 4.1) differ from full-blown or 'strict' conventionalism: the former argue that the description of law as convention is recognized and applied *by virtue of the very vocabulary of law*; the latter, however, adopts an *interpretive* conception of law. So semantic theories are linguistic and logical; conventionalists are willing to concede that we need to interpret the behaviour of lawyers and judges in order to determine what they *should* do.

The importance of Dworkin's attack on conventionalism, in general, and legal positivism, in particular, lies in the failure of such theories to provide either a convincing account of the process of law-making or a sufficiently strong defence of individual rights. He refers to the decision of *McLoughlin* v *O'Brian*[8] in which the plaintiff learned, at home, from a neighbour that her husband and four children had been injured in a car accident. The neighbour drove her to the hospital where she found her husband and sons screaming and seriously injured, and was told that her daughter was dead. She suffered nervous shock and sued, among others, the defendant driver whose negligence had caused the accident. As English law stood, a plaintiff could recover damages for nervous shock only where he or she had actually witnessed the accident or arrived on the scene immediately thereafter. The House of Lords, reversing the decision of the Court of Appeal, unanimously held that, despite precedents to the contrary, the plaintiff, Mrs McLoughlin, *could* recover damages for nervous shock. On 'policy' grounds, the House of Lords held that there was nothing in the law to prevent the plaintiff from succeeding.

Though it is not easy to discern the *ratio* of the case (for there are certain differences between the five judgments in their view of the proper role of policy), it is clear that, in formulating the law, the House of Lords arrived at a decision on the basis of what it regarded as the law. Now, according to Dworkin, a conventionalist would say that in this case (which he uses, along with three others, to illustrate his point) there is *no law* and that the judge must therefore exercise a *discretion* and make new law which is then applied *retrospectively* to the parties in the case. For Dworkin, however, 'propositions of law are true if they figure in or follow from the principles of justice, fairness, and procedural due process that provide the best constructive interpretation of the community's legal practice'.[9] Thus, in *McLoughlin* v *O'Brian* deciding whether the plaintiff should recover involves deciding whether legal practice is seen in a 'better light' if we assume the community has accepted the principle that people in her position are *entitled* to receive compensation. In other words, in Dworkin's vision of 'law as integrity' (see 5.2.7), a judge must think of himself not (as the conventionalist would have it) as giving voice to his *own* moral or political convictions (or even to those convictions

---

[8] [1983] 1 AC 410.     [9] *Law's Empire*, 225.

which he thinks the legislature or the majority of the electorate would approve), but 'as an author in the chain of common law'.[10] As Dworkin puts it:

> He knows that other judges have decided cases that, although not exactly like his case, deal with related problems; he must think of their decisions as part of a long story he must interpret and then continue, according to his own judgment of how to make the developing story as good as it can be.[11]

There is, therefore, 'no law beyond the law'; contrary to the positivist thesis, there are no 'gaps' in the law. Law and morals are inextricably intertwined. There cannot therefore be a rule of recognition by which to identify what is 'law'. Nor does law 'as a union of primary and secondary rules' provide an accurate model, for it fails to account for principles and policies.[12]

## 5.2.1 **Principles and policies**

In addition to rules (which 'are applicable in an all-or-nothing fashion') there are 'principles' and 'policies' which, unlike rules, have 'the dimension of weight or importance'. In other words, if a rule applies, and it is a valid rule, a case must be decided in a way dictated by the rule. A principle, on the other hand, provides a *reason* for deciding the case in a particular way, but it is not a *conclusive* reason: it will have to be *weighed* against other principles in the system. A distinction must, however, be drawn between 'principles' and 'policy'. A 'principle' is 'a standard to be observed, not because it will advance or secure an economic, political, or social situation, but because it is a requirement of justice or fairness or some other dimension of morality'.[13]

A 'policy', on the other hand, is 'that kind of standard that sets out a goal to be reached, generally an improvement in some economic, political, or social feature of the community'.[14] Of course, Dworkin rejects any master rule or rule of recognition by which these principles and policies gain admission to the legal system; indeed such a rule would be an impossibility for such standards 'are numberless, and they shift and change so fast that the start of our list would be obsolete before we reach the middle. Even if we succeeded, we would not have a key for law because there would be nothing left for our key to unlock.'[15]

Principles describe *rights*; policies describe *goals*. It is part of Dworkin's argument for 'taking rights seriously' that he contends that rights have a 'threshold weight' against community goals; this is his theory of 'rights as trumps' (see 10.2.1). If we are to respect individual rights, he argues, they must not be capable of being squashed by some competing community goal. The central question in any litigation is whether the claimant has a 'right to win'; not whether the community's interests should be satisfied. Thus civil cases are, and should be, decided by reference to *principles*. And even

---

[10]  Ibid, 238–9.        [11]  Ibid, 239.
[12]  For a spirited defence of the rule of recognition against Dworkin's attack, see Matthew H Kramer, 'Coming to Grips with the Law' (1999) 5 *Legal Theory* 171.
[13]  *TRS*, 22.        [14]  *TRS*.        [15]  *TRS*, 44.

if a judge appears to be advancing an argument of *policy*, we should read him to be referring to *principle* because he is actually deciding the individual *rights* of members of the community:

> If a judge appeals to public safety or the scarcity of some vital resource, for example, as a ground for limiting some abstract right, then his appeal might be understood as an appeal to the competing rights of those whose security will be sacrificed, or whose just share of that resource will be threatened if the abstract right is made concrete.[16]

In order to refute the model of rules, Dworkin asks us to consider the American case of *Riggs* v *Palmer*.[17] The stark question faced by the court was whether a murderer could inherit under the will of his victim. The will was validly executed and was in the murderer's favour. But the law was uncertain: the *rules* of testamentary succession provided no applicable exception. So, on the face of it, the murderer should have a right to get his money. The New York court held, however, that the application of the *rules* was subject to the *principle* that 'no man should profit from his own wrong'. Hence a murderer could not inherit from his victim. Dworkin argues that this decision demonstrates that, in addition to rules, the law includes *principles*.

### 5.2.2 Hercules and hard cases

Having disposed of the model of rules, Dworkin invites us to concentrate our attention on what actually happens in a 'hard case'. We have already seen that these cases, to which no rule is immediately applicable, require the judge, in Dworkin's thesis, to deploy standards other than rules (since, by definition, no rule applies). For this purpose he appoints Hercules, a judge 'of superhuman skill, learning, patience and acumen'.[18] Hercules is expected to 'construct a scheme of abstract and concrete principles that provides a coherent justification for all common law precedents and, so far as these are to be justified on principle, constitutional and statutory principles as well'.[19] Where the legal materials allow for more than one consistent reconstruction, Hercules will decide on the theory of law and justice which best coheres with the 'institutional history' of his community.

Hercules owes his existence to the image of law as a 'gapless system'. Thus Dworkin's holistic conception of adjudication requires Hercules to seek consistency and integrity (they are not the same thing)[20] in answering the legal question before him. This encourages him to be 'wide-ranging and imaginative in his search for coherence with fundamental principle'.[21] He must treat the law *as if* it were a 'seamless web'. If the claimant has a 'background moral right', Hercules will recognize an *institutional* right and, in turn, his *concrete* right against the defendant. But

---

[16] *TRS*, 100.     [17] 115 NY 506, 22 NE 188 (1889).     [18] *TRS*, 105.     [19] *TRS*, 116–17.
[20] See *Law's Empire*, 219–24.
[21] Ibid, 220. The concept of 'coherence' encapsulates the idea that a legal system should make sense as a whole if it is to be intelligible—a fundamental prerequisite of law if it is successfully to guide our behaviour. A number of writers have elaborated upon the notion with considerable subtlety and sophistication. See, in particular, N MacCormick, *Legal Reasoning and Legal Theory* (Oxford: Clarendon Press, 1994), especially 152–94; J Raz, 'The Relevance of Coherence' in his *Ethics in the Public Domain: Essays in the*

the existence of such a 'background' right will depend on a number of considerations, including the previous decisions of courts faced with similar or analogous problems. This leads to a consideration of the role of the doctrine of precedent in Dworkin's thesis—which has been the subject of some controversy. Essentially Dworkin argues that a precedent may have 'enactment' or 'gravitational' force. The effect on future cases of a judgment or opinion having *enactment* force would be limited to its precise words. A judgment or opinion with *gravitational* force has an influence that falls outside the language of the opinion: it appeals to the fairness of treating like cases alike.

This theory of precedent leads Dworkin back to the crucial distinction between the respective roles of principles and policy in hard cases. In Dworkin's words:

> If an earlier decision were taken to be entirely justified by some argument of *policy*, it would have *no* gravitational force. Its value as a precedent would be limited to its *enactment* force, that is, to further cases captured by some *particular words of the opinion*.[22]

So, in the case of decisions generated by *policy* (which, of course, are, in Dworkin's view, the proper concern of the legislature rather than the courts), there is no need for consistency. If, for example, the government decides to stimulate the economy and is able to do so, with roughly equal efficiency, by expenditure either on new roads or on housing, road construction firms would have no *right* that the former is done. There is no general argument of *fairness* in respect of government decisions which seek to serve a collective goal.

Both Hercules and the notion of a 'hard case' have attracted (as we shall see) a certain amount of criticism. Hercules J is a much misunderstood fellow. Several critics have sought to show that he is both megalomaniac and myth. These allegations will be considered later, but it is important at this stage to recognize Hercules for what he is (or, more accurately, what his creator intends him to be). He is postulated as a hypothetical model; Dworkin does not expect us, save in our imagination, to believe that he inhabits any actual bench. He is a useful *idea* because he sets a standard by which real judges might measure their performance: 'He is more reflective and self-conscious than any real judge need be or, given the press of work, could be.'[23] As for the concept of a 'hard case', you should be clear what Dworkin means by such cases. They are those cases which deal with a fundamental proposition of law, upon which lawyers disagree. Some critics have attacked the primacy which Dworkin accords to such cases in describing the judicial function. What about *easy* cases? But a close reading of Dworkin will reveal that, while Hercules may well deploy his grand theory in easy cases, it is in hard cases when such theory really displays its cutting edge. In other

---

*Morality of Law and Politics* (Oxford: Clarendon Press, 1994); R Alexy, 'Jürgen Habermas's Theory of Legal Discourse' (1996) 17 *Cardozo Law Review* 1027–34; A Peczenik, 'Coherence, Truth and Rightness in the Law' in P Nerhot (ed), *Law, Interpretation and Reality* (Dordrecht and Boston, Mass: Kluwer, 1990), 275; R Alexy and A Peczenik, 'The Concept of Coherence and its Significance for Discursive Rationality' (1990) 3 *Ratio Juris* 130.

[22] *TRS*, 113; emphasis added.     [23] *Law's Empire*, 265.

words, the idea of the 'hard case' is, like Hercules, a paradigm case which focuses our attention on the judicial role in its most graphic and most important form.

### 5.2.3 **One right answer**

The proposition that there is, to every legal problem, only one right answer, never fails to stop students in their tracks. This, they inevitably protest, is nonsense. Surely, they cry, there are at least two possible outcomes, neither of which can be said with any certainty to be the correct one. But (as already pointed out) Dworkin's model of adjudication points unequivocally to the idea that, in his pursuit of coherence and integrity, Hercules will find the best answer to the legal question before him. That answer will be the right one. And there can be only *one* answer that 'fits' most comfortably; there must therefore be only one right answer. It is only a size 8 shoe that fits my foot. Neither a 7½ nor an 8½ is the correct size. There is only one right size.

If my own analogy seems doubtful, try Dworkin's Tal's smile. In the course of a chess tournament one of the players (Tal) smiles inanely at his opponent who (unsmilingly) objects. The referee must decide whether smiling is in breach of the rules of chess. The rule book is silent. He must therefore reflect upon the nature of chess: it is a game of intellectual skill; does this include the use of psychological intimidation? He must, in other words, find the answer that best 'fits' the general theory and practice of chess. To this question there can be only one right answer. And this is equally true of the judge deciding a hard case. What is more, lawyers *accept* that there is only one uniquely correct result to any legal dispute. When giving advice, a lawyer does not say 'This will is neither valid nor invalid'; it is either one or the other. He, too, bases himself on an interpretation of the law (precedents, statutes, doctrine) and this enables him to give an answer that best represents the state of the law as he finds and understands it.

### 5.2.4 **The semantic sting**

Dworkin distinguishes between two sorts of differences lawyers might have with regard to law. While agreeing on the criteria a rule must fulfil in order to be legally valid, they may disagree as to whether these criteria are satisfied by a particular rule. Thus lawyers might agree that a rule is valid if properly enacted by the legislature, but disagree as to whether the rule at issue was indeed actually enacted by the legislature. These sorts of disagreements are empirical—and do not challenge legal positivism. But legal positivism is, according to Dworkin, threatened by a second kind of disagreement. Lawyers frequently agree about the facts surrounding the creation of a particular rule, but disagree about whether those facts are sufficient to vest that rule with legal authority. This sort of disagreement runs deeper than the merely empirical kind, because it relates to the criteria for legal validity which, according to legal positivism, are exhausted by the rule of recognition. This sort of divergence Dworkin labels theoretical disagreement about the law. Theoretical disagreement, Dworkin argues, is inconsistent with the 'pedigree thesis' which accounts for the concept of law, you will recall (see 4.2.3), by reference to the rules of change, adjudication, and recognition. As he says:

> If legal argument is mainly or even partly about pivotal cases, then lawyers cannot all be using the same factual criteria for deciding when propositions of law are true and false. Their arguments would be mainly or partly about which criteria they should use. So the project of the semantic theories, the project of digging out shared rules from a careful study of what lawyers say and do, would be doomed to fail.[24]

In other words, if two lawyers dispute the criteria of legal validity, the basis of legal validity cannot be exhausted by the shared criteria contained in the rule of recognition. The 'semantic sting' entails therefore that the concept of legal validity is more than mere promulgation in accordance with shared criteria embodied in a rule of recognition.

For Hart, of course, the rule of recognition is a social rule and is hence established by the conduct of those who also accept the rule as a justification for disparaging those who fail to observe it. This 'internal point of view', is the basis upon which Hart distinguishes his theory from Austin's imperative account of law. Dworkin claims that this feature of Hart's theory commits him to the proposition that the rule of recognition may be uncertain at particular points. And this undermines Hart's theory, Dworkin argues, because 'if judges are divided about what they must do if a subsequent Parliament tries to repeal an entrenched rule, then it is not uncertain whether any social rule [of recognition] governs that decision; on the contrary, it is certain that none does.'[25]

For Dworkin, the requirements of a social rule cannot be uncertain since a social rule is constituted by acceptance and conforming behaviour by most people in the relevant group: '[T]wo people whose rules differ...cannot be appealing to the same social rule, and at least one of them cannot be appealing to any social rule at all.'[26]

If the rule of recognition is a social rule, then, Jules Coleman contends, Hart's position entails general agreement among the officials of a legal system about what standards constitute the rule of recognition, but it does not follow that there cannot be disagreement as to what those standards may require in any given case:

> The controversy among judges does not arise over the content of the rule of recognition itself. It arises over which norms satisfy the standards set forth in it. The divergence in behaviour among officials as exemplified in their identifying different standards as legal ones does not establish their failure to accept the same rule of recognition. On the contrary, judges accept the same truth conditions for propositions of law...They disagree about which propositions satisfy those conditions.[27]

According to Coleman there are two kinds of disagreement that lawyers may have about the rule of recognition. The first is disagreement about what standards constitute the rule of recognition. The second is disagreement about what propositions

---

[24] Ibid, 43.    [25] *TRS*, 61–2.    [26] *TRS*, 55.
[27] Jules Coleman, 'Negative and Positive Positivism' (1982) 11 *Journal of Legal Studies* 139, 156.

satisfy those standards. Hart's analysis of social rules implies only that the first is impossible. Thus, under Hart's approach, it is perfectly possible for there to be argument about whether a given enactment complies, say, with the constitution.

The semantic sting is central to Dworkin's assault on legal positivism. It challenges the claim that there are common standards that exhaust the conditions for the proper application of the concept of law. This is an important objection for it illustrates Dworkin's unease about all semantic theories: they wrongly assume that important disagreement is impossible unless 'we all accept and follow the same criteria for deciding when our claims are sound, even if we cannot state exactly, as a philosopher might hope to do, what these criteria are'.[28]

For him, semantic theories are inconsistent with theoretical controversy surrounding what he calls 'pivotal cases'. And he believes that the outcome in hard cases often turns on disagreement about pivotal cases.

Hart denies that his theory is semantic, and argues that his theory of law is 'a descriptive account of the distinctive features of law in general as a complex social phenomenon'.[29] In other words, Hart regards *The Concept of Law* as an explanation and description of the distinguishing characteristics of law from other systems of social rules. For him, of course, the quintessential ingredient is the rule of recognition.

In *Justice in Robes*[30] Dworkin reflects upon the appropriate function of morals in legal theory, contending that even when judges attempt to be faithful to the text of the law, their subjective conceptions of justice are fundamental to their decisions. He argues that it is the responsibility of judges to determine the moral principles which underpin the law and employ them as loyally as they would the law itself. Dworkin proffers a hypothetical case in which the plaintiff, Mrs Sorenson, has suffered harm as a result of taking a generic drug. Eleven manufacturers negligently supplied the unsafe drug. Unable to prove which company manufactured it, or even that she took a single pill supplied by any specific manufacturer, she faces the prospect of obtaining no compensation for the harm she has suffered. She argues that each manufacturer is liable in proportion to its share of the market for the drug: 'market share damages'.

Dworkin argues that adopting a Hartian 'sources thesis' (ie, that the law is identified by reference to statutes, precedents, and social practice) would annihilate Mrs Sorensen's action since it fails to include moral principles, and there is no legislation or judicial decision that would satisfy Hart's 'sources thesis' that could come to her aid. Dworkin therefore concludes that in cases such as this one, the question of what is the law is resolved 'by asking whether the best justification of negligence law as a whole contains a moral principle that would require that result in her circumstances.'[31] Moral concerns are always germane—even when officials differ in respect of the outcome. Hence Mrs Sorenson's failure is, Dworkin suggests, far from inevitable.

[28] *Law's Empire*, 45.
[29] HLA Hart, *The Concept of Law*, 2nd edn (Oxford: Clarendon Press, 1994), 246.
[30] Dworkin, *Justice in Robes*.     [31] Ibid, 14.

A number of critics are unconvinced by this conclusion. Brian Leiter, for instance, argues that Dworkin conflates two questions: 'What is the law in this jurisdiction?' with the question 'How ought a particular case to be decided?' In his view,

> Positivists have always been clear that a judge's legal duty to apply valid law can be overridden by moral or equitable considerations in any particular case, and Hart's general theory ('the sources thesis') that 'laws' are distinguished by their source—by their being enacted, for example, by a legislative body or figuring in the holding of a court—is simply silent on how the wronged Mrs. Sorenson should be treated. On Dworkin's Theory of Esoteric Law, however, it seems every moral wrong must have a preordained *legal* remedy—even though no one knew the law required it!— so that forward-looking jurists who craft new legal rules in response to real-world problems are really only 'discovering' a legal remedy that already existed in Dworkinian Heaven.[32]

Whatever view you take of Dworkin's attempt to demonstrate the superiority of his approach over Hart's, this hypothetical nicely exemplifies the Dworkinian attitude towards judges and judging.

### 5.2.5 **The rights thesis**

It should be obvious by now (and this question is further explored in 10.2.1) that Professor Dworkin grounds his legal theory on a version of liberalism which he describes as springing from the proposition that 'government must treat people as equals'. By this he means that it 'must impose no sacrifice or constraint on any citizen in virtue of an argument that the citizen could not accept without abandoning his sense of equal worth'.[33] This leads Dworkin (in a series of essays) not only to adopt a liberal position on a number of specific issues (eg, whether the criminal law should enforce private morality (it should not); whether wealth is a value (it is not); whether reverse discrimination is immoral (it is not)), but also to 'define and defend a liberal theory of law'[34] that informs his assault on positivism, conventionalism, and pragmatism (which he defines as resting on the claim that 'judges do and should make whatever decisions seem to them best for the community's future, not counting any form of consistency with the past as valuable for its own sake').[35] Pragmatists look to efficiency or justice as the guiding light for judges. None of these theories of law provides an adequate defence of individual rights. It is only 'law as integrity' (see 5.2.7) which supplies a proper buttress against the encroachment by instrumentalism upon individual rights and general liberty.

The extent to which you should familiarize yourself with Dworkin's particular jurisprudence on the wide range of contemporary issues he has written about will, of course, depend on the importance attached to them in your course. But they are

---

[32] Brian Leiter, 'The Theory of Esoteric Law', University of Texas Law, Public Law Research Paper No 121. Available at SSRN: http://ssrn.com/abstract=965459. See too Timothy Endicott, 'Adjudication and the Law' (2007) 27 *Oxford Journal of Legal Studies* 311.

[33] 'Why Liberals Should Care about Equality' in *A Matter of Principle*, 205.          [34] *TRS*, vii.

[35] *Law's Empire*, 122.

valuable as practical applications of the rights thesis and therefore, even if they are not explicitly dealt with in your course, your reading at least some of them will give you a better, rounder understanding of Dworkin. Thus, for example, in his book, *Sovereign Virtue*, he addresses the kind of equality a government should preserve and maintain. Liberal egalitarianism, he argues, endeavours to give effect to personal choice over individual luck:

> When and how far is it right that individuals bear disadvantages or misfortunes of their own situations themselves, and when is it right, on the contrary, that others—the other members of the community in which they live, for example—relieve them from or mitigate the consequences of these disadvantages?…[I]ndividuals should be relieved of consequential responsibility for those unfortunate features of their situation that are brute bad luck, but not from those that should be seen as flowing from their own choices.[36]

This formula, Dworkin contends, strikes a proper balance between collective and personal responsibility. He proposes, amongst other ideals, a radical redistribution of wealth, a universal health-care system, a more generous welfare scheme, and more regulation of election campaign expenditures and contributions. He regards the free market as arbitrary and unfair; it is unjust because it rewards not just the choice to perform a useful service, but also one's fortuitous talent for doing it. The book is, in short, another argument for the sort of liberal equality that pervades Dworkin's other works. Equality, however, is far from an uncontested notion: 'People who praise it or disparage it disagree about what they are praising or disparaging.'[37]

### 5.2.6 **Law as literature**

Think of a novel you have recently read. Did you *like* it? Why? What is the author *saying*? What does the novel mean to you? Your answer to these sorts of questions reveal your *interpretation* of the work of art in question. And such interpretation is essentially *constructive*: it seeks to discover the author's *purpose* in writing the book, and to give the *best* account possible. In interpreting a work of art, we are trying to *understand* it in a particular way. We are, moreover, attempting to depict the book (or painting, film, poem) *accurately*—as it really is, not 'through rose-coloured glasses'. We are, in other words, in search of the actual, historical intentions of the author, not foisting our values on the author's creation.

Now, what has all this to do with law? Why this detour into literary theory? A key component of Dworkinian legal theory is its claimed affinity to literary interpretation.[38] When we attempt to interpret a work of art, Dworkin argues, we seek to understand it in a particular way. We try to portray the book, movie, poem, or picture accurately. We want to establish, as far as we are able, the intentions of the author, director, poet,

[36] *Sovereign Virtue: The Theory and Practice of Equality* (Cambridge, Mass: Harvard University Press, 2000).                                                                                    [37] Ibid, 2.
[38] See especially Ch 2 of *Law's Empire*, and 'How Law is Like Literature' in *A Matter of Principle*, 146, and his dazzling account of interpretation (embracing art and literature) in Ch 7 of *Justice for Hedgehogs*.

or painter in a *constructive* manner. Why did Henry James choose to write about these particular characters? What was his purpose? In answering these sorts of questions, we characteristically attempt to give the best account of the novel we can.

Law, claims Dworkin, like a novel or a play, requires interpretation. Judges are like interpreters of a developing story. They 'normally recognise a duty to continue rather than discard the practice they have joined. So they develop, in response to their own convictions and instincts, working theories about *the best interpretation of their responsibilities under that practice*.'[39] We should therefore think of judges as authors engaged in a chain novel, each one of whom is required to write a new chapter which is added to what the next co-novelist receives. Each novelist attempts to make a single novel out of the previous chapters; he or she endeavours to write a chapter so that the ultimate result will be coherent. To accomplish this, the judge requires a vision of the story as it proceeds: its characters, plot, theme, genre, and general purpose, attempting to find the meaning in the evolving creation, and an interpretation that best justifies it.

So, Dworkin seems to be saying, in the same way as you and I might disagree about the *real* meaning intended by a novelist in his work, two judges might disagree about 'the soundest interpretation of some pertinent aspect of judicial practice'.[40]

If this suggestion strikes you as a little obscure or far-fetched, consider Dworkin's 'courtesy' example which seeks to apply this form of interpretation to a *social* practice.[41] He asks us to imagine a community whose members follow a set of rules which they call 'rules of courtesy'. Various such rules exist requiring, for instance, that peasants doff their caps to nobility. Over a period of time members of the society begin to develop certain attitudes toward these rules: they assume that the rules have a certain *value* (ie, they serve some purpose) independent of their mere existence, and they regard the requirements of courtesy as flexible—the strict rules need to be adapted or modified to meet changing needs. Once people have made these two assumptions, they have adopted an 'interpretive' view of courtesy: the institution of courtesy ceases to be mechanical. Members of the community now try to impose some *meaning* on it: to view courtesy in its best light, and then to reinterpret it in the light of that meaning.

If a philosopher wishes to explain this particular social practice, he would not be assisted by a theory which confined itself to a set of semantic rules which declare the proper use of the word 'courtesy'. He would fall prey to the 'semantic sting'. He can explain it only by 'imposing a certain structure on [the] community's practice such that particular substantive theories can be identified and understood as subinterpretations of a more abstract idea'.[42] In other words, his claim is 'interpretive' rather than semantic: it is not a claim about *linguistic* ground rules that everyone must follow to make sense.

And the same, argues Dworkin, is true of law. Semantic theories (such as those proffered by legal positivists) fail to explain the essence of law. Thus the so-called Hart–Fuller debate concerning whether evil 'laws' are indeed 'laws' (see 2.10.2) is sterile if conducted at the *semantic* level: this merely relates to the meaning of 'law' at what

---

[39] *Law's Empire*, 87; emphasis added.     [40] Ibid.     [41] Ibid, 46–86.     [42] Ibid, 71.

Dworkin calls the 'preinterpretive' stage. It becomes a more interesting and important debate at the *interpretive* level, for then the question becomes, not one of mere semantics, but one about the *substance* of law. For someone to claim that Nazi law is not 'law' then represents a 'sceptical interpretive judgment that Nazi law lacked features crucial to flourishing legal systems whose rules and procedures do justify coercion. His judgment is now a special kind of political judgment.'[43]

Judges should therefore be thought of as authors engaged in a 'chain novel', each one of whom is required to write a new chapter which is added to what the next co-novelist receives. Each novelist attempts to make a single novel out of the material he receives; he tries to write his chapter in such a way that the final product will appear to be the creation of a single writer. If he is to do this (and he wants to do the best possible job) he must have a view of the novel as it progresses: its characters, plot, theme, *genre*, objective. He will seek the meaning or layers of meaning in the unfolding work and an interpretation that best explains it. This stimulating analogy is part of Dworkin's vision of 'law as integrity'. It lies at the heart of his vision of the essential nature of law as a moral enterprise.

### 5.2.7 Law as integrity

Hercules is thus a constructive interpreter of the chapters of the law that have been written before him (though, of course, unlike the chain novel analogy, he may have written some of the chapters himself). 'Law as integrity' requires him to ask whether his interpretation of the law could form part of a coherent theory justifying the whole legal system. But where does Dworkin's elemental concept of 'integrity' come in? He does not 'define' it, but provides a picture of its significant features:

> [L]aw as integrity accepts law and legal rights wholeheartedly... It supposes that law's constraints benefit society not just by providing predictability or procedural fairness, or in some other instrumental way, but *by securing a kind of equality among citizens that makes their community more genuine and improves its moral justification for exercising the political power it does.* ... It argues that rights and responsibilities flow from past decisions and so count as legal, not just when they are explicit in these decisions but also when they follow from the principles of personal and political morality the explicit decisions presuppose by way of justification.[44]

Thus, at the core of Dworkin's theory is the age-old problem of the relationship between law and force. Law is inevitably bound up with the extent to which coercion may legitimately be used. This is a continuing theme in legal positivism, natural law, and certain social theories (see, eg, 4.3.4, 2.6, and 7.5). Dworkin argues that a society which accepts integrity as a political virtue does so, in large part, in order to justify its moral authority to assume and deploy a monopoly of coercive force. This sounds an echo of certain aspects of Weber's idea of 'legitimate domination' (see 7.5.2) to whom Dworkin makes no reference. I say 'in large part' because he identifies a number of

---

[43] Ibid, 104.     [44] Ibid, 95–6; emphasis added.

other consequences that flow from the acceptance of integrity, including protection against partiality, deceit, and corruption.

More importantly, integrity promotes the ideal of self-government and participation in democracy. It is, in short, an amalgam of values which form the essence of the liberal society and the rule of law, or, as Dworkin, has now called it, 'legality'. Why do we value the law? Why do we respect those societies that adhere to the law and, more importantly, celebrate their observance of those political virtues that characterize states 'under law'? We do so, Dworkin suggests, because, while an efficient government is laudable, there is a greater value that is served by legality:

> Efficiency of government, on any plausible conception of what that means, is plainly an important product of legality, and any plausible explanation of legality's value must emphasize that fact. No ruler, even a tyrant, survives for long or achieves his goals, even very bad ones, if he altogether abandons legality for whimsy or terror. But there is another important value that legality might also be seen to serve, not in competition with efficiency, but sufficiently independent of it to provide, for those who take it to be of great importance, a distinctive conception of what legality is for. This is political integrity, which means equality before the law, not merely in the sense that the law is enforced as written, but in the more consequential sense that government must govern under a set of principles in principle applicable to all. Arbitrary coercion or punishment violates that crucial dimension of political equality, even if, from time to time, it does make government more efficient.[45]

This preoccupation with the moral legitimacy of the law is a fundamental element of Dworkin's legal philosophy. It is based, in large part, on the somewhat nebulous concept of 'community' or 'fraternity'. It is an idea that continues to receive an unsympathetic reaction from Dworkin's detractors, particularly, of course, the neo-positivists, as they should perhaps be styled. You will need to formulate your own perspective of this question. It will be important for you to decide precisely where you stand on the extent to which Dworkin's moral reading of the law successfully disposes of the main tenets of legal positivism.

### 5.2.8 Community

Dworkin's case for law's legitimacy rests on the idea that a political society that accepts integrity becomes 'a special form of community' in that it asserts its moral authority to use coercion.[46] And 'integrity' requires a sort of reciprocity between citizens, as well as their recognition of the importance of their 'associative obligation'.[47] A community's social practices generate 'genuine' obligations when it is a 'true' rather than

---

[45] R Dworkin, 'Hart's Postscript and the Character of Political Philosophy' (2004) 24 *Oxford Journal of Legal Studies* 1, 29. How does this differ from Fuller's conception of law? See 2.6.

[46] You will find a helpful discussion of Dworkin's account of community in Stephen Guest, *Ronald Dworkin*, 105–14. See too Dworkin's discussion of community, in a rather different context, in his *Sovereign Virtue*. On the relationship between community and the obligation to obey the law, see Stephen Perry, 'Associative Obligations and the Obligation to Obey the Law' in Scott Hershovitz (ed), *Exploring Law's Empire: The Jurisprudence of Ronald Dworkin* (Oxford: Oxford University Press, 2006), 183.

[47] *Law's Empire*, 196.

a 'bare' community. This transformation occurs when its members consider their obligations as 'special' (ie applying specifically to the group), 'personal' (ie flowing between members), and based on the equal concern for the welfare of all. If these four conditions are met, members of a 'bare' community acquire the obligations of a true community, whether or not they want them:

> It is therefore essential to insist that true communities must be bare communities as well. People cannot be made involuntary 'honorary' members of a community to which they do not even 'barely' belong just because other members are disposed to treat them as such. I would not become a citizen of Fiji if people there decided for some reason to treat me as one of them. Nor am I the friend of a stranger sitting next to me on a plane just because he decides he is a friend of mine.[48]

The 'true' community is the foundation upon which Dworkin builds his idea of political legitimacy. He contends that political obligation is an example of associative obligation. In order to create political obligations, a political community must be a 'true' community. And only one that espouses the ideal of integrity is a genuine associative community that is capable of being morally legitimate, because its fraternal decisions relate to obligation rather than naked force.[49]

## 5.3 Equality

The ideal of equality is, as we have seen, central to Dworkin's theory. His analysis of the concept is complex and sporadically highly technical. Some of its key features are summarized here.[50]

Broadly speaking, Dworkin's concept of equality endorses a fairly high degree of state interference in individuals' lives, not only to prevent harm to others but to redistribute wealth and resources. To this end, he distinguishes two core concepts of equality: equality of welfare and equality of resources. In respect of the first, he isolates a number of conceptions of welfare that might be adopted in order to fulfil the ideal of equality of welfare. But none, he contends, provides an adequate ideal. Only a conception of equality of resources will do; this relates to those resources privately owned by individuals. How is this aspect of equality to be measured? Dworkin answers that a division of resources is equal if, when it is complete, no one would prefer another's bundle of resources to his or her own. This is secured by a market mechanism in which the primary market that comprises the resources in question and a secondary market consists of insurance.

---

[48] Ibid, 202.     [49] See Chapter 11.
[50] Dworkin develops the argument in the following articles: 'What is Equality? Part I: Equality of Welfare' (1981) 10 *Philosophy and Public Affairs* 185; 'What is Equality? Part II: Equality of Resources' (1981) 10 *Philosophy and Public Affairs* 283; 'What is Equality? Part III: The Place of Liberty' (1987) 73 *Iowa Law Review* 1; and 'What is Equality? Part IV: Political Equality' (1987) 22 *University of San Francisco Law Review* 1.

Dworkin's primary market is a Walrasian auction which is a sort of simultaneous auction where each agent estimates its demand for the good at every possible price and submits this to an auctioneer who then sets the price in order that the total demand across all agents equals the total amount of the good. A Walrasian auction therefore matches exactly supply and demand. All productive resources are eventually sold. The bidders in Dworkin's hypothetical auction are survivors of a shipwreck on an island who seek to distribute all its resources between them. They are each given an equal number of clamshells with which to bid. On completion of the auction, Dworkin argues, the 'envy test' will have been satisfied. He proposes that a more elaborate version of the auction could be deployed to provide a method for developing or testing equality of resources in a community that has a dynamic economy, with labour, investment, and trade.

The secondary market in insurance is required because other forces come into play once the auction is concluded. These include individuals' variable levels of skill, luck, and the possibility of gambling. These three factors are linked by insurance; in theory, individuals can insure against the exigency of bad luck. Providing equality of opportunity to insure would mean that equality of resources would not require redistribution in the future if, say, bad luck materialized. By this means individuals' physical or mental handicaps can be compensated.

In the case of individuals' talents, on the other hand, the envy test is applied diachronically (that is, over a period of time). It requires that no one envy the occupation and resources at the disposal of anyone else over time, though an individual may envy another's resources at any particular time. We are not, of course, equally endowed with talent. Dworkin therefore argues that the role of talent is to be neutralized by a periodic redistribution of resources through some form of income tax.

But how, one is entitled to ask, can one plan one's life devoid of an awareness of one's talents or handicaps? How, in other words, can one know what to bid for at the auction in order to fulfil one's life plans and ambitions? Dworkin concedes that this problem is especially acute in respect of individual talents. However, Dworkin considers that this objection is most serious for talents, but suggests that the solution is—before the auction gets under way—to stipulate that each individual knows his tastes, ambitions, talents, and his approach toward risk. But he has no knowledge of what income level his personal talents will permit him to achieve. The opportunity to procure insurance is now not against having or not having a talent or handicap, but against not being able to earn an income of a certain level.

As we shall see in Chapter 8, this analysis of equality differs from both Nozick's night-watchman state (see 9.4) and Rawls's theory of justice (see 9.3). For Dworkin, liberty (including specific liberties such as freedom of expression and religion) is derived from the fundamental right to equality. Indeed, he contends that while the conflict may be real in certain cases, in the case of equality of resources, the rights to liberty we regard as basic are an element of 'distributional equality', and are therefore automatically protected whenever equality is achieved. The priority of liberty is realized not at the expense of equality, but in its name. Liberty and equality are, in Dworkin's view, squared by either definitional or rational means.

The first is the more persuasive in that Dworkin maintains that at the heart of all conceptions of equality lies the 'abstract egalitarian principle'. It specifies that government should act to improve people's lives, and show equal concern for the life of every individual. In other words, the egalitarian principle requires government to respect liberty since it obliges it to show equal concern for the lives of those it governs.

In keeping with the widely held liberal view of neutrality in respect of competing conceptions of the good life, Dworkin's hypothetical auction allows no restrictions on the basis of religious or personal morality. Each bidder's subjective conception of his or her social and moral situation required to pursue the good life may be quantified by reference to opportunity costs, in the same way as physical resources are calculated. They may therefore be assessed by enquiring how far these desires can be met within an egalitarian structure that measures their cost to others.

But Dworkin's model permits one constraint on absolute freedom of choice: the rectification of externalities produced by some individuals at the expense of others. The auctioneer would determine the measures that are required to achieve the desired correction. Such constraints on freedom of choice are justified, Dworkin argues, where they improve the extent to which equality of resources secures its objective, namely, a genuinely equal distribution measured by true opportunity costs.

Certain other liberties spring from 'equality in private ownership' including individuals' freedom to engage in actions essential to establishing and revising the convictions, projects, and preferences that they bring to the auction and after the auction, as well as a variety of decisions about production and trade that will alter and reallocate their initial holdings. One can, he suggests, justify special protection to a number of liberties including freedom of religion and expression, and unfettered access to literature and art, freedom of personal, social, and intimate association, and freedom of *non*-expression in the form of freedom from surveillance.

Dworkin also stipulates that the exercise of prejudice must not contravene the 'abstract egalitarian principle'. For if a group of racists organized to purchase tracts of land for housing from which they will subsequently exclude blacks, this would violate the fundamental egalitarian principle—because this fails to treat all members of the community with equal concern. It is therefore necessary to impose on the auction a 'principle of independence' (which seeks to place victims of prejudice in a position as close as possible to that which they would occupy if prejudice did not exist) to achieve equality.

## 5.4 Good lives and living well

Dworkin's *Justice for Hedgehogs* navigates a vast terrain that extends beyond the borders of conventional legal philosophy. While there are obviously echoes of his previous writings, the book also contains a powerful prescription of how to live a moral life, a dignified life.[51]

---

[51] Discussions with Stephen Guest have enhanced my understanding of this magisterial work. I am most grateful to him. Ronald Dworkin was kind enough to respond to my several questions.

Endorsing what he calls 'Hume's principle' (that facts about the world or human nature cannot normally ordain what ought to be; see 2.4), Dworkin contends that his distinction between fact and value, far from encouraging philosophical scepticism, actually weakens it

> because the proposition that it is not true that genocide is morally wrong *is itself a moral proposition*, and, if Hume's principle is sound, that proposition cannot be established by any discoveries of logic or facts about the basic structure of the universe. Hume's principle, properly understood, supports not scepticism about moral truth but rather the importance of morality as a separate department of knowledge with its own standards of inquiry and justification.[52]

This contention is central to Dworkin's theory that moral values are both independent and objective. He insists upon the independence of arguments of value, rejecting the idea that external forces could induce a conflict between our values. Instead we should cleave to our value judgments, justifying them by reference to our more abstract values. Each of us is responsible for rendering our moral views as clear and coherent as we can.

We are, moreover, obliged to make our lives as good as we can:

> Someone lives well when he senses and pursues a good life for himself and does so with dignity: with respect for the importance of other people's lives and for their ethical responsibility as well as his own. The two ethical principles—living well and having a good life—are different. We can live well without having a good life: we may suffer bad luck or great poverty or serious injustice or a terrible disease or premature death. The value of our striving is adverbial; it does not lie in the goodness or impact of the life realized. That is why people who live and die in great poverty can nevertheless live well... You live badly if you do not try hard enough to make your life good.[53]

We must, in other words, live lives of 'dignity'; this requires not merely that we take our lives seriously, but that we also assume responsibility for our lives. Living a life of dignity promotes self-respect. This is a matter of ethics. In addition, we owe moral duties towards others. For Dworkin, moral questions are an extension of ethics. By acknowledging the significance of self-respect, we are obliged—if we are to be logically consistent—to recognize its importance in the lives of others.

The overarching, unrelenting coherence of value has long been a theme of all Dworkin's writings. And the importance of individual dignity is a persistent strain of

---

[52] Dworkin, op cit, 17.; emphasis added.
[53] Dworkin, op cit, 419–20. I asked Dworkin why he appeared to exclude, at least implicitly respect for creatures other than humans. Does a person who devotes his life to the care of a pet, or to rescuing a maltreated animal, not live well? Does his or her kindness and sacrifice not constitute equivalent ethical virtue? I recognised, of course, that Dworkin's conception of living well is premised on the respect with which we treat other humans, but I could not see why concern for non-humans does not render a life equally authentic or worthy. It seemed to me that he intentionally avoids this aspect of obligation or responsibility in his moral reckoning. He replied: 'It follows from what I say that animals can't live well. But not that living well doesn't require concern for animals.' How would you have answered my question?

his legal, political, and moral philosophy. 'Without dignity our lives are only blinks of duration.'[54]

## 5.5 The assault on Dworkin

Dworkin's writing has stimulated a vigorous debate in the literature.[55] His ever-expanding group of detractors adopts a variety of standpoints from which to launch their assault upon what is a large, and occasionally a moving, target. Some criticize the very interpretive project that is at the heart of the Dworkinian project. Scott Shapiro, for example, has suggested that it is a methodology that defeats the purpose of law:

> Having to answer a series of moral questions is precisely the *disease* that the law aims to cure. Dworkinian legal interpretation thus ends up reinfecting the patient after the contagion has been neutralized.[56]

I have already mentioned a number of these attacks; some of the other more significant onslaughts on the central features of Dworkin's theory may briefly be summarized under the following ten heads:

### 1. The attack on Hart

Professor Hart has described Dworkin's claim that judges do not make law as a 'noble dream'.[57] In his posthumously published 'postscript' to the second edition of *The Concept of Law*,[58] Hart sketches his defence against Dworkin. In particular, Hart rejects the charge that his theory is prey to the semantic sting. He responds to this allegation by denying that he ever held 'the mistaken idea that if the criteria for the identification of the grounds of law were not uncontroversially fixed, "law" would *mean* different things to different people'.[59] Nor does he accept that Dworkin's criticism that his theory precludes a non-participant, external observer from describing how participants experience the law from an internal point of view.

This internal standpoint, Hart now appears to accept, includes a belief that there may be *moral* reasons for conforming to the law, and a *moral* justification for coercion.[60]

---

[54] Dworkin, op cit, 423.

[55] For a lively, if iconoclastic, critique of the main elements of the Dworkinian enterprise, see Allan C Hutchinson, 'Indiana Dworkin and Law's Empire' (1987) 96 *Yale Law Journal* 637. I have already mentioned that you should see the essays (and Dworkin's characteristically trenchant response to his critics) in Scott Hershowitz (ed), *Exploring Law's Empire: The Jurisprudence of Ronald Dworkin*.

[56] Scott J Shapiro, *Legality* (Cambridge, Mass, and London: Belknap Press of Harvard University Press, 2011).

[57] HLA Hart, 'American Jurisprudence through English Eyes: The Nightmare and the Noble Dream' in *Essays in Jurisprudence and Philosophy* (Oxford: Clarendon Press, 1983), 123.

[58] HLA Hart, *The Concept of Law*, 2nd edn (Oxford: Clarendon Press, 1994). See the essays collected in Jules Coleman (ed), *Hart's Postscript: Essays on the Postscript to* The Concept of Law (Oxford: Oxford University Press, 2001).

[59] *The Concept of Law*, 2nd edn, 246.          [60] Ibid, 243.

More significantly, Hart is now willing to acknowledge that the rule of recognition 'may incorporate as criteria of legal validity conformity with moral principles or substantive values'.[61] This concession situates Hart, posthumously, in the soft positivist camp.[62]

Other critics have attacked Dworkin's model in three main ways:

(a) *Rules may incorporate principles.* Some critics (notably MacCormick and Sartorius) have sought to rescue Hart's model of rules by arguing that principles interact with rules, underpinning and qualifying them. Sartorius (while otherwise adopting Dworkin's view in this respect) argues that by 'loosening up a bit', Hart's rule of recognition, to take account of 'general results', it would provide an authoritative standard by which to identify principles as well as rules.[63]

(b) *Principles are not 'principles'.* Raz upbraids Dworkin for his failure to distinguish between statements 'of law' and statements 'about the law'. He claims that when we refer generally to a body of legal rules without specifying their detailed content, these are normally statements of principle, rather than statements of 'principle' in the Dworkinian sense. For example, if I state that the law recognizes freedom of speech, I mean that, apart from the limitations on expression contained in the law of libel, laws protecting national security, controlling obscenity, prohibiting breach of confidence, and so on, the law allows a high degree of freedom. This statement is a summary reference to a whole range of laws, not a statement of the content of a single law. You, on the other hand, might describe the position by referring to a specific law that requires the courts to protect freedom of speech in all cases, including those not governed by specific rules. Your statement, says Raz, *is* a statement of the content of one particular law and *is* a 'principle' in the Dworkinian sense, for it imposes an obligation and guides the actions of courts.[64] If this is correct, it undermines Dworkin's thesis that judges decide hard cases by reference to 'principles' in his sense of the term.

(c) *Judges do have a discretion.* Dworkin acknowledges that judges have a 'weak' discretion (their decision determines the outcome of a hard case and they have to apply their judgment). But a number of critics reject the idea that judges lack a

---

[61] Ibid, 250.

[62] See Brian Leiter, 'Legal Realism, Hard Positivism, and the Limits of Conceptual Analysis' in Coleman (ed), *Hart's Postscript: Essays on the Postscript to* The Concept of Law, 355. Kramer argues (convincingly, I think) that Hart's 'wholesale capitulation' was unwise. See Matthew H Kramer, 'Coming to Grips with the Law' (1999) 5 *Legal Theory* 171, 192. See too Kramer, *In Defence of Legal Positivism: Law Without Trimmings* (Oxford: University Press, 1999) 153–61. In particular, Kramer seeks to establish that Dworkin is unable to establish (as he did in *Law's Empire*) that soft positivism, by virtue of accepting that many legal norms may be identified by reference to a moral test, embraces 'moral realism'. (See 2.9 on this theory.) For Dworkin's analysis of objective morality, see R Dworkin, 'Objectivity and Truth: You'd Better Believe It' (1996) 25 *Philosophy and Public Affairs* 87.                    [63] *Individual Conduct and Social Norms*, 192.

[64] J Raz, 'Legal Principles and the Limits of Law' (1972) 81 *Yale Law Journal* 823, 828.

'strong' discretion in the sense of having a *choice* between a decision X and decision Y. Some point to the ambiguity of the very concept of discretion,[65] while others (like Professor Hart) adopt the 'unexciting' middle ground that sometimes judges do and sometimes they don't exercise a discretion. Joseph Raz has even suggested that Dworkin's views do not significantly differ from Hart's.[66] Moreover, Raz argues that Dworkin has misstated the distinction between rules and principles.[67] Raz expounds his own analysis of legal principles, concluding that, far from excluding judicial discretion, as Dworkin claims, they presume its existence and direct it.

(d) *Judges* do *rely on policy*. Several critics (notably Professor Greenawalt) deny Dworkin's claim that judges characteristically decide hard cases on grounds of principle rather than policy. The strongest plank of this argument is the proposition that judges give weight to the interests of third parties (ie, persons who are not parties to the litigation in issue) in hard cases. For instance, Greenawalt argues that certain conduct might be legally justified because the contrary conduct would have violated or risked damage to the established legal rights of non-parties. Thus, the driver of a car who swerves to avoid a baby may argue that if he had not swerved he would have violated the baby's right. On the other hand, it might be argued that certain conduct was *unjustified* because it violated, or risked damage to, the rights of third parties.[68] This argument also raises doubts about Dworkin's distinction between arguments of principle and arguments of policy.

(e) *There is no 'community morality'*. Several critics have questioned Dworkin's assumption that there is, within every legal community, a morality that breathes life into the law. Others have questioned Dworkin's very notion of 'community'. It has fallen prey to a communitarian (see 10.3.1) attack on the ground that, instead of providing fraternity, community produces a sense of 'self identity'.[69] The tolerance that Dworkin prescribes for a community, Michael Sandel appears to believe, would destroy the homogeneity necessary to engender this sense of self-identity. Dworkin rejects this view, but other doubts remain about his nebulous notion of community that seems better suited to describe friendship than society that is, in the last resort, based on coercion. As Michael Freeman asks:

> [I]s Dworkin committed to the view that a state which has to enforce its will upon recalcitrant citizens is not a 'true' community? It would seem that a state which had to enforce laws by means of coercion was undercutting its own foundation which rests

---

[65] See B Hoffmaster, 'Understanding Judicial Discretion' (1982) 1 *Law and Philosophy* 21.

[66] See J Raz, 'Dworkin: A New Link in the Chain' (1986) 74 *California Law Review* 1103, 1115.

[67] J Raz, 'Legal Principles and the Limits of Law' (1972) 81 *Yale Law Journal* 823.

[68] 'Policy, Rights, and Judicial Decision' in M Cohen (ed), *Ronald Dworkin and Contemporary Jurisprudence* (London: Duckworth, 1984) 88–118, at 97.

[69] Michael Sandel, *Liberalism and the Limits of Justice*, 2nd edn (Cambridge: Cambridge University Press, 1998).

on a relationship where there is obligation. But this is to assume that Dworkin has adequately accounted for associative obligations within groups such as family and friends. Do these really rest on reciprocity? Is this how members of a family or friends conceive of obligation? Can love or altruism be reduced to reciprocal obligation? Surely not. And surely there are associative obligations where reciprocity is never in question? Can Dworkin explain the bonds which unite the Irish (think of St Patrick's Day parades in continents far from Ireland...)?[70]

Do you think it is possible for you to support your political community in the way you support your football team?

(f) *He misconstrues the rule of recognition.* For Dworkin, of course, Hart's rule of recognition cannot include substantive moral standards among its criteria of law. This has been vigorously denied, as we have seen, by so-called soft positivists,[71] and even by Hart himself. Kramer identifies another failure by Dworkin in respect of the rule of recognition. He charges him with misunderstanding the essential nature and purpose of Hart's rule of recognition. This arises mainly through Dworkin's error in overlooking the fact that, in both hard and easy cases, judges share a high degree of common understanding about the criteria that determine whether a rule is indeed a legal rule. In other words, in attacking the rule of recognition for neglecting the interpretative divergences that exist between judges, such discrepancies 'cannot go beyond the point where they would bring about substantial indeterminacy and erraticism in the law at the level of concrete results'.[72]

## 2. The law

It is sometimes claimed that Dworkin confuses or conflates 'law' with 'the law'. The criticism alleges, in effect, that he does not adequately distinguish between the theoretical account of the concept of law, on the one hand, and the workings of specific legal systems on the other. As Kramer puts it:

> Dworkin swerves back and forth between speaking about *law* and speaking about *the law*; that is, he equivocates between speaking about a general type of institution and speaking about one instance of that general type.[73]

This, Kramer asserts, is especially problematic because it is used to distance his theory (concerned with 'the law') from positivist theories (concerned with 'law').

## 3. The rights thesis

Dworkin's argument that utilitarianism does not take rights sufficiently seriously is denied by some critics who accuse Dworkin himself of working 'in the shadow

---

[70] MDA Freeman (ed), *Lloyd's Introduction to Jurisprudence*, 8th edn (London: Sweet & Maxwell, 2008), 732.

[71] See, in particular, WJ Waluchow, *Inclusive Legal Positivism* (Oxford: Clarendon Press, 1994).

[72] Kramer, *In Defence of Legal Positivism: Law Without Trimmings*, 144.      [73] Ibid, 129.

of utilitarianism'.[74] In particular, Hart argues that it does not follow (as Dworkin claims) that if X's liberty is curtailed, this shows that he is not being treated as an equal. For Dworkin counting 'external preferences' is a form of double counting (see 10.2.1), a view rejected by Hart and others who are sympathetic to utilitarian versions of justice.

### 4. A 'hard case' is inadequately defined

Dworkin describes a hard case (*inter alia*) as one in which lawyers would disagree about rights, where no settled rule disposes of the case, where the rules are subject to competing interpretations. Some critics have complained that this fails to distinguish sufficiently a hard case from an easy one. The strong version of this argument suggests that Dworkin 'is committed to the view that all cases are "hard cases"'.[75] This startling conclusion is arrived at by identifying Dworkin's allegedly circular reasoning that claims:

- In order to discover which cases are 'hard', Hercules must apply the principles recommended by the 'soundest theory'.

- A 'hard case' is one in which principled (as opposed to syllogistic) reasoning is employed.

- Principled reasoning must therefore be used to identify those cases which are 'hard cases'.

- Thus Hercules is committed to the view that all cases are 'hard cases'.

### 5. Hercules is objectionable

I mentioned earlier that critics have had difficulty in accepting the omniscient Hercules J. Four major objections have been voiced:

(a) *He is a politician.* Some critics charge Hercules with substituting his own political judgment for the politically neutral, correct interpretation of previous decisions.[76]

(b) *He is a fraud.* He *thinks* he has discovered the answer to a hard case, but he is fraudulently offering *his* judgment as the judgment of the law.

(c) *He is a tyrant.* He arrogantly assumes his conception of the law is correct, though he cannot *prove* his opinion is better than that of those who disagree.

(d) *He is a myth.* No real judges can behave in this Utopian style.

Each of these charges against Hercules is adroitly deflected by Dworkin.[77]

---

[74] HLA Hart, 'Between Utility and Rights' in *Essays in Jurisprudence and Philosophy*, 198 at 222.

[75] AC Hutchinson and JN Wakefield, 'A Hard Look at Hard Cases' (1982) 2 *Oxford Journal of Legal Studies* 86, 100.

[76] Scott Shapiro argues that Hercules is being instructed to open up and unsettle the very moral issues that it was the point of having a constitution (a constitutional plan) to settle, Scott J Shapiro, *Legality* (Cambridge Mass, and London: Belknap Press of Harvard University Press, 2011), 311.

[77] See *Law's Empire*, 258–66, 397–9.

### 6. The theory travels badly

A number of commentators point to an important weakness of Dworkin's model of law. It seems to be grounded in a liberal democratic (read American) view of society, and therefore runs into a number of difficulties when it is applied to other kinds of communities, especially 'unjust societies'. It is not easy to apprehend how the theory might work in an unjust or even an undemocratic society. Dworkin argues, as we have seen, from and for a liberal democratic perspective. How well would the theory travel to a fundamentally iniquitous society in which the rights which Hercules would be seeking do *not* figure as part of the law? How, for instance, might Hercules have performed in apartheid South Africa? Dworkin suggests that in a 'wicked society' (and he has in mind Nazi Germany and apartheid South Africa) Hercules may have no choice but to *lie*. If he is to give effect to 'law as integrity', Dworkin seems to be saying, how can Hercules reach a decision which is its very antithesis? But this is a complex matter which raises a number of difficulties.

To test the Dworkin model in an unjust society such as apartheid South Africa, is bedevilled by at least three problems. First, Dworkin's theory is primarily an argument from democracy; his concern to eliminate strong judicial discretion is premised on the offensiveness of judges—unelected officials unanswerable to the electorate—wielding legislative or quasi-legislative power. This argument has an embarrassingly hollow ring in apartheid South Africa. The imposition of law upon a disfranchised majority who can change neither the law nor the lawmaker renders any misgivings about the untrammelled power (real or putative) of an unelected judiciary fairly trivial.

Secondly, in reaching his decision in a hard case, Hercules J is expected to find the uniquely correct answer by reference to the 'community's morality' and thereby to give effect to individual rights. Such an approach in apartheid South Africa would be more likely to be destructive of rights than to be protective of them.

Thirdly, Dworkin argues that judicial decisions in civil cases characteristically are (and ought to be) generated by principle rather than policy. The judge, since he does not legislate, may not legitimately have recourse to policy considerations. It would plainly be folly to suggest that judges do not take account, explicitly or implicitly, of policy. But when they do, Dworkin asks us to read such appeals to policy as, in effect, statements about rights, that is, references to principles. This 'substitutability' of arguments of principle and arguments of policy is a further dimension of Dworkin's justification of adjudication by unelected officials—a preoccupation more genuinely held in an elective democracy. There was, nevertheless, an undeniable proclivity amongst South African judges to invoke, for example, what may broadly be called 'apartheid' or 'separate development', in order to justify a decision in a hard case dealing with race laws. Apartheid, on Dworkin's account, is manifestly a 'policy' (though he does, on occasion, suggest that policies advance 'some overall benefit for the community as a whole', a description hardly apposite here), but we are to understand such references as an appeal to the competing rights of the parties to the dispute (ie a reference to 'principles').

But yet again the assumptions about an essentially just legal system intrude. For Dworkin, as we have seen, legal principles 'must be moral principles'.[78] He is, however, by no means clear about this, referring occasionally to principles which are 'morally defective',[79] 'unattractive',[80] 'very nasty',[81] and recognizing that there 'is no persuasive analysis...that insures that the principle that blacks are less worthy of concern than whites can be rejected as not a principle at all'.[82] But his conclusions in respect of the position of a judge in a wicked legal system dispel to some extent the uncertainty as to whether the policy of apartheid, and the principles, however unjust, that are deployed in adjudication, do indeed conform to Dworkin's general typology.[83] References, then, by Hercules J to the 'policy' or 'principle' of racial discrimination (or 'national security') are, of course, contrary to Dworkin's expectation, more likely to be destructive of rights than to be protective of them.

(This question has, I think, potentially far-reaching implications, not only for Dworkin's account of law, but for legal theory in general, and was therefore considered in greater detail in 2.11.)

## 7. One right answer

Several critics argue that it is not true that to every legal question there is one right answer. Dworkin's claim in support of the right-answer thesis is a fairly complex one,[84] but you should have a grasp of its main elements. Note that it may be presented in *two* forms. The *first* argues that the surface linguistic behaviour of lawyers is misleading because it suggests that there is no 'logical space' between the proposition 'this is a valid contract', and the counter-proposition that 'this contract is invalid'. It does not, in other words, contemplate that *both* propositions may be false. And they could be: it might be an 'inchoate' contract. Thus the question whether the contract is valid or invalid may have *no* right answer.

The *second* version does not suppose that there is any 'logical space' between the propositions that a contract is valid and that it is invalid. It does not, in other words, suppose that there is any third option. Yet it denies that one of the two possibilities *always* applies—because neither may. Dworkin employs formal logic to express these alternatives. But it is unlikely that you will be expected to be a trained logician. You should, however, be able to show whether Dworkin has refuted the claim that there is no right answer.

---

[78] Dworkin, *TRS*, 343.      [79] Ibid, 339.      [80] Ibid, 342.      [81] Ibid, 341.
[82] Ibid, 343.
[83] But doubts remain. It cannot be denied that Dworkin's orientation is in many respects a distinctly American one, located in the tradition of a Supreme Court vested with considerable 'political' power. The application of the thesis to other legal systems must (despite Dworkin's confidence) be treated with caution.
[84] 'Is There Really No Right Answer in Hard Cases?' in *A Matter of Principle*, 119.

## 8. Law and literature

Dworkin's depiction of law as an interpretive concept has been attacked by a number of critics.[85] Stanley Fish argues that interpretation is a 'social construct': the meaning of a text of both law and literature is a function of 'interpretive communities'.[86] Fish denies that there can be 'theory' unconnected to a *particular* field of activity, but sufficiently general to be thought of as a constraint on (and explanation of) *all* fields of activity. There cannot be, says Fish, a theorist who is able to survey the world dispassionately. We are all trapped within our own belief systems. The most we can do is express our individual rhetorical positions and, perhaps, persuade others of their force. But is it the case that statements about law are true because an 'interpretive community' of lawyers agree about justice? As JW Harris puts it:

> 'Justice' is not something about which there is a simple consensus among lawyers or anyone else, in the way that you can find common agreement about the type to which a piece of writing belongs. On the other hand, all lawyers suppose that, among other things, the canonical meaning of legal materials enters into the grounds of true legal propositions. Income tax rates are whatever they are, not because of an interpretive community which is convinced that such and such is the just rate, but because (justly or otherwise) the legislature has so laid it down.[87]

Needless to say, Dworkin rejects Fish's assault. He does not deny that interpretation is socially constructed, but he argues that interpretation that seeks to 'fit' the existing materials limit one's view of their substantive meaning. In other words, there are two kinds of interpretation: 'convictions about integrity' (which relate to 'fit'), and convictions about 'artistic merit' (which relate to the dimensions of value). While these two interact, they are 'sufficiently insulated to give friction and therefore sense to anyone's interpretive analysis'.[88]

Dworkin responds to Fish also by distinguishing between internal and external scepticism. The former is a scepticism from *within* the enterprise of interpretation. The latter is scepticism *outside* and *about* that enterprise. Dworkin gives the example of a claim made that *Hamlet* is best understood as a play about 'obliquity, doubling, and delay'. An 'internal' sceptic might retort, 'You are wrong. *Hamlet* is too confused and jumbled to be about anything at all.' An 'external' sceptic might reply, 'I agree with you; I too think this is the most illuminating reading of the play. Of course, that is only an opinion we share; we cannot sensibly suppose that *Hamlet*'s being about delay is an objective fact we have discovered locked up in the nature of reality, "out there" in some

---

[85] See eg AD Woozley, 'No Right Answer' in Cohen, *Ronald Dworkin and Contemporary Jurisprudence*, 173–81. See too Stanley Fish, 'Working on the Chain Gang: Interpretation in Law and Literature' (1982) 60 *Texas Law Review* 551 and 'Wrong Again' (1983) 62 *Texas Law Review* 299.

[86] Stanley Fish, *Doing What Comes Naturally: Rhetoric and the Practice of Theory in Literary and Legal Studies* (Durham, NJ: Duke University Press, reprint 1990), 14.

[87] JW Harris, *Legal Philosophies*, 2nd edn (London: Butterworths, 1997), 194–5.

[88] Dworkin, *A Matter of Principle*, 171. Marmor argues that 'Fish's sceptical conclusions are inescapable', Andrei Marmor, *Interpretation and Legal Theory* (Oxford: Clarendon Press, 1992), 84.

transcendental metaphysical world where the meanings of plays subsist.'[89] This nicely encapsulates the polarity. The internal sceptic relies on the soundness of a general interpretive attitude to call into question all possible interpretations of a particular object of interpretation. He assumes that his general view is correct. The external scep-tic, on the other hand, does not challenge any particular moral or interpretive claim. He does not say that it is wrong to describe *Hamlet* as about delay; he claims instead that this account cannot be objectively proved. His scepticism is 'external' because it leaves the actual conduct of interpretation undisturbed. And, Dworkin concludes, such scepticism is irrelevant: 'The only scepticism worth anything is scepticism of the internal kind.'[90]

This fails to satisfy Marmor, for whom it is inconsistent with Dworkin's holistic theory of interpretation.[91]

## 9. Integrity and 'fit'

The consensual model of society implicit in the ideal that '. . . we should try to conceive our political community as an association of principle'[92] is likely to draw the fire of those who adopt a conflict model of society or who conceive the rule of law as an elaborate trick to conceal the oppressive nature of 'liberal' society (see 7.6). Nor does it appeal to those crit-ics who reject the interpretive enterprise as naive, Utopian, or simply wrong. Some regard it as a poor explanation for political obligation.[93]

Andrei Marmor launches a wholesale onslaught against Dworkin's 'interpretive' pro-ject, which includes an attack on law as integrity. In interpreting the legal materials, the judge, according to Dworkin, is guided by basic evaluative judgments like 'integrity'. But the value of integrity is rendered futile in the absence of an assumption that legal texts somehow *constrain* the meanings available. Otherwise Hercules could simply make it all up. As Marmor declares:

> This gives rise to the crucial question, can we distinguish between interpretation and invention? Are people justified in holding a 'right–wrong' picture of interpretation, and assuming that it makes sense to speak about 'the correct interpretation' of a given text? In other words, what is Dworkin's answer to the charge that 'anything goes' in interpretation?[94]

His answer is, of course, that it does not—because there is a body of legal doctrine (pre-cedents, statutes, etc) that restricts the choice of interpretations available to the judge. But this does not placate Marmor, who contends that the two methods adopted by the judge—'fit' and moral evaluation—are almost indistinguishable. How can Hercules separate the exercise of 'fit' from his moral and political values?

---

[89] *Law's Empire*, 78.
[90] Ibid, 86. 'External scepticism should disappear from the philosophical landscape. We should not regret its disappearance. We have enough to worry about without it,' Dworkin, *Justice for Hedgehogs*, 68.
[91] Marmor, *Interpretation and Legal Theory*, 81.          [92] *Law's Empire*, 411.
[93] See P Soper, 'Dworkin's Domain' (1987) 100 *Harvard Law Review* 1166, 1183.
[94] Marmor, *Interpretation and Legal Theory*, 70. See too NE Simmonds, 'Imperial Visions and Mundane Practices' (1987) 46 *Cambridge Law Journal* 465.

And even if he can, how is he to weigh one against the other? These values are impossible to quantify, they are 'incommensurable'. Hercules cannot simply place two incommensurable criteria on the scales, and hope that one weighs more than the other. As Finnis says:

> Two incommensurable criteria of judgment are proposed in Dworkin's theory, 'fit' (with past political decisions) and 'justifiability' (inherent substantive moral soundness). A hard case is hard (not merely novel) when not only is there more than one answer which violates no applicable rule, but the answers thus available are ranked in different orders along each of the available criteria of evaluation: brevity, humour, Englishness, fit (integrity), romance, inherent 'quality', profundity, inherent 'justifiability' and so forth.[95]

To this criticism, Dworkin's rejoinder is that in most cases the right answer to a hard case can be found through this process of evaluative choice, to which the incommensurability argument is inapplicable.

### 10. A 'semantic' theory?

You will recall that central to Dworkin's assault on legal positivism (or 'conventionalism') is the semantic sting. But if legal positivism is indeed preoccupied with semantic squabbles about the meaning of 'law' it would, Marmor points out, lead to 'an embarrassing dilemma':

> If lawyers and judges share semantic rules which determine the meaning of law, any further theoretical argument over what the law is would not make much sense. It would boil down to two alternatives. One would be to admit to facing a semantically borderline example in which case the argument would become rather silly (like one over whether a large pamphlet is a book or not). The other would be to concede that, contrary to the rhetoric, the argument was not really about what the law is, but about whether to follow the law or change it.[96]

In other words, Marmor argues, theoretical disagreements are either silly, or a sort of pretence. Since we would not wish to insult judges with silliness, we appear to be left with a pretence: disagreements about the conditions of legal validity are camouflaged arguments over what the law should be, how it is to be changed, and so on. But if this is the case, why should we not simply take legal rhetoric at face value? Why is the pretence necessary?

Marmor's main point, however, is that Hart's is not a semantic theory at all. Hart insists that 'law' has several possible meanings, and expressly eschewed verbal wrangles of this kind.[97]

There are countless other attacks on the Dworkinian citadel. And Dworkin defends his theory, with his characteristic dexterity, against most of them. For some stimulating exemplars of his proficiency in combat, see his 'Reply to Critics' in *Taking Rights*

---

[95] JM Finnis, 'On Reason and Authority in *Law's Empire*' (1987) 6 *Law and Philosophy* 357, 372.
[96] Marmor, *Interpretation and Legal Theory*, 6.
[97] Ibid, 6–7. See too Soper, 'Dworkin's Domain', 1171–6.

*Seriously,* 'A Reply by Ronald Dworkin' in Marshall Cohen (ed), *Ronald Dworkin and Contemporary Jurisprudence,* and his responses in Scott Hershovitz (ed), *Exploring Law's Empire: The Jurisprudence of Ronald Dworkin.* And he is doubtless prepared to defend his theory against the growing band of adversaries at the gate. You will, of course, have your own appraisal to add to the list.

## Questions

1. Is Dworkin's distinction between policies and principles a satisfactory one?

2. Does Dworkin adequately define a 'hard case'? Is his attack on the 'model of rules' convincing?

3. Does his description of 'rules' oversimplify their nature and function?

4. What are the main distinctions between rules and other standards?

5. How convincing is Dworkin's argument that judges discover the 'community's morality' by reasoning in terms of rights? What consequences might such an approach have in a 'wicked legal system'?

6. Does Dworkin really differ with the positivists?

7. Could Hercules J really exist? Why should we assume that his answer to the question about the contested concept of law should incorporate the rights thesis?

8. According to Dworkin, 'law as integrity' secures 'a kind of equality among citizens that makes their community more genuine and improves its moral justification for exercising the political power it does…' (*Law's Empire,* 95)

   Analyse this claim.

9. Is law really like literature?

10. Are you persuaded by Dworkin's argument that positivism falls prey to the 'semantic sting'?

11. What might a feminist legal theorist make of Dworkin's theory of equality?

12. 'The moment now seems opportune to step back and ask whether the Hart/Dworkin debate deserves to play the same organizing role in the jurisprudential curriculum of the twenty-first century that it played at the close of the twentieth. I am inclined to answer that question in the negative, though not, to be sure, because I can envision a jurisprudential future without Hart's masterful work at its center. Rather, it seems to me—and, I venture, many others by now—that on the particulars of the Hart/Dworkin debate, there has been a clear victor, so much so that even the heuristic value of the Dworkinian criticisms of Hart may now be in doubt.' (Brian Leiter, 'Beyond the Hart–Dworkin Debate' (2003) 48 *American Journal of Jurisprudence* 17, 18)

   Do you agree? Is Hart really the victor?

13.  Why is *Justice for Hedgehogs* so titled?

14.  'Legal philosophers argue...about an ancient philosophical puzzle of almost no practical importance that has nevertheless had a prominent place in seminars on legal theory: the puzzle of evil law.' (Ronald Dworkin, *Justice for Hedgehogs*, 410)

     Do you agree that this subject is 'of almost no practical importance'? See 2.11.

15.  In what ways is Dworkin's thesis in *Justice for Hedgehogs* consistent with his interpretivist argument in *Taking Rights Seriously*?

## Further reading

COHEN, MARSHALL (ed), *Ronald Dworkin and Contemporary Jurisprudence* (London: Duckworth, 1984).

DWORKIN, RONALD, *Taking Rights Seriously*, new impression with a reply to critics (London: Duckworth, 1978).

DWORKIN, RONALD, *A Matter of Principle* (Cambridge, Mass and London: Harvard University Press, 1985).

DWORKIN, RONALD, *Law's Empire* (Cambridge, Mass and London: Belknap Press, 1986).

DWORKIN, RONALD, *Life's Dominion: An Argument about Abortion and Euthanasia* (London: HarperCollins, 1993).

DWORKIN, RONALD, 'Hart's Postscript and the Character of Political Philosophy' (2004) 24 *Oxford Journal of Legal Studies* 1.

DWORKIN, RONALD, *Justice in Robes* (Cambridge, Mass and London: Harvard University Press, 2006).

DWORKIN, RONALD, *Justice for Hedgehogs* (Cambridge, Mass and London: Harvard University Press, 2011).

FISH, STANLEY, 'Working on the Chain Gang: Interpretation in Law and Literature' (1982) 60 *Texas Law Review* 551.

FISH, STANLEY, 'Wrong Again' (1983) 62 *Texas Law Review* 299.

GUEST, STEPHEN, *Ronald Dworkin*, 3rd edn (Stanford: Stanford Law and Politics, 2012).

HART, HLA, 'American Jurisprudence through English Eyes: The Nightmare and the Noble Dream' in *Essays in Jurisprudence and Philosophy* (Oxford: Clarendon Press, 1983).

HERSHOWITZ, SCOTT (ed), *Exploring Law's Empire: The Jurisprudence of Ronald Dworkin* (Oxford: Oxford University Press, 2006).

HUNT, ALAN (ed), *Reading Dworkin Critically* (New York and Oxford: Berg, 1992).

HUTCHINSON, AC and WAKEFIELD, JN, 'A Hard Look at Hard Cases' (1982) 2 *Oxford Journal of Legal Studies* 86.

KRAMER, MATTHEW H, 'Coming to Grips with the Law' (1999) 5 *Legal Theory* 171.

KRAMER, MATTHEW H, '*In Defense of Legal Positivism: Law Without Trimmings* (Oxford: Oxford University Press, 1999).

MARMOR, ANDREI, *Interpretation and Legal Theory* (Oxford: Clarendon Press, 1992).

RAZ, J, 'Dworkin: A New Link in the Chain' (1986) 74 *California Law Review* 1103.

RIPSTEIN, ARTHUR (ed), *Ronald Dworkin* (Cambridge: Cambridge University Press, 2007).

SOPER, P, 'Dworkin's Domain' (1987) 100 *Harvard Law Review* 1166.

WALUCHOW, WJ, *Inclusive Legal Positivism* (Oxford: Clarendon Press, 1994).

# 6

# Legal realism

Those who declare allegiance to the banner of legal realism might just as easily be called sceptics (and they sometimes are) or even cynics. Indeed, many students—especially after their gruelling journey through legal positivism—find that they are in good company. The realists, they are relieved to discover, eschew the ponderous metaphysics which they discern in talk of legal concepts—be they 'commands', 'rules', 'norms', or indeed any construct which has no foundation in 'reality'. If you have been disposed to feel similarly unhappy with the 'formalism' of juristic thinking in the work of Bentham, Austin, Hart, or Kelsen, you may well find succour in the movement which is (rather loosely) described as legal realism.

## 6.1 What are realists realistic about?

It is at once apparent that though they are both 'realists' in a general sense, there are important differences (which will be returned to) between the American and the Scandinavian realists. Indeed, some go so far as to suggest that any similarity is a purely verbal one.

Broadly speaking, three related distinctions may be identified. First, while the Americans are, in general, pragmatist and behaviourist, emphasizing 'law in action' (as opposed to legal conceptualism), the Scandinavians launch a philosophical assault on the metaphysical foundations of law; where the Americans are 'rule-sceptics', they are 'metaphysics-sceptics'. This is sometimes explained by locating American Realism within the tradition of English empiricist philosophy, while the Scandinavians are more closely associated with the European tradition of philosophy. The deeper hostility of the Scandinavians to any conceptual thinking about law, especially natural law, may perhaps be connected either to the absence of any significant Catholic influence in Scandinavia, or, more plausibly, the greater influence of logical positivism in Europe, as compared with the US.

Secondly, the Americans are far more concerned with courts and their operation, while the scope of the Scandinavians' jurisprudence is far broader, embracing the legal system as a whole. The Americans, thirdly, were more empirically minded than the Scandinavians, who, in Lloyd's words 'appear to rely mainly on argument of an *a priori* kind to justify particular legal solutions or developments'.[1]

---

[1] *Lloyd's Introduction to Jurisprudence*, 8th edn (London: Sweet & Maxwell, 2008), 1052.

Yet we may legitimately group the two 'schools' together in one important respect: they both declare war on all absolute values (such as 'justice') and they are both empirical, pragmatic, and, of course, 'realistic'. Nothing captures this approach better than the (oft-repeated) aphorism by one of the leading exponents of American Realism, Oliver Wendell Holmes, which comes at the end of this striking extract from 'The Path of the Law':

> Take the fundamental question, What constitutes the law? You will find some text writers telling you that it is something different from what is decided by the courts of Massachusetts or England, that it is a system of reason, that it is a deduction from principles of ethics or admitted axioms or what not, which may or may not coincide with the decisions. But if we take the view of our friend the bad man we shall find that he does not care two straws for the axioms or deductions, but that he does want to know what the Massachusetts or English courts are likely to do in fact. I am much of his mind. *The prophecies of what the courts will do in fact, and nothing more pretentious, are what I mean by the law.*[2]

'Well said!' many a student is tempted to cry. 'Enough of this metaphysical nonsense! The law is what the courts say it is!' Or, as the Scandinavian realist, Alf Ross, put it, to invoke 'justice' is equivalent to banging on a table: it is an emotional expression which turns one's demand into an absolute postulate. This 'realism', then, is an impatience with theory, a concern with law 'as it is', and a preoccupation with the actual operation of law *in its social context*. Legal realism is suspicious of theories that treat law as a lifeless phenomenon. And yet, realists are—paradoxically—considered to be positivists. Their preoccupation with the law 'as it is' and their almost obsessive pragmatism and empiricism mark them as advocates of what Alan Hunt describes as 'a rather simplistic positivism'.

But, though they accept, along with the positivists, the need for a scientific analysis of law, the realists reject the single avenue of logic and seek to apply the numerous avenues of scientific enquiry, including sociology and psychology. Realism, in Llewellyn's words, 'is not a philosophy—it is a technology'.

## 6.2 American Realism

The jazz age produced its jazz jurisprudence. The turn of the twentieth century saw a dismissal of a good deal of the theories of Austin, Bentham, Mill, and Hume. In their place, the realists sought to put a more sociological account of the 'law in action'. Consider the following arresting extracts from a remarkable article by Felix Cohen:

> Valuable as is the language of transcendental nonsense for many practical legal purposes, it is entirely useless when we come to study, describe, predict, and criticize legal phenomena. And although judges and lawyers need not be legal scientists, it is of some practical importance that they should recognize that the traditional language of argument and opinion neither explains nor justifies court decisions. When the vivid fictions and metaphors of traditional

[2] (1897) 10 *Harvard Law Review* 460–1; emphasis added.

jurisprudence are thought of as reasons for decisions, rather than poetical or mnemonic devices for formulating decisions reached on other grounds, then the author, as well as the reader, of the opinion or argument, is apt to forget the social forces which mold the law and the social ideals by which the law is to be judged…Our legal system is filled with supernatural concepts, that is to say, concepts which cannot be defined in terms of experience, and from which all sorts of empirical decisions are supposed to flow. Against these unverifiable concepts modern jurisprudence presents an ultimatum. Any word that cannot pay up in the currency of fact, upon demand, is to be declared bankrupt, and we are to have no further dealings with it.[3]

This captures the essence of the realist onslaught on 'transcendental' metaphysics. The article (which is written with a lightness of touch, and should be read by all serious students) not only underlines the American realists' impatience with conceptual 'nonsense', but demonstrates the programmatic, educational objectives of the movement.

Few jurisprudence courses devote significant (or even any) time to realism. Where it is taught, the focus tends to be on the approaches of the three leading members of the group: Oliver Wendell Holmes, Karl N Llewellyn, and Jerome Frank. You should be aware not only that, in addition to these three celebrated jurists, there were many *other* important realists, but also know a little about their work. In particular, you should, at the very least, have a passing knowledge of the writing of some of the following (magnificently named) realists: John Chipman Gray (1839–1915), Herman Oliphant (1884–1939), William Underhill Moore (1879–1949), Walter Wheeler Cook (1873–1943), Arthur Linton Corbin (1874–1966), and Wesley Newcomb Hohfeld (1879–1917; see 10.1), all of whom were pioneers of the realist movement. Professor William Twining's *Karl Llewellyn and the Realist Movement*,[4] contains not only an admirable account of its eponymous hero, but also a trenchant analysis of the leading protagonists of the movement itself. It will certainly give you a much rounder picture of the genesis, history, and contribution of the American realists than the general jurisprudence textbooks. Similarly, Neil Duxbury's incisive *Patterns of American Jurisprudence*[5] includes a skilful analysis of the movement which he describes in the following terms:

American legal realism is one of the great paradoxes of modern jurisprudence. No other jurisprudential tendency of the twentieth century has exerted such a powerful influence on legal thinking while remaining so ambiguous, unsettled and undefined.[6]

For a more philosophical, sympathetic, revisionist reading of American Realism, see Brian Leiter's dazzling, if difficult, collection of essays in his *Naturalizing*

---

[3] Felix Cohen, 'Transcendental Nonsense and the Functional Approach' (1935) 35 *Columbia Law Review* 809, 812 and 823.

[4] William Twining, *Karl Llewellyn and the Realist Movement* (London: Weidenfeld & Nicholson, 1973).

[5] (Oxford: Clarendon Press, 1997).

[6] Duxbury, op cit, 65. A good history of the movement may be found in Laura Kalman, *Legal Realism at Yale: 1927–1960* (Chapel Hill, NC: University of North Carolina Press, 1986). See too John Henry Schlegel, 'American Legal Realism and Empirical Social Science: From the Yale Experience' (1979) 28 *Buffalo Law Review* 459.

*Jurisprudence: Essays on American Realism and Naturalism in Legal Philosophy*, especially those in Part I of the book. See note 8 below.

The realists were preoccupied with empirical questions (ie, attempting to identify the sociological and psychological factors influencing judicial decision-making), yet their implicit conceptual loyalties were distinctly positivist. Though they did not reject completely the notion that courts may be constrained by rules, the realists argued that they exercise discretion much more often than is generally supposed. They deny the naturalist and positivist view that judges are influenced mainly by legal rules; realists attach greater significance to political and moral intuitions about the facts of the case. In fact, in the 1930s their irritation with rules led some to stigmatize realism as nihilistic. Its detractors saw in the movement a rejection not only of morality, but even of legal rules, in the adjudication process. Some critics went so far as to brand realists as anti-democratic and totalitarian. This attack, according to Duxbury, rested on a caricature 'which bore little relation to the professional, pedagogic and general sociological concerns which motivated realist legal thought'.[7]

Their 'core claim', according to Leiter, is that judges respond primarily to the stimulus of *facts*. In other words, decisions are reached on the basis of a judicial consideration of what seems fair on the facts of the case, rather than on the basis of the applicable legal rule.[8] To understand this claim, Leiter identifies the following three elements:

- In deciding cases, judges react to the underlying facts of the case—whether or not they are legally significant, ie, whether or not the facts are relevant by virtue of the applicable rules.

- The legal rules and reasons generally have little or no effect, especially in appellate decisions.

- Many of the realists advanced the 'core claim' in the hope of reformulating rules to render them more fact-specific.[9]

The first claim proposes that judicial decisions in indeterminate cases are influenced by the judge's political and moral convictions—not by legal considerations. The second could be said to suggest that the law is indeterminate (along the lines later to be pursued by the Critical Legal Studies movement, see 13.1). It suggests that in most

[7] Duxbury, op cit, 161. This point is further explored in Neil Duxbury, 'The Reinvention of American Legal Realism' (1992) 12 *Legal Studies* 137. For other critiques of the realists' conservatism, see Laura Kalman, *Legal Realism at Yale: 1927–1960*; Grant Gilmore, *The Ages of American Law* (New Haven, Conn: Yale University Press, 1977); Grant Gilmore, 'Legal Realism: Its Cause and Cure' (1961) 70 *Yale Law Journal* 1037. According to Michael Stephen Green, '[r]ather than being the embarrassment that the philosophers have made it out to be, realism is, I believe, a respectable competitor in the jurisprudential marketplace', Michael Stephen Green, 'Legal Realism as Theory of Law' (2005) 46 *William and Mary Law Review* 1915. See too Hanoch Dagan, 'The Realist Conception of Law' (2007) 57 *University of Toronto Law Journal* 607.

[8] Brian Leiter, 'Rethinking Legal Realism: Toward a Naturalized Jurisprudence' in Brian Leiter, *Naturalizing Jurisprudence: Essays on American Realism and Naturalism in Legal Philosophy* (Oxford: Oxford University Press, 2007), 21–2.

[9] Brian Leiter, 'American Legal Realism' in W Edmundson and M Golding (eds), *Blackwell Guide to the Philosophy of Law and Legal Theory* (Oxford: Blackwell, 2003).

appellate decisions, the available legal materials are insufficient logically to produce a unique legal outcome.

Legal realism was, of course, a reaction against formalism, a mode of legal reasoning that assimilates legal reasoning to syllogistic reasoning. The formalist pattern of deductive reasoning takes the following syllogistic form:

1. Legal rule (major premise).
2. Relevant facts (minor premise).
3. Judgment.

Realists consider that formalism understates the power of the judge to make law by representing legal judgments as *entailed* syllogistically by the pertinent rules and facts.[10] If legal decisions are indeed logically implied by propositions that bind judges, it follows that judges lack the legal authority to reach conflicting outcomes.

For present purposes it will suffice to consider briefly the Big Three. This will be followed by a short consideration of the theory and methodology of the movement and its influence. A sensible starting point is Llewellyn's important essay 'Some Realism about Realism'[11] in which he identifies nine 'points of departure' common to the realists. This is a valuable statement (by one of the movement's leading exponents) of its 'manifesto' which may be summarized as follows:

1. The conception of *law in flux*, of moving law, and of judicial creation of law.
2. The conception of law *as a means to social ends*, and not as an end in itself.
3. The conception of *society in flux*—faster than law.
4. The *temporary divorce of 'is' and 'ought' for the purpose of study*.
5. *Distrust of traditional legal rules and concepts* as descriptive of what courts or people actually do.
6. *Distrust of the theory that traditional prescriptive rule formulations are the main factor* in producing court decisions.
7. The belief in grouping cases and legal situations into *narrower categories*.
8. An insistence on evaluating the law in terms of its *effects*.
9. An insistence on *sustained and programmatic attack* on the problems of law.

### 6.2.1 **Oliver Wendell Holmes Jr**

Holmes (1841–1935) was very much the intellectual, and perhaps even the spiritual, father of American Realism. 'The common law,' he famously declared, 'is not a

---

[10] For Horwitz this attack on deductive legal reasoning was the realists' most 'original and lasting contributions to legal thought', M Horwitz, *The Transformation of American Law, 1870–1960* (Oxford: Oxford University Press, 1992), 200.                    [11] (1931) 44 *Harvard Law Review* 1222.

brooding omnipresence in the sky, but the articulate voice of some sovereign or quasi-sovereign that can be identified…'[12] Any analysis of his work (that is not confined to his several provocative and colourful maxims about logic, experience, bad men, and prophecies) must include at least three central elements. First, Holmes, as a Supreme Court Justice, was (not surprisingly) a profound believer in defining the law by reference to what the courts actually said it was. This is especially evident in his famous address, 'The Path of the Law' which he delivered to law students in 1897. He warned them to distinguish clearly between law and morality: consider what the law is, not what it ought to be (shades of legal positivism).

Secondly, in developing this view, he introduces the device of the 'bad man' (see 6.1): 'If you want to know the law and nothing else, you must look at it as a bad man, who cares only for the material consequences which such knowledge enables him to predict.'[13] Thirdly, Holmes firmly believed that legal developments could be scientifically justified: the 'true science of law', he argued, 'consists in the establishment of its postulates from within upon accurately measured social desires instead of tradition.'[14] For him history was less important than economics.

### 6.2.2 **Karl Llewellyn**

Karl Nickerson Llewellyn (1893–1962) was an extraordinary individual (he was an accomplished poet, pugilist, and linguist). His contribution to American Realism was formidable. Consult Twining's book for a careful and sympathetic portrait, but if this is, as Holmes described the study of Roman law, 'high among the unrealities', you should, at the very least, read the extracts from Llewellyn's writing in Twining's book. See too 8.2.1.2.

The most significant aspect of Llewellyn's contribution to realism is his *functionalism*. This approach, which runs through his major works, *The Bramble Bush*,[15] *The Cheyenne Way*,[16] and *The Common Law Tradition*[17] at its simplest, perceives law as serving certain fundamental functions: 'law-jobs'. We should, he argues, regard law as an engine 'having purposes, not values in itself'.[18] If society is to survive, certain basic needs must be satisfied; this engenders conflict which must be resolved. Six 'law-jobs' are identified:

---

[12] *Southern Pacific Co v Jensen* 244 US 205 (1917) at 222 (dissenting).
[13] *Collected Legal Papers*, 171, quoted by Twining, *Karl Llewellyn and the Realist Movement*, 17. His pragmatic and progressive ideas coalesce in some of his famous dissents such as *Lochner v New York* 198 US 45 (1905).                                     [14] *Collected Legal Papers* (London: Constable & Co, 1920), 225–6.
[15] Karl N Llewellyn, *The Bramble Bush* (New York: Oceana: 1930). See too Karl N Llewellyn, *Jurisprudence: Realism in Theory and Practice* (Chicago, Ill and London: University of Chicago Press, 1962).
[16] Karl N Llewellyn and E Hoebel, *The Cheyenne Way: Conflict and Case Law in Primitive Jurisprudence* (Norman, Okla: University of Oklahoma Press, 1941) (*The Civilization of the American Indian Series*, Vol 21).
[17] Karl N Llewellyn, *The Common Law Tradition: Deciding Appeals* (Boston, Mass: Little, Brown & Co, 1960).                    [18] 'A Realistic Jurisprudence—The Next Step' (1930) *Columbia Law Review* 431.

1. Adjustment of trouble cases.

2. Preventive channelling of conduct and expectations.

3. Preventive rechannelling of conduct and expectations to adjust to change.

4. Allocation of authority and determination of procedures for authoritative decision-making.

5. Provision of direction and incentive within the group.

6. 'The job of the juristic method'.

The focal concept of this functionalist account of law is the 'institution' of law which performs various jobs: an institution is, for Llewellyn, an organized activity built around the doing of a job or cluster of jobs. And the most important job the law has is the disposition of trouble cases. As he puts it in *The Bramble Bush*:[19]

> This doing of something about disputes, this doing of it reasonably, is the business of law. And the people who have the doing in charge, whether they be judges or sheriffs or clerks or jailers or lawyers, are officials of the law. *What these officials do about disputes is, to my mind, the law itself.*

Though he was later to revise this radical assertion, it captures his preoccupation with law as a 'technology' rather than a 'philosophy'.

In addition to *major* institutions (which are concerned with *fundamental* jobs or job clusters upon which the existence of society depends), there are also *minor* institutions such as *crafts*. These consist of the skills that are held by a body of specialists; the practice of the law is a craft. In *The Common Law Tradition* he applies the concept of a craft to the juristic method of the common law. From your study of Llewellyn's work you will be familiar with his famous distinction between the grand style and the formal style of judicial opinions. The former is 'the style of reason' which is informed by 'policy' considerations, while the latter is logical and formal and seeks refuge in rules of law. He, needless to say, prefers the grand style and the 'situation sense' which is its hallmark. It is not part of his argument that either of these styles is to be found in pure form at any point in history. Instead, he paints a picture in which there is an oscillation between the two.

Thus, in the early part of the nineteenth century, when American law was at its creative height, the grand style was employed. From the middle of the nineteenth century, however, Llewellyn detects a shift toward the formal style. In the middle of the twentieth century, Llewellyn finds evidence of a swing back to the grand style, a development he applauds as 'the best device ever invented by man for drying up that free-flowing spring of uncertainty, conflict between the seeming commands of the authorities and the felt demands of justice'.[20]

Llewellyn's work has attracted criticism from a variety of standpoints. Thus, by insisting on the universality of his 'law-jobs', Hunt argues that he 'stumbles into a major theoretical deficiency of functionalism of imposing on disparate phenomena,

---

[19] At 3.    [20] *The Common Law Tradition*, 37–8.

from different societies and different historical periods, an a priori unity'.[21] And even Twining concedes that the grand style/formal style dichotomy has its drawback for 'it may be as dangerous and misleading to pigeon-hole judges or courts into styles as it is to lump jurists into schools'.[22] What are we to understand by 'situation sense', which is the pot of gold at the end of the grand style of judicial reasoning? Note that Llewellyn does not suggest (contrary to Ronald Dworkin: see 5.2.3) that there is 'one right answer' to every legal question. Indeed, he devotes a large section of *The Common Law Tradition*[23] to rejecting this idea. The subject is not without difficulty and his concept has been widely misunderstood.[24] According to Llewellyn, the result of a case is to be judged by reference to whether it is 'something which can be hoped, or thought, to look reasonable to any thinking man'.[25] There is an element of vagueness and specula- tion in Llewellyn's analysis here. Or at least that is what it seems to one reader. You will have your own views.

### 6.2.3 Jerome Frank

Frank (1889–1957) was the most 'radical' of the American realists. He is gener- ally associated with the distinction he drew—first in *Law and the Modern Mind*[26] (1930: the same year as Llewellyn's *The Bramble Bush*), but developed in later works such as *Courts on Trial*)[27]—between 'rule-sceptics' (who include Llewellyn, and who were afflicted with 'appellate court-itis') and 'fact-sceptics' (among whom he counted himself), who were concerned to uncover the unconscious forces that affect the discovery and interpretation of the *facts* of the case. For Frank, most real- ists, in their preoccupation with appellate courts, missed the important aspect of unpredictability in the judicial process: the elusiveness of *facts*. Thus the various prejudices of judges and jurors ('for example, plus or minus reactions to women, or unmarried women, or red-haired women, or brunettes, or men with deep voices, or fidgety men, or men who wear thick eyeglasses, or those who have pronounced ges- tures or nervous tics'[28]) often crucially affect the outcome of a case. The main thrust of Frank's attack was directed against the idea that certainty could be achieved through legal rules. This, in his view, was absurd. If it were so, he argued, why would anyone bother to litigate? Even where there is an applicable rule, one of two opposite conclusions is possible.

To illustrate the point he gives the example of the division that existed among members of the United States Supreme Court in 1917 concerning the validity of a particular statute. In 1923 the court, by a majority, ruled that the statute was invalid. But between these two dates the membership of the court had changed several

---

[21] *The Sociological Movement in Law* (London: Macmillan, 1978), 50.
[22] *Karl Llewellyn and the Realist Movement*, 212.      [23] At 226–32.
[24] See Twining, *Karl Llewellyn and the Realist Movement*, 216–29.
[25] *The Common Law Tradition*, 277.
[26] Jerome Frank, *Law and the Modern Mind* (New York: Brentano's, 1930).
[27] Jerome Frank, *Courts on Trial* (Princeton, NJ: Princeton University Press, 1949).
[28] *Law and the Modern Mind*, xiii.

times. Indeed, had the matter been heard between November 1921 and June 1922, the outcome would have been the opposite. In other words, the answer to the question of the statute's validity turned, not on the certainty of the applicable rule, but on the personnel of the court. We *want* the law to be certain, he suggested, because of our deep need for security and safety which is endemic to children. In the same way as a child places his trust in the wisdom of his father, so we seek in the law and other institutions a similar comforting security. We should, he urged, grow up!

Frank is certainly the most accessible of the realists, indeed, as Twining puts it, 'clever rather than wise, a dilettante intellectual rather than a scholar, a brilliant controversialist, but somewhat erratic in his judgments, in his juristic writings Frank exhibited the strengths and weaknesses of a first-class journalist.'[29] Few students will complain about this.

### 6.2.4 **The American realist method**

American Realism, as Hunt points out, is powerfully informed by a behaviourist view of law. This 'behaviour orientation' is evident in the work of all the leading members of the movement. Thus Llewellyn suggests that the focus of study should be 'shifted to the area of contact, of interaction, between official regulatory *behavior* and the *behavior* of those affecting or affected by official regulatory *behavior*'.[30] And similar declarations are to be found in the writings of Frank, Oliphant, and Yntema.

What does this mean? Behaviourism concentrates on the attempt to describe and explain *outward manifestations* of mental processes and other phenomena that are not directly observable and measurable. Thus behavioural psychology is concerned principally with the measurement of legal, and especially, judicial *behaviour*. And this is especially evident in the realists' near-obsession with 'prediction'. Have a look at Moore, Underhill et al, 'Law and Learning Theory: A Study in Legal Control'.[31] The modern development of judicial behaviouralism in the 1960s is well described by Glendon Schubert, in his book, *Judicial Behavior*.[32]

While, in Duxbury's words, realism 'marked the marriage of social science and law',[33] it is hard to deny Hunt's observation that in their quest for a 'legal science', the American realists (with the exception of Llewellyn) exhibited a narrow empiricism: 'a vast amount of energy was burnt up in the collection of data'.[34] According to Hunt, empiricists believe incorrectly that the collection of data is a sufficient condition for the development of a social science method. 'Data collection becomes an end in itself; it becomes a purposeless and undirected activity.'[35] And charges of 'naive

---

[29] *Karl Llewellyn and the Realist Movement*, 379.
[30] 'A Realistic Jurisprudence—The Next Step' (1930) 30 *Columbia Law Review* 431, more easily found in Llewellyn, *Jurisprudence: Realism in Theory and Practice*, 3–41, at 40; emphasis added.
[31] (1943) 53 *Yale Law Journal* 1.
[32] Glendon A Schubert, *Political Culture and Judicial Behavior Vol 2: Subcultural Analysis of Judicial Behavior: A Direct Observational Study* (Lanham, Md: University Press of America, 1985).
[33] Duxbury, op cit, 92.  [34] *The Sociological Movement in Law*, 55.  [35] Ibid, 55–6.

realism', 'barefoot empiricism', and, most recently, 'pragmatic instrumentalism'[36] and 'profound conservatism'[37] are levelled at the realists from other quarters as well. It would be a good idea for you, in your reading of the leading realists, to consider how valid these criticisms are. What of Lloyd's observation in earlier editions (but omitted from the latest) that 'nothing very startlingly fresh has emerged…beyond what the reasonably progressive and socially-minded lawyer might already have accepted as axiomatic'?[38] Or Hunt's remark that: 'In a very real sense we *are* all realists now if only in the most general context of recognising the need to view law in its social context'?[39]

The realist challenge to the autonomy of law was certainly an important precursor of the critical legal studies and postmodernist approaches to law and the legal system discussed in Chapter 13. The relationship between the realist movement and sociological jurisprudence is also a strong one (see 7.1). Indeed, in Twining's view:

> [T]he main achievement of the realist movement was to concretise sociological jurisprudence.... Perhaps the most important lesson to be learned from a study of realism is a partial answer to the question: What difference can it make in practice to adopt a sociological (or realist or contextual) approach to law?[40]

You cannot therefore see realism in a vacuum. Its connections with psychology, anthropology, economics, and sociology are clear enough, but it has even been provocatively suggested (by Professor Twining) that there is more in common between Bentham and Llewellyn than may at first appear. A *rapprochement* of this kind is not only intellectually challenging, but it presents some fertile ground for the more imaginative jurisprudence examiner! Realism resonates also in the pragmatism of Richard Posner who, in an extensive collection of writings,[41] contends that the economic analysis of law is the quintessence of pragmatism (see 9.2).

In the early 2000s a new movement emerged at the University of Wisconsin, Madison, styling itself the 'New Legal Realism' or 'NLR'. According to its web site, it seeks 'to develop rigorous, genuinely interdisciplinary approaches to the empirical study of law'.[42] But, as Brian Leiter points out, their professed predecessors, while they

---

[36] See R Summers, *Instrumentalism and American Legal Theory* (Ithaca, NY and London: Cornell University Press, 1982), 20.

[37] See B Ackerman, *Reconstructing American Law* (Cambridge, Mass: Harvard University Press, 1984).

[38] *Lloyd's Introduction to Jurisprudence*, 5th edn (London: Sweet & Maxwell, 2001), 687.

[39] *The Sociological Movement in Law*, 59. He is echoing the widely quoted aphorism (which, as far as I know, is unattributed): 'Realism is dead; we are all realists now' which (like Hunt's comment) was uttered in relation to American Realism.

[40] *Karl Llewellyn and the Realist Movement*, 383. Critics of a more radical persuasion applaud the political perspective of the realists. See, in particular, Horwitz, *The Transformation of American Law*, and J Singer 'Legal Realism Now' (1988) 76 *California Law Review* 465.

[41] See, eg, Richard Posner, *The Problematics of Moral and Legal Theory* (Cambridge, Mass: Harvard University Press 1999); *Overcoming Law* (Cambridge, Mass: Harvard University Press, 1995).

[42] http://www.newlegalrealism.org/about.html.

'paid homage to the social sciences, even adopting the rhetoric of the then-dominant behaviourism...their actual scholarly practice was almost entirely insulated from the social science of the day'. He concludes: 'As some commenters have already pointed out, it is not entirely clear what this project has to do with American Legal Realism. I'd like to suggest an answer: essentially nothing.'[43]

### 6.2.4.1 A philosophical joke?

How seriously should American Realism be taken today? Brian Leiter has sought to remedy many of the myths and misconceptions surrounding American Realism, and, though his writings tend toward the taxing, his constructive re-interpretation of the central tenets of the movement is both stimulating and provocative.[44] Hart's rather sweeping dismissal of rule scepticism as 'the claim that talk of rules is a myth, cloaking the truth that law consists simply of the decisions of courts and predictions of them',[45] is plainly an unfair misrepresentation of its members' contribution to legal theory. By demonstrating the limitations of a doctrinal account of law without a proper empirical investigation of the manner in which legal doctrine functions in society, the American realists unquestionably paved the way to the sociological approach to law considered in Chapter 7.

## 6.3 The Scandinavian realists

A deep distrust of metaphysical concepts (which was exhibited by both the American realists and legal positivists) reaches its *apogee* with the Scandinavian realists. In the words of one of its leading (and more accessible) members, Professor Alf Ross (1899–1979), 'all metaphysics are a chimera and there is no cognition other than empirical'. We have already encountered some of the limitations of empiricism; in the case of the Scandinavians, it is not so much that they are empiricists, but that they are more than willing to consign anything that smacks of metaphysics (especially 'justice') to the category of 'meaningless'. This, as Hart points out, leads to some 'absurdities':

> Surely it is wrong to say...that the words 'just' and 'unjust' applied to a legal rule as distinct from a particular decision are 'devoid of meaning.' When we assert that a rule forbidding black men to sit in the public park is unjust we no doubt use, as our criterion of just treatment, the

[43] http://leiterlawschool.typepad.com/leiter/2006/06/the_socalled_ne.html. See Thomas J Miles and Cass R Sunstein. 'The New Legal Realism' (2008) 75 *University of Chicago Law Review* 831 for an account of the group's programme and preliminary achievements.

[44] Leiter, op cit, 59 where he challenges the view that realism is a 'jurisprudential joke, a tissue of philosophical confusions'. He maintains that 'it is time for legal philosophers to stop treating Realism as a discredited historical antique, and start looking at the movement with the sympathetic eye it deserves', ibid, 80.          [45] HLA Hart, *The Concept of Law*, 2nd edn (Oxford: Clarendon Press, 1994), 133.

unstated principle that, in the distribution of rights and privileges among men, differences in colour should be neglected.[46]

Few students will want to dissent from Hart's comment. But it seems to dispose, far too easily, of the position adopted (and defended with remarkable tenacity) by the Scandinavian realists and, in particular, their founding father, Axel Hägerström (1868–1939).

Hägerström went so far as to deny that any legal rule could be said to 'exist'. Such a statement presupposes that things could exist in a non-natural sense. And this, in his view, is nonsense. Talk of 'rights' and 'duties', is therefore meaningless since these phenomena are not rooted in actual experience, but are hangovers from primitive law in which they were imbued with magical significance. His refusal to regard legal concepts as anything more than fantasies of the mind is at the heart of the philosophies of his leading disciples, Alf Ross (1899–1979), Karl Olivecrona (1897–1980), and AV Lundstedt (1882–1955). It is most unlikely that you will be expected to have a detailed knowledge of all of these jurists (who have passed out of fashion). It will probably suffice to have a general grasp of the principal tenets of the two writers (Ross and Olivecrona) who have had a reasonably influential 'reception' in English-speaking countries. (I must confess that, save for the welcome—though entirely unintended—laughs that his book, *Legal Thinking Revised*, evokes, I have never required my own students to devote much of their time attempting to unravel the impenetrable thoughts of Lundstedt. The laughs, incidentally, spring from this jurist's breathtaking conceit and self-importance. Read the opening pages for some hilarious examples.)[47]

Essentially, Lundstedt regarded law as little more than the fact of social existence in organized groups, and the conditions that enable us to co-exist. All metaphysical thinking is rejected. Legal rules are merely 'labels' which, torn from their context of legal machinery, are meaningless scraps of paper. It cannot be said that *because* of a certain rule, a legal duty arises, for this is to support a *metaphysical* or normative relationship which can never be proved. All jurists (save him) are guilty of a fundamental error: they regard the sense of justice as inspiring the law, whereas, in fact, the opposite is true. Law is determined by 'social welfare' (which includes the minimum requirements of material life, security of person and property, and freedom of action). Jurisprudence must be a *natural* science based on empiricism.

The most obvious criticism of Lundstedt is that his concept of 'social welfare' is no less metaphysical than any of the notions he attacks. For Friedmann there is little new in Lundstedt's view 'except the author's claim to originality'.[48]

It is the work of Alf Ross that has proved to be of most interest and importance.

---

[46] In his review of Ross's *On Law and Justice* [1959] *Cambridge Law Journal* 233, reprinted in Hart, *Essays in Jurisprudence and Philosophy* (Oxford: Clarendon Press, 1983), 161.

[47] Nevertheless, for a sympathetic, and very useful, analysis (especially of his notion of 'social welfare'), see C Munro, 'The Swedish Missionary: Vilhelm Lundstedt' [1981] *Juridical Review* 55.

[48] W Friedmann, *Legal Theory*, 5th edn (New York: Columbia University Press, 1967), 310.

### 6.3.1 **Alf Ross**

In the light of the impact of his work outside Scandinavia, you would be well advised to look at Ross's leading work, *On Law and Justice*,[49] though there is much of value in *Directives and Norms*[50] and his essay 'Tu-tu'.[51]

Ross asks us to imagine a game of chess.[52] A third person is watching the two players. If he is ignorant of the rules, he will probably realize some kind of game is being played, but he will not be able to follow what is happening: the moves mean nothing, there is no connection between them. Social life, argues Ross, is like chess in that many individual actions are connected to a set of common conceptions of rules. It is this consciousness of the rules that facilitates our understanding of (and even our ability to predict) the course of events. The primary rules of chess (eg, that a pawn may move only forward) are *directives* which are accepted by each player as socially binding: he knows that he can only move his pawns according to the rules, and he knows that if he does not abide by this rule he will be met by a protest by his opponent. If, however, he merely makes a poor move no protest is likely to follow! The primary rules are therefore distinguished from the 'rules of skill contained in the theory'.

Ross then asks how we can establish *which* directives govern the game of chess. Merely to watch games being played (ie, to adopt a behaviourist approach) would clearly be inadequate: 'Even after watching a thousand games it would still be possible to believe that it is against the rules to open with a rook's pawn.'[53] The easiest method would be to consult textbooks on chess or rulings given at chess congresses. But this might not be adequate either: such declarations might not be adhered to in practice.

The only way, therefore, to find out which rules govern chess is to adopt an 'introspective method': we need to know which rules are actually felt by the players to be binding on them. And we can test this by watching to see whether such rules are actually effective in the game and are outwardly visible as such. The concept of 'validity' in chess thus contains two elements: the effectiveness of the rule as established by observation, and the extent to which the rules are regarded as binding. Ross recognizes, of course, that the rules of chess have no 'reality' apart from the experience of the two players. Thus in the concept 'rule of chess' we have two elements: the experienced ideas of certain patterns of behaviour, and the abstract contents of those ideas (the 'norms' of chess). He concludes that the norms of chess 'are the abstract idea content (of a directive nature) which make it possible, as a scheme of interpretation, to understand the phenomena of chess…as a coherent whole of meaning and motivation, a game of chess; and, along with other factors, within certain limits to predict the course of the game'.[54]

What has all this to do with law? No one with any degree of perception would seek to reduce the complex concept of law to the level of a game—or would they? Game

---

[49] Alf Ross, *On Law and Justice*, transl Margaret Dutton (London: Stevens & Sons, 1958).
[50] Alf Ross, *Directives and Norms* (London: Routledge & Kegan Paul, 1968).
[51] (1957) 70 *Harvard Law Review* 812. Useful extracts from these works may be found in *Lloyd's Introduction to Jurisprudence*, 8th edn (London: Sweet & Maxwell, 2008), 1065–76.
[52] *On Law and Justice*, 13–18.      [53] Ibid, 15.      [54] Ibid, 16.

theory has a reasonably respectable place in economics and other social sciences (see 9.2) and the Cambridge philosopher, Wittgenstein, employed 'language games' as a means of illuminating the use of words. In developing his central idea of 'valid law', Ross argues that the concept 'valid norm of chess' provides a useful model. In the same way as the seemingly random moves of chess acquire a coherence once we apply the 'scheme of interpretation' of the valid norms of chess, many human activities have meaning only when we apply the 'scheme of interpretation' of valid legal norms. Thus he defines 'valid law' as 'the abstract set of normative ideas which serve as a scheme of interpretation for the phenomena of law in action, which again means that these norms are effectively followed, and followed because they are experienced and felt to be socially binding'.[55]

This attempt to exclude metaphysical questions from the determination of 'valid law' is justified by Ross by saying that no one would:

> think of tracing the valid norms of chess back to an *a priori* validity, a pure idea of chess, bestowed upon man by God or deduced by man's eternal reason. The thought is ridiculous, because we do not take chess as seriously as law.... But this is no reason for believing that logical analysis should adopt a fundamentally different attitude in each of the two cases.[56]

This sideswipe at the theory of natural law is not, however, particularly persuasive. Surely, there is nothing in the rules of chess (as opposed to those of law) which could conceivably *prompt* such an analysis; the players are happy to accept the rules and thus metaphysical questions are irrelevant.

You will have noticed that in drawing this analogy, Ross acknowledges the normative character of law, but uses the term 'directives' to describe legal propositions. He nevertheless insists that such directives refer only to the law *actually in force*; other statements that purport to describe the law (eg, in legal textbooks) are merely propositions *about* the law, not *of* law. And therefore the study of the rules of law in action consists of assertions even though it is normative—for it is *about* norms.

His notion of 'valid law' is not, however, confined to the issuing of directives. There is, in addition, a 'psychological point of view'[57] which is experienced by officials (especially judges)—it is not necessary for the people at large to experience this acceptance of validity. This recognition of the 'internal' aspect of law ought to sound echoes in your mind of Hart's 'critical reflective attitude' (see 4.2.4). But Hart has himself pointed to an important distinction between the two: Ross 'misrepresents the internal aspect of rules as a matter of "emotion" or "feeling"—as a special psychological "experience"'.[58] Ross was strongly influenced by Hägerström's logical positivism: the view that statements have meaning only if the propositions they express are capable of proof or verification. This, of course, accounts for Ross's hostility to metaphysical questions. And, more than any of his Scandinavian colleagues, he focuses a good deal of his analysis on judicial behaviour and its predictability. In this respect he seems to be working the same seam as his American counterparts. But, as JW Harris points out,

---

[55] Ibid, 18.     [56] Ibid.     [57] *Directives and Norms*, 90.
[58] *Essays in Jurisprudence and Philosophy*, 166.

Ross differs from them by his insistence that decisions which concur with pre-existing rules demonstrate that the rules effectively control the decisions: if they did not, they could not be verified. Harris puts the distinction well:[59]

> Ross and Frank agree that it is my lawyer's business to predict what courts will do; but Frank says that they are to beware of rules as grounds for prediction, whilst Ross says rules 'exist' just because they are good grounds for prediction.

Of course, as several critics have been quick to point out, when *a judge* declares that the law is X, *he* is not predicting anything.

### 6.3.2 **Karl Olivecrona**

A more radical attack on metaphysics is to be found in Olivecrona's *Law as Fact*,[60] which, as its title suggests, argues that law 'exists' in a *factual* sense only: words are printed on pieces of paper or internalized in people's minds, but their significance is that they form a link in the chain of causation which results in certain courses of behaviour. In simple terms, law is little more than a form of psychology—it is a *symbolic expression* for the fact that the human mind responds in certain ways to various forms of social pressure. Given our psychological make-up and educational conditioning, certain behaviour patterns result. Lawyers and officials read the laws enacted by the legislature and, by virtue of their conditioning, they are induced to act in particular ways: the judge decides X, the policeman enforces X. When a revolution takes place, the revolutionaries seize the legal machinery and exert, through propaganda, psychological pressures on the people. As a result of their conditioning, members of society simply carry on as before. He concedes (with Kelsen) that a monopoly of force is required in order for the psychological basis of law to be *effective*, but suggests that once the new regime is established, the coercive element may be pushed into the background and applied only in exceptional circumstances. In most cases the psychological conditioning suffices.

This account of the nature of law also provides Olivecrona with an ingenious explanation of both the origin of law and the relationship between law and morality.

Law is, as we have just seen, originally coercive—sanctions are provided for infractions of rules. Individuals are then faced with the choice between compliance and disobedience. In time, this process becomes too onerous for most of us so that both the temptation of committing the act in question, on the one hand, and the fear of the possible sanction, on the other, are sublimated or repressed into our subconscious mind. In our conscious mind we simply retain an imperative *symbol* such as 'You shall not!' The rule has therefore been internalized and there is now normally no need for the threat of coercion. As soon as the idea of, say, stealing, enters our head, an

---

[59] *Legal Philosophies*, 102.
[60] Karl Olivecrona, *Law as Fact* (Copenhagen: Einar Munksgaard; London; Humphrey Milford, 1939); Karl Olivecrona, *Law as Fact*, 2nd edn (London: Stevens & Sons, 1971). See Torben Spaak, 'Karl Olivecrona's Legal Philosophy. A Critical Appraisal' (2011) 24 *Ratio Juris* 156.

unconditional order rings in our ears: 'Stealing is wrong!' This, of course, implies that the creation of new imperatives assumes that some legal system *already exists*. Hence it is, in his view, a futile enterprise to attempt to trace law to its ultimate source; the origin of law is simply a matter of *fact*. And to the argument that what jurists generally seek is not law's actual historical origin as much as the source of its *validity*, Olivecrona replies that this is a meaningless, metaphysical abstraction which has no foundation in *fact*.

This (somewhat idiosyncratic) account of the genesis of law leads him, secondly, to reverse the usual view that the law reflects moral values. Olivecrona suggests that the law is, in fact, the progenitor of many of our moral standards. We are, at an early age, conditioned into accepting that certain conduct is unlawful—the stamp of 'illegality' lends these rules a particular power. We quickly learn to internalize these rules and they then come to be our standards of morality. But surely, you will want to cry, the reform of our laws often springs from a genuine, unselfish desire to improve the lot of society—morality thereby affecting law rather than the reverse. Olivecrona's reply seems to be that law reformers are moved by enlightened self-interest. He could, I suppose, even claim that they are themselves subjected to the same psychological propaganda issuing from the law—thus completing the vicious circle!

For Olivecrona, rules of law are 'independent imperatives': propositions in imperative form (as opposed to statements of fact) but they do not issue—like commands—from particular persons (cf Austin and Bentham, 3.3.1 and 3.4.3). He gives the example of the Ten Commandments: it cannot be said that *Moses* is issuing the commands—the words are said to be the commands of God. But, as he puts it:

> In reality the Decalogue is a bundle of imperative sentences, formulated several thousand years ago and carried through the centuries by oral tradition and in writing. *They are nobody's commands, though they have the form of language that is characteristic of a command.* The rules of law are of a similar character.[61]

This is not, however, a crucial element in his theory as, for him, laws only 'exist' in the sense already described (words on paper or in minds).

### 6.3.3 Critique

The above is, I need hardly point out, only a sketch of the essential features of the jurisprudence of Ross and Olivecrona. You will have several points of your own (negative as well as positive) to make about their theories—especially after reading their work in the original. I have already suggested some of the possible limitations of Ross's theory. As far as Olivecrona is concerned, there are at least four targets to aim at. First, his psychological hypothesis is presented *a priori* without any empirical proof. Ask a friend who is studying psychology whether the rigours of that discipline would allow the theory to stand—in the absence of proof. Secondly, even if the theory were valid,

---

[61] In the 1939 edition of *Law as Fact* at 43 (the passage seems to be omitted from the second edition of 1971); emphasis added.

can descriptions of 'the law' be reduced to statements about the psyches and senses of citizens?

Thirdly, Olivecrona's account of the part played by coercion strikes many as somewhat naive: force is, of course, the background of law (he gives the examples of execution, eviction, imprisonment), but does it really operate in the way he describes? Fourthly, his analysis of the connection between law and morality is, at best, suspect. There are, of course, several other criticisms, that have been levelled at both Olivecrona (eg, his insistence on formality in law does not always apply in autocratic systems, and his idea of the state as an 'organization' rules out any form of conceptual thinking) and Ross (eg, his assertion that a decision is at variance with valid law if future courts are unlikely to follow it misunderstands the doctrine of precedent, and it is too dogmatic to confine experience to what is experienced through the senses—we do experience things morally), but you will need to explore their work more deeply before accepting or rejecting these, and other, attacks.

## 6.4 Realism and psychology

It is sometimes suggested that the realists developed a 'psychological school of jurisprudence'. While some of the American realists were strongly influenced by developments in psychology and psychiatry (Jerome Frank drew on Freud and Piaget, and Moore and Oliphant both adopted the methods of behavioural psychology), it is the Scandinavians (and especially Olivecrona) who (as we saw) might be considered to have initiated a psychological approach to legal theory. As he said, 'the "binding force" of the law is a reality merely as an idea in human minds'.[62] The purpose of lawgivers is to influence the actions of individuals in society, 'but this can only be done through influencing their minds. How the influence works on the individual mind is a question for psychology.'[63] Certainly Olivecrona stressed psychological conditioning and its effect on the relationship between law and morality.

Though Ross, in *On Law and Justice*, rejected Olivecrona's 'psychological realism', he does, in his later work, *Directives and Norms*, adopt a form of this approach himself. Whereas, in the first work, he argued that a legal norm was principally directed to courts rather than to citizens, in his later account of 'valid law' he distinguishes between a 'logical' and a 'psychological' point of view: legal rules are indeed directed to officials (and hence the rule 'exists' only in the sense that—logically—it depends on the existence of a rule directed to the officials). In other words, the *primary* rule that certain behaviour is prohibited requires a *secondary* rule specifying what sanction the judge is to apply when faced by such a violation. *Logically*, therefore, there is only *one* set of rules—the *secondary* rules, because primary rules contain nothing that is not already *implied* in secondary rules. However, he concedes that from a *psychological* point of view, there are *two* sets of norms: rules addressed to citizens are 'felt

---

[62] *Law as Fact* (1939 edn), 17.     [63] Ibid, 52.

psychologically to be independent entities which are grounds for the reactions of the authorities...primary rules must be recognised as actually existing norms, in so far as they are followed with regularity and experienced as being binding'.[64]

It is fair to conclude that, though realism, in general, could not be said to have developed a 'psychological school of jurisprudence', the legal theories of the Scandinavian realists, Olivecrona and Ross, are rooted in psychology.

# Questions

1. 'In [the realists'] view the concepts of "legal obligation" and "the law" are myths, invented and sustained by lawyers for a dismal mix of conscious and subconscious motives. The puzzles we find in these concepts are merely symptoms that they are myths. They are unsolvable because unreal, and our concern with them is just one feature of our enslavement. We would do better to flush away the puzzles and the concepts altogether, and pursue our important social objectives without this excess baggage.' (Ronald Dworkin, *Taking Rights Seriously*, 15)

   Is this a fair assessment?

2. What's wrong with Holmes's 'bad man' as a tool of analysis?

3. Are Llewellyn's 'law jobs' a helpful description of the functions of law? Are his 'trouble cases' hard cases?

4. Is it true that, '[u]ntil a court has passed judgment on [the] facts no law on that subject is yet in existence'?

5. Alan Hunt says that American Realism provided 'the bridge between sociological jurisprudence and the sociology of law'. You cannot be expected to evaluate the validity of this claim in full, but does it strike you as an accurate or useful one?

6. American Realism is characterized both as a conservative and a radical movement. How is this possible?

7. The American realists have been described as barefoot empiricists. Is this a reasonable criticism?

8. Consider the claim that the realists were the progenitors of critical legal theory (especially CLS, feminist, and postmodernist theory). You will want to pursue this idea after you have read Chapters 13 and 14.

9. Twining says 'the main achievement of the Realist movement was to concretise sociological (or contextual) jurisprudence.' (Twining, *Karl Llewellyn and the Realist Movement*, 383)

   What does realism teach us that we did not already know?

---

[64] *Directives and Norms*, 92. Echoes of Hart's 'internal point of view' as experienced by officials? See 4.2.8.

10. 'If my interpretation is correct, the American legal realists were similar to the Scandinavian legal realists, especially Alf Ross. The Scandinavian realists shared with the Americans a commitment to empiricism that motivated them to reject legal obligations. A judge's only reasons for a decision are those that are subjectively recommended by her attitudes. Furthermore, much like the Americans, the Scandinavians thought a prediction theory of law followed once legal obligation was rejected.' (Michael Steven Green, 'Legal Realism as Theory of Law' (2005) 46 *William and Mary Law Review* 1915/1998)

Is it fair to treat the American and Scandinavian realists as members of the same 'school'? What do they share? How do they differ?

11. Is it possible or desirable to expunge all metaphysical thinking from law?

12. Is social life, as Alf Ross contends, really like chess in that many of our acts are connected to a set of common conceptions of rules?

13. What does Ross mean by his assertion that to invoke 'justice' is equivalent to banging on a table?

14. Is Olivecrona correct that the law is the source of many of our moral standards?

15. Is it possible to conclude that Realism in general developed a 'psychological school of jurisprudence'?

# Further reading

COHEN, FELIX, 'Transcendental Nonsense and the Functional Approach' (1935) 35 *Columbia Law Review* 809.

DAGAN, HANOCH, 'The Realist Conception of Law' (2007) 57 *University of Toronto Law Journal* 607.

DAGAN, HANOCH, *Reconstructing American Legal Realism and Rethinking Private Law Theory* (New York: Oxford University Press, 2013).

DUXBURY, NEIL, *Patterns of American Jurisprudence* (Oxford: Clarendon Press, 1995).

FISHER, WW, HORWITZ, MJ, and REED, TA (eds), *American Legal Realism* (Oxford: Oxford University Press, 1993).

FRANK, JEROME, *Courts on Trial* (Princeton, NJ: Princeton University Press, 1949).

FRANK, JEROME, *Law and the Modern Mind*, 2nd edn (New York: Bretano's, 1930/1963).

FULLER, LON LUVOIS, 'American Legal Realism' (1934) 92 *University of Pennsylvania Law Review* 429.

GRANT, G, 'Legal Realism: Its Cause and Cure' (1961) 70 *Yale Law Journal* 1037.

GREEN, MICHAEL STEVEN, 'Legal Realism as Theory of Law' (2005) 46 *William and Mary Law Review* 1915.

HOLMES, OLIVER WENDELL, *Collected Legal Papers* (London: Constable & Co, 1920).

HORWITZ, MORTON, *The Transformation of American Law, 1860–1960* (Oxford: Oxford University Press, 1992).

LEITER, BRIAN, 'American Legal Realism' in W Edmundson and M Golding (eds), *Blackwell Guide to the Philosophy of Law and Legal Theory* (Oxford: Blackwell, 2003).

LEITER, BRIAN, *Naturalizing Jurisprudence: Essays on American Realism and Naturalism in Legal Philosophy* (Oxford: Oxford University Press, 2007).

LEWIS, JU, 'Karl Olivecrona: "Factual Realism" and Reasons for Obeying a Law' (1970) 5 *University of British Columbia Law Review* 281.

LLEWELLYN, KARL N, *The Bramble Bush* (New York: Oceana, 1930).

LLEWELLYN, KARL N, 'Some Realism about Realism' (1931) 44 *Harvard Law Review* 1222.

LLEWELLYN, KARL N, 'The Normative, the Legal and the Law Jobs: The Problem of Juristic Method' (1940) 49 *Yale Law Journal* 1355.

LLEWELLYN, KARL N, *The Common Law Tradition: Deciding Appeals* (Boston, Mass: Little, Brown & Co, 1960).

LLEWELLYN, KARL N, *Jurisprudence: Realism in Theory and Practice* (Chicago, Ill and London: University of Chicago Press, 1962).

LLEWELLYN, KARL N, and HOEBEL, E ADAMSON, *The Cheyenne Way: Conflict and Case Law in Primitive Jurisprudence* (Norman, Okla: University of Oklahoma Press, 1941) (*The Civilization of the American Indian Series*, Vol 21).

LUNDSTEDT, A VILHELM, *Legal Thinking Revised: My Views on Law* (Stockholm: Almqvist & Wiksell, 1956).

MACCORMACK, G, 'Hägerström on Rights and Duties' [1970] *Juridical Review* 59.

MACCORMACK, G, 'Scandinavian Realism' [1970] *Juridical Review* 33.

OLIVECRONA, KARL, *Law as Fact* (Copenhagen: Eniar Munksgard: London Humphrey Milford, 1939).

OLIVECRONA, KARL, 'The Imperative Element in Law' (1964) 18 *Rutgers Law Review* 794.

OLIVECRONA, KARL, *Law as Fact*, 2nd edn (London: Stevens & Sons, 1971).

POUND, R, 'The Call for a Realist Jurisprudence' (1931) 44 *Harvard Law Review* 697.

ROSS, ALF, *On Law and Justice*, transl Margaret Dutton (London: Stevens & Sons, 1958).

ROSS, ALF, *Directives and Norms* (London: Routledge & Kegan Paul, 1968).

RUMBLE, WILFRED E, *American Legal Realism: Skepticism, Reform, and the Judicial Process* (Ithaca, NY: Cornell University Press, 1968).

SCHUBERT, G, 'Behavioral Jurisprudence' (1968) 2 *Law and Society Review* 407.

SIMMONDS, NE, 'The Legal Philosophy of Axel Hägerström' (1976) *Juridical Review* 210.

SINGER, J, 'Legal Realism Now' (1988) 76 *California Law Review* 465.

SUMMERS, ROBERT S, *Instrumentalism and American Legal Theory* (Ithaca, NY and London: Cornell University Press, 1982).

SUMMERS, ROBERT S (ed), *American Legal Theory* (Aldershot: Dartmouth, 1992).

TWINING, WILLIAM, *Karl Llewellyn and the Realist Movement* (London: Weidenfeld & Nicholson, 1973).

# 7

# Law and social theory

To claim that law cannot be understood save in its social context sounds like a platitude. But this proposition encompasses a great deal more than this apparently simple assertion. It maintains that properly to comprehend and explain the concept of law requires a sociological analysis that is rooted in the social conditions in which the law and legal ideas are fashioned and employed. Such a sociological account of law normally rests on three closely related claims: that we cannot truly grasp the meaning of law except as a 'social phenomenon', that an analysis of legal concepts provides only a partial explanation of 'law in action', and that law is merely one form of social control.

None of these arguments is especially startling; indeed, we have already seen (in 6.2) that in their 'revolt against formalism' the American realists (and more recently, the Critical Legal Studies and postmodernist movements described in Chapters 13 and 14) exhibited a profound impatience with traditional legal theory and its preoccupation with the 'law in books'. Thus Alan Hunt is able to describe American Realism as 'the bridge between sociological jurisprudence and the sociology of law'.[1]

It is most likely that if your course includes this aspect of jurisprudence (and several do not) it will deal with both ends of this spectrum, and you will be expected to demonstrate an understanding of how the early sociological jurists—especially Roscoe Pound laid the foundation of the contemporary, full-blown sociology of law. You will also be referred to the works of the leading sociologists (particularly Durkheim, Weber, and Ehrlich) who had a great deal to say about the law. And (as if this were not enough) you will be urged to read important modern empirical and theoretical studies of legal institutions (principally lawyers, courts, and the police).

So rapidly has this field developed that a number of law schools now offer specific courses in 'law and society' and the sociology of law. And 'socio-legal studies' are alive and fairly well in several universities, as is the subject of law and anthropology (see Chapter 8). The treatment of sociological jurisprudence and the sociology of law in the context of an already crowded jurisprudence course therefore tends to be of the synoptic variety. Nevertheless, as with every other strand in the fabric of legal theory, nothing you study is ever 'wasted', and, particularly in the case of the sociological approach to law, you will derive considerable benefit from devoting a fair amount of effort to this part of your course. This is not only because all the substantive law

---

[1] *The Sociological Movement in Law* (London: Macmillan, 1978), 37.

subjects which you have studied *belong* in a social context, but because a 'sociological perspective' (see 7.1) will enhance your appreciation of the nature of law and its operation.

The scale of the subject is formidable: there is a prodigious literature generated by 'legal sociologists' (or 'sociologists of law') which is of great importance to the 'sociological jurist'. Moreover, a proper understanding of 'law in society' or 'law as a social phenomenon' requires the adoption (or, at least, a sympathetic grasp) of a 'sociological perspective'. The student of jurisprudence—yet again—is called upon to don another hat. Not content with his aspiring to be an amateur historian, philosopher, economist, and political scientist, his teacher now expects him or her to become part-time sociologist. But help is at hand! This chapter will (I hope) identify and clarify the major areas of student difficulty.[2]

## 7.1 What is a sociological perspective?

Beware of catchphrases. It is, however, possible to identify certain essential features of a 'sociological perspective' in general, and of its application to law, in particular. Sociologists tend to employ three important concepts which, to most legal theorists, are alien. They are the ideas of social structure, social stratification, and social function. The first suggests that in any society there are a number of institutions (legal, cultural, political, economic, etc) which form the *social structure* and which interact in a variety of complex ways: thus one institution or group may exert greater political or economic influence than another, hence the idea of *social stratification* (which includes problems of class conflict, sex, and race discrimination). These institutions and groups may be analysed in terms of their particular *social function* (eg, sociologists may seek to explore the function of the church in Serbia).

Sociologists, using these central ideas, who have sought to explain the nature and operation of law in society, regard law as merely one (albeit an important and ubiquitous) feature of that society. They generally reject the idea (most closely associated with legal positivism) that there can be a value-free explanation of law. I say 'generally' because there are certain sociologists (notably Donald Black in *The Behavior of Law*)[3] who purport to give a value-free sociology of law.[4] The question of a 'value-free' sociology is, however, a difficult and controversial one: some might

---

[2] See too Roger Cotterrell, *The Sociology of Law: An Introduction* (London: Butterworths, 1984); Hunt, *The Sociological Movement in Law*; Kahei Rokumoto (ed), *Sociological Theories of Law* (Aldershot: Dartmouth, 1994); W Chambliss and R Seidman, *Law, Order and Power*, 2nd edn (Reading, Mass and London: Addison-Wesley, 1982).

[3] *The Behavior of Law* (New York: Academic Press, 1976). See too Glendon A Schubert (ed), *Judicial Behavior: A Reader in Theory and Research* (Chicago, Ill: Rand McNally, 1964).

[4] For an attack on Black, see A Hunt, 'Dichotomy and Contradiction in the Sociology of Law' (1981) 8 *British Journal of Law & Society* 47, an extract from which may be found in *Lloyd's Introduction to Jurisprudence*, 8th edn (London: Sweet & Maxwell, 2008), 909–16.

argue that we can never escape our own values when we describe anything. The best we can hope for is that we should *recognize* this fact and make *explicit* our own moral or ideological values.

The sociologist of law, therefore, is concerned to analyse and interpret the part played by law and legal administration in effecting certain observable forms of conduct or behaviour. He or she will attempt to present certain 'types' of society in which the role or function of law may be examined. Thus, as will be shown in a moment, Durkheim, in seeking to explain the problem of 'social cohesion', postulates two 'types' of society in which law performs significantly different purposes. Or, to take a few more modern examples, an influential dichotomy is drawn by Ferdinand Tönnies[5] between societies which conform to the *Gemeinschaft* type (community) and the *Gesellschaft* type (association). The former is based on shared, common interests in which the public and private are indistinguishable. The latter, on the other hand, assumes a society of atomistic individuals with private interests. To these types, Kamenka and Tay have famously added a third, the 'bureaucratic-administrative' type.[6] Yet another tripartite typology is proposed by Nonet and Selznick.[7] They suggest a threefold classification based on the models of 'repressive law', 'autonomous law', and 'responsive law' as phases through which law passes.

## 7.2 Roscoe Pound

Pound (1870–1964), the leading exponent of 'sociological jurisprudence', lived a long and productive life. His prolific output, with its propensity for 'classification' (he was, in his early years, a botanist) is, to a large extent, consolidated in his five-volume work, *Jurisprudence*, which was published in 1959. It constitutes a powerful reaction against British analytical legal theory, and demonstrates a knowledge of and sympathy for Continental juristic thought. But Pound's assault on traditionalism was part of a wider movement in the social sciences which laid siege on what Jhering (1818–92) called the 'jurisprudence of conceptions'.

Pound emphasizes the importance of the distinction between 'law in books' and 'law in action'. His purpose was not, however, confined to identifying the tension between the two, but he wanted to show how they could be *harmonized*. He sought, in other words, to make the latter conform to the former. As he put it, 'In a conflict between the "law in books" and the national will, there can be but one result, let us not be legal monks.'[8]

---

[5] In *Community and Association*, transl and supplemented by Charles P Loomis (London: Routledge & Kegan Paul, 1974).

[6] See, eg, 'Beyond Bourgeois Individualism: The Contemporary Crisis in Law and Legal Ideology' in E Kamenka and RS Neale (eds), *Feudalism, Capitalism and Beyond* (London: Edward Arnold, 1973), 48.

[7] *Law and Society in Transition: Toward Responsive Law* (New York: Octagon Books, 1978).

[8] 'Law in Books and Law in Action' (1910) 44 *American Law Review* 12.

### 7.2.1 Social interests and 'jural postulates'

For Pound the task of lawyers and legislators is 'social engineering'. The law, by identifying and protecting certain 'interests', ensures social cohesion. An 'interest' is defined as a 'demand or desire which human beings, either individually or through groups or associations or in relations, seek to satisfy'. It is legally protected by attributing to it the status of a legal right. The purpose of social engineering is to construct as efficient a society as possible, one which ensures the satisfaction of the maximum of interests with minimal friction and waste of resources.

Pound's elaborate theory of interests includes, for example, what he calls 'individual interests' comprising interests of the personality (the physical person, freedom of will, honour and reputation, privacy; and belief and opinion), 'domestic relations', and 'interests of substance' (property, freedom of industry and contract, freedom of association, and similar interests). There are also 'public interests' which include 'interests of the State as juristic person', and 'social interests' (including the interest in general security, covering those branches of the law which deal with safety, health, peace and order, the conservation of social resources, and so on).

This is merely part of his labyrinthine scheme that perhaps demonstrates how Pound as botanist may have influenced Pound as jurist! But this is not the end of his complex taxonomy, for in the next phase of the argument, having categorized these manifold interests recognized by the law, Pound proceeds to examine the various legal means (including the concepts of rights and duties) by which they are secured. He then argues that when interests conflict, they may be 'weighed' or 'balanced' only against other interests 'on the same plane'. Thus, an *individual* interest must not be weighed against a *public* interest, and so on. He also presents a classification of the institutions of law: he distinguishes between: rules, principles, conceptions, doctrines, and standards.

The business of the law, in Pound's view, therefore consists in satisfying as many interests as possible. But, how are we to know whether *new* interests qualify for recognition? He suggests that they might be tested by reference to certain 'jural postulates of civilization'. These consist of those (changing) assumptions which exist in 'civilised society': no intentional aggression; beneficial control over what people acquire under the existing social and economic order; good faith in dealings; due care not to injure; control over dangerous activities; and so on.

If you find this attempt at precise categorization too formalistic or even artificial, that is the least of the criticisms that it has attracted.

### 7.2.2 Critique of Pound

Eleven main sorts of criticism may be identified. First, Pound's 'objective' classification of interests and accompanying jural postulates 'reads like a political manifesto in favour of a liberal and capitalist society'.[9] It also rests on a *consensus* model of society

---

[9] *Lloyd's Introduction to Jurisprudence*, 851.

in which there is a considerable degree of shared values. Many sociologists regard a *conflict* model as a more accurate description of reality: see 7.6.6. Secondly, his model of competing interests 'pressing for recognition and security' overlooks the extent to which the law recognizes *vested* rights. Thirdly, he assumes that it is a simple matter to know the *real* interests of people, but we are all manipulated, to a greater or lesser extent, by advertising and other forms of persuasion. Fourthly, how do we actually set about *establishing* people's interests: is it a matter of psychology or market research? Fifthly, should we, in any event, seek to satisfy people's wants? There may be good reason to protect certain interests regardless of whether people want them (eg, paternalistic legislation relating to pornography or drugs). Sixthly, his inventory seems almost irretrievably vague and nebulous. For instance, what, even in these troubled times of terror, is to be accommodated by the social interest in 'peace and order'? What are we to understand by the interest in 'self-assertion'?

Seventhly, even if we regard the list as helpful, it raises a plethora of difficulties: is there really any fundamental distinction between public and social interests? Is the difference between individual and social interests not one between different *types* of interest as much as one between interests that exist on different *levels*? Are the three types of interest equal in status? Eighthly, the idea of 'balancing' notwithstanding, when it comes to a judge selecting between competing interests, 'each situation has a pattern of its own, and the different types of interest and activities that might be involved are infinitely various. It is for the judge to translate the activity involved in the case before him in terms of an interest and to select the ideal with reference to which the competing interests are measured.'[10] In other words, the listing of interests is less important than the judicial attitudes towards particular activities. Ninthly, Pound assumes that claims pre-exist law, but certain claims actually result from law (eg, welfare legislation). Tenthly, what does it mean to 'recognize' an interest? There is a grey area in which an activity may be permitted without being 'recognized' by the law. Finally, Pound establishes his jural postulates by generalizing a value which is *already legally protected*; but if new claims are, as he proposes, to be judged by reference to jural postulates, they will be recognized only if similar claims already receive legal protection. This hardly suggests a particularly dynamic process of law reform. There are many more criticisms in the literature. You will want, in addition to reading these critiques and adding your own evaluation, to compare Pound with others who adopted a sociological standpoint as well as with those jurists who have considered the role of interests and rights. See 10.2.

Critics are hard on Pound. Even if, as Hunt puts it, he 'used sociology when he saw fit; he cannot be regarded as having developed a sociological theory of law'.[11] He undoubtedly exerted a considerable influence on sociological jurisprudence. More than that, he laid the foundation for an approach to law that looked beyond traditionalism to an alternative perspective rooted in 'law in action'.

---

[10] RWM Dias, *Jurisprudence*, 5th edn (London: Butterworths, 1985), 435.
[11] *The Sociological Movement in Law*, 34.

## 7.3 Eugen Ehrlich

It is sometimes said that Pound's theory has much in common with the views of Eugen Ehrlich (1862–1922). (See Table 7.1.) In particular, it is suggested that there is a strong resemblance between Pound's 'law in action' and Ehrlich's idea of 'living law'.[12] This question is returned to later.

Ehrlich, like Pound, recognized that the formal sources of law provide an incomplete picture of what law is really like—the 'living law'. This is to be distinguished from what he called 'norms of decision' (rules found in the civil codes, judicial decisions, and statutes) which are the norms to be enforced by the courts when parties resort to litigation. 'Living law' is 'the law which dominates life itself even though it has not been posited in legal propositions'.[13] As he says:

> To attempt to imprison the law of a time or of a people within the sections of a code is about as reasonable as to attempt to confine a stream within a pond. The water that is put in the pond is no longer a living stream but a stagnant pool.[14]

So, for example, the law of contract is better understood by empirical studies than by reading textbooks and judicial decisions. This might be illustrated by the well-known research conducted by Stewart Macauley into commercial practices in Wisconsin. He showed that, instead of concerning themselves with the rules of offer and acceptance, consideration, etc, hardened businessmen were frequently not only ignorant of those rules, but found ways of avoiding the law and lawyers whenever possible. As one respondent put it, 'One doesn't run to lawyers if he wants to stay in business because one must behave decently.'[15] For business people the law of contract is far less important than the actual operation of commercial practice. In brief terms, therefore, if we wish to obtain a reliable insight into the actual practice of law, we need to penetrate the social context in which it is played out.

Ehrlich's work has not assumed a major place in the sociology of law (though he coined the phrase), and critics have found a number of flaws in his theory of the 'living law'. In particular, he fails to provide a coherent theory of the relationship between the 'living law' and the state (which plays a significant part in the development of the 'living law').

David Nelken[16] raises several difficulties with the very concept of the 'living law': what, if anything, do the various norms of the 'living law' (relating to families, organizations, and business activity) actually have *in common*? To what extent do these organizations and associations reproduce within themselves Ehrlich's two types

---

[12] The limitations of the equation are examined in D Nelken, 'Law in Action or Living Law? Back to the Beginning in Sociology of Law' (1984) 4 *Legal Studies* 157.

[13] *Fundamental Principles of the Sociology of Law*, transl WL Moss (Cambridge, Mass: Harvard University Press, 1936), 493.          [14] Ibid, 488.

[15] S Macauley, 'Non-contractual Relations in Business' (1963) 28 *American Sociological Review* 55 at 61. A British survey reached similar conclusions: H Beale and T Dugdale, 'Contracts between Businessmen' (1975) 2 *British Journal of Law & Society* 45.          [16] (1984) 4 *Legal Studies* 157, 173.

**Table 7.1** Pound and Ehrlich compared

| Pound | Ehrlich |
| --- | --- |
| He conceives of society as groups of individuals united in their pursuit of the interest in diminishing resources. | He adopts a less individualistic approach: individual behaviour is channelled by norms of social groups. |
| His principal concern is to harmonize the 'law in books' and the 'law in action'. | He does not regard 'norms for decision' and 'living law' as in competition: they are applied under different conditions: the former in disputes, the latter in normal circumstances. |
| His conception of law is largely rule-based. | His distinction between 'norms for decision' and 'living law' reveals a more complex conception of law. |
| His distinction between 'law in books' and 'law in action' is confined to actions by citizens. | His distinction between 'norms for decision' and 'living law' extends to decision-making by judges, lawmakers, and other officials. |
| He regards law as a method of 'social control', a tool for social engineering. | He sees law as a development from social forces rather than a tool for social engineering. |
| Norms are the claims made by competing groups in society. | His theory of norms is more complex: they reflect shared feelings, behaviour, and identity. |

of law, having *both* 'norms for decision' and 'living law'? Can groups and associations be defined *apart* from the norms that constitute them? How do the norms of 'living law' *arise*? What are the relationships of opposition, incorporation, and symbiosis between *state* 'norms for decision' and the 'living law' of groups? How do the norms of some groups affect the norms held dear in other associations? Nelken says that the answers to these questions depend on the development of a 'sociology of norms' rather than a sociology of law. If so, perhaps Ehrlich may be forgiven for failing to provide the answers, though it does render his theory narrower than it might otherwise have been. Still, his influence has not been inconsiderable (especially in anthropology), and his ideas are described by Cotterrell[17] as 'a powerful challenge to lawyers' typical assumptions about the nature and scope of law and of its importance'.

## 7.4 Émile Durkheim

Among the leading figures of sociology, Durkheim (1858–1917) stands tall. It is likely that you will be expected to have a fairly detailed knowledge of his contribution to the sociology of law.[18]

---

[17]  *The Sociology of Law*: An Introduction, 31.
[18]  You will find Ch 4 of Alan Hunt, *The Sociological Movement in Law*, admirably clear. Durkheim's various writings on law have been (for the first time) collected and edited in a very useful book (with a good introduction) by S Lukes and A Scull, *Durkheim and the Law* (Oxford: Martin Robertson, 1983).

Durkheim's general concern may be simply stated: what is it that holds society together? Throughout his major works (especially *The Division of Labour in Society*, first published in French in 1893)[19] he is preoccupied with 'social solidarity'—and the law plays a central role in the transition from mechanical to organic solidarity; it is an 'external' index which 'symbolizes' the nature of social solidarity (see 7.4.1). Though his *sociologie du droit* is complex, there are essentially two major claims that he makes. First, he argues that as society develops from religion to secularism, from collectivism to individualism, law becomes less penal and more 'restitutive' in character. Secondly, he claims that the function of punishment is an expression of collective sentiments by which social cohesion is maintained. Each claim is now briefly examined.

### 7.4.1 **Law and social solidarity**

For Durkheim, society produces two distinct forms of social solidarity: 'mechanical' solidarity and 'organic' solidarity. The former is to be found in simple, homogeneous societies which have a uniformity of values and lack any significant division of labour. 'Collectivism' is highly developed while 'individualism' is barely present. The latter, on the other hand, is to be found in societies which have a developed division of labour and, hence, exhibit a strong degree of 'interdependence'. Instead of homogeneity there is considerable differentiation; 'individualism' replaces 'collectivism'.

The law reflects 'all the essential varieties of social solidarity'. As he says in an oft-quoted statement:

> Since law reproduces the principal forms of social solidarity, we have only to classify the different types of law to find therefrom the different types of social solidarity which correspond to it.[20]

Durkheim identifies also an important relationship between *mechanical* solidarity and *repressive* law; and between *organic* solidarity and *restitutive* law. This is explained by reference to the features of these two forms of cohesion described above. Law in the former is essentially penal, but, with increasing differentiation, disputes tend to be resolved by recourse to restitutive law (which includes all civil law, procedural law, and major parts of constitutional and administrative law).

In this analysis, Durkheim treats law and morality as virtually synonymous. Law is derived from and is an expression of society's morality. In the absence of moral commitment to support it, law ceases being a part of society.

### 7.4.2 **The function of punishment**

For Durkheim crime is closely connected to the social values expressed in the 'collective conscience': an act is criminal

---

[19]  É Durkheim, *The Division of Labour in Society*, transl George Simpson (London: Collier-Macmillan, 1964).                                                    [20]  *The Division of Labour in Society*, 68.

when it offends strong and defined states of the collective conscience...[W]e must not say that an action shocks the common conscience because it is criminal, but rather that it is criminal because it shocks the common conscience.[21]

Crime is an inevitable feature of social life; indeed, it is a factor in public health, an integral part of all healthy societies. And *punishment* is a crucial element in his notion of crime: the state acts to reinforce the 'collective conscience' by punishing those who offend against the state itself. Punishment is defined as 'a passionate reaction of graduated intensity that society exercises through the medium of a body acting upon those of its members who have violated certain rules of conduct'.[22] He is in no doubt that the function of punishment is vengeance and that it is a necessary 'act of defence'.[23]

In his essay 'Two Laws of Penal Evolution'[24] he propounds the following two 'laws':

> The intensity of punishment is the greater the more closely societies approximate to a less developed type—and the more the central power assumes an absolute character.
>
> Deprivations of liberty, and of liberty alone, varying in time according to the seriousness of the crime, tend to become more and more the normal means of social control.

The former is qualitative, the latter quantitative. His argument, in relation to the first, is that in primitive societies the death penalty is 'augmented' by a variety of gruesomely imaginative 'torments': 'death by ashes' (suffocation under a pile of ashes), crucifixion, burning alive, being cooked alive, being crushed under an elephant, and other similarly grisly methods. Durkheim's point is that as societies progress, the form of punishment becomes less violent and less harsh. But since punishment results from *crime*, he identifies a correlation between the evolution of crime and the forms of social solidarity. He distinguishes between two types of crime: 'religious criminality' (acts 'which are directed against collective things') and 'human criminality' (acts 'which only injure the individual'). Each type will attract its own form of punishment, and it will therefore change according to the type of crime. He concludes:

> Seeing as, in the course of time, crime is reduced more and more to offences against persons alone, while religious forms of criminality decline, it is inevitable that punishment on the average should become weaker.[25]

### 7.4.3 **Critique of Durkheim**

You will (again) want to attach almost as much importance to the criticism that Durkheim's theory has attracted as to the theory itself. Here—for starters—is a very brief sketch of ten major criticisms. You may expand on each of them. First, his account is too narrow: his treatment of law as 'a completely moral phenomenon' neglects the extent to which law and morality often conflict. Secondly, his views of

[21] Ibid, 80–1: see Chapter 12.      [22] Ibid, 96.
[23] Ibid, 87. On various approaches to punishment, see Chapter 12.
[24] Translated by T Anthony Jones and Andrew Scull in Lukes and Scull, *Durkheim and the Law*, 102.
[25] Ibid, 126.

primitive societies are *a priori*, and there is empirical evidence that tends to refute his assumption that, for example, they lack a division of labour.[26] Thirdly, his theory of how law becomes increasingly restitutive does not, in the view of several critics, provide a coherent account of this development. Fourthly, in his explanation of the transition from mechanical to organic solidarity, he gives no description of the *intermediate* stages between primitive and modern societies. Fifthly, it has been argued by modern social scientists that, contrary to Durkheim's thesis, repressive law was actually *less* important in simple or primitive societies. Sixthly, his concept of the state has been attacked: he regards the state as the expression of the collectivity; it is treated merely as an instrumental organ—as a means by which offenders are punished. Seventhly, Durkheim's insistence on reducing punishment to its retributive features has not met with critical acclaim; it is sometimes considered to ignore the deterrent, rehabilitative, reformist aspects of punishment. On the other hand, eighthly, he neglects the punitive dimension of *civil* law and, at the same time, fails to account for the growing intrusiveness of the criminal law into, for example, labour relations. Ninthly, his suggestion that crime 'is a factor in public health' has been denied by several writers who, in general, find it unconvincing on a number of grounds.[27] Finally, Durkheim's 'two laws of penal evolution' have been attacked on several counts. In particular, the basis of the distinction between 'religious' and 'human' crimes has been questioned: on what ground, for instance, are some acts treated as attacks upon the collective, while others (simply because they cause injury to persons) are not?

Despite these (and many other) misgivings, few deny Durkheim's influence on the sociology of law. Indeed, 'the persistent sociologism of Durkheim ensures that his work will remain a significant point of reference'.[28] Like the curate's egg, Durkheim's theory seems to be regarded as good in parts. In the view of Lukes and Scull:[29]

> Current research may continue to endorse the value of Durkheim's insistence on studying law in its social and historical context, and on the need to tease out the connections between law and the forms of social relations. Such research may also reiterate his emphasis on the central importance of law to the understanding of social life in general.... It does so, however, only while rejecting the larger theoretical system within which these propositions were once embedded.

You ought to be able to answer a question with a quotation such as this as its *aperitif*.

## 7.5 Max Weber

A trained lawyer, Weber (1864–1920) devotes to the law a rigorous and systematic social and historical analysis which occupies a central position in his general sociological theory. He is unquestionably the most prominent and influential social

---

[26] See Hunt, *The Sociological Movement in Law*, 70–1.
[27] See Hart's essay 'Social Solidarity and the Enforcement of Morality' in his *Essays in Jurisprudence and Philosophy* (Oxford: Clarendon Press, 1983), 248, for the connections between this thesis and Lord Devlin's 'disintegration thesis'.      [28] Hunt, *The Sociological Movement in Law*, 92.
[29] *Durkheim and the Law*, 27.

theorist, and it is not uncommon to find him revered by his contemporary successors. Every serious student of jurisprudence will at least attempt to read Weber's great works, especially *Economy and Society: An Outline of Interpretive Sociology*[30] and *Max Weber on Law in Economy and Society*.[31] His writings are rich in their intellectual and social investigation of law and legal history, and you will be richer in knowledge and understanding through studying them. But, if this is to dwell in the realm of the fantastic, you will find an excellent guide in AT Kronman's *Max Weber*,[32] and Hunt's *The Sociological Movement in Law* contains a lucid account in Chapter 5.[33]

Essentially, Weber's project was to explain the development of capitalism in Western societies. And a key element in his explanation is the existence of a 'rational' legal order. He employs certain 'ideal types' along with the development of particular concepts of rationality to demonstrate the movement toward capitalism. His starting point is the *individual*: social action can be understood only by reference to its meaning, purpose, and intention for the individual. This method he calls *Verstehen*.[34] His sociology of law may be considered under three heads: his typology of law, his theory of legitimate domination, and his analysis of the relationship between capitalism and law. Each element is now briefly discussed.

### 7.5.1 **Weber's typology of law**

Weber's definition of law resembles the traditional positivist, formal conception:

> An order will be called *law* if it is externally guaranteed by the probability that coercion (physical or psychological), to bring about conformity or avenge violation, will be applied by a *staff* of people holding themselves specially ready for that purpose.[35]

His typology of law is based on the various types of legal thought, and 'rationality' is the key. Thus he distinguishes between 'formal' systems and 'substantive' systems. It is important to note that the crux of this distinction is the extent to which the system is 'internally self-sufficient', that is, the rules and procedures required for decision-making are available within the system. The second distinction is between 'rational' and 'irrational': these terms describe the manner in which the materials (rules, procedures) are applied in the system. Thus the highest stage of rationality is

---

[30] Max Weber, *Economy and Society: An Outline of Interpretive Sociology*, ed Guenther Roth and Claus Wittich (New York: Bedminister Press, 1968).

[31] Max Weber, *Max Weber on Law in Economy and Society*, transl Edward Shils and ed Max Rheinstein (Cambridge, Mass: Harvard University Press, 1954) (*20th Century Legal Philosophy Series*, Vol 6).

[32] Anthony R Kronman, *Max Weber* (London: Edward Arnold, 1983; hereinafter '*Max Weber*').

[33] Frank Parkin's little book, *Max Weber* is also a useful general introduction. See too Cotterrell, *The Sociology of Law: An Introduction*, 148–61. You will find extracts from Weber in *Lloyd's Introduction to Jurisprudence*, 881–90.

[34] The term was first used by nineteenth-century philosophical anthropologists. For a perceptive analysis of the strengths and weaknesses of *Verstehen*, see William Lucy, *Understanding and Explaining Adjudication* (New York: Oxford University Press, 1999).

[35] From *Max Weber on Law in Economy and Society*, 5.

**Table 7.2** Weber's internal typology of law

|  | Rational | Irrational |
| --- | --- | --- |
| SUBSTANTIVE | Substantively rational | Substantively irrational |
| FORMAL | Formally rational | Formally irrational |

reached where there is an 'integration of all analytically derived legal propositions in such a way that they constitute a logically clear, internally consistent, and, at least in theory, gapless system of rules, under which, it is implied, all conceivable fact situations must be capable of being logically subsumed.'[36]

Taken together, these two distinctions yield a fourfold scheme of law-making and adjudication which may be illustrated as in Table 7.2.

Examples of each type of legal thought are given by Weber, as follows:

- *Substantively irrational law.* Weber calls this 'Khadi justice' (after the procedure used in Islamic law) where decisions are made *ad hoc*, based on ethical, emotional, and political considerations; cases are decided on their own merits without reference to general principles.

- *Substantively rational law.* This is exemplified by certain theocratic legal systems and 'the patriarchal system of justice' which recognizes no separation between law and morals. There is some attempt to construct a doctrinal system of rules and principles.

- *Formally rational law.* This is exemplified by the codes of civil law countries which are derived from Roman law. It is a gapless legal system which contains answers to all legal problems.

- *Formally irrational law.* Examples are to be found in primitive systems which employ trial by ordeal or oracle. Decisions are made on the basis of tests beyond the control of human intellect.

Weber then proposes a second typology based on:

- the mode of law-creation;
- the formal qualities of the law so created; and
- the type of justice attained.

He argues that law passes through the following four phases:

- Charismatic legal revelation through 'law prophets'.
- Empirical creation and finding of law by legal *honoratiores* (those who have a specialized expert knowledge and occupy a position of social prestige by virtue of their economic situation, and who receive little or no remuneration for this).

---

[36] Ibid, 62. Shades of Dworkin? See 5.1.

**Table 7.3** Weber's typology of legal development

| Mode of creation | Formal qualities | Types of justice |
| --- | --- | --- |
| Charismatic | Magical, irrational | Charismatic |
| Empirical | Reliance on *honoratiores* | Khadi justice |
| Secular, theocratic | Theocratic substantive rationality | Empirical |
| Professionalized | 'Sublimation of concepts' | Rational |

- Imposition of law by secular or theocratic powers.
- Systematized elaboration of law and professionalized administration of justice.

The relationship between the two typologies may be illustrated as in Table 7.3.

This representation squeezes a long and complicated analysis into a very small space.[37] For instance, the idea of the 'sublimation of concepts' occurs in Weber's account of legal thought (in the important chapter in *Max Weber on Law in Economy and Society*, 'The Legal *honoratiores* and the Types of Legal Thought'). Describing the development of the legal profession in Roman and English law, he remarks that the 'sublimation of juristic thinking' (by which he seems to mean systematization or rationalization) requires a bureaucratic framework. Thus, in Rome:

> the necessity of systematic juristic studies was greatly increased by the imperial system of legal administration through appointed officials and its rationalisation and bureaucratisation, especially in the provincial service.... The systematic rationalisation of the law in England, for example, was retarded because no bureaucratisation occurred there. As long as the juris-consults dominated the Roman legal administration of justice as the legal *honoratiores*, the striving for systematisation was feeble, and no codifying and systematising intervention by the political authority occurred.[38]

Weber's general thesis is that the formal rationalization of law in Western societies is a result of 'capitalism ... interested in strictly formal law and legal procedure' and 'the rationalism of officialdom in absolutist States [which] led to the interest in codified systems and in homogeneous law'.[39] This is *not*, however, an economic explanation (he is therefore sometimes called 'the bourgeois Marx'). There are, in his view, a number of factors that account for this development, including, in particular, the growth of *bureaucracy* which established, as we saw above, the basis for the administration of a rational law conceptually systematized. Other causal factors are the legal profession and legal education (which stressed the conceptual and rational elements of law) and 'natural law' (which results from the tension between formal law and substantive justice).

---

[37] Adapted from Hunt, 107. Table 7.4 is adapted from Hunt, 119.    [38] At 222.
[39] *The Religion of China* (Glencoe, Ill: The Free Press, 1951), 149.

## 7.5.2 **Weber's theory of legitimate domination**

Weber's attempt to explain why people believe they are obliged to obey the law leads him to draw his well-known distinction between three types of legitimate domination: *traditional* (where 'legitimacy is claimed for it and believed in by sanctity of age-old rules and powers'), *charismatic* (based on 'devotion to the exceptional sanctity, heroism or exemplary character of an individual person'), and *legal-rational* domination (which rests on 'a belief in the legality of enacted rules and the right of those elevated to authority under such rules to issue commands'). It is, of course, this third type that is a central feature of Weber's account of law. And, though the concept of legal-rational authority is bound up with his theory of value (which argues for the sociologist of law adopting a detached view of his subject), the important correlation is between this form of domination and the modern bureaucratic state. Under the other forms of domination, authority resides in *persons*; under bureaucracy it is vested in *rules*.

The hallmark of legal-rational authority is its so-called *impartiality*. But it depends upon what Weber calls the principle of 'formalistic impersonality': officials exercise their responsibilities 'without hatred or passion, and hence without affection or enthusiasm. The dominant norms are concepts of straightforward duty without regard to personal considerations.'[40] I shall resist the temptation to examine this fascinating subject in any detail—but you should not! Try to read Kronman, *Max Weber*, Chapter 3.[41] Essentially, Weber argues, as I have said, that while the legitimacy of the first two types depends on a specific relationship between ruler and subject, the source of the legitimacy of legal-rational domination is *impersonal*: obedience is therefore owed to the *legal order*. The importance of Weber's sociology of law—at least for students of jurisprudence—is the correlation between the various typologies: see Table 7.4.

But there are a host of important claims that Weber makes in pursuit of the basis of legitimate domination. The detail with which you explore this important (and extremely influential) aspect of Weber's sociology of law will, of course, depend on the approach adopted in your course.

It is important to note that for Weber political domination draws its legitimacy from the existence of a system of rationally made laws which stipulate the circumstances under which power may be exercised. This form of legitimacy is, in Weber's view, the core of all stable authority in modern societies. Thus, legal rational rules determine the scope of power and provide its legitimacy:

> In Weber's view, in order to understand political legitimacy under conditions of legal domination it is not necessary to evaluate the *content* of the law. The existence of law—in particular

---

[40] *Economy and Society*, 225.
[41] An interesting essay is R Cotterrell, 'Legality and Political Legitimacy in the Sociology of Max Weber' in D Sugarman (ed), *Legality, Ideology and the State* (London: Academic Press, 1983), 69.

**Table 7.4** Weber's analysis of law and legitimacy

| Domination | Legitimation | Legal thought | Justice | Judicial process | Obedience | Administration |
|---|---|---|---|---|---|---|
| Traditional | Traditional | Formal irrationality substantive rationality | Secular or theocratic empirical | Empirical and/or substantive and/or personal (Khadi justice) | Traditional (personal) duty to, eg, king | Patrimonial (hereditary) |
| Charismatic | Charismatic | Formal irrationality substantive irrationality | Charismatic | Revelation: empirical | Response to charisma of leader | None in pure ideal type |
| Legal-rational | Legal-rational | Logical formal rationality | Rational | Rational | Owed to legal order | Bureaucratic-professional |

conditions and in a particular form—provides *its own ideological basis whatever its substantive content*. And the action of the State, in accordance with law, derives legitimacy from law.[42]

In other words, legal domination is not dependent upon the extent to which the law reflects the *values* to which people who accept its legitimacy subscribe.

### 7.5.3 Capitalism and law

Weber is commonly associated with the view that economic forces do not affect the law. But, while this does not misrepresent his argument, it is a crude oversimplification. What Weber actually seeks to show is that law is affected only *indirectly* by economic circumstances. He conceives of law as being 'relatively autonomous'. He claims that 'generally it appears...that the development of the legal structure has by no means been predominantly determined by economic factors.'[43] It is more accurate, therefore, to say that for Weber, law is *fundamentally related to*, but not *determined by* economic factors.

His argument may be summarized as follows: rational economic conduct ('profit-making activity' and 'budgetary management') is at the heart of the capitalist system; this rationalism is facilitated by the certainty and predictability of logically formal rational law. Hence, the presence of this type of law *assists* but does not *cause* the advance of capitalism. He uses the example of England to prove (or, in the view of some critics, to disprove) his thesis that only where the law is systematized so as to ensure the predictability of economic relations, can capitalism develop. By his own admission, however, the emergence of capitalism in England occurred *without* a formally rational legal system. Weber shows how, in many respects, the English common

---

[42] Cotterrell in Sugarman (ed), *Legality, Ideology and the State*, 71; emphasis added.
[43] *Max Weber on Law in Economy and Society*, 131.

law was, during the development of the capitalist economy, highly *irrational*. In particular, unlike the logical, systematic codification and procedure of the *Corpus Juris* formulated under the direction of the Roman emperor, Justinian, English law was a hit-and-miss affair, with a reliance on legal fictions and an archaic procedure based on writs, oaths, and irrational modes of proof. He is therefore forced to conclude that 'England achieved capitalistic supremacy among the nations not because but rather in spite of its judicial system.'[44] How are we to interpret Weber's apparent ambiguity?

For Weber, of course, formally rational law is considered one of the preconditions of capitalism because it provides the necessary certainty and predictability that is an essential if entrepreneurs are to pursue profit-making enterprises. The achievement of this formal rationality required, in Weber's view, the systematization of the legal order, a systematization which he found singularly absent in the English law. How, then, does he explain the emergence of capitalism in England?

This question has exercised many sociologists who offer a variety of explanations for this apparent contradiction in Weber's work. First, it is clear that although English law lacked the systematic order of the Roman law, it was, as Weber himself recognized, a highly *formalistic* legal order. Indeed, Weber characterized such formalism (exhibited, for instance, in proceedings under the writ system) as irrational. And this formalism, says Weber, effected a stabilizing influence on the legal system which produced a greater degree of security and predictability in the economic marketplace.

A second feature of the English legal system to which Weber ascribes considerable significance in the advancement of capitalism is the legal profession. He shows how lawyers in England traditionally served as advisers to businessmen and corporations. This enabled and encouraged them to modify the law to suit the interests of their commercial clients. Coupled with the centralization of the Bar in London, close to the City, and the monopolization of legal education by the Inns of Court, this ensured that lawyers were a group which was 'active in the service of propertied, and particularly capitalistic, private interests and which has to gain its livelihood from them'.[45]

Another factor was that, unlike Continental practice, lawyers in England approximated to 'craft guilds' in their education, training, and specialization which 'naturally produced a formalistic treatment of the law, bound by precedent'.[46] This led to what Weber calls, following Roman law, 'cautelary jurisprudence': emphasis is laid on drafting instruments and devising new clauses to prevent or avoid future litigation. This phenomenon resulted in a close relationship between lawyers and their (mostly commercial) clients. In other words, this feature of legal practice compensated for the lack of systematization in the law itself.

Perhaps therefore what Weber is really saying is that England developed a capitalist economic system despite the absence of legal systematization, because other

---

[44] Ibid, 231.        [45] Ibid, 318.        [46] Ibid, 201.

important components of the legal system engendered it, but that it may have developed even more rapidly and more efficiently if the common law had been less irrational and unsystematic. Yet (as Kronman shows)[47] it sometimes seems as if Weber suggests that capitalism flourished in England precisely *because* the common law was never rationally systematized! Such a view has a certain ring of logic for it is arguable that rational consistency of the law may actually impede the economic pragmatism that suits the economic needs of capitalism. But this does not seem to be an accurate representation of Weber's thesis, and a number of difficulties remain in respect of the extent to which he actually makes *causal* connections between economic and legal factors. Kronman[48] describes as 'causal agnosticism' Weber's refusal to assign causal primacy to either economic or legal conditions. This seems to me to be an important (and neglected) aspect of the question.

He further describes how Weber identifies three ways in which the law influences economic factors.[49] First, it provides a relatively stable set of rules for the protection of contractual expectations. Secondly, certain legal concepts (eg, agency and negotiability) are crucial to economic development. Thirdly, specific economic legislation may encourage certain forms of enterprise or economic organization. On the other hand, economic factors may influence law; a good example is the manner in which lawyers in England placed themselves at the disposal of commercial clients.

In his analysis of this reciprocal relationship, Weber frequently points to exceptions, limitations, or even contradictions of this connection:

> Every strong claim that he makes regarding the influence of one or the other is qualified, somewhere in the text, by an assertion that the influence has only been partial or indirect and has in any case been exerted in the opposite direction as well. To some extent, this agnostic conclusion is unilluminating.[50]

And, Kronman might have added, frustrating! But perhaps this is the mark of a genuine scientist: he is not merely seeking to prove his hypothesis, but, in the search for truth, he pays equal attention to those phenomena that may refute it. Real life is acknowledged to be too complex to admit of simple or comforting causative links.

### 7.5.4 **Critique of Weber**

It is impossible here to do justice to the vast sweep of Weber's sociology of law. His many insights are penetrating: the law of contract, 'natural law', religion, leadership, beliefs, and social action. It is easy to see why he remains so important a sociologist—despite (or is it because of?) the appearance of so many 'new' and more exotic social theories. As far as his 'jurisprudence' is concerned, it would not be difficult to devise an entire course based upon the richness of his writings about law. This is

---

[47] *Max Weber*, 123.     [48] Ibid, 125.     [49] Ibid, 125–30.     [50] Ibid, 129.

not to say, of course, that Weber lacks his detractors. His work has been subjected to close and sustained scrutiny by generations of sociologists. Eight main kinds of criticism may be mentioned, though many other general and particular critiques have been made.

At the most general level, Hunt[51] identifies three central 'problematics' which Weber poses for the sociology of law. Each points up certain limitations of his theory. First, his treatment of the relationship between law and domination is restricted and even distorted by his reduction of domination to the personal relationship between ruler and ruled. It leads him to view 'the ideological form of the legal order...as the real form of legal or political relations'.[52] This is a profound point which I take to mean that the process of domination is more complex than its formal, legal manifestation. Secondly, Weber's analysis of the relation between law and the bureaucratic state is distorted by his concern with legitimacy: this accords unwarranted primacy to this aspect of the political structure. Thirdly, in his discussion of the relationship between law and the economic order, Weber adopts an excessively empiricist view. Fourthly, his sociology is sometimes considered to be incapable of answering many of the questions of modern law; thus Lloyd asks how the problems of the contemporary welfare state can be solved by reference to a theory 'irreversibly committed to a model of capitalism tied to *laissez-faire* economics'.[53] Fifthly, his concept of legal domination exhibits an unduly positivist view of law: 'the highly complex ideological elements of law must be analysed in ways that cannot utilise the ideal type method, if conditions of legitimacy are to be understood in relation to social change.'[54]

A sixth criticism is aimed at another feature of Weber's theory of domination: why should 'bureaucracy' qualify as a type of 'domination'? In the case of traditional or charismatic leaders it is clear that they are 'dominating', since no one has the authority to tell them what to do. But bureaucrats, almost by definition, are told by someone what to do. The conundrum is well expressed by Parkin:[55]

> If bureaucracy does attempt to exercise domination it usurps the authority of a nominally superior body. In other words it uses its power illegitimately. Thus, in the light of Weber's own account, bureaucracy can hardly be an example of 'legitimate domination.' If it acts legitimately it is not dominant; if it exercises domination it ceases to be legitimate.

Seventhly, the 'England problem' has, as we saw, attracted its share of criticism. In addition to the difficulties of its (apparent, though misunderstood) causal claim, it posits a model in which law remains fairly static. If (as Weber suggests) law provides a commonsense context in which rational purposive action is taken, this implies that should the law change it would cease having this function. And the nature of law *is* constantly changing; for persuasive evidence of such change in relation to the 'rule of law' and 'discretionary regulation'.[56] Eighthly, contemporary critics doubt

[51] *The Sociological Movement in Law*, 130–3.      [52] Ibid, 131.
[53] *Introduction to Jurisprudence*, 8th edn (London: Sweet & Maxwell, 2008), 842.
[54] Cotterrell in Sugarman (ed), *Legality, Ideology and the State*, 88.
[55] Parkin, *Max Weber*, 89.      [56] See Cotterrell, *The Sociology of Law*, 168–87.

the applicability today of Weber's claim that in the late nineteenth century the *Rechtsstaat* (the state whose legitimacy is based on the 'rule of law') formal rationality triumphed over substantive rationality. He argues that this lent modern law a neutrality which made the basis of authority independent of acceptance by citizens of particular moral or political values. Critics suggest that modern law exhibits a fundamental reversal towards *substantive* rationality. This takes the form of the growing acceptance of discretionary regulation which is influenced by substantive questions of policy.

## 7.6 Karl Marx

The theories of Karl Marx (1818–83) and Friedrich Engels (1820–95) continue to exert a declining influence on political theory and practice. Marxist interpretations of history, art, and literature are now commonplace. And a Marxist approach to law could belong in Chapter 9 on theories of justice. Although neither Marx nor Engels provide a comprehensive or systematic account of law, there are, scattered throughout their numerous writings, several observations about the relationship between law and economics (or material conditions). These have been hunted down and edited in a useful collection, M Cain and A Hunt under the title *Marx and Engels on Law*.[57] For an admirably lucid and concise introduction to the subject consult Hugh Collins's *Marxism and Law*.[58] The usual problem arises of doing justice to a large and expanding subject within a crowded jurisprudence course. Thus, though you will be expected to have a knowledge of the essentials of Marxist political philosophy, you may (and should) legitimately concentrate on its application to the law and the state.

Marxism, as I said, offers no explicit theory of justice, but both Marx and Engels argue that there is no *absolute* concept of justice; justice is what is acceptable in and necessary for a given mode of production. On this question, see S Lukes, *Marxism and Morality*. In his analysis of capitalism, Marx eschews moral judgments; he claims that his account is a scientific one. Yet his writings bristle with moral condemnations of the exploitation and alienation that are endemic to the capitalist system: he refers, for instance, to it 'stultifying human life into a material force'. At the same time, however, both he and Engels reject the view that there is any objective standard of justice which transcends the economic relations of a society.

[57] See too P Phillips, *Marx and Engels on Law and Laws* (Oxford: Robertson, 1980).
[58] As general accounts of Marx's general political theory, it is hard to find a better text than S Avineri, *The Social and Political Thoughts of Karl Marx* (Cambridge: Cambridge University Press, 1968). I also recommend R Miliband's *Marxism and Politics* (Oxford: Oxford University Press, 1977). An accessible general collection is D McLellan (ed), *Karl Marx: Selected Writings* (Oxford: Oxford University Press, 1977). You will also find a helpful discussion of the principal features of Marxist theories of law in Ch 13 of *Lloyd's Introduction to Jurisprudence*, including several well-chosen extracts from Marx, Engels, and leading Marxist theorists.

Thus, for one leading political philosopher, Marx is saying that 'justice' does 'not provide a set of independent rational standards by which to measure social relations, but must itself always in turn be explained as arising from and controlling those relations'.[59]

### 7.6.1 Historicism

A central feature of Marxist theory developed in his great work *Capital* is its historicism: social evolution is explained in terms of inexorable historical forces. Replacing Hegel's dialectical theory of history, Marx and Engels expounded the well-known theory of 'dialectical materialism'. Hegel explained the unfolding of history in terms of the development of a thesis, its opposite (or antithesis) and, out of the ensuing conflict, its resolution in a synthesis which absorbs and transcends, negates, and preserves both thesis and antithesis. Marx argues that each period of economic development has a corresponding *class* system. Thus during the period of hand-mill production, the feudal system of classes existed. When steam-mill production developed, capitalism replaced feudalism. Under a capitalist system, three principal social classes exist: the landowners, capitalists, and wage labourers. But he foresaw the crystallization of just two classes: the 'bourgeoisie' (those who own the means of production) and the 'proletariat' or 'working class' (who are forced to sell their labour).

Classes are determined by the means of production, and therefore an individual's class is dependent on his relation to the means of production. Marx's 'historical materialism' is based on the fact that the means of production are materially determined; it is dialectical, in part, because he sees an inevitable (ie necessary, logically determined) conflict between those two hostile classes. A revolution would eventually occur because the bourgeois mode of production, based on individual ownership and unplanned competition, stands in contradiction to the increasingly non-individualistic, social character of labour production in the factory. The proletariat would seize the means of production and establish a 'dictatorship of the proletariat' which would, in time, be replaced by a classless, communist society in which law would eventually 'wither away'.

Note the meaning of these two (often misused) terms:

- 'Relations of production': men enter into these relations in order to exploit natural resources by whatever technology is available at a given time in history.

- 'Productive forces': the combination of the 'relations of production' (which depend on the nature of the available natural resources) and the knowledge of technologies for their exploitation.

---

[59] S Lukes, 'Marxism, Morality and Justice' in GHR Parkinson (ed), *Marx and Marxisms* (Cambridge: Cambridge University Press, 1982), 177 at 197.

## 7.6.2 **Base and superstructure**

This metaphor has generated lively debate. In his preface to *A Contribution to the Critique of Political Economy*, Marx draws an important distinction between the economic or material 'base' or 'infrastructure' of a society and its social 'superstructure'. The material base, Marx argues, determines the form and content of the superstructure. Three major problems have arisen in respect of this crucial aspect of Marx's historical materialism. First, is the material base confined to economic factors or does it include *the law*? One modern answer is (following J Plamenatz in, eg, *Man and Society*)[60] that economic relations cannot be described without reference to legal rules. In other words, capitalism, or any other mode of production, depends on the law and legal system for the establishment of economic relations. But this view is opposed: GA Cohen (in *Karl Marx's Theory of History: A Defence*) has argued that we should regard the base as consisting exclusively of material factors. This is because we ought to read any reference in the base to legal 'rights' and 'duties' to refer to 'powers', which are not 'legal'. The debate simmers.[61] Secondly, what is meant by the 'superstructure'? It seems to have a number of uses in Marx's writing, including the legal and political institutions which express the relations of production and the forms of consciousness which reflect a particular class view of the world.

However, as far as the law is concerned, there is no doubt that Marx conceived it (along with various political and cultural phenomena) as belonging to the superstructure of any society. Thirdly (and most importantly), what is the relationship between base and superstructure? This subject has occupied a central place in Marxist theory. It is, of course, linked to the first question above concerning the extent to which law constitutes a part of the material base, but, whatever view is taken on that matter, it is essential to know precisely *how* the base affects the superstructure. You will not be expected to have a detailed grasp of this intriguing problem but you should have some view regarding the position of law.

There are broadly two views concerning the nature of the relationship between base and superstructure and the position of law. The first has been labelled 'crude materialism' for it claims that the law simply 'reflects' the economic base: the form and content of legal rules correspond to the dominant mode of production. This is generally regarded as providing a simplistic and incoherent explanation of *how* law does so. The second view is known as 'class instrumentalism' for it argues that the law is a direct expression of the will of the dominant class. Its implausibility resides in the claim that the dominant class actually has a united or corporate 'will' of which it is conscious. These, and other, difficulties have led certain Marxist theorists (including Collins, *Marxism and Law*)[62] to recommend the abandonment of the base-superstructure model. An alternative explanation for the crucial relationship between economic conditions and the law may lie with Marx's theory of ideology.

[60]  Vol 2 (London: Longman, 1963), 280 ff.
[61]  For a summary, see H Collins, *Marxism and Law* (Oxford: Clarendon Press, 1982), 77–85.
[62]  At 81.

### 7.6.3 Ideology

The argument shifts to the manner in which individuals develop a 'consciousness' of their predicament. In an equally famous passage of the preface to *A Contribution to the Critique of Political Economy* Marx declared: 'It is not the consciousness of men that determines their being, but, on the contrary, their social being that determines their consciousness.' That is to say that our ideas are not arbitrary or fortuitous, they are a result of economic conditions. We absorb our knowledge from our social experience of productive relations. This provides, in part, an explanation of the way in which *law* comes to maintain the social order that (as a matter of the 'natural order of things' rather than as a corporately willed desire) represents the interests of the dominant class.

How does this 'dominant ideology' come to be tacitly accepted by members of society as the 'natural order of things'? One answer is that through a variety of social institutions an 'ideological hegemony' is established, which ensures that (educationally, culturally, politically—and legally) this dominant set of values prevails. This explanation first appears in the prison writings of the Italian Marxist, Antonio Gramsci and is developed (to a high level of sophistication) in the writings of Louis Althusser among whose—several—influential ideas is that of Ideological State Apparatuses (ISAs) that form our values, preferences, and desires. Institutions that shape us include the family, the media, religious organizations, and especially our system of education and the ideas it disseminates.[63]

If you wish to pursue these fascinating subjects further there are two books which devote a fair amount of space to the relationship between law and ideology: P Hirst, *On Law and Ideology*,[64] and C Sumner, *Reading Ideologies*.[65] The law's role in this process is subtle and complex. It is a sort of 'symbolic framework' within which individuals and groups interpret their rights, interests, and conflicts. Collins puts it well:

> The legal system plays a vital role.... In particular the legal framework of rules and doctrines provides a comprehensive interpretation and evaluation of social relationships and events which is in tune with the main themes in the dominant ideology. Because the legal system is encountered frequently in daily life, its systematic articulation and dissemination of a dominant ideology are some of the chief mechanisms for the establishment of ideological hegemony.[66]

As Cotterrell explains: 'Legal ideology can be thought of... not as legal doctrine itself but as the "forms of social consciousness" reflected in and expressed through legal doctrine.'[67]

Marxism's materialist account of law is often met with the claim that it appears to be refuted by reformist legislation which advances the interests of the working class. How, it is asked, can such laws represent the dominant ideology or interests? One popular answer (associated with Nicos Poulantzas, *Political Power and Social Classes*)

---

[63] 'Ideology and Ideological State Apparatuses' in *Lenin and Philosophy* (London: NLB, 1971), 121–73.
[64] Chs 2 and 3.          [65] Chs 1, 2, and 6.          [66] *Marxism and Law*, 50.
[67] *The Sociology of Law*, 122.

is to describe the state as 'relatively autonomous'. It argues that the capitalist state is not entirely free to act as it pleases (in the interests of the ruling class), but is constrained by certain social forces. Nevertheless it will not allow any fundamental challenge to the capitalist mode of production; it is, at bottom, 'a committee for managing the common affairs of the whole bourgeoisie'.[68]

### 7.6.4 Goodbye to law?

Law is a vehicle of class oppression. In a classless society there is therefore no need for law. This is the essence of the argument first implied by Marx in his early writings (especially *The Critique of the Gotha Programme*), popularized by Engels in *Anti-Dühring* and restated by Lenin in *The State and Revolution*. In its more refined version the thesis claims that, following the proletarian revolution, the *bourgeois* state would be swept aside and replaced by the dictatorship of the proletariat. Society, after reactionary resistance has been defeated, would have no further need for law or state: they would 'wither away'. A major difficulty with this prognosis is its bland equation of law with the coercive suppression of the proletariat. It neglects the fact not only that a considerable body of law serves other functions, but that, even (or especially) a communist society requires laws to plan and regulate the economy. To assert that these are not 'law' is to invite scepticism.

A more sophisticated version of this theory is to be found in the work of the Soviet jurist Evgeny Pashukanis (1891–1937). His so-called commodity-exchange theory of law regards law as protecting the rights of individuals in a *contractual relationship*. All law, he argued, could be explained as reflections of this contractual commodity exchange—even criminal law (with its 'contract' between state and citizen under which a tariff of punishments is provided if the individual should offend the law). In a communist society there could be no law: law would eventually disappear to be replaced by administration.[69] To Stalin in 1936 these limitations were so grave as to result in Pashukanis's liquidation:[70] Pashukanis's argument that law would disappear became, under Stalin, an embarrassment. So Stalin made Pashukanis disappear. He was executed in September 1937.

### 7.6.5 Legal fetishism

Neglect at your peril one important conclusion of Marxist legal theory: there is nothing special about law. The root of historical materialism is the proposition that law is (to paraphrase ID Balbus) 'the result of one particular kind of society' rather than that society is the result of the law.[71] 'Legal fetishism' is the condition, in Balbus's words,

[68] Marx and Engels, *Manifesto of the Communist Party*, transl S Moore in *Collected Works*, Vol 6 (London: Lawrence and Wishart, 1976).

[69] A lucid exposition of his theory may be found in R Warrington, 'Pashukanis and the Commodity Form Theory' in Sugarman (ed), *Legality, Ideology and the State*, 43.

[70] See E Kamenka and A Tay, 'The Life and Afterlife of a Bolshevik Jurist' (1970) 19(1) *Problems of Communism* 72 (Jan–Feb).

[71] 'Commodity Form and Legal Form: An Essay on the "Relative Autonomy of the Law"' (1977) 11 *Law and Society Review* 571, 582.

where 'individuals affirm that they owe their existence to the Law, rather than the reverse'. Just as there is a form of commodity fetishism, there is a form of legal fetishism which obscures from legal subjects the origins of the legal system's powers and creates the impression that the legal system has a life of its own. As Balbus says:

> Commodity fetishism and legal fetishism are…two inseparably related aspects of an inverted, 'topsy-turvy' existence under a capitalist mode of production in which *humans are first reduced to abstractions, and then dominated by their own creations.*[72]

The best defence against this affliction is the vulgar model which consigns law (along with literature and politics) to 'part of the superstructure'. But if (as was suggested earlier) this model is to be rejected and law is regarded as part of the material base, how is Marxist theory to resist the malady? Collins provides the following answer:

> Marxists need not follow legal fetishism into the wider excesses of that ideology. Marxists can accept that other social rules as well as laws serve to constitute the foundation for a social formation and to preserve social order…it is wrong for Marxists to ridicule political philosophies which assume the necessity for law, though they need not concur with them in their entirety.[73]

There thus seems to be a limited degree of legal fetishism intrinsic in the more sophisticated version of the base-superstructure model.

But many Marxists *do* unequivocally reject the legal fetishism which regards law as a distinct, special, or identifiable phenomenon which has a unique and autonomous form of reasoning and thought. It has to be said, however, that developments in contemporary Chinese Marxism raise considerable doubts about the continued application of this approach to law in these societies.

### 7.6.6 **Conflict or consensus?**

Classical Marxist theory rejects, in particular, the idea that the law can be a neutral body of rules which guarantees liberty and legality. It spurns, in short, the idea of the rule of law. Indeed, in the opening words of Collins's book: 'The principal aim of Marxist jurisprudence is to criticise the centrepiece of liberal political philosophy, the ideal called the rule of law.'[74] Equally, the concept of 'justice' is largely contingent upon material conditions. To espouse the idea of the rule of law would be to accept the image of law as a neutral arbiter which is above political conflict and remote from the control of particular groups or classes. But Marxists reject this 'consensus' model of society. Of course, the choice between a 'consensus' and 'conflict' model of society is at the core of our understanding of society. Implicit in almost all theories of law is a consensus view. It perceives society as essentially unitary: the legislature represents the common will, the executive acts in the common interest, the law is a neutral referee that is administered 'without fear or favour' for the common good. There are no fundamental conflicts of values or interests. Any conflicts that arise do so at the *personal* level: A sues B for damages for breach of contract, etc. Structural conflicts between

---

[72] Ibid, 584.          [73] *Marxism and Law*, 98.          [74] At 1.

*groups* (if they exist at all) are transposed into questions about the enforcement of *individual* obligations.

At the other end of the spectrum is the 'conflict' model which conceives of society as divided between two opposing camps: those who have property and power, and those who do not. Conflict lies at the heart of society so that individuals or smaller groups have their position defined by the very *structure* of the society: they exist as components of one or other of the two sides. Law in this image, far from being a neutral referee, is actually *the means* by which the dominant group maintains its domination. Closely related to this problem is the subject of individual rights and Marxism. Recent jurisprudential debate has focused on the question: can a socialist accept rights? Much of the discussion has been generated by a few pages in the book, *Whigs and Hunters*, by the well-known British Marxist historian, EP Thompson.[75] It is often argued that the very notion of individual rights is *incompatible* with socialism. In very broad (and perhaps rather crude) terms, this argument generally rests on the irreconcilable conflict between the egoism of liberal theory and the communitarianism of socialism. Some Marxists therefore explicitly reject the concept and language of rights (except perhaps for advancing short-term tactical objectives). They argue that social change does not occur as a consequence of our moralizing about rights. Neither Marx nor Engels addressed themselves *explicitly* to the nature of rights in a socialist society; they were more concerned to uncover the deception of bourgeois ideas and institutions. There are, however, a number of (sometimes ambiguous) statements in their work which may be read to suggest that in a socialist society individual rights *will not be necessary*.

It is very important to grasp the fact that for Marx (at least in his early writing) the achievement of political revolution would be to end the separation between 'civil society' and the state. As he declares in *On the Jewish Question*:

[T]he citizen is proclaimed the servant of egoistic man...the sphere in which man behaves as a communal being is degraded to a level below the sphere in which he behaves as a partial being...[M]an as a member of civil society counts for true man, for man as distinct from the citizen, because he is man in his sensuous, individual, immediate existence, while political man is only the abstract fictional man, man as an allegorical or moral person...[T]he actual individual man must take the abstract citizen back into himself and, as an individual man in his empirical life, in his individual work and individual relationships become a species-being; man must recognise his own forces as social forces, organise them, and thus no longer separate

---

[75] A more nuanced analysis of the question appears in Tom Campbell, *The Left and Rights: A Conceptual Analysis of the Idea of Socialist Rights* (London: Routledge & Kegan Paul, 1983). The matter has been further developed by NE Simmonds, 'Rights, Socialism and Liberalism' (1985) 5 *Legal Studies* 1, to which Professor Campbell has responded: (1985) 5 *Legal Studies* 14. You should also try to read essays by I Markovits, 'Socialist vs Bourgeois Rights' (1978) 45 *University of Chicago Law Review* 612; C Sypnowich, *The Concept of Socialist Law* (Oxford: Clarendon Press, 1990), and 'Law as a Vehicle of Altruism' (1985) 5 *Oxford Journal of Legal Studies* 276; and A Merritt, 'The Nature and Function of Law: A Criticism of EP Thompson's *Whigs and Hunters*' (1980) 7 *British Journal of Law and Society* 194. Though these works are, in the light of political changes in Eastern Europe and the former Soviet Union, a little dated, there is much of value in them. On the question of the theoretical approaches to rights in China, see Albert HY Chen, 'Developing Theories of Rights and Human Rights in China' in Raymond Wacks (ed), *Hong Kong, China and 1997: Essays in Legal Theory* (Hong Kong: Hong Kong University Press, 1993).

social forces from himself in the form of political forces. Only when this has been achieved will human emancipation be completed.

Marx argues that democratic participation is the only way of ending the alienation of the people from the state. His own view of socialist rights (or rights under socialism) therefore seems to rest upon his rejection of the essential characteristics of a capitalist society: the exploitation and alienation it causes. He contrasts the 'rights of citizens' with the 'rights of man'. The former are *political* rights exercised *in common* with others and involve *participation* in the community. The latter, on the other hand, are *private* rights exercised *in isolation* from others and involve *withdrawal* from the community. In the same essay he says, 'Not one of the so-called rights of man goes beyond egoistic man... an individual withdrawn into himself, his private interests and his private desires.' And, most importantly, from the point of view of Marx's central argument concerning private property: 'The practical application of the right of man to freedom is the right of man to private property.' Some commentators have argued that Marx should not be taken to mean here that these 'rights of man' (equality before the law, security, property, liberty) are *not important*; but rather that the very *concept* of such rights is endemic to a society based on *capitalist* relations of production. This is a difficult argument to sustain for in much of his writing Marx sought to show that these rights had no independent significance.

You should also note the Marxist claim that capitalism is destructive of *real* individual liberty. According to Marx, private property represents the dominance of the material world over the 'human element', while communism represents the triumph of the human element over the material world. Marx used the concept of 'reification' to describe the process under which social relations assume the form of relations between *things*. In a capitalist society, he saw this 'reification' as the result of the 'alienation' of workers from the product of their work: the 'general social form of labour appears as the property of a thing'; it is 'reified through the "fetishism of commodities"'. Capitalist relations *seem* to protect individual freedom (eg, 'freedom of contract') but the reality is very different: equality before the law is merely a *formal* property of exchange relations between private property owners: 'This equal right... is... a right of inequality in its content, like every right.'[76]

Revolutionary Marxists have little truck with rights (largely because they are an expression of a capitalist economy and will not be required in a classless, socialist society). This rejection appears to be based on four objections to rights.[77] They may be very briefly stated as follows:

- *Their legalism.* Rights subject human behaviour to the governance of *rules*.

- *Their coerciveness.* Law is a coercive device. Rights are tainted for they protect the interests of capital.

---

[76] *Critique of the Gotha Programme.* Your understanding of socialist rights will clearly be aided by your understanding of 'rights' in general: see Chapter 10.

[77] Identified by Campbell in *The Left and Rights.*

**Table 7.5** Bourgeois and socialist rights compared

| Bourgeois rights | Rights under socialism |
| --- | --- |
| They are entitlements. | They are policy pronouncements. |
| They are ends. | They are a means to some end. |
| They are political. | They are more organizational. |
| They are less so. | They are positive. |
| They depend on the activation of the right-holder. | They are less so. |
| They protect individuals against the attacks of others. | They advance harmonious communal life. |
| They are conditional on right-holders fulfilling their own obligations. | They are dependent on others fulfilling their correlative obligations. |
| They relate to a supporting set of sanctions. | They relate to mandatory rules but not to supporting sanctions. |
| They are (or seek to be) clearly defined. | They are intentionally vague. |
| Their exercise and violation are private affairs. | These are public affairs. |
| They are not so. | They are largely economic. |
| They are 'legalistic' and individualistic. | They are not. |

- *Their individualism*. They protect self-interested atomized individuals.
- *Their moralism*. They are essentially moral and Utopian, and hence irrelevant to the economic base.

Professor Campbell, however, suggests that by adopting an *interest-based* theory of rights (as opposed to power- or contract-based theories) socialist rights become an important element in ensuring democracy. He argues that any form of socialism will require *authoritative rules*—if only to facilitate cooperative and educational activities.[78] Some of these rules will be directed toward the protection of the *individual*—ie rights are constituted. The *interests* (and therefore the rights) of the individual are distinguishable from the acceptance of society as an 'aggregate of competitive and egoistic individuals'. This permits an accommodation of human rights in a socialist society.

Drawing on the writing of Campbell and the interesting comparison by Markovits[79] between East and West Germany, Table 7.5 may be used as a summary of the major differences between so-called 'socialist rights' and 'bourgeois rights'.

The view that rights are necessarily 'individualistic' in the sense intended by Campbell has been attacked from a number of perspectives. Simmonds contends that his description of liberal theory as implying a society of 'competitive and egoistic

---

[78] Ibid, 123.      [79] (1978) 45 *University of Chicago Law Review* 612.

individuals' is too crude.[80] Sypnowich[81] attacks, *inter alia*, Campbell's equation of individual rights and alienated society:

> In the search for a vehicle which mediates the relations of individuals with the community, socialists should look to law, which upon its restructuring in the transformation of economic and political relations, will better fulfil the bourgeois promises of liberty and equality.

This sort of critique is strongly reminiscent of EP Thompson's view of the rule of law expressed in *Whigs and Hunters*.[82] After a detailed investigation of the effects of the so-called Black Act in the eighteenth century in England, Thompson considers some of the threats to civil liberties and democratic rights emanating from the modern state. He argues that Marxists tend to dismiss *all* law as merely an instrument of class rule and to treat civil liberties as no more than an illusion which obscures the realities of class rule. But law, he says, is not merely an instrument of class domination, but also a 'form of mediation' between and within the classes. Its *function* is not only to serve power and wealth, but also to impose 'effective inhibitions upon power' and to subject 'the ruling class to its own rules'.

He rejects the Marxist isolation of law as a distinctive part of the superstructure separate from its base; in his study of the Black Act he says[83] he discovered that law 'was deeply imbricated within the very basis of productive relations.... [W]e cannot... simply separate off all law as ideology, and assimilate this also to the State apparatus of a ruling class' (here he differs from Althusser). And, with a resounding, rhetorical flourish, he concludes:

> [T]he rule of law itself, the imposing of effective inhibitions upon power and the defence of the citizen from power's all-intrusive claims, seems to me to be an unqualified human good. To deny or belittle this good is, in this dangerous century when the resources and pretensions of power continue to enlarge, a desperate error of intellectual abstraction. More than this, it is a self-fulfilling error, which encourages us to give up the struggle against bad laws and class-bound procedures, and to disarm ourselves before power. It is to throw away a whole inheritance of struggle *about* law, and within the forms of law, whose continuity can never be fractured without bringing men and women into immediate danger.[84]

How is it possible for a distinguished, self-confessed Marxist historian to embrace the rule of law as an 'unqualified human good'? We have already seen that the 'principal aim of Marxist jurisprudence is to criticize the centrepiece of liberal political philosophy, the ideal called the rule of law'.[85] And Collins adds that 'Marxists are... inconsistent when they both uphold the virtues of legality and liberty and at the same time criticise the rule of law.'[86] Has something gone badly wrong here?

One answer is that 'Thompson is not a Marxist historian'.[87] But at least six other responses may briefly be made. First, to argue for restraints on authoritarian rule does not commit Marxists to a wholesale adulation of the rule of law. Secondly, some critics

---

[80]  (1985) 5 *Legal Studies* 1. See Campbell's reply (1985) 5 *Legal Studies* 14.
[81]  (1985) 5 *Oxford Journal of Legal Studies* 276, 284.
[82]  At 258–69.      [83]  *Whigs and Hunters* (London: Penguin, 1975), 261.      [84]  Ibid, 266.
[85]  Collins, *Marxism and Law*, 1.      [86]  Ibid, 145.
[87]  A Merritt (1980) 7 *British Journal of Law & Society* 194, 210.

have argued that Thompson commits the very offences which he lays at the door of those whom he describes as 'modern Marxists', namely reductionism and functionalism; yet he is himself both reductionist (for he reduces all law to a restraint on power) and functionalist (for he describes law as a means of mediating between and within the classes). But law is not the only method of inhibiting state power; what of political institutions, the press, trade unions, etc? Thirdly, to define law as an inhibition of power presupposes the existence of a power alienated from the people which *needs* to be inhibited. But this is to accept the bourgeois state as given and unchangeable when, to paraphrase Balbus, law is a result of one particular kind of society, rather than society being the result of law.

Fourthly, Thompson appears to accept[88] that there is an 'essential' notion (or core meaning) of law which is *outside* the base-superstructure model and which is unrelated to class-bound instrumentalism; yet he seeks to eradicate 'essentialism' from his own work. Fifthly, one is never entirely clear what he means by the 'rule of law'; his definition oscillates between a formal and substantive notion. Constitutional lawyers may find this ambiguity about so important a concept a little hard to swallow! Sixthly, it is sometimes alleged that Thompson's own historical account of the Black Act contradicts his conclusion about the rule of law.[89] To some critics, Thompson's embrace of the rule of law constitutes part of his attack on the 'new' theoretical Marxism (associated especially with the works of Althusser and Poulantzas), an attack which he continues in his important book, *The Poverty of Theory*.[90] It is unlikely that you will be expected to enter this perilous territory, but if you are you will find a useful map in Perry Anderson's *Arguments Within English Marxism*.[91] I discuss rights in Chapter 10.

## 7.7 Michel Foucault

An incisive analysis of the individual and society characterizes the remarkable scholarship of the French thinker, Michel Foucault (1926–84).[92] His complex account of society and human nature is deeply embedded in actual historical practices and institutions, and his theories therefore have a number of implications for the law and legal system. Yet it would be unwise to attempt to uncover specific facets from the intricate network of his ideas that relate to, or even bear on, the law. His ideas defy such simplistic interpretation or application, for his 'vocabulary, preoccupations, and methods of analysis...systematically flout the scholarly conventions'.[93] This is not music to the ears of the beleaguered jurisprudence student, though few courses will have the space to admit more than Foucault's essential philosophy, or what, in his later work, he

---

[88] *Whigs and Hunters*, 268.        [89] See Merritt at 211–14.

[90] EP Thompson, *The Poverty of Theory and Other Essays* (London: Merlin Press, 1978).

[91] Perry Anderson, *Arguments Within English Marxism* (London: Verso Editions, 1980).

[92] See generally Ben Golder and Peter Fitzpatrick, *Foucault's Law* (Abingdon: Routledge, 2009).

[93] Anne Barron, 'Foucault and Law' in J Penner, D Schiff, and R Nobles (eds), *Jurisprudence and Legal Theory: Comment and Materials* (London: Butterworths, 2002), Ch 19. This is an able, scholarly summary of Foucault's principal, often difficult, ideas. See too Paul Rabinow (ed), *The Foucault Reader* (Harmondsworth: Penguin Books, 1984).

prefers to call 'genealogy',[94] and then, more than likely, they will focus on the extent to which it contributes to an understanding of the law in society.

An immediate problem in relation to his account of law is the claim that Foucault failed to acknowledge its significance in modern society. It is even argued by several theorists that he 'expelled' law from his analysis of power relations. But this 'expulsion thesis' is robustly contested by Golder and Fitzpatrick, who argue:

> Whilst law in Foucault's account is indeed made subordinate to disciplinary formations...such [a view]...does not *pace* those proponents of the 'expulsion thesis', betoken the end or the subsumption of law in modernity. Rather, if on occasion the 'counter-law [disciplinary power] becomes the effective and institutionalized content of the juridical forms',[95] then this movement and investment attest to law's necessary responsiveness, to its orientation towards an outside.[96]

### 7.7.1 Power

For Foucault power is distinct from either physical force or legal regulation. Nor is it antipathetic to freedom or truth. Instead, in works such as *Discipline and Punish*,[97] he demonstrates how, beginning in the eighteenth century, the human body was subjected to a new 'microphysics' of power through the 'geography' of institutions such as factories, hospitals, schools, and prisons. Discipline consists of four 'practices', each of which generates consequent effects on those who are subjected to it. Thus this control creates in those who are its subjects an 'individuality' that contains the following four characteristics:

1. 'Cellular': By the 'play of spatial distribution'.
2. 'Organic': By the 'coding' of activities.
3. 'Genetic': By the accumulation of time.
4. 'Combinatory': By the 'composition of forces'.

In doing so, it 'operates four great techniques':

1. It draws up tables.
2. It prescribes movements.
3. It imposes exercises.
4. It arranges 'tactics' in order to obtain the combination of forces.

---

[94] 'Genealogy is gray, meticulous, and patiently documentary. It operates on a field of entangled and confused parchments, on documents that have been scratched over and recopied many times...[I]t rejects the metahistorical deployment of ideal significations and indefinite teleologies. It opposes itself to the search for "origins"', Foucault, *The Archaeology of Knowledge*, transl AM Sheridan Smith (London: Tavistock, 1972), Ch 1. He is here influenced by Nietzsche.

[95] Michel Foucault, *Discipline and Punish: The Birth of the Prison*, transl A Sheridan (Harmondsworth: Penguin, 1991), 224.          [96] Golder and Fitzpatrick, op cit, 130.

[97] See note 95.

He concludes:

> Tactics, the art of constructing, with located bodies, coded activities and trained aptitudes, mechanisms in which the product of the various forces is increased by the calculated combination are no doubt the highest form of disciplinary practice.[98]

By applying these methods, the social order is rendered more manageable. Disciplinary power, moreover, induces us to act in ways that we come to think of as natural. We are thus manipulated and controlled by these 'technologies': we become 'docile bodies'—and, as a result, capitalism is able to develop and flourish. Foucault refers to Jeremy Bentham's conception of a Panopticon as a paradigm of disciplinary control. This was a prison building he designed in 1785 that permits an observer to survey inmates without their being aware of being observed. Through its spatial command, it combines power, control of the body and of groups, and knowledge (the prisoner is systematically monitored in his cell)—and 'normalization'. In the nineteenth century this normative rationality, according to Foucault, eroded legal regulation through the entry of medicine, psychiatry, and social sciences into the legal system. This occurred when 'normal' behaviour began to be measured, not by absolute moral standards of right or wrong, but by appeals to statistical yardsticks of normality.

His investigation of power (of which this is merely a précis) leads Foucault to question liberalism, with its preoccupation with centralized *state* power. Indeed, he regards this misconstruction as a means by which liberalism actually fosters the very domination it seeks to diminish.

## 7.7.2 **The law**

Since the Foucauldian world is one in which disciplinary power pervades almost every element of social life, the law has no special claim to primacy, though, as pointed out earlier, it is not to be altogether 'expelled' from an account of contemporary society. Nevertheless, because discipline constructs the individuals against whom it is deployed, it cannot be accounted for by a theory that presumes that each of us is:

> an embodied, living creature, an inhabitant of a particular environment, with a unique set of needs, interests, abilities and aptitudes; it seeks to administer and normalize the conduct of these discrete and disparate persons with a view to ordering a multiplicity of persons and making each and all of them more useful. Far from being the 'given' of power, individual capacities are in this modality the effect of power; far from being universal, they are irreducibly particular and endlessly differentiated.[99]

This is a piquant depiction of our postmodern regulatory state in which government policy is directed towards controlling the various threats to the maintenance of social order. The law has thus become 'sociologized'. Formal equality is camouflage; it obscures the domination that is the hallmark of our social condition.

---

[98] Ibid, 167.   [99] Barron, 'Foucault and Law', 983.

### 7.7.3 Critique

Among the chief criticisms of Foucault's work is its impenetrability, especially the difficulties of locating its author in any tradition or ideology. He has been described, amongst other things, as a Marxist, an 'irrationalist', a nihilist, an anarchist, and a conservative. But he defies pigeon-holing; he is, one might argue, all and none of these things. This frustrates, even annoys, those who seek to place him in an unambiguous category of political or philosophical thought. Secondly, critics are unable to discern a specific 'message' that he articulates; he waves no bright activist banner. Thirdly, issues are infuriatingly discussed with little regard for any logical sequence, questions of causality are neglected or reversed, different levels of analysis are often confused, his use of metaphor sometimes impedes, rather than assists, his argument. Fourthly, a number of critics allege that Foucault both disparages and relies on Enlightenment values. Fifthly, his historical method has been attacked as unreliable, sloppy, or even fabricated. For example, historians have contended that his account in *Madness and Civilization* of what he dubs the 'Great Confinement' occurred not in the seventeenth century, as Foucault claims, but, in the nineteenth century, thereby undermining his claim that the confinement of madmen was linked to the Age of Enlightenment.

## 7.8 Jürgen Habermas

The social theory of Jürgen Habermas (1922– ), the influential German social theorist, incorporates subtle cultural, political, and economic analyses that are not always easy to amalgamate into a coherent whole.[100] Drawing on the writings of Marx, Weber, Durkheim, and Parsons, amongst others, he develops a complex account of modern society. Central to his theory, as expressed especially in *The Theory of Communicative Action*, is the question of the rationality of action. Distinguishing between (a) cognitive-instrumental rationality (conduct that seeks to achieve a specific objective) and (b) communicative rationality (interactions that seek mutual understanding), Habermas contends that both forms of rationality must be understood as ideal types to be applied to various social formations at different stages of development. This leads him to argue that human interaction is symbolically mediated through the use of language. He therefore concentrates on the use of language or 'speech-acts' that pursue mutual understanding, proposing that language that is sufficiently well formed to be comprehensible, and generates three claims: (a) a claim that the speech-act is

---

[100] Among his huge output, most important among Habermas's work are *The Theory of Communicative Action, Vol 1: Reason and the Rationalization of Society* (Boston, Mass: Beacon, 1984), *The Theory of Communicative Action, Vol 2: Lifeworld and System: A Critique of Functional Reason* (Boston, Mass: Beacon, 1987), *Critique of Functionalist Reason*, translated by Thomas McCarthy (Cambridge: Polity Press, 1989), and see K Raes, 'Legalisation, Communication and Strategy: A Critique of Habermas' Approach to Law' (1986) 13 *Journal of Law & Society* 183.

true as corresponding to a certain state of affairs; (b) that the speech-act is correct with regard to a specified or implied normative context; and (c) that the speech-act is expressed truthfully by the speaker.

Habermas maintains that communicative actions (including signs, gestures, the written word) imply that all three claims are accepted or, on the other hand, that any one or more of the claims will be queried and hence develop into a matter for further discussion (ie communicative action) about the legitimacy of the implied claims. Habermas describes this form of communication as 'discourse', and distinguishes between (a) *theoretical* discourse concerning truth; (b) *practical* discourse on rightness; and (c) *expressive and evaluative* discourse concerning authenticity and sincerity.

Habermas attempts to show that the Western combination of capitalism and a bureaucratic state produces a society that operates through money and power. The rationality of the former (financial transactions) places a premium on the value of productivity, while bureaucratic power seeks political efficacy in decision-making.

It is when social institutions interfere or undermine the 'lifeworld' (the sphere of common norms and identities) that, Habermas argues, difficulties arise. Communicative actions are then redefined in instrumental terms, and actions that pursue mutual understanding degenerate into conduct that is instrumentally directed toward success. Contemporary society, he argues, suffers from just these types of problems: *anomie* and alienation occur when economic and political systems invade the 'lifeworld'.

We need concentrate here only on his post-Kantian project of the defence of reason. In particular, Habermas attempts to show that despite the inexorable march of instrumental-technocratic consciousness, and the domination of the 'lifeworld' that it brings in its wake, the capitalist state also presents opportunities for greater 'communicative action'.

### 7.8.1 The modern state

Habermas describes four stages in the 'juridification' of sovereignty, as set out in Table 7.6.

Table 7.6 Habermas: modern forms of sovereignty

| | |
|---|---|
| Bourgeois state | Sovereign state with monopoly of coercive force as sole source of domination |
| Constitutional state | Power limited by constitutional norms |
| Democratic constitutional state | Political participation of electorate |
| Social and democratic constitutional state | Juridifies inequalities by enactment of labour laws and social security |

The modern state's combination of capitalism and a strong, centralized authority results in the 'lifeworld' being intruded upon. This generates, in Habermas's view, atomization and alienation (echoes of Marx, see 7.6). Because the 'lifeworld' is established by processes whose existence depends on communication and social solidarity, this intrusion undermines the 'lifeworld' itself and reduces the prospects for collective self-determination. But he recognizes the opportunity for rational communicative discourse in respect of facts, values, and inner experience.

### 7.8.2 The law

Since his concept of 'communicative reason' rests on the principles of freedom and equality, we should expect Habermas to embrace some version of liberalism. But his approach is more complex. He distinguishes between 'law as medium' and 'law as institution'. The former describes law as a body of formal, general rules that control the state and the economy. The latter inhabits the 'lifeworld' and hence expresses its shared values and norms in institutional form, for example, parts of the criminal law that touch on morality. Unlike 'law as medium', 'law as institution' requires legitimation. In fact, argues Habermas, in our pluralistic, fragmented society, these institutions are a powerful source of normative integration. Barron expresses this nicely:

> [S]ince law also speaks the language of the system, it can function as a bridge between lifeworld and system, and a vehicle for the former's defence and reinvigoration. In particular, law can serve as the 'transformer' that converts the 'communicative power' generated by discursive processes in the lifeworld into the 'administrative power' of the state.[101]

For Habermas, therefore, the legitimacy of the law depends crucially on the effectiveness of the process of discourse by which the law is made. Freedom of speech and other fundamental democratic rights thus appear to be decisive. Indeed, he seems at times to be advocating a Utopian system approximating to Greek democracy!

At the heart of his legal theory is the connection between law and morality. Law thus has a fundamentally moral or normative element. Notwithstanding the increased drift towards instrumental technological efficiency, the law requires moral legitimacy which, procedurally, is achieved through rational discussion and communication. Furthermore, law plays a vital role in institutionalizing the independent operation of money and power in a society's economic and administrative structures, respectively.[102]

---

[101] Anne Barron, '(Legal) Reason and its "Others": Recent Developments in Legal Theory' in Penner, Schiff, and Nobles (eds), *Jurisprudence and Legal Theory: Comment and Materials*, 1083.

[102] In *Between Facts and Norms*, Habermas modifies his general theory to recognize that while the law depends on state coercion, it also requires the support of individual rights.

If you wish to explore how Habermas demonstrates the historical development of law, have a look at the last chapter of *The Theory of Communicative Action* where he traces the origins of the welfare state.

### 7.8.3 Critique

The writings of Habermas have generated an enormous literature. And his theories have been widely applied (or misapplied) to a host of jurisprudential and philosophical approaches to law, politics, and sociology. Thus, for example, his account of communicative action is deployed by a number of Critical Legal Studies adherents (see Chapter 13). Among the criticisms that have been levelled against him are, first, that he places excessive faith in the law as a means of achieving social integration.[103] Secondly, his discourse principle (that only those legal norms are valid to which all persons affected have assented as participants in rational discourse) is impractical and idealistic. Thirdly, he fails adequately to identify which laws in particular function to reinforce social integration. Fourthly, it has been suggested by some that he neglects sociological studies of law, especially those that examine its legitimacy.

## 7.9 Autopoiesis

The question of legal 'closure' is a recurring theme in critical theory (see Chapter 13). The concept describes the way in which the law operates autonomously from other disciplines or practices, and the fact that the law often reproduces and validates itself. Professor Cotterrell provides a useful summary:

> To adopt an idea of legal closure is to claim that law is self-standing and irreducible or has an independent integrity which is normally unproblematic, natural or self-generated, not dependent on contingent links with an extralegal environment of knowledge or practice.[104]

The law is a law unto itself. This self-referential notion has recently been developed to offer a full-blown sociological account of the legal system by the German theorists Niklas Luhmann and Gunther Teubner who, employing a biological metaphor, have called their theory 'autopoiesis'. In this vision of the law (as some sort of physiological process), extralegal information (economics, science, etc) is received, but the law somehow ingests it and, as if by some biological process, transforms it into a form that is legal. In this way the law is constantly reproducing its own normative form. Thus the law's self-absorbed autonomy does not rule out the receipt of data cognitively. This,

---

[103] See Brian Z Tamanaha, 'Socio-Legal Positivism and a General Jurisprudence' (2001) 21 *Oxford Journal of Legal Studies* 1.

[104] 'Sociological Perspectives on Legal Closure' in Alan Norrie (ed), *Closure or Critique: New Directions in Legal Theory* (Edinburgh: Edinburgh University Press, 1993), 175.

more or less, enables law to acquire an autonomous sovereignty over all its views. More than that, the law develops an ability to *think* independently, thereby achieving almost complete closure, at least normatively.

This complex (and, at times, slightly obscure) sociological theory seeks to deny the possibility of authentic normative change in the law. It is explained instead by Luhmann as 'the structural coupling of system and environment'.[105] In other words, there is no direct causative link between the extralegal world and the law itself; there is no noisy 'input', merely the gentle hum of the legal system reproducing itself. But if the law is, as Teubner puts it, 'an autonomous epistemic subject that constructs a social reality of its own', are we not in danger of reifying it, treating the law as an object? Do we not risk abandoning the power of human beings to control and change legal norms? Moreover, as Freeman asks, if legal systems are autopoietic, how are they born? Where do they come from, and why did they appear? 'Unless the first legal system was not autopoietic or not a legal system (by what test?), it seems it must have had its source in the extralegal environment, whether this was religion, morality, or power.'[106]

## 7.10  Whither the sociology of law?

While the sociology of law is generally acknowledged to have come of age, a number of doubts have been expressed about its future. Generally regarded as the 'second phase' (after the emergence of sociological jurisprudence) in the development of the sociological movement in law, it is frequently doubted whether the sociology of law has an adequate 'theoretical' grounding. By this is meant that, though there has been a considerable growth in *socio-legal studies* (eg, there have been numerous empirical studies of the courts, the jury, the police, the legal profession, etc), not enough attention has been paid to the difficulties inherent in the concept of 'law' and the 'legal system'. They are, in the course of these projects, treated as 'unproblematic' when (as I hope is by now clear!) they are anything but. On the other hand, it is sometimes argued that sociologists of law are, in some instances, narrowly 'positivistic' in their preoccupation with legal 'definition'. You will form your own conclusions. Certainly, in the work of Roberto Unger (especially *Law in Modern Society*)[107] and Jürgen Habermas (especially in *Legitimation Crisis*)[108] there is a wealth of sociological and political 'theory'.

---

[105] Large extracts from Luhmann, *Law as a Social System* may be found in G Teubner, R Nobles, and D Schiff, 'The Autonomy of Law: An Introduction to Autopoiesis' in Penner, Schiff, and Nobles (eds), *Jurisprudence and Legal Theory: Comment and Materials*, 903–8, 921–34, and Teubner, *Altera pars audiatur: Law in the Collision of Discourse* (Berlin: Walter de Gruyter, 1987), 934–54.

[106] *Lloyd's Introduction to Jurisprudence*, 879.

[107] Roberto Unger, *Law in Modern Society: Toward a Criticism of Social Theory* (London: Collier-Macmillan, 1977).

[108] See K Raes, 'Legalisation, Communication and Strategy: A Critique of Habermas' Approach to Law' (1986) 13 *Journal of Law & Society* 183.

Alan Hunt complains that:

[A]t root the contemporary status of sociology of law is marked precisely by a lack of clarity as to its nature, purpose and direction; it is a hot-house plant, the forced offspring of the deficiencies of sociological jurisprudence and the jurisprudential tradition in general.[109]

# Questions

1. In what ways does a sociological account advance our understanding of the law?

2. What are the main achievements of Roscoe Pound?

3. What do you understand by the 'living law'?

4. Durkheim's most important achievement, according to Cotterrell, may be 'his single-minded search for a sociological grounding for moral bonds in societies that, to many observers, appear to have become far too complex, chaotic, secular, and atomistic for any such moral frameworks to exist.' (*Law's Community: Legal Theory in Sociological Perspective* (Oxford: Clarendon Press, (1995), 203)

   Evaluate this claim.

5. Can Weber's account of legitimate domination explain Saddam Hussein?

6. Does Weber solve the 'England problem'?

7. Explain 'dialectical materialism', 'relations of production', 'means of production', 'base', 'superstructure', and 'legal fetishism' in Marxist theories of law and state.

8. Can a Marxist believe in the rule of law or human rights? See also 10.3.

9. What is 'legal closure'?

10. Does Foucault have anything important to say about law in society?

11. A critic of Habermas refers to the 'alienating, excluding effect of, and the irony of, a theory which makes an extensive case for open and accessible discourse, but is presented in a form and manner that is comprehensible only to the initiated.' (BZ Tamanaha, 'The View of Habermas From Below: Doubts About the Centrality of Law and the Legitimation Enterprise' (1999) 76 *Denver University Law Review* 989, 1003)

    Do you agree?

# Further reading

ALTHUSSER, LOUIS, *Lenin and Philosophy, and Other Essays*, transl Ben Brewster (London: NLB, 1971).

ANDERSON, PERRY, *Arguments within English Marxism* (London: Verso Editions, 1980).

---

[109] *The Sociological Movement in Law*, 137. For further and better particulars read Hunt's Ch 6; it contains a penetrating diagnosis of, and prognosis for, the sociological movement in legal theory.

AVINERI, SHLOMO, *The Social and Political Thought of Karl Marx* (Cambridge: Cambridge University Press, 1968).

BANAKER, REZA and TRAVERS, MAX (eds), *An Introduction to Law and Social Theory* 2nd edn (Oxford: Hart Publishing, 2013).

BARRON, ANNE, 'Foucault and Law' in J Penner, D Schiff, and R Nobles (eds), *Jurisprudence and Legal Theory: Comment and Materials* (London: Butterworths, 2002), Ch 19.

BLACK, DONALD, *The Behavior of Law* (New York and London: Academic Press, 1976).

CAIN, MAUREEN and HUNT, ALAN, *Marx and Engels on Law* (London: Academic Press, 1979).

CAMPBELL, CM and WILES, PAUL (eds), *Law and Society* (London: Martin Robertson, 1979).

CAMPBELL, TOM, *The Left and Rights: A Conceptual Analysis of the Idea of Socialist Rights* (London: Routledge & Kegan Paul, 1983).

CHAMBLISS, WILLIAM and SEIDMAN, ROBERT, *Law, Order, and Power*, 2nd edn (Reading, Mass and London: Addison-Wesley, 1982).

COHEN, GA, *Karl Marx's Theory of History: A Defence* (Oxford: Clarendon Press, 1978).

COLLINS, HUGH, *Marxism and Law* (Oxford: Clarendon Press, 1982).

COTTERRELL, ROGER, *The Sociology of Law: An Introduction* (London: Butterworths, 1984).

COTTERRELL, ROGER, *Law's Community: Legal Theory in Sociological Perspective* (Oxford: Clarendon Press, 1995).

COTTERRELL, ROGER, *Law, Culture and Society: Legal Ideas in the Mirror of Social Theory* (Aldershot: Ashgate, 2006).

COTTERRELL, ROGER, (ed), *Law in Social Theory* (Aldershot: Ashgate, 2006).

COTTERRELL, ROGER, *Living Law: Studies in Legal and Social Theory* (Aldershot: Ashgate, 2008).

DURKHEIM, ÉMILE, *The Division of Labour in Society*, transl George Simpson (London: Collier-Macmillan, 1964).

EHRLICH, EUGEN, *Fundamental Principles of the Sociology of Law*, transl WL Moss (Cambridge, Mass: Harvard University Press, 1936) *(Harvard Studies in Jurisprudence*, Vol 5).

ENGELS, FRIEDRICH, *Anti-Dühring* (Moscow: Foreign Languages Publishing House, 1954).

GOLDER, BEN and FITZPATRICK, PETER, *Foucault's Law* (Abingdon: Routledge, 2009).

HIRST, PAUL, *On Law and Ideology* (London: Macmillan, 1979).

HUNT, ALAN, *The Sociological Movement in Law* (London: Macmillan, 1978).

HUNT, ALAN, 'Dichotomy and Contradiction in the Sociology of Law' (1981) 8 *British Journal of Law & Society* 47.

KAMENKA, E and NEALE, RS (eds), *Feudalism, Capitalism and Beyond* (London: Edward Arnold, 1973).

KRONMAN, ANTHONY R, *Max Weber* (London: Edward Arnold, 1983).

LUKES, STEVEN, *Marxism and Morality* (Oxford: Clarendon Press, 1985).

LUKES, STEVEN and SCULL, ANDREW (eds), *Durkheim and the Law* (Oxford: Martin Robertson, 1983).

MCLELLAN, DAVID (ed), *Karl Marx: Selected Writings* (Oxford: Oxford University Press, 1977).

MARX, K, 'Critique of the Gotha Programme' in D McLellan, *The Thought of Marx* (London and Basingstoke: Macmillan, 1971).

MARX, K, 'Preface to a Contribution to the Critique of Political Economy' in *Early Writings*, ed L Colletti (Harmondsworth: Penguin Books/NLB, 1975).

MARX, K, *Capital*, transl B Fowkes and D Fembach (Harmondsworth: Penguin Books/Random House, 1976).

MARX, K, 'On the Jewish Question' in D McLellan (ed), *Karl Marx: Selected Writings* (Oxford: Oxford University Press, 1977).

MARX, K and ENGELS, F, *Manifesto of the Communist Party*, transl S Moore, in *Collected Works*, Vol 6 (London: Lawrence and Wishart, 1976).

MERRITT, A, 'The Nature and Function of Law: A Criticism of EP Thompson's *Whigs and Hunters*' (1980) 7 *British Journal of Law and Society* 194.

MILIBAND, RALPH, *Marxism and Politics* (Oxford: Oxford University Press, 1977).

NELKEN, D, 'Law in Action or Living Law? Back to the Beginning in Sociology of Law' (1984) 4 *Legal Studies* 157.

NELKEN, D, 'Blinding Insights? The Limits of a Reflexive Sociology of Law' (1998) 25 *Journal of Law and Society* 107.

NONET, PHILIPPE and SELZNICK, PHILIP, *Law and Society in Transition: Toward Responsive Law* (New York: Octagon Books, 1978).

PARKIN, FRANK, *Max Weber* (Chichester: Ellis Horwood, 1982).

PARKINSON, GHR, *Marx and Marxisms* (Cambridge: Cambridge University Press, 1982) (Royal Institute of Philosophy Lecture Series, No 14).

PHILLIPS, PAUL, *Marx and Engels on Law and Laws* (Oxford: Robertson, 1980).

PLAMENATZ, JP, *Man and Society: A Critical Examination of Some Important Social and Political Theories from Machiavelli to Marx* (London: Longman, 1963).

POULANTZAS, NICOS, *Political Power and Social Classes*, transl/ed Timothy O'Hagan (London: Verso Editions, 1978).

POUND, ROSCOE, *Jurisprudence* (St Paul, Minn: West Publishing, 1959).

ROKUMOTO, KAHEI (ed), *Sociological Theories of Law* (Aldershot: Dartmouth, 1994).

SCHUBERT, GLENDON A (ed), *Judicial Behavior: A Reader in Theory and Research* (Chicago, Ill: Rand McNally, 1964).

SYPNOWICH, C, 'Law as a Vehicle of Altruism' (1985) 5 *Oxford Journal of Legal Studies* 276.

SYPNOWICH, C, *The Concept of Socialist Law* (Oxford: Clarendon Press, 1990).

TAMANAHA, BRIAN Z, *Realistic Socio-Legal Theory* (Oxford: Oxford University Press, 1997).

TEUBNER, GUNTHER (ed), *Autopoietic Law: A New Approach to Law and Society* (Berlin: Walter de Gruyter, 1987).

TEUBNER, GUNTHER, *Law as an Autopoietic System* (Oxford: Blackwell, 1993).

TEUBNER, GUNTHER, NOBLES, R, and SCHIFF, D, 'The Autonomy of Law: An Introduction to Autopoiesis' in J Penner, D Schiff, and R Nobles (eds), *Jurisprudence and Legal Theory: Comment and Materials* (London: Butterworths, 2002).

THOMPSON, EDWARD, *Whigs and Hunters* (London: Penguin, 1975).

TÖNNIES, FERDINAND, *Community and Association*, transl and supplemented by Charles P Loomis (London: Routledge & Kegan Paul, 1974).

TURNER, STEPHEN P and FACTOR, REGIS A, *Max Weber: The Lawyer as Social Thinker* (London: Routledge, 1994).

WEBER, MAX, *The Religion of China: Confucianism and Taoism*, transl/ed Hans H Gerth (Glencoe, Ill: The Free Press, 1951).

WEBER, MAX, *Max Weber on Law in Economy and Society*, ed Max Rheinstein, transl Edward Shils and Max Rheinstein (Cambridge, Mass: Harvard University Press, 1954) (*20th Century Legal Philosophy Series*, Vol 6).

WEBER, MAX, *Economy and Society: An Outline of Interpretive Sociology*, ed Guenther Roth and Claus Wittich (New York: Bedminister Press, 1968).

# 8

# Historical and anthropological jurisprudence

Unlike manna, the law does not fall from the sky. It tends to develop as an expression of a society's peculiar culture, values, and mores. This historical view of the genesis of law was highly influential in nineteenth-century Germany, and its adherents are often described as belonging to the so-called Romantic Movement. This school shared the positivists' misgivings about the abstractions of natural law, though it rejected their view that law was manufactured by calculated or deliberate preference. Law, it contended, was the result of historical development.

A related theory of the nature of law is based on the contention that it should be examined not just in modern states but also in primitive ones as well as in 'non-state' contexts such as voluntary clubs and societies, religious institutions, universities, and even international organizations. Legal theory should take account of the development of law in these other contexts or risk being incomplete. It is this concern that has led some theorists to the subject of anthropological jurisprudence which investigates 'simple' societies in order to discover the nature of law and legal systems.

## 8.1 Why do legal systems differ?

Before embarking on this historical and anthropological expedition, it is worth pausing to reflect briefly on what special characteristics distinguish the Western legal tradition from other systems. Western legal systems have at least the following distinctive features:

- A reasonably clear differentiation between legal institutions (including adjudication, legislation, and the rules they generate), on the one hand, and other types of institutions, on the other; legal authority in the former exerting supremacy over political institutions.
- The nature of legal doctrine which comprises the principal source of the law and the basis of legal training, knowledge, and institutional practice.
- The concept of law as a coherent, organic body of rules and principles with its own internal logic.
- The existence and specialized training of lawyers and other legal personnel.

While some of these factors may arise in other legal traditions, they differ in respect of the importance they accord to, and their attitude towards, their precise role in society. Law, especially the rule of law, in Western Europe is a fundamental element in the formation and significance of society itself. This reverence for law and the legal process shapes also the exercise of government, domestically and internationally, by contemporary Western democracies.

The civil law system of codified law that obtains in most of Europe, South America, and elsewhere, exhibits several significant differences from the common law of England, former British colonies, the United States, and most of Canada. Though the two traditions have, in the last century, grown closer, there are at least five important divergences.

- The common law is essentially unwritten, non-textual law that was fashioned by medieval lawyers and the judges of the Royal courts before whom they submitted their arguments. Indeed, it may be this entrenched oral tradition supported by a strong monarchy, developed by experts before the revival in the study of Roman law, that explains why that system was never 'received' in England. Codification has been resisted by generations of common lawyers, though this hostility has been weaker in the United States.

- The common law is casuistic: the building blocks are cases rather than, as in the civil law system, texts. The consequence of the common lawyer's preoccupation with what the judges say—rather than what the codes declare—is a more pragmatic, less theoretical approach to legal problem-solving.

- In the light of the centrality of court decisions, the common law elevates the doctrine of precedent to a supreme position in the legal system.

- While the common law proceeds from the premise, 'where there is a remedy, there is a right', the civilian tradition adopts the opposite position: 'where there is a right, there is a remedy'. This is largely a consequence of the so-called writ system under which, from the twelfth century in England, litigation could not commence without a writ issued on the authority of the king. Every claim had its own formal writ. So, for example, the writ of debt was a prerequisite to any action to recover money owing, and the writ of right existed to recover land. In the seventeenth century, the writ of *habeas corpus* (literally 'you must produce the body') was a vital check on arbitrary power for it required the production of a person detained without trial to be brought before a court. In the absence of a legal justification for his imprisonment, the judge could order the individual to be liberated. It took a century for civilian jurisdictions to accept this essential attribute of a free society.

- In the thirteenth century the common law introduced trial by jury in both criminal and civil cases. The jury decides on the facts of the case; the judge determines the law. Trial by jury has remained a fundamental feature of the common law; this separation between facts and law was never adopted by civil law systems. It illustrates also the importance of the oral tradition of common law as against the essential role of written argument employed by the civil law.

This is not an exhaustive comparison, but it captures the essence of the distinction, one which evolved historically, even if result in the case of the common law often seems, especially to the civil law, eccentric, anachronistic, and incomprehensible:

> [W]hat the Continental lawyer sees as being a single problem and solves with a single institution is seen by the common lawyer as being a bundle of more specific problems which he solves with a plurality of legal institutions, most of them of ancient pedigree…One should be frank enough to say, however, that though the English system has a certain antiquarian charm about it, it is so extremely complex and difficult to understand that no one else would dream of adopting it.[1]

It would be folly to deny the role of local factors in the nature and development of law. Moreover, generalizations of an historical or even anthropological nature are a central element in the most important positivist account of law. You will recall that Hart's 'minimum content of natural law' acknowledges that in order to survive as a community certain rules prohibiting force, theft, and deception are required. And these generated primary rules (see 4.2.3). But the two schools that I survey in this chapter go further: they place indigenous culture, custom, and tradition at the very heart of their exposition of the concept of law.

## 8.2 The historical school

The German Romantic Movement, influenced by the ideas of Hegel and Herder, found its most powerful spokesman in the jurist, Friedrich Karl von Savigny (1779–1861). In England, its foremost champion was Sir Henry Maine (1822–88).

### 8.2.1 Savigny

His fundamental belief was that the law is located in the spirit of the people: the *Volksgeist*. Like language, a society's law materializes spontaneously from its way of life: culture, traditions, and customs. It is therefore not a distant, arbitrary phenomenon, but a fundamental feature of the 'common consciousness' of the inhabitants of a country. Though, as pointed out earlier, he eschewed natural law, his account also differs markedly from the positivist position (discussed in Chapters 3 and 4), which portrays law as a distinct, premeditated act by the lawgiver. Law, he sought to show, is an integral element of the social fabric.

#### 8.2.1.1 Codification

In the early part of the nineteenth century there was a powerful movement in support of the codification of the law of the German states. It should be obvious to you why

---

[1] K Zweigert and H Kötz, *An Introduction to Comparative Law*, 3rd edn (Oxford: Oxford University Press, 1998), 37.

Savigny should resist this development. First, it is important to appreciate the origin of codification, what it means, and entails.

During the Classical Period of Roman Law (between the first century BC and the middle of the third century AD), so productive were the leading jurists (Gaius, Ulpian, Papinian, Paul, and several others) that their huge output became desperately unwieldy. Between AD 529 and 534 therefore the Eastern emperor, Justinian, ordered that these multiple texts be condensed into a systematic, comprehensive codification. The three resulting books, the *Corpus Juris Civilis* (comprising the Digest, Codex, and Institutes) were to be treated as definitive: a conclusive statement of the law that required no interpretation.

But the delusion of categorical clarity soon became evident: the codification was both exceptionally lengthy and too detailed to admit of easy application. These short-comings, ironically, turned out to be its strength. More than 600 years after the fall of the Western Roman Empire, Europe witnessed a revival in the study of Roman law. And Justinian's codification, which had remained in force in parts of Western Europe, was the ideal specimen upon which European lawyers could conduct their experiments. With the establishment in about AD 1088 in Bologna of the first university in Western Europe, and the burgeoning of universities throughout Europe in the succeeding four centuries, students of law were taught Justinian's law alongside canon law. Roman civil law thus extended throughout most of Europe—in the face of its detractors during the Renaissance and the Reformation.

By the eighteenth century, however, it was acknowledged that more succinct codes were required. Justinian's codification was replaced by several codes that sought concision, convenience, and completeness. The Napoleonic code of 1804 came close to fulfilling these lofty aspirations. It was exported by colonization to large tracts of Western and Southern Europe and thence to Latin America, and exerted a huge influence throughout Europe. In the common law world, however, codification never took off, even though it had an influential devotee in Jeremy Bentham who extolled the virtues of codification in the following enthusiastic terms:

> [A] man need but open the book in order to inform himself what the aspect borne by the law bears to every imaginable act that can come within the possible sphere of human agency: what acts it is his duty to perform for the sake of himself, his neighbour or the public: what acts he has a right to do, what other acts he has a right to have others perform for his advantage.... In this one repository the whole system of the obligations which either he or any one else is subject to are recorded and displayed to view.[2]

The logic of Savigny's organic, historical approach logically led him to have little truck with those who advanced the cause of codification in Germany.[3] It would, in his view,

---

[2] Jeremy Bentham, *Of Laws in General*, Ch 19, para 10, quoted in Gerald J Postema, *Bentham and the Common Law Tradition* (Oxford: Oxford University Press, 1986), 148.

[3] Fruitlessly—for a more technical, abstract, and extraordinarily comprehensive code was enacted in Germany in 1900. Generally called the BGB, its influence has also been considerable: it provided a model for the civil codes of China, Japan, Taiwan, Greece, and the Baltic states.

freeze the development of the law at the moment of its codification. No historical explanation of the growth of law could countenance its 'wrapping up' in the finality of a code. He conceded, however, that codification might be appropriate when a society's culture had reached its summit. But at that point the dynamism and vitality of the law would render a code redundant! Indeed, he argued that codification normally occurred at the wrong time: either when a society is in the process of developing its law (when the required skill of gleaning key legal concepts is unlikely to be present), or when the society is in decline, as was the case in the Roman Empire when Justinian undertook his great codification.

### 8.2.1.2 Legislation

Savigny regarded the enactment of legislation as inferior to the expression by the people of its common consciousness.[4] This metaphysical conception of community and its relation to the law mirrors to some extent the classical common law notion that legal thought is the manifestation of the collective will—well captured by Roger Cotterrell:

> The authority and legitimacy of the common law as a legal order entitled to the highest respect was seen as residing not in the political system but in the community...[T]he authority of the judge is not as a political decision-maker...but as representative of the community. Hence he has authority only to *state* the community's law, not to impose law upon the community as if he were a political ruler or the servant of one. And the community is to be thought of here as something uniting past and present, extending back through innumerable past generations as well as encompassing the present one.[5]

Such abstract claims (including the idea that the common law consists of immutable custom or that it is derived from divine reason) provide an inadequate explanation of the role of legislation, especially in contemporary society. Yet, unlike classical common lawyers, Savigny recognizes the importance of legislation in the development of law. When a society reaches a higher level of cultural maturity, its 'common consciousness' is no longer capable of creating law—and legislation becomes inevitable. Nevertheless he insists on maintaining that the authority of such legislation is the same as other communal sources. In other words, the lawmaker—along with academic jurists (who were, and still are, highly influential in Germany)—represents the *Volksgeist*.

### 8.2.1.3 Critique

Savigny's concept of the *Volksgeist* gives rise to a number of fundamental difficulties. First, to postulate the existence of a collective 'spirit' of a 'people' is starry-eyed, if not simply misguided. Whether it was possible to describe earlier societies in this way is,

---

[4] FK von Savigny, *Of the Vocation of Our Age for Legislation and Jurisprudence* (1831), transl A Hayward (New York: Arno Press, reprint 1975).

[5] Roger Cotterrell, *The Politics of Jurisprudence: A Critical Introduction to Legal Philosophy* (London: Butterworths, 1989), 27.

at best, doubtful, but in today's multicultural, multilingual, multi-faith nations such an account is problematic.

Secondly, it overlooks the subjugation of minorities, or even majorities, by war, invasion, or occupation, and the peaceful infiltration of foreign law and custom, as occurred in the case of the adoption of the German Civil Code in, for instance, China, Japan, and Taiwan.

Thirdly, his undifferentiated notion of 'culture' is hard to accept. He appears to regard the culture of all societies as susceptible to the same process of development and change. This is simply not the case.

Fourthly, his analysis of the nature and purpose of legislation undervalues its significance—especially, of course, in contemporary, complex societies. Today we take for granted the statute as the stereotypical source of law that seeks to introduce new rules, or to amend old ones—generally in the name of reform, progress, or the alleged improvement of our lives. Savigny should not, perhaps, be blamed for failing to foresee the explosion of legislative energy by lawmakers who frequently owe their election to a manifesto of promises that presumes the existence of an unrelenting statutory assembly line. In most advanced societies, it is not easy to think of any sphere of life untouched by the dedication of legislators to manage what we may or may not do.

## 8.3  Sir Henry Maine

Rare is the law student who has not encountered Maine's famous aphorism in his celebrated book, *Ancient Law*, published in 1861, that 'the movement of progressive societies has hitherto been a movement from *Status to Contract*'.[6] The proposition (by which Maine meant that in early law an individual's social position was determined at birth by his or her status, whereas modern law afforded individuals the contractual freedom to alter their standing) is frequently contradicted by the claim that nowadays the law increasingly attaches rights and duties according to one's status (as, eg, an employee, a tenant, and so on). It is contended, in other words, that Maine's maxim has been inverted. But this neglects the presence of the word 'hitherto' in Maine's generalization. He was not predicting the future, merely describing how the law had evolved in the past. And it is his evolutionary account of law for which Maine is rightly admired,[7] though his ground-breaking writing is wide-ranging. The following

---

[6] HS Maine, *Ancient Law* (London: Dent edn, 1917), 100. This is his most famous work published in 1861 'it was written in the era in which the principal intellectual excitement had been provided by the recently published masterpiece of the biologist Charles Darwin, *The Origin of the Species* (1859), and thus reflects to some extent the current interest in evolution…', JM Kelly, *A Short History of Western Legal Theory* (Oxford: Clarendon Press, 1992), 326.

[7] 'By 1871 *Ancient Law* was widely used in the law school of Europe and America. Maine reported that an eminent American attorney had told him that "he thought almost every attorney in the States has a copy…" The book went through eleven editions in twenty five years', Cotterrell, op cit, 48. I suspect it is little read today, though I would recommend that you at least browse its fascinating pages at http://en.wikisource.org/wiki/Ancient_Law.

discussion touches only on this, and two other elements of his historical analysis of the origin and development of law.

### 8.3.1 **The evolution of law**

Maine was almost certainly the first to apply a scientific, empirical methodology to a subject that had, until then, been dominated by a conceptual approach. His scope of sources is impressively broad, including Greek, English, Hindu, Roman, Irish, and Biblical law. He sought to show how our legal concepts and institutions are rooted in earlier times such as the Roman Empire or beyond. This was sometimes rather speculative, though his description of the six phases through which the form of law in 'progressive' societies passes has a certain ring of truth. The stages are:

- Kingly rule
- Customary law
- Codes
- Fictions
- Equity
- Legislation.

This development traces the progress from ancient society founded on kinship, through bigger entities comprising groups of families, to the complex modern state based on territorial proximity.

### 8.3.2 **Natural law**

His reservations about natural law (see 2.1) were based on a misunderstanding of its substance by its Roman interpreters. Disputes involving foreigners living in Rome were subject to the *ius gentium* which had developed from rules that were shared by Italian tribes. But Greek influence had resulted in its being identified with *naturalis ratio*. This, Maine argued, was mistaken. He pointed to the concept of *occupatio* which was one of several methods by which one could acquire rights over property under the *ius gentium*. To contend, therefore, that individuals in a state of nature attained property over things that hitherto no one owned was incorrect. He showed that, in fact, common ownership was the earliest form of title, and that the archetypal form of ownership was that acquired through adverse possession. Moreover, the concept of a social contract (see 9.3.2) was ahistorical: individuals lacked the capacity to change their legal status or acquire duties until much later.

He nevertheless acknowledged that natural law theory was constructive in one important respect:

> [S]implicity and symmetry were kept before the eyes of a society whose influence on mankind was destined to be prodigious from other causes, as the characteristics of an ideal and

absolutely perfect law. It is impossible to overrate the importance to a nation or profession of having a distinct object to aim at in the pursuit of improvement.[8]

Apart from this contribution, he had little time for the metaphysical and mystery of the natural law philosophy.

### 8.3.3 Fictions

The use of fictions is a vital element in the development of English common law. Maine defined a fiction as an assumption that conceals, or affects to conceal, the fact that a rule of law has been altered: its letter remains unchanged, while its operation has been modified. In other words, it is a supposition or postulation that something is true regardless of whether or not it is. English courts employed fictions to extend their jurisdiction, to circumvent unwieldy procedures, and to facilitate the provision of remedies that would otherwise be unavailable. For example, originally the action in 'trover' was based on the defendant finding and taking the plaintiff's goods. Eventually, the requirement of the plaintiff to prove 'finding' became superfluous: it was assumed that he had found them—by means of a fiction—and he needed to show only that the goods were his and that the defendant had taken them.

Maine vividly explains their historical significance, indeed their indispensability:

> *Fictio*, in old Roman law, is properly a term of pleading, and signifies a false averment on the part of the plaintiff which the defendant was not allowed to traverse; such, for example, as an averment that the plaintiff was a Roman citizen, when in truth he was a foreigner...But I now employ the expression 'Legal Fiction' to signify any assumption which conceals, or affects to conceal, the fact that a rule of law has undergone alteration, its letter remaining unchanged, its operation being modified....At a particular stage of social progress they are invaluable expedients for overcoming the rigidity of law, and, indeed, without one of them, the Fiction of Adoption which permits the family tie to be artificially created, it is difficult to understand how society would ever have escaped from its swaddling clothes, and taken its first steps towards civilization.[9]

> The earliest and most extensively employed of legal fictions was that which permitted family relations to be created artificially, and there is none to which I conceive mankind to be more deeply indebted. If it had never existed, I do not see how any one of the primitive groups, whatever were their nature, could have absorbed another, or on what terms any two of them could have combined, except those of absolute superiority on one side and absolute subjection on the other.[10]

The idea of legal fictions sticks in the throat of legal reformers. Their very name speaks of deception. Indeed Bentham pronounced that 'fictions are to law what fraud is to trade'. Yet they have survived in the face of arguments in support of their legislative abolition, though they exert considerably less influence on modern law, as even Maine conceded.

---

[8]  *Ancient Law*, 38.
[9]  Ibid, 13.     [10]  Ibid.

### 8.3.4 **Critique**

Though he is overlooked by contemporary jurisprudence (most of the leading text-books omit him altogether), it is hard to overstate the importance of Maine as a Victorian jurist who sought to explain the origin and growth of law with a coherent historical account. And, even if some of his many empirical sources have been questioned,

> [F]or the first time in English legal scholarship a theory is offered which clearly links law and culture, does so with a wealth of specific empirical reference, shows processes of law-making other than legislation as of great historical significance, and emphasizes the gradual pace of legal development and the roots of modern legal ideas in history.[11]

A second criticism stigmatizes Maine's elitism in that he tends to analyse law from the standpoint of authority 'lacking in sympathy with the feelings and aspirations of the mass of mankind'.[12] Thirdly, a related critique contests his—cosy—explanation of the evolution of law based on the progress of civilization under the direction of the privileged few. Indeed he has been condemned for glorifying European culture. Fourthly, as Cotterrell points out, though Maine's works were prescribed for examinations in the English Inns of Court, British and colonial universities, as well as the Indian Civil Competitive Examination, the contours of legal doctrine that they draw are extremely generous, extending to considerable tracts of historical and cultural knowledge from many parts of the world. They were thus of little assistance to prospective lawyers who were sometimes advised to look elsewhere for their legal information!

## 8.4 Anthropological jurisprudence

Maine exercised a significant influence over what has come to be called anthropological jurisprudence or legal anthropology. This approach to law which developed in the twentieth century was recognized as essential to an understanding of law by no lesser authority than the great American realist judge, Oliver Wendell Holmes Jr (see 6.2.1) who declared in 1895: 'If your field is Law, the roads are plain to Anthropology.' While in an article in the *Harvard Law Review* of 1899 he wrote: 'It is perfectly proper to regard and study the law simply as a great anthropological document.'

### 8.4.1 **'Law' in tribal societies**

Primitive, tribal societies appear, at first blush, to lack 'law' in the form that it exists in so-called advanced societies. The apparent absence of the institutions that we normally associate with legal systems—courts, law enforcement authorities, prisons, legal codes—led to the conclusion that these communities were governed by custom

---

[11] Cotterrell, op cit, 44.
[12] JW Burrow, *Evolution and Society: A Study in Victorian Social Theory* (Cambridge: Cambridge University Press, 1966), 177–8.

rather than law. These ethnocentric assumptions, however, have been shown, in many instances, to be erroneous. The advent of empirical anthropological research reveals that, though their precise form, structure, and function may differ from the model of law depicted in the works of Western legal theorists, the institutions of primitive societies are not as dissimilar from those of advanced societies. The considerable literature on legal anthropology is a discipline in its own right;[13] its central contributions to legal theory can only be abbreviated in this chapter. The simplest and, I hope, the most coherent means by which to highlight the key features of this branch of legal theory, is to identify some of its key contributors and how they have shaped the nature and direction of the discipline. This should give you a flavour of its influence and protean character.

### 8.4.2 Bronislaw Malinowski

The influential British anthropologist, Bronislaw Malinowski (1884–1942), rejected Maine's evolutionary approach (see 8.3) for its failure to comprehend the nature of governance and social control in primitive societies.[14] Instead he advanced an ethnographic analysis that required extensive field work in order to 'study by direct observation the rules of custom as they function in actual life'.[15] His contribution to the study of order in simple societies was trail-blazing; his 'research strategy, and the novel perspective on the questions of order which he advocated, proved immensely influential with other scholars. It would not be an exaggeration to say that his work represented a watershed in the study of social control in small-scale societies.'[16]

While Maine regarded primitive societies, such as existed on the Trobriand Island, off Papua New Guinea, as subject to stagnant custom, Malinowski's meticulous ethnographic methodology yielded an intricate arrangement of criminal and civil regulation, as well as a system of enforcement.[17] In addition to examining and recording the Trobrianders' specific system of legal rules, he attempted also to investigate the cultural milieu of their law, and to understand its rationality: '[W]e are met by law, order, definite privileges and a well-developed system of obligations.'[18]

The Trobriand Islanders' society, he showed, was organized around the concept of 'reciprocity'. Notwithstanding the lack of 'central authority, codes, courts and constables',[19] order was maintained by, for example, ostracizing an individual who failed to make a payment that was due:

> The rules of law stand out from the rest in that they are felt and regarded as the obligations of one person to the rightful claims of another. They are sanctioned not by a mere psychological

---

[13] For an admirably accessible introduction to the subject, see James Donovan, *Legal Anthropology: An Introduction* (Lanham, Md: AltaMira Press, 2008).

[14] B Malinowski, *Crime and Custom in Savage Society* (London: Rowman & Littlefield, 1926), 56.

[15] Ibid, 126.

[16] S Roberts, *Order and Dispute: An Introduction to Legal Anthropology* (Harmondsworth: Penguin, 1979), 191.     [17] Op cit, 58–9.     [18] Ibid, 121.     [19] Ibid, 14.

motive, but by a definite social machinery of binding force based…upon *mutual dependence, and realised in the equivalent arrangement of reciprocal services.*[20]

In other words, the essence of 'law' is its observance of habit or practice: function rather than form. For example, he observed that among the islanders each of those who engaged in fishing carried out a specific job in manning the boat that they jointly owned. As a result each acquired a right to a share of the catch. Should a fisherman constantly fail to attend the fishing trip, he would lose his portion of the catch. The fishermen were connected to those who grew yams, the other staple food on the island. They provided yams in return for fish. Should a member of either group persistently fail to perform his side of the agreement, there would be no supply of the other's product. Where a breakdown endures for a significant period, Malinowski indicates, the wayward islander would be forced to toe the line or feel obliged to live elsewhere.

### 8.4.3 **E Adamson Hoebel**

Though not, strictly speaking, a legal anthropologist, Hoebel (1906–93), in collaboration with the American realist, Karl Llewellyn (1893–1962), see 6.2.2, published one of the most important interdisciplinary studies of tribal law: *The Cheyenne Way.*[21] It is significant for at least three reasons. First, it provides a lucid account of the case study as the principal method by which to analyse tribal law. Secondly, it closely examines the manner and form in which disputes are settled, investigating specific examples of disagreements or 'trouble cases' and demonstrating how 'law-jobs' were carried out in society. (See 6.2.2.)[22] And thirdly, it seeks to distinguish law from other related forms of social regulation, such as religious norms.

Their starting point is that law seeks to channel behaviour so as to avoid or prevent conflict. But, they argue, law has the additional role of 'cleaning up social messes'. Indeed they claim that anything that achieves this end should be regarded as law. The resolution of disputes is thus the cardinal feature of law—a proposition that has been central to anthropological jurisprudence ever since. Ironically, however, 'they did not themselves observe and record any actual cases. Instead, they relied completely on informants' recalled accounts…'[23]

In 1954 Hoebel published *The Law of Primitive Man: A Study in Comparative Legal Dynamics Law of Primitive Man*, in which he formulated his notion of the diverse categories of legal systems, and evaluated their degree of complexity and perfection—an echo of Maine's evolutionary approach (see 8.3).

---

[20] Ibid, 55; emphasis added.
[21] Karl Llewellyn and E Adamson Hoebel, *The Cheyenne Way: Conflict and Case Law in Primitive Jurisprudence* (Norman, Okla: University of Oklahoma Press, 1941).
[22] See S Roberts, *Order and Dispute: An Introduction to Legal Anthropology* (Harmondsworth: Penguin, 1979), 198–206.          [23] Donovan, op cit, 91.

### 8.4.4 Max Gluckman

Developing the 'trouble case' approach pioneered by Llewellyn and Hoebel, the study of the Barotse of Northern Rhodesia (now Zambia), by the South African anthropologist Max Gluckman (1911–75) revealed a number of surprising similarities between the conceptual tools of this primitive tribe and those of advanced Western legal systems.[24] In particular, it emerged that there existed in their judicial process the idea of the 'reasonable man'—a lynchpin of the common law. Indeed, he went further and discerned a number of other parallels, including the role of courts as regulators of established relationships and creators of new ones, the maintenance of certain behavioural norms, the punishment of offenders, the notions of right, duty, and injury, the distinction between custom and statute, responsibility, negligence, guilt, ownership, and trespass.

His discovery of this cornucopia of resemblances was, needless to say, controversial, and has attracted a fair degree of criticism. In particular, it is thought that he rather exaggerated the similarities, especially since the colonial administration has, to a large extent, 'contaminated' the Lozi legal system through its system of customary law under which the Lozi lived. In the words of James Donovan:

> Far from being a pristine, precontact legal system, the Lozi system may have looked like European law because European law had left its mark on the Lozi system. Gluckman was not able to eliminate this possibility, and therefore his conclusions should be couched in more qualified tones.[25]

The cultural or conceptual prejudices of the anthropologist are a persistent danger against which critics have not been slow to caution.

### 8.4.5 Paul Bohannan

In his analysis of the Tiv of Nigeria, Paul Bohannan (1920–2007), like Gluckman, focuses on the judicial process, but his principal contribution is his idea of 'double institutionalization' by which law is distinguished from norms and custom. In simple terms, customs are norms that have been 'institutionalized' to achieve certain social tasks.[26] But it is impractical for society to continue for an extended period with several competing independent institutions. It therefore becomes necessary for legal institutions to deal with the problems that inevitably arise. Bohannan contends that laws are actually customs that have been extracted from their normal habitat through a process of 'reinstitutionalization'. This constitutes a switch from the social to the legal when specific customs are chosen by legal institutions to supply the standards according to which disputes which endanger the effective operation of other social institutions may be resolved. In other words, 'double institutionalization' selects certain norms that

---

[24] Max Gluckman, *The Judicial Process among the Barotse of Northern Rhodesia* (Manchester: University of Manchester Press, 1955).                                                                 [25] Donovan, op cit, 106.

[26] Paul Bohannan, *Justice and Judgment Among the Tiv* (Oxford: Oxford University Press, 1957), and Paul Bohannan, 'The Differing Realms of Law' (1965) 67 *American Anthropologist* 33.

become laws that govern *all* social institutions. Custom is incapable of realizing this goal; only law can.

### 8.4.6 **Leopold Pospisil**

A resolute pursuit of the principal features of law characterizes the work of another Realist, Leopold Pospisil (b 1923) who, in attempting to distinguish law from custom, identifies a group of four elements manifested by law: authority, universality, 'obligatio',[27] and sanction.[28] Law exists when these four attributes are present. After investigating different societies, he arrives at the conclusion that 'there is no basic qualitative difference between primitive and civilized law'.[29] Whether a rule is law or custom depends not on its source, but the extent to which it exhibits these characteristics. In other words, it does not follow that a rule that exists in a Western society is necessarily law, while merely because it occurs in a non-Western society does not mean it is automatically custom.

Another important aspect of Pospisil's analysis is his insistence that provided the above four elements are evident, law exists notwithstanding the fact that the source of the law is not the state but a criminal gang whose 'ethics' contain all four legal attributes. This notion of 'legal levels' foreshadows the theory of legal pluralism (see 8.5).

### 8.4.7 **Other theorists**

Among contemporary legal anthropologists the writings of a number of distinguished theorists are worthy of your close attention.[30] These include Laura Nader,[31] William O'Barr and John Conley,[32] and Sally Falk Moore.[33]

## 8.5 **Legal pluralism**

The mainspring of this increasingly recondite theory (presaged by Pospisil's idea of 'legal levels', see 8.4.6) is the notion that within a single jurisdiction a number of legal

---

[27] By which he refers to the establishment of a new relationship by the decision of an authority that determines the rights of one party and the obligations of another.

[28] Leopold Pospisil, *Anthropology of Law: A Comparative Theory* (New York: Harper & Row, 1971); Leopold Pospisil, *Kapauku Papuans and Their Law* (New Haven, Conn: Yale University Press, 1958).

[29] Pospisil, *Anthropology of Law: A Comparative Theory*, 341.

[30] Their theories are lucidly described by James Donovan, op cit.

[31] See Laura Nader, *The Life of the Law: Anthropological Projects* (Berkeley, Calif: University of California Press, 2002); Laura Nader (ed), *Law in Culture and Society* (Berkeley, Calif: University of California Press, 1969); and Laura Nader and Harry Todd (eds), *The Disputing Process: Law in Ten Societies* (New York: Columbia University Press, 1978).

[32] William O'Barr and John Conley, *Just Words: Law, Language, and Power*, 2nd edn (Chicago, Ill: University of Chicago Press, 2005); William O'Barr and John Conley, *Rules versus Relationships: Ethnography of Legal Discourse* (Chicago, Ill: University of Chicago Press, 1990).

[33] Sally Falk Moore, *Law as Process: An Anthropological Approach* (London: Routledge & Kegan Paul, 1978).

systems can co-exist along with the 'official' state law. It seeks to demonstrate how a multiplicity of legal systems can operate, interact, and even compete within a single society. There is nothing especially novel in this condition: think of colonial systems with their parallel imported and indigenous laws.[34] But, with the march of economic globalization, certain economic norms relating to contract, property, and credit may conflict with established customary or religious conventions. For example, the Islamic Sharia prohibits usury; this may clash with the modern banking practice of charging interest. Concepts of collective ownership may also collide with banking approaches to loans.

Equally, the importation of Western liberal, individual values—increasingly expressed as human rights—often conflict with non-liberal cultural and religious norms. A conspicuous instance is the position and treatment of women in certain societies that, for example, ordain or even encourage child or arranged marriages.

As Tamanaha justly cautions, we should avoid falling into either of two opposite errors. The first is to accord untrammelled primacy to state law. The second is to believe that other legal or normative systems are parallel to state law. In other words, in every social sphere we ought to examine particular official legal systems and normative systems on their own terms to establish their relationship with other normative systems, their facility to exercise authority, and their actual application or acceptance by individuals and groups. Naturally, though state law is not uniformly powerful, it is normally highly important, and distinguishable from other competing official legal or normative systems.

But the subject of legal pluralism is problematic. It has, in particular, been dogged by the conceptual debate concerning the very meaning of 'law' which is plainly a fundamental starting-point for any constructive analysis of completing or parallel systems of 'law'. Other theoretical and practical difficulties have beset this discipline; indeed, even some of its original advocates have expressed serious doubts about its soundness:

> Today [John] Griffiths admits—to his credit as an intellectual—that his conception of legal pluralism was a mistake. He finally became convinced that it is impossible to adequately conceptualise law for social scientific purposes. Griffiths now agrees with critics that what he previously identified as 'legal pluralism' is better conceptualised as 'normative pluralism'...The originator of the concept most widely adopted by legal pluralists to identify law, Sally Falk Moore, rejects this application of her idea. The most ardent promoter of the concept of legal pluralism for more than two decades, John Griffiths, now renounces legal pluralism. Nonetheless, the notion of legal pluralism continues to spread.[35]

It is by no means a clear or 'scientific' theory.[36]

---

[34] See generally Sally Falk Moore, ibid; Sally Engle Merry, 'Legal Pluralism' (1988) 22 *Law and Society Review* 869; John Griffiths, 'What is Legal Pluralism?' (1986) 24 *Journal of Legal Pluralism and Unofficial Law*.

[35] Brian Z Tamanaha, 'Understanding Legal Pluralism: Past to Present, Local to Global' (2008) 30 *Sydney Law Review* 375, 395–6.

[36] See Brian Z. Tamanaha, 'The Folly of the "Social Scientific" Concept of Legal Pluralism' (1993) 20 *Journal of Law and Society* 192.

# Questions

1. Is a codified system of law necessarily superior to the common law?

2. What are the principal differences between the two systems?

3. '*Ubi ius, ibi remedium.*' What do you understand by this maxim, and to what extent does it accurately capture the essence of the civilian legal tradition?

4. In what ways is the concept of a '*Volksgeist*' problematic?

5. How might Maine's observation that hitherto the movement of progressive societies has been one from status to contract be falsified?

6. Why is Maine's work held in such high regard by legal historians and anthropologists?

7. Are Malinowski's conclusions based on his account of the Trobriand Islanders ethnocentric?

8. What can legal theory learn from anthropological jurisprudence.

9. Can you identify any similarities between Hart's concept of law and the theories of legal anthropologists?

10. Explain the concept of 'legal pluralism'.

11. Max Gluckman has been criticized for exaggerating the parallels between the law of the Lozi and various concepts used by advanced Western legal systems. Is this criticism fair?

12. Why do you think legal anthropologists tend to focus on disputes and their settlement?

13. How would you distinguish between custom and law?

14. Compare the approach of Hoebel with that of Pospisil.

15. Bohannan charges legal anthropology with an inclination to elevate 'the law' of the observer's jurisdiction to the position of an analytical system and then attempting to arrange the 'raw social data' from other societies into its categories. Have you identified such a tendency? If so, in respect of which particular features of law?

16. What's wrong with legal pluralism?

# Further reading

ABEL, RICHARD L, 'A Comparative Theory of Dispute Institutions in Society' (1972) 8 *Law and Society Review* 218.

AMSTERDAM, ANTHONY and BRUNER, JEROME, *Minding the Law* (Cambridge, Mass: Harvard University Press, 2002).

AN-NA'IM, ABDULLAHI AHMED, *Human Rights in Cross-Cultural Perspectives: A Quest for Consensus* (Philadelphia, Pa: Temple University Press, 1992).

ANLEU, SHARYN LR, *Law and Social Change* (London: Sage Publications, 2000).

AUERBACH, JS, *Justice without Law?* (New York: Oxford University Press, 1983).

BLACK, DONALD J, 'The Boundaries of Legal Sociology' (1972) 81 *Yale Law Journal* 1086; reprinted in K Rokumoto (ed), *Sociological Theories of Law* (New York: New York University Press, 1994).

BLACK, DONALD J, 'The Relevance of Legal Anthropology' (1981) 10 *Contemporary Sociology* 43.

BOHANNAN, PAUL, *Justice and Judgment Among the Tiv* (Oxford: Oxford University Press, 1957).

BOHANNAN, PAUL, 'The Differing Realms of Law' (1965) 67 *American Anthropologist* 33; reprinted in K Rokumoto (ed), *Sociological Theories of Law* (New York: New York University Press, 1994).

CHANOCK, MARTIN, *Law, Custom and Social Order: The Colonial Experience in Malawi and Zambia* (New York: Cambridge University Press, 1985).

COMAROFF, JOHN L and ROBERTS, SIMON A, *Rules and Processes: The Cultural Logic of Dispute in an African Context* (Chicago, Ill: University of Chicago Press, 1981).

DANIELSEN, DAN and ENGLE, KAREN (eds), *After Identity: A Reader in Law and Culture* (New York: Routledge, 1995).

DIAMOND, STANLEY (ed), *Primitive Views of the World: Essays from Culture in History* (New York: Columbia University Press, 1960).

DONOVAN, JAMES, *Legal Anthropology: An Introduction* (Lanham, Md: AltaMira Press, 2008).

DONOVAN, JAMES and ANDERSON, H EDWIN, *Anthropology and Law* (New York: Berghahn Books, 2003).

EPSTEIN, AL, 'The Reasonable Man Revisited: Some Problems in the Anthropology of Law' (1973) 7 *Law and Society Review* 643.

EPSTEIN, AL (ed), *Contention and Dispute: Aspects of Law and Social Control in Melanesia* (Canberra: Australian National University Press, 1974).

EVAN, WILLIAM M, *Social Structure and Law: Theoretical and Empirical Perspectives* (London: Sage Publications, 1990).

FITZPATRICK, PETER, *Law and State in Papua New Guinea* (London: Academic Press, 1980).

FITZPATRICK, PETER, 'Law and Societies' (1984) 22 *Osgoode Hall Law Review* 115; reprinted in M Mundy (ed), *Law and Anthropology* (Burlington, Vt: Ashgate Publishing, 2002).

FITZPATRICK, PETER, 'Is It Simple to be a Marxist in Legal Anthropology?' (1985) 48 *Modern Law Review* 472.

FRENCH, REBECCA R, 'Of Narrative in Law and Anthropology' (1996) 30 *Law and Society Review* 417.

GEERTZ, CLIFFORD, 'Local Knowledge: Fact and Law in Comparative Perspective' in *Local Knowledge: Further Essays in Interpretive Anthropology* (New York: Basic Books, 1983).

GLUCKMAN, MAX, *The Judicial Process among the Barotse of Northern Rhodesia* (Manchester: University of Manchester Press, 1955).

GLUCKMAN, MAX, *Politics, Law and Ritual in Tribal Society* (Chicago, Ill: Aldine, 1965).

GLUCKMAN, MAX, *Ideas and Procedures in African Customary Law* (Oxford: Oxford University Press, 1969).

GULLIVER, PH, *Disputes and Negotiations: A Cross-Cultural Perspective* (New York: Academic Press, 1979).

HAMNETT, IAN (ed), *Social Anthropology and Law* (New York: Academic Press, 1977).

HARRIS, OLIVIA (ed), *Inside and Outside the Law: Anthropological Studies of Authority and Ambiguity* (London: Routledge & Kegan Paul, 1996).

HARRISON, LAWRENCE E and HUNTINGTON, SAMUEL P, *Culture Matters: How Values Shape Human Progress* (New York: Basic Books, 2000).

HOEBEL, E ADAMSON, *The Law of Primitive Man: A Study in Comparative Legal Dynamics* (Cambridge, Mass: Harvard University Press, 1954).

KAHN, PAUL W, *The Cultural Study of Law: Reconstructing Legal Scholarship* (Chicago, Ill: University of Chicago Press, 1999).

KAHN, PAUL W, 'Freedom, Autonomy, and the Cultural Study of Law' in Austin Sarat and Jonathan Simon (eds), *Cultural Analysis, Cultural Studies, and the Law* (Durham, NC: Duke University Press, 2003).

LLEWELLYN, KARL and HOEBEL, E Adamson, *The Cheyenne Way: Conflict and Case Law in Primitive Jurisprudence* (Norman, Okla: University of Oklahoma Press, 1941).

MACCORMACK, G, 'Anthropology and Legal Theory' (1978) *Juridical Review* 216; reprinted in Peter Sack and Jonathon Aleck (eds), *Law and Anthropology* (New York: New York University Press, 1992).

MAINE, SIR HENRY, *Ancient Law* [1861] (New York: Dutton, 1960).

MALINOWSKI, BRONISLAW, *Crime and Custom in Savage Society* (London: Routledge & Kegan Paul, 1926).

MALINOWSKI, BRONISLAW, 'A New Instrument for the Interpretation of Law—Especially Primitive' (1942) 51 *Yale Law Journal* 1237.

MERRY, SALLY E, 'Legal Pluralism' (1988) 22 *Law and Society Review* 869; reprinted in Peter Sack and Jonathon Aleck (eds), *Law and Anthropology* (New York: New York University Press, 1992).

MERRY, SALLY E (ed), *Law and Anthropology: A Reader* (Oxford: Blackwell, 2004).

MOORE, SALLY F, *Law as Process: An Anthropological Approach* (London: Routledge & Kegan Paul, 1978).

MOORE, SALLY F, *Law and Anthropology: A Reader (Blackwell Anthologies in Social and Cultural Anthropology)* (Oxford: Wiley/Blackwell, 2004).

MUNDY, MARTHA (ed), *Law and Anthropology* (Burlington, Vt: Ashgate Publishing, 2002).

NADER, LAURA, 'The Anthropological Study of Law' (1965) 67 *American Anthropologist* 3; reprinted in Peter Sack and Jonathon Aleck (eds), *Law and Anthropology* (New York: New York University Press, 1992).

NADER, LAURA (ed), *Law in Culture and Society* (Berkeley, Calif: University of California Press, 1969).

NADER, LAURA, *The Life of the Law: Anthropological Projects* (Berkeley, Calif: University of California Press, 2002).

NADER, LAURA and TODD, HARRY (eds), *The Disputing Process: Law in Ten Societies* (New York: Columbia University Press, 1978).

O'BARR, WILLIAM and CONLEY, JOHN, *Just Words: Law, Language, and Power*, 2nd edn (Chicago, Ill: University of Chicago Press, 2005).

O'BARR, WILLIAM and CONLEY, JOHN, *Rules versus Relationships: Ethnography of Legal Discourse* (Chicago, Ill: University of Chicago Press, 1990).

POSPISIL, LEOPOLD, *Anthropology of Law: A Comparative Theory* (New York: Harper & Row, 1971).

POTTAGE, ALAIN and MUNDAY, MARTHA (eds), *Law, Anthropology, and the Constitution of the Social: Making Persons and Things (Cambridge Studies in Law and Society)* (Cambridge: Cambridge University Press, 2004).

ROBERTS, SIMON, *Order and Dispute: An Introduction to Legal Anthropology* (Harmondsworth: Penguin, 1979).

ROKUMOTO, KAHEI (ed), *Sociological Theories of Law* (New York: New York University Press, 1994).

ROSEN, LAWRENCE, *The Anthropology of Justice: Law as Culture in Islamic Society* (Cambridge: Cambridge University Press, 1989).

SACK, PETER and ALECK, JONATHON (eds), *Law and Anthropology* (New York: New York University Press, 1992).

SARAT, AUSTIN and SIMON, JONATHAN (eds), *Cultural Analysis, Cultural Studies, and the Law* (Durham, NC: Duke University Press, 2003).

STARR, JUNE and COLLIER, JANE F (eds), *History and Power in the Study of Law: New Directions in Legal Anthropology* (Ithaca, NY: Cornell University Press, 1989).

STEIN, PETER, *Legal Evolution: The Story of an Idea* (New York: Cambridge University Press, 1980).

TAMANAHA, BRIAN Z, 'The Folly of the "Social Scientific" Concept of Legal Pluralism' (1993) 20 *Journal of Law and Society* 192; reprinted in M Mundy (ed), *Law and Anthropology* (Burlington, Vt: Ashgate Publishing, 2002).

TAMANAHA, BRIAN Z, 'Understanding Legal Pluralism: Past to Present, Local to Global' (2008) 30 *Sydney Law Review* 375.

WHITE, JAMES B, *Justice as Translation: An Essay in Cultural and Legal Criticism* (Chicago, Ill: University of Chicago Press, 1990).

WILSON, RICHARD A (ed), *Human Rights, Culture and Context: Anthropological Perspectives* (London: Pluto Press, 1997).

# 9

# Theories of justice

What is justice? How is it to be secured? Is there a necessary connection between law and justice? Questions like these have exercised the minds of thinkers since Plato and Aristotle. Theories of justice are a significant, and abiding, concern of moral, political, and legal theory. You will be told of the contributions of these great Greek philosophers to the problem of justice and, after studying their modern counterparts (Bentham, Rawls, Nozick), you may be inclined to wonder whether we have got any closer to defining this elusive ideal. There is, as you might expect, a large body of literature on the general question of justice.[1]

It requires little perception to recognize the injustice that afflicts individuals and societies. Discrimination on the grounds of race, gender, religion, and belief remain an intractable obstacle in the path towards justice. Moreover, as we saw in Chapter 1, the huge inequalities in wealth between rich and poor countries creates the need for what is now called 'global justice' that extends the analysis of the questions pursued in this chapter beyond individual states to the world at large. The statistics are disturbing and distressing: 1,020 million people are chronically undernourished; 884 million lack access to safe drinking water; 2,500 million lack access to basic sanitation; 2,500 million lack access to basic medicines; 924 million lack adequate shelter; and 1,600 million have no electricity. There are 218 million child labourers. It is appalling that in the twenty-first century, one-third of deaths, 18 million a year, are due to poverty-related causes which are easily preventable through improved nutrition, clean drinking water, vaccines, antibiotics, and other medicine.[2] In an age of globalization, such a development is critically important, though this subject does not yet appear to feature in many university courses on jurisprudence.

---

[1] Useful collections of essays may be found in T Morawetz (ed), *Justice* (Aldershot: Dartmouth, 1991), and E Kamenka and A Tay (eds), *Justice* (London: Edward Arnold, 1979). A careful discussion of various theories of justice is to be found in C Perelman, *The Idea of Justice and the Problem of Argument* (London: Routledge & Kegan Paul, 1963); JR Lucas, *On Justice* (Oxford: Clarendon Press, 1980); Michael J Sandel (ed), *Justice: A Reader* (New York: Oxford University Press, 2006); Tom Campbell, *Justice*, 2nd edn (Basingstoke: Palgrave Macmillan, 2000); Serena Olsaretti (ed), *Desert and Justice* (Oxford: Clarendon Press, 2007).

[2] The figures are quoted in Thomas Pogge, 'What is Global Justice?' http://www.yale.edu/macmillan/globaljustice/docs/gjlecture.pdf. See too, his *World Poverty and Human Rights* (Cambridge: Polity, 2002), and Thomas Nagel, 'The Problem of Global Injustice' (2005) *Philosophy and Public Affairs* 113.

Before embarking on a consideration of the different approaches to justice, mention needs to be made of the two most influential philosophers whose theories are the starting-point for any discussion of the question: Aristotle and Kant.

Aristotle's analysis of the subject in Book 5 of his *Nicomachean Ethics* which still forms the starting point for most discussions of justice. Note, however, that his analysis of justice is merely a part of his detailed account of ethics, law, politics, and a good deal more. In respect of the former, for example, he postulates a theory of how we ought to live. Following Plato, he conceives of the ethical virtues (including justice, temperance, and courage) as rational, emotional, and social skills. To live well, he argues, we need to understand the manner in which goods like friendship, pleasure, virtue, wealth, and honour form a coherent whole. You cannot acquire practical wisdom—which is required in order to recognize in specific cases what action is the most rational—only through learning general rules. You need also the emotional and social skills that allow you to put your general understanding of well-being into practice in each instance.

His account of virtue is a pursuit of the Golden Mean. If justice is a virtue, then, he contends, it must be a type of mean: a kind of midway point between two extremes, one of excess and the other of deficiency. So, for example, the virtue of courage—if present in excess—would transform into recklessness; and if deficient, it would present as cowardice.

'The good', he declares, 'is final and self-sufficient; happiness is defined.' The supreme good, he argued, is 'eudaimonia' or happiness. To achieve eudaimonia, one must be virtuous: the inclination and readiness to act with excellence in every situation. Aristotle thus emphasizes the importance of character and virtue. Character is a state of being. So, for example, if I am a kind person I possess the proper feelings toward others. But character also relates to action. I will act in accordance with my virtuous inner temperament which will also involve being moved to act in accordance with them. While, as we shall see, both consequentialism and deontology are concerned with the right action, virtue ethics associated with Aristotle is preoccupied with the question of what constitutes a good life, and what sort of person we ought to be—in general.

We are constantly faced with moral dilemmas.[3] But since there is unlikely to be a single rule that applies to the various moral questions we encounter, we can learn how to behave in a just or virtuous way from experience, reason, perception, sensitivity, and so on. Our ethical obligations cannot be codified in an overarching policy or principle. This is at the heart of the 'doctrine of the mean'. Virtue ethics thereby avoids the inflexible forms of obligation espoused by both Kant and consequentialism.[4] To put

---

[3] For a provocative assortment of such problems, see Michael Sandel's popular and accessible, *Justice: What's the Right Thing to Do?* (London: Penguin, 2010).

[4] Some feminist theorists (see Chapter 14) adopt a slightly different version of virtue ethics known as the 'ethics of care', which argues that while men tend to adopt 'masculine' virtues like justice, women embrace feminine values such as caring, patience, self-sacrifice, nurturing and so on. They argue that these virtues have been neglected thanks to society's marginalization of women. See, eg, Carol Gilligan, *In a Different Voice: Psychological Theory and Women's Development* (Cambridge, Mass: Harvard University Press, 1982).

it simply, consequentialism is outcome-based, deontology is agent-based, and virtue ethics is character-based.

Aristotle acknowledges that the concept of justice is imprecise, and therefore seeks to specify the features of injustice, and work backwards from there to an understanding of the elements of justice. We adopt a similar approach when we attempt to determine what constitutes a 'healthy' person: we recognize when someone is unhealthy, we are therefore able to identify its opposite. Hence a lawless individual or one who is greedy is unjust; it follows that a just person is one who obeys the law and does not seek more than his fair share.

Justice, he says, consists in treating equals equally and unequals unequally, in proportion to their inequality. He recognizes that the equality implied in justice could be arithmetical—based on the identity of the persons concerned, or geometrical—based on maintaining the same proportion. This is Aristotle's famous distinction between *corrective* or *commutative* justice, on the one hand, and *distributive* justice, on the other. The former was, in his view, the justice of the courts which was applied in the redress of crimes or civil wrongs. It required that all men were to be treated equally. Distributive justice is concerned with giving each according to his desert or merit. This, in Aristotle's view, was principally the concern of the legislator.

An altogether different view is propounded by Immanuel Kant (1724–1804) who, in *Groundwork for the Metaphysics of Morals*, states, 'A good will is good not because of what it effects or accomplishes, nor because of its fitness to attain some proposed end; it is good only through its willing, i.e., it is good in itself.' In other words, good will is the basis of moral worth which depends not on the specific act, but on the principle upon which the act is done. Good will is good in itself, not the result of anything else. It is the ability to carry out acts for their sole purpose and duty.

Such duties Kant divides between the hypothetical and the categorical. *Hypothetical* imperatives are those that spring from a particular purpose or end. For example, 'I must read this book if I am to pass my jurisprudence exam'. *Categorical* imperatives, on the other hand, prompt us to act for the sake of the act itself. They are universal in that they apply to all rational beings. It takes the following form: 'Act only according to that maxim whereby you can at the same time will that it should become a universal law.' In other words, act as if your values should apply to all. So, categorical imperatives, unlike hypothetical imperatives, tell us what to do regardless of our desires. Morality does not state: 'If you want to avoid imprisonment do not steal.' It declares instead: 'Do not steal.' We should refrain from theft whether or not we wish to avoid jail.

What this means is that unless you accept that your moral rule can be applied to everyone, including you, it is not a valid moral rule. For example, if I wonder whether I should commit adultery, I should ask whether I believe that there should be a universal rule that says 'marital infidelity is OK'. If not, I should conclude that my proposed adultery is wrong.

For Kant, therefore, the only valid justification for doing the right thing was that you were under a *duty* to do so. This is the essence of deontology (from the Greek 'deon' meaning 'duty'). When you act from some other motive (eg, fear of the consequences) you are not acting morally. This, as we shall see, differs from the consequentialist position adopted most prominently by the English Utilitarian, Jeremy Bentham.

In *The Concept of Law*, Professor Hart argues that the idea of justice:

> consists of two parts: a uniform or constant feature, summarised in the precept 'Treat like cases alike' and a shifting or varying criterion used in determining when, for any given purpose, cases are alike or different.[5]

He suggests that today the principle that, *prima facie*, human beings are entitled to be treated alike has become so widely accepted that racial discrimination is usually defended on the ground that those discriminated against are not 'fully human'.

The subject of justice is, needless to say, an extraordinarily large one. It is normally beyond the scope of most jurisprudence courses to pursue the complex philosophical debates that have raged for so long. This chapter is therefore devoted to four central theories of justice. First, utilitarianism; secondly, the economic analysis of law; thirdly, John Rawls's influential theory of 'justice as fairness'; and, fourthly, Robert Nozick's radical approach to the question.

## 9.1 Utilitarianism

On one level, utilitarianism represents an assault on the metaphysics that characterized a good deal of eighteenth-century political philosophy. Indeed, as discussed in 3.2, Bentham expends much of his energy fulminating against natural rights (which he called 'nonsense on stilts') and, in particular, Blackstone. But it is much more. It has a profound moral basis which takes as its premise the proposition that the fundamental objective of morality and justice is that happiness should be maximized. Though there are a number of classical utilitarian theories (including those of John Stuart Mill and Henry Sidgwick) it is Jeremy Bentham's formulation that tends to be the one that is most familiar to students of jurisprudence. This sometimes leads to an equation of Bentham and utilitarianism which is to overlook the fact that his form of utilitarianism is what JJC Smart calls 'hedonistic' and may be contrasted with GE Moore's 'non-hedonistic' utilitarianism, and Mill's intermediate position. You should therefore be circumspect when discussing utilitarianism, to recognize its different forms. In practice, however, most jurisprudence courses tend to confine their study to classical utilitarianism as represented by Jeremy Bentham. His general view is well captured in this famous passage from *An Introduction to the Principles of Morals and Legislation*:[6]

> Nature has placed mankind under the governance of two sovereign masters, *pain* and *pleasure*. It is for them alone to point out what we ought to do, as well as to determine what we shall do. On the one hand the standard of right and wrong, on the other the chain of causes and effects, are fastened to their throne…The *principle of utility* recognises this subjection, and assumes it for the foundation of that system, the object of which is to rear the fabric of

---

[5] At 156.    [6] Ch 1, para 1.

felicity by the hands of reason and of law. Systems which attempt to question it, deal in sounds instead of sense, in caprice instead of reason, in darkness instead of light.

To this end Bentham devised his 'felicific calculus' by which we might test the 'happiness factor' of any action. This much is reasonably straightforward. But too many students are so impressed (or amused) by Bentham's classification of 12 pains and 14 pleasures and its attractive (or crude) simplicity that they barely progress beyond generalities about the defects of the theory. Serious students will want to read JJC Smart and Bernard Williams' *Utilitarianism: For and Against*[7] in which these two distinguished philosophers present both sides of the argument in a sustained analysis of the theory's merits and demerits. A helpful discussion of the subject may also be found in Chapter 1 of NE Simmonds, *Central Issues in Jurisprudence*.

The essence of utilitarianism is its *consequentialism*. It is important therefore to distinguish consequentialist from *deontological* systems of ethics. The former is self-explanatory, the latter is its opposite: it holds that the rightness or wrongness of an action is logically independent of its consequences—'Let justice be done though the heavens fall!' is one of its proud slogans. Utilitarianism therefore looks to the future; it is concerned to maximize happiness or welfare or some other 'good'. Philosophers distinguish two forms of utilitarianism: 'act utilitarianism' and 'rule utilitarianism'. The former adopts the position that the rightness or wrongness of an action is to be judged by the consequences, good or bad, of the *action itself*. The latter argues that the rightness or wrongness of an action is to be judged by the goodness or badness of *the consequences of a rule that everyone should perform the action in like circumstances*.[8]

Most discussions of utilitarianism (including this one) concern themselves with act utilitarianism, though in the context of legal theory it is not uncommon to find appeals made to 'ideal rule utilitarianism' which provides that the rightness or wrongness of an action is to be judged by the goodness or badness of a rule which, *if observed*, would have better consequences than any other rule governing the same action. This version of rule utilitarianism has obvious advantages in the context of a judge who is called upon to decide whether the claimant should be awarded damages against the defendant: clearly he should ignore the effect of his judgment on the *particular* indigent defendant. It may be contrasted with 'actual rule utilitarianism' which holds that the rightness of an action is to be judged by reference to a rule which is *actually observed* and whose acceptance would maximize utility.

### 9.1.1 Consequences

What does it mean to say that a utilitarian is concerned to evaluate the *consequences* of our actions? Consider the following illustration:[9] I am stranded on a desert island

---

[7] (Cambridge: Cambridge University Press, 1973).

[8] JJC Smart and Bernard Williams, *Utilitarianism: For and Against* (Cambridge: Cambridge University Press, 1973), 9.

[9] Adapted from NE Simmonds, *Central Issues in Jurisprudence*, 4th edn (London: Sweet & Maxwell, 2014), 26.

with no one but a dying man who, in his final hours, entrusts me with $10,000 which he asks me to give to his daughter, Rita, if I ever manage to return to the United States. I promise to do so, and, after my rescue, I find Rita living in a mansion; she has married a millionaire. The $10,000 will now make little difference to her financial situation. Should I not instead donate the money to charity? As a utilitarian, I consider the possible *consequences* of my action. But what *are* the consequences? I must weigh the result of my broken promise against the benefit of giving the $10,000 to an animal welfare charity. Would keeping my promise have better consequences than breaking it? If I break my promise, I may be less likely to keep other promises I have made, and others may be encouraged to take their own promise-keeping less seriously. I must, in other words, attempt to calculate *all* the likely consequences of my choice. But a non-consequentialist Kantian might argue that the reason why I should give the money to Rita is that I have *promised* to do so. My action ought to be guided not by some uncertain *future* consequence, but by an unequivocal *past* fact: my promise. My reply might be that I *do* consider the past fact of my promise—but only to the extent that it affects the *total consequences* of my action of giving the money to the charity instead of to Rita. I might also say that it is absurd to argue that I am obliged to keep *every* promise I make.

Suppose, I argue, I promise to meet you at a bar at 8 pm. On the way I am run over by a bus and end up in hospital. You would (I hope) not regard me as immoral because I fail to keep my promise to you. It is surely *implied* that my promise is subject to certain (unspecified) exceptions. We begin to see the complexity of the utilitarian/deontological debate.

### 9.1.2 **Preferences**

Bentham's version of hedonistic act utilitarianism is generally considered too quaint for modern tastes, while the 'ideal' act utilitarianism of Moore (who, broadly speaking, thought that certain states of mind, such as those of acquiring knowledge, had an *intrinsic* value independent of their pleasantness) and JS Mill (who argued that there are higher and lower pleasures—implying that pleasure is a necessary condition for goodness, but that goodness depends on qualities of experience other than pleasantness and unpleasantness) are regarded as somewhat elitist. This is largely because these writers tend to substitute their own preferences for the preferences they thought people *ought* to have. Modern utilitarians therefore talk of maximizing the extent to which people may achieve what they *want*; we should seek to satisfy people's *preferences*. This has the merit of not imposing any conception of 'the good' which leaves out of account individual choice: you may prefer backgammon to Bach, or billiards to Beethoven. But it raises certain difficulties of its own; see 9.2.

### 9.1.3 **Critique of utilitarianism**

Moral philosophers have spilled a good deal of ink disputing the value of consequentialism in general and utilitarianism in particular. It is unlikely that there will be time in your jurisprudence course to treat the subject in detail, but you will need to know its essence, if only to understand its modern outgrowth, the economic analysis of law, and also to appreciate theories, especially Rawls's, which seek to avoid the drawbacks of utilitarianism. The attacks on utilitarianism are many and varied. I shall identify eight such criticisms. A fundamental assault on utilitarianism is made by those—who include Bernard Williams[10] and Rawls himself[11]—who argue that it fails to recognize the 'separateness of persons'. It suggests that utilitarianism, at least in its pure form, treats human beings as means rather than ends in themselves. This important attack consists, in Professor Hart's view[12] of four main points which may be summarized as follows:

- Separate individuals are important to utilitarians only in so far as they are 'the channels or locations where what is of value is to be found'.

- Utilitarianism treats individual persons equally, but only by effectively treating them as having *no* worth, for their value is not *as persons*, but as 'experiencers' of pleasure or happiness.

- Why should we regard as a valuable moral goal the mere increase in totals of pleasure or happiness abstracted from all questions of *distribution* of happiness, welfare, etc?

- The analogy used by utilitarians, of a rational single individual prudently sacrificing present happiness for later satisfaction, is false for it treats my pleasure as replaceable by the greater pleasure of others.

These four criticisms contain most of the issues that lie at the heart of many of the other attacks, of which the following may be mentioned. Why *should* we seek to satisfy people's desires? Certain desires are unworthy of satisfaction (eg, the sadist who wants to torture children). Note that Bentham's catalogue includes 'the pleasure of malevolence'.

A third attack is one made by Rawls: he argues that utilitarianism defines what is right in terms of what is 'good'; but this means, he says, that it begins with a conception of what is 'good' (eg, happiness) and then concludes that an action is *right* in so far as it maximizes that 'good'.[13] Fourthly, utilitarianism is concerned only with maximizing welfare; many regard the more important question as the just *distribution* of welfare. Fifthly, many critics point to the impracticability of *calculating* the consequences of one's actions: how can we know in advance what results will follow from what we propose to do. Sixthly, are our wants and desires not manipulated by persuasion, advertising, and the like? If so, can we separate our 'real' preferences from our 'conditioned' ones? Should we, as utilitarians, then set about trying to suggest to people that they *should* prefer reading Kelsen to drinking beer? If so, how do we justify doing this? If we

[10] In Smart and Williams, *Utilitarianism: For and Against*.
[11] See J Rawls, *A Theory of Justice* (Harmondsworth: Penguin, 1973), 194 ff.
[12] Expressed in his essay, 'Between Utility and Rights', in his *Essays in Jurisprudence and Philosophy* (Oxford: Clarendon Press, 1983), 198 at 200–2.          [13] See his alternative, 169.

answer that the principle of utility requires us to do it, we are saying that the 'felicific calculus' includes not only what we *want*, but also what we may one day *decide* to want as a result of persuasion or 're-education'!

Seventhly, is it possible (and, if it is, is it desirable?) to balance my pleasure against your pain? On a larger scale, can judges or legislators, when faced with a choice between two or more courses of action, realistically (or even sensibly) weigh the majority's happiness against a minority's misery? Eighthly, how far into the future do (or can) we extend the consequences of our actions? Or to put it slightly differently, as Williams does,[14] 'No one can hold that everything, of whatever category, that has value, has it in virtue of its consequences. If that were so, one would just go on for ever, and there would be an obviously hopeless regress.'

There are many other arguments and counter-arguments. Note, too, that utilitarianism may be treated as a system of *personal* morality or as one of *social or political* decision. As far as legal theory is concerned it is usually the latter. Bentham, of course, sought to show that, on the basis of the former, we could generalize outwards to the latter. And many of the important law reforms of the nineteenth century are attributable to its influence as a political theory. But it has few supporters today. Instead, it appears in the nether garments of the so-called 'economic analysis of law'.

## 9.2 The economic analysis of law

This modern form of utilitarianism has, as its launching pad, the proposition that the rational man or woman always chooses to do what will maximize his or her satisfactions. And if they want something badly enough they will be prepared to *pay* for it. But the relationship between law and economics has deeper roots.[15]. There is an obvious connection between a good deal of private law (contract, tort, labour law, property) and the economy. The law has a direct impact upon the economy; governments in most countries seek, through law, to regulate the market, facilitate trade and investment, engage in wealth redistribution, and so on. Economic theory contributes significantly to the role and function of law. The influence, especially of transaction cost economics, is evident in the writings of the judge and legal theorist, Richard Posner. Though he denies that he adopts a utilitarian position, Posner argues (especially in his *Economic Analysis of Law*[16] and *The Economics of Justice*[17]) that much of the common law can be explained by this simple fact of life. Courts frequently decide hard cases by choosing an outcome which will maximize the wealth of society. By 'wealth maximization' Posner means a situation in which goods and other resources are in the hands of those people who *value them most*; that is to say, those people who are willing (and able) to

---

[14]  In Smart and Williams, *Utilitarianism: For and Against*, 82.

[15]  You will find an excellent discussion of this subject in Chs 11 and 12 of Suri Ratnapala, *Jurisprudence*, 2nd edn (Melbourne: Cambridge University Press, 2013). I draw on Ch 12 here.

[16]  Richard A Posner, *Economic Analysis of Law*, 6th edn (New York: Aspen, 2003).

[17]  Richard A Posner, *The Economics of Justice* (Cambridge, Mass: Harvard University Press, 1983).

*pay* more to have them. So, for example, if I buy your copy of *The Concept of Law* for $5 when the most I was *willing* to pay for it was $6, my wealth has been increased by $1. In the same way, society maximizes its wealth when all its resources are distributed in such a way that the sum of everyone's transactions is as high as possible.

And this, argues Posner, is as it *should* be; his analysis, though essentially descriptive, is also to some extent normative. Moreover, in a series of essays, he and other members of the so-called Chicago School that emerged in the 1960s, attempt to demonstrate how common law judges have (mostly unconsciously) been guided by these economic considerations. Posner rejects the autonomy of law on two grounds. First he denies that law develops independently of social and economic forces. Law, he argues, has no inner logic. Secondly, he asserts that non-legal disciplines (especially economics) have an essential role to play in our understanding of the law. His argument in support of the importance of economic factors is therefore both descriptive (economics actually determines judicial outcomes) and normative (the efficient allocation of resources ought to guide judges in their judgments).

Thus, in the development of the law of negligence, for example, Posner argues, the imposition of liability normally depends on what is most efficient economically. In his words:

> The common law method is to allocate responsibilities between people engaged in interacting activities in such a way as to maximise the joint value, or, what amounts to the same thing, minimise the joint cost of the activities.[18]

And how does it do this?

> It may do this by redefining a property right, by devising a new rule of liability, or by recognising a contract right, but nothing fundamental turns on which device is used.[19]

Posner analyses several aspects of the common law in this manner. So, for example, he argues that in seeking to withhold or limit the circulation of 'personal information', an individual is engaged in a form of deception, especially where the information depicts him in an unfavourable light. This is the burden of Posner's application of his economic analysis of law to the subject of personal information.[20] As he contends, 'To the extent that people conceal personal information in order to mislead, the economic case for according legal protection to such information is no better than that for permitting fraud in the sale of goods.'[21]

---

[18] *The Economic Analysis of Law*, 2nd edn (Boston, Mass: Little, Brown, 1977), 179.    [19] Ibid.

[20] See Richard A Posner, 'The Right of Privacy' (1978) *Georgia Law Review* 393; reproduced in Raymond Wacks (ed), *Privacy*, The International Library of Essays in Law and Legal Theory, Vol I (Aldershot: Dartmouth, and New York University Press, 1993) 423; 'An Economic Theory of Privacy' in FD Schoeman (ed), *Philosophical Dimensions of Privacy: An Anthology* (Cambridge: Cambridge University Press, 1984). Cf RA Epstein, 'A Taste for Privacy? Evolution and the Emergence of a Naturalistic Ethic' (1980) 9 *Journal of Legal Studies* 665; reproduced in Wacks (ed), op cit, 453; CE Baker, 'Posner's Privacy Mystery and the Failure of the Economic Analysis of Law' (1978) 12 *Georgia Law Review* 475; EJ Bloustein, 'Privacy is Dear at Any Price: A Response to Professor Posner's Economic Theory' (1978) 12 *Georgia Law Review* 429; reproduced in Wacks (ed), op cit, 471.

[21] Posner, 'The Right of Privacy' (1978) *Georgia Law Review* 393, 401.

But even if one were to accept the 'economic' perspective, it does not follow that one need accept the assessment of the economic 'value' of withholding personal information; individuals may be willing to trade off their interest in restricting the circulation of such information against their 'societal' interest in its free flow. In other words Posner has not shown, and may be unable to show, that his calculation of 'competing' interests is necessarily the correct, or even the most likely, one. This analysis cannot be pursued here, but it is worth noting that Posner's claim that his economic theory 'explains' the operation of law produces a certain dissonance if one compares the protection of 'privacy' in the United States with that prevailing in England.

Posner also argues that transaction-cost considerations may militate against the legal protection of personal information. Where the information is discrediting and accurate, there is a social incentive to make it generally available: accurate information facilitates reliance on the individual to whom the information relates. It is therefore socially efficient to allow a society a right of access to such information rather than to permit the individual to conceal it. In the case of non-discrediting or false information, the value to the individual of concealment exceeds the value of access to it by the community. Information which is false does not advance rational decision-making and is therefore of little use.

An important aspect of this thesis is that the common law tends to generate more economic efficiency than legislation. Moreover, Posner contends, the adversarial system mirrors the market, and engenders impartiality.

Much of this provocative post-utilitarian revisionism employs the jargon of economics; the innocent jurisprudence student is therefore expected to understand (and use) terms such as 'optimality', 'transaction costs', 'damage costs', 'precaution costs'. But don't panic; most of these apparently intimidating concepts actually stand for fairly straightforward ideas.

Thus, 'Pareto efficiency' (named after the Italian economist, Vilfredo Pareto) is achieved when at least one person is made better off, and no one is made worse off. For example, I am willing to sell you my bicycle for £100. But you reckon it is worth £200, but are happy to pay me £150 which I accept. We are both better off, and neither of us is worse off. The test of 'Pareto optimality' describes a situation which cannot be altered without making at least one person worse off than he was prior to the change.

The problem with this test is that rarely are decisions made in which Pareto efficiency is obtained; someone generally suffers. A refinement of this standard was therefore proposed by two British economists, the so-called Kaldor–Hicks test, which is satisfied when the alteration in the allocation of resources produces enough money to compensate those who are losers. In other words, any gains made ought to be sufficient to enable those who benefit to compensate those who do not.

Transaction costs are those incurred in the course of effecting a transaction. Suppose that my shop sells olive oil for €12 a litre. You find a Tuscan farm that sells the same quality oil directly to consumers for only €8 a litre. Your (understandable) decision might be to buy from the cheaper source, believing I am making an excessive profit. But this is to ignore my numerous transaction costs which would include seeking a supplier (information costs), bargaining with them (bargaining costs), ensuring that they honour their contract (enforcement costs), complying with EU regulations (regulatory costs), insuring the product against damage or loss (legal costs), and so on.

The significance of transaction costs was first identified by the Nobel laureate, Ronald Coase (1910–2013), whose name is synonymous with the widely used Coase theorem which postulates a situation in which one outcome is the most 'efficient'. For example, a factory emits smoke which causes damage to laundry hung outdoors by five nearby residents. In the absence of any corrective measures, each resident would suffer £75 in damages, a total of £375. The smoke damage may be prevented in one of two ways: either a smoke-screen could be installed on the factory's chimney, at a cost of £150, or each resident could be provided with an electric tumble drier at a cost of £50 per resident. The *efficient* solution is obviously to install the smoke-screen since it eliminates total damage of £375 for an outlay of only £150, and it is cheaper than purchasing five electric driers for £250. But the question raised by Coase is whether the efficient outcome would result if the right to clean air were assigned to the residents or if the right to pollute is given to the factory. In the case of the former, the factory has three choices: pollute and pay £375 in damages, install a smoke-screen for £150, or buy five tumble driers for the residents at a total cost of £250. The factory would, naturally, install the smoke-screen: the efficient solution. If there is a right to pollute, the residents have three choices: suffer their collective damages of £375, buy five driers for £250, or buy a smoke-screen for the factory for £150. They, too, would choose to buy the smoke-screen. The efficient outcome would therefore be achieved *regardless of the assignment of the legal right*. This simple hypothesis assumes that the residents would incur no costs in coming together in order to negotiate with the factory. Coase calls this 'zero transaction costs'. But real life is more complex: certain costs would be incurred in this process. The simple version of the Coase theorem may therefore be stated as follows: where there are zero transaction costs, the efficient outcome will occur regardless of the choice of legal rule. You can see why, for 'economists of law', the Coase theorem (which has a more complex version where there are 'positive transaction costs') is so important.[22]

The *raison d'être* of Posnerian theory is the notion of wealth-maximization which, he claims, provides the benefits of utilitarianism without its drawbacks. It would, moreover, be chosen as the most attractive option by most people. But the goal of wealth-maximization is far from uncontroversial and has been contested by, among others, Ronald Dworkin (see 9.2.1).

---

[22] A useful, non-technical introduction to the subject (from which I have borrowed the above example) is AM Polinsky, *An Introduction to Law and Economics* (Boston, Mass: Little, Brown & Co, 1983). Guido Calabresi and A Douglas Melamed emphasize the importance of 'entitlements' or property rights to valuable resources. They identify three grounds upon which they are created: efficiency, distribution, and justice. In recognizing and protecting entitlements, the law determines which of the competing parties should succeed. This, they argue, avoids a society in which might is right. They identify three types of entitlements: those protected by property rules, by liability rules, and by inalienable entitlements. See their article 'Property Rules, Liability Rules and Inalienability: One View of the Cathedral' (1972) 85 *Harvard Law Review* 1089.

I cannot here explore these interesting questions (which have become an integral feature of many jurisprudence courses) further. But there is much in the economic analysis to stimulate lawyers into thinking about just solutions—at least where it is possible to place an economic value on costs and benefits. It has therefore been applied, with some success, to the problem of measuring the efficiency of our systems of accident compensation.

Allied to the 'law and economics' approach is the application of game theory and 'public choice theory' to issues of justice. The former postulates models in which participants choose a strategy where the outcome depends on the available strategies.[23] In other words, how do I, as a player in the game, maximize my opportunities in the light of other players' possible choices and actions? So, for example, game theory has been deployed to assess the efficacy of the law in accident prevention. It underlines also the game element in the law: we do not always act in a rational manner in deciding, for instance, whether to enter into contractual relations. Factors such as the likelihood or otherwise of litigation or the prospects of losing face often influence what may appear to be a decision based exclusively on legal rules and principles. And, game theorists contend, since law possesses several features of a game, it ought to acknowledge this fact in the formulation of legal rules.

Public choice theory applies game theory to the process of law creation by legislation, regulation, and judicial decision.[24] In particular, the theory seeks to expose the self-interest that frequently explains the actions of public officials. It regards with suspicion the notion that legislators, judges, and other officials act in the public interest or genuinely seek to advance the common good. Acknowledging the function of these selfish motives (personal advancement, money, power), in the creation and interpretation of the law, suggests to these theorists that the legal system be arranged in such a way as to reduce their impact.

### 9.2.1 Critique

Two principal attacks are made on the foundation of the theory. First, it is argued that it rests on the assumption of economic and social equilibrium. In other words, the analysis is pursued on the basis that time is frozen: it overlooks the inevitable truth that individual preferences are not fixed or constant—they change over time. The Law and Economics movement, it is contended, oversimplifies the complex, fluid nature of the market.[25]

---

[23] See Douglas Baird, Robert Gertner, and Randal Picker, *Game Theory and the Law* (Cambridge, Mass: Harvard University Press, 1994).

[24] See Daniel Farber and Philip Frickey, *Law and Public Choice* (Chicago, Ill: University of Chicago Press, 1991), and JM Buchanan and G Tulloch, *The Calculus of Consent* (Ann Arbor, Mich: University of Michigan Press, 1962).

[25] This attack is most powerfully advanced by the so-called Austrian school of economists. See, eg, LA Schwartzstein, 'An Austrian Economic View of the Legal Process' (1994) 55 *Ohio State Law Journal* 1049.

A second criticism is a moral one launched by, amongst others, Ronald Dworkin. Two of his essays, in particular, may be consulted with benefit: 'Is Wealth a Value?' and 'Why Efficiency?'—both of which are reproduced in *A Matter of Principle*.[26] Judge Posner has attempted to defend his economic analysis (and is further attacked by Dworkin).[27] Note the ambitious claim Posner makes for his theory:

> I have tried to develop a moral theory that goes beyond classical utilitarianism and holds that the criterion for judging whether acts and institutions are just or good is whether they maximise the wealth of society. This approach allows reconciliation among utility, liberty, and even equality as competing ethical principles.[28]

And it is, of course, Posner's view that judges have proceeded on this assumption in the development of the common law, a thesis which Dworkin comprehensively dismisses: 'It has not achieved the beginning of a beginning.'[29]

Economic analysis is now used fairly widely by policy-makers and even courts, especially in the United States. It sits more comfortably in the case of the former, where legislators attempt to predict the outcome of competing policies and thereby better to reform the law. In respect of the adjudicative process, however, one may query whether many judges have the requisite training and skill to determine the validity or otherwise of the arguments presented to them. Not all judges are Richard Posner.

It is not possible to do justice to this debate here, but five major criticisms of the economic analysis of law may be briefly identified. Each, of course, stands in need of elaboration. First, the theory rests on the assumption that wealth maximization is a value (in itself or instrumentally) that a society would regard as worth trading off against justice, but as Dworkin puts it, 'increasing social wealth does not in itself make the community better'.[30] Secondly, the theory oversimplifies what is a complex matter; in the words of one critic, ' "What people want" is presented in such a way that while in form it is empirical it is almost wholly non-falsifiable by anything so crude as fact.'[31] Thirdly, the analysis merely reflects a particular ideological preference: it reinforces and advances the capitalist, free-market system.[32] Fourthly, it may be queried what the theory has to do with *justice*?[33] It presupposes an *initial* distribution of wealth—which may be wholly unjust. 'Efficiency' therefore becomes a means of rationalizing, and sustaining, existing inequalities. Fifthly, is it possible to reduce life to the solitary consideration of money?[34]

[26] At 237 and 267, respectively.
[27] In Marshall Cohen (ed), *Ronald Dworkin and Contemporary Jurisprudence* (London: Duckworth, 1984), 238 and 295.     [28] *The Economics of Justice*, 115.
[29] *A Matter of Principle* (Cambridge, Mass: Harvard University Press, 1985), 265.
[30] *Law's Empire* (Cambridge, Mass and London: Belknap Press, 1973), 288.
[31] A A Leff, 'Economic Analysis of Law: Some Realism about Nominalism' (1974) 60 *Virginia Law Review* 451, 456.
[32] See M Horwitz, 'Law and Economics: Science or Politics?' (1981) 8 *Hofstra Law Review* 905.
[33] Or with concern for our fellow creatures. The trade in bear gall could presumably be justified by the existence of a market for this substance—regardless of the appalling cruelty suffered by the bears. See 10.5.
[34] See Martha Nussbaum, 'Flawed Foundations: The Philosophical Critique of (a Particular Type of) Economics' (1997) 64 *University of Chicago Law Review* 1197.

## 9.3 John Rawls

The contribution of John Rawls (1921–2002) to legal and political theory is immense. His substantial book, *A Theory of Justice* is, by the admission of one of its most vehement critics, Robert Nozick:

> a powerful, deep, subtle, wide-ranging, systematic work in political and moral philosophy which has not seen its like since the writings of John Stuart Mill, if then. It is a fountain of illuminating ideas, integrated together into a lovely whole. Political philosophers now must either work within Rawls' theory or explain why not.[35]

Ronald Dworkin's praise is no less generous:

> No theorist has made a greater contribution to legal philosophy in modern times than the political philosopher, John Rawls.[36]...I offer you a confession, but with no apology. Each of us has his or her own Immanuel Kant, and from now on we will struggle, each of us, for the benediction of John Rawls. After all the books, all the footnotes, all the wonderful discussions, we are only just beginning to grasp how much we have to learn from that man.[37]

You would be well advised to pay close attention to this important revival of social contractarianism (see 2.3). In an ideal world, you should read the book itself. This is not, sadly, an ideal world and even the most conscientious student will find neither the time nor the patience to plough through its 600 (often difficult) pages. There are several admirable commentaries on *A Theory of Justice* to which you will doubtless be referred. My own preference—from a student's point of view—is *Reading Rawls*, edited by N Daniels, which contains a helpful introduction and a number of illuminating essays (especially those by T Nagel, R Dworkin, TM Scanlon, R Miller, and HLA Hart).[38] Many of the criticisms made of the book are answered in Rawls's book *Political Liberalism*[39] published in 1993, where he develops his theory of justice into a comprehensive political and institutional theory of democracy. I shall here provide a sketch of the four most important general aspects of the original theory, followed by a brief critique.

### 9.3.1 The rejection of utilitarianism

Like Nozick and Dworkin, Rawls regards utilitarianism as an unsatisfactory means by which to measure justice. His attack on utility is, however, different from both of theirs. He refuses to accept inequalities even if they secure maximum welfare; his conception

[35] *Anarchy, State, and Utopia* (Oxford: Wiley–Blackwell, 2001), 183.

[36] Ronald Dworkin, *Justice in Robes* (Cambridge, Mass and London: Harvard University Press, 2006), 34.

[37] Ibid, 261. Cf Ronald Dworkin, *Justice for Hedgehogs* (Cambridge, Mass and London: Harvard University Press, 2011), 63–5, 267–9. See too Thomas Pogge, *John Rawls: His Life and Theory of Justice*, transl M Kosch (Oxford: Oxford University Press, 2007).

[38] Norman Daniels (ed), *Reading Rawls: Critical Studies on Rawls' A Theory of Justice* (Oxford: Basil Blackwell, 1975).          [39] (New York: Columbia University Press, 1993).

of welfare is not concerned with benefits, but 'primary social goods' which includes self-respect; he regards the liberty contained in the first principle as non-negotiable—even in order to maximize welfare. Some critics argue, however, that there are fewer differences than Rawls appears to realize.[40]

Suffice it to say here that Rawls's hostility toward utilitarianism is based largely on two features of the theory. First, that it fails to recognize the separateness or distinctness of individual persons; this is an aspect that many anti-utilitarians (including Dworkin and Nozick) find unacceptable. Secondly, Rawls argues that questions of justice are *prior to* questions of happiness. In other words, it is only when we regard a particular pleasure as just that we can say whether it has any value. How do we know whether John's enjoyment of torture should be counted as having any value *before* we know whether the practice of torture is itself *just*? (See the discussion of utilitarianism in 9.1.) Thus, whereas utilitarianism defines what is right in terms of what is good, Rawls regards what is right as prior to what is good.

### 9.3.2 Social contractarianism

Rawls's theory of justice as fairness is rooted in the idea of the social contract (see 2.3). In *A Theory of Justice*,[41] he expresses the objective of his project as follows:

> My aim is to present a conception of justice which generalises and carries to a higher level of abstraction the familiar theory of the social contract as found, say, in Locke, Rousseau, and Kant. In order to do this we are not to think of the original contract as one to enter a particular society or to set up a particular form of government. Rather, the guiding idea is that the principles of justice for the basic structure of society are the object of *the original agreement*. They are the principles that *free and rational persons* concerned to further *their own interests* would accept in an *initial position of equality* as defining the fundamental terms of their association. These principles are to regulate all further agreements; they specify the kinds of social cooperation that can be entered into and the forms of government that can be established. This way of regarding the principles of justice I shall call *Justice as fairness*.

Read this passage again. It captures, I think, the essence of Rawls's theory of justice. The phrases I have italicized are key elements in his social contractarian argument, the attraction of which is the objectivity it seeks to present. We must, Rawls argues, distinguish between people's genuine judgments about justice and their subjective, self-interested views. In doing so, it is plain that the position adopted by a hypothetical neutral outsider concerning what is just is likely to be fairer than that which we hold as parties who have a vested interest in the outcome. Once we have arrived at those objective principles, we should measure them against our own judgments. The inevitable distinction between the two must be corrected by our modifying our own judgments in such a way that we eventually reach a situation in which the two are similar: this is the position of 'reflective equilibrium'.[42]

---

[40] See F Michelman in Daniels (ed), *Reading Rawls*, 319.     [41] At 11; emphasis added.
[42] *A Theory of Justice*, 20 and 48–51.

**Table 9.1** Rawls's gain and loss table

| Decisions | Circumstances | | |
|---|---|---|---|
| | C1 | C2 | C3 |
| D1 | –£700 | £800 | £1,200 |
| D2 | –£800 | £700 | £1,400 |
| D3 | £500 | £600 | £800 |

### 9.3.3 **The original position**

Most students enjoy Rawls's imaginary picture of the POP (people in the 'original position') sitting ('under a tree' according to at least one!), each shrouded in a 'veil of ignorance', debating the principles of justice. This ignorance prevents them from knowing to which sex, class, religion, or social position they belong. Each person represents a social class, but they do not know whether they are clever or stupid, strong or weak. Nor do they know in which country or in what period they are living. They possess only certain elementary knowledge about the laws of science and psychology. In this state of blissful ignorance they must unanimously decide upon the general principles that will define the terms under which they will live as a society. And, in doing so, they are moved by rational self-interest: each seeks those principles which will give him or her (but they do not know their sex!) the best chance of attaining his or her chosen conception of the good life (whatever that happens to be). So stripped of their individuality, the POP will opt, says Rawls, for a 'maximin' principle. This strategy may be explained by Rawls's own gain and loss table (slightly adapted, see Table 9.1).[43]

I must choose from among several possible circumstances. So, if I choose D1, and C1 occurs, I will lose £700, but if C2 occurs I will gain £800 and, if I am really lucky and C3 should occur, I will gain £1,200. And similarly in respect of decisions D2 and D3. Gain $g$ therefore depends on the individual's decision $d$ and the circumstances $c$. Thus $g$ is a function of $d$ and $c$. Or, to express it mathematically $g = f(d, c)$. Which decision would I choose? The maximin principle dictates that I opt for D3 because in this case the *worst* that can happen to me is that I gain £500—which is better than the worst for the other actions (in which I stand to lose either £800 or £700).

Similarly, the POP, as rational individuals, would choose principles which guarantee that the worst condition one might find oneself in, when the veil of ignorance is lifted, is the least undesirable of the available alternatives. In other words, I will select those principles which, *should I turn out to be at the bottom of the social pile*, will be in my best interests. So, argues Rawls, the POP will choose the following two principles.

---

[43] Ibid, 153.

### 9.3.4 **The two principles of justice**

*First principle.* 'Each person is to have an equal right to the most extensive total system of equal basic liberties compatible with a similar system of liberty for all.'

*Second principle.* 'Social and economic inequalities are to be arranged so that they are both:

(a)  to the greatest benefit of the least advantaged, consistent with the just savings principle, and

(b)  attached to offices and positions open to all under conditions of fair equality of opportunity.'

You should know these two principles intimately, but a most important feature is that the first has 'lexical priority' over the second. Or, to put it simply, the POP put *liberty above equality*—because of the 'maximin' strategy described above: no one would wish to risk his or her liberty when the veil of ignorance is removed and it is revealed they are among the least well-off members of society. By the same token of maximin reasoning, they will opt for clause (a) of the second principle—the so-called 'difference principle'. This ensures that the worst anyone could be is 'least advantaged' and, if they do belong to this group, they will benefit from this clause. It would be rational for them to choose this principle rather than either total equality or some form of greater inequality, because of the respective risks of being worse off or reducing the prospects of improving their lot. And, they will be better able to 'improve their lot' in a society which places liberty above equality; this is because various 'social primary goods' (which Rawls defines to include rights, liberties, powers, opportunities, income, wealth, and especially self-respect) are more likely to be attained in a free society.

Another reason why Rawls argues that the difference principle will appeal to the POP is that it is preferable to its two chief competitors: the 'system of natural liberty' and the idea of 'fair equality of opportunity'. The former consists in an untrammelled market economy which makes no attempt to redistribute wealth. The POP would reject this principle, he argues, because it 'permits distributive shares to be improperly influenced by…factors so arbitrary from a moral point of view'. Thus the accident of being born into a wealthy family would be relevant, whereas, morally speaking, it ought not to be. The latter bases people's prospects on their natural talent and the energies they expend in applying them effectively. This is clearly preferable to the system of natural liberty, but it is, in Rawls's view open to a similar objection: why should an individual's talents be any more morally relevant than the fact that he is the son of a millionaire? In neither case do these accidents have anything to do with *desert*. Choosing the difference principle, however, means that individuals who have natural talents may increase their wealth only if, in the process, they also increase the wealth of the *least advantaged*.

The second principle contains two important limitations that ensure that the least advantaged benefit from the social arrangements selected. First, the 'just savings principle': this refers to the need for the POP (who do not, of course, know which stage of civilization their society has reached: are they in the First World or the Third?) to ask themselves how much they would be willing to save at each stage of advance, on the assumption that all other generations will save at the same rates. The principle therefore:

> assigns an appropriate rate of accumulation to each level of advance. Presumably this rate changes depending upon the state of society. When people are poor and saving is difficult, a lower rate of saving should be required; whereas in a wealthier society greater savings may reasonably be expected since the real burden is less. Eventually once just institutions are firmly established, the net accumulation required falls to zero.[44]

The POP will therefore save some of their resources for future generations.

The second limitation refers to the fact that all offices should be open to all (and not, as one examination candidate suggested that 'offices should be open at all hours'!). Rawls is here referring to job opportunities.

### 9.3.5 Reconsideration

In the decades since the publication of *A Theory of Justice* in 1972, Rawls revised, refined, and modified his ideas in a number of essays, culminating in 1993 in the publication of his book *Political Liberalism*.[45] In this work he seeks to eradicate some of the universalist assumptions present in *A Theory of Justice*. He adopts a more communitarian approach, arguing that his idea of the person as impartial citizen offers the best account of liberal-democratic political culture, and his objective is to establish the rules for consensus in political communities where citizens seek such.

In 1999 he further re-evaluated his views in *Law of Peoples*,[46] where he goes so far as to concede that liberalism may not be appropriate to all societies, and proffers a model of what he calls a 'decent, well-ordered society' that liberal societies ought to accept, even if it is undemocratic, provided it abstains from aggression against other societies, and exhibits a 'common good conception of justice', a 'reasonable consultation hierarchy', and protects basic human rights.

In *Political Liberalism*, he considers the plethora of criticism (and misunderstanding) that his earlier work (itself the outcome of a similar process) provoked. While there are numerous amendments and explanations, I shall mention only those that strike me as the most significant.[47]

First, it is clear that, although many critics regarded his principles of justice as a sort of Archimedean point in ethics which would provide a universal standard of social justice, Rawls intended no such thing. His theory is meant to apply to modern constitutional democracies. Secondly, he demonstrates another feature of the modesty of

---

[44]  Ibid, 287.
[45]  John Rawls, *Political Liberalism* (New York: Columbia University Press, 1993).
[46]  John Rawls, *The Law of Peoples; with The Idea of Public Reason Revisited* (Cambridge, Mass: Harvard University Press, 1999).
[47]  See Martha Nussbaum, 'Rawls's Political Liberalism. A Reassessment' (2011) 24 *Ratio Juris* 1.

his thesis: the idea of 'justice as fairness' is a *political* rather than an epistemological or metaphysical task. It is, in other words, a conception of justice that is fundamentally practical. It is supposed to be philosophically neutral, to transcend philosophical controversy.

Thirdly, in pursuit of an elusive 'overlapping consensus', Rawls posits his principles of justice as the terms under which members of a pluralistic, democratic community with competing interests and values might achieve political accord. His conception of political liberalism acknowledges that this consensus may be challenged by the establishment by the state of a shared moral or religious doctrine. But the community's sense of justice would prevail over the state's interpretation of the public good.[48]

Fourthly, the first principle of justice which originally requires that each person have an equal right to 'the most extensive total system of equal basic liberties' now consists in an equal right to 'a fully adequate scheme of equal basic liberties'. Fifthly, Rawls demonstrates how the two principles of justice might, following the 'original position', be adopted constitutionally (the first principle is enshrined in the constitution), legislatively (the second principle may be accepted by democratic decision), and, judicially (the courts ensure that the supreme law of the constitution is defended against the vagaries of legislative activity).

This may seem a slightly romantic, Utopian vision of social and political harmony, an allegation Rawls refutes:

> [A]n initial acquiescence in a liberal conception of justice as a mere *modus vivendi* could change over time first into a constitutional consensus and then into an overlapping consensus. In this process I have supposed that the comprehensive doctrines of most people are not fully comprehensive, and this allows scope for the development of an independent allegiance to the political conception that helps to bring about a consensus...[which] leads people to act...in accordance with constitutional arrangements, since they have reasonable assurance (based on past experience) that others will also comply. Gradually, as the success of political cooperation continues, citizens gain increasing trust and confidence in one another. This is all we need to say in reply to the objection that the idea of overlapping consensus is Utopian.[49]

Persuaded? Some are not. It has been argued that the new emphasis on 'real people' and 'overlapping consensus' actually makes the difference principle harder to accept. Is it possible to apply the principle without some normative judgment about what 'equality' is? What, he asks, is 'equal pay'? Is it to be related to need, production, effort, or value of the work? '[C]an we believe that consensus could actually be achieved once people were aware of the normative ambiguities within equality?'[50]

Broadly speaking, therefore, Rawls re-formulates his earlier ideas to take greater account of competing social values and pluralist conceptions of the good life. In other

---

[48] See his article, 'The Idea of an Overlapping Consensus' (1987) 7 *Oxford Journal of Legal Studies* 1.
[49] *Political Liberalism* (New York: Columbia University Press, 1993), 168.
[50] *Lloyd's Introduction to Jurisprudence*, 8th edn (London: Sweet & Maxwell, 2008), 593.

words, he proposes a less comprehensive form of political liberalism that rests on collectively agreed notions of fairness, freedom, equality, and order. His revised theory of justice is presented as one pertaining to political life rather than (as in *A Theory of Justice*) to life in general.

### 9.3.6 **Critique of Rawls**

Some of the earlier doubts persist. As I have already said, his original book has generated a prodigious body of critical literature. And the criticism relates both, in the most general sense, to Rawls's project as a whole (his social contractarianism, his 'deep theory') and to specific attacks upon detailed aspects of the conceptual tools he employs (the 'original position', the 'difference principle', 'reflective equilibrium', the 'maximin rule', and so on). I shall mention only seven main sorts of criticisms that have been made. Each requires detailed elaboration.

First, as we have seen, some (notably Nozick) attack the very notion of any patterned distribution of social goods. Secondly, the 'original position' has been criticized both as a hypothetical device (it is highly artificial; can people *really* be stripped of their values?) and, more importantly, as necessarily supplying the outcome that Rawls postulates. Thus Ronald Dworkin argues that at the core of Rawls's 'deep theory' is the right of each individual to equal concern and respect.[51] But, says Dworkin, this right is a consequence not of the social contract but a presupposition of Rawls's *use* of the contract. Similarly, several critics have doubted whether the POP would *necessarily* opt for Rawls's two principles and, even if they did, why should they prefer liberty to equality?[52] What about the winner-takes-all philosophy that many have? Why should the POP not prefer this more adventurous alternative? Critics have also argued that it is unclear how conflicts between basic liberties are to be resolved. Some have even detected a conflict between Rawls's first and second principle themselves: 'Is it not the case that inequalities in wealth and power always produce inequalities in basic liberty?'[53]

Fourthly, an important criticism relates to the alleged 'bias' that is exhibited by the theory. This ranges from the presupposed 'deep theory' identified by Dworkin (above) to the ideological bias implicit in Rawls's assumptions about the POP. Thus, from a Marxist point of view, it has been argued by several writers[54] that Rawls makes several traditional, bourgeois, liberal assumptions. For instance, he regards people as naturally 'free'; but they are largely a product of their class interests. Similarly, his conception of the state is a consensus rather than a conflict model (see 7.6.6). As Richard Miller shows, in a class-divided society (in which no institutional arrangement acceptable to

---

[51] 'The Original Position' in Daniels (ed), *Reading Rawls*, 16.

[52] See, in particular, Professor Hart's essay, 'Rawls on Liberty and its Priority' in both his *Essays in Jurisprudence and Philosophy*, 223 and Daniels (ed), *Reading Rawls*, 230.

[53] *Lloyd's Introduction to Jurisprudence*, 592.

[54] See M Fisk, 'History and Reason in Rawls' Moral Theory' in Daniels (ed), *Reading Rawls*, 53; Miller, 'Rawls and Marxism', ibid, 206; W Lang, 'Marxism, Liberalism and Justice' in Kamenka and Tay (eds), *Justice*, 116.

the best-off class is acceptable to the worst-off) the difference principle is unlikely to be chosen by the representatives of the best-off class.[55] Rawls's theory therefore assumes a non-egalitarian structure of society. As HA Bedau puts it, it 'provides the nearest thing we have to a rational assessment of why the poor should allow the wealthy to keep most of that wealth and not, as in Marxist ideology, seek to expropriate it without so much as a thank you'.[56]

Fifthly, the difference principle has itself been subjected to criticism from a variety of standpoints. It assumes that natural talents are a 'collective asset'; is this acceptable? If they are, Nozick argues, the same could be said for bodily organs; is this accept-able? Does the difference principle really promote equality or simply make everyone worse off? Sixthly, Rawls's conception of 'social primary goods' is attacked: would the POP necessarily choose these things (rights, power, money, etc) in preference to, say, a caring society in which all are treated as equals? Does it not assume that people are acquisitive, greedy and selfish? Finally, some have doubted whether Rawls has pro-vided a theory of justice at all! According to certain critics, justice is about *deserts*: it is just that we should get what we *deserve*. Thus, if you work hard at studying jurispru-dence you deserve the reward of doing well. But, in Rawls's theorem, hard work need be rewarded in order only to secure that the worst-off do as well as possible. Finally, the theory, Martha Nussbaum has cogently argued, neglects three problems of social jus-tice: the problem of justice for the disabled, to 'all world citizens', and to non-human animals (see 10.5).[57]

Among the criticisms levelled at Rawls's *Political Liberalism* is the charge by com-munitarians that his conception of the person is unduly individualistic. We are, so the communitarian argument goes (see 10.3.1), to an important extent defined by—and attached to—our communities. We are social animals, rather than the selfish, atomis-tic individuals conceived by Rawls. This censure may strike you as unjust.

## 9.4 **Robert Nozick**

The free-market libertarianism of Robert Nozick (1938–2002)[58] along with the writings of certain other theorists (notably FA Hayek in a number of works, particularly *The Road to Serfdom* and *The Constitution of Liberty*),[59] represents another challenge to the very idea of wealth distribution as postulated, in particular, by John Rawls (see 9.3). The springboard of libertarianism is limiting the power of the state to protecting our secur-ity and administering justice through the courts. Other functions (such as health care,

---

[55] Op cit.

[56] 'Inequality, How Much and Why?' (1975) 6 *Journal of Social Philosophy* 25.

[57] See Martha C Nussbaum, *Frontiers of Justice: Disability, Nationality, Species Membership* (Cambridge, Mass: Belknap Press, 2006).  [58] Especially in his celebrated book, *Anarchy, State, and Utopia*.

[59] Friedrich von Hayek, *The Road to Serfdom* (London: Routledge & Kegan Paul, 1986); *The Constitution of Liberty* (London: Routledge & Kegan Paul, reprinted 1963). See too *Law, Legislation and Liberty, Volume I: Rules and Order, Volume II: The Mirage of Social Justice* (London: Routledge & Kegan Paul, reprinted 1982).

education, welfare) that we associate with a modern society ought to be undertaken by the private sector. In arguing their case, libertarians generally appeal to economic and sociological factors such as the virtues of competition, the intrinsic mechanisms that generate the inefficiency and incompetence of state bureaucracies, as well as the imperfect records of governments in overcoming social problems, including those of an economic and environmental nature. While Nozick endorses these arguments, his principal defence of libertarianism is a moral one: it values individual rights.

One assault on the Nozickian approach comes from the political right who regard his emphasis on the *individual* as inhospitable to the nationalism that is the hallmark of much of the philosophy of the so-called 'New Right' or 'neo-cons'.

Secondly, Nozick's profound individualism leads him to reject any form of paternalism; he therefore argues that since individuals own their bodies, they should be free to use them for whatever purpose they choose. This notion of 'self-ownership', according to Nozick, extends to the talents we possess, and the use to which we put them. Taxing my income is therefore a form of forced labour.

By the same token, we own our bodily organs; no one should be compelled to donate a kidney to one who desperately needs it. By extension therefore the enforced redistribution of wealth from the rich to the poor is unacceptable.

For Nozick liberty and equality are irreconcilable: we cannot, he argues, interfere with the distribution of resources in society without interfering with the liberty of individuals. Any attempt at 'patterned' distribution (like the one advocated by Rawls; see 9.3) presupposes a state with excessive powers. The state, in Nozick's view, is 'intrinsically immoral';[60] therefore he proposes a 'minimal State' whose functions are limited to the 'night-watchman' protection against force, theft, and fraud, the enforcement of contracts, and a few other essentials. A state that goes beyond this narrow model is an infringement of individual freedom which is based on the 'separateness of persons'.

We should be concerned not with redistributing resources, but with protecting individuals' rights to *what they already have*. In other words, the question of whether a particular distribution of goods is just should be answered by reference to whether the *initial acquisition* was just. So, where I acquired my property by freely entering into a contract, I am entitled to keep it, hence Nozick's 'entitlement theory' of justice.

The theory is based on the following three sets of principles:

- *Principles of acquisition*: they determine the circumstances under which persons are able to acquire ownership of previously unowned resources.

- *Principles of transfer*: they determine the methods by which the ownership of resources may be transferred between persons.

- *Principles of rectification*: they determine how an *unjust* acquisition or transfer of property should be rectified (eg, where property has been acquired fraudulently).

Nozick illustrates his entitlement theory by asking us to imagine a society in which the distribution of wealth conforms to a non-entitlement conception of justice, say one

---

[60] *Anarchy, State, and Utopia*, 51.

which favours an equal distribution, though it could equally be one based on desert or enterprise, for example). Let us call it D1. A challenger to Nozick's theory would be bound to accept this as a just distribution, since Nozick has permitted his adversary to select it. Suppose that amongst the members of this society is the celebrated basketball player, Wilt Chamberlain, who has as a condition of his contract with his team that he will play only if every spectator places 25 cents into a special box at the entrance of the stadium, the contents of which will be paid to him. Suppose also that over the course of the season, a million fans part with 25 cents to see him play. The result will be a new distribution, D2, in which Chamberlain is richer by $250,000, making him wealthier than any other member of the society. This distribution plainly violates the original pattern established in D1. Is D2 just? Is Chamberlain entitled to his cash?

Nozick answers both questions in the affirmative. Since everyone in D1 was, *ex hypothesi*, entitled to what he had, there is no injustice in the starting point that resulted in D2. What is more, the spectators who paid 25 cents in the shift from D1 to D2 did so freely—and hence cannot complain. Nor can those who had no desire to watch Chamberlain, for they have lost nothing. There is, in other words, no injustice at all. This demonstrates in Nozick's view the flaw in all non-entitlement theories of justice. These theories, he argues, postulate that it is a necessary condition for a just distribution that it contain a certain structure or fit a certain pattern. His Wilt Chamberlain example illustrates that a distribution, such as D2, can be just even though it does not have a particular structure or pattern. In addition, it demonstrates that 'liberty upsets patterns'—that permitting individuals to employ their holdings as they choose inevitably defeats any distribution championed by non-entitlement theories, whatever their ideological basis—egalitarian, liberal, socialist, etc. As a corollary, Nozick contends that any pattern is destructive of freedom. To impose a pattern of distribution requires an intolerable level of coercion, denying individuals the right to employ their talents and labour as they see fit. Hence distributive justice, according to Nozick, far from requiring a redistribution of wealth, actually prohibits it. The minimal state is therefore the best method by which to secure distributive justice.

An immediate question arises about this comforting historical entitlement theory: what if the distribution of goods in society at large is manifestly unjust? Nozick's reply is that 'If each person's holdings are just, then the total set (distribution) of holdings is just.'[61] This cavalier hostility toward a fairer redistribution of social goods sticks in the throats of many who value social justice. But, however abhorrent you may find Nozick's theory, be sure to attack it on stronger grounds than the student who, in an examination, asserted that 'Nozick is a crypto-fascist'. The publication of *Anarchy, State, and Utopia* excited a fair amount of controversy (partly because its late author was, at the time, a relatively young Harvard professor who was taught by John Rawls) and the book has been subjected to a good deal of (often indignant) criticism. Depending on how much time is spent on Nozick in your course, you will want to read some of this criticism: you will find a useful collection of essays in Jeffrey Paul (ed),

---

[61] Ibid, 153.

*Reading Nozick.*[62] Here I shall mention only six criticisms of Nozick's views (the merest outline of which has been sketched above). First, his account rests on an oversimplified conception of the individual who is isolated from society; moreover his

> world not only excludes the ever-growing role of the State within contemporary capitalism; it is also radically pre-sociological, without social structure, or social or cultural determinants of, and constraints upon, the voluntary acts and exchanges of its component individuals.[63]

Secondly, Nozick's assault on utilitarianism is, as Hart shows, paradoxical:

> [I]t yields a result identical with one of the least acceptable conclusions of an unqualified maximising utilitarianism, namely that given certain conditions there is nothing to choose between a society where few enjoy great happiness and very many very little, and a society where happiness is more equally spread.[64]

A utilitarian would regard the aggregate or average welfare in both societies as the same. Nozick, of course, treats the condition as a historical one. But neither, Hart seems to be suggesting, is willing to disturb the existing pattern of distribution, however unequal. A third sort of criticism concerns the Nozickian model of the minimal 'night-watchman' state. How does this state *emerge* from a state of nature, as Nozick argues it does, without infringing individual rights? Moreover,

> How is the minimal State to be controlled? How is it to be kept minimal? How are the economically advantaged to be stopped acquiring political power? The minimal State and an alert citizenry [are] supposed to stop this happening. How is destitution to be prevented and relieved? Nozick's answer, naïve in the extreme, points to the free operation of the market, voluntary uniting and private philanthropy.[65]

Fourthly, Nozick's comparison of income tax to forced labour has been attacked by a number of critics[66] who question the legitimacy of treating the two as remotely equivalent. In HLA Hart's words:

> Is taxing a man's earnings or income, which leaves him free to choose whether to work and to choose what work to do, not altogether different in terms of the burden it imposes from forcing him to labour? Does it really sacrifice him or make him or his body just a resource for others?[67]

Fifthly, why should we accept Nozick's limitation of rights to those of property and the negative right to liberty? What of rights to welfare? Nozick would, of course, reply that to recognize such rights implies that individuals have a right to the assistance *of others*; this would undermine his whole premise which is based on the 'separateness' of persons. But we are surely entitled to object that this entirely neglects the interests of the weaker members of society.

---

[62] Jeffrey Paul (ed), *Reading Nozick: Essays on Anarchy, State, and Utopia* (Oxford: Basil Blackwell, 1982).
[63] S Lukes, 'State of Nature' in *Essays in Social Theory* (London: Macmillan, 1977), 194.
[64] 'Between Utility and Rights' in *Essays in Jurisprudence and Philosophy*, 205.
[65] *Lloyd's Introduction to Jurisprudence*, 600.
[66] Including Hart, *Essays in Jurisprudence and Philosophy*, 206.          [67] Ibid.

Sixthly, Nozick's reliance on Locke's theory of individual property seems misguided. We saw in 2.3.2 that Locke argues that we acquire ownership over a thing by mixing our labour with it. But, as NE Simmonds[68] asks, can this apply to *natural resources*? If I apply my labours to extracting oil from beneath the ocean, the Lockean theory would presumably permit me to claim ownership of the oil I have extracted. But, unlike a table I build, I did not bring the oil into being: on what ground should I be able to assert an exclusive right over the full value of the oil? Note that, though Nozick mounts a frontal attack on Rawls's theory of justice, they share hostility to utilitarianism. It would be a useful exercise to compare how and why each comes to reject utility as a basis for a just society.

## Questions

1. Is Kant's deontological approach unrealistic?

2. What objections can you identify to virtue ethics?

3. What are the main differences between the approaches to morality and justice of Aristotle and Kant?

4. What are the main drawbacks of consequentialism?

5. Why does Dworkin object to utilitarianism?

6. Does the economic analysis of law overcome the difficulties of utilitarianism?

7. What is 'Pareto optimality'?

8. Explain the Coase theorem.

9. Is wealth a value?

10. Can we accurately measure individuals' preferences?

11. '[C]entral to the Economic Analysis of Law is the assumption, or thesis, that there is no difference of principle between buying the right to inflict injury intentionally and buying the right not to take precautions which would eliminate an equivalent number of injuries causes accidentally.' (John Finnis, 'Natural Law and Legal Reasoning' in Robert P George (ed), *Natural Law Theory: Contemporary Essays* (Oxford: Oxford University Press, 1992), 151)

    Is this a fair and accurate criticism?

12. What are Rawls's main objections against utilitarianism? Does his theory of justice overcome these problems?

13. How can Rawls be so sure that the people in the original position would agree on his two principles of justice?

---

[68] *Central Issues in Jurisprudence*, 99.

14. Is the 'difference principle' workable?

15. Is liberty more important than equality?

16. Can there ever be an objective standard of justice?

17. Why should feminists not support Rawls's theory of justice?

18. What is wrong with Nozick's theory of the minimal state?

19. Are you persuaded by Nozick's Wilt Chamberlain example?

20. Should the law promote justice or should it adopt a neutral stance, leaving citizens free to choose their own conception of virtue and the good life?

# Further reading

BUCHANAN JM and TULLOCH G, *The Calculus of Consent* (Ann Arbor, Mich: University of Michigan Press, 1962).

CAMPBELL, TOM, *Justice*, 2nd edn (Basingstoke: Palgrave Macmillan, 2000).

COHEN, G A, *Self-Ownership, Freedom and Equality* (Cambridge: Cambridge University Press, 1995).

CRISP, R AND M SLOTE, *Virtue Ethics* (New York: Oxford University Press, 1997).

DANIELS, NORMAN (ed), *Reading Rawls: Critical Studies on Rawls' A Theory of Justice* (Oxford: Basil Blackwell, 1975).

FISK, MM, 'History and Reason in Rawls' Moral Theory' in Daniels (ed), *Reading Rawls*, see above.

HART, HLA, 'Between Utility and Rights' in HLA Hart, *Essays in Jurisprudence and Philosophy* (Oxford: Clarendon Press, 1983).

HAYEK, FA, *The Constitution of Liberty* (London: Routledge & Kegan Paul, 1960).

HAYEK, FA, *The Road to Serfdom* (London: Routledge & Kegan Paul, 1976).

KAMENKA, E and TAY, A (eds), *Justice* (London: Edward Arnold, 1979).

LEFF, AA, 'Economic Analysis of Law: Some Realism about Nominalism' (1974) 60 *Virginia Law Review* 451.

LUCAS, JR, *On Justice* (Oxford: Clarendon Press, 1980).

LUKES, STEVEN, *Essays in Social Theory* (London: Macmillan, 1977).

MACINTYRE, A, *After Virtue* (London: Duckworth, 1985).

MORAWETZ, THOMAS (ed), *Justice* (Aldershot: Dartmouth, 1991).

NOZICK, ROBERT, *Anarchy, State, and Utopia* (Oxford: Wiley–Blackwell, 2001).

NUSSBAUM, M, *The Fragility of Goodness* (Cambridge: Cambridge University Press, 1986).

OLSARETTI, SERENA (ed), *Desert and Justice* (Oxford: Clarendon Press, 2007).

PAUL, JEFFREY (ed), *Reading Nozick: Essays on Anarchy, State, and Utopia* (Oxford: Basil Blackwell, 1982).

PERELMAN, C, *The Idea of Justice and the Problem of Argument* (London: Routledge & Kegan Paul, 1963).

POGGE, THOMAS, *John Rawls: His Life and Theory of Justice*, transl M Kosch (Oxford: Oxford University Press, 2007).

POLINSKY, AM, *An Introduction to Law and Economics* (Boston, Mass: Little, Brown & Co, 1983).

POSNER, RICHARD A, *The Economic Analysis of Law*, 2nd edn (Boston, Mass: Little, Brown & Co, 1977).

POSNER, RICHARD A, *The Economics of Justice* (Cambridge, Mass and London: Harvard University Press, 1981).

RAWLS, JOHN, *A Theory of Justice* (Harmondsworth: Penguin, 1973).

RAWLS, JOHN, *Political Liberalism* (New York: Columbia University Press, 1993).

RAZ, JOSEPH, *The Authority of Law: Essays on Law and Morality* (Oxford: Clarendon Press, 1979).

ROUSSEAU, JEAN-JACQUES, *The Social Contract and Discourses*, transl GDH Cole, revised JH Brumfitt and JC Hall (London: Dent, 1973).

SADURSKI, WOJCIECH (ed), *Ethical Dimensions of Legal Theory* (Amsterdam and Atlanta, Ga: Rodopi, 1991) (Poznan Studies in the Philosophy of the Sciences and the Humanities).

SANDEL, MICHAEL J (ed), *Justice: A Reader* (New York: Oxford University Press, 2006).

SARTORIUS, ROLF E, *Individual Conduct and Social Norms: A Utilitarian Account of Social Union and the Rule of Law* (Encino, Calif: Dickenson, 1975).

SCANLON, TM, *What We Owe Each Other* (Cambridge, Mass: Harvard University Press, 1998).

SIMMONDS, NE, *Central Issues in Jurisprudence: Law, Justice, Law and Rights*, 4th edn (London: Sweet & Maxwell, 2013).

SLOTE, M, *Morals from Motives* (Oxford: Oxford University Press, 2001).

SMART, JJC and WILLIAMS, BERNARD, *Utilitarianism: For and Against* (Cambridge: Cambridge University Press, 1973).

STATMAN, D (ed), *Moral Luck* (New York: State University of New York Press, 1993).

STATMAN, D (ed), *Virtue Ethics* (Edinburgh: Edinburgh University Press, 1997).

SUGARMAN, DAVID (ed), *Legality, Ideology and the State* (London: Academic Press, 1983).

SUMNER, COLIN, *Reading Ideologies: An Investigation into the Marxist Theory of Ideology and Law* (London: Academic Press, 1979).

SWANTON, C, *Virtue Ethics* (New York: Oxford University Press, 2003).

SYPNOWICH, CHRISTINE, *The Concept of Socialist Law* (Oxford: Clarendon Press, 1990).

THOMPSON, EP, *Whigs and Hunters: The Origin of the Black Act* (London: Allen Lane, 1975).

THOMPSON, EP, *The Poverty of Theory, and Other Essays* (London: Merlin Press, 1978).

VARGA, CSABA (ed), *Marxian Legal Theory* (Aldershot: Dartmouth, 1992).

WILLIAMS, B, *Ethics and the Limits of Philosophy* (London: Fontana, 1985).

# 10

# Rights

Among the most significant and contentious concepts to perplex legal and moral philosophers is that of a 'right'. To talk of rights, however, immediately raises the distinction between what a right *is*, on the one hand, and what rights people actually *have* or should have, on the other. This is the distinction between *analytical* and *normative* jurisprudence respectively. It is hard to see how the two questions can be kept apart when it comes to seeking to understand the nature of rights (and attempts to do so may give rise to several difficult philosophical problems). Nevertheless it is a convenient separation which assists, I think, in clarifying our thinking about rights. We should, however, recognize that the two are obviously closely related.

This chapter will examine the concept of rights, various theories and types of rights (including human and animal rights), and conclude with another brief exercise in 'applied jurisprudence' that demonstrates how ostensibly competing approaches to a central democratic right are played out.

## 10.1 What is a right?

It is not only lawyers who employ the term 'right' with more enthusiasm than precision. The concept invariably insinuates itself into discourses on ethics as well as in ordinary conversation. For the Scandinavian realists (see 6.3) a 'right' was a mystical figment of one's imagination. You will find a concise, lucid statement of their position (and much else) in Professor White's excellent short book, *Rights*.[1] We have, already, in 2.3, encountered the idea of 'natural rights'. The nature and scope of its modern formulation as 'human rights' is considered later in 10.3.

This is a large subject and, for most students of jurisprudence, a fairly forbidding one. The seam has been worked by generations of legal and moral philosophers and the literature is enormous. You will benefit from a reading of the non-legal expositions of rights, but most jurisprudence courses concentrate on the (sufficiently taxing) subject of legal rights, and the starting point of most expositions is the analysis by Wesley Hohfeld. You should know how Hohfeld sought to elucidate the concept of a right, and the extent to which he succeeded. Most of the leading textbooks deal with his account,

---

[1] Alan R White, *Rights* (Oxford: Clarendon Press, 1984), 2–4. See too Carlos S Nino (ed), *Rights* (Aldershot: Dartmouth, 1992), Tom Campbell, *Rights: A Critical Introduction* (London: Routledge, 2005).

**Table 10.1** Hohfeld's scheme of 'jural relations'

| | | | | |
|---|---|---|---|---|
| *Opposites* | {right | privilege | power | immunity |
| | {no-right | duty | disability | liability |
| *Correlatives* | {right | privilege | power | immunity |
| | {duty | no-right | ability | disability |

but (as always) it would be a good idea to read his own words in *Fundamental Legal Conceptions as Applied in Judicial Reasoning*.[2]

Hohfeld sought to clarify the proposition 'X has a right to do R' which may, in his view, mean one of four things:

- That Y (or anyone else) is under a duty to allow X to do R; this means, in effect, that X has a *claim* against Y. He calls this claim right simply a 'right'.

- That X is free to do or refrain from doing something; Y owes *no duty* to X. He calls this a 'privilege' (though it is often described as a 'liberty').

- That X has a power to do R; X is simply free to do an act which alters legal rights and duties or legal relations in general (eg, sell his property) whether or not he has a claim right or privilege to do so. Hohfeld calls this a 'power'.

- That X is not subject to Y's (or anyone's) power to change X's legal position. He calls this an 'immunity'.

Hohfeld conceived of these four 'rights' having both 'opposites' and 'correlatives' (ie the other side of the same coin) as shown in Table 10.1.

Thus, to use Hohfeld's own example, if X has a *right* against Y that Y shall stay off X's land, the *correlative* (and equivalent) is that Y is under a *duty* to keep off the land. A *privilege* is the *opposite* of a *duty*, and the *correlative* of a '*no-right*'. Hence, whereas X has a *right* (or *claim*) that Y should stay off his land, X himself has the *privilege* of entering on the land, or, in other words, X does not have a duty to stay off.

It is important to note that, for Hohfeld, claim rights (ie rights in the normal sense) are strictly *correlative* to duties. To say that X has a claim right of some kind is to say that Y (or someone else) owes a certain duty to X. But to say that X has a certain liberty is *not* to say that anyone owes him a duty. Thus if X has a *privilege* (or liberty) to wear a hat, Y does not have a *duty* to X, but a *no-right* that X should not wear a hat. In other words, the *correlative* of a liberty is a no-right. Similarly the correlative of a power is a liability (ie, being liable to have one's legal relations changed by another), the correlative of an immunity is a disability (ie, the inability to change another's legal relations).

[2] An extract may be found in *Lloyd's Introduction to Jurisprudence*, 8th edn (London: Sweet & Maxwell, 2008), 569–74. A helpful introduction to Hohfeld is Hamish Ross, 'Hohfeld and the Analysis of Rights' in J Penner, D Schiff, and R Nobles, *Introduction to Jurisprudence and Legal Theory: Commentary and Materials* (London: Butterworths, 2002), Ch 13.

But is Hohfeld correct? Is it true that whenever I am under some duty someone else has a corresponding right? Or vice versa? In the first case, surely it is possible for me to have a duty without you (or anyone else) having a right that I should perform it. In the criminal law certain duties are imposed upon me, but no one has a correlative right to my performing these duties. This is because it is possible for there to be a duty to do something which is not a duty to *someone*; for instance, the duty imposed on a policeman to report offenders—he owes this duty to no one in particular, and, hence, it gives rise to no right in anyone. And even where someone owes a duty to *someone* to do something, the person to whom he owes such a duty does not necessarily have any corresponding right. Thus, a professor has certain duties toward her students, but this does not necessarily confer any rights upon them. Similarly we commonly accept that we owe certain duties to infants or animals; yet many argue that it does not follow from this that they have rights (see 10.5). You will have encountered several examples of the absence of correlativity of rights and duties in criminal law: the duty, say, to observe road signs contains no reference to any duty to others and therefore implies no rights vested in anyone.

On the other hand, it is, of course, common for me to have a right to do something, without you (or anyone else) having a corresponding duty. Lawyers, however, often assume that right and duty are correlatives. Hohfeld[3] quotes Lord Lindley's dictum in *Quinn* v *Leatham*[4] that the plaintiff had a right to earn his living as he pleased provided he did not infringe the law or the rights of others:

> This liberty is a right recognised by law; its correlative is the general duty of every one not to prevent the free exercise of this liberty except so far as his own liberty of action may justify him in so doing.[5]

But this seems mistaken. And similar attacks have been made on Hohfeld's treating a power as a correlative of a liability, an immunity of a disability, and so on.

Yet these criticisms may miss the point of Hohfeld's purpose. JW Harris offers a spirited defence of Hohfeld's position.[6] It is true that, in order to make sense of legal relations between persons, correlativity is part of the law's lowest common denominator—because every judicial issue involves at least two persons. In practice, therefore, *litigation* gives rise to opposing parties—even where, strictly speaking, the defendant does not owe a duty to the claimant. Thus my duty to pay tax on my income does not necessarily give rise to a right held by another; but the taxman will pursue me in the courts in order to recover tax owing. Hence, the court has to answer the question: does the defendant owe a duty *to the claimant*? Similarly, in those recent decisions in which the courts have had to consider whether private individuals have *locus standi* to enforce the duties imposed by the criminal law, or the duty of public authorities to

---

[3] *Fundamental Legal Conceptions as Applied in Judicial Reasoning*, ed WW Cook (New Haven, Conn and London: Yale University Press, 1964), 42.          [4] [1901] AC 495, 534.

[5] Emphasis added by Hohfeld.

[6] *Legal Philosophies*, 2nd edn (London: Butterworths, 1997), 81–3.

provide various facilities such as health care and housing, the question is whether the defendant's conduct was in some way privileged—in relation to *the claimant*.[7]

In other words, *someone* has to bring the action or, indeed, be sued. Correlatives seem a convenient way of describing the relationship between the claimant's action and the defendant's conduct. But, as Harris concedes, where a court holds[8] that in certain rare circumstances an injunction may be granted by a civil court to restrain a threatened breach of the criminal law) that a private person may bring an action only where he has a 'private right', this must mean that he has a 'private interest'—a non-Hohfeldian, non-relational conception of right. And, on the other hand, there will be cases where a general, uncorrelated 'duty' is the basis for recognizing a certain relationship. So, in *Johnson* v *Phillips*[9] the duty of the police to promote the free flow of traffic was held to justify a constable, in an emergency, ordering a motorist to drive the wrong way down a one-way street. Here no correlative right arises. Perhaps the answer is that 'judicial reasoning [is] necessarily infused with moral and political ideas about private right and public duty, for which some non-Hohfeldian analysis is essential'.[10]

All four of Hohfeld's rights (which, in modern accounts, are usually called claim rights, liberties, powers, and immunities) are rights *against a specific person or persons*. As NE Simmonds points out, students are often confused by the fact that, in Hohfeld's scheme, X's liberty does not entail any *duty* on Y's part not to interfere. Thus the fact that X has a liberty (as against Y) to wear a hat does *not* entail that Y is under a duty not to interfere with X's wearing a hat. Y would therefore be entitled to *prevent* X from wearing a hat (eg, by buying up the supply of hats and refusing to sell X one).[11]

You may discover other defects with the correlativity thesis; Professor MacCormick, for example, argues that duties are often imposed in order to *protect* rights rather than merely being correlative to such rights. And it is surely true that when we talk of imposing duties on people (such as the duty to wear seatbelts) we do not think of this duty as being owed to some person or persons. We do not, in other words, normally think that where there is a duty there is a right.

You should also consider the validity of the more general attack on Hohfeld: that he fails adequately to analyse the essential *nature* of rights and other legal concepts. JW Harris argues persuasively[12] that we cannot understand the totality of any legal concept frozen in time in a 'momentary legal system'. We employ legal concepts in legal reasoning as part of what he calls the 'doctrine model of rationality'. In other words, all legal concepts exist in a historical context which requires reference to certain fundamental features of the legal system (eg, our conception of property rights). In addition, criticism is frequently made of Hohfeld's treatment of the concepts of 'duty' and

---

[7] See, for instance, *Gouriet* v *Union of Post Office Workers* [1978] AC 435 and *Attorney-General (ex rel McWhirter)* v *Independent Broadcasting Authority* [1973] QB 629.

[8] As it did, in, say, *Gouriet* v *Union of Post Office Workers*.          [9] [1976] 1 WLR 65.

[10] Harris, *Legal Philosophies*, 83.

[11] *Central Issues in Jurisprudence*, 4th edn (London: Sweet & Maxwell, 2014) 298.

[12] *Law and Legal Science: An Enquiry into the Concepts, Legal Rule and Legal System* (Oxford: Clarendon Press, 1979), sect 3.

'power'. In particular, it is argued that he fails to distinguish the various *types* of duty and power: we use these terms in several ways which his analysis tends to neglect.[13]

## 10.2 Theories of rights

There are two major theories of rights: the so-called 'will' (or 'choice') theory and the 'interest' theory. The former (advanced especially by Professor Hart),[14] holds that when I have a right to do something, what is essentially protected is my *choice* whether or not to do it. It stresses the freedom and individual self-fulfilment that are regarded as essential values which the law ought to guarantee. The 'interest' theory, on the other hand (most effectively espoused by MacCormick),[15] claims that the purpose of rights is to protect, not individual choice, but certain *interests* of the right-holder. It should be noted that the advocates of both theories (though not MacCormick) normally accept the *correlativity* of rights and duties; indeed, this is (as we shall see) often central to their arguments.

In attacking the will theory, proponents of the interest theory raise two main arguments. First, they reject the view (at the heart of the will theory) that the essence of a right is the power to waive someone else's duty. Sometimes, they argue, the law *limits* my power of waiver without destroying my substantive right (eg, I cannot consent to murder or contract out of certain rights). Secondly, there is a distinction between the substantive right and the right to *enforce* it. MacCormick gives the example of children: their rights are exercised by their parents or guardians; how can it be said, therefore, that the right-holder (ie, the child) has any choice whether or not to waive such rights? It must, he argues, be concluded that children have no rights—which is absurd.

While the will theory, by arguing that the enforcement of Y's duty requires the exercise of will by X (or someone else), rests on the assumption of the correlativity of rights and duties, it is possible to postulate the interest theory (as MacCormick does) independently. Thus, it may be argued that conferring a right on someone (eg, to housing) constitutes an acceptance that the interest represented by that right ought to be recognized and protected. There are two main versions of this theory. One asserts that X has a right whenever he is in a position to benefit from the performance of a duty. The other claims that X has a right whenever the protection of his interest is recognized as a reason for imposing duties—whether or not they are *actually* imposed. You should examine the virtues and deficiencies of both theories.[16]

---

[13] For an interesting alternative analysis of legal rights, see J Raz, 'Legal Rights' (1984) 4 *Oxford Journal of Legal Studies* 1. A lucid exposition of rights as 'excess baggage' in the case for protecting animals is RG Frey, *Interests and Rights: The Case Against Animals* (Oxford: Clarendon Press, 1980).

[14] See *Essays on Bentham: Studies on Jurisprudence and Political Theory* (Oxford: Clarendon Press, 1982), Ch 7.

[15] See *Legal Right and Social Democracy: Essays in Legal and Political Philosophy* (Oxford: Clarendon Press, 1982), Ch 8, and 'Rights in Legislation' in PMS Hacker and J Raz (eds), *Law, Morality and Society* (Oxford: Clarendon Press, 1977).

[16] A useful account may be found in Tom Campbell, *The Left and Rights: A Conceptual Analysis of the Idea of Socialist Rights* (London: Routledge & Kegan Paul, 1983), Chs 6 and 9. And see Chapter 9 above.

## 10.2.1 **Right-based theories**

Rights are 'in'. Human rights, animal rights, moral and political rights have assumed a central place in contemporary jurisprudence (to say nothing of moral and political philosophy). Indeed, it is not unreasonable to suggest that the profligate service which the concept is asked to perform has drained it of much of its meaning. I return briefly to this disquieting issue in 10.3.

A modern trilogy, first introduced by Dworkin, of legal and moral theories which are *right-based, duty-based*, and *goal-based* has emerged. A helpful reader is J Waldron's *Theories of Rights.*[17] Waldron, in his introduction, provides an example which illuminates this (sometimes elusive) distinction. We are opposed to torture. If our opposition is based on the suffering of the victim, our approach is *right*-based. If we believe that torture debases the torturer, our concern is *duty*-based. If we regard torture as unacceptable only when it affects the interests of those other than the parties involved, our approach is utilitarian *goal*-based.

Our principal concern is, of course, with right-based theories. Professor Dworkin's 'rights thesis' argues for the primacy of rights over considerations of the general welfare. This view of 'rights as trumps' justifies their protection on a complex exclusion of 'external preferences'. I mentioned, in 9.1.2, the distinction between 'personal' and 'external' preferences. The former refers to those things that I want for *myself*; the latter are the things I want for *others*. So, for example, I may want to be affluent, but not wish others to be. Dworkin argues that when we seek to improve the general welfare, external preferences should be excluded—because they undermine the 'basic right to equal concern and respect' which, in his theorem, is a fundamental political right—'a postulate of political morality'.[18] Why do they have this effect? Because any imposition of external preferences is equivalent to a judgment that those on whom they are imposed are inferior, not to be treated as equals or 'with equal concern and respect'. I cannot here trace the elaborate argument which Dworkin deploys in support of this rejection of utilitarianism (or the counter-arguments which it has generated), but you will get a good idea of Dworkin's general conception of rights as trumps from Chapters 7 and 12 of *Taking Rights Seriously.*[19] Dworkin expresses his view so clearly in his reply to Sartorius that I think it is worth quoting the following passage at length:

> Rights cannot be understood as things people have, come what may, no matter what general justification for political decisions is in play. We construct political theories as a package, and the rights that package assigns individuals must vary with what else is in the package. The idea of rights as trumps is a *formal* idea: it fixes the general function of rights within any particular theory that uses the idea at all. We can therefore think about the content of rights at two different levels of analysis. When we are engaged in constructing a general political theory, we must consider what package—what general justification for political decisions together with what rights—is most suitable. . . . But on other occasions we must take the general scheme

---

[17] J Waldron (ed), *Theories of Rights* (Oxford: Oxford University Press, 1984).
[18] *Taking Rights Seriously* (London: Duckworth, 1978), 272.
[19] I recommend also the essays by Hart and Sartorius in M Cohen (ed), *Ronald Dworkin and Contemporary Jurisprudence* (London: Duckworth, 1984).

of some political theory as fixed and consider what rights are necessary as trumps over the general background justification that theory proposes.[20]

In other words (to use one of Dworkin's own examples) my strong preference for pistachio ice cream is a reason for society producing pistachio, and it is a stronger reason than others that may be found for not producing it (such as your mild preference for vanilla). But it is pointless to speak of my *right* to have pistachio (or even my more general right to have my strong preferences satisfied) unless we mean that my preference provides a reason for producing pistachio even if the *collective* preferences of the community would be better served by producing vanilla. A political right, in Dworkin's account, arises only when the reasons for giving *me* what I want are stronger than some *collective* justification which normally provides a full political justification for a decision.

For Dworkin, therefore, no utilitarian view offers an adequate foundation for a theory that takes rights seriously, and only a restricted form of utilitarianism (which excludes external preferences) provides some support for the egalitarianism that is the main appeal of utilitarianism. Both Hart and Sartorius (and indeed other writers) accuse Dworkin of effectively adopting a utilitarian position, a charge which, as you will see, Dworkin adroitly refutes. Doubts do, however, remain. Dworkin concedes that 'to prevent a catastrophe or even to obtain a clear and major benefit',[21] it may be necessary for individual rights to be overridden. Thus my right to free speech may have to give way when the public interest requires it (say, during a state of emergency). But this suggests that there is an implicit recognition that even the most fundamental rights are not immune to the claims of utility—the public interest.

This, in turn, raises the question whether utilitarianism is itself inevitably hostile to individual rights. A utilitarian is committed to the proposition that all actions are to be judged according to the extent to which they advance or contribute to the general welfare. Does this mean that he is unable to accommodate rights into his felicific calculus? This is a controversy that cannot easily be resolved one way or the other. It has been argued that utilitarianism is compatible with individual rights because when an interest is shown, by reference to the general good, to be worthy of protection, a *right* to that interest may be recognized. But this means, first, that rights are at the mercy of the felicific calculus (a pretty fragile guarantee) and, secondly, that rights will always succumb to considerations of the general welfare.

Another way out of the apparent impasse has been offered by Alan Gewirth.[22] Briefly, he argues that we cannot justify—in the interests of the general welfare—the denial of rights to others without accepting the importance of rights. At the very least, in order to persuade another that his rights should be denied, the latter should be accorded the right to freedom of thought—so that he can consider the argument against his right that is sought to be denied! You should be able to show the effects of this conflict on

---

[20]  Ibid, 281.      [21]  *Taking Rights Seriously*, 192.
[22]  See, in particular, Alan Gewirth, *Reason and Morality* (Chicago, Ill: University of Chicago Press, 1978).

the protection of rights; your discussion will, of course, draw on the moral basis of act and rule utilitarianism, discussed in 9.1.

## 10.3 Human rights

The concept of human rights has been described as 'one of the greatest inventions of our civilisation [which] can be compared in its impact on human social life to the development of modern technological resources and their application to medicine, communication, and transportation'.[23] Similar acclaim abounds. Though the concept (in the form of 'natural rights' see Chapter 2) first emerges in the Middle Ages, the recognition in the seventeenth and eighteenth centuries of the secular notion of human rights was plainly a significant intellectual moment in history. The concept makes little sense unless it is understood as fundamental and inalienable, whether or not such rights are legally recognized and regardless of whether they emanate from a 'higher' natural law (see Chapter 2).

The legal recognition of human rights in the twentieth century occurred when the United Nations, in the grim shadow of the Holocaust, adopted the Universal Declaration of Human Rights in 1948. This document and the International Covenants on Civil and Political Rights, and Economic, Social and Cultural Rights in 1976, demonstrate, even to the most sceptical observer, a commitment by the international community to the universal conception and protection of human rights. This so-called International Bill of Rights, with its inevitably protean and slightly kaleidoscopic ideological character, reflects an extraordinary measure of cross-cultural consensus among nations.

Over the centuries, the idea of human rights has passed through three generations. The first generation comprises the seventeenth- and eighteenth-century, mostly negative civil and political rights. The second generation consists in the essentially positive economic, social, and cultural rights that include the right to housing, education, adequate living standards, and health. They are recognized by various international and regional human rights instruments. The third generation rights are primarily collective rights which are foreshadowed in Article 28 of the Universal Declaration which declares that 'everyone is entitled to a social and international order in which the rights set forth in this Declaration can be fully realized'. These 'solidarity' rights include the right to social and economic development and to participate in and benefit from the resources of the earth and space, scientific and technical information (which are especially important to the Third World), the right to a healthy environment, peace, and humanitarian disaster relief.

Of course, not all political rights are human rights. Human rights, it seems safe to say, are sufficiently important to justify international intervention when they are violated. But does the breach of any human right validate the imposition by the United Nations of sanctions or even military intervention by NATO or other states as we have

---

[23] C Nino, *The Ethics of Human Rights* (Oxford: Clarendon Press, 1991), 1. See Charles R Beitz, *The Idea of Human Rights* (New York: Oxford University Press, 2009).

recently witnessed in a number of African and Middle Eastern countries? Would the infringement of economic and social rights permit such a breach of national sovereignty? The answer must be in the negative:

> It would be…wrong for the community of nations, even if licensed by the Security Council and likely to be successful, to march into any nation to establish equal pay for women or more adequate schools or to invade Florida to shut down its gas chambers or establish gay marriages there. Economic or military sanctions that inevitably inflict great suffering…are justified only to stop truly barbaric acts: mass killing or jailing or torturing of political opponents or widespread and savage discrimination.[24]

This suggests that certain human rights are more fundamental, more essential, and more universal, than others. If this is the case, these 'positive', socio-economic rights, though frequently included in human rights declarations and bills of rights, are of a different order from 'negative' political rights. This is a question that has long plagued the argument, especially since, even if socio-economic rights were justiciable (which may be doubted), should judges have the authority to determine how the economic resources should be distributed?[25] Is this not, some claim, the proper province of elected members of parliament?

Indeed, despite its appeal and importance, the idea of human rights remains exasperatingly vague, if not incoherent. It is difficult to disagree with James Griffin's sombre appraisal:

> The term 'human right' is nearly criterionless. There are unusually few criteria for determining when the term is used correctly and when incorrectly—not just among politicians, but among philosophers, political theorists, and jurisprudents as well. The language of human rights has, in this way, become debased.[26]

Does it matter? I believe it does. When the currency of a concept, especially one as fashionable and significant as 'human rights', is degraded by wanton excess, it not only reduces its utility, but creates a risk that it will generate derision for the idea itself. To assert that a particular pursuit is a human right or that its preclusion is a violation thereof does not make it so. Nor, of course, is there a necessary connection between what is just and its being a human right.[27] The 'globalization' of human rights engendered by the large corpus of United Nations and other international conventions facilitates the identification and recognition of such rights in diverse societies and cultures.

---

[24] Ronald Dworkin, *Justice for Hedgehogs* (Cambridge, Mass: The Belknap Press, 2011), 224.

[25] The constitutions of some jurisdictions include such rights and declare them to be justiciable. The 1996 post-apartheid constitution of South Africa is a conspicuous example; it provides several means by which these rights (eg, housing, health care, food, and water) might be secured. And the South African Constitutional Court has grappled with these provisions; see, eg, *Government of the Republic of South Africa v Grootboom* (2001) 1 SA 46 (CC). See David Bilchitz, 'Giving Socio-economic Rights Teeth: The Minimum Core and its Importance' (2002) 118 *South African Law Journal* 484, and his *Poverty and Fundamental Rights: The Justification and Enforcement of Socio-economic Rights* (Oxford: Oxford University Press, 2008).

[26] James Griffin, *On Human Rights* (Oxford: Oxford University Press, 2008), 14–15.

[27] 'Some international lawyers write as if the domains of justice and human rights are identical. But they are clearly not. Human rights do not exhaust the whole domain of justice or fairness', Griffin, ibid, 198.

A measure of generosity and even perhaps imprecision is perhaps inevitable, probably even desirable. Yet the danger remains that their amplitude and ambiguity drains
human rights of real meaning and hence undermines the very protection such declarations seek to secure. This is particularly worrying in view of the cynicism which the
discourse of human rights increasingly attracts, for there is no shortage of detractors
and sceptics. Some see human rights as a Machiavellian plot by international capital
to enslave the Third World. Others, of a more conservative persuasion, adopt Edmund
Burke's reactionary view that spurns human rights on the ground that they inspire
'false ideas and vain expectations in men destined to travel in the obscure walk of
laborious life'.

Here I want to sketch some of the more important theoretical challenges. I have
identified the following six.[28] It is, I think, important to have a good understanding of
these attacks, for they seem increasingly to insinuate themselves into jurisprudential
debates about human rights in a post-communist world. I concentrate on the first, for
it constitutes a significant, though often misunderstood, assault on the very idea of
individual rights.

### 10.3.1 **Communitarianism**

Community and communitarianism have assumed considerable importance, most
conspicuously among legal and political theorists—and politicians—in the United
States. The communitarian ideal is a bit of a Trojan horse, containing a number of
other associated ideas. Among communitarians, the individualism of theories of
rights has generated widespread unease concerning the extent to which such theories
neglect the interests of the community, civic virtue, and social solidarity. The notions
of rights (and justice) feature prominently in the theory of deontological liberalism
which owes much to Kant. It is this political theory which communitarians so strongly
invoke; the idea that:

> [S]ociety, being composed of a plurality of persons, each with his own aims, interests, and con-
> ceptions of the good, is best arranged when it is governed by principles that do not *themselves*
> presuppose any particular conception of the good; what justifies these regulative principles
> above all is not that they maximise the social welfare or otherwise promote the good, but
> rather that they conform to the concept of *right*, a moral category given prior to the good and
> independent of it.[29]

Or, to put it simply, the right is prior to the good. And this priority is, according to
Kant, derived entirely from the concept of freedom in the relations between individuals; it has nothing to do with achieving happiness. Justice and right are antecedent
to all other values which depend on want-satisfaction because justice and right stem
from the idea of freedom which, in turn, is a prerequisite of all human ends. In Kant's

---

[28]  See Raymond Wacks, 'The End of Human Rights?' (1994) 24 *Hong Kong Law Journal* 372.
[29]  Michael Sandel, *Liberalism and the Limits of Justice* (Cambridge: Cambridge University Press, 1982), 1.

words in his *Critique of Practical Reason*, 'the concept of good and evil must be defined after and by means of the [moral] law'.

I mention only one aspect of liberal, and particularly Kantian, epistemology: the concept of the human subject, for it goes to the heart of liberal theory and hence is central to the communitarian (and, as is considered in 13.2.6, the postmodern) attack on human rights. It is an atomistic conception of the autonomous individual—which is found in 'those philosophical traditions which come to us from the seventeenth century and which started with the postulation of an extensionless subject, epistemo-logically a *tabula rasa* and politically a presuppositionless bearer of rights'.[30] In other (simpler) words, as used by Sandel, for Kant, the subject of practical reason has an autonomous will which enables him to participate in an ideal, unconditioned realm which is independent of our teleological, social, and psychological inclinations.

This conception of the individual (which plainly has important consequences for liberal theories of rights and justice) is rejected by communitarians who conceive of persons, as Michael Sandel puts it, echoing the arguments of Hegel against Kant, as 'situated selves rather than unencumbered selves'. The communitarian response, developed most effectively by Sandel, and Charles Taylor, is that individuals are partly defined by their communities. Moral obligation springs therefore from what Hegel called the '*Sittlichkeit*' of the society. The subject of deontological liberalism is thus a transcendental, detached, independent, and autonomous agent. He or she 'stripped of all possible constitutive attachments, is less liberated than disempowered'.[31] We cannot, in the view of communitarians, be understood as persons without reference to our social roles in the community: as citizens, members of a family, group, or nation.

This is a powerful idea which has exerted considerable influence in moral, political, and legal theory. And it appears to inflict serious damage on the concept of human rights. But is it possible to preserve a broadly Kantian moral system of universal rights without adopting Kant's transcendental idealism? Keep the moral baby and throw out the metaphysical bathwater? This is precisely what John Rawls seems to have attempted in his social contractarian theory of justice discussed in 9.3. You will recall that 'people in the original position' determine principles of justice beneath a veil of ignorance which insulates them from their social condition.

In fact, according to Stephen Gardbaum,[32] the communitarian claim seems to break down into three relatively discrete positions, and the adoption of one does not logic-ally require the adoption of either or both of the others. First, the problem of 'agency' (which entails the arguments about individual and community which I have just men-tioned). The atomistic thesis may be traced to Hobbesian social contract theory. In legal theory the communitarian move is central to both the critical legal studies (CLS) project, outlined in 13.1, and the recent republican revival in the United States. It argues that the relationship between individual and community is constitutive, rather

---

[30] Charles Taylor, 'Atomism' in his *Philosophical Papers*, vol 2, 210, quoted in Steven Lukes, *Moral Conflict and Politics* (Oxford: Clarendon Press, 1991), 73.          [31] Sandel, 178.
[32] See his admirable essay, 'Law, Politics, and the Claims of Community' (1992) 90 *Michigan Law Review* 685, which I follow closely here.

than merely contingent and instrumental. Legal republicanism rejects the dominant instrumental conception of politics as an arena in which self-interest is advanced, and argues instead for the transformative potential of dialogue in public space.[33] CLS adherents depict the law as constitutive of key social relationships: marriage, employment, and so on.[34] But there is a second strand of the communitarian claim. It goes to the origin and form of normative structures generally and attempts, as Gardbaum puts it, to resolve the class tensions between universalism and particularism, foundationalism and contextualism, objectivism and relativism, rationalism and historicism. It contends that 'the particular moral and political context in which values are affirmed is always crucial to their validity'.[35]

Two forms of this argument exist. The first (which I briefly consider in 13.2) is postmodern in origin and generally regards appeals to universal values as redundant if not meaningless. Writers such as Jürgen Habermas and Richard Rorty belong here. A second argument—advanced, for example, by Michael Walzer—conceives of universal values as having 'no self-executing authority in the autonomous sphere of politics which has its own distinct criteria of validation based on the requirements of the political value of self-rule'.[36]

In legal theory this form of community is most conspicuously, and successfully, articulated by Ronald Dworkin (see 5.2.8) in which the community is the source or the author of law. Right answers are products not of universal legal truths or the personal predilections of judges, but of interpreting 'community morality' as expressed in legal doctrine. Nonetheless if we are to take rights seriously they must, Dworkin argues, trump collective goals.

The third form of communitarianism explicitly attacks liberalism and (unlike the other two communitarian positions) postulates the substantive claim that the communitarian is a superior form of association. This position is taken by writers such as Sandel and Alasdair MacIntyre.[37]

Substantive communitarian ideas constitute a direct, postmodern challenge to liberalism and rights that is sceptical of the rationality of the individual human subject, and rejects Enlightenment foundationalist and universalistic modes of normative argument.

## 10.3.2 Relativism

Are human rights really universal? To what extent are they 'relative' to local culture, history, and social and political conditions? Cultural relativists, for example, claim that human rights declarations overlook parochial diversity, and although this approach has a fairly long pedigree in anthropology, it is only fairly recently that it has

---

[33] Read Frank Michelman's influential essay, 'Law's Republic' (1988) 97 *Yale Law Journal* 1493.
[34] See JM Balkin, 'Ideology as Constraint' (1991) 43 *Stanford Law Review* 1133, and, if you have the stamina, RW Gordon, 'Critical Legal Histories' (1984) 36 *Stanford Law Review* 57, 111.
[35] S Gardbaum, 'Law, Politics, and the Claims of Community' (1992) 90 *Michigan Law Review* 685, 694.
[36] Ibid.    [37] *After Virtue: A Study in Moral Theory*, 3rd edn (London: Duckworth, 2007).

rejoined the assault on the human rights citadel. The doctrine maintains that 'there is an irreducible diversity among cultures because each culture is a unique whole with parts so intertwined that none of them can be understood or evaluated without reference to the other parts and so to the cultural whole, the so-called pattern of culture'.[38]

The thesis implies *ethical* relativism which claims that 'the moral rightness and wrongness of actions varies from society to society and that there are no absolute moral standards binding on all men at all times'.[39] Allowing the theory its most constructive interpretation, it appears to rest on the view that since moral beliefs depend on culture, language, economy, and so on, and since such factors vary from society to society, morality is relative to each society.

Two principal arguments may be mobilized against the relativist. The first denies that morality depends on social factors at all; this may therefore be described as the absolutist position. The second denies the assertion that there has always been a diversity of cultures, etc and a diversity of moral beliefs. This is known as universalism. The absolutist position was held by Plato and claims that the validity of moral beliefs is logically independent of the social or cultural background of the person who accepts them; ethics is no less a scientific enterprise than mathematics. This so-called cognitivist position arises in two forms: *intuitionism* (which holds that ethical truths are known by *a priori* cognition, ie, intuitions), and *naturalism* (which holds that ethical truths are known empirically). Discrimination is wrong in the same way as $1 + 1 = 2$.

Cognitivism in ethics (as we saw in 2.4) has had something of a rough ride from philosophers. It is particularly vulnerable to the charge that it divorces moral thinking from the 'real world'; it compels us to think about morality in a vacuum. The universalist position is stigmatized as ethnocentric for its failure to apprehend cultural practices from the perspective of the culture in which a particular practice is transacted.

### 10.3.3 Utilitarianism

The utilitarian repudiation of the idea of individual rights, indeed the essential inconsistency between the two philosophies, continues to dominate political, moral, and legal thinking about rights. This hostility to rights springs from the utilitarian concern to maximize general welfare (see 9.1). Individual interests may therefore be sacrificed at the altar of utility: so, for example, free speech is to be protected only where it will maximize the general welfare of the community. Rights are stigmatized as individualist. They operate formally but do not necessarily assist those (the poor, oppressed, alienated) who most need them. They are merely 'excess baggage', superfluous in the condemnation of cruelty or exploitation. All we need, it is argued, is a fully developed theory of right and wrong. Moreover, as Hart puts it, in uncharacteristically forthright terms:

---

[38] J Ladd, 'Introduction' in J Ladd (ed), *Ethical Relativism* (Belmont, Calif: Wadsworth, 1973), 2.
[39] Ibid, 1.

Except for a few privileged and lucky persons, the ability to shape life for oneself and lead a meaningful life is something to be constructed by positive marshalling of social and economic resources. It is not something automatically guaranteed by a structure of negative rights. Nothing is more likely to bring freedom into contempt and so endanger it than failure to support those who lack, through no fault of their own, the material and social conditions and opportunities which are needed if a man's freedom is to contribute to his welfare.[40]

Utilitarianism's detractors considerably outnumber its supporters, and the attacks take numerous forms. As far as its approach to individual rights are concerned, it is criticized by both free-market libertarians such as Robert Nozick (see 9.4) for overriding what John Rawls calls 'the distinction between persons' and liberals like Ronald Dworkin (see Chapter 5) for neglecting individuals' claims to equal concern and respect.

### 10.3.4 Socialism

The incompatibility of individual rights and socialism has become something of a truism as was pointed out in 7.6.6. There, I suggested that, put simply, the argument normally rests on both the irreconcilable conflict between the egotism of liberal theory and the communitarianism of socialism, and the denial that conditions of morality are inherent in human life. Against this position, Steven Lukes[41] argues that there are four conditions which combine to make rights necessary: scarcity, egoism, conflicting conceptions of the good, and imperfect knowledge and understanding.

### 10.3.5 Legal positivism

Though they are not synonymous, the ideas of natural and human rights share certain common ground. The notion that certain rights are 'natural' is expressed most cogently in the social-contractarian political philosophies of Rousseau and Locke which inspired the French and American revolutions.

The lofty rhetoric of the Declaration of Independence of 1776 appealed to the natural rights of all Americans to 'life, liberty and the pursuit of happiness'. As the Declaration put it: 'We hold these truths to be self-evident, that all men are created equal, that they are endowed by their Creator with certain unalienable rights.' Similar sentiments were incorporated into the French 'Declaration of the Rights of Man and the Citizen' of 1789.

The moral scepticism that informs the writings especially of David Hume in the eighteenth century sought to deny the existence of objective values and, hence, natural rights which were founded on what GE Moore was much later to call the 'naturalistic fallacy': deriving an 'ought' from an 'is'. To Jeremy Bentham natural rights were 'bawling upon paper'.[42] In his characteristically colourful prose, he describes rights-talk

---

[40] 'Between Utility and Rights' in his *Essays on Bentham*, 207–8.
[41] Stephen Lukes, *Marxism and Morality* (Oxford: Oxford Paperbacks, 1987), 56–7.
[42] J Bentham, *Anarchical Fallacies*, quoted in HLA Hart, 'Between Utility and Rights' in his *Essays on Bentham*, 199.

as 'the effusion of a hard heart operating on a cloudy mind. When a man is bent on having things his own way and gives no reason for it, he says: I have a right to have them so.' They are, moreover, a contradiction in terms: 'a son that never had a father', 'a species of cold heat, a sort of dry moisture, a kind of resplendent darkness', 'nonsense on stilts'.[43] Much positivist and non-cognitivist analysis therefore rejects rights-talk as meaningless or, at best, irrational 'emotional ejaculations'. See 3.2 and 4.1.

### 10.3.6 Critical theory

As is discussed in Chapter 13, a full-frontal assault on the concept of rights is an important feature of both the critical legal studies movement and of postmodern accounts of society. For example, Costas Douzinas concludes his comprehensive historical and theoretical analysis of the concept of human rights with the following warning:

> As human rights start veering away from their initial revolutionary and dissident purposes, as their end becomes obscured in ever more declarations, treaties and diplomatic lunches, we may be entering the epoch of the end of human rights and of the triumph of a monolithic humanity. If human rights have become the 'realised myth' of postmodern societies, this is a myth realised only in the energies of those who suffer grave and petty violations in the hands of the powers that have proclaimed their triumph . . . The end of human rights comes when they lose their utopian end.[44]

An attack is also waged by radical feminists (see 14.3.2) and some adherents of Critical Race Theory (see 14.5) who generally argue that rights mask the real inequalities, and may actually serve to preserve and maintain them.

## 10.4 The future of human rights

Stripped of the polemic that seems to characterize much of the debate, the matter ultimately and, perhaps, inescapably, boils down to the question of what it is to be a human being. (This is, of course, a profoundly *un*postmodern view.) I do not deny that the notion is culturally or historically contingent, but reflection on what John Finnis calls the 'basic forms of human flourishing' (see 2.7) may reveal not only a considerable measure of common ground, but also that the competing perspectives are not nearly as irreconcilable as they may appear. Thus the tension between communitarian and individualistic conceptions of rights need not take the stark form it so readily assumes. In particular, the idea of human rights does not require a selfish, individual-centred rejection of community. The so-called International Bill of Rights, despite its imperfections and the claim that it does not enunciate justiciable rights, represents—even for the agnostic—a formidable, authoritative foundation for human rights norms. If

---

[43] See J Waldron (ed), *Nonsense upon Stilts: Bentham, Burke and Marx on the Rights of Man* (London: Methuen, 1987), 73.

[44] Costas Douzinas, *The End of Human Rights* (Oxford: Hart Publishing, 2000).

human rights are an integral feature of both international law and custom, several of the challenges outlined earlier may be seriously undermined. So-called cultural imperialism, neo-colonialism, and ethnocentricity are not to be lightly dismissed; international human rights must be mediated through local cultural circumstances.

You should ask whether it is not disingenuous to invoke the claim of relativism or contextualism to frustrate the legitimate and lawful expectations of individuals. Why is it almost always the oppressor, rather than the victim who cites local culture in support of an unjust practice? These questions are unlikely to go away. A proper grasp of the theories underpinning rights and human rights will help to clarify the arguments on all sides.

## 10.5 Animal rights

Are animals merely replaceable commodities? If not, the question of their welfare and, hence, our responsibility for it, is ultimately a moral one.[45] Take an extreme example: bear farming in China and Vietnam. The plight of thousands of endangered Asiatic black bears makes horrifying reading. After being trapped in the wild, they are confined in tiny wire cages no bigger than the size of their own bodies. Metal catheters up to seven inches long are inserted into their abdomens in order to 'milk' them of their bile for use in Oriental medicines and preparations. Many spend their entire lives (which may last twenty years) subjected to this torture. In the minds of some otherwise intelligent people, this appalling practice is defended on the ground that these creatures are mere objects; therefore the question of their well-being, let alone whether they can be said to have rights, simply does not arise.

The issue of our moral and legal obligations toward animals will, I hope, prove instructive both in respect of the problems raised by animal cruelty itself (which extends, of course, to a plethora of practices including vivisection, hunting, battery farming, trapping, rodeos, circuses, bull-fighting, some zoos, the fur trade, and the conditions under which animals are transported to the abattoir), but also as an exercise in applied ethics and legal theory.[46] The subject has generated a vast literature; what follows is a consideration of some of the central issues.

---

[45] I draw here on Raymond Wacks, 'Sacrificed for Science: Are Animal Experiments Morally Defensible?' in Gerhold K Becker (ed), in association with James P Buchanan, *Changing Nature's Course: The Ethical Challenge of Biotechnology* (Hong Kong: Hong Kong University Press, 1996), and Raymond Wacks, 'Do Animals Have Moral Rights?' in Raymond Wacks, *Law, Morality, and the Private Domain* (Hong Kong: Hong Kong University Press, 2000). See too Cass R Sunstein and Martha C Nussbaum (eds), *Animal Rights: Current Debates and New Directions* (New York: Oxford University Press, 2004), and JM Coetzee, *The Lives of Animals* (London: Profile Books, 2000). See Elisa Aaltola, *Animal Suffering: Philosophy and Culture* (London: Palgrave 2012); Gary L Francione, *Animals as Persons: Essays on the Abolition of Animal Exploitation* (New York: Columbia University Press, 2008).

[46] Two admirable introductions to the major moral and practical elements of the subject are David DeGrazia, *Animal Rights: A Very Short Introduction* (Oxford: Oxford University Press, 2002), and Gary L Francione, *Introduction to Animal Rights: Your Child or the Dog?* (Philadelphia: Temple University Press, 2005).

### 10.5.1 **Early philosophical influences**

Aristotle and the Stoics distinguished animals from humans on the ground that while we possess *logos* (reason or language), animals are *aloga* (without *logos*). This led to the moral conclusion of the superiority of humans. Descartes regarded animals as mere biological mechanisms lacking subjective awareness. John Locke took issue with this view, arguing animals have feelings, and that unnecessary cruelty toward them was morally wrong, but that the right not to be harmed vested in the owner of the animal or to the person who was being impaired by such cruelty. A similar view was expressed by St Thomas Aquinas and Immanuel Kant, who repudiated the notion that humans have direct duties toward non-humans. Cruelty to animals is wrong, Kant argues, only because of its negative effects on humans.

The echoes of these standpoints persist in contemporary debates about our duties, if any, to avoid animal cruelty and suffering. At the heart of the discussion is the extent to which animals ought to be protected by granting them rights or some other means by which their welfare might be protected. Those who champion animal rights generally argue that because animals are sentient creatures and hence enjoy a subjective good, they have a certain moral status and therefore warrant certain rights, especially the right to life and the right not to be exploited for human benefit. Against this view, it is asserted that in order to be a rights-bearer, sentience is inadequate; there needs to be some cognitive ability such as rationality or the capacity to reason morally. Since only humans appear to have this facility, we are free to exploit those who do not. To this argument, those who support animal rights reply that it is both arbitrary and inconsistent with modern rights theory to limit rights to those who enjoy cognitive capacity. We now regard rights as particularly important in the protection of the weakest and most vulnerable members of society.

### 10.5.2 **Utilitarianism**

As you will recall (I hope) from the discussion in 9.1, utilitarians argue that the morally correct action is the one that maximizes utility, ie increases overall benefit while minimizing detriment. Thus, the pain of a few may in principle be justified by the pleasure of (or at least the benefits to) the many. The utilitarian objection to killing a conscious being therefore rests on the destruction of the prospect of future pleasures. Killing an animal is wrong, not because it harms the animal killed, but because its death diminishes the sum of the utilitarian calculus.[47]

A prominent text on animal welfare, Peter Singer's *Animal Liberation*,[48] proceeds from an act-utilitarian standpoint. His central argument is that in calculating the

---

[47] But see RG Frey, *Interests and Rights: The Case Against Animals* (Oxford: Clarendon Press, 1980) for a rejection of the argument, from a utilitarian position, that animals can be said to have either rights or interests.

[48] See also Singer's *Practical Ethics* (Cambridge: Cambridge University Press, 1979). For a similar argument regarding pain and suffering see S Clarke, *The Moral Status of Animals* (Oxford: Clarendon Press, 1977).

consequences of our actions, the pain suffered or pleasure enjoyed by animals counts no less than our own. To regard their experience as in some way inferior to ours is 'speciesism'. Animals have moral worth; their lives are not simply expendable or to be exploited for our own ends. Singer does not claim that the lives of humans and animals have equal worth or that they call for identical treatment—except in respect of the capacity to experience pleasure and pain. Animals need not be *treated* equally, but they are entitled to equal *consideration*.

Thus, animal experiments are justifiable, provided pain is restricted to a minimum and the research is highly likely to produce aggregate benefits outweighing individual pain. His test is whether it would be morally acceptable to perform such experiments on mentally retarded human orphans.[49] If it would not, it would be 'speciesist' to inflict pain on animals of similar intelligence.

The strength of this utilitarian argument lies in its focus upon actual suffering, a concern that seems to accord with our intuitive view of animals, captured two centuries ago in Bentham's observation that the question to ask about animals 'is not Can they reason? nor Can they talk? but, Can they suffer?' Its weakness lies in its neglect of individual animals and its willingness to accept the use of animals where expected benefits outweigh the costs of suffering.[50]

### 10.5.3 Can animals have rights?

The utilitarian, in order to prove his case for treating animals humanely, must show that the consequences of such humanity outweigh the consequences of any of a number of alternatives, and this may stretch his empirical evidence to breaking-point. The proponent of a right-based argument, on the other hand, needs to overcome not only the objection that animals cannot really be said to possess rights, but also that talk of moral rights is, in Bentham's words 'nonsense on stilts'. To invoke the categorical imperative that cruelty to animals is simply *wrong*, the Kantian is more likely to enable a dog to have his day.[51]

---

[49] See *Practical Ethics*, 59. Orphans in order to exclude the possibility of vicarious suffering to relatives.

[50] Another feature of utilitarianism sometimes viewed as helpful in developing a sound moral approach towards animals is Mill's view (advanced in a more sophisticated form by RM Hare (see *Moral Thinking* (Oxford: Clarendon Press, 1983)) that our primary duty is to develop certain qualities of character which would promote the greatest overall utility. But this may impose unreasonable demands on moral actors. It is not impossible to reconcile consequentialism with rights, see, eg, LW Sumner, *The Moral Foundation of Rights* (Oxford: Clarendon Press, 1987).

[51] A strong case for animals as right-bearers is made by Tom Regan, *The Case for Animal Rights* (London: Routledge, 1984). For assaults on this view, see RG Frey, *Rights, Killing and Suffering: Moral Vegetarianism and Applied Ethics* (Oxford: Basil Blackwell, 1983) which I reviewed in (1986) 49 *Modern Law Review* 403, and P Carruthers, *The Animals Issue: Moral Theory in Practice* (Cambridge: Cambridge University Press, 1992). Other anthropocentric arguments are based on the alleged irrationality of the case for animal rights. See RA Posner, 'Animal Rights: Legal, Philosophical, and Pragmatic Perspectives' and RA Epstein, 'Animals as Objects or Subjects of Rights', in Sunstein and Nussbaum (eds), *Animal Rights: Current Debates and New Directions*. For a compelling attack on this view, see Gary Steiner, *Animals and the Limits of Postmodernism* (New York: Columbia University Press, 2013), 134–47.

As the clamour in support of animal rights grows louder, many countries have become increasingly polarized in respect of the extent to which a variety of practices, ranging from fox-hunting to vivisection can be justified in a compassionate society. Many shrink from the very notion that an animal is capable of being vested with rights. Yet consider the following conclusion reached in a judgment by an Indian court:

> [W]e hold that circus animals . . . are housed in cramped cages, subjected to fear, hunger, pain, not to mention the undignified way of life they have to live, with no respite and the impugned notification has been issued in conformity with . . . the values of human life, philosophy of the Constitution . . . Though not homosapiens, [sic] they are also beings entitled to dignified exist-ence and humane treatment sans cruelty and torture . . . Therefore it is our fundamental duty to show compassion to our animal friends, but also to recognise and protect their rights . . . If humans are entitled to fundamental rights, why not animals?[52]

Is the idea really so implausible? To assert that since animals cannot be the subject of duties, they cannot be 'moral agents' and are thus incapable of being objects of rights is to beg the question about what it takes to be a right-holder. In particular, it presumes a choice-based rather than an interest-based theory of rights.[53]

Rights talk immediately raises the distinction between what a right is, on the one hand, and what rights people actually have or should have, on the other—this is, loosely, the distinction between moral rights and legal rights. The two are often con-fused, and it is by no means certain that even Hohfeld's influential analysis of rights (see 10.1) is applicable to moral rights. It probably is not.[54]

What of moral rights? A *moral* right is an entitlement which confers moral liberties on those who have them to do certain things, and the moral constraint on others to abstain from interference.[55] A *legal* right is one recognized by the law. Statutes impos-ing a duty on persons not to inflict cruelty on animals (with their normal sanctions for violation)[56] could be said to confer on animals a legal right to humane (ie non-cruel) treatment.[57] Does the same follow in respect of *moral* rights? I shall briefly consider this difficult question and then address the problem of whether, notwithstanding my confidence in respect of legal rights, animals, or, to enable me to put the strongest case, 'higher' animals, can be bearers of rights.

The following reasoning, by the philosopher, HJ McCloskey, is representative of a position that is fairly widely held. He contends that '[t]o show that animals possess moral rights, moral rights against persons, it is not sufficient to establish that persons have duties in respect of animals'.[58] His argument rests on the view that there is no

---

[52]  *Nair v Union of India* (2000) Kerala High Court No 155/1999, quoted by Martha C Nussbaum, *Frontiers of Justice: Disability, Nationality Species Membership* (Cambridge, Mass: Belknap Press, 2006), 325.
[53]  In any event, is it wholly implausible that animals may indeed be subjects of certain duties (eg, a sheepdog or watchdog)?          [54]  See J Raz, 'Legal Rights' (1984) 4 *Oxford Journal of Legal Studies* 1.
[55]  See HJ McCloskey, 'Moral Rights and Animals' (1978) 22 *Inquiry* 23, 27–8.
[56]  Among the most comprehensive statutes is the Austrian legislation.
[57]  See J Feinberg, 'Human Duties and Human Rights', 188–9, and 'The Rights of Animals and Unborn Generations', 159, both reproduced in his *Rights, Justice and the Bounds of Liberty: Essays in Social Philosophy* (Princeton, NJ: Princeton University Press, 1980).          [58]  McCloskey, op cit, 27–8.

strict correlativity of rights, a position accepted earlier in respect of legal rights. It warrants closer examination. The claim proceeds along the following lines:

1. Central to the concept of moral rights is the notion of *exercising* such rights. The paradigm possessor of a right is an actor or potential actor who can act by doing what he is entitled to do, or act by demanding, claiming, requiring what he is entitled to demand or claim, require. In the absence of the possibility of such action in the being towards whom duties are owed, and where the being is not a member of a kind which is normally capable of action, we withhold talk of rights and confine ourselves to talk of duties. Moral rights are ascribed to beings that are capable of moral autonomy, moral self-direction, and self-determination.

2. We can therefore deny the capacity for rights to 'ex-persons' (the brain damaged, or extremely senile) and 'non-persons' (those born with damaged or under-developed brains), but not to 'potential persons' (infants who will become persons). We also deny this capacity to inanimate objects and plants, even though they (like ex-persons and non-persons) may be the object of duties. This is because they cannot exercise rights or have them exercised for them.

3. The capacity to have interests is insufficient to establish a capacity to bear rights. This is because, though non-humans (including corporate bodies, churches, states, clubs, etc), may be said to have interests, the idea that non-human animals have interests relies on an equation of interests with desires, aims, and beliefs, and it would therefore still need to be shown that the possession of *these* capacities is a ground for the attribution of rights. Moreover, 'rights and interests are completely different things'.[59] There will be circumstances where a right-bearer may wish to exercise his rights *against* his own interests. Equally it may be in his interests to deprive him of his freedom to exercise rights. And where a putative right-bearer is incapable of expressing his wishes (if he has any) his mind would have to be read. Where he has no mind or will to be read, he cannot be a representation of his rights or the exercising or waiving of moral rights.

4. Since most animals lack the relevant moral capacity, they do not have moral rights. Some animals (whales and dolphins) may be found to have such capacity: it may therefore be 'morally appropriate for us meanwhile to act towards (whales and dolphins) *as if* they are possessors of rights'.[60]

This is an important and careful argument, but it does not seem to be a particularly convincing one. Indeed, some of its claims do not appear to advance its own case.

---

[59]  Ibid, 39. Here McCloskey departs from his earlier view expressed in 'Rights' (1965) 15 *Philosophical Quarterly* 115. See also Tom Regan, 'McCloskey on Why Animals Cannot Have Rights' (1976) 26 *Philosophical Quarterly* 251. Joseph Raz argues (as part of a larger and sophisticated defence of freedom) that '[A]ll rights are based on interests', J Raz, *The Morality of Freedom* (Oxford: Clarendon Press, 1986), 191.

[60]  McCloskey, 42–3. McCloskey proposes, instead of a rights-based argument, a justice-based argument in support of animals. A full account would require an analysis of how considerations such as desert, merit, well-being, needs, wishes, and so on figure in the structure of a theory of justice towards animals.

Thus, it is difficult to see how a right-bearer's inability to express his wishes leads ineluctably to the conclusion (in point 3) that he has no rights that can be represented. To argue (as McCloskey does)[61] that the paternalism it involves would offend liberal values may call for an examination of those values. Nor is the speculative empirical move (in point 4) a particularly solid foundation for the benevolence towards a limited range of creatures.

Non-human animals have interests and needs. In particular, they have a clear interest in avoiding pain and probably also an untimely death. But this does not dispose of the matter. It enables one to reject one of the two main theories of rights (the 'choice' theory) which is plainly less congenial to animals than the 'interest' theory. Both theories are discussed at 10.2. The main virtue of an interest-based theory is that it enables us more easily to ground *duties* toward animals,[62] but, as I shall try to show, it has a considerably wider application.

MacCormick offered, as we saw, the example of children: their rights are exercised by their parents or guardians; it cannot therefore be argued that the child has a *choice* whether or not to waive its rights. This would lead to the specious conclusion that children have no rights. And a similar point could, of course, be made in relation to animals.

Tom Regan's so-called 'sentimental anthropomorphism' argues for the similarities between a human and an animal life. In particular, animals, like us, are 'subjects-of-a-life'. They have inherent, not merely instrumental, value or worth. This entitles them to the absolute right to live their lives with respect and autonomy:

> The most reasonable criterion of right-possession . . . is not that of sentience or having interests, since neither of these by themselves can account for why it is wrong to treat humans who are not irreversibly comatose merely as means; rather the criterion that most adequately accounts for this is the criterion of inherent value: All those beings (and only those beings) which have inherent value have rights.[63]

Hence, no amount of benefit to humans (from, say, vivisection) can justify the violation of this absolute right:

> The laudatory achievements of science, including the many genuine benefits obtained for both humans and animals, do not justify the unjust means used to secure them . . . [T]he rights view does not call for the cessation of scientific research. Such research should go on—but not at the expense of laboratory animals.[64]

While the idea of rights lends support to the animal case (as it does to several causes), it is often rejected by many who might otherwise be enlisted to the animal cause. Hence

---

[61] McCloskey, 39.

[62] This is not, of course, to say either that all duties derive from rights or that morality is rights-based. See Raz, *The Morality of Freedom*, Ch 7.

[63] Regan, *The Case for Animal Rights* (Berkeley, Calif: University of California Press, 1983), 397. But he would justify sacrificing the lives of a million dogs to save a single human life (351). Singer is to similar effect: since a dog lacks the cognitive ability to imagine the distant future, he asserts, it has less to lose by dying than we do. But Gary Francione counterclaims that a dog's sentience implies an interest in its continued existence, Francione, 6, 17.          [64] Ibid.

communitarians stigmatize rights as individualist. They are seen to operate formally not necessarily to assist those (the poor, oppressed, alienated) who most need them. They are disparaged as 'excess baggage' superfluous in the condemnation of cruelty or exploitation. All we need, it is argued, is a fully developed theory of right and wrong. Moreover, as I shall suggest below, Regan's argument that animals have an inherent value does not lead ineluctably to a rights-based conclusion.[65]

A second attack conceives of rights as weapons of last resort: 'the really desperate word'.[66] And the source of Regan's notion of inherent value is sometimes questioned; is his theory simply a form of sophisticated intuitionism?[67] Though Regan seeks to distinguish his case from that held by classic intuitionists like GE Moore, there is always the danger that your intuition might lead in the opposite direction to mine. How are we to determine who is right? Some rights-sceptics therefore prefer to prescribe duties without recourse to the precarious problems generated by animal rights through the mechanism of a social contract which I shall now briefly examine.

### 10.5.4 Social contractarianism

In essence, contractarianism seeks to establish a moral system on the basis of what rational agents would agree under ideal circumstances. John Rawls's version of the social contract was examined in 9.3.2. He explicitly excludes animals as rational agents.[68] But it is not altogether implausible that, in pursuit of objectivity (even though we do not ask them to imagine themselves members of another species) the people in the original position, behind their veil of ignorance, might choose a moral system which included respect for animals. At most, the social contract may require indirect duties to animals because of the (contingent) characteristics of the social contract struck in any particular society, or out of respect for the feelings of humans. But this

[65] On the other hand, Steiner argues '[g]iven the world in which we live, and given the extraordinary affliction that animals suffer at our hands, the language of rights would appear to be absolutely indispensable in the endeavor to release animals from their state of affliction', Steiner, 162. Jacques Derrida, regards as 'stupidity' the classification of different species under the abstract heading of 'animal', arguing that this is the source of violence toward these creatures, culminating in the industrialized cruelty they suffer, Jacques Derrida, *The Animal That Therefore I Am*, transl David Willis (New York: Fordham University Press 2008).

[66] Mary Midgley, *Animals and Why They Matter: A Journey Around the Species Barrier* (Harmondsworth: Penguin, 1983), 61–4.

[67] See P Carruthers, *The Animals Issue: Moral Theory in Practice* (Cambridge: Cambridge University Press, 1992).

[68] As an alternative to Rawls's theory of justice (which neglects the interests of, inter alia, disability and non-human animals) Martha Nussbaum has developed what she calls the 'capabilities approach' which focuses on human capabilities that has as its object, the recognition of human dignity. This idea is extended to non-human animals so that 'no sentient animal should be cut off from the chance of a flourishing life, a life with the type of dignity relevant to that species, and that all sentient animals should enjoy certain positive opportunities to flourish,' Nussbaum, *Frontiers of Justice: Disability, Nationality, Species Membership*. There are echoes of the 'basic forms of human flourishing' described by John Finnis (see Chapter 2) to whom Nussbaum makes no reference. On the difficult subject of sentience see DeGrazia's suggested 'sliding-scale model', DeGrazia, *Animal Rights: A Very Short Introduction*, op cit, 34–8.

seems too delicate a foundation upon which to construct a protective framework for non-humans.[69]

## 10.5.5 Intrinsic worth

Resting the welfare of animals on any of the arguments canvassed briefly above is unlikely to supply a convincing case. Perhaps, in the same way as the heated debate about abortion has missed the central issue, this controversy has lost its way. Ronald Dworkin distinguishes between two positions that are taken by those who oppose abortion.[70] The first he calls a derivative objection, for it derives from the rights and interests that it assumes all human beings, including *foetuses*, have. A second objection rests on the claim that human life has an intrinsic value, that it is sacred or inviolable; abortion is therefore wrong because it infringes this value even in the case of an unborn human being. This he calls the detached objection.

Dworkin contends that the critical question in the abortion debate is the violation, not of the rights or interests of the *foetus* (an impossibly difficult metaphysical problem anyway) but of the importance of life itself:

> Abortion wastes the intrinsic value—the sanctity, the inviolability—of a human life and is therefore a grave moral wrong unless the intrinsic value of other human lives would be wasted in a decision *against* abortion.[71]

The sterility of the disagreement concerning whether an animal may be said to be a 'person',[72] or (if it is) whether it can or should have rights, gives rise to similar difficulties. And to a similar solution. The determination of the circumstances under which it is morally defensible to subject a living creature to pain or death seems to require coherent detached arguments that seek to show why the inherent worth of other lives (human and animal) are more valuable. The arguments sketched above appear, as

---

[69] A more promising form of (indirect) contractarianism is to be found in the approach of Thomas Scanlon. He argues that through the concept of trustees, acting on behalf of the animals, they might be asked to accept certain proposed principles. See TM Scanlon, *What We Owe to Each Other* (Cambridge, Mass: Belknap Press, 1998).

[70] R Dworkin, *Life's Dominion: An Argument about Abortion and Euthanasia* (London: HarperCollins, 1993, paperback edn, 1995), 11 and *passim*.          [71] Ibid, 60.

[72] At the time of writing (October 2014), a New York court is considering an application to recognize Tommy, a 26-year-old chimpanzee, as the first animal to be considered a person under the law. The Boston-based Nonhuman Rights Project is seeking a declaration that would free him from what they describe as a 'small, dank, cement cage in a cavernous dark shed'. It contends that 'in law, science and history' the chimp has the right of habeas corpus - the ancient writ that requires a person under detention to be brought before a judge so that he may be released. Also in October the French parliament amended its civil code to accept that animals can no longer be conceived as 'furniture', but as 'living beings capable of sensitivity'. The Privy Council has accepted that a bronze Hindu idol has legal personality and *locus standi*: *Union Bank of India v Bumper Development Corporation Ltd* (1988) QBD (17 Feb, unreported) cited in LV Prott and PJ O'Keefe, *Law and the Cultural Heritage*, vol 3 (London: Butterworths, 1989) 546–7. See also A D'Amato and SK Chopra, 'Whales: Their Emerging Right to Life' (1991) 85 *American Journal of International Law* 21. Some African legal systems recognize the juristic personality of trees, rocks, and even spirits. For a powerful argument (adopted by three Supreme Court judges) in support of legal rights for natural objects, see CD Stone, 'Should Trees Have Standing?—Towards Legal Rights for Natural Objects' (1972) 45 *Southern California Law Review* 450. Are these claims a little extravagant?

in the case of the dispute concerning abortion, to generate a good deal of vitriol and rhetoric, and little in the way of constructive results.

## 10.5.6 The rights of animals

In moral discourse the power of rights is formidable. Moral claims are routinely translated into moral rights: individuals assert their rights to life, work, health, education, housing, and so on. Communities and putative nations demand a right to self-determination, sovereignty, free trade. In the legal context rights have assumed a prominence so great that they are sometimes regarded as synonymous with law itself;[73] declarations of political rights are often conceived to be the hallmark of the modern democratic state. And the inevitable contest between competing rights is one of the self-justifying characteristics of a liberal society. Whether the choice or the interest model of rights is adopted, 'it is quite inconceivable that the extension of any right should coincide exactly with the boundaries of our species'.[74]

The harm that scientific and economic 'progress' can inflict on our environment and all who share it is plain. The attraction of rights as a weapon by which both to safeguard the interests of living things against harm, and to promote the circumstances under which they are able to flourish is understandable. Yet the traditional concept of rights is problematic and, in any event, may be unable to deliver these goods. The case for a fundamental shift in our social and economic systems and structures may be the only way in which to secure a sustainable future for our planet and its inhabitants. The importance of the sanctity of all life and its flourishing offers a powerful means to this end.

The argument is sometimes heard that concern for animals is misplaced. Human beings, it is contended, are manifestly more important than non-humans. Energy spent on animal causes is better directed against human suffering. Indeed one writer asserts that the popular movement in support of animal rights is a 'reflection of moral decadence'.[75] This argument seems to be driven by the idea that those who are engaged in animal rights or welfare activities either subordinate human interests to animal interests, or that they have a pathological indifference towards human beings.[76] In my experience, at least, the opposite tends to be true. Individuals involved in the animal welfare movement are frequently dedicated as well to the alleviation of suffering of oppressed or disadvantaged humans.[77] And even if this were not so, our concern for animals is inseparable from our anxiety about the ravages we continue to inflict on our environment, and the consequences of this damage on all living things. In relation to the use of live animals in experiments, one occasionally hears it said that science is somehow

---

[73] See R Dworkin, *Taking Rights Seriously* (Cambridge, Mass: Harvard University Press, 1977).

[74] Sumner, *The Moral Foundation of Rights*, 206.    [75] Carruthers, *The Animals Issue*, xi.

[76] For one philosopher 'there is no real difference in the basic grounds on which we should condemn man's inhumanity to animals and man's inhumanity to man', TLS Sprigge, 'Metaphysics, Physicalism, and Animal Rights' (1979) 22 *Inquiry* 101, 103.

[77] There is a strong connection between the feminist and the anti-vivisection campaigns of the nineteenth century in Britain. See O Banks, *Faces of Feminism* (Oxford: Blackwell, 1986), 81–2, quoted in L Birke, *Women, Feminism and Biology: The Feminist Challenge* (Brighton: Harvester, 1986), 120. See the discussion of the 'ethics of care' in Chapter 14.

value-neutral.[78] This provides a handy device by which scientists may be blinded from the suffering of animals and deny them subjective awareness and moral status.[79]

Cruelty to animals and indifference to the extinction of endangered species, is sometimes defended in the name of cultural or ethical relativism. This is a neglected issue that warrants close attention. It is true that, as in the case of human rights, 'since people are more likely to observe normative propositions if they believe them to be sanctioned by their own cultural standards, observance of human rights standards can be improved through the enhancement of the cultural legitimacy of those standards'.[80] Yet, all too often, these arguments merely camouflage injustice. Where suffering is caused (and especially where international norms are infringed) we should resist such claims.

If the argument about our treatment of animals is best considered as an aspect of our attitude towards the planet we inhabit, it requires an understanding of the circumstances that give rise to the numerous ways in which we mistreat animals. The recognition of their 'rights' would almost certainly reduce their suffering. But the theoretical arguments in support of the case are far from straightforward.[81]

## Questions

1. Are rights and duties, as Hohfeld argues, necessarily correlative?

2. Does the fact that A has a liberty (as against B) to wear a tie entail that B is under a duty not to interfere with A's wearing a tie?

3. Compare the 'will' and 'choice' theories of rights.

4. Dworkin claims that no utilitarian view offers an adequate basis for a theory that takes rights seriously, and only a limited version of utilitarianism (which excludes external preferences) offers some support for the egalitarianism that is the main appeal of utilitarianism. Do you agree?

---

[78] 'It is in the name of science, and with the specious bribe of release from all our ills, that we have been cajoled and threatened and insulted into permitting the continued torture of our kindred and the continued blunting of the sensibilities of those who come to work in our laboratories. Let no-one rely on common decency in such a situation: the pressure of one's professional peer-group, the atmosphere of dismissive tolerance of all outside the clan, the calm assumption that this is what we do, are all far too strong for most of us to resist', S Clark, *The Moral Status of Animals*, 141–2.

[79] '[A]nimals have been allowed to suffer in research not through cruelty, but rather, because consideration of suffering is forgotten in the thrill of the pursuit, by nature ultimately ruthless, complemented by an ideology which discounts the cogency of moral reflection in scientific activity and denies the meaningfulness of attributing feelings to animals, and is coupled with practical pressures', Bernard E Rollin, *The Unheeded Cry: Animal Consciousness, Animal Pain and Science* (Oxford: Oxford University Press, 1989).

[80] AA An'Naim, 'Problems of Universal Cultural Legitimacy for Human Rights' in AA An'Naim and F Deng (eds), *Human Rights in Africa: Cross-Cultural Perspectives* (Washington DC: Brookings Institution, 1990), 331.

[81] Why should animals, particularly domesticated animals, not be accorded citizenship? For a cogent argument in support of this view, see Sue Donaldson and Will Kymlicka, *Zoopolis: A Political Theory of Animal Rights* (Oxford: Oxford University Press, 2011), and 'Animals and the Frontiers of Citizenship' (2014) 34 *Oxford Journal of Legal Studies* 201.

5. What's the difference between 'civil liberties' and 'human rights'?

6. 'The idea of human rights . . . when extended beyond a few very general and negative rights, does not liberate us; it turns us into feral egotists who are at the same time dependent. This effect can be seen in our schools, where children do as they please because, with the native cunning of youth, they have realised the permissive possibilities inherent in the notion of their rights. I can only say how relieved I am that I shall not be around to see the full flowering of the human-rights culture in the years to come.' (Theodore Dalrymple, 'Wronged By Our Rights,' *Spectator*, 24 Apr 2004)

   How would you respond to this argument?

7. Why do communitarians oppose human rights?

8. '[T]here is nothing in democratic liberal theory which necessarily excludes legal protection for positive social and economic rights.' (David Feldman, *Civil Liberties and Human Rights in England and Wales*, 2nd edn (Oxford: Oxford University Press, 2002), 17)

   Why not?

9. Is the concept of human rights inescapably fuzzy?

10. Is James Griffin correct in his claim that justice requires considerably more than the non-violation of human rights? (James Griffin, *On Human Rights* (Oxford: Oxford University Press, 2008) 249.)

11. Are socio-economic rights justiciable?

12. Are you persuaded by McCloskey's argument that since most animals lack the relevant moral capacity, they do not have moral rights?

13. Does Regan's view that animals have an inherent value lead inevitably to the conclusion that they can and do enjoy rights?

14. 'Why should the law refuse its protection to any sensitive being? The time will come when humanity will extend its mantle over everything which breathes. We have begun by attending to the condition of slaves; we shall finish by softening that of all the animals which assist our labours or supply our wants.' (Jeremy Bentham, quoted in A Brown, *Who Cares for Animals?* (London: Heinemann, 1974))

   Do you agree?

# Further reading

BALKIN, JM, 'Ideology as Constraint' (1991) 43 *Stanford Law Review* 1133.

BILCHITZ, DAVID, *Poverty and Fundamental Rights: The Justification and Enforcement of Socio-economic Rights* (Oxford: Oxford University Press, 2008).

CARRUTHERS, P, *The Animals Issue: Moral Theory in Practice* (Cambridge: Cambridge University Press, 1992).

CLARKE, S, *The Moral Status of Animals* (Oxford: Clarendon Press, 1977).

DeGrazia, David, *Taking Animals Seriously: Mental Life and Moral Status* (Cambridge: Cambridge University Press, 1996).

DeGrazia, David, *Animal Rights: A Very Short Introduction* (Oxford: Oxford University Press, 2002).

Douzinas, Costas, *The End of Human Rights* (Oxford: Hart Publishing, 2000).

Dworkin, Ronald, *Taking Rights Seriously*, new impression with a reply to critics (London: Duckworth, 1978).

Dworkin, Ronald, *A Matter of Principle* (Cambridge, Mass and London: Harvard University Press, 1985).

Dworkin, Ronald, *Law's Empire* (Cambridge, Mass and London: Belknap Press, 1986).

Dworkin, Ronald, *Life's Dominion: An Argument about Abortion and Euthanasia* (London: HarperCollins, 1993).

Dworkin, Ronald, 'Hart's Postscript and the Character of Political Philosophy' (2004) 24 *Oxford Journal of Legal Studies* 1.

Dworkin, Ronald, *Justice for Hedgehogs* (Cambridge, Mass and London: The Belknap Press of Harvard University Press, 2011).

Feinberg, J, 'Human Duties and Human Rights' in J Feinberg, *Rights, Justice and the Bounds of Liberty: Essays in Social Philosophy* (Princeton, NJ: Princeton University Press, 1980).

Feinberg, J, 'The Rights of Animals and Unborn Generations' in J Feinberg, *Rights, Justice and the Bounds of Liberty: Essays in Social Philosophy*, see above.

Francione, Gary L and Robert Garner, *The Animal Rights Debate: Abolition or Regulation?* (New York: Columbia University Press, 2010).

Frey, RG, *Interests and Rights: The Case Against Animals* (Oxford: Clarendon Press, 1980).

Frey, RG, *Rights, Killing, and Suffering: Moral Vegetarianism and Applied Ethics* (Oxford: Basil Blackwell, 1983).

Gardbaum, Stephen, 'Law, Politics, and the Claims of Community' (1992) 90 *Michigan Law Review* 685.

Gewirth, Alan, *Reason and Morality* (Chicago, Ill and London: University of Chicago Press, 1978).

Gewirth, Alan, *Human Rights: Essays on Justification and Applications* (Chicago, Ill and London: University of Chicago Press, 1983).

Gordon, RW, 'Critical Legal Histories' (1984) 36 *Stanford Law Review* 57.

Griffin, James, *On Human Rights* (Oxford: Oxford University Press, 2008).

Guest, Stephen, *Ronald Dworkin*, 3rd edn (Stanford, Calif: Stanford Law and Politics, 2012).

Harris, JW, *Law and Legal Science: An Enquiry into the Concepts, Legal Rule and Legal System* (Oxford: Clarendon Press, 1979).

Hart, HLA, 'American Jurisprudence through English Eyes: The Nightmare and the Noble Dream' in *Essays in Jurisprudence and Philosophy* (Oxford: Clarendon Press, 1983).

Hills, Alison, *Do Animals Have Rights?* (Cambridge: Icon Books, 2005).

Hohfeld, Wesley Newcomb, *Fundamental Legal Conceptions as Applied in Judicial Reasoning*, ed WW Cook (New Haven, Conn and London: Yale University Press, 1964). Also in (1913) 23 *Yale Law Journal* 28.

LADD, J (ed), *Ethical Relativism* (Belmont, Calif: Wadsworth, 1973).

LOCKE, JOHN, *Two Treatises of Government*, ed P Laslett (Cambridge: Cambridge University Press, 1964).

LUKES, STEPHEN, *Moral Conflict and Politics* (Oxford: Clarendon Press, 1991).

MACCORMICK, NEIL, *Legal Rights and Social Democracy: Essays in Legal and Political Philosophy* (Oxford: Clarendon Press, 1982).

MACINTYRE, ALASDAIR, *After Virtue: A Study in Moral Theory* (London: Duckworth, 1982).

MACKIE, JL, *Ethics: Inventing Right and Wrong* (Harmondsworth: Penguin, 1977, reprinted 1990).

MCCLOSKEY, HJ, 'Moral Rights and Animals' (1978) 22 *Inquiry* 23.

MICHELMAN, FRANK, 'Law's Republic' (1988) 97 *Yale Law Journal* 1493.

NINO, CARLOS S, *The Ethics of Human Rights* (Oxford: Clarendon Press, 1991).

NINO, CARLOS S (ed), *Rights* (Aldershot: Dartmouth, 1992).

NUSSBAUM, MARTHA C, *Frontiers of Justice: Disability, Nationality, Species Membership* (Cambridge, Mass: Belknap Press, 2006).

RAZ, JOSEPH, 'Legal Rights' (1984) 4 *Oxford Journal of Legal Studies* 1.

RAZ, JOSEPH, *The Morality of Freedom* (Oxford: Clarendon Press, 1988).

RAZ, JOSEPH, *Ethics in the Public Domain: Essays in the Morality of Law and Politics* (Oxford: Clarendon Press, 1994).

REGAN, TOM, 'McCloskey on Why Animals Cannot have Rights' (1976) 26 *Philosophical Quarterly* 251.

REGAN, TOM, *The Case for Animal Rights* (London: Routledge, 1984).

REGAN, TOM, *Defending Animal Rights* (Chicago, Ill: University of Illinois Press, 2007).

RORTY, RICHARD, *Philosophy and the Mirror of Nature* (Oxford: Basil Blackwell, 1990).

ROSS, HAMISH, 'Hohfeld and the Analysis of Rights' in J Penner, D Schiff, and R Nobles, *Introduction to Jurisprudence and Legal Theory: Commentary and Materials* (London: Butterworths, 2002), Ch 13.

SANDEL, MICHAEL, *Liberalism and the Limits of Justice* (Cambridge: Cambridge University Press, 1982).

SANDEL, MICHAEL and MACINTYRE, ALASDAIR, *After Virtue: A Study in Moral Theory*, 3rd edn (London: Duckworth, 2007).

SCRUTON, ROGER, *Animal Rights and Wrongs* (London: Continuum, 2006).

SCULLY, MATTHEW, *Dominion: The Power of Man, the Suffering of Animals, and the Call to Mercy* (London: Souvenir Press, 2011).

SIMMONDS, NE, *Central Issues in Jurisprudence: Law, Justice, Law and Rights*, 4th edn (London: Sweet & Maxwell, 2014).

SINGER, PETER, *Animal Liberation*, 4th edn (London: Pimlico, 1995).

SINGER, PETER (ed), *In Defence of Animals: The Second Wave*, 2nd edn (Oxford: Blackwell Publishing, 2005).

SPRIGGE, TLS, 'Metaphysics, Physicalism, and Animal Rights' (1979) 22 *Inquiry* 101.

SUMNER, LW, *The Moral Foundation of Rights* (Oxford: Clarendon Press, 1989).

SUNSTEIN, CASS R and NUSSBAUM, MARTHA C (eds), *Animal Rights: Current Debates and New Directions* (New York: Oxford University Press, 2004).

WALDRON, JEREMY (ed), *Theories of Rights* (Oxford: Oxford University Press, 1984).

WALDRON, JEREMY, *Nonsense upon Stilts: Bentham, Burke and Marx on the Rights of Man* (London: Methuen, 1987).

WHITE, AR, *Rights* (Oxford: Clarendon Press, 1984).

# 11

# Why obey the law?

Is there a moral duty to obey the law? In other words, do we have a moral obligation to comply with legal rules merely because they are legal rules? What of plainly unjust laws? Or laws that make unreasonable demands on us?

The question of whether we have a duty to abide by the law is something of an old jurisprudential chestnut. Nevertheless its pursuit reveals some important theoretical elements of the nature of law and its moral claims. This chapter very briefly sketches the principal arguments. But note that the matter under consideration pertains to the situation in just or nearly just societies. The issue assumes a rather different complexion in iniquitous societies such as Nazi Germany or apartheid South Africa (see 2.10.2). In such cases, the principle *lex iniusta non est lex* may render the argument more delicate, and more complex.[1]

## 11.1 The terms of the debate

Few, if any, on either side of the argument adopt an absolutist position. In other words, it is rare to find supporters of the view that the duty to obey is absolute. It is generally acknowledged that under certain circumstances it is morally acceptable to break the law or even that one might actually be under a duty to do so. Nor, on the other hand, would many who are doubtful of the duty maintain that it does not arise at all, and that we are at liberty to flout the law.

The doubters nevertheless concede that we are frequently under a moral duty to comply with the law regardless of its specific demands. We have, for example, a duty not to steal or deceive, or to adhere to recognized standards of behaviour where not to do so would be unsafe, such as driving on the correct side of the road. But they think that non-compliance is tolerable only when there is no independent moral reason to

---

[1] See John Finnis, *Natural Law and Natural Rights*, 2nd edn (Oxford: Oxford University Press, 2011), 354–66, where he contends that the natural law tradition 'accords iniquitous rules legal validity, whether on the ground that these rules are accepted in the courts as guides to judicial decisions…or [that] they satisfy the criteria of validity laid down by constitutional or other legal rules…or both…' In his postscript, he refines the first clause of this quotation by adding that where such evil rules satisfy the legal system's criteria of validity, natural law theory 'does not seek to deny that fact unless the system itself provides a juridical basis for treating these otherwise valid rules as legally valid by reason (directly or indirectly) of their iniquity,' (476). What 'juridical basis' do you think Finnis has in mind?

observe the law or when the weight of such reasons supports disobedience. And they appreciate the advantages generated by a legally ordered society and hence that it warrants general support and compliance. In short, therefore, the debate seems to revolve around whether there is a *prima facie* duty to obey that law, for:

> [N]o respectable theory of political obligation ever claimed that a person is obligated no matter what to obey the laws of a legal system to which he or she is subject. Every minimally plausible theory sets out certain conditions under which such an obligation is said to arise...[2]

And the general question of legal obedience is inevitably related to wider considerations of political obligation. Thus, as is evident in earlier chapters, especially Chapter 2, the extent to which law is distinct from morality is a central theme of a significant portion of legal theory. The debate between natural lawyers and legal positivists turns largely on the status and function of morality in the very definition of law. So, for example, Lon Fuller speaks of the 'internal morality' of law. Dworkin goes further and appears to treat the question of legal obedience as indistinguishable from his general theory of law. In other words, his concept of law as integrity presumes a theory of political obligation. For him, one has an obligation to obey the law when a legal system possesses the particular political value of integrity. See 5.2.7.

### 11.1.1 A *prima facie* duty?

What does it mean to assert that we are under a *prima facie* duty to obey the law?[3] Consider the following arresting example:

> If I have in my left hand a book of Jubbub etiquette—something totally unknown to you—and in my right hand a book of your country's law, and I announce that I am going to open each at random, will you allow that there are moral reasons indicating obedience to whatever comes out of my right hand which plainly do not obtain in the case of the left-hand book? Or is your conscience equipoised between the two books—that is, until you hear the prescription read out, there is no way of knowing whether there will be moral reasons to comply?...For one to be able to affirm that a *prima facie* moral duty to obey English law exists, one must be satisfied that, whatever comes out of the English law book, there are reasons (stateable in advance) why it is morally right to comply—albeit that, once the prescription is known, other moral reasons may tell against.[4]

---

[2] Stephen Perry, 'Associative Obligations and the Obligation to Obey the Law' in Scott Hershovitz (ed), *Exploring Law's Empire: The Jurisprudence of Ronald Dworkin* (Oxford: Oxford University Press, 2006), 183. A stimulating debate between a supporter and a doubter of the duty is to be found in Christopher Heath Wellman and A John Simmons, *Is There a Duty to Obey the Law?* (New York: Cambridge University Press, 2005). Wellman bases his argument in support of a moral duty on Samaritan obligations to perform effortless rescues, arguing that we have a moral duty to obey the law as our just contribution to the communal Samaritan task of rescuing our fellow citizens from the hazards of the state of nature. Simmons, on the other hand, contends that there is no strong moral presumption in favour of obedience to or compliance with any existing state.

[3] A lucid—now classic—account of the issues is MBE Smith, 'Is There a Prima Facie Obligation to Obey the Law?' (1973) 82 *Yale Law Journal* 950.

[4] JW Harris, *Legal Philosophies*, 2nd edn (London: Butterworths, 1997), 227.

In other words, to claim that one has a *prima facie* duty to obey the law is to assert that the obligation arises independently of the precise legal provisions involved—unless there are grounds to justify a specific exception. The authority of law dictates a duty to obey. To put it bluntly: law is to be obeyed because it is the law. The duty is *prima facie* in the sense that it may be overridden by a more pressing moral obligation.

## 11.1.2 Justifying the duty

Reasons to obey might be prudential or moral. Prudential reasons are those that arise from self-interest. One may, for instance, obey the law out of fear of punishment or habit. These considerations are not in issue here. This question is normally concerned only with reasons that have some sort of moral basis. These might spring from one or more of the following four principal sources.

### 11.1.2.1 Fair play

One might feel morally obliged to obey the law because the legal and political system is fundamentally fair and just. The price to be paid for the benefits bestowed by the law (security, order, justice, etc) is obedience of its requirements. This is expressed by Hart as follows:

> [W]hen a number of persons conduct any joint enterprise according to rules and thus restrict their liberty, those who have submitted to these restrictions when required have a right to a similar submission from those who have benefited by their submission.[5]

One immediate difficulty with this view is that some might deny that the legal system as a whole is indeed beneficial. Or it might be argued that my obedience does not, in fact, benefit anyone. A familiar example in the literature is the predicament of the driver who approaches an intersection on a deserted road at three o'clock in the morning. Failing to stop presents no risk to others, and the violation is unlikely to be discovered. But failure to obey the law is arguably immoral since the majority of drivers adhere to it, and hence my disobedience is wrong since I am taking an unfair advantage. This is a genuine moral argument.

Another problem with the fairness position is that to impose a moral duty on me, I should be an active participant in the collaborative social arrangement or at least have considered the consequences of accepting the social benefits. Yet few have a choice; we do not ask for or have the opportunity to accept or reject the purported benefits. Can a

---

[5] HLA Hart, 'Are There Any Natural Rights?' (1955) 64 *Philosophical Review* 175, 185. See too John Rawls, 'Legal Obligation and the Duty of Fair Play' in S Hook (ed), *Law and Philosophy* (New York: New York University Press, 1964), 3. As mentioned in Chapter 9, Rawls argues that in a just or nearly just society one is under a 'natural duty' to support just institutions. Since the POP behind the veil of ignorance would agree to such a norm, the duty exists independently of any promise to obey the law. Where, however, the law crosses the threshold and, for example, makes unjust demands of a minority into injustice conscientious refusal is justified. When the law is manifestly unjust, Rawls accepts that civil disobedience may be warranted. He defines this activity as 'a public, non-violent, conscientious yet political act contrary to law usually done with the aim of bringing about a change in the law or policies of the government', Rawls, *A Theory of Justice* (Harmondsworth: Penguin, 1973), 364.

moral duty therefore be based upon reciprocity for something we have no real freedom to accept or refuse?

### 11.1.2.2 Consent

The argument here is that by virtue of my membership of society, I implicitly consent to an obligation to obey its laws. As one leading theorist puts it:

> [T]he model of promise lends clarity and credibility to a theory of political obligation; for promising is surely as close to being an indisputable ground of moral requirement as anything is. Basing a theory of political obligation on consent, then, lends it plausibility unequalled by rival theories.[6]

But is this so? While consent may be evidenced by my paying taxes, participating in elections, or simply residing in the jurisdiction,[7] as with the fairness line of reasoning, is it reasonable to regard such actions as constituting consent since it is unlikely to be understood by individuals as representing acceptance of the duty? Nor do they have a genuine choice of an alternative. Moreover, it is difficult to see how, say, my paying my taxes ineluctably generates a moral obligation to obey all other laws. Consent seems too fragile a reed to support a general moral duty of obedience.

### 11.1.2.3 The common good

'The stipulations of those in authority,' John Finnis contends from a natural law perspective,

> have presumptive obligatory force (in the eyes of the reasonable person thinking unrestrict-edly about what to do) only because of what is needed *if the common good is to be secured and realized.*[8]

In other words, any reasonable person would understand that the likelihood of one's failure to obey the law is damage to the common good.

This argument need not be grounded in natural law theory; it is frequently based on the ostensibly compelling consequentialist view that the effect of widespread disobedience would be pandemonium. You will recall Hobbes's view that without general deference to the law, society would descend into turmoil and conflict (see 2.3.1). This claim draws also on the argument from 'bad example'. When I break the law, others may follow suit, and I too may be tempted to repeat my own example. So if I fraudulently fail to declare some of my income when completing my tax form, others may be disposed to do the same. The fact that I know that most taxpayers cheat in this way is immaterial, for my children may learn of my evasion and rather fancy the

---

[6] A John Simmons, *Moral Principles and Political Obligations* (Princeton, NJ: Princeton University Press, 1979), 70, quoted by Margaret Gilbert, *A Theory of Political Obligation* (Oxford: Clarendon Press, 2006), 57 n 7.

[7] According to Blackstone, '[N]o subject of England can be constrained to pay any aids or taxes, even for the defence of the realm or the support of government, but such as are imposed by his own consent, or that of his representatives in parliament', W Blackstone, 2 *Commentaries* §135.

[8] See Finnis, op cit, 358; emphasis added.

utilitarian calculation involved: the law may legitimately be flouted when the cost to oneself exceeds any material benefit to others. On this reckoning they can effortlessly justify helping themselves to goods off the shelves of Wal-Mart since the company's loss is negligible compared with their gain.

This approach is grounded in 'act-utilitarianism' (see 9.1), and, like all utilitarian arguments, it encounters several hurdles. In the present context, for example, it needs to establish that the wrongness of an action will always (or at least frequently) result in bad consequences if everyone did the same. This outcome is rarely susceptible to empirical proof and seems, in any event, highly implausible.

### 11.1.2.4 Gratitude

The least successful argument in support of a moral duty of obedience to the law is that it is immoral to bite the hand that feeds you. One's duty springs from gratitude towards the state for the benefits it confers on you: security, education, social welfare, and so on, depending on the society in which you happen to reside. All that is asked of you in return for these benefits is that you obey the law in the same way that you show gratitude to your parents (or should!) in return for their sacrifices. The obvious distinction is that while your parents' munificence and kindness may well give rise to a *prima facie* duty to observe their directives, the same duty cannot sensibly be extended to the state.

## Questions

1. Jeremy Bentham advised 'Obey punctually, censor freely'. Why would such a fervent critic of the common law counsel adherence to this recommendation?

2. What's wrong with exceeding the speed limit on a well-lit, empty road at 3 am?

3. Is the common good of a fair society really advanced by the recognition of a moral duty to obey the law?

4. To what extent can the notion of consent or promise-keeping as applied to a club or association society be extended to the legal system?

5. Is it ever morally acceptable to contravene the law—even in an unjust society?

6. Distinguish between consequentialist and non-consequentialist arguments in support of a moral duty to obey the law. Which position is the more convincing?

7. What is the difference between 'conscientious objection' and 'civil disobedience'? Under what circumstances is either justified?

8. How does Rawls justify the duty to obey the law?

9. Dworkin maintains that there is a general obligation of obedience to law. On what grounds?

10. How might the arguments in support of a moral duty to obey the law differ between a legal positivist, on the one hand, and a natural lawyer, on the other?

# Further reading

CHRISTIE, GA, 'On the Moral Obligation to Obey the Law' (1990) *Duke Law Journal* 1311.

DEVLIN, P, *The Enforcement of Morals* (Oxford: Oxford University Press, 1963).

DWORKIN, R, *Law's Empire* (Cambridge, Mass: Harvard University Press, 1986).

FINNIS, J, *Natural Law and Natural Rights*, 2nd edn (Oxford: Oxford University Press, 2011).

GILBERT, MARGARET, *A Theory of Political Obligation* (Oxford: Clarendon Press, 2006).

GREEN, L, *The Authority of the State* (Oxford: Oxford University Press, 1990).

GREENAWALT, K, *Conflicts of Law and Morality* (Oxford: Oxford University Press, 1987).

HART, HLA, 'Are There Any Natural Rights?' (1955) 64 *Philosophical Review* 175.

HONORÉ, AM, 'Must We Obey? Necessity as a Ground of Obedience' (1981) 67 *Virginia Law Review* 39.

HONORÉ, AM, *Making Law Bind* (Oxford: Clarendon Press, 1987).

LYONS, D, *Ethics and the Rule of Law* (Cambridge: Cambridge University Press, 1984), Ch 7.

MACKIE, JL, *Ethics: Inventing Right and Wrong* (Harmondsworth: Penguin Books, 1977).

MACKIE, JL, 'Obligations to Obey the Law' (1981) 76 *Virginia Law Review* 143.

PERRY, STEPHEN, 'Associative Obligations and the Obligation to Obey the Law' in Scott Hershovitz (ed), *Exploring Law's Empire: The Jurisprudence of Ronald Dworkin* (Oxford: Oxford University Press, 2006).

RAWLS, J, *A Theory of Justice* (Harmondsworth: Penguin, 1973).

RAZ, J, *The Authority of Law: Essays on Law and Morality* (Oxford: Oxford University Press, 1979), 233–49.

ROSS, W, *The Right and the Good* (Oxford: Oxford University Press, 1930).

ROSS, W, *The Foundations of Ethics* (Oxford: Oxford University Press, 1938).

SARTORIUS, R, *Individual Conduct and Social Norms* (Encino, Calif: Dickenson, 1975).

SIMMONS, A JOHN, *Moral Principles and Political Obligations* (Princeton, NJ: Princeton University Press, 1979).

SINGER, P, *Democracy and Disobedience* (Oxford: Clarendon Press, 1973).

SMITH, MBE, 'Is There a Prima Facie Obligation to Obey the Law?' (1973) 82 *Yale Law Journal* 950.

THOMSON, J, *The Realm of Rights* (Cambridge, Mass: Harvard University Press, 1990).

WALKER, A, 'Political Obligation and the Argument from Gratitude' (1988) 17 *Philosophy and Public Affairs* 191.

WASSERSTROM, RA, 'The Obligation to Obey the Law' in Robert S Summers (ed), *Essays in Legal Philosophy* (Oxford: Basil Blackwell, 1968).

WELLMAN, CHRISTOPHER HEATH and A JOHN SIMMONS, *Is There A Duty to Obey the Law?* (New York: Cambridge University Press, 2005).

WOOZLEY, A, *Law and Obedience* (Chapel Hill, NC: University of North Carolina Press, 1979).

# 12

# Why punish?

Few subjects inflame public passion as much as the punishment of offenders. Whether it is a court's failure adequately to penalize a convicted criminal or its imposition of an excessive sentence, opinions are generously offered—especially by the media—on the appropriate sentence a lawbreaker should receive. Nor is the sentencing policy of many jurisdictions immune to censure. The sometimes cushy conditions of modern penitentiaries[1] (gymnasia, swimming pools, TV, Internet access, and similar indulgences), the apparent ease with which prisoners receive early release or parole, and the trend toward 'open' prisons are increasingly perceived as a preference for the rights of criminals over their victims.

These shifts in social policy (evident especially in Western societies) cannot sensibly be divorced from a serious philosophical analysis of the purpose of punishment. Some of the—extensive—literature on the subject therefore tends to be unduly abstract.[2] In the context of the subject of jurisprudence, however, this is perhaps defensible, though it would be prudent to evaluate the arguments about punishment in the context of these hard empirical facts.

It is self-evident that any appraisal of the criminal sanction requires a consideration of the ends that it is thought to serve. Those of a benevolent (or sanguine) disposition generally tend to support the proposition that even the most malevolent offender is capable of reform or rehabilitation and hence that the rationale of punishment ought to be forward-looking, attempting to persuade the criminal to recognize the error of his or her ways and, where possible, to return him or her to society with a new outlook on life—or at least to deter the wrongdoer—and others—from offending or re-offending. Those, on the other hand, who have less faith in the potential of human improvement, or who believe that a delinquent deserves to be chastised for his crime, tend to espouse a retributive approach to punishment.

Whatever stance one adopts, punishment (which is, after all, state coercion) necessitates some sort of justification, and this chapter sketches how its exercise—in pursuit

---

[1] Minimum security comfortable Federal prisons in the United States which frequently house white-collar criminals and other non-violent offenders have been derisively dubbed 'Club Fed'.

[2] Amongst the vast anthology, there are some valuable introductory texts including RA Duff and D Garland (eds), *A Reader on Punishment* (Oxford: Oxford University Press, 1994), T Honderich, *Punishment: The Supposed Justifications Revisited* (London: Pluto Publishing, 2005), and CL Ten, *Crime, Guilt and Punishment* (Oxford: Oxford University Press, 1987).

of the enforcement of the criminal law—might be validated. It is worth recognizing that punishment is not an *inevitable* feature of social life, that it imposes substantial costs, and that its exercise is open to abuse. It should also be acknowledged that, despite the best efforts of theorists, some wonder whether punishment can be justified at all!

You will recall that Durkheim sought to demonstrate the close connection between crime and the social values expressed in the 'collective conscience'. He contended that an act is criminal when it offends strongly held community values, pronouncing the memorable maxim that we must not say that an act shocks the common conscience because it is criminal, but that it is criminal because it shocks the common conscience. (See 7.4.2.)

Crime is therefore an unavoidable fact of social life, and punishment is the means by which the state reinforces the collective conscience by punishing those who offend against the state itself. Its purpose, according to Durkheim, is vengeance.

## 12.1 Justifying punishment

Punishing those who break the law would appear, at first blush, to require no major defence. It is, most would assert, little more than the inevitable consequence of one's being convicted of an offence. But the precise grounds upon which the exercise of state power to inflict suffering or deprivation on an individual has always been controversial, especially in a liberal democracy.[3]

In search of a justification for this ubiquitous activity, legal and political theorists tend to refer to 'theories' of punishment, but they seem to lack the defining characteristics of a true theory, as Hart points out:

> They are not, as scientific theories are, assertions or contentions as to what is or what is not the case; the atomic theory or the kinetic theory of gases is a theory of this sort. On the contrary, those major positions concerning punishment which are called deterrent or retributive or reformative 'theories' of punishment are moral *claims* as to what justifies the practice of punishment—claims as to why, morally, it *should* or *may* be used.[4]

In other words, debates about punishment are really arguments concerning the moral justification, if any, of a variety of sanctions ranging from the imposition of a fine to the deprivation of liberty—or even of life. And while, as should become clear, the justifications advanced tend either to be retributive or consequentialist in nature, there

---

[3] An influential account of the political role of punishment is to be found in Michel Foucault's now classic analysis of prisons. He conceives of the practice of punishment under law as an element of forces that reflect the governing forms of social and political power: the power to threaten, coerce, suppress, destroy, and transform. Nor is he persuaded that modern society has tempered the cruelty of punishment that existed in earlier periods. The claimed objectives of punishment (justice, moderation) camouflage other less attractive purposes. See Michel Foucault, *Discipline and Punish: The Birth of the Prison* (New York: Pantheon, 1977). For a useful discussion of Foucault's approach to punishment, see Ben Golder and Peter Fitzpatrick, *Foucault's Law* (London and New York: Routledge, 2009), Ch 2. See too 7.7.

[4] HLA Hart, *Punishment and Responsibility*, 2nd edn (originally published in 1969), with an introduction by John Gardner (Oxford: Oxford University Press, 2008), 72.

are a number of approaches that seek to amalgamate the best of each position or to transcend this often rigid division.

Before exploring these views, it is important that you understand what most theorists agree are the starting points for any rational discussion of this complex subject. Happily, two of the most gifted minds in legal and political theory have attempted to illuminate the matter. Both Hart[5] and Rawls[6] have delineated with characteristic clarity the dispassionate conceptual and analytical distinctions that might assist our arriving at a coherent conclusion on the matter. Four fundamental points arise from their respective accounts.

First it is essential to separate the concept of punishment from its justification. Any definition of punishment should be value-neutral. This entails that we do not smuggle into our definition norms that might justify what is incorporated in the definition itself. This would result in treating whatever constitutes 'punishment' as automatically justified.

Secondly, it is important to distinguish between the justification of the *practice* or institution of punishment and the justification of any given *act* of punishment. One might have a certain form of punishment available without having an occasion to mete it out on a specific individual. Moreover, it is perfectly possible that a particular practice of punishment is justified even though a given act of punishment is not.

Thirdly, as mentioned above, the practice of punishment may be justified by reference either to forward-looking or to backward-looking factors.[7] Where the former is applied, the approach is *consequentialist* and thus adopts some version of utilitarianism. This dictates that the goal of the practice of punishment is to increase the general social welfare by reducing (or, ideally, preventing) crime. Where, on the other hand, the approach is retrospective, one is assuming a *deontological* standpoint. This involves regarding punishment either as a good in itself or as a practice required by justice. Such a position tends to give rise to a retributive justification, as should become clear.[8]

Fourthly, punishing a wrongdoer should be by reference to the *norms* that define the institutional practice such as the Roman maxim *nulla poena sine lege* (no punishment without law). To justify the actual practice, however, requires a consideration of other matters, including community values (see Dworkin 5.2.8).

Hart distinguishes three related questions. First, what is the 'general justifying aim' of a system of punishment; in other words, what justifies the establishment and

---

[5] HLA Hart, 'Prolegomenon to the Principles of Punishment' in *Punishment and Responsibility*, n 4 above.          [6] John Rawls, 'Two Concepts of Rules' (1955) 64 *The Philosophical Review* 3.

[7] Though, as John Gardner observes: 'All justifications for punishment, indeed all justifications for anything, are forward-looking in the sense that they explain how the justified thing promises to make the world a better place, or at least to avoid its getting any worse... The special feature of the retributive view... is that it finds some intrinsic—not merely instrumental—value in a certain type of suffering, namely in suffering that is deserved', *Introduction* to HLA Hart, *Punishment and Responsibility*, xv.

[8] Attempts have been made to adopt a 'third way' under which these two approaches coalesce. See Ten, op cit; Jean Hampton, 'The Moral Education Theory of Punishment' (1984) 13 *Philosophy and Public Affairs* 208; Alan Goldman, 'Toward a New Theory of Punishment' (1982) 1 *Law and Philosophy* 57.

maintenance of such a system: what good can it accomplish, what duty can it fulfil, and what moral demand can it satisfy? Secondly, who may legitimately be punished: what principles or objectives should determine the allocation of punishment to individuals? Thirdly, how should the appropriate sentence be determined?

Since punishment cannot sensibly be justified without stating its purpose, it is crucial that its goal be clearly acknowledged. And we need to demonstrate not only that the sanction in question actually achieves the objectives claimed, but that they cannot be attained without punishment rather than in some other way.

It is important to recognize that few adopt either approach in a wholesale manner. While an unadulterated consequentialist approach would regard punishment as justified to the extent that its exercise accomplishes certain specific goals such as the common good or the public interest, consequentialists generally seek a variety of limitations or constraints on this instrumentalist approach. Equally, retributivism is rarely supported in its pure form. While the approach rests principally on the normative view that those convicted deserve punishment, it is readily conceded that this may not be true in every case.

## 12.2 Retributivism

The oldest, and perhaps the most instinctive, attitude towards a wrongdoer is that he deserves punishment in order to 'pay' for his crime. It is thought perfectly just that a convicted criminal warrants an appropriate sanction. Its most extreme form is the *lex talionis* (the law of retaliation), which, in the words of the Hebrew scriptures, demands 'an eye for an eye, a tooth for a tooth, an arm for an arm, a life for a life'.[9] A murderer, under this code, should himself be killed. This approach, however, has its obvious limitations. Should a rapist be raped, a torturer tortured? And what of conduct that causes no tangible harm, such as driving with excessive alcohol in one's blood? Moreover, what punishment should be visited upon fraudsters, blackmailers, and the like? Nor is it obvious how this penal tit-for-tat distinguishes between intentional, reckless, and negligent behaviour.

Retributivism was famously—and resolutely—championed by Kant:

Even if a civil society were to be dissolved by the consent of all its members (e.g., if a people inhabiting an island decided to separate and disperse throughout the world), the last murderer remaining in prison would first have to be executed, so that each has done to him what his deeds deserve and blood guilt does not cling to the people for not having insisted upon this punishment; for otherwise the people can be regarded as collaborators in his public violation of justice.[10]

---

[9] It is sometimes suggested that the biblical exhortation 'an eye for an eye' was actually intended to restrict punishment to the infliction of comparable injury rather than insisting that the requirements of justice mandated vengeance.

[10] *Die Metaphysik der Sitten* (1797) translated as *Introduction to the Metaphysics of Morals*, xx.

Kant's moral universe is, of course, governed by the notion that we are rational agents who know what we are doing and hence may legitimately be held responsible for our actions. Our rational nature means we are dedicated to the proposition that what applies to me should apply to all. This 'categorical imperative' dictates: 'Act only on that maxim through which you can at the same time will that it should become a universal law.' In other words, you may treat me as I treat you. If I am kind to others, I consent to their being kind to me. If I exploit them, I authorize my suffering the same mistreatment. Thus my deceit, for example, invites chastisement; I have brought it on myself.

Kant's moral theory recognizes the offender's state of mind, the standard to be applied in fixing moral responsibility, and a rationale for punishing breaches of those standards.

The retributive approach, though until quite recently deprecated as callous and vindictive, has become increasingly attractive as a coherent objective of punishment. The increase in recidivism has generated among criminologists and penologists significant disillusionment about the efficacy of rehabilitation or reform as practical goals of penal policy. Nor is there much evidence that either general or special deterrence has been particularly effective. This scepticism has produced a growing recognition that at the heart of the very act of punishment is the notion of retribution, whether or not it is a legitimate justification. Contemporary retributivists attempt to demonstrate that without the threat and the practice of punishment, social order would be compromised for it is unjust to expect victims of crime simply to endure their suffering. The imposition of the criminal sanction must naturally conform to legal controls.

### 12.2.1 **Weak and strong retributivists**

The concept of desert is fundamental to all retributivist approaches. It is well expressed by one distinguished philosopher:

> Punishment is punishment only when it is deserved. We pay the penalty, because we owe it, and for no other reason; and if punishment is inflicted for any other reason whatever than because it is merited by wrong, it is a gross immorality, a crying injustice, an abominable crime, and not what it pretends to be.[11]

But there is a difference between weak and strong versions of retributivism.[12] The former believe that desert is a necessary, but not a sufficient, condition for justifying punishment. They require, in addition, that punishment produces positive effects, such as deterring crime or reforming or incapacitating offenders. Strong retributivists, on the other hand, regard desert as a sufficient threshold to justify punishment; desirable consequences are immaterial. Some in this camp hold that desert allows but does not

[11] FH Bradley, *Ethical Studies*, 2nd edn (Oxford: Oxford University Press, 1927), 26–7.
[12] Following Larry Alexander, 'The Philosophy of Criminal Law' in Jules Coleman and Scott Shapiro (eds), *The Oxford Handbook of Jurisprudence and Philosophy of Law* (Oxford: Oxford University Press, 2002), 816–17.

require punishment, while others maintain that there is a moral duty to punish those who deserve it, though there is a divergence in respect of the extent to which this moral duty should prevail over competing moral considerations.

## 12.2.2 **Critique**

The retrospectivity of retributivism is often stigmatized as vindictive, anachronistic, and lacking in genuine moral content. But though the approach does indeed look backwards, it is an oversimplification to criticize it on this ground for it attempts to justify an element of a structure that incorporates the establishment of norms relating to *future* conduct. Nevertheless it is the case that traditional versions of retributivism are indifferent as to whether punishment realizes any social or other benefits. Indeed, they contend that the state has not merely a right, but a duty to punish that arises solely from the fact of a crime having been committed. Thus it rejects a non-punitive response even where this might be demonstrated to be a superior remedy.

But there are a number of other compelling arguments against retributivism. Five will suffice here. First, since retributivism appears to require that *all* moral misconduct be punished, this strikes many as extreme: it may, for example, simply be too expensive to penalize certain misbehaviour. Secondly, certain criminal offences, say the violation of arbitrary car parking regulations, do not represent the breach of ethical values, and hence the imposition of punishment cannot be based on the contravention of some moral duty. Thirdly, punishment is required by considerations of justice, yet, as David Lyons points out, moral guilt and desert are not the only relevant factors:

> Retributive theories appear to fail because they justify too much or too little. If they justify any punishment at all, they seem to justify punishment in too many cases, and by too many people. But it is unclear that they succeed in justifying any punishment at all, especially by legally constituted authorities, because they either do not show why anyone has the right to punish or why right to punish should be reserved to the state. They also fail to acknowledge some of the reasons that seem to justify coercive legal rules, reasons that accordingly seem to play an essential role in the justification of punishment under those rules.[13]

Fourthly, the concept of desert is less than precise:

> What does it really mean, for example, to say that a criminal 'deserves' to suffer or be penalized for the crime? Does it mean any more than that we believe he ought to suffer for it? If so, how does this 'ought' mysteriously arise from the fact or nature of the crime? Why should it not be derived from, for example, the need to prevent and deter other such crimes?[14]

The retributivist response is that it is fair to punish offenders in proportion to the gravity of their crime. In other words, it would be unjust to punish a petty thief more severely than a rapist. But, while this is unquestionably true, the water becomes murky when we attempt to measure the seriousness of offences that admit of a less obvious

---

[13] David Lyons, *Ethics and the Rule of Law* (Cambridge: Cambridge University Press, 1984), 154.
[14] Mark Tebbit, *Philosophy of Law: An Introduction*, 2nd edn (London: Routledge, 2005), 199.

ranking. Does robbery warrant a heavier sentence than defrauding many individuals of large sums of money?

Fifthly, it is argued that retributivism is based on rhetoric rather than reason, on sentiment rather than sense. The most likely—and plausible—response to this charge is that while the retributivist position may not be entirely rational, it is justifiable on moral grounds in that, when regulated by the law, it accords with the popular reaction to serious crime.

## 12.3 Consequentialism

A consequentialist—or instrumentalist—justification seeks to show that punishment is a cost-effective method by which to achieve certain independently identifiable goods, such as the prevention or reduction of crime, or the protection of personal safety or security. Should it fail to accomplish these or similarly desirable social objectives then, according to the consequentialist view, the infliction of punishment is unjustified.

Locking up a convicted offender, not only eliminates him from society, but his incarceration may deter him from re-offending, as well as deterring others from engaging in criminal activity. A custodial sentence may also have the instrumental purpose of rehabilitating the offender so that when he leaves prison he might be reintegrated into society.

## 12.4 Critique

Consequentialism was discussed in 9.1 where it was distinguished from deontology which, you will recall, holds that one has a duty—that derives from the nature of the act itself—to perform or refrain from certain types of actions. Its consequences are irrelevant. You may have come across Kant's famous dictum that one is under a moral duty always to tell the truth—even to a murderer who asks how to find his would-be victim. Note, however, that the two theories are necessarily mutually exclusive. Hence it has been argued that the 'deontological' concept of human rights can be justified only by reference to the consequences of enjoying such rights. And Robert Nozick (see 9.4) proposes an essentially consequentialist theory which is subject to uninfringeable 'side-constraints' that limit the kinds of actions agents are permitted to take.

The consequentialist is frequently called upon to defend his position against the criticism that the theory fails to treat individuals as individuals, but merely as means to an end. In the context of punishment, among the most compelling objections to consequentialism is, first, the claim that—without desert as a criterion—punishment loses its purchase; offenders are punished, not because they deserve to endure, say, a deprivation of liberty, but on the ground that it may achieve some advantageous social purpose. This, critics contend, may result in unsuitably lenient sentences.

Secondly, a consequentialist position renders the protection of the innocent against injustice dependent upon its instrumental achievement of certain goals. Thus punishment that is plainly undeserved (of, say, the objectively innocent) or that is extremely harsh might well prove effective in preventing or deterring crime, and a consequentialist would then be bound, in principle, to consider such punishments as justifiable, despite their injustice. This recurrent complaint is generally met by adopting what is referred to as a 'side-constrained consequentialism'. It proceeds from the assumption that, as Hart puts it, the 'general justifying aim' of any system of punishment resides in its constructive consequences, but the pursuit of that objective is subject to non-consequentialist constraints which prohibit, for example, the intentional punishment of the innocent, or the disproportionately severe punishment of the guilty.[15] Hart argues that while retribution is an objectionable rationale of punishment, 'retribution in distribution' is morally acceptable since guilt is a necessary precondition of its exercise. In other words, reducing crime is a justifiable objective, but not at the cost of moral principle.

Similarly, John Rawls distinguishes between justifying a practice and justifying a particular action falling under it. The practice of punishment, he contends, may be justified only in consequentialist terms, but the meting out of a specific sentence to a specific offender can be justified only by reference to his guilt. In this way, he attempts to unite the two approaches.[16]

## 12.5 Restorative justice

The mainspring of this standpoint is the proposition that, instead of retribution, we ought to institute a process of restoration between the offender, the victim, and other concerned individuals by programmes of reconciliation or mediation that assemble the affected parties in order to consider how best to address the crime and its aftermath. It champions, in other words, repair above reprimand.[17]

## 12.6 Critique

The obvious difficulty with this charitable approach is its failure to recognize that it is not merely the material injury that is produced by the commission of the offence, but the wrong itself. What stands in need of repair is, as Duff points out, the fractured relationship between offender and victim, as well as the community. Reconciliation requires a proper recognition—especially by the offender—that a misdeed has been perpetrated and evidence of authentic penitence and contrition. Can the criminal justice system really achieve this sort of restoration?

[15] Hart, op cit, 8–11. See too N Lacey, *State Punishment: Political Principles and Community Values* (London: Routledge, 1988).

[16] J Rawls, 'Two Concepts of Rules' (1955) 64 *The Philosophical Review* 3.

[17] See, eg, A von Hirsch, AJ Ashworth, and C Shearing, 'Restorative Justice: A "Making Amends" Model?' in A von Hirsch and AJ Ashworth (eds), *Proportionate Sentencing* (Oxford: Oxford University Press, 2005). Cf RA Duff, *Punishment, Communication, and Community* (New York: Oxford University Press, 2001).

## 12.7 Communication

Reproving or censuring a wrongdoer is an obviously important element in the practice of punishment both from the standpoint of desert (see 12.2.1) and from the
position that since crimes are public wrongs they warrant society's reproof. It is,
moreover, a kinder, gentler, rational means of dissuading offenders from repeating
their misdeeds, thus countering the criticism that consequentialism is unduly harsh
and coercive.

Such reprobation is, of course, implicit in a court's denunciation through its
conviction of the offender. But there is always the possibility of censure through
so-called 'hard treatment': incarceration, fines, community service, which, it
must be said, is likely to convey a louder message to the convict, though, if so,
is the result less one of communication than naked deterrence? Critics point out
that, unlike the side-constrained consequentialist accounts discussed earlier (see
12.3) this approach assumes that the message is one of bare threat rather than
restrained communication. Its logic thus collapses into simple deterrence, thereby
forfeiting much of its moral flavour. But can this be realistically avoided when
it must be the case that for communication to be effective it ought to resonate
successfully with an individual who, by definition, frequently rejects the moral
claims of the law? Should he not, in other words, be required to do penance for his
transgression?

## 12.8 Critique

The primary purpose of communication is the attempt to treat the offender as a
responsible and rational agent at liberty to repudiate the values of the social order that
he has infringed. Indeed, to have any genuine worth his remorse ought to be voluntary, nor, as Duff points out, should a liberal society take this sort of intrusive interest
in its citizens' moral characters.[18]

## Questions

1. Why do we need to punish offenders?

2. Can retributivism be justified in a liberal society?

3. What are the principal defects of a consequentialist approach to punishment?

---

[18] Duff, op cit.

4. Robert Nozick argues that 'retributive punishment is an act of communicative behavior' that informs the offender: 'this is how wrong what you did was'. He proposes the formula: $r \times H$ (extent of responsibility multiplied by actual harm done) as a guide to determine the appropriate punishment (R Nozick, *Philosophical Explanations* (Cambridge, Mass: Harvard University Press, 1981), 370). Analyse this approach.

5. Nozick's communicative idea is developed by Jean Hampton who views punishment in a Kantian light as an intrinsically defensible response to the antisocial conduct of the offender (JG Murphy and J Hampton, *Forgiveness and Mercy* (Cambridge: Cambridge University Press, 1988). What is wrong with this approach?

6. Is the concept of desert useful in justifying punishment or in the application of penal policy?

7. 'Weak punishment induces contempt for the law—especially by the offender.' Do you agree?

8. How might capital punishment for murder be justified?

9. Hegel argued that deterrence, instead of addressing an offender as a responsible moral agent, threatens him coercively as a self-interested being 'like a dog instead of with the freedom and respect due to him as a man'. What could he mean?

10. Can retributivist and consequentialist approaches be reconciled? Should they?

## Further reading

CRUFT, ROWAN, KRAMER, MATHEW H, and REIFF, MARK R (eds), *Crime, Punishment, and Responsibility: The Jurisprudence of Antony Duff* (Oxford: Oxford University Press, 2011).

DAVIS, MICHAEL, *To Make the Punishment Fit the Crime: Essays in the Theory of Criminal Justice* (Boulder, Colo: Westview, 1992).

DUFF, A, *Intention, Agency and Criminal Liability: Philosophy of Action and the Criminal Law* (Oxford: Blackwell, 1990).

DUFF, A, *Punishment* (Aldershot: Dartmouth, 1993).

DUFF, A and GARLAND, D (eds), *A Reader on Punishment* (Oxford: Oxford University Press, 1994).

FEINBERG, JOEL, *Doing and Deserving* (Princeton, NJ: Princeton University Press, 1970).

FEINBERG, JOEL and GROSS, HYMAN (eds), *Punishment: Selected Readings* (Encino, Calif: Dickenson, 1975).

FOUCAULT, MICHEL, *Discipline and Punish: The Birth of the Prison* (New York: Pantheon, 1977).

GARLAND, DAVID, *Punishment and Modern Society* (Chicago, Ill: University of Chicago Press, 1990).

GIBBS, JACK P, *Crime, Punishment, and Deterrence* (New York: Elsevier, 1975).

GOLDMAN, ALAN, 'Toward a New Theory of Punishment' (1982) 1 *Law and Philosophy* 57.

GROSS, HYMAN, *A Theory of Criminal Justice* (New York: Oxford University Press, 1979).

GRUPP, SE, *Theories of Punishment* (Bloomington, Ind: Indiana University Press, 1971).

HAMPTON, JEAN, 'The Moral Education Theory of Punishment' (1984) 13 *Philosophy and Public Affairs* 208.

HARDING, CHRISTOPHER and IRELAND, RICHARD W, *Punishment: Rhetoric, Rule, and Practice* (London: Routledge, 1989).

HART, HLA, *Punishment and Responsibility*, 2nd edn, with an introduction by John Gardner (Oxford: Oxford University Press, 2008; originally published 1969).

HONDERICH, TED, *Punishment: The Supposed Justifications*, rev edn (Harmondsworth: Penguin, 1976).

JOHNSTONE, GERRY, *Restorative Justice: Ideas, Values, Debates* (London: Routledge, 2001).

LACEY, NICOLA, *State Punishment: Political Principles and Community Values* (London: Routledge, 1988).

LYONS, DAVID, *Ethics and the Rule of Law* (Cambridge: Cambridge University Press, 1984).

MOORE, MICHAEL S, 'The Moral Worth of Retribution' in Ferdinand Schoeman (ed), *Responsibility, Character, and the Emotions: New Essays in Moral Psychology* (Cambridge: Cambridge University Press, 1987).

MURPHY, JG and HAMPTON, J, *Forgiveness and Mercy* (Cambridge: Cambridge University Press, 1988).

NOZICK, ROBERT, *Philosophical Explanations* (Cambridge, Mass: Harvard University Press, 1981), 366–74.

OLSARETTI, SERENA (ed), *Desert and Justice* (Oxford: Oxford University Press, 2003).

PRIMORATZ, IGOR, *Justifying Legal Punishment* (Atlantic Highlands, NJ: Humanities Press, 1989).

RAWLS, JOHN, *A Theory of Justice* (Cambridge, Mass: Harvard University Press, 1971).

SCANLON, TM, *What We Owe To Each Other* (Cambridge, Mass: Harvard University Press, 1998).

SEMPLE, JANET, *Bentham's Prison: A Study of the Panopticon Penitentiary* (Oxford: Clarendon Press, 1993).

SIMMONS A JOHN, COHEN, MARSHALL, COHEN, JOSHUA, and BEITZ, CHARLES R, *Punishment: A Philosophy and Public Affairs Reader* (Princeton, NJ: Princeton University Press, 1995).

SINGER, RICHARD G, *Just Deserts: Sentencing Based on Equality and Desert* (Cambridge, Mass: Ballinger, 1979).

STRAWSON, PETER F, 'Freedom and Resentment', reprinted in Strawson, *Freedom and Resentment and Other Essays* (London: Methuen, 1974).

TEBBIT, MARK, *Philosophy of Law: An Introduction*, 2nd edn (London: Routledge, 2005), Ch 12.

TEN, CL, *Crime, Guilt, and Punishment* (Oxford: Clarendon Press, 1987).

VON HIRSCH, ANDREW, *Doing Justice: The Choice of Punishments* (New York: Hill & Wang, 1976).

VON HIRSCH, ANDREW, *Past or Future Crimes: Deservedness and Dangerousness in the Sentencing of Criminals* (New Brunswick, NJ: Rutgers University Press, 1985).

WALKER, NIGEL, *Why Punish?* (Oxford: Oxford University Press, 1991).

# 13

# Critical legal theory

Why 'critical'? Is all legal theory not in some respects critical? Bentham was critical of natural law. Hart's legal theory is critical of Austin; Dworkin is critical of legal positivism, and so on. The theories under consideration in this chapter, however, are critical in a rather different, more radical sense. They reject what is taken to be the natural order of things, be it the free market (in the case of Critical Legal Studies (CLS), see 13.1), or 'meta-narratives' (postmodernism, see 13.2), patriarchy (in the case of feminist jurisprudence, see 14.3), or the conception of 'race' (Critical Race Theory (CRT) see 14.5).

Critical legal theorists share a profound scepticism about many of the enterprises that have long been assumed to be at the heart of jurisprudence. This chapter touches on the first two of these movements; Chapter 14 surveys the last two.[1]

The central theme of critical legal theory is to doubt the prospect of uncovering a universal foundation of law based on reason. It repudiates the very project of jurisprudence which it generally perceives as clothing the law and legal system with a bogus legitimacy. Moreover, its acceptance of law as a distinctive and discrete discipline buttresses the concept of law as autonomous—independent from politics and morality. The myth of determinacy is a significant element of the critical assault on law. Far from being a determinate, coherent body of rules and doctrine, the law is portrayed by critical legal theorists as uncertain, ambiguous, and unstable. And far from expressing rationality, the law reflects political and economic power. Moreover, as many of the adherents of CLS seek to demonstrate, the law is neither neutral nor objective.

In pursuit of neutrality, the law deploys a number of fictions or illusions. In particular, the exalted idea of a liberal society under the rule of law in which all are treated equally, is treated with deep suspicion by CLS. Social justice is an empty promise. Since the law is irretrievably wedded to power, it cannot transcend this power which is therefore chiefly ideological: social relations based on power are made to appear legitimate—because they seem to be beyond power. Postmodernist critics of the law generally proceed from the starting point that all claims of truth are questionable.

---

[1] Be warned. These are large subjects that frequently roam well beyond the frontiers of most conventional jurisprudence courses. In this chapter I provide only the bare essentials; you will find helpful prologues and readings in *Lloyd's Introduction to Jurisprudence*, 8th edn (London: Sweet & Maxwell, 2008), and especially J Penner, D Schiff, and R Nobles (eds), *Introduction to Jurisprudence and Legal Theory: Commentary and Materials* (London: Butterworths, 2002).

No particular reading of a text is 'privileged' or authoritative. It is merely one of any number of possible interpretations.

These contentions should become intelligible in the course of this chapter.

## 13.1 Critical Legal Studies

CLS developed in the United States in the 1970s. It expressed a broadly Marxist critique of the substantive doctrines of the law. The movement, in its early stages, was distinctive in two respects, First, it was located within legal scholarship (as opposed to sociology or political science), and secondly, it sought to address the inequities of legal doctrine. Its original focus was on Blackstone's *Commentaries*, the Wagner Acts, and on tort and contract. Later it reflected also the wider tendency of leftist thought towards culture, literature, and aesthetics.

Another important feature of CLS is its interdisciplinary approach. It draws on politics, philosophy, literary criticism, psychoanalysis, linguistics, and semiotics to expound its critique of law, and continues to exert a—declining—influence on ideas about the politics of rights, which sometimes borders on the nihilistic. If American Realism was 'jazz jurisprudence', CLS may be its 'rock' successor.[2] CLS is, in many ways, an outgrowth of the American realist movement, though even some of its critics concede that, in important respects, it extends beyond the scepticism of its alleged progenitor.[3] Ronald Dworkin puts the matter succinctly (but without much evidence of the constructive interpretation he generally advocates) when he declares that in most of its programme:

> save in its self-conscious leftist posture and its particular choice of other disciplines to celebrate, critical legal studies resembles the older movement of American legal realism, and it is too early to decide whether it is more than an anachronistic attempt to make that dated movement reflower. Much of its rhetoric, like that of legal realism, is borrowed from external scepticism: its members are fond of short denunciations of 'objectivism' or 'natural law metaphysics' or of the idea of values 'out there' in the universe.[4]

CLS was greeted by many scholars as a breath of fresh air in the sometimes stultifying atmosphere of legal theory. It has certainly excited controversy and rancour (Harvard Law School, where CLS had a significant following, still feels its fallout—though perhaps it has merely brought into the open the inevitable ideological differences that exist between teachers of law in most law schools). It has generated a

---

[2] See the dialogue between Duncan Kennedy and Peter Gabel: 'Roll over Beethoven' (1984) 36 *Stanford Law Review* 1.

[3] Duxbury, however, demonstrates that 'critical legal studies—for all that it may have progressed little further than did legal realism in grappling with law as a political phenomenon—is not simply realism repeated', Neil Duxbury, *Patterns of American Jurisprudence* (Oxford: Hart Publishing, 2000), 425. See 435 ff for an excellent account of the historical roots and theoretical preoccupations of CLS.

[4] *Law's Empire* (Cambridge, Mass and London: Belknap Press, 1973), 272. But for a brief demonstration that the nature and ends of CLS and realism are fundamentally different, see Jeffrey A Standen, 'Critical Legal Studies as an Anti-Positivist Phenomenon' (1986) 72 *Virginia Law Review* 983.

prodigious literature which, at best, is both challenging and stimulating. But see for yourself. A useful starting point is the book, *The Politics of Law*, edited by D Kairys.[5] It is very much a 'manifesto' of the movement's creed, and contains several short essays—all written from a 'critical' standpoint—on a variety of branches of substantive law. So, for example, in their essay 'Contract Law as Ideology', Peter Gabel and Jay M Feinman aver:

> [C]ontract law today constitutes an elaborate attempt to conceal what is going on in the world....Contract law, like the other images constituted by capitalism, is a denial of [the] painful feelings [of isolation, passivity, unconnectedness, and impotence] and an apology for the system that produces them.[6]

You will at once realize that this is no half-hearted 'criticalness'; CLS is a direct attack on the orthodoxy of legal theory, scholarship, and education. More than that, it is an important intellectual assault on the very organization of modern society itself. Another helpful launching pad for your reading is the collection of leading essays, edited (with a lively and lucid introduction) by James Boyle, *Critical Legal Studies*.[7]

There are (following Trubek) three important ideas that inform CLS: 'hegemonic consciousness' (a concept derived from the writings of the Italian Marxist, Antonio Gramsci); 'reification' (a concept used by Marx and developed in the writings of the Hungarian Marxist, György Lukács); and 'denial' (a concept used in Freudian psychology). By 'hegemonic consciousness' Gramsci meant that social order is maintained by a system of beliefs; in a capitalist society these beliefs are accepted as 'common sense' and part of the natural order by those who are actually subordinated

---

[5] David Kairys (ed), *The Politics of Law: A Progressive Critique* (New York: Pantheon Books, 1982). See too Charles M Yablon, 'The Indeterminacy of the Law: Critical Legal Studies and the Problem of Legal Explanation' (1985) 6 *Cardozo Law Review* 917; Morton J Horowitz, *The Transformation of American Law, 1870–1960: The Crisis of Legal Orthodoxy* (New York: Oxford University Press, 1992); Robert W Gordon, 'Critical Legal Histories' (1984) 36 *Stanford Law Review* 270; G Edward White, 'The Inevitability of Critical Legal Studies' (1984) 36 *Stanford Law Review* 649. An amusing discussion of critical scholarship which itself manages to be both critical and light-hearted is Arthur Austin, 'The Top Ten Politically Correct Law Review Articles' (1999) 27 *Florida State University Law Review* 233.

[6] In Kairys (ed), see n 5 above, at 183.

[7] *International Library of Essays in Law and Legal Theory* (Aldershot: Dartmouth, 1992). See also M Kelman, *A Guide to Critical Legal Studies* (Cambridge, Mass: Harvard University Press, 1987), and Ch 14 of *Lloyd's Introduction to Jurisprudence*. A helpful symposium is to be found in (1984) 36 *Stanford Law Review* (I particularly recommend the essays by Trubek and by Hutchinson and Monahan), and Alan Hunt has produced a bibliography of CLS in (1984) 47 *Modern Law Review* 369 and has attempted to assess the importance of the movement in 'The Theory of Critical Legal Studies' (1986) 6 *Oxford Journal of Legal Studies* 1. An intelligent account of the movement's nature and objectives is Alan Hutchinson's *Dwelling on the Threshold* (Toronto: Carswell, 1988). Most students enjoy Duncan Kennedy's piece on 'Legal Education as Training for Hierarchy' (from Kairys (ed), *The Politics of Law*, and extracted in *Lloyd's Introduction to Jurisprudence*, 1267–71), especially his proposal to abolish grading and classification of degrees. Roberto Unger's huge and, at times impenetrable, essay, 'The Critical Legal Studies Movement' (1983) 96 *Harvard Law Review* 561, is not for beginners! On the nihilist strand in CLS, a stimulating essay is JW Singer, 'The Player and the Cards: Nihilism and Legal Theory' (1984) 94 *Yale Law Journal* 1. See too J Stick, 'Can Nihilism be Pragmatic?' (1986) 100 *Harvard Law Review* 332. For a useful comment on the Singer/Stick exchange, see S Fuller, 'Playing Without a Full Deck: Scientific Realism and the Cognitive Limits of Legal Theory' (1988) 97 *Yale Law Journal* 549.

to it. In other words, these ideas are treated as eternal and necessary whereas they really reflect only the transitory, arbitrary interests of the dominant elite. This system of ideas is then 'reified' (a term used by Marx, see 7.6), that is, becomes a material thing: it is presented as essential, necessary, and objective when, in fact, it is contingent, arbitrary, and subjective. Legal thought is also a form of 'denial': it is a means of coping with perceived contradictions that are too painful for us to hold in our conscious mind. It therefore *denies* the contradiction between the promise, on the one hand of, say, equality and freedom, and the reality of oppression and hierarchy, on the other.

Drawing on the work of Roberto Unger (especially his important book, *Law in Modern Society*),[8] CLS generally subscribes to the view that the following four ideas prevail in society:

- *Law is a 'system'.* This body of 'doctrine', properly interpreted, supplies the answer to all questions about social behaviour.

- A *form of reasoning* exists that may be used by specialists to find answers from 'doctrine'.

- This 'doctrine' reflects *a coherent view* about the relations between persons and the nature of society.

- *Social action reflects norms generated by the legal system* (either because people *internalize* these norms or actual *coercion* compels them to do so).

Each of these four ideas is challenged by CLS:

- It denies that law is a system. 'Doctrine' never provides a determinate answer to questions, nor can it cover all conceivable situations. This is described as the principle of *indeterminacy.*

- It rejects the view that there is an autonomous and neutral mode of legal reasoning. This is described as the principle of *antiformalism.*

- It disputes the idea that 'doctrine' encapsulates a single, coherent view of human relations; instead CLS argues that 'doctrine' represents several different, often competing views, none of which is sufficiently coherent or pervasive to be called dominant. This is described as the principle of *contradiction.*

- It doubts that even where there is consensus, there is reason to regard the law as a decisive factor in social behaviour. This is described as the principle of *marginality.*

If these four principles (indeterminacy, antiformalism, contradiction, and marginality) are accepted, then as Trubek puts it, '[t]he law, in whose shadow we bargain, is itself a shadow'.[9] If law is indeterminate, all legal scholarship on what the

---

[8] Roberto Unger, *Law in Modern Society: Toward a Criticism of Social Theory* (London: Collier–Macmillan, 1977). The book is roundly criticized by W Ewald, 'Unger's Philosophy: A Critical Legal Study' (1988) 5 *Yale Law Journal* 665.          [9] (1984) 36 *Stanford Law Review* 575, 579.

law is becomes merely a form of advocacy; if there is no distinct form of legal reasoning, such scholarship becomes a political debate; if legal 'doctrine' is essentially contradictory, legal argument cannot rely on legal materials if it is not to result in a tie; and if law is marginal, social life must be ordered by norms outside of the law.

As Boyle demonstrates, there are five major aspects of critical legal theory:[10]

1. *Legal rules and legal reasoning.* This has two principal strands. The first is largely inspired by Unger, mainly in his book *Knowledge and Politics*, where he seeks to show that the liberal theory of the state is based on the view that all values are relative; the market economy and democracy therefore become the natural institutions in a liberal society.

2. The second proceeds from a sceptical realism which rejects the conventional view, for example, that courts can sensibly interpret language, the division between private and public law, the neutrality of rules, and the centrality of rights. The writings of Duncan Kennedy and Peter Gabel have been particularly influential here.[11]

3. *Legal history.* There are a number of important CLS writings on the history of legal concepts and institutions and their relationship with ideological factors. In 'Critical Legal Histories', for instance, Robert Gordon shows how the traditional evolutionary approach neglects the extent to which we have control over our lives:

   > We invent shorthand labels like 'modernisation' as a way of summarising what has happened in and trying to generalise about particular societies. Then, by trick of the mind, we suddenly reify our label into a process that *had* to happen the way it did. The next thing you know, we start explaining the whole contingent miscellany of contemporary social practices (especially the nasty ones) as the *natural* outcomes of the 'modernisation process'. But if there is no such single process, there can't be any set of functional responses to it either.[12]

4. *Substantive law.* As already pointed out, CLS does not merely traverse the lofty peaks of abstract theory, but seeks to apply its insights to actual 'black letter' legal issues. There are numerous examples of such work. Boyle provides a substantial list which indicates the broad sweep of the analysis.[13]

5. *Legal practice.* A major line of attack concentrates on the manner in which law consists of symbols (eg, 'contracting parties') reified to represent the social order. This, in turn, produces an alienated world of repression by rules and authority.

---

[10] *Critical Legal Studies* (Aldershot: Dartmouth, 1992).
[11] Try to read Kennedy's penetrating essay, 'Freedom and Constraint in Adjudication' reprinted in Boyle (ed), *Critical Legal Studies.*          [12] Quoted in Boyle, *Critical Legal Studies*, xxiii.
[13] *Critical Legal Studies*, 1, n 57.

CLS latterly moved towards a full-blown epistemological onslaught on legal thought and the manner in which 'text' stands in need of deconstruction:

> [I]n common with deconstructive literary philosophy, post-Wittgensteinian linguistics and the contemporary philosophy of science, [CLS shares] a concern with the 'politics of reason', the connection between epistemology and social power.[14]

Each of these large claims warrants closer examination.

The CLS movement, though it has its roots in realism, is not, as suggested earlier, to be regarded merely as a 'new realism'. Both movements are antiformalist and sceptical; both seek to demystify the law: to reveal the law 'in action'. But in at least four important respects CLS differs from realism. First, it is largely uninterested in the pragmatic or empirical concerns (what courts, lawyers, legislators actually 'do') that preoccupied the realists. For CLS the law is regarded as 'problematic' in the sense that it reproduces the oppressive character of society. Secondly, unlike the American realists who accepted the distinction between legal reasoning and politics, CLS views it as axiomatic that *law is politics*: there is nothing special about legal reasoning to distinguish it from other forms of reasoning.

Thirdly, CLS exhibits a much deeper concern with *theory* than was ever the case with the realists. There is a fairly strong tie with the critical theory of the so-called Frankfurt School and its leading contemporary figure, Jürgen Habermas (13.2.5), as well as writers like Foucault (13.2.5), Unger, and, more recently, deconstructionists such as Jacques Derrida (13.2.4). Fourthly, though the realists were determined to differentiate between legal rules and their actual operation in society, they generally embraced the neutrality of law and the ideology of liberalism. CLS, of course, rejects both.

### 13.1.1 **Trashing CLS?**

The movement, though it now shares a good deal with postmodernist legal theory, to be discussed in a moment, seems to have been eclipsed by it. Fashion is, alas, like that. References to CLS tend now to use the past tense. What went wrong? After an astute evaluation of CLS, David Jabbari concludes that the American theorists failed 'to move beyond criticism to the construction of new conceptions of law which show law to be capable of both effecting and regulating social change ... [D]espite its reconstructive aims, the existing components of US critical theory do not overcome a nihilistic attitude to law as a means of changing society.'[15] This is contrasted with what the writer calls the European critical theory of law which 'seeks to transcend nihilism by encouraging a greater degree of participation in the processes by which legal and other decision-making is carried on'.[16]

Many adherents of both Critical Race Theory (see 14.5) and feminist legal theory (see 14.1) share an unease with CLS. According to Duxbury, they have in common

---

[14]  Ibid, xxxvii.
[15]  'From Criticism to Construction in Modern Critical Legal Theory' (1992) 12 *Oxford Journal of Legal Studies* 508, 542.                                                                          [16]  Ibid.

a similar sense of disquiet regarding the purpose of critical legal studies. While critical legal scholars have attacked the quest for consensus which has dominated post-realist American jurisprudence, their transformative agenda, feminists and critical race theorists argue, betrays their faith in the possibility of a society founded on some sort of alternative consensus. Yet this new society, with its alternative consensus, would not necessarily fare any better than does liberal legalism in accommodating the experiences, values and concerns of women and minority groups. Taken together, feminist jurisprudence and critical race theory may be read as a call for an end to the quest for consensus.[17]

As he explains, CLS, on the one hand, and CRT and feminism, on the other, evince an important difference. CLS is founded on the idea that it is possible to formulate an alternative composition of political and legal arrangements that would attract general support. CRT and feminist theory, however, question the very notion of consensus, and contend that the law ought to be based not on the possibility of consensus but on the reality of difference. Though they endorse CLS's transformative agenda, it does not, they argue, incorporate or express their distinctive experience.[18] Thus Patricia Williams claims:

> [W]hile the goals of CLS and of the direct victims of racism may be much the same, what is too often missing is acknowledgment that our experiences of the same circumstances may be very different; that the same symbol may mean different things to each of us.[19]

There is no question, however, that CLS has played a major role in revealing the yawning gap between rhetoric and reality. This continues to drive many of the debates in critical legal theory in general. This is no mean achievement. In the words of Robert Gordon:

> On the scene, one confronts issues of race and gender and class inequality, of democratic procedure, of relations with clients and the communities they affect, that can be the subject of small initiatives involving small risks. And that is finally what may be the most infuriating and subversive message of the Crits—not at all their supposed 'nihilism', but their insistence, to those who have come to equate maturity and realism with a cynical resignation, that there are grounds for hope.[20]

The radically programmatic, often Utopian, vision of CLS moves much of its writing beyond the more practical, reformist concerns of the American realist movement. The transformative possibilities of law often seem to be undercut by the destructive, even nihilistic, tendencies that characterize some of the more dogmatic adherents of CLS. Neil MacCormick captures this unease:

> It is certainly good advice to scholars and practitioners that they should always be ready to turn any question upside down and to see whether underplayed principles cannot be played up to create a seriously arguable counter to the view which one has initially entertained. The danger of mere dogmatism in legal dogmatics comes from a failure to take seriously the possibility that another view might be argued just as well as one's own initial one and insightful

---

[17] Duxbury, *Patterns of American Jurisprudence*, 509.          [18] Ibid.
[19] Patricia J Williams, *The Alchemy of Race and Rights* (Cambridge, Mass: Harvard University Press, 1991), 149.                                  [20] 'Law and Ideology' (1988) 3(1) *Tikkun* 14.

CLS writings at the level of concrete doctrine rather than general programmatics demonstrate this.[21]

Moreover, as MacCormick contends (no tongue in cheek), that for all its radicalism, several CLS claims about law's indeterminacy and the role of ideology may be found in the work of one of its principal demons, Hans Kelsen! (See the last chapter of *Pure Theory of Law*.)

## 13.2 Postmodern legal theory

Postmodernism, originally a movement in art, came late to legal theory where it continues to exert considerable influence. It is a very broad church that both inspires and accommodates theorists of many kinds and disciplines: language, literature, psychology, history, linguistics, art, and so on. Now law.

Some writers in this genre seem eager to impress readers with the self-conscious sweep of their erudition. Reading their work is often heavy going. The effort to comprehend may produce less pleasure than pain. But help is at hand. A number of collections, such as *Postmodern Jurisprudence* by Douzinas and Warrington, shed considerable light on the darker reaches of this often tenebrific subject.[22] The symposium 'Postmodernism and Law'[23] is also a useful seam which I have worked in some of what follows. There are also some stimulating, if challenging, essays in Douzinas, Goodrich, and Hachamovitch, *Politics, Postmodernity and Critical Legal Studies*.[24]

### 13.2.1 What is it?

In his influential book, *The Postmodern Condition: A Report on Knowledge*, Jean-François Lyotard (one of the movement's most important standard-bearers) declares: 'I define *postmodern* as incredulity toward meta-narratives'.[25] Sweeping concepts, universal values, 'master narratives' are regarded by postmodernists, iconoclastically, as redundant, if not meaningless. The great historical epochs, developments, and ideas (especially those associated with the Enlightenment (and the Enlightenment itself)) are treated with deep suspicion. The conventional assumption that human 'progress' is 'evolving' toward 'civilization' or some other end is repudiated in postmodern

---

[21] 'Reconstruction after Deconstruction: Closing in on Critique' in A Norrie (ed), *Closure or Critique: New Directions in Legal Theory* (Edinburgh: Edinburgh University Press, 1993).

[22] C Douzinas and R Warrington (with S McVeigh), *Postmodern Jurisprudence: The Law of the Text in the Texts of the Law* (London: Routledge, 1991).

[23] (1991) 62 *University of Colorado Law Review* 439.

[24] C Douzinas, P Goodrich, and Y Hachamovitch, *Politics, Postmodernity and Critical Legal Studies* (London: Routledge, 1994). See too the helpful reader, D Patterson (ed), *Postmodernism and Law* (Aldershot: Dartmouth, 1994).

[25] Jean-François Lyotard, *The Postmodern Condition: A Report on Knowledge* (Manchester: Manchester University Press, 1984), xxxiv.

thinking. Interpretation and understanding is to be sought in the experience of individuals:

> [I]nstead of fixing the a priori priority of a historical subject, as orthodox Marxism did, or instead of sweeping the question of the subject under the carpet of social knowledge, as both structuralists and post-structuralists have done, the task ahead consists of analysing, in concrete terms, our historical trajectories as subjects both at the biographical and the macrolevel. Modern men and women are configurations or networks of different subjectivities...contemporary capitalist societies consist of four structural places to which four structural subjectivities correspond: the subjectivity of the family corresponds to the *householdplace*; the subjectivity of the class corresponds to the *workplace*; the subjectivity of the individual corresponds to the *citizenplace*; the subjectivity of the nation corresponds to the *worldplace*.[26]

In its onslaught on the Enlightenment, much postmodernist thought rejects the Kantian preoccupation with individual rights, equality, and justice that are among the hallmarks of modernism.[27] Nor is the espousal of these values embraced only by those who champion the idea of natural rights (see 2.3), for they pervade the majority of post-Enlightenment legal theory, including positivism (see Chapters 3 and 4). The assault on rationalism was already part of the empirical tradition of British philosophers such as Locke and Hume (see 2.3.2 and 2.4), but it is only with the recent development of postmodernist legal philosophy (and its continental European flavour) that the intensity campaign has been evident. Drawing on elements of 'cultural theory', and the writings of Foucault, Derrida, Lacan, and other, principally French and German theorists, the development may also be seen as an attempt to invalidate, or at least to contest, the methods, assumptions, and ideas of the analytical, Anglo-American philosophical tradition.

A leading postmodernist political theorist, Chantal Mouffe, also stresses the anti-essentialist, anti-foundationalist rejection of 'metanarratives' and the crisis of confidence in reason:

> [W]hat one means when one refers to postmodernity in philosophy is to recognise the impossibility of any ultimate foundation or final legitimation that is constitutive of the very advent of the democratic form of society and thus of modernity itself. This recognition comes after the failure of several attempts to replace the traditional foundation that lay within God or nature with an alternative foundation lying in man and his reason. These attempts were doomed to failure from the start because of the radical indeterminacy that is characteristic of modern democracy. Nietzsche had already understood this when he proclaimed that the death of God was inseparable from the crisis of humanism.[28]

---

[26] Boaventura de Sousa Santos, 'The Postmodern Transition: Law and Politics' in A Sarat and TR Kearns (eds), *The Fate of Law* (Ann Arbor, Mich: University of Michigan Press, 1991) and in *Lloyd's Introduction to Jurisprudence*, 1465–73, 1308–16.

[27] For a lucid and incisive analysis of Kant's central ideas, see Anne Barron, '(Legal) Reason and its "Others": Recent Developments in Legal Theory' in Penner, Schiff, and Nobles, *Introduction to Jurisprudence and Legal Theory: Commentary and Materials*, 1038–63.

[28] C Mouffe, 'Radical Democracy: Modern or Postmodern' in A Ross (ed), *Universal Abandon? The Politics of Postmodernism* (Minneapolis, Minn: University of Minnesota Press, 1988), 34, quoted by Richard M Thomas, 'Milton and Mass Culture: Toward a Postmodernist Theory of Tolerance' (1991) 62 *University of Colorado Law Review* 525, 527–8.

Thus, postmodernist accounts of society (and the role of law within it) reveal a disenchantment with formalism, essentialism, statism, Utopianism, and even democracy. But they question a great deal more. Critical theory, aesthetic or ethical, seeks to subvert 'foundational' ideas of truth 'whether founded in transcendental conceptions of truth or in an acceptance of the self's unchallenged place at the centre of any analysis'.[29] This attack proceeds from a variety of standpoints and employs several methods. The breadth of this formidable scholarship extends well beyond the boundaries of any course in jurisprudence or legal theory, and includes works by Michel Foucault, Jacques Derrida, Jacques Lacan, Jürgen Habermas, Richard Rorty, Charles Taylor, Michael Walzer, and Alasdair MacIntyre, to name but a few. Anne Barron expresses well the ambitions of cultural theory, acknowledging that its numerous questions transcend the idiom of conventional jurisprudence:

> How does law make sense of the world as it orders and regulates 'reality'? How does law establish the truth of its world picture, or bolster the truth claims of the other knowledges that it admits to itself? What 'fantasies' underpin these narratives? What other representations of reality, and other normative orders, are excluded or denied in this process? How do these excluded meanings and values 'return' to de-stabilise the legal text, or the other social 'texts' (i.e. discursive formations) that law helps to write?[30]

### 13.2.2 The death of the subject

Postmodernists claim that both the subject and object are fantasies. The postmodern preoccupation with the 'subject' generates, especially in the context of the law, some interesting analyses of the individual as moral agent, as rights-bearer, or simply as player in the legal system.[31] Several accounts are explicitly psychological or linguistic, with the structural psychoanalytical theories of Lacan and the poststructuralist ideas of Derrida exerting considerable influence. These are merely touched on below.

### 13.2.3 Jacques Lacan

Lacan is generally regarded as the architect of postmodern psychoanalytic semiotics. Drawing on the work, in particular, of Freud, Saussure, and Levi-Strauss, he claims that the unconscious is structured like a language; it is therefore essential to identify the inner workings of that discourse that takes place within the unconscious. The unconscious is the repository of knowledge, power, agency, and desire. He argues that we do not control what we say; rather the structure of language is pre-determined by thought and desire. Lacan employs a psychoanalytical, Freudian conception of the divided human subject (ego, superego, and the unconscious) to demonstrate that the

---

[29] D Tallack (ed), *Critical Theory: A Reader* (Hemel Hempstead: Harvester Wheatsheaf, 1995), 358.
[30] Barron, op cit, 1070–1.
[31] See James Boyle, 'Is Subjectivity Possible? The Postmodern Subject in Legal Theory' (1991) 62 *University of Colorado Law Review* 489.

'I' expressed by language (which he calls the 'subject of the statement') can never represent an individual's 'true' identity (which he calls the 'subject of enunciation'). This disjunction between identity and its representation occurs in the first eighteen months of our lives, and is forever lost. We create a semblance of individual and social stability only by fantasy—which cannot be maintained.[32]

The subject is thus, he argues, divided or decentred. The language of the unconscious is, he contends, the arbiter of all experience, knowing, and living.

### 13.2.4 Jacques Derrida

Jacques Derrida[33] expounds the idea of 'deconstruction' to explain the operation of '*différance*'. This neologism describes the state of interdependence and difference between the hierarchical oppositions. '*Difference*' is based on the French word '*differer*', which means both to differ and to defer. He replaces an 'e' with the 'a' in '*différance*'. The words are indistinguishable in spoken French.

Adopting the Swiss linguist, Ferdinand de Saussure's semiotics, Derrida distinguishes between 'signifiers' and 'signified'. Saussure distinguished between '*langue*', the deep structure of linguistic rules, and '*parole*', the set of speech acts made by members of a linguistic community. The former is, in the understanding of language, the more important element because it is the system of relations among various signs that constitutes a language. So, for example, the word 'dog' does not correspond to the creature we know and love. But we understand it by virtue of its difference from similar sounds such as 'bog', 'cog', or 'fog'. This leads him to postulate that, since the meaning of 'dog' emerges from this combat of differences between signifiers, its meaning, like the meaning of all signifiers, is infinitely deferred. For Saussure, linguistic structures are the cause, not the effect, of subjectivity and identity. Thus, Derrida concludes, stability can be achieved only by 'deconstructing' language in order to show how the meaning of one signifier includes within it another signifier (the 'other').

Deconstruction entails the identification of hierarchical opposition, followed by a temporary reversal of the hierarchy. Derrida gives the following example: if the history of Western civilization has been characterized by a prejudice in favour of speech over writing, we should consider what it might be like if writing were more important than speech. We try to regard speech as a kind of writing, as ultimately parasitic upon writing, rather than the other way around. In so doing, we have reversed the privileged position of speech over writing, and temporarily substituted a new priority. But this new priority is merely temporary, because it may in turn be reversed using the same technique. The purpose is not to create a new conceptual basis, but, in pursuit of fresh

---

[32] J Lacan, *The Four Fundamental Concepts of Psychoanalysis*, transl A Sheridan (London: Penguin, 1979).

[33] See J Derrida, 'The Force of Law: The "Mystical Foundation of Authority"' (1990) 11 *Cardozo Law Review* 919. Derrida questions whether deconstruction allows any just action, or indeed any discourse on the subject of justice at all. Is it, he asks, a threat to law and to the very prospect of justice; can it offer explicit criteria by which we can distinguish between law and justice? His enigmatic conclusion is that 'deconstruction is justice'.

understanding, to test what happens when the 'common sense' position is turned on its head. These hierarchies of thought are, Derrida argues, ubiquitous. One simple form is: A is the rule and B is the exception. Reversing this hierarchy—by deconstruction—may demonstrate that, in fact, the opposite is true: B is the rule and A is the exception. At any rate, the process of deconstruction reveals elements of both A and B that might otherwise have gone unnoticed.

Derrida's task is the ambitious one of exposing the 'metaphysics of presence' in Western philosophy. By this he means that in every set of oppositions one kind of 'presence' is privileged over a corresponding kind of 'absence'. Western philosophy, he argues, is based on the hidden premise that what is most apparent to our consciousness—what is obvious or immediate—is most real, foundational, or important.

In other words, if language is a system of relational differences lacking a core, then meaning is not immediately apparent in any single sign because,

> [T]he play of differences involves synthesis and referrals that prevent there from being at any moment or in any way a simple element that is present in and of itself and refers only to itself…Nothing…in the system is anywhere simply present or absent. There are only, everywhere, differences and traces of traces.[34]

Derrida's unsettling conclusion is that since language emerges from this unstable system of differences, it will always be indeterminate. The prospect of the subject of identity—and hence of an individual right-holder—is therefore weak.

### 13.2.5 **Foucault and Habermas**

The extensive and complex social theories of Michel Foucault and Jürgen Habermas are more appropriately considered in the context of law and social theory, and were therefore canvassed in 7.7 and 7.8.

While the postmodern subject is sometimes described as dead, it is perhaps more accurate to describe him or her as moribund: 'dispersed, decentered network of libidinal attachments, emptied of ethical substance and psychical inferiority, the ephemeral function of this or that act of consumption, media experience, sexual relationship, trend or fashion'.[35] It has been suggested by James Boyle,[36] following Foucault, that contemporary political and legal argument 'can best be understood as a debate over the essential characteristics of the subjects whose actions those arguments describe and prescribe':

> The subjects of our economic theories and the legal subjects of corporate law, the subjects behind [Rawls's] veil of ignorance and the subjects of civil society all mingle uneasily, finding

---

[34] Jacques Derrida, *Positions*, transl Alan Bass (London: Athlone Press, 1981), 10–12, quoted by William MacNeil, 'Righting and Difference' in Raymond Wacks (ed), *Human Rights in Hong Kong* (Hong Kong: Hong Kong University Press, 1992), 117–18.

[35] Terry Eagleton, 'Capitalism, Modernism and Postmodernism' (1985) 152 *New Left Review* 71.

[36] 'Is Subjectivity Possible? The Postmodern Subject in Legal Theory' (1991) 62 *University of Colorado Law Review* 489.

little in common, like guests at a bad cocktail party. If postmodernism has anything to offer here, it is by giving us another stylistic prejudice, which might offer a new arrangement of our material…a riotously clashing collage of subjects…Bizarre as it may seem, the way we handle the legal subject could offer us a vision of postmodern practice—a practice that could simultaneously use and transform its raw material.[37]

JM Balkin[38] attempts to uncover the true nature of the legal subject. He argues that it is neglected or even effaced by conventional legal theory. The argument appears to be that when we as individuals attempt to understand the law, its content, nature, and objectives, we bring our subjective experience to bear on what we encounter. And this fundamental process is allegedly missing from accounts of the law offered by Hart, Dworkin, and other mainstream jurists. Do you agree? It would make an interesting essay or examination question.

### 13.2.6 **The postmodern agenda**

Postmodernist legal thought has an important political object. Impatience with the modern state's bureaucratic suffocation of the individual, the overarching presence of government, the increasing globalization of markets, and universalizing of values, has provoked a need to redefine and nurture the individual. It has also (perhaps inevitably) witnessed a new pragmatism:

Pragmatism attracts postmodernists for several reasons. It rejects foundationalism: knowledge is radically contingent; the test of knowledge is efficacy; thinking is instrumental, functional, problem-solving. Secondly, in its contemporary reinterpretation at least, pragmatism is progressive, emancipatory and democratic. Pragmatists are concerned with the relationship of knowledge and power and the ways in which discourse, whether in science, politics or ethics, is linked to structures of domination.[39]

A down-to-earth set of goals (economic, ecological, political) is accompanied by the advocacy of a more inclusive community that emphasizes the special predicament of women, minorities, the dispossessed, and the poor. A popular expression (to be found also among CLS and feminist theorists) is 'empowerment'. But the radical postmodern political agenda is a complex one which may generate confusion or what has been called a 'multiplication of ideologies'.

### 13.2.7 **Language**

Much of what we do is transacted through words, written and spoken. These 'signs' are an essential feature of social intercourse and their meaning and interpretation are inseparable from our understanding of the world. The subject of semiotics is devoted

---

[37] *Critical Legal Studies*, 524.
[38] 'Understanding Legal Understanding: The Legal Subject and the Problem of Legal Coherence' (1993) 103 *Yale Law Journal* 105. See too Jennifer Wicke, 'Postmodern Identity and the Legal Subject' (1992) 62 *University of Colorado Law Review* 455.           [39] *Lloyd's Introduction to Jurisprudence*, 1415.

to the study of the uses of language and, in particular, its ideological content and consequences. Umberto Eco has said (somewhere) that 'semiotics is, in principle, the discipline studying everything which can be used in order to lie'.

The inspiration for modern semiotics is the work of Ferdinand de Saussure whose model of language, developed in the early part of the last century, was used by a number of structuralists (especially Roland Barthes) in the 1960s to 'decode' restaurant menus, advertisements, fashion, and several other linguistic expressions of the modern age. The following famous extract from Saussure's work launched a thousand structuralists. It will, I think, help you to grasp the essentials of this strand in critical theory:

> [I]n language there are only differences. Even more important: a difference generally implies positive terms between which the difference is set up; but in language there are only differences *without positive terms*. Whether we take the signified or the signifier, language has neither ideas nor sounds that existed before the linguistic system, but only conceptual and phonic differences that have issued from the system. The idea or phonic substance that a sign contains is of less importance than the other signs that surround it.[40]

Language, according to Saussure, creates the subject (me, you), not the other way around. The possibilities of this fascinating insight have been explored in a variety of ways by several theorists (Barthes, Derrida, Paul de Man, Foucault, Julia Kristeva).

The law is, of course, expressed by and through language. And legal semiotics has much to offer legal theory in its pursuit not only of the interpretation of text, but also in understanding some of the central questions of jurisprudence, as a leading scholar in the field, Bernard Jackson, persuasively argues.[41] Should your teacher be bold enough to venture down this interesting jurisprudential path, you will almost certainly be referred to Jackson's work as well as that of another distinguished British semiotician, Peter Goodrich, especially his books, *Reading the Law: A Critical Introduction to Legal Method and Techniques*,[42] and *Languages of Law*.[43]

Semiotic analysis proceeds beyond mere interpretation of the law's words and symbols and their meaning. It attempts to uncover ('demystify'), the political, psychological, and social functions of legal language. The nature of legal discourse, in other words, may, in many instances, turn out to be little different from political or moral debate. An important distinction, of course, is that, like Alice in Wonderland, courts or legislatures decide what a word or phrase shall mean. Jackson makes several ambitious claims for the rapidly developing discipline of legal semiotics, including its ability to clarify problems concerning legal validity, truth, the debate between normativism and realism, the concept of the unity of a legal system, the sociology of law,

---

[40] Ferdinand de Saussure, *Course in General Linguistics*, transl W Baskin, C Bally, and A Sechehaye with A Reidlinger (New York: McGraw Hill, 1966).

[41] Bernard Jackson, 'On Scholarly Developments in Legal Semiotics' (1990) 3 *Ratio Juris* 415. See too his book *Semiotics and Legal Theory* (Liverpool: Deborah Charles, 1985).

[42] (Oxford: Basil Blackwell, 1986).    [43] (London: Weidenfeld & Nicolson, 1990).

and the 'sensitive' reading of legal texts. The last-mentioned activity is perceptively pursued by Peter Goodrich in his *Reading the Law*.

### 13.2.8 Critical theory and individual rights

Critical scholarship is generally hostile to the concept of individual rights. It tends to take rights sceptically. A wholesale assault on the concept of rights is an important feature of all three accounts of society that we have considered in this chapter. The lowest common denominator resides in a deconstructive critique of both the indeterminacy of rights and their tendency to shore up prevailing social and political hierarchies.[44]

Adherents of CLS regard rights as one of the features of liberalism which appear to be objective, neutral, and protective of freedom, whereas, in reality, rights perpetuate the individualism that is actually destructive of true freedom. This rights-scepticism engenders either an outright rejection of the concept of rights or the formulation of an alternative vision of rights that extends beyond the communitarian to what the Brazilian social theorist, Roberto Unger, champions as an element in a programme of 'empowered democracy'.[45]

Much feminist legal theory shuns rights as formal, hierarchical, and patriarchal. Law in general, and rights in particular, reflect a male viewpoint (see 14.3). The postmodern assault on rights lies primarily in its hostility towards the possibility of an autonomous, rational individuated subject. This controlling idea of rights discourse in the liberal tradition is 'trashed' by poststructuralists, and looks instead to 'what is negated and denied in the process of its construction: a poststructuralist critique of the totalising narratives of liberal political and legal thought would therefore expose how the latter tend to constitute the domain in which the subject may express itself politically in such a way as to effect a closure around the realm of the political itself'.[46] In other words, the rights-bearing subject has been bled both of meaning and authentic existence. The structural, psychological, and linguistic patterns of this offensive constitute, through the analysis of social theorists like Michel Foucault, Louis Althusser, and Jacques Lacan, a serious threat to the idea of the universal subject. The poststructuralist onslaught of, in particular, Jacques Derrida, denies the very idea of the subject having an 'essence', and hence the impossibility (indeed, meaninglessness) of rights discourse.

---

[44] There is, as we saw in Chapter 10, little support among postmodernist writers for animal rights, although some, notably Derrida, denounce the cruelty and violence inflicted on animals, see Jacques Derrida, *The Animal That Therefore I Am*, transl D Wills, M-L Mallet, ed (New York: Fordham University Press, 2008, 88 ff; Gary Steiner, *Animals and the Limits of Postmodernism* (New York: Columbia University Press, 2013).

[45] Rejecting traditional concepts of rights (see Chapter 10), Unger advances four 'super-liberal rights': 'market rights', 'immunity rights', destabilization rights', and 'solidarity rights' which are supposed to create a society in which individuals are more likely to attain self-fulfilment. See Hugh Collins, 'Roberto Unger and the Critical Legal Studies Movement' (1987) *Law and Society* 387.

[46] A Barron, 'The Illusion of the "I": Citizenship and the Politics of Identity' in Norrie (ed), *Closure or Critique: New Directions in Legal Theory*; see 21.

## 13.2.9 **Critique**

[P]ostmodernists just want to have fun. Postmodernist strategies and styles are often playful, jokey, and ironical…Intellectual and artistic life can be boring, pretentious, and ponderous. Postmodernists help us to lighten up.[47]

Levity is not to be dismissed, but you may wonder whether postmodernists achieve this ideal.

The expansiveness of postmodernism makes it hard to criticize. Certainly, there are those who at least call themselves (or are described by others as) postmodernists whose writing may be condemned for its apocalyptic or Utopian drift. Also some indulge in the very generalities they are supposed to reject: 'equality', 'democracy', 'empowerment', and so on. These are sitting ducks. The more than occasional collapse into subjectivity should be watched. Also the friendly tolerance of virtually any argument in the name of postmodernism (with proper credentials and citations) is a disquieting feature of an 'anything goes' philosophy that sometimes wallows in self-contradiction and even nihilism.[48] More frustrating is the tendency to co-opt the opposition. As a result:

According to postmodernism, because of the 'instability of meaning', the 'surplus of meaning', the 'deferral of the subject', or the 'failure of a metaphysics of presence', there is no distinction between reading or misreading a text…Other distinctions, such as those between logic and rhetoric, and between argument and entertainment are denied or dissolved as well.[49]

Is this fair? If so, the project may amount to an intellectual dead-end which—to mix metaphors—paralyses rather than promotes analysis, let alone serious normative enquiry. If the truth is always contingent, contextual, and shifting, how are we to decide how to live, what is right or wrong? The death of the subject seems also to undermine the political project that much postmodern thought seeks to advance. If my identity as a person is so unstable or if I am merely the site of conflicting ideas and images, then how can I be held responsible for my actions?

Postmodernism is not a homogeneous movement. Nor, as with any 'school', is the quality or writing evenly distributed. The best of postmodernist legal theory is, as you will discover, highly sophisticated, provocative, unsettling. Its catholic sweep— literature, psychology, semiotics—generates flashes of genuine insight which illuminate with their novelty and perception. Many of the arguments, though their shape and object are necessarily different, have already been contested in other arenas, most conspicuously art and literature. We should not lament this; postmodernist literary theory is rich in ideas and intelligence. Law and legal practice are always in need of scrupulous deconstruction. But be wary of imitation and spectacle.

---

[47] D Jamieson, 'The Poverty of Postmodernist Theory' (1991) 62 *University of Colorado Law Review* 577, 579.
[48] Nihilism is not, however, an entirely negative philosophy. You will find a good summary of its chief claims by Peter Goodrich in *Reading the Law*, 210–17.          [49] Jamieson, 582–3.

# Questions

1. What is 'critical' about CLS? Is it not merely raising similar questions to those asked by the American realists?

2. What are 'hegemonic consciousness', 'reification', and 'denial'?

3. Unger identifies four important principles: indeterminacy, antiformalism, contradiction, and marginality. What are they, and how do they help to explain the way in which law and the legal system operate?

4. 'Although a lot of superficial and amateurish work was done under the banner of CLS, that hardly distinguishes it from many other trendy movements that legal academia absorbed more peacefully (e.g. "policy science", postmodernism, pragmatism, Critical Race Theory, "feminist jurisprudence" and the like). It was the anti-capitalist policies of much of CLS that set it apart.' (Brian Leiter, *Naturalizing Jurisprudence: Essays on American Realism and Naturalism in Legal Philosophy* (Oxford: Oxford University Press, 2007), 99)

   Examine the validity of this claim.

5. 'Law is politics' is a central theme of CLS adherents. What does it mean? How might it be applied to your law and legal system?

6. 'The project of CLS is to demystify the legal ideas which obscure the contradictions of liberal capitalist society...CLS gives legal doctrine (and presumably the normative legal theory which helps to rationalise it) the backhanded compliment of asserting its great social importance—an importance which makes a concerted attack on its pretensions all the more necessary.' (Roger Cotterrell, *The Politics of Jurisprudence: A Critical Introduction to Legal Philosophy*, 2nd edn (London: Butterworths, 1992) (1989), 211)

   Investigate this view, examining the contributions and limitations of the Critical Legal Studies movement.

7. Postmodernism is defined by Lyotard as 'incredulity toward metanarratives'. Can we describe life satisfactorily without universal values expressed in sweeping terms: democracy, freedom, the rule of law, and so on?

8. Lacan, Derrida, and Foucault are among leading postmodernist thinkers who speak of the death of the subject. Does the 'orthodox' legal theory you have studied neglect or even destroy the legal subject?

9. 'Every time that something comes to pass or turns out well, every time that we placidly apply a good rule to a particular case, to a correctly subsumed example, according to a determinant judgment, we can be sure that law (droit) may find itself accounted for, but certainly not justice. Law (droit) is not justice. Law is the element of calculation, and it is just that there be law, but justice is incalculable, it requires us to calculate with the incalculable; and aporetic experiences are the experiences, as improbable as they are necessary, of justice, that is to say of moments in which

the decision between just and unjust is never insured by a rule.' (Jacques Lacan, 'The Force of Law: The "Mystical Foundation of Authority"' in D Cornell, M Rosenfeld, and DG Carlson (eds), *Deconstruction and the Possibility of Justice* (New York: Routledge, 1992), 16)

Why does Derrida believe that 'law is not justice'? (Note that an 'aporia' is a philosophical conundrum or an apparently unfathomable stalemate. It may also signify the state of being confused by such a problem or impasse.)

10.   What relevance does postmodern legal theory have for lawyers and judges?

# Further reading

BALKIN, JM, 'Understanding Legal Understanding: The Legal Subject and the Problem of Legal Coherence' (1993) 103 *Yale Law Journal* 105.

BARRON, ANNE, 'The Illusion of the "I": Citizenship and the Politics of Identity' in A Norrie (ed), *Closure or Critique: New Directions in Legal Theory* (Edinburgh: Edinburgh University Press, 1993).

BARRON, ANNE, '(Legal) Reason and its "Others": Recent Developments in Legal Theory' in J Penner, D Schiff, and R Nobles (eds), *Introduction to Jurisprudence and Legal Theory: Commentary and Materials* (London: Butterworths, 2002), 1038–63.

BOYLE, JAMES, 'Is Subjectivity Possible? The Postmodern Subject in Legal Theory' (1991) 62 *University of Colorado Law Review* 489.

BOYLE, JAMES (ed), *Critical Legal Studies* (Aldershot: Dartmouth, 1992).

DAVIES, MARGARET, *Asking the Law Question*, 3rd edn (Sydney: The Law Book Company, 2008), Chapter 5.

DE SOUSA SANTOS, BOAVENTURA, 'The Postmodern Transition: Law and Politics' in A Sarat and TR Kearns (eds), *The Fate of Law* (Ann Arbor, Mich: University of Michigan Press, 1991).

DERRIDA, J, 'The Force of Law: The "Mystical Foundation of Authority"' (1990) 11 *Cardozo Law Review* 919.

DONALDSON, M, 'Some Reservations About Law and Postmodernism' (1995) 40 *American Journal of Jurisprudence* 335.

DOUZINAS, COSTAS, *The End of Human Rights* (Oxford: Hart Publishing, 2000).

DOUZINAS, COSTAS and WARRINGTON, R (with McVeigh, S), *Postmodern Jurisprudence: The Law of the Text in the Texts of the Law* (London: Routledge, 1991).

DOUZINAS, COSTAS, GOODRICH, PETER, and HACHAMOVITCH, YIFAT, *Politics, Postmodernity and Critical Legal Studies* (London: Routledge, 1994).

DUXBURY, NEIL, *Patterns of American Jurisprudence* (Oxford: Clarendon Press, 1997).

EAGLETON, TERRY, 'Capitalism, Modernism and Postmodernism' (1985) 152 *New Left Review* 71.

EWALD, F, 'Unger's Philosophy: A Critical Legal Study' (1988) 5 *Yale Law Journal* 665.

FISH, STANLEY, *There's No Such Thing as Free Speech* (New York: Oxford University Press, 1994).

FITZPATRICK, P (ed), *Dangerous Supplements: Resistance and Renewal in Jurisprudence* (London: Pluto Press, 1991).

FITZPATRICK, P and HUNT, A (eds), *Critical Legal Studies* (Oxford: Basil Blackwell, 1987).

FOUCAULT, MICHEL, *The Order of Things: An Archaeology of Human Sciences* (New York: Pantheon, 1973).

FULLER, S, 'Playing Without a Full Deck: Scientific Realism and the Cognitive Limits of Legal Theory' (1988) 97 *Yale Law Journal* 549.

GOODRICH, PETER, *Reading the Law: A Critical Introduction to Legal Method and Techniques* (Oxford: Basil Blackwell, 1986).

GOODRICH, PETER, *Languages of Law* (London: Weidenfeld & Nicolson, 1990).

HIRST, PAUL, *On Law and Ideology* (London: Macmillan, 1979).

HUNT, ALAN, 'The Theory of Critical Legal Studies' (1986) 6 *Oxford Journal of Legal Studies* 1.

HUTCHINSON, ALAN, *Dwelling On The Threshold* (Toronto: Carswell, 1988).

HUTCHINSON, ALAN, *Critical Legal Studies* (New York: Rowman & Littlefield, 1989).

JABBARI, DAVID, 'From Criticism to Construction in Modern Critical Legal Theory' (1992) 12 *Oxford Journal of Legal Studies* 508, 542.

JACKSON, BERNARD, 'On Scholarly Developments in Legal Semiotics' (1990) 3 *Ratio Juris* 415.

JAMIESON, D, 'The Poverty of Postmodernist Theory' (1991) 62 *University of Colorado Law Review* 577, 579.

KAIRYS, DAVID (ed), *The Politics of Law: A Progressive Critique* (New York: Pantheon Books, 1982).

KELMAN, MARK, *A Guide to Critical Legal Studies* (Cambridge, Mass: Harvard University Press, 1987).

KENNEDY, DUNCAN, 'Law and Ideology' (1988) 3(1) *Tikkun* 14.

KENNEDY, DUNCAN, 'Legal Education as Training for Hierarchy' (from David Kairys (ed), *The Politics of Law*, see above, and extracted in *Lloyd's Introduction to Jurisprudence*, 8th edn (London: Sweet & Maxwell, 2008), 1267–71.

KENNEDY, DUNCAN and GABEL, PETER, 'Roll over Beethoven' (1984) 36 *Stanford Law Review* 1.

LACAN, J, *The Four Fundamental Concepts of Psychoanalysis*, transl A Sheridan (London: Penguin, 1979).

LYOTARD, JEAN-FRANÇOIS, *The Postmodern Condition: A Report on Knowledge* (Manchester: Manchester University Press, 1984).

MACINTYRE, ALASDAIR, *After Virtue: A Study in Moral Theory* (London: Duckworth, 1982).

MACNEIL, WILLIAM, P, 'Righting and Difference' in Raymond Wacks (ed), *Human Rights in Hong Kong* (Hong Kong: Oxford University Press, 1992), 117–18.

MACNEIL, WILLIAM, P, *Lex Populi: The Jurisprudence of Popular Culture* (Stanford, Calif: Stanford University Press, 2007).

MOUFFE, C, 'Radical Democracy: Modern or Postmodern' in A Ross (ed), *Universal Abandon? The Politics of Postmodernism* (Minneapolis, Minn: University of Minnesota Press, 1988).

NORRIE, ALAN (ed), *Closure or Critique: New Directions in Legal Theory* (Edinburgh: Edinburgh University Press, 1993).

PATTERSON, DENNIS (ed), *Postmodernism and Law* (Aldershot: Dartmouth, 1994).

RORTY, RICHARD, *Philosophy and the Mirror of Nature* (Oxford: Basil Blackwell, 1990).

SINGER, W, 'The Player and the Cards: Nihilism and Legal Theory' (1984) 94 *Yale Law Journal* 1.

STICK, J, 'Can Nihilism be Pragmatic?' (1986) 100 *Harvard Law Review* 332.

TALLACK, DOUGLAS (ed), *Critical Theory: A Reader* (Hemel Hempstead: Harvester Wheatsheaf, 1995).

THOMAS, RICHARD M, 'Milton and Mass Culture: Toward a Postmodernist Theory of Tolerance' (1991) 62 *University of Colorado Law Review* 525, 527–8.

UNGER, ROBERTO, *Knowledge and Politics* (New York: Free Press, 1975).

UNGER, ROBERTO, *Law in Modern Society: Toward a Criticism of Social Theory* (London: Collier–Macmillan, 1977).

UNGER, ROBERTO, 'The Critical Legal Studies Movement' (1983) 96 *Harvard Law Review* 561.

UNGER, ROBERTO, *False Necessity: Anti-Necessitarian Social Theory in the Service of Radical Democracy* (Cambridge: Cambridge University Press, 1987).

WACKS, RAYMOND, *Personal Information: Privacy and the Law* (Oxford: Clarendon Press, 1989).

WACKS, RAYMOND (ed), *Hong Kong, China and 1997: Essays in Legal Theory* (Hong Kong: Hong Kong University Press, 1993).

WACKS, RAYMOND, *Law, Morality, and the Private Domain* (Hong Kong: Hong Kong University Press, 2000).

WALDRON, JEREMY, 'Did Dworkin Ever Answer the Crits?' in Scott Hershovitz (ed), *Exploring Law's Empire: The Jurisprudence of Ronald Dworkin* (Oxford: Oxford University Press, 2006).

WARD, IAN, *An Introduction to Critical Legal Theory* (London: Cavendish, 1998).

# 14

# Feminist and critical race theory

Sexism and racism have long been abhorrent facts of life. White males generally dominate political and legal discourse. This chapter considers two relatively recent challenges to this state of affairs. First, it examines key elements of feminist legal theories; it then outlines the principal claims of critical race theory.

## 14.1 Feminist legal theories

Most conventional legal theory claims to be gender-blind. But, in neglecting or even ignoring the position of women, it condemns them and their experience to oblivion. So, for example, one leading feminist has pointed out that in the liberal theory of Ronald Dworkin (see Chapter 5) 'questions of membership and power are quite simply not on the theoretical agenda'.[1] Such questions might upset Dworkin's notion of law as integrity which turns, as we saw, on the existence of a single 'interpretive community' from which the law draws its shared meaning and legitimacy.

The response of feminist jurisprudence to this silence has been deafening, and this is reflected in the extraordinary impact this branch of legal theory has had, not only on university courses,[2] but on the law itself; the role and function of the law are, not surprisingly, key questions in feminist legal theory. Nor is the analysis confined to the purely academic. Feminist writers examine the inequalities to be found in the criminal law, especially rape and domestic violence,[3] family law,[4] contract,[5] tort, property, and other branches of the

---

[1] Nicola Lacey, 'Community in Legal Theory: Idea, Ideal or Ideology?' in Nicola Lacey (ed), *Unspeakable Subjects: Feminist Essays in Legal and Social Theory* (Oxford: Hart Publishing, 1998), 232.

[2] In a survey of British and Australian institutions published in 1995, almost half of those questioned covered the subject 'in depth'. This compared with zero only ten years before, H Barnett, 'The Province of Jurisprudence Determined—Again!' (1995) 15 *Legal Studies* 88.

[3] See N Lacey, C Wells, and D Meure, *Reconstructing Criminal Law: Critical Perspectives on Crime and the Criminal Process* (London: Weidenfeld & Nicholson, 1990); Ngaire Naffine, 'Possession: Erotic Love in the Law of Rape' (1994) 57 *Modern Law Review* 10.

[4] See Katherine O'Donovan, *Family Law Matters* (London: Pluto Press, 1993).

[5] See Mary Jo Frug, 'Rescuing Impossibility Doctrine: A Postmodern Feminist Analysis of Contract Law' (1992) 140 *University of Pennsylvania Law Review* 1029.

substantive law, including aspects of public law[6] and public international law.[7] The literature is gargantuan.[8]

Feminist writing is often unashamedly polemical. Since its focus is injustice, this is hardly surprising. 'The personal is political' was the powerful slogan adopted by early feminists. It constituted in part a rejection of the ostensible radicalism of social movements that failed to address the routine subjugation of women at home or at work.

Feminists do not speak with a single voice. Why should they? This chapter will attempt to identify the main strands in this luxuriant tapestry, and the achievements of the feminist movement in theory and practice.

Recent advances in so-called 'difference feminism' (see 14.3.4) share a number of elements, concerns, and theoretical approaches with American 'critical race theory' (CRT). In particular, they share uneasiness with the dominance of white men. A brief account of this movement is included in this chapter (see 14.4) in the hope that it may illuminate the transformative goals of both projects. The 'critical' and postmodern turn taken, to a greater or lesser extent by both groups, will be better grasped after reading the previous chapter which surveys these two approaches.

## 14.2 Origins of feminism

Early opposition to the subordination of women, expressed famously in Mary Wollstonecraft's *A Vindication of the Rights of Women* of 1792, was founded on the notion that women were rational and thus able to perform civic duties. She did not, however, maintain that this entitled women to exercise full political rights. Indeed, early feminism did not pursue the right of political equality that came to dominate both the philosophy and the demands of modern feminism in the 1960s. The egalitarian genesis of feminism has, however, been replaced by a broad and complex range of feminisms that are sharply antagonistic and yet intricately bound together in respect of both their ideological approach and political objectives.

---

[6] See Catharine MacKinnon, *Towards a Feminist Theory of the State*, (Cambridge, Mass: Harvard University Press, 1989); Deborah Rhode, 'Feminism and the State' (1994) 107 *Harvard Law Review* 1181.

[7] See, eg, Katherine Franke, 'Gendered Subjects of Transitional Justice' (2006) 15 *Columbia Journal of Gender and Law* 813.

[8] See Francis E Olsen (ed), *Feminist Legal Theory, International Library of Essays in Law and Legal Theory* (Aldershot: Dartmouth, 1994). I recommend also Katharine Bartlett and Roseanne Kennedy (eds), *Feminist Legal Theory: Readings in Law and Gender* (Boulder, Colo: Westview Press, 1991, which contains an invaluable guide to further reading), and Patricia Smith, *Feminist Jurisprudence* (New York: Oxford University Press, 1993). See too Emily Jackson and Nicola Lacey, 'Introducing Feminist Legal Theory' in J Penner, D Schiff, and R Nobles (eds), *Introduction to Jurisprudence and Legal Theory: Commentary and Materials* (London: Butterworths, 2002), 780–853. An allied philosophy is 'queer theory' that developed in the early 1990s out of feminism and gay and lesbian studies. It draws on deconstructionists, especially the writings of Foucault (see 7.7) and Derrida (see 13.2.4). Queer theorists, like feminists, contest the notion that gender is an essential element of the self. It also examines the socially constructed nature of sexual acts and identities. Though gay and lesbian studies explore the idea of 'natural' and 'unnatural' behaviour in regard to homosexuality, queer theory extends its analysis to any type of sexual activity or identity that falls into normative and deviant categories. See generally Martha Albertson Fineman, Jack E Jackson, and Adam P Romero

For example, even the apparently uncomplicated concept of equality has generated a vigorous debate between 'liberal' feminists, who contend that the equality of
women as rational beings entails a single, undifferentiated, gender-neutral conception of citizenship, and other feminists, who regard the claim of human rationality as
neglecting the social and biological differences between the sexes. These differences, it
is argued, reduce women's opportunities to exercise their political and legal rights. In
other words, it does not follow that even acknowledging equal rationality between the
sexes, and hence establishing formal equality, is an effective means of ending women's
subordination. Indeed, some feminists have doubted whether the appeal to rationality is a valid basis on which to base equal treatment. Rationality, it is maintained, is
itself a gendered claim that, rather than embodying a universal truth, merely expresses
an idea of Enlightenment philosophy. The adoption by feminists of this strategy, it is
argued, is tantamount to accepting that a woman has a right to be like a man.

Feminist theory and practice is peppered with a host of similar taxing quandaries.
Indeed, many feminists recognize that the enterprise of a feminist jurisprudence that
seeks to obliterate women's subservience must find an impartial concept of 'woman'
in a society that adopts an oppressive view. Attempts to avoid generalizing what it is
to be a woman often gives rise to the difficulty of 'essentialism'—reducing women to a
universal essence and thereby overlook the particulars of female diversity.

Another aspect of essentialism relates to the practices of some non-Western societies. How should Western feminists react to clitoridectomy or the wearing of veils in
Islamic societies? Does a rejection of these practices rest on Western conceptions of
gender oppression? On the other hand, when these practices are tolerated, are feminists implicitly holding non-Western cultures to a lower standard?

Essentialism also neglects other sources of subjugation, including class, race, sexual
preference, and nationality. Naffine puts this well:

> [A] person's sex may not always be the most fundamental marker of either their oppression
> or advantage. Sometimes race, for example, might assume a greater priority and so a woman
> might feel a greater allegiance with a man of her own race than a woman from another.[9]

The relationship between feminist jurisprudence and critical race theory (considered
in 14.5.1) is in part a recognition, and rejection, of the preoccupation of feminists with
a stereotypical white, middle-class, educated woman.[10]

The dread of essentialism has also generated the expression of highly personal accounts
by women of their experience of subordination. But the fear of essentialism evident in
both these autobiographical narratives and the wider 'retreat from grand theory'[11] have,
in turn, led to a different form of essentialism: that the 'true' female predicament can
be experienced only by, say, working-class, black women. This subjectivist standpoint,

---

(eds), *Feminist and Queer Legal Theory: Intimate Encounters, Uncomfortable Conversations* (Farnham,
Surrey; Burlington, VT: Ashgate, 2009).

[9] Ngaire Naffine, 'In Praise of Legal Feminism' (2002) 22 *Legal Studies* 71, 88. This essay contains a
perspicuous and frank account of the theories, methodology, successes, and failures of legal feminism.

[10] See Drucilla Cornell, 'Convention and Critique' in Drucilla Cornell (ed), *Transformations: Recollective
Imagination and Sexual Difference* (New York: Routledge, 1993).          [11] Naffine, 90.

though it may illuminate the condition of suppressed women, presents another danger: 'It can entail a reluctance to condemn other cultural practices which harm women and consequently generate ethical relativism, rather than ethical vigour.'[12]

You will at once recognize that the question of which particular feminist stance is embraced has important consequences for legal theory and, indeed, the law in general. And in this chapter I attempt to describe the special features that characterize each of these approaches. But this is no simple matter. While there is a degree of dissonance between feminists, the arguments are subtle and elaborate. The division below into four major 'schools' is designed to highlight the richness and intricacy of feminist legal theory. It should not be regarded as a complete or straightforward summary of feminist jurisprudence. It would be foolhardy to suppose that the fairly discrete standpoints may easily be accommodated within the rubric of feminist jurisprudence.

## 14.3  Legal feminisms

At least four major strands of feminist thought may be identified.[13] They are:

- Liberal feminism.
- Radical feminism.
- Postmodern feminism.
- Difference feminism.

### 14.3.1  Liberal feminism

At the heart of liberalism is the importance of individual rights, both civil and political. Liberals insist on an extensive sphere of personal freedom (including freedom of speech, conscience, association, and sexuality) that ought not to be intruded upon by the state, save to protect others from harm. In contemporary legal theory, though liberals such as Ronald Dworkin (see Chapter 5), HLA Hart (see 4.3), and John Rawls (see 9.3) emphasize the significance of liberty, equality, and individual rights, they do so, as we have seen, in different ways, according diverse priorities to at least these elements.

In liberal feminism all persons are regarded as autonomous, rights-bearing agents, and the values of equality, rationality, and autonomy are accentuated. Its central claim is that since women and men are equally rational, they ought to have the same opportunities to exercise rational choices. This focus on equality is, however, stigmatized by

---

[12]  Ibid, 93. It has even been contended that the fear of essentialism may produce an 'utter paralysis of political reflection', Anne Barron, 'Feminism, Aestheticism and the Limits of Law' (2000) 8 *Feminist Legal Studies* 275, 276.

[13]  See M Cain, 'Feminism and the Limits of Equality' (1990) 24 *Georgia Law Review* 803, who concedes that the categories are not airtight. Other feminist points of departure include post-colonial feminist theory, black feminism, lesbian feminism, and world feminism. See J Conaghan, 'Reassessing the Feminist Theoretical Project in Law' (2000) 27 *Journal of Law and Society* 351.

radical feminists (see 14.2.2) as misguided for 'to argue on the basis of women's simi-larity to men merely assimilates women into an unchanged male sphere. In a sense, the result is to make women into men'.[14]

But most liberal feminists, while acknowledging that the legal and political system is patriarchal, resist the wholesale onslaught that is a central, though not a universal, feature of the radical agenda. They prefer to wage war within the existing institu-tional framework of discrimination, especially in the field of employment. This is well expressed by one of the leading liberal feminists, Wendy Williams, who prefers equal to differential treatment of women on the ground that the latter inevitably results in more inequality. After analysing the law relating to statutory rape, the male-only draft, and pregnancy, she concludes that there are two choices available to women: to claim equality on the ground of similarity to men, or to seek special treatment on the basis of their essential differences:

> My own feeling is that, for all its problems, the equality approach is the better one. The special treatment model has great costs. First...is the reality that conceptualising pregnancy as a spe-cial case permits unfavourable as well as favourable treatment of pregnancy...Second, treat-ing pregnancy as a special case divides us in ways that I believe are destructive in a particular political sense as well as a more general sense...Third...what appear to be special 'protec-tions' for women often turn out to be, at best a double-edged sword...Fourth...our freedom of choice about the direction of our lives is more limited than that of men in significant ways.[15]

Bluntly put, liberal feminism emphasizes *equality*, while radical feminism is con-cerned with *difference*.

One of the most crucial issues for liberal feminists is the public–private division. A fundamental constituent of this assault on liberal values is its demarcation of pub-lic and private spheres. The division between a public and private sphere is a main tenet of liberalism. Indeed, 'liberalism may be said largely to have been an argument about where the boundaries of [the] private sphere lie, according to what principles they are to be drawn, whence interference derives and how it is to be checked'.[16] The extent to which the law might legitimately intrude upon the 'private' is a recurring theme, especially in nineteenth-century liberal doctrine: 'One of the central goals of nineteenth-century legal thought was to create a clear separation between consti-tutional, criminal and regulatory law—public law—and the law of private transac-tions—torts, contracts, property and commercial law.'[17] The question of the limits of

[14] Cain, 804. A robust case in support of an individualistic, liberal approach is made by Martha C Nussbaum, *Sex and Social Justice* (Oxford: Oxford University Press, 1999). See too Martha Minow, 'Justice Engendered' (1987) 101 *Harvard Law Review* 10.

[15] W Williams, 'The Equality Crisis: Some Reflections on Culture, Courts and Feminism' (reproduced in the collection by Bartlett and Kennedy, 15–34), 26.

[16] S Lukes, *Individualism* (Oxford: Basil Blackwell, 1973), 62. See too E Kamenka, 'Public/Private in Marxist Theory and Marxist Practice' in Stanley I Benn and GF Gaus (eds), *Public and Private in Social Life* (London: Palgrave Macmillan, 1983), 267, 273–4. For a general discussion, see Raymond Wacks, *Personal Information: Privacy and the Law* (Oxford: Clarendon Press, 1989), Ch 1, and Raymond Wacks, *Law, Morality, and the Private Domain* (Hong Kong: Hong Kong University Press, 2000).

[17] Martin J Horwitz, 'The History of the Public/Private Distinction' (1982) 130 *University of Pennsylvania Law Review*, 1423.

the criminal law in enforcing 'private morality' also continues to vex legal and moral philosophers,[18] but radical feminists have in this dichotomy, discerned the failure of the law to intrude into the home to address crimes of so-called 'domestic' violence on women, or to intervene in the home, notwithstanding the exploitation of women that routinely occurs in that private domain. Latterly, however, this assessment has been moderated by a recognition that increasing regulation of the private sphere (in the case, for instance, of social security) is an inexorable feature of the modern welfare state and hence of the actual subjugation of women.

The public–private division highlights also the fact that it assists the subordination of women by virtue of the fact that political equality is largely a function of the public sphere—one from which women tend to be excluded. Hence, these features of liberalism may themselves be implicated in the subjugation of women, and they are therefore questioned by radical feminists.[19]

### 14.3.2 Radical feminism

The preoccupation with difference, expressed most coherently by the leading radical feminist, Catharine MacKinnon in her books, *Feminism Unmodified*[20] and *Towards a Feminist Theory of the State*,[21] challenges the view that, since men have defined women as different, women can ever achieve equality. And since men dominate women, the issue is ultimately one of power.[22]

There are, moreover, significant differences between men and women. These 'dualisms', according to Olsen, are 'sexualized'. One half is considered masculine (and therefore superior). They include (on the left side of Table 14.1) features associated with men. The other half (on the right) are terms associated with women.[23]

For MacKinnon and Christine Littleton,[24] the question seems to be one of redefining 'woman', and seeking to explain and understand the world from her perspective. A good deal of this world is manufactured by males. It is 'phallocentric' and oppressive, especially in the manner in which it encourages or allows violence against women.

---

[18] This is illustrated by the Hart–Devlin debate concerning, in particular, the issue of homosexual acts between consenting adults. The liberal position is, of course, exemplified by the Wolfenden Report (*Report of the Committee on Homosexual Offences and Prostitution*, Cmnd 247, 1957), which based itself on JS Mill's 'harm principle' expressed in *On Liberty* (1859). See too the *Report of the Committee on Obscenity and Film Censorship* (Chairman: Bernard Williams), Cmnd 7772, 1979. See Chapter 2.

[19] They (especially MacKinnon, see n 20) contend, eg, that the legal concept of privacy, by sheltering the home from state intrusion, has facilitated domestic violence, rape, and the exploitation of women.

[20] Catharine MacKinnon, *Feminism Unmodified: Discourses on Life and Law* (Cambridge, Mass: Harvard University Press, 1987).            [21] (Cambridge, Mass: Harvard University Press, 1989).

[22] Or as Robin West puts it—somewhat less delicately (but perhaps more arrestingly)—in her aphorism: 'the important difference between men and women is that women get fucked and men fuck', Robin West, 'Jurisprudence and Gender' (1988) 55 *University of Chicago Law Review* 1.

[23] F Olsen, 'Feminism and Critical Legal Theory: An American Perspective' (1990) 18 *International Journal of the Sociology of Law* 199, 200–1.

[24] Extracts from both works may be found in *Lloyd's Introduction to Jurisprudence*, 1175–84, and 1184–97, respectively.

**Table 14.1** Male/female dualisms

| Male | Female |
| --- | --- |
| Rational | Irrational |
| Active | Passive |
| Thought | Feeling |
| Reason | Emotion |
| Culture | Nature |
| Power | Sensitivity |
| Objective | Subjective |
| Abstract | Contextualized |

This leads her, controversially, to advocate a ban on pornography for its depiction of women as sex objects:

> The mass production of pornography universalises the violation of women in it, spreading it to all women, who are then exploited, used and abused and reduced as a result of men's consumption of it. In societies pervaded by pornography, all women are defined by it: this is what a woman wants, this is what a woman is.[25]

Yet, despite her attack on the untrammelled free speech that sustains the debasement of women, and her criticism of the existing patriarchal legal system, and scepticism about debates concerning equality and difference (on the ground that they fail to dislodge the fundamental dominance of men and male values), MacKinnon does not repudiate the law as a vehicle of radical change.

This may be contrasted with the view of other radical feminists who, like Carol Smart in *Feminism and the Power of Law*,[26] deny that the law can effect genuine equality. Resisting the charms of the law is, in fact, a recurring theme in radical feminism. The extent to which reforming the law can satisfy the demands of women at work, in the home, or simply as human beings, is regarded as moot. Thus, Christine Littleton, in challenging the conventional concept of equality, proposes instead 'equality as acceptance' which stresses the consequences rather than the sources of difference. This has obvious legal implications in respect of equal pay and conditions of work. Ann Scales is eloquent in her dismissal of change through the form of law:

> We should be especially wary when we hear lawyers, addicted to cognitive objectivity as they are, assert that women's voices have a place in the existing system…The injustice of sexism is not irrationality; it is domination. Law must focus on the latter, and that focus cannot be achieved through a formal lens.[27]

It is by 'asking the woman question' that radical feminists seek to expose this and other forms of the domination of women. The 'woman question', 'is designed to identify the

---

[25] C MacKinnon, *Towards a Feminist Theory of the State*, 247.
[26] Carol Smart, *Feminism and the Power of Law* (London: Routledge, 1989).
[27] 'The Emergence of Feminist Jurisprudence: An Essay' (1986) 95 *Yale Law Journal* 1373, 1385.

gender implications of rules and practices which might otherwise appear to be neutral or objective… [I]t reveals the ways in which political choice and institutional arrangement contribute to women's subordination.'[28] These, and other, disagreements are, as you will see, subtle, complex, and wide-ranging. They frequently take us to the heart of some of the significant concerns of jurisprudence in general.

### 14.3.3 Postmodern feminism

Some of the main elements of postmodernism are sketched in 13.2. In the present context, it need only be observed that postmodernists generally reject the idea of the 'subject'. It is necessary to understand the unacceptability to postmodernists of any objective truths. Concepts such as 'equality', 'gender', and even 'woman' are treated with profound scepticism. Indeed, the very idea that things have properties which they must possess if they are to be that particular thing (ie, that they have 'essences') is repudiated by many postmodernists. This so-called 'essentialism' is detected by postmodern feminists in the work of radical feminists such as MacKinnon who argues that beneath the surface of women lies 'precultural woman'. Similarly, essentialist concepts like 'the law' or 'patriarchy' are suspect.

The critical feminist project is well described by Deborah Rhode:

> What distinguishes feminist critical theories from other analysis is both the focus on gender equality and the conviction that it cannot be obtained under existing ideological institutional structures. This theoretical approach partly overlaps, and frequently draws upon other critical approaches, including CLS and critical race scholarship. At the most general level, these traditions share a common goal: to challenge existing distributions of power.[29]

Leading postmodernist feminists, such as Drucilla Cornell and Frances Olsen, draw on the work of Jacques Derrida and Julia Kristeva to create what Cornell calls an 'imaginative universal' which transcends the essentialism of real experience and enters the realm of mythology.[30] The maleness of law, the phallocentrism of society, are important themes in postmodern feminist writing.

In an influential essay, Katherine Bartlett attempts to show that in analysing the practice of law by courts and lawyers, at least three 'feminist legal methods' are used: 'asking the women question', 'feminist practical reasoning', and 'consciousness-raising'.[31] The first seeks to uncover 'the gender implications of rules and practices which might otherwise appear to be neutral or objective'. Discriminatory rules and practices are thereby revealed and attacked. Feminist practical reasoning 'challenges the legitimacy of the norms of those who claim to speak, through rules, for the community'. In particular, it emphasizes the women's perspective in, say, rape and domestic violence

---

[28] Katherine T Bartlett, 'Feminist Legal Methods' (1990) 103 *Harvard Law Review* 829, *Lloyd's Introduction to Jurisprudence*, 1197–215, 1198–9.

[29] Rhode, 'Feminist Critical Theories' (1990) 42 *Stanford Law Review* 617.

[30] Drucilla Cornell, 'The Doubly-prized World: Myth, Allegory and the Feminine' (1990) 75 *Cornell Law Review* 644.

[31] Katherine T Bartlett, 'Feminist Legal Method' (1990) 103 *Harvard Law Review* 829.

cases. Finally, consciousness-raising is 'an interactive and collaborative process of articulating one's experiences and making meaning of them with others who also articulate their experiences'. In other (simpler) words, it attempts to understand and reveal their oppression.

In seeking an appropriate feminist epistemology Bartlett argues for what she calls 'positionality' which recognizes the contingency of values and knowledge. Even the political commitment of feminists is provisional and requires critical evaluation and revision:

> Like the postmodernist position…positionality rejects the perfectibility, externality of truth. Instead the positional knower conceives of truth as situated and partial. Truth is situated in that it emerges from particular involvements and relationships. These relationships, not some essential or innate characteristic of the individual, define the individual's perspective and provide the location for meaning, identity, and political commitment.[32]

This would seem to be the case with most human experience, but it serves to drive feminist method away from essentialism and, perhaps, relativism, though I am less sure about the latter (see 14.4).

### 14.3.4 **Difference feminism**

Radicals are uncomfortable with the acceptance by liberal feminism of a male standard of achievement against which women's equality is to be measured. Acknowledging the validity of this claim, difference (or 'cultural') feminism rejects a sympathetic view of formal equality and gender which, it is argued, undermine the differences between men and women. Instead it seeks to uncover the unstated premises of the law's substance, practice, and procedure. In pursuit of this objective, difference feminists expose the diverse forms of discrimination implicit in the criminal law, the law of evidence, tort law, and the process of legal reasoning itself. This includes an attack on, for example, the concept of the 'reasonable man', the male view of female sexuality deployed in rape cases, and the very language of the law itself. For Luce Irigaray:

> The written law is a law established for a society of men—amongst—themselves. The trend for women to work outside the home and family, their entry into the world of work and public relationships, is raising questions about the current legal system, especially as far as human rights are concerned. The pretext of the neutral individual does not pass the reality test: women get pregnant, not men; women and little girls are raped, boys very rarely; the bodies of women and girls are used for involuntary prostitution and pornography, those of men infinitely less; and so on. And the exceptions to the rule or custom are not valid objections as long as society is for the most part run by men, as long as men are the ones who enact and enforce the law.[33]

---

[32] Katherine T Bartlett, 'Feminist Legal Methods' (1990) 103 *Harvard Law Review* 829, *Lloyd's Introduction to Jurisprudence*, 1197–215, 1212.

[33] L Irigaray, *Thinking the Difference: For A Peaceful Revolution*, transl K Montin (London: Athlone Press, 1994), 59. See too Ngaire Naffine, *Law and the Sexes: Explorations in Feminist Jurisprudence* (London: Allen & Unwin, 1990).

The thrust of this important branch of feminist thinking is that equality is a more complex and ambiguous aspiration than liberals appear to acknowledge. This aspect of feminist writing is well captured by the title of Carol Gilligan's seminal study, *In a Different Voice: Psychological Theory and Women's Development*.[34] In this influential work, Gilligan, a psychologist, seeks to show how women's moral values tend to stress responsibility, whereas men emphasize rights. Women look to context, where men appeal to neutral, abstract notions of justice. In particular, she argues, women endorse an 'ethic of care' which proclaims that no one should be hurt. This morality of caring and nurturing identifies and defines an essential difference between the sexes.[35] But it has been criticized, for instance, for its essentialism, and for treating these characteristics as natural when they are a *consequence* of male domination.[36]

Much feminist legal theory eschews rights as formal, hierarchical, and patriarchal. Law in general, and rights in particular, reflect a male viewpoint 'characterized by objectivity, distance and abstraction'.[37] In the words of leading feminist legal theorist, Catharine MacKinnon: 'Abstract rights...authorise the male experience of the world.'[38] But, although Elizabeth Kingdom recommends 'abandoning the concept of rights as a means of pressing feminist claims in law',[39] she restricts that rejection to the appeal to women's right to choose and the right to reproduce, resisting 'any extrapolation from that argument a kind of policy essentialism to the effect that every and any mention of rights must be expunged from the feminist dictionary of legal politics'.[40] Her argument is that appeals to rights often conceal inadequate theories of law in respect of women's social position. Such theories tend to be essentialist and therefore unacceptable to many feminist theorists.

According to Patricia Cain, difference and radical feminists differ in that the former focus upon a positive aspect of women's 'special bond' to others, while the latter concentrate on a negative dimension: the sexual objectification of women. Moreover, certain cultural feminists (she mentions Robin West)[41] embrace the idea that 'woman' has a 'discoverable natural essence'. West contends that the maleness of the law derives

[34] (Cambridge, Mass: Harvard University Press, 1982).

[35] See M Drakopoulou, 'The Ethic of Care: Female Subjectivity and Feminist Legal Scholarship' (2000) 8 *Feminist Legal Studies* 199; Luce Irigaray, *Thinking the Difference: For a Peaceful Revolution*, transl Karin Montin (London: Athlone Press, 1994).

[36] For lively discussions of these and other difficulties with the difference approach, see C MacKinnon, *Towards a Feminist Theory of the State*, Ann Scales, op cit, J Williams, 'Dissolving the Sameness/Difference Debate: A Post-Modern Path Beyond Essentialism in Feminist and Critical Race Theory' (1991) *Duke Law Journal* 296, and A Harris, 'Race and Essentialism in Feminist Legal Theory' (1990) 42 *Stanford Law Review* 581.

[37] EM Schneider, 'The Dialectic of Rights and Politics: Perspectives from the Women's Movement' in KT Bartlett and R Kennedy (eds), *Feminist Legal Theory: Readings in Law and Gender*, 319.

[38] C MacKinnon, 'Feminism, Marxism, Method and the State: Toward Feminist Jurisprudence' (1983) 8 *Signs: Journal of Women, Culture & Society* 63.

[39] Quoted in C Smart, 'Feminism and the Law: Some Problems of Analysis and Strategy' (1986) 14 *International Journal of Sociology of Law* 109.

[40] EF Kingdom, *What's Wrong with Rights? Problems for Feminist Politics of Law* (Edinburgh: Edinburgh University Press, 1991).

[41] See her important essay, 'Jurisprudence and Gender' (1988) 55 *University of Chicago Law Review* 1.

from an assumption of separateness. But, unlike men, women are more 'connected'—through the biology of pregnancy, breastfeeding, and even sex. This has powerful moral consequences. In the words of Carol Gilligan:

> The moral imperative…[for] women is an injunction to care, a responsibility to discern and alleviate the 'real and recognisable trouble' of this world. For men, the moral imperative appears rather as an injunction to respect the rights of others and thus to protect from interference the rights to life and self-fulfilment.[42]

### 14.3.5 Other feminisms

Though the above taxonomy accounts for the major strands in contemporary feminist jurisprudence, the richness of feminist legal thought extends beyond it to include, among others, Marxist, socialist, existentialist, structuralist, post-structuralist, deconstructionist, and linguistic schools.

The involvement of feminism in psychoanalytic theory has already been noted. The oppression of women plainly lends itself to a cornucopia of explanations and this is evident in the range of available theories. But it is more than that. Questions of biology, language, politics, and economics cannot simply be roped off and designated 'male' or 'female'; they provide important tools by which to understand social life. Thus, your study of feminist theory is bound to lead you well beyond the traditional boundaries of jurisprudence—if they still exist.

## 14.4 Critique

Criticism of feminism is not necessarily hostile to the goals of the movement. Indeed, as we have seen, feminists are often their own fiercest opponents. So, for example, echoing the unease expressed by a number of writers, Carol Smart, a leading British feminist theorist, declares that the form that the movement took in the 1980s 'has been defined by the interests largely of white, North American, feminist legal scholars…Feminist jurisprudence tends to be limited by the very paradigm it seeks to judge. In criticizing law for being male, it cannot escape the related criticism of promoting a (classless, white) female point of view as the solution.'[43] Smart, it will be recalled, doubts the power of the law to achieve social change, and disparages 'law's overinflated view of itself'.[44]

The alleged exclusion of black, lesbian, and working-class women from the feminist canvas seems to have been corrected in recent years by a vast literature, especially by and about black women in the United States.[45] But this sort of critique is internal

---

[42] *In A Different Voice*, 159–60.

[43] 'Feminist Jurisprudence' in P Fitzpatrick (ed), *Dangerous Supplements: Resistance and Renewal in Jurisprudence* (London: Pluto Press, 1991), 156.          [44] *Feminism and the Power of Law*, 3.

[45] See Marlee Kline, 'Race, Racism, and Feminist Legal Theory' (1989) 12 *Harvard Women's Law Journal* 115.

rather than external: radical feminists obviously join issue on several matters with liberal feminists. Thus the former's individualism is often the main the target of its detractors. In particular, critics complain that liberal feminists, by embracing individual rights, treat the distribution of such rights in society as unproblematic. In other words, they fail to expose the injustices against women that are legitimated by a liberal conception of the social order. This is, of course, a critique that might be made of liberalism in general. But some radical feminists, such as MacKinnon, go further and express misgivings about liberal feminism's acceptance of gender-neutrality in the law.

On the other hand, radical feminists are criticized for their preoccupation with sex and reproduction, neglecting the political and economic oppression of women. Nor, it is argued by, for example, Drucilla Cornell, is the feminist cause advanced by the radical repudiation of 'the feminine', especially by MacKinnon:

> For MacKinnon, feminism must involve the repudiation of the feminine; for me, feminism *demands* the affirmation of the feminine within sexual difference, and the challenge to women's shame of their 'sex' which flows inevitably from the repudiation of the feminine. Without this challenge, we are left with the politics of revenge and lives of desolation, which make a mockery of the very concept of freedom.[46]

It is not merely radical feminists who differ with their liberal counterparts. Inevitable, understandable divergences exist in this field of legal theory, no less than in others. Thus psychoanalytic theorists proceed from a different standpoint than from Marxist feminists. Carol Gilligan's views on women's values and Catharine MacKinnon's views on pornography have generated a huge debate among feminists. And there are, of course, disputes about the nature and function of the law in achieving equality (if that is indeed what is sought: another contentious question). There are a number of studies of the efficacy of the legal system in this regard.[47]

The postmodern tendency towards contextualism (which is sometimes hard to distinguish from relativism) seems, in my view, to provide a convenient mask for injustice enacted in the specious name of 'local culture'. Thus Katharine Bartlett's notion of 'positionality' (mentioned 14.3.3) all too easily slides into ethical relativism: if truth is socially constructed, oppression becomes simpler to justify.[48]

Some would deny the utility or integrity of the feminist legal enterprise as a whole. It has been argued, more or less, that the house of jurisprudence has many rooms, and rather than hiving off the 'special interests' of certain groups, however

---

[46] D Cornell, *Transformations: Recollective Imagination and Sexual Difference* (London: Routledge, 1993), 132.

[47] See, for instance, Deborah Rhode, *Justice and Gender: Sex Discrimination and the Law* (Cambridge, Mass: Harvard University Press, 1989); S Atkins and B Hoggett, *Women and the Law* (Oxford: Basil Blackwell, 1984).

[48] But see her essay, 'Tradition, Change, and the Idea of Progress in Feminist Legal Thought' [1995] *Wisconsin Law Review* 303, in which this standpoint appears not to feature.

oppressed, the perennial questions of law and human existence are universal and transcend these differences. The exclusivity of feminist jurisprudence may defeat its noble purpose. The Utopianism of some feminist writing has also attracted criticism, as has the occasional confusion between theory and practice; the strategy (eg, to outlaw sexual harassment) may be more successful than the 'grand' theory upon which it is built.

## 14.5 Critical race theory

CRT has been described as 'the heir to both Critical Legal Studies [CLS, see 13.1] and traditional civil rights scholarship'.[49] A central feature of its intellectual, institutional, and political development is the fact that this American movement originated as a reaction against what it saw as the deconstructive excesses of CLS.[50] Yet CRT is sceptical of many Enlightenment concepts such as 'justice', 'truth', and 'reason' since they 'reveal their complicity with power'.[51] It also attempts to expose the manner in which these ideas are 'racialized' in American law.[52]

The movement traces its origin to a conference held in Madison, Wisconsin in 1989. This 'outsider jurisprudence' or 'jurisprudence of construction' (phrases coined by Mari Matsuda[53]) is, in Angela Harris's words:

> aided by their engagement of what I call the 'politics of difference.' One benefit of this engagement is a long and rich tradition of wrestling at a practical level with the questions of identity that legal postmodernists have raised in the abstract. A second, deeper benefit is a commitment to the tension itself. For people of color, as well as for other oppressed groups, modernist conceptions of truth, justice, and objectivity have always been both indispensable and inadequate. The history of these groups—the legacy of the politics of difference—is a primer on how to live, and even thrive, in philosophical contradiction.[54]

---

[49] Angela P Harris, 'The Jurisprudence of Reconstruction' (1994) 82 *California Law Review* 741, 743. Harris's essay is a 'foreword' to a symposium in this number of the journal. It is a useful starting point. See too in (1990) 103 *Harvard Law Review* 1745.

[50] See Symposium, 'Minority Critique of the Critical Legal Studies Movement' (1987) 22 *Harvard Civil Rights—Civil Liberties Law Review* 297 (1987), quoted in Derek P Jinks, 'Essays in Refusal: Pre-Theoretical Commitments in Postmodern Anthropology and Critical Race Theory' (1997) 107 *Yale Law Journal* 1.

[51] Angela P Harris, 'Foreword: The Jurisprudence of Reconstruction' (1994) 82 *California Law Review* 741, 743.

[52] Derrick Bell, *And We Are Not Saved: The Elusive Quest for Racial Justice* (New York: Basic Books, 1987); Derrick A Bell, Jr, '*Brown v. Board of Education* and the Interest-Convergence Dilemma' (1980) 93 *Harvard Law Review* 518 (1980); 'Richard Delgado, Derrick Bell and the Ideology of Racial Reform: Will We Ever Be Saved?' (1988) 97 *Yale Law Journal* 923 (book review). The ideas of CRT have resonated in the United Kingdom and some of its former colonies (notably Australia, Canada, and India) where the racial shadow of post-colonialism continues to provide significant scope for legal and sociological analysis.

[53] 'Public Response to Racist Speech: Considering the Victim's Story' (1989) 87 *Michigan Law Review* 2320, 2323.                    [54] (1994) 82 *California Law Review* 741, 744.

In a leading inaugural CRT essay, Kimberlé Crenshaw argues that the American civil rights movement, despite its important victories against discrimination, left racist ideology intact.[55] According to Harris:

> The deeper race-crits dig, the more embedded racism seems to be; the deeper the race-crit critique of Western culture goes, the more useful postmodernist philosophy becomes in demonstrating that nothing should be immune from criticism. By calling everything taken for granted into question, postmodernist critique potentially clears the way for alternative accounts of social reality, including accounts that place racism at the centre of Western culture.[56]

Similar faith in deconstructive methods of exposing racism is expressed by Robert Chang[57] and by Cheryl Harris in her interesting essay, 'Whiteness as Property'.[58]

The privileged position occupied by mostly white, middle-class academics is perceived by CRT scholars as a significant obstacle to a wholesale exposure of the racism that permeates the law, its rules, concepts, and institutions. Those who have themselves suffered the indignity and injustice of discrimination are the authentic voices of marginalized racial minorities. The law's formal constructs reflect, it is argued, the reality of a privileged, elite, male, white majority. It is this culture, way of life, attitude, and normative behaviour that combine to form the prevailing 'neutrality' of the law. A racial minority (or in the case, say, of apartheid South Africa, see 2.11, majority) is consigned to the margins of legal existence.

Where CRT departs most significantly from full-blown postmodernist accounts (see 13.2) is in the acknowledgement by at least some of its members of the relevance of conventional 'rights talk' in the quest for equality and freedom. Its critique of contemporary society and law therefore appears, in some cases, to be a partial one. This seems to mark something of a retreat from the postmodernist hostility towards rights, and a willingness to embrace modernist normative concerns with liberty, equality, and justice. Kimberlé Crenshaw is unequivocal in endorsing the centrality of individual rights in the past and the future: 'Rights have been important. They may have legitimated racial inequality, but they have also been the means by which oppressed groups have secured both entry as formal equals into the dominant order and the survival of their movement in the face of private and State repression.'[59] There is, however, among

---

[55] Kimberlé Crenshaw, 'Race, Reform, and Retrenchment: Transformation and Legitimation in Antidiscrimination Law' (1988) 101 *Harvard Law Review* 1331.

[56] Angela P Harris (1994) 82 *California Law Review* 741, 749.

[57] 'Toward an Asian American Legal Scholarship: Critical Race Theory, Poststructuralism, and Narrative Space' (1993) 81 *California Law Review* 1243.

[58] (1993) 106 *Harvard Law Review* 1707. See too on Latino-Critical Studies (so-called 'Lat-Crit') R Delgado and J Stefanic (eds), *The Latino Condition: A Critical Reader* (New York: New York University Press, 1998), and R Delgado and J Stefanic (eds), *Critical White Studies: Looking Behind The Mirror* (Philadelphia, Penn: Temple University Press, 1997).

[59] Kimberlé Crenshaw, 'Race, Reform and Retrenchment' (1988) 101 *Harvard Law Review* 1331, 1348. For another argument along these lines (of which there are now several) see Patricia Williams, 'Alchemical Notes: Reconstructing Ideals from Deconstructed Rights' (1987) 22 *Harvard Civil Rights—Civil Liberties Review* 401. The Re-Enlightenment?

other CRT adherents, a deep suspicion of liberalism and the formal equality it aspires to protect, and aversion to individual rights and other features of liberal philosophy.[60]

CRT presents a range of concepts for analysis, particularly the concept of 'race' itself. It sometimes appears to revive some of the values and methods 'trashed' by CLS (see 13.1). These include a return to modernism and a *renaissance* of normative jurisprudence.

An important feature of CRT scholarship is the use of 'auto/biography' to analyse and criticize social and legal relations. For example, Patricia Williams in *The Alchemy of Race and Rights*[61] combines legal analysis with personal narrative in order to criticize legal subjectivity. This method seeks to obscure the distinction between law and social relations. This auto/biography enables Williams to explore 'how both literary knowledge—in the sense of autobiography as a literary genre—and legal knowledge are produced to make possible a postcolonial mimicry of these dominant discourses'.[62] The reference to postcolonial discourse denotes an offshoot of CRT that takes as its point of departure the fact that the dismantling of colonial governments and formally segregated social institutions has not ended the racial structures and assumptions of colonial and racially segregated societies.[63] The hostility of traditional legal scholarship to the auto/biographical is perceived by CRT as a means by which to dissociate the law from the very social relations, especially racial and gender discrimination, that it mediates.

The following nine themes may be identified as central to CRT scholarship. Each is followed by an example of the sort of issues that is pursued:[64]

1. *Critique of liberalism.* This may include an attack on liberal ideas such as affirmative action and colour blindness.

2. *Storytelling.* Subjective accounts of experiences of racism serve to challenge mainstream cultural assumptions.

3. *Revisionism.* This relates especially to questioning the efficacy of anti-discrimination law.

---

[60] See R Delgado and J Stefanic, 'Critical Race Theory: An Annotated Bibliography' (1993) 79 *Virginia Law Review* 461.

[61] (Cambridge, Mass: Harvard University Press, 1991).

[62] Richard Schur, 'Critical Race Theory and the Limits of Auto/biography: Reading Patricia Williams's 'The Alchemy of Race and Rights Through/Against Postcolonial Theory' (2002) 25 *Biography* 2002. This 'storytelling' approach is an important feature of CRT publications. These include Derrick Bell, *Confronting Authority: Reflections of an Ardent Protester* (Boston, Mass: Beacon Press, 1994), Gloria Anzaldua, *Borderlands/La Frontera* (San Francisco, Calif: Aunt Lute Books, 1987), bell hooks, *Bone Black: Memories of Girlhood* (London: The Women's Press, 1997), and David Mura, *Turning Japanese: Memoirs of a Sansei* (New York: Anchor Books, 1992).

[63] The colonial legacy has spawned a spirited analysis of the imperial practices of racism and expropriation of aboriginal land in many former colonies. See Peter Fitzpatrick, *The Mythology of Modern Law* (London: Routledge, 1992).

[64] These are employed as criteria for inclusion in the CRT bibliography produced by R Delagado and J Stefanic, 'Critical Race Theory: An Annotated Bibliography' (1993) 79 *Virginia Law Review* 461. I have adapted them here.

4. *Understanding race and racism.* These enquiries attempt to explain the social and cultural roots and nature of discrimination.

5. *Structural determinism.* How does the structure of legal concepts and thought influence its content, often in support of the status quo?

6. *Race, sex, and class.* How do these factors intersect? Are black women's interests adequately advanced by the women's movement?

7. *Anti-essentialism.* Is the black community a single one or several communities?

8. *Cultural nationalism.* Are the interests of black persons best promoted by nationalism or separation from the majority?

9. *Legal institutions.* Why are black persons under-represented in legal practice and education?

### 14.5.1 CRT and feminist theory

CRT shares a certain political pedigree with feminism. Both grew out of a dissatisfaction with mainstream legal theory that was perceived as an expression of dominant theoretical accounts of law and the legal system. And, while feminism is rooted in the subjugation of women, CRT is a product of the forces of slavery, segregation, and the civil rights movement in the United States.

In 14.1 it was suggested that the relation between feminist jurisprudence and critical race theory is in part an acknowledgement, and a refutation, of the preoccupation of feminists with white, middle-class, educated women. 'Discrimination against a white female,' Kimberlé Crenshaw declares, 'is the standard sex discrimination claim.'[65] This essentialist view of women, it has been contended, neglects the many other 'axes' of identity and oppression, especially that of race.[66] Thus Crenshaw demonstrates how black women do not fit the categories of sex discrimination because they are unable to show that the basis of discrimination against them is exclusively on the grounds of sex. Nor do they fit the categories of racial discrimination because they are unable to show that the basis of discrimination against them is exclusively on the grounds of race. She therefore argues for a change of perspective that locates those most marginalized at the centre of analysis.

CRT thus shares certain objectives of radical feminism, but it has larger ambitions. Not unlike the radical feminists discussed in 14.3.2 (in respect of men and women), CRT reveals the polarized categories that characterize Western thought. An illustration of these antinomies is set out in Table 14.2.[67]

---

[65] Kimberlé Crenshaw, 'Demarginalising the Intersection of Race and Sex: A Black Feminist Critique of Anti-Discrimination Doctrine, Feminist Theory and Antiracist Politics' (1989) *University of Chicago Legal Forum* 139, 145.                                                                                    [66] Op cit.

[67] Adapted from Kimberlé Crenshaw, 'Race, Reform and Retrenchment: Transformation and Legitimation in Antidiscrimination Law' (1988) 101 *Harvard Law Review* 1331.

**Table 14.2** Black and white images

| White images | Black images |
| --- | --- |
| Industrious | Lazy |
| Intelligent | Unintelligent |
| Moral | Immoral |
| Knowledgeable | Ignorant |
| Enabling Culture | Disabling Culture |
| Responsible | Shiftless |
| Virtuous/Pious | Lascivious |
| Law-Abiding | Criminal |

The centrality of public–private partition was alluded to in 14.3.1. It will be recalled that radical feminists detect in this partition the reluctance of the law to encroach upon the domestic environment in order to tackle crimes of domestic violence on women, or to intervene in the home, despite the routine exploitation of women that takes place in that private sphere. For CRT, however, the dichotomy depicts the position of white women; poor black women have tended to work outside the home. Thus the picture of a domesticated, passive, ineffectual woman may accurately convey the plight of white, middle-class women; it distorts the predicament of economically deprived black women. In this anti-essentialist spirit, CRT has uncovered several other white-oriented models of females, femininity, and sexuality.[68]

## 14.5.2 **CRT and postmodernism**

As discussed in Chapter 13, postmodernism generally confronts some of the key ideas and ideals of the Enlightenment, and a good deal of postmodernist thought spurns the Kantian anxieties about individual rights, equality, and justice that are significant features of modernism. There is also, as we saw, an uneasiness in postmodern thought about the 'subject'. In certain respects, CRT espouses a postmodernist view of the law, and deploys postmodern tools such as deconstruction to reveal its racist entrails.[69] It is also less willing to jettison either the concept of the subject or of legal rights.[70] Indeed, some CRT scholars embrace the modernist values of equality and rights. This ambiguity has generated a discussion of the extent to which CRT may legitimately be described as postmodern.

[68] See Crenshaw, n 58.

[69] See Gary Minda, *Postmodern Legal Movements: Law and Jurisprudence at Century's End* (New York: New York University Press, (1995); Douglas E Litowitz, 'Some Critical Thoughts on Critical Race Theory' (1997) 72 *Notre Dame Law Review* 503; Gary Peller, 'The Discourse of Constitutional Degradation' (1992) 81 *Georgia Law Review* 313.

[70] See, eg, Ratna Kapur, '"A Love Song to Our Mongrel Selves": Hybridity, Sexuality and the Law' (1999) 8 *Social and Legal Studies* 353.

# Questions

1. '[Feminism] ... is a range of committed inquiry and activity dedicated first, to describing women's subordination—exploring its nature and extent; dedicated second, to asking both *how*—through what mechanisms, and *why*—for what complex and interwoven reasons—women continue to occupy that position; and dedicated third to change.' (Clare Dalton, 'Where We Stand: Observations on the Situation of Feminist Legal Thought' (1987–88) 3 *Berkeley Women's Law Journal* 1)

   Consider the approach of feminist legal theory to these questions.

2. Distinguish the claims of liberal, radical, cultural, postmodern, and difference feminism.

3. 'The injustice of sexism is not irrationality; it is domination.' Does this assertion by Ann Scales suggest that legislative attempts to prevent sexual discrimination are a waste of time and money?

4. Are radical feminists excessively preoccupied with sex and reproduction, neglecting the political and economic oppression of women?

5. Can legal feminist theory progress without the concept of rights?

6. 'MacKinnon insists that feminism does not require prioritizing of oppressions, and that "male domination" or "patriarchy" must be construed as the systemic and founding source of oppression for women. And though this may appear true for some economically advantaged white women, to universalize this presumption is to effect a set of erasures, to cover over or "subordinate" women who "are" sites of competing oppressions, and to legislate through a kind of theoretical imperialism feminist priorities that have produced resistances and factionalizations of various kinds.' Judith Butler, 'Disorderly Woman' (1991) 63 *Transitions* 86.

   Is this a fair criticism?

7. What is the principal rationale for the development of critical race theory?

8. Does CRT 'story-telling' elucidate or inhibit the claims of the movement?

9. Evaluate the suggestion that CRT is 'postmodern' (see 13.2) or 'nihilistic'.

# Further reading

ATKINS, S. and HOGGETT, B., *Women and the Law* (Oxford: Basil Blackwell, 1984).

BARRON, ANNE, 'The Illusion of the "I": Citizenship and the Politics of Identity' in A Norrie (ed), *Closure or Critique: New Directions in Legal Theory* (Edinburgh: Edinburgh University Press, 1993).

BARRON, ANNE, '(Legal) Reason and its "Others": Recent Developments in Legal Theory' in J Penner, D Schiff, and R Nobles (eds), *Introduction to Jurisprudence and Legal Theory: Commentary and Materials* (London: Butterworths, 2002).

BARTLETT, KATHERINE, 'Feminist Legal Method' (1990) 103 *Harvard Law Review* 829.

BARTLETT, KATHERINE, 'Tradition, Change, and the Idea of Progress in Feminist Legal Thought' (1995) *Wisconsin Law Review* 303.

BARTLETT, KATHERINE and KENNEDY, ROSEANNE (eds), *Feminist Legal Theory: Readings in Law and Gender* (Boulder, Colo: Westview Press, 1991).

CAIN, M, 'Feminism and the Limits of Equality' (1990) 24 *Georgia Law Review* 803.

CHANG, ROBERT, 'Toward an Asian American Legal Scholarship: Critical Race Theory, Poststructuralism, and Narrative Space' (1993) 81 *California Law Review* 1243.

CONAGHAN, JOANNE, 'Reassessing the Feminist Theoretical Project in Law' (2000) 27 *Journal of Law and Society* 351.

CORNELL, DRUCILLA, 'The Doubly-Prized World: Myth, Allegory and the Feminine' (1990) 75 *Cornell Law Review* 644.

CORNELL, DRUCILLA, *Beyond Accommodation* (London: Routledge, 1991).

CORNELL, DRUCILLA, *Transformations: Recollective Imagination and Sexual Difference* (London: Routledge, 1993).

CRENSHAW, KIMBERLÉ, 'Race, Reform, and Retrenchment: Transformation and Legitimation in Antidiscrimination Law' (1988) 101 *Harvard Law Review* 1331.

CRENSHAW, KIMBERLÉ, 'Demarginalising the Intersection of Race and Sex: A Black Feminist Critique of Anti-Discrimination Doctrine, Feminist Theory and Antiracist Politics' (1989) *University of Chicago Legal Forum* 139.

DAVIES, MARGARET, *Asking the Law Question*, 3rd edn (Sydney: The Law Book Company, 2008), Chapters 6 and 7.

DELGADO, R and STEFANIC, J, 'Critical Race Theory: An Annotated Bibliography' (1993) 79 *Virginia Law Review* 461.

DELGADO, R and STEFANIC, J (eds), *Critical White Studies: Looking Behind The Mirror* (Philadelphia, Penn: Temple University Press, 1997).

DELGADO, R and STEFANIC, J (eds), *The Latino Condition: A Critical Reader* (New York: New York University Press, 1998).

DRAKOPOULOU, MARIA, 'The Ethic of Care: Female Subjectivity and Feminist Legal Scholarship' (2000) 8 *Feminist Legal Studies* 199.

FRUG, MARY JOE, 'Rescuing Impossibility Doctrine: A Postmodern Feminist Analysis of Contract Law' (1992) 140 *University of Pennsylvania Law Review* 1029.

GILLIGAN, CAROL, *In a Different Voice: Psychological Theory and Women's Development* (Cambridge, Mass: Harvard University Press, 1982).

GRAYCAR, REGINA and MORGAN, JENNY, *The Hidden Gender of Law* (Sydney: Federation Press, 1990).

HARRIS, ANGELA P, 'Race and Essentialism in Feminist Legal Theory' (1990) 42 *Stanford Law Review* 581.

HARRIS, ANGELA P 'The Jurisprudence of Reconstruction' (1994) 82 *California Law Review* 741.

HARRIS, CHERYL, 'Race, Reform, and Retrenchment: Transformation and Legitimation in Antidiscrimination Law' (1988) 101 *Harvard Law Review* 1331.

HUNTER, R, MCGLYNN, C, and RACKLEY, E (eds), *Feminist Judgments: From Theory to Practice* (Oxford: Hart Publishing, 2010).

IRIGARAY, L, *Thinking the Difference: For a Peaceful Revolution*, transl K Montin (London: Athlone Press, 1994).

JACKSON, EMILY and LACEY, NICOLA, 'Introducing Feminist Legal Theory' in J Penner, D Schiff, and R Nobles (eds), *Introduction to Jurisprudence and Legal Theory: Commentary and Materials* (London: Butterworths, 2002).

KINGDOM, ELIZABETH F, *What's Wrong with Rights? Problems for Feminist Politics of Law* (Edinburgh: Edinburgh University Press, 1991).

KLINE, MARLEE, 'Race, Racism, and Feminist Legal Theory' (1989) 12 *Harvard Women's Law Journal* 115.

KRAMER, MATTHEW H, *Critical Legal Theory and the Challenge of Feminism* (Lanham, Md: Rowman & Littlefield, 1995).

LACEY, NICOLA (ed), *Unspeakable Subjects: Feminist Essays in Legal and Social Theory* (Oxford: Hart Publishing, 1998).

LACEY, NICOLA, WELLS, C, and MEURE, D, *Reconstructing Criminal Law: Critical Perspectives on Crime and the Criminal Process* (London: Weidenfeld & Nicholson, 1990).

MACKINNON, CATHARINE, 'Feminism, Marxism, Method and the State: Toward Feminist Jurisprudence' (1983) 8 *Signs: Journal of Women, Culture & Society* 63.

MACKINNON, CATHARINE, *Feminism Unmodified: Discourses on Life and Law* (Cambridge, Mass: Harvard University Press, 1987).

MACKINNON, CATHARINE, *Towards a Feminist Theory of the State* (Cambridge, Mass: Harvard University Press, 1989).

MATSUDA, MARI, 'Public Response to Racist Speech: Considering the Victim's Story' (1989) 87 *Michigan Law Review* 2320.

NAFFINE, NGAIRE, *Law and the Sexes: Explorations in Feminist Jurisprudence* (London: Allen & Unwin, 1990).

NAFFINE, NGAIRE, 'Possession: Erotic Love in the Law of Rape' (1994) 57 *Modern Law Review* 10.

O'DONOVAN, KATHERINE, *Sexual Divisions in Law* (London: Weidenfeld & Nicholson, 1985).

O'DONOVAN, KATHERINE, *Family Law Matters* (London: Pluto Press, 1993).

OLSEN, FRANCES E, 'Feminism and Critical Legal Theory: An American Perspective' (1990) 18 *International Journal of the Sociology of Law* 199.

OLSEN, FRANCES E (ed), *Feminist Legal Theory* (Aldershot: Dartmouth, 1994).

RACKLEY, ERIKA, *Women, Judging and the Judiciary: From Difference to Diversity* (London: Routledge-Cavendish, 2014).

RHODE, DEBORAH, *Justice and Gender: Sex Discrimination and the Law* (Cambridge, Mass: Harvard University Press, 1989).

RHODE, DEBORAH, 'Feminist Critical Theories' (1990) 42 *Stanford Law Review* 617.

SCALES, ANNE, 'The Emergence of Feminist Jurisprudence: An Essay' (1986) 95 *Yale Law Journal* 1373.

SCHNEIDER, EM, 'The Dialectic of Rights and Politics: Perspectives from the Women's Movement' in KT Bartlett and R Kennedy (eds), *Feminist Legal Theory: Readings in Law and Gender* (Boulder, Colo: Westview Press, 1991).

SMART, C, 'Feminism and the Law: Some Problems of Analysis and Strategy' (1986) 14 *International Journal of Sociology of Law* 109.

SMART, C, *Feminism and the Power of Law* (London: Routledge, 1989).

SMART, PATRICIA, *Feminist Jurisprudence* (Oxford: Clarendon Press, 1993).

# 15

# Jurisprudence understood?

Or at least *better* understood. Each of the fourteen preceding chapters—which (I trust) you have pored over—endeavour to elucidate the central themes of legal philosophy. There is, of course, no substitute for reading the primary sources. While scholarly secondary texts—books and articles—to which I have made copious references, afford invaluable analysis and insight, the process of engaging directly with the writing of the theorists themselves is an indispensable path to both comprehension and appreciation of their work. There was a time when Hart's *The Concept of Law* was prescribed reading for almost every university jurisprudence course. How many students now read this seminal work?

Responsibility for this lamentable state of affairs could perhaps be laid at the door of books such as this. Am I (and the authors of similar volumes) guilty of steering students away from the fundamental works of legal theory? Should introductory texts like this one be banned, or at least shunned? Naturally I think not. A *vade mecum* properly used can only assist the reader in his or her quest for advice, guidance, and understanding. And I am deeply gratified that this has indeed been the substance of the reaction that I have received from students in many parts of the world. It is certainly the spirit in which the book was written.

I cannot repeat too often that this is not a textbook in the conventional sense. Two overriding criteria determined what I included in its pages. First, I consulted, wherever possible, the syllabuses of undergraduate jurisprudence and legal philosophy courses offered by major law schools. There is, as you might expect, a considerable degree of diversity in both the content and the method of teaching legal theory. Yet I discovered a discernable core of subjects common to a great many of these courses. It is these that I identified as essential for inclusion in the book. Secondly, there are a number of topics with which I found, in teaching jurisprudence for almost thirty years in three jurisdictions, my students encountered particular difficulty (Kelsen is one example). I therefore devoted more space to them in an attempt at illumination and explanation.

My selection has not, however, proved uncontroversial. Among the distinguished anonymous readers of the second edition, for instance, one urged me to eliminate altogether Chapters 6, 7, 8, and sections of Chapters 13 and 14 because they were 'mainly empirical'—and insufficiently intellectual. Another thought these 'sociological' questions, including the material covered in Chapters 13 and 14 should be considerably expanded! And some of the reviewers of the manuscript for this edition suggested that I drop Chapters 7, 9, 10, 11, and 12! These disagreements are understandable. The focus of several courses tends toward the explicitly philosophical, with a predictable emphasis placed on 'theory'. Other syllabuses, however, are considerably more extensive, embracing social and political theory in substantial detail. The theories of writers such as Nietzsche, Machiavelli, Leo Strauss, and others fall within their compass. And there are still other jurisprudence syllabuses that extend their reach to incorporate globalization, judicial review, liberalism, the rule of law, post-colonialism, religion, and anarchism—some of which are only touched upon in this book.

Despite these incursions into what, for many teachers of jurisprudence, is alien and inhospitable terrain, the primary questions persist. What is law? Does it consist of universal moral values in accordance with nature? Or is law merely a collection of predominantly man-made rules, commands, or norms? Does the law have a specific purpose such as justice, the protection of individual rights, or economic, political, gender, and racial equality? Can the law be understood without a proper appreciation of its social, historical, or anthropological context? What of unjust law: do we have an obligation to obey its directives? How do we justify punishing offenders?

While these—and myriad related—subjects vivify a good deal of legal theory, the apparently intractable problem of the relationship between law and morals continues to dominate current academic debate. Can law be value-free as legal positivists seek to demonstrate, or is law marked by an inescapable morality? Recently published, weighty volumes by Ronald Dworkin and Scott Shapiro crystallize this persistent dispute that defies simple resolution.[1] The former position, as we have seen, defends the unity of value; the latter adopts an instrumental model of law. You will need to decide which best captures this thing we called law. Is the pursuit of objectivity by legal positivists—from Austin and Bentham to their contemporary followers—ultimately illusory? Is a 'science of law' embodied in Kelsen's 'Pure Theory' a chimera? Should we heed Sir Neil MacCormick's warning?

> The fear is that…reference to value deprives legal theory…of any pretensions to scientific character. Were this true, law schools, so far as they are anything more than trade schools teaching skills and tricks of a sometimes questionable kind of job, would be purveyors of ideology, not disseminators of knowledge and learning. Were it true, jurisprudence would become, or be seen as what it has been all along, an exercise in legitimation of the actual state and its mode of government. Were it true, law professors would be mere apologists for the established order of things, interpreting that in the most attractive possible light…[H]uman artefacts and contrivances, including any rules by which people try to live, or get others to live, have to be understood functionally. What is their point, what is the final cause to which they are oriented?…Failure to confront and account openly for values involved, and to defend one's own proposals as to what the relevant values are, may confer work about law an apparently greater objectivity than if a proper open-ness were practised. But it is the concealment of value-orientation, not its open avowal, that is ideological in a sinister sense. Honest interpretation that is open about the values it presupposes and that is as alert to system-failures as to system-successes judged against those values is the best objectivity that is available to the human sciences, jurisprudence included.[2]

---

[1] See 4.5 and Chapter 5.
[2] Neil MacCormick, *Institutions of Law: An Essay in Legal Theory* (Oxford: Oxford University Press, 305.

What, after studying the many theories discussed in this book, do you believe law is? Can law be analytically severed from morality? Does law have a purpose? If so, what might that purpose be? Can it secure greater justice for all who share our troubled planet? Is this the *raison d'être* of theorizing about law?

None of these questions, as you will know by now, is susceptible to a simple answer. But it is in their asking—and careful reflection upon them—that the nature of law might be revealed, and thereby the path toward understanding jurisprudence.

# Glossary

This list includes the less familiar philosophical terms you are most likely to encounter in your study of jurisprudence. Many have been discussed in detail in the preceding chapters. The definitions are as brief as I could make them; they are designed both to remind you of their meaning, and to facilitate an understanding of them when their appearance occurs before their more comprehensive exposition in the text. I am concerned principally with the sense of these terms when employed in legal theory. Some will obviously have a different significance when used in other contexts or disciplines.

ABSOLUTISM The theory that certain acts are always wrong regardless of their consequences. Compare with 'consequentialism'. See also 'deontological'.

COGNITIVISM See 'non-cognitivism'.

COLLECTIVISM The theory and practice that opposes individualism, and regards the collective as the social, political, and economic unit. See 'individualism'.

COMMUNITARIANISM The theory that it is not the individual or the state or any other entity, but the community that ought to be the focus of our values and legal and political analysis. See 'individualism'.

CONSEQUENTIALISM The belief that whether an act is morally right depends exclusively upon its consequences or of some quality related to the act, eg, the motive behind it, or the existence of a general rule requiring acts of the same kind.

CONVENTIONALISM Used principally by Ronald Dworkin to describe the theory that the law is a function of social conventions that are designated as legal conventions, such as the doctrine of precedent. It closely resembles legal positivist semantic theories.

DEONTOLOGICAL The view that certain acts are intrinsically right or wrong,

regardless of their consequences. See also 'absolutism' and 'consequentialism'.

DIALECTICAL MATERIALISM The theory expounded by Engels that history develops by the material (physical) forces that transform nature. The process is dialectical in the sense that it unfolds by generating oppositions (thesis and antithesis) between conflicting powers. These contradictions resolve themselves and produce new material systems. Ultimately, though class conflict would, Engels believed, result in a proletarian revolution, the dialectic would persist in directing social transformation.

EMOTIVISM The theory, associated with David Hume, that moral judgments are based, not on reason, but on emotion. See also 'non-cognitivism' and 'moral realism'.

EMPIRICISM The idea that all knowledge of factual matters is derived from experience. It claims that *a priori* knowledge does not exist; we can know only what our five senses tell us.

EPISTEMOLOGY The theory of knowledge; it is concerned with how we know and what it is to know.

ESSENTIALISM Used especially by legal feminists to describe the tendency to reduce women to a universal essence and thereby to overlook the particulars of female diversity.

EXISTENTIALISM The idea that individuals themselves create the meaning and essential nature of their lives rather than it being constructed for them by the state or by religious doctrine. The philosophy is most closely associated with the writings of Nietzsche, Kierkegaard, Heidegger, Jaspers, Camus, and Sartre.

FORMALISM Treats law like mathematics or science. Formalists believe that a judge identifies the relevant legal principles, applies them to the facts of a case, and logically deduces a rule that will govern the outcome of the dispute.

FOUNDATIONALISM The theory that knowledge of the world is based on a foundation of incontrovertible beliefs from which other truths may be derived to construct a superstructure of recognized truths.

HISTORICISM The theory (a) that, as in the Weberian idea of *Verstehen* (see 7.5), every period of history can be understood only by attempting to comprehend the ideas and context of that period or (b) that historical forces inevitably determine social developments, as in the case, eg, of Marxist social theory.

INCOMMENSURABILITY The idea that moral dilemmas are incapable of resolution since they cannot be measured against a common standard. How, eg, is one to measure 'truth' against 'love'? Compare with 'utilitarianism' (which avoids this problem by claiming that all values may be reduced to one: happiness).

INDETERMINACY The proposition that there is no uniquely right answer to a legal problem until it has been determined by legislation or a judicial decision. Also used by critical legal theorists, especially CLS, to deny that law is a system (see 13.1).

INDIVIDUALISM The theory that individuals be accorded primary moral importance, and, as Kant argued, be regarded as ends in themselves with autonomy and inviolable rights. Compare with 'collectivism' and 'communitarianism.' See also 'Kantianism.'

INTUITIONISM The view (often called moral or ethical intuitionism) that incorporates moral realism (qv), ethical non-naturalism (the idea that evaluative facts cannot be reduced to natural facts), and the notion that the basis of ethics is our intuitive knowledge of evaluative facts.

KANTIANISM In ethics, the thesis that moral judgments are expressions of practical, rather than theoretical, reason. Practical reason, according to Kant, is derived from its own rational nature. The 'autonomy of the will' is the capacity to use practical reason to produce standards of conduct and it constitutes the basis of human dignity. This will is autonomous only if the principles it generates are capable of being universal laws and so create 'categorical imperatives', ie, unconditionally binding duties. Importantly, Kant insists that persons are ends in themselves, and must not be used instrumentally as utilitarianism appears to do. Compare with 'utilitarianism'. See 'prescriptivism'.

META-ETHICS Concerned with the meaning of moral propositions and the grounds upon which moral judgments are justified.

METANARRATIVE Stories used to legitimate the tools of social control. For postmodernists, especially Lyotard, they are to be distrusted.

METAPHYSICS The branch of philosophy that attempts to provide a comprehensive account of the most general features of reality and of 'being'. This includes the 'big' questions about God, space, time, the nature and existence of minds, identity, causality, and so on.

METHODOLOGY Normally used broadly to denote merely 'method'.

MORAL REALISM The view that moral judgments can be objectively true or false, and are not simply produced by emotional attitudes or desires; in this sense they are 'real' (see 2.8).

NATURALISM The belief that everything can be explained by reference to factual or causal properties of the world, without reference to supernatural powers. Ethical naturalism denies that ethics involves special forms or methods of argument.

NATURALISTIC FALLACY The error of identifying moral good with any natural property. GE Moore contended that the question whether something is good always remains an open one; it can never be correct. Thus fact and value are fundamentally distinct.

NIHILISM The comprehensive rejection and denial of the existence of human values, including morality.

NON-COGNITIVISM The view that moral judgments are not objectively true or subject to rational determination, and cannot be 'known'. Values, as opposed to facts, are neither true nor false, but merely express feelings, desires, attitudes, or demands. See 'emotivism' and 'moral realism'.

NORMATIVE ETHICS The branch of ethics concerned with advancing grounds by which to distinguish right from wrong, good from bad. See 'deontological' and 'consequentialism'.

ONTOLOGY A branch of metaphysics concerned with identifying the kinds of things that actually exist, including the nature of reality itself.

POSTMODERNISM A broad multi-disciplinary assault on the values of the Enlightenment, especially the idea of objective human knowledge achieved through reason in pursuit of universal objective truths.

PRAGMATISM The theory that attempts to explain meaning and truth in terms of the application of ideas or beliefs to the performance of actions that have practical or effective outcomes.

PRESCRIPTIVISM The view espoused by RM Hare that the use of moral terms like 'good' and 'bad' conveys an implicit imperative to act accordingly.

RATIONALISM The belief that reason, rather than sensory experience, is crucial to our understanding of the world. Weber uses the term to describe the 'legal–rational' mode of domination, as compared with traditional and customary modes (see 7.5.2).

REDUCTIONISM The belief that statements of one kind can be replaced systematically by statements of a simpler or more certain kind.

REIFICATION The treating of something as if it were an object. Thus in Marxist theory, reification is used to describe the process of using human beings as commodities (see 7.6.6).

RELATIVISM The general view that our judgments are conditioned by the specific social context of a particular individual, time, or place. Ethical relativism denies the existence of universal standards of moral value, and claims that moral judgments depend on the cultural norms of particular societies.

SCEPTICISM Doubts whether human knowledge is possible.

SUBJECTIVISM Regards moral judgment as depending on the arbitrary, personal, or individual, rather than rational, objective standards.

**Syllogism** An important form of deductive reasoning in which a conclusion follows from two or more premises.

**Teleology** The study of the end, purpose, or goal of something. See 'consequentialism'.

**Utilitarianism** The approach to morality that regards pleasure or the satisfaction of desire as the exclusive element in human good, and treats the morality of acts and rules as wholly dependent on the consequences for human welfare. See 'consequentialism', and 9.1.

# Index

References such as '178–9' indicate (not necessarily continuous) discussion of a topic across a range of pages. Wherever possible in the case of topics with many references, these have either been divided into sub-topics or only the most significant discussions of the topic are listed. Because the entire work is about 'jurisprudence' and 'legal theory', the use of these terms (and certain others which occur constantly throughout the book) as entry points has been restricted. Information will be found under the corresponding detailed topics.